COLLECTION OF APPLICATIONS

Einsatz und *Anwendung*
von Fairchild Halbleiter-Bauelementen

D1719406

te-wi Verlag GmbH
München

1

IMPRESSUM

Dieses Buch ist eine Sammlung der aktuellsten Artikel, die von der Division Semiconductors der Firma Fairchild als Applikationsberichte oder innerhalb des Firmenmagazins "Progress" laufend veröffentlicht werden.

HERAUSGEBER:

Fairchild Camera and Instrument (Deutschland) GmbH
Daimlerstraße 15
8046 Garching bei München

REDAKTION:

te-wi Verlag GmbH, Waldfriedhofstraße 30
8000 München 70, Tel. 089/376239

GESAMTHERSTELLUNG:

technik marketing, München
tm2306/0878 1. Auflage, August '78
Printed in W-Germany
ISBN-3-921803-01-2

A Word to the Reader

This book is a collection of the most important articles which are regularly published by the Semiconductor Division of Fairchild as individual "Application Notes" or within the company's journal "Progress". As Fairchild is a leading participant in most innovations of the SC industry the reader will get a first hand view of the technological evolution of this industry and its impact on a variety of circuit families such as Operational Amplifiers, Voltage Regulators, Digital Circuits (LPS, CMOS, ECL 100K), MOS and Bipolar Memories, CCD Shift Registers and Delay Lines, Interface and Consumer Circuits, Optoelectronics and Fairchild's powerful Microprocessor Families.

Beside the description and application of individual circuits this book gives practical guidelines for the system designer; it explains why and where a specific circuit family should be preferably used. The book is supplemented by basic considerations e.g. on Operational Amplifiers, Signal Transmission Lines and criteria for the quality and reliability of SC components. The study of this book helps gaining a better visibility in the problem solving and the progress of the innovative SC industry.

Due to the speedy development of the SC market, some device numbers have been changed and some types have been replaced by new ones. The "DEVICE INDEX/REFERENCE" on pages 4+5 shows a complete list of the types mentioned in this book and their replacements. On the final selection of a device our sales offices and distributors are ready to assistance.

Fairchild Camera and Instrument
Semiconductor Division, August '78

Wort an den Leser

Dieses Buch ist eine Sammlung der aktuellsten Artikel, die von der Division Semiconductors von Fairchild als Applikationsberichte oder innerhalb des Firmenmagazins "Progress" laufend veröffentlicht werden.
Da Fairchild an den meisten Innovationen der Halbleiterindustrie führend beteiligt ist, erhält der Leser aus erster Hand Einblick in die technologische Entwicklung dieser Industrie und ihren Einfluß auf eine Vielzahl von Schaltkreisfamilien wie Operationsverstärker, Spannungsregler, Digitalschaltkreise (LPS, CMOS, ECL 100K), MOS und Bipolar-Speicher, CCD-Schieberegister und Verzögerungsleitungen, Interface- und Consumerschaltkreise, optoelektronische Bauelemente und Fairchild's leistungsfähige Mikroprozessorfamilien.

Neben der Beschreibung und Anwendung einzelner Schaltungen gibt das Buch praktische Richtlinien für den Systementwickler; es erläutert warum und wo eine spezielle Schaltkreisfamilie sinnvoll eingesetzt werden kann. Das Buch wird ergänzt durch grundlegende Betrachtungen, z.B. über Operationsverstärker, Signalübertragungsleitungen und Kriterien für die Qualität und Zuverlässigkeit von Halbleiterbauelementen. Das Studium dieses Buches gibt in hohem Maße Aufschluß über die Problemlösungen und den Fortschritt der innovativen Halbleiterindustrie.

Da bei der stürmischen Entwicklung des Halbleitermarktes sich einige Typenbezeichnungen geändert haben, bzw. einige Typen durch neue abgelöst wurden, ist auf Seiten 4 + 5 (DEVICE INDEX/REFERENCE) eine komplette Liste der in diesem Buch angesprochenen Bauelemente und deren Ersatztypen angegeben. Bei der endgültigen Typenauswahl stehen Ihnen unsere Vertriebsbüros und Vertragshändler gerne beratend zur Seite.

Fairchild Camera and Instrument
(Deutschland) GmbH
Division Semiconductors, August '78

4

Device No.	Family	Description	Replacement *	Page
9401	Bi µP	CRC Generator/Checker		57, 66, 86
9403	"	FIFO Buffer Memory		87, 155-157
9404	"	Data Path Switch		89, 93, 101, 104, 110
9405	"	Arith. Logic Register Stack	9405 A	88, 93, 101, 104, 110
9406	"	Program Stack		89, 93, 101, 104, 110
9407	"	Data Access Register		90, 93, 101, 104
9408	"	Microprogram Sequencer/Controller		101-112
9410	"	16x4 RAM Register Stack		91, 93, 101, 104
9440	"	16 Bit Microprocessor (FIRE)		119-125
9601	Interface	Retriggerable Monostable		55-57, 162, 170, 410-412, 421
96L02	"	Dual Retriggerable Monostable		55
9614	"	Dual Line Driver	9638	391
9616	"	Triple RS232 Line Driver	9636	427-432
9617	"	Triple RS232 Line Receiver	9637	427-432
9660-63	"	Digit Segment Drivers	obsolete	424-425
9937	DTL	Hex Inverter	74LS05	410, 412, 416
9N13	TTL	Dual 4 Input Schmitt Trigger	74LS13	203
9N32	"	Quad 2 Input NOR Gate	74LS32	170
CCD 321	CCD	Dual 455 Bit Anal. Shift Register	CCD 321A	295-298, 307
CCD 110	CCD	Lin. Image Sensor (256 element)		212
CCD 121	"	Lin. Image Sensor (1024 element)		212
CCD 131	"	Lin. Image Sensor (1728 element)		212
CCD 1100	CCD	Line Scan Camera Subsystem (256)		213
CCD 1300	"	Line Scan Camera Subsystem (1024)		208-211, 213
CCD 1400	"	Line Scan Camera Subsystem (1728)		213-214
F 100K Series	ECL	Subnanosecond Unsaturated Logic		31-36
F 3850	MOS µP	8 Bit Microprocessor (CPU)		70-76, 79
F 3851	"	Program Storage Unit		70-76, 79
F 3852	"	Dyn. Memory Interface		70-76, 80
F 3853	"	Static Memory Interface		70-76, 80
F 3854	"	Direct Memory Access Unit		70-76, 81
F 3856	"	Program Storage Unit		81
F 3857	"	PSU/SMI		82
F 3861	"	Peripheral I/O Device		82
F 3870	"	8 Bit Microcomputer (1 Chip)		98
F 460	CCD Mem	16 K LARAM	F 464	145
F 464	"	64 K Dyn. Shift Register		148-154
F 6800	MOS µP	8 Bit Microprocessing Unit		83
F 6810	"	128x8 Static RAM		83
F 6820	"	Peripheral Interface Adapter		84
F 6850	"	Async. Data Adapter		84
FCD 820	Opto	Opto Coupler		202-203
FLC 3503/05/07	Opto	LCD Watch Displays	available on	207
FLC 5505	"	LCD Watch Displays	special request	207
FLC 6005	"	LCD Watch Displays	for large	207
FLC 8004/06	"	LCD Watch Displays	quantities	207
FNA 30	Opto	LED Numeric Display	obsolete	424
FNA 45	"	LED Numeric Display	obsolete	424
FND 70	"	LED Numeric Display	FND 357	424
FND 500	"	LED Numeric Display		424
FND 507	"	LED Numeric Display		423
FT 317	Trans.	NPN Power Transistor		370
FT 324	"	NPN Power Transistor		370
FT 417	"	PNP Power Transistor		370
FT 424	"	PNP Power Transistor		370
OCM -1	MOS µP	One Card Microcomputer (8 Bit)		98-99
SE 9301	Trans.	NPN Power Transistor		365-366
SE 9304	"	NPN Power Transistor		365-366
SE 9401	"	PNP Power Transistor		365-366
SE 9404	"	PNP Power Transistor		365-366
SH 1549	Hybrid	Tuner Control/Memory Circuit	obsolete	299-303
TBA 820	Linear	Audio Power Amplifier		282
µA 2240	Linear	Programmable Timer/Counter		276-277
µA 555	"	Single Timer		272-275
µA 556	"	Dual Timer		272-275
µA 706	"	Audio Power Amplifier	TDA 2002	358-363
µA 715	"	High Speed Op Amp		309-312, 344
µA 721	"	AM/FM Radio IC		279-283
µA 725	"	High Performance Op Amp	µA 714	313-317
µA 740	"	FET Input Op Amp	µAF 356	327-329
µA 741	"	Op Amp		259, 263, 323-326
µA 742	"	Zero Crossing AC Trigger Triac		353-357
µA 750	"	Dual Comparator Subsystem	obsolete	346-352
µA 758	"	PLL Stereo Decoder	µA 1310	374-384
µA 759	"	Power Op Amp (0,3 A)		241-246
µA 760	"	High Speed Diff. Comparator		338-345
µA 775	"	Quad Comparator (Single Supply)	µA 339	301
µA 777	"	Precision Op Amp		330-337
µA 7800 Series	"	Fixed Pos. Voltage Regulators (1 A)		247-251, 267
µA 7805	"	5 V Regulator (1 A)		421
µA 78H05	"	High Power 5 V Regulator (5 A)	µA 78H05A	260-263, 267
µA 78L82	"	8,2 V Pos. Voltage Regulator (0,1 A)		283
µA 78M00 Series	"	Fixed Pos. Voltage Regulators (0,5 A)		247-251, 267
µA 78MG	"	Adjust. Pos. Voltage Regulator (0,5 A)		252-259, 267, 278
µA 78S40	"	Switching Voltage Regulator		284-294
µA 791	"	Power Op Amp (1 A)		240-246
µA 798	"	Dual Op Amp		301
µA 79HG	"	High Power Adjust. Neg. Voltage Reg. (5 A)		385-386
µA 79MG	"	Adjust. Neg. Voltage Regulator		252-259, 267, 278
µA 9708	"	6 Channel, 8 Bit A/D Converter		399-402

* The types shown as replacement are in some cases only functional equivalents and not always pluck-in replacements.
Please contact your Fairchild sales office or distributor for latest developments.

Fairchild Semiconductors, August 1978

TABLE OF CONTENTS

DIGITAL

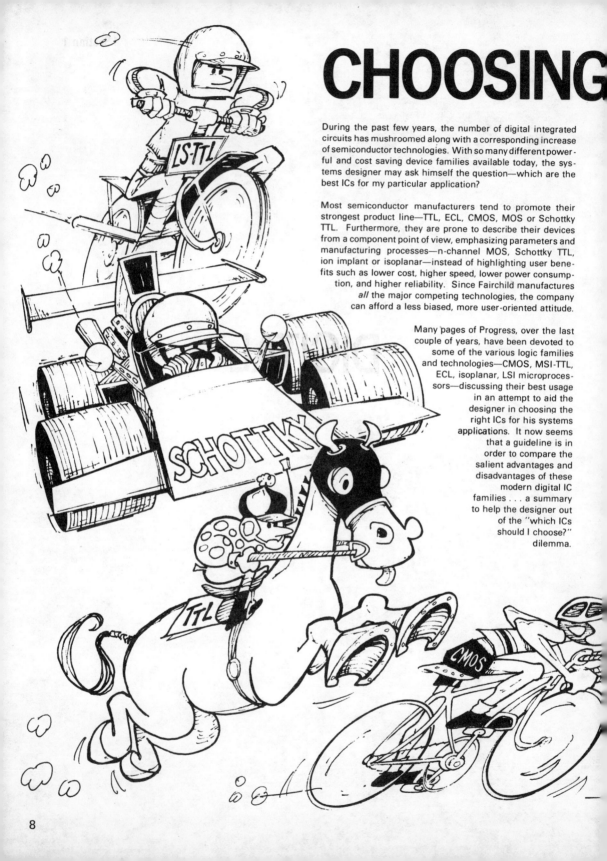

CHOOSING

During the past few years, the number of digital integrated circuits has mushroomed along with a corresponding increase of semiconductor technologies. With so many different powerful and cost saving device families available today, the systems designer may ask himself the question—which are the best ICs for my particular application?

Most semiconductor manufacturers tend to promote their strongest product line—TTL, ECL, CMOS, MOS or Schottky TTL. Furthermore, they are prone to describe their devices from a component point of view, emphasizing parameters and manufacturing processes—n-channel MOS, Schottky TTL, ion implant or isoplanar—instead of highlighting user benefits such as lower cost, higher speed, lower power consumption, and higher reliability. Since Fairchild manufactures *all* the major competing technologies, the company can afford a less biased, more user-oriented attitude.

Many pages of Progress, over the last couple of years, have been devoted to some of the various logic families and technologies—CMOS, MSI-TTL, ECL, isoplanar, LSI microprocessors—discussing their best usage in an attempt to aid the designer in choosing the right ICs for his systems applications. It now seems that a guideline is in order to compare the salient advantages and disadvantages of these modern digital IC families . . . a summary to help the designer out of the "which ICs should I choose?" dilemma.

THE BEST

The easiest way to do this is to present the pros and cons of the various logic families in simple table form so that the relative trade offs are readily obvious. Since the first thing a designer must do is establish the required component speed characterized by the clock rate of registers and counters, this discussion is divided into four groups based on the wide range of possible clock rates.

Very High Speed	Clock Rate	>100 MHz	ECL
High Speed	Clock Rate	30 to 100 MHz	ECL, S-TTL
Medium Speed	Clock Rate	5 to 50 MHz	LS-TTL, TTL
Low Speed	Clock Rate	<5 MHz	LS-TTL, CMOS

VERY HIGH SPEED SYSTEMS—Clock Rate 100 MHz

There is only one reasonable IC logic family for use in very high speed systems—Emitter Coupled Logic, ECL. Originally, this technology presented considerable electrical problems such as voltage and temperature sensitivity and fast edge rates that caused reflection and cross-talk problems. In recent years, however, ECL development has become more user-oriented and there is better compatibility between circuit characteristics and interconnection techniques.

The modern popular ECL line is the 10,000 series, manufactured in uncompensated, in voltage-compensated, or in both voltage and temperature-compensated forms by several manufacturers. The latter form of compensation assures that significant parameters such as logic levels, noise margins and speed remain constant over a wide range of temperature and power supply voltage. These 10K and 95K logic circuits have deliberately slowed-down edge rates to make them easier to use and they can also drive terminated transmission lines whenever required by the interconnection length. Extensive literature is available on the use of 10K-type circuits; the Fairchild ECL handbook is a good reference. Future ECL trends include the following.

● A series of dedicated, communications-oriented circuits, like prescalers up to 1.2 GHz, oscillators, phase comparators for phase locked loops, etc.

● A faster digital logic family with gate propagation delays below 1 ns mainly intended for computer CPU applications.

HIGH SPEED SYSTEMS—Clock Rate 30 to 100 MHz
(Table I)

Here, the designer has a choice between ECL and Schottky TTL. H-TTL is really obsolete since it consumes more power than Schottky TTL, has similar interconnection problems and offers only half the speed. Also, it is not significantly faster than the best Low Power Schottky TTL. So, this narrows down the choice to ECL and Schottky TTL.

MEDIUM SPEED SYSTEMS—Clock Rate 5 to 50 MHz
(Table II)

Standard TTL has been the obvious choice for medium speed systems for many years. Many designs will increasingly use Low Power Schottky TTL as it becomes more available, multiple sourced, and as the price premium decreases. An intelligent mix of standard and LS-TTL can solve most fan-out problems.

SLOW SPEED SYSTEMS—Clock Rate < 5MHz (Table III)

The designer of slow speed systems is faced with the largest number of attractive alternatives. Traditionally, he has used TTL and DTL. Now he can save power and cost and avoid heat and reliability problems by changing to LS-TTL, without affecting the logic design and perhaps not even changing the PC board layout.

If the system speed permits, the designer can switch to CMOS and save even more power and simplify the power supply; but now he must cope with a family of different logic elements and a hodgepodge of MSI elements, far less systems oriented than the better TTL circuits. He will also notice wide parameter differences between the "same" products from different vendors.

The greatest challenge, however, is to examine the traditional hard-wired system design and decide whether or not it can be

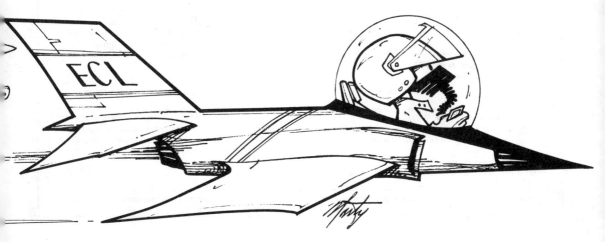

implemented with a microprocessor. If the requirements are both complicated and slow enough, this approach might save manufacturing cost, design time, and service time, as well as improve reliability, provide additional flexibility, and perhaps allow additional features at no extra cost.

MOS (p-channel, n-channel, either metal or silicon gate, also silicon on sapphire) does not compete directly with LS-TTL and CMOS. The MOS logic elements (gates and flip-flops) are very small but the input and output buffers are so large and relatively slow that MOS cannot be cost/performance competitive at MSI complexity (below 200 gates). MOS is therefore meaningful only in LSI circuits, as listed below, where it has proven to be not only competitive, but dominating.

- LSI memories, RAMs, ROMs, and shift registers of 500 to 4096 bits at clock rates below 5 MHz.

- Specialized, inherently slow LSI functions produced in very large volume (calculators, clocks, some instrument circuits like DVMs).

- Custom LSI circuits where the manufacturing volume is high enough or the weight/space saving valuable enough to absorb the development cost.

- Microprocessors, where a very carefully designed, standard circuit performs specialized tasks through ROM-stored programming.

TABLE I. COMPARISON OF DIGITAL LOGIC FAMILY CHARACTERISTICS FOR HIGH SPEED SYSTEMS (CLOCK RATE 30 TO 100 MHz)

10K AND 95K SERIES ECL	SCHOTTKY TTL
Advantages	Disadvantages
Short delays allow propagation through more logic levels in a clock cycle. Compatibility with even faster families currently in development makes future system upgrading easy.	Component delays are about twice as long as with ECL and will not be improved in the foreseeable future.
Low output impedance easily drives all types of interconnections including terminated transmission lines.	Outputs are not capable of driving terminated transmission lines without causing severe fan-out compromises.
High output drive capability and complementary outputs accommodate differential transmission over tested pairs.	
Slow edge rate minimizes reflection problems.	Has the fastest output transitions of any logic family, causing reflection problems even with relatively short interconnection lengths, and causing crosstalk problems.
Complementary outputs on many elements add design flexibility.	
Wired-OR capability simplifies logic design.	
Compensated circuits simplify power supply and temperature regulation.	Generates fast power supply load changes, requires good decoupling.
High input impedance minimizes loading, allows high fan-out.	Input thresholds and output low levels are slightly offset from conventional TTL, causing some loss of noise immunity.
Disadvantages	Advantages
Unfamiliar type of circuitry, logic, nomenclature, and pinouts.	Compatible with popular TTL, same supply voltage, almost identical signal levels, same SSI and MSI logic, nomenclature, pinouts.
Not level-compatible with TTL and CMOS, requires additional interface elements.	
Requires external pull-down resistors on all used outputs.	Outputs require no pull-up (or down) resistors.
Has less absolute noise margin.	Large signal swing and large absolute noise immunity cause less problems with temperature or supply voltage variations and gradients, resistive drops along supply lines, and outside noise.
Higher ground current requires heavier distribution busses.	
Has one less logic pin per package due to double ground.	
Has higher power consumption at low frequencies than equivalent S-TTL circuits.	Has lower system power consumption at moderate speed.

SUMMARY

The proliferation of digital circuits and technologies gives the designer a new degree of freedom, but it also challenges his judgement and imagination. The system designer is faced with an almost overwhelming number of competing technologies, each with its strong and weak points. The basic component speed requirement and the available power will quickly narrow the choice down to two or three different logic families; the tables presented here will make the final decision easier.

The designer should not forget, however, that the component speed requirement is also affected by his choice of architecture. A parallel approach requires more, but slower components, while a serial architecture requires fewer but faster components. The versatility of modern MSI circuits makes it easy to explore these alternatives. It is very important to choose the IC logic family at an early stage in the system design, since the full cost, speed and reliability advantages can only be gained by designing in accordance with the device features, taking advantage of their logic and organization.

TABLE II. COMPARISON OF DIGITAL LOGIC FAMILY CHARACTERISTICS FOR MEDIUM SPEED SYSTEMS (CLOCK RATE 5 TO 50 MHz)

STANDARD TTL	LOW POWER SCHOTTKY TTL
Advantages	Disadvantages
Large number of SSI and MSI functions.	Fewer device types available.
Low prices.	Presently higher priced than standard TTL.
Available from many suppliers.	Presently available from only a few suppliers.
Disadvantages	Advantages
High power consumption (10 mW per gate, 200 to 500 mW per MSI package.)	Saves 75% of the power of equivalent standard TTL.
Large, heavy, expensive, hot power supply and regulator.	Smaller, lighter, cheaper, cooler power supply and regulator.
Heat density problems when using predominantly MSI.	No heat density problem. Cooler, therefore more reliable.
	May eliminate the need for fans and filters.
Not fully compatible with most CMOS and MOS.	Compatible with CMOS and MOS.
	Generates less noise than standard TTL.

TABLE III. COMPARISON OF DIGITAL LOGIC FAMILY CHARACTERSTICS FOR LOW SPEED SYSTEMS (CLOCK RATE 5 MHz)

STANDARD OR LOW POWER SCHOTTKY TTL	CMOS
Advantages	Disadvantages
Well designed, systems-oriented MSI.	Some of the original CMOS circuits are poorly defined and not systems oriented.
Adequate speed, tight tolerances.	Low speed, delays depend on supply voltage and capacitive loading.
Low impedance outputs give good immunity against capacitively coupled noise.	Poor current noise immunity (capacitively coupled noise.)
Familiar functions, logic, pinouts.	New functions, logic pinouts.
Standard TTL available from many suppliers, low cost.	Large parameter variations between different vendors.
Disadvantages	Advantages
Relatively high static consumption and heat generation.	Extremely low static power consumption, very little heat generated at moderate speed.
Tight power supply voltage requirements (5 V + 5% commercial, ± 10% military grade).	Very wide range of supply voltages (theoretically 3...15 V, practically 5...12 V).
Not well-suited for portable battery operation.	Ideally suited for battery operation.
More expensive power supply.	Low cost power supply. Less cost, weight, heat, size than for any other family.
Lower voltage noise immunity.	High voltage noise immunity, an advantage with inductively coupled noise.
LS-TTL available from only a few suppliers.	Available from many suppliers.

CMOS

Complementary MOS digital logic building blocks of SSI and MSI complexity have been hailed as the ideal logic family. They are rapidly gaining popularity as more and more manufacturers introduce increasing numbers of parts at reasonable prices. There are now over 20 suppliers offering more than 150 functions. The worldwide consumption of CMOS devices has jumped from $50M in 1973 to over $100M in 1974 and is expected to exceed $300M in 1977, growing faster than any other integrated circuit family.

Originally designed for aerospace applications, CMOS now finds its way into portable instruments, industrial and medical electronics, automotive applications and computer peripherals, besides dominating the electronic watch market.

In late 1973, Fairchild introduced the 34000 CMOS family, using Isoplanar technology to achieve superior electrical performance. Most of these devices are functional equivalents and pin-for-pin replacements of the well-known 4000 series; some are equivalent to TTL circuits and some are proprietary logic designs.

A few CMOS devices, such as bidirectional analog switches, exploit the unique features of CMOS technology; some take advantage of the smaller device size and higher potential packing density to achieve true LSI complexity; but most of the available CMOS elements today are of SSI and MSI complexity and perform logic functions that have been available in DTL or TTL for many years. Therefore, it is both helpful and practical to compare the performance of CMOS with that of the more familiar DTL/TTL *(Figure 1)*. The function selector guide at the end of this article lists

YOU'VE COME A LONG WAY

by Peter Alfke and Bill Harmon

	STANDARD TTL	74L	DTL	9LS LOW POWER SCHOTTKY	74LS LOW POWER SCHOTTKY	CMOS 5 V SUPPLY	CMOS 10 V SUPPLY
PROPAGATION DELAY	10 ns	33 ns	30 ns	5 ns	10 ns	35 ns	25 ns
FLIP-FLOP TOGGLE FREQUENCY	35 MHz	3 MHz	5 MHz	80 MHz	40 MHz	5 MHz	10 MHz
QUIESCENT POWER	10 mW	1 mW	8.5 mW	2 mW	2 mW	10 nW	10 nW
NOISE IMMUNITY	1 V	1 V	1 V	0.8 V	0.8 V	2 V	4 V
FAN OUT	10	10	8	20	20	50*	50*

*OR AS DETERMINED BY ALLOWABLE PROPAGATION DELAY

Fig. 1. CMOS Compared to Other Logic Families

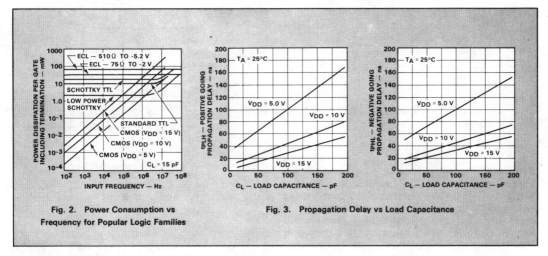

Fig. 2. Power Consumption vs Frequency for Popular Logic Families

Fig. 3. Propagation Delay vs Load Capacitance

numerous CMOS circuits that are identical to their TTL counterparts right down to pinout, others that are functionally identical only, still others that are similar and, in most cases, offer added features.

CMOS speed is comparable to 74L-TTL and DTL, and about three to six times slower than TTL or Low Power Schottky (LS-TTL). Voltage noise immunity and fanout are almost ideal, supply voltage is noncritical, and the quiescent power consumption is close to zero—several orders of magnitude lower than for any competing technology.

POWER CONSUMPTION

Under static conditions, the p-channel (top) and the n-channel (bottom) transistors are not conducting simultaneously, thus only leakage current flows from the positive (V_{DD}) to the negative (V_{SS}) supply connection. This leakage current is typically 0.5 nA per gate, resulting in very attractive low power consumption of 2.5 nW per gate (at 5 V).

Whenever a CMOS circuit is exercised, when data or clock inputs change, additional power is consumed to charge and discharge capacitances (on-chip parasitic capacitances as well as load capacitances). Moreover, there is a short time during the transition when both the top and the bottom transistors are partially conducting. This dynamic power consumption is obviously proportional to the frequency at which the circuit is exercised, to the load capacitance and to the square of the supply voltage. As shown in *Figure 2*, the power consumption of a CMOS gate exceeds that of a Low Power Schottky gate somewhere between 500 kHz and 2 MHz of actual output frequency.

At 100 transitions per second, the dynamic power consumption is far greater than the static dissipation; at one million transitions per second, it exceeds the power consumption of LS-TTL.

SUPPLY VOLTAGE RANGE

CMOS is guaranteed to function over the unprecedented range of 3 to 18 V supply voltage. Characteristics are guaranteed for 5, 10, and 15 V operation and can be extrapolated for any voltage in between. Operation below 4.5 V is not very meaningful because of the increase in delay (loss of speed) and the increase in output impedance. Operation above 15 V is not recommended because of high dynamic power consumption and risk of noise spikes on the power supply exceeding the breakdown voltage (typ >20 V), causing SCR-latch-up and destroying the device unless the current is externally limited.

Low static power consumption combined with wide supply voltage range make CMOS the ideal logic family for battery operated equipment.

PROPAGATION DELAY

Compared to TTL and LS-TTL, all CMOS devices are slow and very sensitive to capacitive loading. The Fairchild 34000 family uses both advanced processing (Isoplanar) and improved circuit design (buffered gates) to achieve propagation delays and output rise times that are superior to any other junction-isolated CMOS design. (Silicon-on-sapphire, SOS, can achieve similar performance but at a substantial cost penalty).

Isoplanar processing achieves lower parasitic capacitances which reduce the on-chip delay and increase the maximum toggle frequency of flip-flops, registers and counters. Buffering all outputs, even on gates, results in lower output impedance and thus reduces the effect of capacitive loading.

Propagation delay is affected by three parameters: capacitive loading, supply voltage, and temperature.

Capacitive Loading Effect

Historically, semiconductor manufacturers have always specified the propagation delay at an output load of

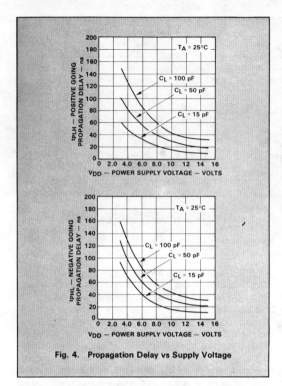

Fig. 4. Propagation Delay vs Supply Voltage

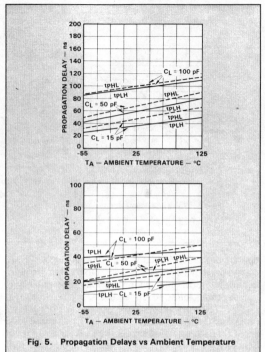

Fig. 5. Propagation Delays vs Ambient Temperature

15 pF, not because anybody considers this a representative systems environment, but rather because it was the lowest practical test-jig capacitance. It also generated the most impressive specifications. TTL with an output impedance less than 100 Ω is little affected by an increase in capacitive loading; a 100 pF load increases the delay by only about 4 ns. CMOS, however, with an output impedance of 1 kΩ (worst case at 5 V) is 10 times more sensitive to capacitive loading. *Figure 3* shows the positive and negative going delays as a function of load capacitance. It should be noted that the older, unbuffered gates have an even higher output impedance, a larger dependence on output loading, and do not show the same symmetry.

Supply Voltage Effect

Figure 4 shows propagation delay as a function of supply voltage and again indicates the symmetry of the positive and negative going delays. Increasing the supply voltage from 5 to 10 V more than doubles the speed of CMOS gates. Increasing the supply voltage to 15 V almost doubles the speed again, but, as mentioned before, results in a significant increase in dynamic power dissipation.

> The best choice for slow applications is 5 V. For reasonably fast systems, choose 10 or 12 V. Any application requiring 15 V to achieve short delays and fast operation should be investigated for excessive power dissipation and should be weighed against an LS-TTL approach.

Temperature Effect

Figure 5 shows propagation delay as a function of ambient temperature. The temperature dependence of CMOS is much simpler than with TTL, where three factors contribute—increase of beta with temperature, increase of resistor value with temperature, and decrease of junction forward voltage drop with increasing temperature. In CMOS, essentially only the carrier mobility changes, thus increasing the impedance and hence the delay with temperature. For 34000 devices, this temperature dependence is less than 0.3% per °C, practically linear over the full temperature range. Note that the commercial temperature range is –40 to +85°C rather than the usual 0 to +75°C.

> CMOS delays increase with temperature. They are very sensitive to capacitive loading but can be reduced by increasing the supply voltage to 10 or even 15 V.

NOISE IMMUNITY

One of the most advertised and also misunderstood CMOS features is noise immunity. The input threshold of a CMOS gate is approximately 50% of the supply voltage and the voltage transfer curve is almost ideal. As a result, CMOS can claim very good voltage noise immunity, typically 40% of the supply voltage, *i.e.*, 2 V in a 5 V system, 4 V in a 10 V system. Compare this with the TTL transfer curve in *Figure 6* and its resultant 1 V noise immunity in a lightly loaded system and only 0.4 V worst case.

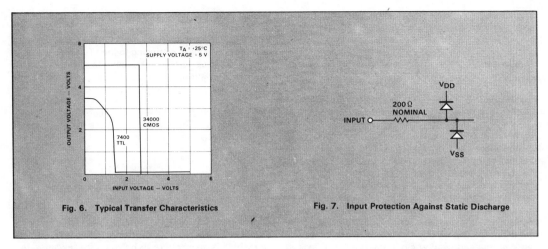

Fig. 6. Typical Transfer Characteristics

Fig. 7. Input Protection Against Static Discharge

Since CMOS output impedance, output voltage and input threshold are symmetrical with respect to the supply voltage, the LOW and HIGH level noise immunities are practically equal. Therefore, a CMOS system can tolerate ground or V_{DD} drops and noise on these supply lines of more than 1 V, even in a 5 V system. Moreover, the inherent CMOS delays act as a noise filter; 10 ns spikes tend to disappear in a chain of CMOS gates, but are amplified in a chain of TTL gates. Because of these features, CMOS is very popular with designers of industrial control equipment that must operate in an electrically and electromagnetically "polluted" environment.

Unfortunately these impressive noise margin specifications disregard one important fact: the output impedance of CMOS is 10 to 100 times higher than that of TTL. CMOS interconnections are therefore less "stiff" and much more susceptible to capacitively coupled noise. In terms of such current injected crosstalk from high noise voltages through small coupling capacitances, CMOS has about six times *less* noise margin than TTL. It takes more than 20 mA to pull a TTL output into the threshold region, but it takes only 3 mA to pull a CMOS output into the threshold of a 5 V system.

> The nearly ideal transfer characteristic and the slow response of CMOS circuits make them insensitive to low voltage, magnetically coupled noise. The high output impedance, however, results in a poor rejection of capacitively coupled noise.

INPUT PROTECTION
The gate input to any MOS transistor appears like a small (< 1 pF) very low leakage ($< 10^{-12}$ A) capacitor. Without special precautions, these inputs could be electrostatically charged to a high voltage, causing a destructive breakdown of the dielectric and permanently damaging the device. Therefore, all CMOS inputs are protected by a combination of series resistor and shunt diodes. Various manufacturers have used different approaches; some use a single diode, others use

two diodes, and some use a resistor with a parasitic substrate diode.

Each member of the 34000 family utilizes a series resistor, nominally 200 Ω, and two diodes, one to V_{DD}, and the other to V_{SS} *(Figure 7)*. The resistor is a polysilicon "true resistor" without a parasitic substrate diode. This insures that the input impedance is always at least 200 Ω under all biasing conditions, even when V_{DD} is short circuited to V_{SS} (selective power-down). A parasitic substrate diode would represent a poorly defined shunt to V_{SS} in this particular case.

The diodes exhibit typical forward voltage drops of 0.9 V at 1 mA and reverse breakdowns of 20 V for D1 and 26 V for D2. For certain special applications such as oscillators, the diodes actually conduct during normal operation. However, currents must be limited to 10 mA.

CMOS devices are shipped in anti-static containers and should be handled with more care than TTL. In extremely hostile environments, an additional series input resistor (10 to 100 kΩ) provides even better protection at a slight speed penalty.

A WORD TO THE TTL DESIGNER
Welcome to CMOS land! You will find it easy to adjust to this pleasant environment. The language is familiar, the climate milder and more stable and working conditions more flexible. Life is slower, but quieter, in CMOS land. It will be a relief to throw away old design inhibitions for the new found freedoms—let's look at some of them.

Fan-out—It is practically unlimited from a dc point of view and is restricted only by delay and rise time considerations.

Power Supply Regulation—Anything between 3 V and 15 V goes, as long as all communicating circuits are fed from the same voltage.

Ground and V_{CC} Line Drops—The currents are normally so small that there is no need for heavy supply line bussing.

V_{CC} Decoupling—It can be reduced to a few capacitors per board.

Heat Problems—They do not exist, unless an attempt is made to run CMOS very fast and from more than 10 V.

But watch out! Be careful when you enter CMOS land! Don't get too carried away by the permissiveness in this country; the relaxed morals may appear fascinating and tempting to you but there are new restrictions that you must learn and obey if you want to be a success. Don't expect everything to be the same as back home, only easier; this country has its own set of rules, regulations and hang-ups. Before you think you have found the Garden of Eden where you can forget all your hard-earned good engineering practices, look at these new problems and challenges.

Unused Inputs—They must be connected to V_{SS} or V_{DD} (V_{CC} or ground) lest they generate a logical "maybe". The bad TTL habit of leaving unused inputs open is definitely out.

Oscillations—Slowly rising or falling input signals can lead to oscillations and multiple triggering. A poorly regulated and decoupled power supply magnifies this problem since the CMOS input threshold varies with the supply voltage.

Timing Details—Even slow systems require a careful analysis of worst case timing delays, derated for maximum temperature, minimum supply voltage and maximum capacitive loading. Many CMOS flip-flops, registers and latches have a real hold time requirement, *i.e.*, inputs must remain stable even after the active clock edge; some require a minimum clock rise time. This hasn't been a problem with TTL since the 8280 was redesigned many years ago. CMOS systems, even slow ones, are prone to unsuspected clock skew problems, especially since a heavily loaded clock generator can have a poor rise time.

Compatibility—The TTL designer knows that devices sold by different manufacturers under the same generic part number are electrically almost identical. There is hardly any difference between a SN7400 from TI, a DM7400 from National, a N7400 from Signetics and a 9N00/7400 from Fairchild. Even more sophisticated devices like the SN74S181 from TI, the Am74S181 from AMD and the 93S41/74S181 from Fairchild are almost identical.

The same electrical compatibility is not yet achieved in CMOS. Many semiconductor houses manufacture 4000-type devices with wide variations in output drive capability and speed. Sometimes even the functions are different and incompatible; two cases in point are the 1-of-10 decoder (CD4028A and MC14028) and the magnitude comparator (MC14585 and MM74C85).

Data Sheet Format—The original CD4000 series data sheets may appear confusing to the TTL user because a range of input voltage requirements is not specified. Rather, this information is contained in a "noise immunity" specification and is not immediately obvious.

Both TTL and CMOS tolerate deviations from the ideal LOW and HIGH input voltages. TTL is therefore specified as follows:

	MIN	MAX	
V_{IH}	2.0	-	V
V_{IL}	-	0.8	V

Any voltage below 0.8 V is considered LOW; any voltage above +2.0 V is considered HIGH. The actual threshold is somewhere in between these values, depending on manufacturing tolerances, supply voltage, and temperature.

Fairchild's 34000 CMOS is specified in a similar way. For V_{DD} = 5 V;

	MIN	MAX	
V_{IH}	3.5	-	V
V_{IL}	-	1.5	V

The CD4000 data sheets, on the other hand, do not call out V_{IH} and V_{IL} but specify a "noise immunity" which is somewhat arbitrarily defined relative to the appropriate supply voltage.

For V_{DD} = 5 V, therefore

V_{NL} = 1.5 V min is equivalent to V_{IL} = 1.5 V max

V_{NH} = 1.4 V min is equivalent to V_{IH} = 3.6 V min, etc.

Systems Oriented MSI—Available CMOS circuits, especially the original 4000 series, are not as well suited for synchronous systems as are the 9300/7400 TTL families. Control polarities are inconsistent; many circuits cannot be cascaded or extended synchronously without additional gates, etc. This will improve as more good synchronous building blocks, like the 340160 are introduced.

CONCLUSION

CMOS has come a long way in six short years, and has taken over many applications previously performed by DTL and TTL or by relays and stepping motors. Most significantly, it has opened up new application areas in sophisticated electronic control. The future for CMOS looks very promising. Minor problems like poor standardization and non-optimal functions will be overcome. The functional complexity will be raised to several hundred gates per IC; many standard LSI "subsystems-on-a-chip" will be introduced and CMOS will be the obvious choice for all slow speed systems.

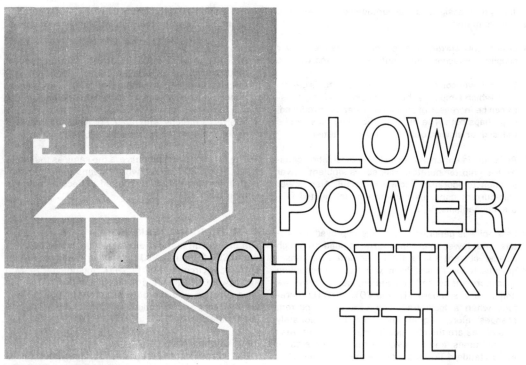

LOW POWER SCHOTTKY TTL

by Peter Alfke and Charles Alford

For many years TTL has been the most popular digital integrated circuit technology, offering a good compromise between cost, speed, power consumption and ease of use. As the price of TTL circuits decreased and the average IC complexity increased to MSI (medium scale integration), the cost and size of the power supply and the difficulty of removing the heat dissipated in the TTL circuits became increasingly important factors. Recent improvements in semiconductor processing have made it possible to not only reduce TTL power consumption significantly, but also to improve the speed over that of standard TTL.

The 9LS low power Schottky TTL family combines a current and power reduction by a factor of 5 (compared to 7400 TTL) with anti-saturation Schottky diode clamping and advanced processing. Shallower diffusions and higher sheet resistivity are used to achieve circuit performance better than conventional TTL. With a full complement of popular TTL functions available in 9LS and in the new, more complex and powerful LSI MACROLOGIC™ TTL circuits,* low power Schottky is destined to become the dominating TTL logic family.

9LS represents more than just a conventional speed versus power trade-off. This is best illustrated by *Figure 1* which compares 9LS to other TTL technologies. Note that 9LS dissipates eleven times less power than 9S or 74S, suffering a delay increase of only 1.7 times.

*Macrologic, PROGRESS, Vol. 3, No. 2, March/April 1975.

The 9L low power non-Schottky family by comparison also dissipates eleven times less power than 74H, and 74L dissipates ten times less power than 74N, but both suffer a delay increase of 3.4 times.

The performance of 9LS is not just the result of Schottky clamping. 9LS is four times faster than 9L at the same power dissipation, while 9S and 74S are only two times faster than 74H at the same power. The new and higher level of efficiency exhibited by 9LS is the result of advanced processing, which provides better switching transistors with no sacrifice in manufacturability.

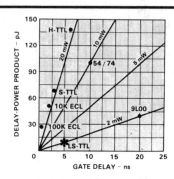

Fig. 1. Delay-Power Product for Popular Logic Families

To the system designer the advantages of this new TTL family are many:

● Less supply current allows smaller, cheaper power supplies, reducing equipment cost, size and weight.

● Lower power consumption means less heat is generated, which simplifies thermal design. Packing density can be increased or cooling requirements reduced, or perhaps both. The number of cooling fans can be reduced, or slower, quieter ones substituted.

● Reliability is enhanced, since lower dissipation causes less chip temperature rise above ambient; lower junction temperature increases MTBF. Also, lower chip-current densities minimize metal related failure mechanisms.

● Less noise is generated, since the improved transistors and lower operating currents lead to much smaller current spikes than standard TTL; consequently, fewer or smaller power supply decoupling capacitors are needed. In addition, load currents are only 25% of standard TTL and 20% of HTTL; therefore, when a logic transition occurs, the current changes along signal lines are proportionately smaller, as are the changes in ground current. Rise and fall times, and thus wiring rules, are the same as for standard TTL and more relaxed than for HTTL or STTL.

● Simplified MOS to TTL interfacing is provided, since the input load current of LSTTL is only 25% of a standard TTL load.

● Ideally suited for CMOS to TTL interfacing. All Fairchild CMOS and most other 4000 or 74C CMOS are designed to drive one 9LS input load at 5.0 V. The

9LS can also interface directly with CMOS operating up to 15 V due to the high voltage Schottky input diodes.

● Best TTL to MOS or CMOS driver. With the modest input current of MOS or CMOS as a load, any 9LS output will rise up to within 1 V of V_{CC}, and can be pulled up to 10 V with an external resistor.

● Interfaces directly with other TTL types, as indicated in the input and output loading tables.

● The functions and pinouts are the same as the familiar 7400/9300 series, which means that no extensive learning period is required to become adept in their use.

CIRCUIT CHARACTERISTICS

The 9LS circuit features are easiest explained by using the 9LS00 2-input NAND gate as an example. The input/output circuits of all 9LS TTL, including, SSI, MSI and MACROLOGIC TTL are almost identical. While the logic function and the base structure of 9LS circuits are the same as conventional TTL, there are also significant differences.

Input Configuration

LSTTL is considered part of the TTL family, but it does not use the multi-emitter input structure that originally gave TTL its name. All 9LS TTL, with the exception of some early designs*, employ a DTL-type input circuit with Schottky diodes to perform the AND function. Compared to the classical multi-emitter structure, this circuit is faster and it increases the input breakdown voltage to 15 V. Each input has a Schottky clamping diode that conducts when an input signal goes negative, as indicated by the input characteristic of *Figure 3*.

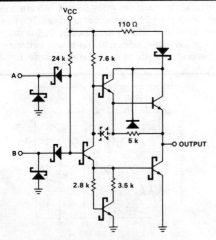

Fig. 2. 2-Input NAND Gate

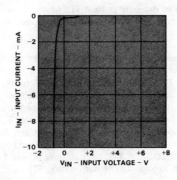

Fig. 3. Typical Input Current-Voltage Characteristic

*The 9LS03, 05, 22, 74, 109, 112, 113 and 114 use transistor inputs at present, but will be redesigned by the first part of 1976 to incorporate diode inputs.

This helps to simplify interfacing with those MOS circuits whose output signal tends to go negative. For a long TTL interconnection, which acts like a transmission line, the clamp diode acts as a termination for a negative-going signal and thus minimizes ringing. Otherwise, ringing could become significant when the finite delay along an interconnection is greater than one-fourth the fall time of the driving signal.

The effective capacitance of an LSTTL input is approximately 3.3 pF. For an input that serves more than one internal function, each additional function adds 1.5 pF.

Output Configuration

The output circuits of 9LS low power Schottky TTL have several features not found in conventional TTL. A few of these features are discussed below.

● The base of the pull-down output transistor is returned to ground through a resistor-transistor network instead of through a simple resistor. This squares up the transfer characteristics since it prevents conduction in the phase-splitter until base current is supplied to the pull-down output transistor. This also improves the propagation delay and transition time. (See *Figure 4*)

● The output pull-up circuit is a 2-transistor Darlington circuit with the base of the output transistor returned through a 5 kΩ resistor to the output terminals, unlike 74H and 74S where it is returned to ground which is a more power consuming configuration. This configuration allows the output to pull up to one V_{BE} below V_{CC} for low values of output current.

● As a unique feature, the 9LS outputs have a Schottky diode in series with the Darlington collector resistor.

This diode allows the output to be pulled substantially higher than V_{CC}, e.g., to +10 V, convenient for interfacing with CMOS. For the same reason, the parasitic diode of the base-return resistor is connected to the Darlington common collector, not to V_{CC}. Some early 9LS designs — the 9LS00, 02, 04, 11, 20, 32, 74, 109, 112, 113 and 114 — do not have the diode in series with the Darlington collector resistor. These outputs are, therefore, clamped one diode drop above the positive supply voltage V_{CC}. These older circuits also contain a "speed-up" diode that supplies additional phase-splitter current while the output goes from HIGH to LOW, and also limits the maximum output voltage to one diode drop above V_{CC}. Since this is the fastest transition even without additional speed-up, this diode is omitted in all new designs.

Output Characteristics

Figure 5 shows the LOW state output characteristics. For low I_{OL} values, the pull-down transistor is clamped out of deep saturation to shorten the turn-off delay. The curves also show the clamping effect when I_{OL} tends to go negative, as it often does due to reflections on a long interconnection after a negative-going transition. This clamping effect helps to minimize ringing.

The waveform of a rising output signal resembles an exponential, except that the signal is slightly rounded at the beginning of the rise. Once past this initial rounded portion, the starting-edge rate is approximately 0.5 V/ns with a 15 pF load and 0.25 V/ns with a 50 pF load. For analytical purposes, the rising waveform can be approximated by the following expression.

$$v(t) = V_{OL} + 3.7 \,[1 - \exp(-t/T)]$$

where

T = 8 ns for C_L = 15 pF and 16 ns for C_L = 50 pF

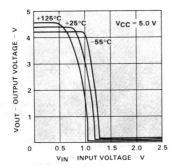

Fig. 4. Typical Output vs Input Voltage Characteristic

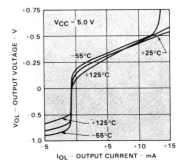

Fig. 5. Typical Output Current-Voltage Characteristic

The waveform of a falling output signal resembles that part of a cosine wave between angles of 0° and 180°. Fall times from 90% to 10% are approximately 4.5 ns with a 15 pF load and 8.5 ns with a 50 pF load. Equivalent edge rates are approximately 0.8 and 0.4 V/ns respectively. For analytical purposes, the falling waveform can be approximated by the following.

$$v(t) = V_{OL} + 1.9\,u(t)\,[1 + \cos \omega t] - 1.9\,u(t-a)\,[1 + \cos \omega(t-a)]$$

where
$$u(t) = 0 \text{ for } t < 0$$
$$\quad\; = 1 \text{ for } t > 0$$

and
$$u(-a) = 0 \text{ for } t < a$$
$$\quad\quad\; = 1 \text{ for } t > a$$

For t in nanoseconds and C_L = 15 pF, a = 7.5 ns, ω = 0.42

For C_L = 50 pF, a = 14 ns, ω = 0.23

AC Switching Characteristics

Low power Schottky TTL gates have an average propagation delay of 5 ns measured under the traditional 15 pF load. At higher capacitive loads, the delay increases at a rate of less than 0.1 ns/pF, as shown in *Figure 6*. Although some drive capability is lost by using high value resistors and small transistor geometries in LSTTL, actually more drive is gained by using non-gold doped transistors with much higher current gain than those in conventional TTL. Even at 200 pF load, TTL circuits are still faster than "full power" TTL such as 9000, 7400, 5400.

Figure 7 shows the power dissipation of various logic families as a function of the input frequency. Under static conditions, only CMOS uses less power than LSTTL, but CMOS loses this advantage when operating at more than a few 100 kHz. At speeds over 1 MHz, LSTTL is the most efficient logic.

The delay times of LSTTL are rather insensitive to variations in temperature and supply voltage, as shown in *Figures 8* and *9*. The average propagation delay changes less than 2 ns over the full military temperature range, less than 1 ns over the commercial temperature range, less than 1 ns over the military supply voltage range, and less than 0.5 ns over the commercial voltage range. Compare this to standard TTL where changes of 6 ns over temperature and several ns over supply voltage are typical. As a result, the designer can use the guaranteed maximum delay values with much more confidence and less additional worst-case derating.

INTERCONNECTION DELAYS

For those parts of a system in which timing is critical, designers should take into account the finite delay along the interconnections. This delay ranges from about 0.12 to 0.14 ns/inch for the type of interconnections normally used in TTL systems. Exceptions occur when using ground planes with STTL to reduce ground noise during a logic transition; ground planes give higher distributed capacitance and delays of about 0.15 to 0.22 ns/inch.

Most interconnections on a logic board are short enough that the wiring and load capacitance can be treated as a lumped capacitance for purposes of estimating their effect on the propagation delay of the driving circuit. When an interconnection is so long that its delay is one-fourth to one-half of the signal transition time, the driver output waveform exhibits noticeable slope changes during a transition. This is evidence that during the initial portion of the output voltage transition, the driver sees the characteristic impedance of the interconnection (normally 150 Ω to 200 Ω) which, for transient conditions, appears as a resistor returned to the quiescent voltage existing just before the beginning of the transition. This characteristic impedance forms a voltage divider with the driver output impedance, tending to produce a signal transition having the same rise

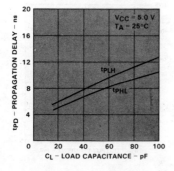

Fig. 6. Typical Propagation Delay vs Load Capacitance

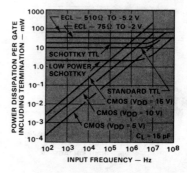

Fig. 7. Typical Power Dissipation vs Input Frequency for Several Popular Logic Families

or fall time as in the no-load condition but with a reduced amplitude. This attenuated signal travels to the far end of the interconnection, which is essentially an unterminated transmission line, whereupon the signal starts doubling. Simultaneously, a reflection voltage is generated which has the same amplitude and polarity as the original signal; *e.g.*, if the driver output signal is positive-going, the reflection will be positive going and, as it travels back toward the driver, it adds to the line voltage. At the instant the reflection arrives at the driver, it adds algebraically to the still-rising driver output, accelerating the transition rate and producing the noticeable change in slope.

If an interconnection is of such length that its delay is longer than half the signal transition time, the attenuated output of the driver has time to reach substantial completion before the reflection arrives. In the limit, the waveform observed at the driver output is a 2-step signal with a pedestal. In this circumstance, the first load circuit to receive a full signal is the one at the far end, because of the doubling effect, while the last one to receive a full signal is the one nearest the driver since it must wait for the reflection to complete the transition. Thus, in a worst-case situation, the net contribution to the overall delay is twice the delay of the interconnection because the initial part of the signal must travel to the far end of the line and the reflection must return.

When load circuits are distributed along an interconnection, the input capacitance of each will cause a small reflection having a polarity opposite that of the signal transition; and each capacitance also slows the transition rate of the signal as it passes by. The series of small reflections, arriving back at the driver, is subtractive and has the effect of reducing the apparent amplitude of the signal. The successive slowing of the transition

rate of the transmitted signal means that it takes longer for the signal to rise or fall to the threshold level of any particular load circuit. A rough but workable approach is to treat the load capacitances as an increase in the intrinsic distributed capacitance of the interconnection. Increasing the distributed capacitance of a transmission line reduces its impedance and increases its delay. A good approximation for ordinary TTL interconnections is that distributed load capacitance decreases the characteristic impedance by about one-third and increases the delay by one-half.

Another advantage of LSTTL is its higher output impedance during a positive-going transition. Whereas the low output impedance of STTL and HTTL allows these circuits to force a larger initial swing into a low impedance interconnection, the low output impedance also has a disadvantage. It makes the reflection coefficient negative at the driven end of the interconnection whenever a transmission line is terminated by an impedance lower than the characteristic impedance. Therefore, when the reflection from the essentially open end of the interconnection arrives back at the driver, it will be "re-reflected" with the opposite polarity. The result is a sequence of reflected signals which alternate in sign and decrease in magnitude, commonly known as ringing. The lower the driver output impedance, the greater the amplitude of the ringing and the longer it takes to damp out.

On the other hand, the output impedance of LSTTL is closer to the characteristic impedance of the interconnections commonly used with TTL, and ringing is practically non-existent. Thus no special packaging is required. This advantage, combined with excellent speed, modest edge rates and very low transient currents, are some of the reasons that designers have found LSTTL extremely easy to work with and very cost effective.

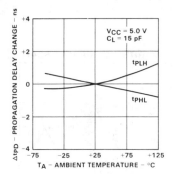

Fig. 8.   Propagation Delay Change with Temperature

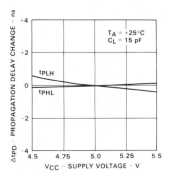

Fig. 9.   Propagation Delay Change with Supply Voltage

UNUSED INPUTS

For best noise immunity and switching speed, unused AND or NAND-gate inputs should not be left floating, but should be held between 2.4 V and the absolute maximum input voltage. Two possible ways of handling these unused inputs are:

Connect an unused input to V_{CC}. Most 9LS inputs have a breakdown voltage > 15 V and require, therefore, no series resistor. For all multi-emitter conventional TTL inputs, a 1 to 10 kΩ current-limiting series resistor is recommended to protect against V_{CC} transients that exceed 5.5 V.

Connect an unused input to the output of an unused gate that is forced HIGH.

Note, do not connect an unused LSTTL input to another input of the same NAND or AND function. This method, although recommended for normal TTL, increases the input coupling capacitance and therefore reduces the ac noise immunity.

WHAT IS A SCHOTTKY DIODE?

A Schottky diode, also called a "hot carrier diode", offers two big advantages over the conventional pn-junction diode — very high speed due to extremely short recovery time and a substantially lower forward-voltage drop for a given current, or an order-of-magnitude higher current for the same voltage.

The more familiar pn-junction diode that exists at the boundary of two differently doped sections inside a semiconductor crystal relies on *minority* carriers for current transport. In contrast, a Schottky diode is formed by the metal-to-semiconductor contact at the surface of the semiconductor crystal and relies on *majority* carriers for current transport (electrons in the case of n-type semiconductor). Charge storage is negligible and forward-to-reverse recovery is extremely fast.

Metal-semiconductor contacts can be classifed into two groups according to their current/voltage characteristics. Those contacts with a *linear* characteristic are called ohmic and are used extensively in monolithic integrated circuits for interconnecting the various components on a chip. Those with a *non-linear* rectifying characteristic are called Schottky barrier diodes. Whether a metal-semiconductor contact is ohmic or rectifying, *i.e.*, has linear or non-linear characteristics, depends on the properties of the metal and on the doping level and the type of the semiconductor.

The rectifying non-linearity of a Schottky diode results from the presence of a potential barrier at the metal-semiconductor interface, which the carriers must surmount by thermionic emission before they can flow through the junction. The barrier potential can be reduced by forward bias (metal more positive than the n-type semiconductor) to increase the carrier flow from the semiconductor into the metal. Under reverse bias, the Schottky diode behaves similarly to a pn-junction diode; the reverse current is small and almost voltage independent unless the breakdown voltage is exceeded.

The Schottky barrier height is always less than the energy gap of the semiconductor. Thus, for a given voltage, the current flowing in a Schottky barrier diode is orders-of-magnitude larger than in a pn diode of the same area; but, the forward current follows the same exponential law, doubling for every increase of 18 mV in forward voltage, *i.e.*, increasing tenfold for every voltage increase of 60 mV (See Figure).

Rectifying metal-semiconductor contacts were discovered and investigated by Ferdinand Braun in 1874. Despite many attempts to understand their current-flow mechanism, the correct physical model was not discovered until half a century later by Walter Schottky. Researchers at Bell Labs in the late forties were investigating metal-semiconductor interfaces when they accidentally discovered the transistor. From then on, most efforts in the semiconductor industry have been directed toward pn-junction devices. Only in the past six or seven years have manufacturers gained the understanding of surface phenomena and developed the metallization techniques required to produce reliable Schottky barrier diodes.

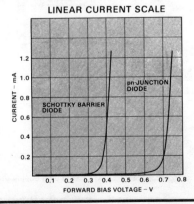

LINEAR CURRENT SCALE

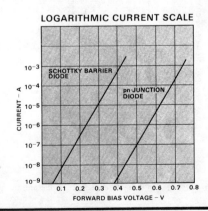

LOGARITHMIC CURRENT SCALE

WHY SCHOTTKY TTL?

With the use of Schottky diodes, the saturation delay normally encountered in saturated logic (TTL, DTL and RTL) can be avoided. These logic families operate by turning their transistors either fully on or fully off. The amount of base current applied to turn on a transistor is critical. Too little current will not turn the transistor on sufficiently. Too much current will turn the transistor on quickly; however, when the base current is interrupted, the transistor continues to conduct until the excess charge in the base disappears, usually through thermal recombination.

The designer of saturated logic circuits therefore faces a problem. He must design the circuit parameters so that each transistor receives sufficient base current even under the worst-case combination of manufacturing tolerances—positive resistor tolerances and low transistor current gain(beta)—and environmental conditions —low supply voltage, low temperature that reduces beta and increases V_{BE}, and high fan-out that increases the collector current of the output stage. On the other hand, he must be concerned about overdriving the transistor and causing excessive saturation delays under the opposite worst-case conditions—negative resistor tolerances, high beta, low V_{BE}, high temperature, high supply voltage and low fan-out—where the transistor may receive ten times more base current than required.

Conventional TTL circuits use gold doping to increase the probability of thermal base-charge recombination, thus decreasing saturation delay; but, this also lowers beta and makes the circuit less efficient. As early as 1955, an elegant circuit trick, the Baker clamp, was developed to overcome this problem. A diode is connected between the base and the collector; originally a germanium diode was used. If this diode has a very low forward-voltage drop, it starts conducting when the collector becomes slightly forward biased with respect to the base. The excess current applied to the base terminal of the transistor then flows through this diode into the collector. The transistor only receives the base current necessary to pull the collector into the "soft saturation" region. There is no excess charge storage and the saturation delay is non-existent.

At first, monolithic integrated circuits could not use this trick, since no pn-junction diode was available with a voltage drop significantly lower than that of the base-emitter diode. The Schottky barrier diode, however, has this desirable characteristic. By 1970, a great deal of progress had been made in the understanding and manufacturing of these diodes. Metal-silicide and refractory-metal contacts assured high temperature stability and the surface effects of silicon were better understood and controlled. All the major TTL manufacturers introduced a line of Schottky TTL circuits where all the transistors that normally would be saturated are equipped with anti-saturation Schottky barrier clamp diodes. These Schottky TTL circuits are very fast; but, since the emphasis is on speed, they consume more power than normal TTL and their short rise and fall times cause interconnection problems.

Low power Schottky TTL consumes one-quarter the current and power of conventional TTL and uses Schottky diode clamping and advanced processing to regain the speed that is lost because of the lower internal charging currents. The 9LS family offers performance superior to conventional TTL while saving 75% of the power dissipation.

WHO IS MR. SCHOTTKY?

"Schottky" has become a semiconductor household word, yet how many engineers know the man behind the name? Is he

1. a famous soviet scientist, inventor of **ТТЛ ЛОГІК**?
2. one of the three Nobel prize winners from Bell Labs who invented the transistor in 1948?
3. a German physicist who invented the screen-grid tube in 1915?
4. a research scientist with one of the leading U.S. semiconductor manufacturers?

If you checked 1, 2 or 4, you are wrong, but this would not be surprising for we researched several libraries before we found only the briefest biographical information on Walter Schottky.

He was born in June 1886 in Zürich, Switzerland, where his father, a well known German mathematician, had a teaching assignment. Walter Schottky received doctorates in engineering and natural sciences from the University of Berlin and spent several years as a professor at the universities of Würzburg and Rostock. He also worked in the research department of Siemens, the German telecommunications giant.

Most of his early research dealt with electrons and ions in vacuum tubes. He invented the screen-grid tube in 1915 and later discovered an irregularity in the emission of thermions, known as the "Schottky effect"— the reduction in the minimum energy required for electron emission under the influence of an electrical field. During the thirties, Walter Schottky worked mainly on the theory of semiconductor physics which, at that time, had the bad reputation of being the "physics of dirt effects" or the study of "order-of-magnitude effects". Semiconductors such as selenium and copper-oxide rectifiers, overvoltage protectors and photovoltaic cells were used commercially but there was no clear understanding of their theory of operation. Walter Schottky established the boundary-layer theory for crystal rectifiers that explains how special concentration and potential conditions exist in the boundary layer of the semiconductor and how these conditions depend on the current through the rectifying junction.

Walter Schottky remained active in semiconductor research for several decades until his death in 1956. He wrote several books, few if any translated into English, and published many articles in scientific journals, *e.g.*, Zeitschrift für Physik and Annalen der Physik.

High Frequency Digital PLL Synthesizer

By Eric G. Breeze

When the FCC first considered increasing the number of CB channels, it was thought that the final number would be 80 or more. Expansion of the crystal-plexing technique, used in CB transceivers for generating the required frequencies, was impractical because of cost, complexity and size. These circumstances led to the digital synthesizer in a phase locked loop (PLL) to generate the necessary frequencies.

The PLL circuit is one of the basic circuits that takes advantage of RF, linear and digital techniques and combines them into a total system. It provides a convenient method for selecting a large number of frequencies with crystal stability without the burden or cost of many crystals and associated switching circuitry. As a result, many features may be added, at moderate cost, to the transceiver: remote electronic channel selection; channel scanning for incoming signals, etc.

BASIC PLL CIRCUIT

The basic PLL block diagram, shown in *Figure 1*, consists of four circuits — a voltage controlled oscillator (VCO), divide-by-N programmable counter (÷N), frequency/phase detector (Ø), integrator/amplifier — and a reference frequency source. Since all of these circuits influence PLL-circuit performance in one way or another, careful attention must be paid to each circuit design to achieve optimum performance.

The *VCO* should have excellent short-circuit stability, should be free from harmonics, and have a predictable voltage-to-frequency curve to ensure that an increase in voltage always causes an increase in output frequency. Long-term stability is unimportant in that the loop automatically compensates for any drift, providing it is within the VCO dc control-voltage range. Note, for this discussion, VCO refers to actual VCO plus the buffer/amplifier stages used to feed the divide-by-N counter and the receiver. Since the VCO is usually an LC oscillator with a varactor diode to control the frequency, it is very sensitive to noise. Therefore, careful attention must be given to supply decoupling and to the grounding points to assure good performance.

The *divide-by-N counter* must have enough drive to avoid miscounting. Ideally, the digital divider stages should have minimum switching noise to avoid affecting the supplies and causing electromagnetic radiation that creates problems in the low-level stages of the receiver.

There are a number of digital *frequency/phase detector* systems but the most widely used type locks on to one of the edges of the two compared frequency waveforms. When the loop is locked, the output of the frequency/phase detector is ideally zero. Moreover, the ideal phase detector always gives an output for very small changes in phase between the two waveforms. If leakage currents exist, the detector supplies either narrow pump-up or pump-down pulses to the integrator to compensate for the leakage. Leakage can occur both at the integrator and in the phase-detector output.

The ideal *integrator/amplifier* has no leakage current and very low noise. Any leakage current shows up on the VCO output as sidebands at the reference frequency and noise appears as random sidebands close to the VCO frequency. The integrator/amplifier time constants and the divide-by-N ratio determine the loop lock-up time.

The VCO output frequency is divided down by the divide-by-N counter and then fed into the frequency/phase detector where the frequency and phase are compared to a reference frequency. The frequency/phase detector output circuit has three modes — it can be an open circuit, or it can supply a series of pump-up or pump-down pulse charges to the integrator/amplifier. The output of the integrator/amplifier supplies dc feedback control voltage to the VCO. When the loop is locked and operating at the desired frequency, the two frequencies fed into the frequency/phase detector are the same and are essentially in phase.

Under these conditions, the frequency/phase detector supplies only sufficient charge to maintain loop lock. When the loop is not locked, the two frequencies at the input to the frequency/phase detector differ. The detector supplies a charge of sufficient amplitude and proper direction to the

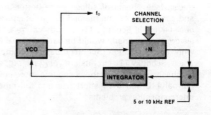

Fig. 1 Basic PLL Circuit

integrator/amplifier to generate a voltage that will drive the VCO to a frequency that will cause the loop to lock.

TRANSCEIVER REQUIREMENTS

The design of CB transceivers takes many different forms — dual IF, single IF, high or low local oscillator mixing, different IF frequencies, transmit frequency generated either by direct frequency or derived by mixing. If a PLL circuit is to cover all these eventualities, it must have a large range of divide-by-N values and must be able to handle the frequencies involved.

Almost all the basic PLL circuits for CB transceivers use a 5 or 10 kHz reference frequency because the CB frequencies have a 10 kHz spacing and are allocated on an odd 5 kHz grid. As the name implies, the reference frequency is the reference to which the PLL locks. Therefore, the PLL circuit cannot be any more stable than the reference frequency source. The reference frequency is therefore usually obtained by digitally dividing down a stable high frequency crystal oscillator to the required 5 or 10 kHz frequency.

TRANSMIT FREQUENCY

The block diagram in *Figure 2* shows two different methods for generating the transmit frequency — direct frequency and derived frequency.

Direct Frequency — The synthesizer VCO operates at the final 27 MHz CB frequency. With this system, the VCO must shift frequency by the IF difference (10.7 MHz in the dual-conversion receiver) between receive and transmit. This requires switching inductors and adds to the difficulties of building a clean VCO circuit. Another problem is that when the transmitter is voice modulated, feedback into the VCO occurs, causing FM modulation unless extensive decoupling and shielding is used.

Derived Frequency — In this system, the actual transmit frequency is derived by mixing the synthesizer VCO output frequency with another frequency usually provided by a crystal oscillator. The VCO frequency needs only to change by 455 kHz; this can be done easily by switching a small capacitance in and out. VCO design is somewhat simpler than that of the direct-drive approach. The main disadvantage with the derived frequency system is that expensive filters are required to eliminate the sum and difference mixing products.

11C85 DESIGN OBJECTIVES

After viewing all the PLL systems and available technologies, it was decided that a high frequency PLL system could best be accomplished using low power Schottky technology.

The design objectives were as follows:

- Mask programmable ($\div$ ratios from 2000 to 9500) for almost any conceivable CB radio configuration — different IF frequencies, single conversion, dual conversion, high injection, etc.

- Binary-coded-decimal (BCD) input channel selection

- Control of transmit/receive modulo changes on chip

- 5-kHz input offset control for SSB applications

- PLL out-of-lock output to detect out-of-lock conditions of the loop

- Minimum peripheral component requirements

Combining a dual modulo prescaler with a counter overcomes many of the difficulties in designing a programmable divider for high frequency operation *(Figure 3)*. This technique is sometimes referred to as *pulse swallowing**. The control or intelligence — used to inform the dual modulo prescaler when to change, say, from 10 to 11 or vice versa — is at a low frequency. Therefore, the remainder of the divide-by-N counter can operate at low speeds, only one-tenth or less of the VCO input frequency.

For example, using a 10/11 prescaler and requiring a PLL frequency of 25.005, 25.010, 25.015 MHz and so on, and using a 5 kHz reference, N is as follows.

N for 25.005 MHz = 5001   The 10/11 prescaler is controlled to count 500 times ten plus one times eleven $(499 \times 10) + (1 \times 11)$

N for 25.010 MHz = 5002 = $(498 \times 10) + (2 \times 11)$

N for 25.015 MHz = 5003 $(497 \times 10) + (3 \times 11)$ and so on.

After considering the stringent VCO requirements — very clean, harmonic-free outputs — it was concluded that discrete components offer more flexibility and better performance than anything that could be built on a chip. Therefore, the VCO was omitted, as was the integrator since it requires very low leakage and noise.

Simultaneously with the design of the programmable 11C85 PLL circuit, a programmed version for a specific CB transceiver was developed — the 11C84. It is a 40-channel CB

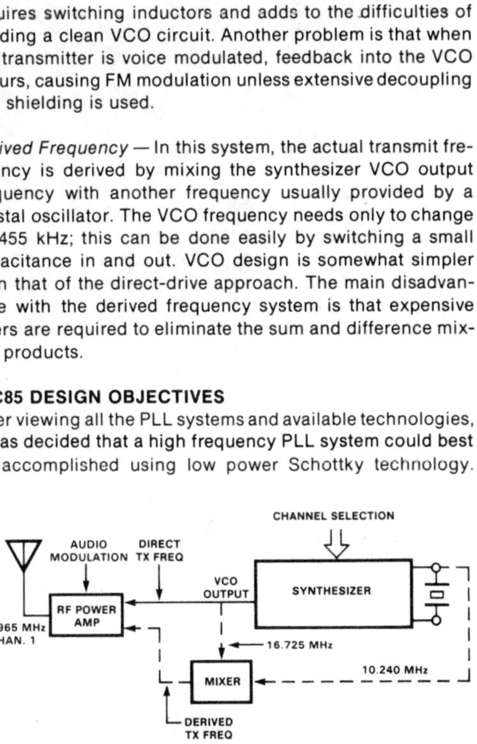

Fig. 2   **Direct Versus Derived Method of Generating Transmit Frequency**

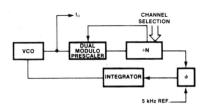

Fig. 3   **High-Frequency Loop using Dual Modulo Prescaler**

* See 11C90 data sheet

digital synthesizer for a single-crystal dual-conversion transceiver with a first IF of 10.695 MHz and second IF of 455 kHz. The receiver section uses a low-injection local-oscillator frequency of approximately 16.3 MHz and the transmit frequency is derived by mixing a 10.24 MHz crystal reference with approximately 16.8 MHz. Channel select is accomplished by BCD addressing.

11C85 OPERATION

The 11C85 monolithic IC consists of three essential blocks — the divide-by-N counter, the reference-frequency divider and the frequency/phase detector.

Divide-By-N Counter *(Figure 4)*

The design of the divide-by-N counter takes advantage of the channel spacing which is always the same, whether in transmit or receive. Only the base number changes between the two frequencies as shown in *Figure 5*. This block consists of a programmable counter and a ROM (224 x 4), which is factory mask programmable and may be considered a 4-bit slice microprogram that controls the programmable counter. The counter includes the following features.

- 10/11 high-frequency prescaler, logically similar to the 95H90 or 11C90.

- 4-bit presettable shift-register counter

- ÷ 2 mode-control flip-flop

- 5-bit (÷ 32) binary counter

- Input multiplexer

The 10/11 prescaler output clocks the 4-bit presettable shift register counter, which is synchronously loaded with a count (modulo 1 through 16) from the ROM output. This occurs when the counter reaches terminal count TC1. Therefore, the 10/11 prescaler must complete that preloaded number of divide-by-10 or 11 cycles before the next terminal count can occur. TC1 also clocks the divide-by-2 mode-control flip-flop which changes the 10/11 prescaler from the divide-by-10 mode to the divide-by-11 mode, or vice versa, and changes the ROM input address.

A 5-bit binary counter (÷ 32) follows the mode-control flip-flop. Its terminal count TC2 is decoded for one of the 32 states and is used to control the select input of the quad 2-input multiplexer. The input multiplexer determines which data is fed to the ROM.

- Channel select inputs — A_0-A_3 or internal codes

- Status of the Tx/Rx input

- Enable input which loads the 4-bit shift register counter enabled by TC1

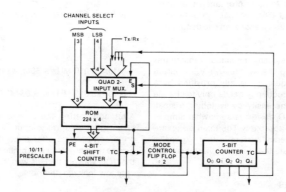

Fig. 4   Divide-By-N Counter

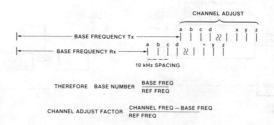

Fig. 5   Base Frequencies and Channel-Select Frequencies

Divide-by-N Algorithm (Figure 6) — The total counter divide ratio ($\div$ N) is split into three products — X and Y for establishing the base value, and Z as the channel adjust factor — each having its own location in the ROM. Therefore, $N_t = X + Y + Z$. The 5-bit binary counter determines which of these products is operational at any one instant. An example for a dual conversion transceiver with the following characteristics is given in the chart below.

1st IF = 10.695 MHz

2nd IF = 455 kHz

Crystal reference frequency = 10.24 MHz

1st local oscillator low injection $\simeq$ 16.3 MHz

2nd local oscillator low injection $\simeq$ 10.24 MHz

Reference frequency = 5 kHz

Transfer frequency derived by mixing PLL output with 10.24 MHz

Frequency/Phase Detector *(Figure 7)*
The digital frequency/phase detector compares the negative edges of the two waveforms, one from the output of the divide-by-N counter, the other from the reference-frequency divider. It consists of the following.

- Digital frequency/phase comparator
- Output circuit
- Anti-backlash circuit
- Out-of-lock output

CB SYNTHESIZER FREQUENCIES					
CHANNEL	FREQUENCIES	-10.24 (Tx)	-10.695 (RxLO)	$\div N_{Tx}$	$\div N_{Rx}$
1	26.965	16.725	16.270	3345	3254
2	26.975	16.735	16.280	3347	3256
:	:	:	:	:	:
40	27.405	17.165	16.710	3433	3342

$$N_T = 16 (10_{a1} + 11_{b1}) + 15 (10_{a2} + 11_{b2}) + 1 (10_{a3} + 11_{b3})$$

RECEIVE

1   $N_{T(Rx)} = 16 ((7 \times 10) + (2 \times 11)) + 15 ((10 \times 10) + (1 \times 11)) + 1 ((4 \times 10) + (7 \times 11))$

    $3254 = (16 \times 92) + (15 \times 111) + (117)$

2   $3256 = (16 \times 92) + (15 \times 111) + (119)$

:   :

40   $3342 = (16 \times 92) + (15 \times 111) + (205)$

TRANSMIT

1   $N_{T(Tx)} = 16 ((6 \times 10) + (3 \times 11)) + 15 ((5 \times 10) + (6 \times 11)) + 1 ((4 \times 10) + (7 \times 11))$

    $3345 = (16 \times 93) + (15 \times 116) + (117)$

2   $3347 = (16 \times 93) + (15 \times 116) + (119)$

:   :

40   $3343 = (16 \times 93) + (15 \times 116) + (205)$

Example Using Divide-By-N Algorithm

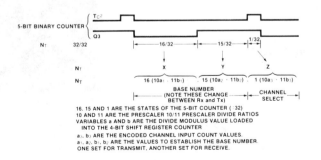

Fig. 6   Divide-By-N Counter Waveforms

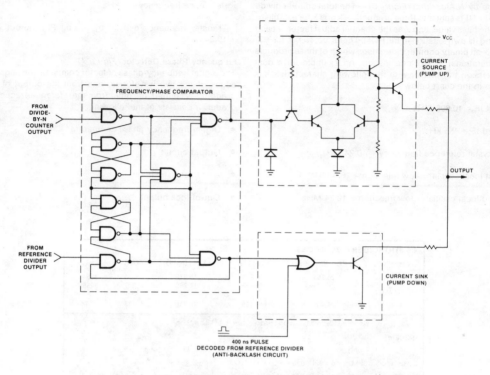

Fig. 7   Digital Frequency/Phase Detector

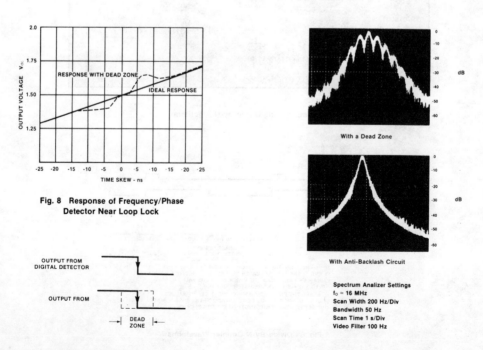

Fig. 8   Response of Frequency/Phase Detector Near Loop Lock

With a Dead Zone

With Anti-Backlash Circuit

Spectrum Analizer Settings
$f_0 \approx 16$ MHz
Scan Width 200 Hz/Div
Bandwidth 50 Hz
Scan Time 1 s/Div
Video Filter 100 Hz

Fig. 9   Frequency/Phase Comparator Dead Zone

Fig. 10   PLL Circuit Spectral Output

The ideal frequency/phase detector will give a linear output (Figure 8) for small differences in phase between the two edges. To date, however, digital frequency/phase detectors have had problems with dead zones of a few nanoseconds due to propagation delays inherent in the design (Figure 9). This would seem to be insignificant in a system but, because of the stringent requirements of the PLL-circuit VCO, these dead zones are important. When the VCO output is closely observed on a spectrum analyzer, 200 cycles/cm on either side of the fundamental frequency, the frequency spectrum shows up as a Christmas-tree display instead of a clean peaked spectral output. (Figure 10)

For example, if the loop is locked and operating in a dead zone, the VCO frequency drifts down slowly; but, before it can be compared, it must be divided down N times by the divide-by-N counter. The detector generates a very small correction signal, "up", and the integrator slowly charges causing the VCO frequency to gradually increase. It then takes a number of complete divide-by-N cycles for the detector to go through the dead zone and generate a new correction signal "down". Hence, the Christmas-tree spectrum. In effect, the dead-zone width is magnified by the divide-by-N counter ratio.

One simple way to stop this problem is to deliberately add leakage to the integrator. However, this has the undesirable effect of raising the sidebands at the reference frequency. A new patented circuit, called an anti-backlash circuit, has been incorporated on the 11C85 chip to better counteract the dead-zone problem.

Frequency/Phase Comparator — The comparison of the negative edges of the waveforms from the divide-by-N counter and the frequency divider is performed by the digital frequency/phase comparator. The comparator contains several latches and steering logic and is so arranged to provide a linear unambiguous output over 360 degree phase between the two waveforms and will not give a false output for multiples of either frequency. When the loop is locked and no integrator leakage exists, both negative edges of the two compared waveforms are in phase.

Output Circuit — The output circuit is designed to provide three modes (Figure 11) — current sourcing (pump-up), current sinking (pump-down) or high impedance (open circuit). The current-sinking section consists of an npn transistor and a resistor, while the current sourcing consists of a Darlington transistor and a resistor. The remaining components are used to compensate for temperature effects. When used in the PLL application, the detector output is fed into a simple external integrator/amplifier to drive the VCO.

Anti-Backlash Circuit — The purpose of this circuit is to eliminate the dead-zone problems apparent in other frequency/phase detectors. A narrow pulse is injected into the pump-down circuit to cause a loop error. The loop automatically compensates by making another error pulse of equal and opposite magnitude (Figure 12). Both errors are closely related in time and can be easily filtered out by small filter capacitors. This technique simplifies the frequency/phase comparator design by minimizing the importance of propagation delays and eliminating the need to match the latches.

Out-Of-Lock Detector (Figure 13) — This circuit is used to detect an out-of-lock condition, either due to a malfunction or a channel change. It can also be used to inhibit the transmitter, mute the audio during channel changes, or it can be connected to a LED display for indication of loop malfunction and for use during loop set-up and test.

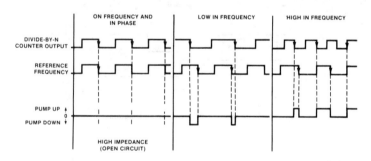

Fig. 11 Output Waveforms from Frequency/Phase Detector

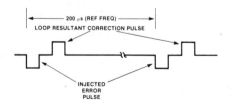

Fig. 12 Output of Frequency/Phase Detector with Anti-Backlash Circuit

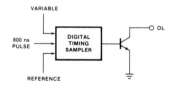

Fig. 13 Out-Of-Lock Circuit

In operation, an 800 ns window signal is decoded off the reference-frequency divider chain (Figure 14). When the loop is locked, the negative edge of the output waveform from the divide-by-N counter rests in the middle of the window. If it strays outside the ±400 ns window for two 5 kHz reference cycles, a latch is set and an out-of-lock condition is indicated. The ±400 ns tolerance allows for small leakage in the integrator and assures that response is made to only true out-of-lock conditions. The circuit output is an npn transistor which is turned on for out-of-lock conditions.

11C85 INPUTS (Figure 15)

Since the chip is manufactured using low power Schottky technology, the 11C85 operates at 5 V ± 0.25 V. However the inputs and outputs have been designed to interface with other circuits as MOS, CMOS and TTL operating up to 12 V.

The channel-control inputs and the Tx/Rx input each have a low power Schottky diode in series with the pull-up resistor to V_{CC}. This allows the inputs to be pulled above 5 V without damaging the chip. Furthermore, there is no need for external pull-up resistors when a switch is used for channel selection. The reference frequency can be obtained from an external oscillator or by using the on-chip inverter stages along with an external 10.24 MHz crystal. The divide-by-N input is connected to the internal reference voltage. The counter input is biased in the active region using an 8 k resistor to facilitate capacitance coupling from the VCO. It accepts sinusoidal or square waveforms and responds to 300 to 500 mV peak-to-peak.

CONTROLLER SCANNER

A new controller/scanner IC, the FCB8010, has recently been developed to provide channel information to the PLL circuit and to drive the LED display. It replaces the awkward 40-channel rotary switch thereby simplifying the transceiver channel selection and control functions. It also provides a variety of extra features.

- Up/down operation at two speeds

- Search mode for busy or vacant channels

- Scan mode for locating busy channels

- Automatic Scan 9 while using priority channel

- Emergency 9 for immediate channel-9 access

- Stores any five channels

- Recalls stored channels

- Serial and parallel outputs for synthesizer channel selection

- Brightness control for LED display

- Single-side-band selection

A remote system can be built with the CB transceiver tucked safely in a trunk or other secure spot and only the mike, the FCB8010 and the display contained in a hand-held push-button unit. The controller/scanner may be used in either serial or parallel operation. Use of the controller's serial output reduces the number of wires from seven to two. □

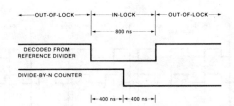

Fig. 14   Out-Of-Lock Timing Diagram

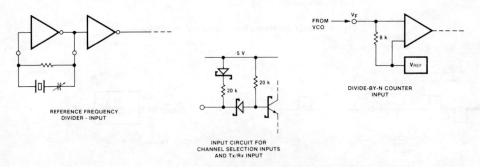

Fig. 15   Input and Output Configurations

F100K, a standard family of SUBNANOSECOND

By J. W. Hively, H. H. Muller and W. K. Owens

Competitive pressure in the data processing industry, with ever-increasing data volumes and new architectures, has stimulated the need for faster processing rates, higher machine densities, and greater system reliability. These requirements can only be met by the use of higher speed integrated circuits with more on-chip integration and multipurpose logic functions. Advanced packaging techniques and optimum system interconnects must be applied to take full advantage of this increased circuit performance. To facilitate system architecture, these high performance integrated circuits also must be less sensitive to environmental influence, i.e., easier to use and have a tighter ac window.

The new F100K standard subnanosecond ECL family has been designed to meet all these requirements. It was planned to provide next-generation system performance and density without total use of LSI while still being compatible with LSI approaches. Fully compensated ECL is used to eliminate most of the traditional ECL limitations while retaining all the advantages.

SELECTION OF CIRCUIT APPROACH

Many circuit implementations were carefully considered prior to selecting the optimum gate configuration for the F100K family. Some of the circuits studied are shown in *Figure 1*. The emitter-follower current-switch (E²CL) and current-mode logic (CML) gates were eliminated mainly because of poor capacitive drive and lack of output wired-OR capability. The CML gate also has low noise margins. The

2-1/2D, EFL, DCTTL and hysteresis gates were eliminated due to the lack of simultaneous complementary outputs along with difficult temperature and voltage compensation characteristics that lead to the loss of system noise immunity.

The choice narrowed down to the current-switch emitter-follower ECL gate which offers the following characteristics:

High fan-out capability
Simultaneous complementary outputs
Excellent ac characteristics
Compatability with existing ECL logic and memories
Series gating capability
Good noise immunity
Amenable full compensation and extended temperature characteristics
External wired-OR capability

F100K circuits operate with a V_{EE} power supply of −4.5 V ±7% to reduce power dissipation. However, a −5.2 ±10% power supply can be used if desired since these circuits are fully voltage and temperature compensated. Therefore F100K directly interfaces with the widely available 2-ns ECL circuits. It should be emphasized that F100K is a *standard ECL family* with subnanosecond switching speed. Major segments of the computer industry were involved in its definition to ensure its acceptance as a standard product family.

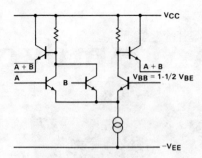

a. ECL Current-Switch Emitter-Follower

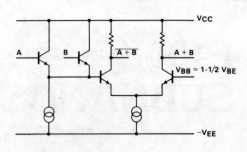

b. E^{2}CL Emitter-Follower Current Switch

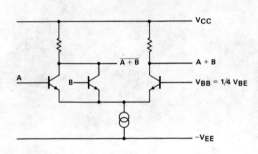

c. CML Current Mode Logic

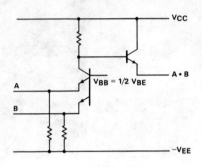

d. EFL Emitter-Follower Logic

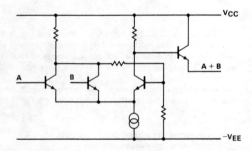

e. FBG Feedback Gate, Hysteresis Gate

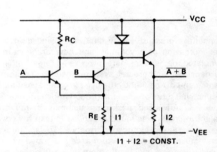

f. 2-1/2 Diode Logic

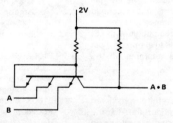

g. DCT^{2}L AND Gate

Fig. 1. Gate Configuration Options

32

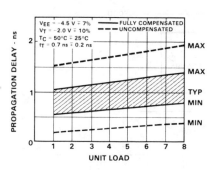

Fig. 2. Comparison of Propagation Delays

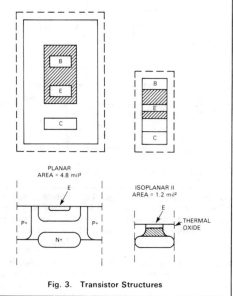

PLANAR
AREA = 4.8 mil²

ISOPLANAR II
AREA = 1.2 mil²

Fig. 3. Transistor Structures

F100K PHILOSOPHY
The four key features of F100K are high speed at reduced power, high level of on-chip integration, most flexible logic functions available to date, and optimum I/O pin assignment.

The high speed is obtained by the use of ECL design techniques and the advanced Isoplanar II process. All circuit inputs have similar loading characteristics to ease drive requirements, i.e., buffers are incorporated where an input pin would normally drive more than one on-chip gate. The on-chip delay incurred by buffering is less than the system delay caused by an output which drives a capacitance of higher than 3 unit loads. Full compensation was selected for the F100K family to provide improved switching characteristics. Full compensation results in constant signal levels, constant thresholds and improved noise margins over temperature and voltage variations from chip to chip, and thus a tighter ac window in the system environment. A comparison of fully compensated ECL to conventional ECL shows a 2:1 improvement in system ac performance due solely to full compensation (*Figure 2*). And, the improved speed has been achieved

at reduced power. This power reduction is accomplished by the use of advanced process technology that reduces parasitic capacitances and improves tolerances, by optimum circuit designs using series gating and collector and emitter dotting, and by designing for the use of a −4.5 V V_{EE} power supply.

Higher on-chip integration is made possible by using the 24-pin package to increase the number of pins available for logic by 62% over the conventional 16-pin package. The emphasis in F100K is to minimize the number of SSI functions and maximize the use of MSI and LSI to reduce wiring delays and thus make more efficient use of the fast on-chip switching technology. Only 10 SSI functions are needed to serve all the system needs presently requiring 25 functions in the ECL 10K family.

The logical extension of the F100K family is LSI and already a function providing the equivalent of up to 285 gates, *i.e.*, a 16 x 4 read/write register file, is being developed.

F100K was planned to minimize the total number of logic functions by increasing the flexibility of each function and by making use of more I/O pins. Since next-generation system performance and ease of system designs are major F100K goals, pin assignment is important and was planned to minimize crosstalk, noise coupling and feedthrough, to facilitate OR-ties and ease power-bus routing. Some of the key considerations in selecting the F100K pin assignments were:

- Locate power pins in the center on opposite sides of the package to ease system design and chip layout and to provide low inductance connections.

- Provide two V_{CC} pins, one for the circuit reference and one for the outputs to minimize noise coupling and maximize logic flexibility.

- Locate in-phase outputs adjacent to input pins, where possible, to prevent slowdown due to feedback.

- Locate inverting outputs of logically independent gates adjacent to each other for the shortest possible wired-emitter OR-ties. This provides an AOI function.

- Locate common pins such as common reset and common clock at pin number 22 and address or control inputs at pins 19 and 20. This is to maximize use of CAD for board layouts.

- When feasible, to create multipurpose functions, mode control pins are used to change the character of the functions. These pins can either be controlled by standard logic levels or hard wired, *i.e.*, tied to V_{CC} or left open

REALIZATION
The fabrication technology of the F100K family is the advanced Isoplanar II process which provides transistors with very high, well controlled switching speeds, extremely small parasitic capacitances and f_T in excess of 5 GHz.

The technology can best be described by comparing the integrated circuit transistor structures of the conventional Planar* process and that of the Isoplanar II process *(Figure 3)*. The top view shows the area needed for each structure; the dashed area is the center of the isolation area.

*Planar is a patented Fairchild process.

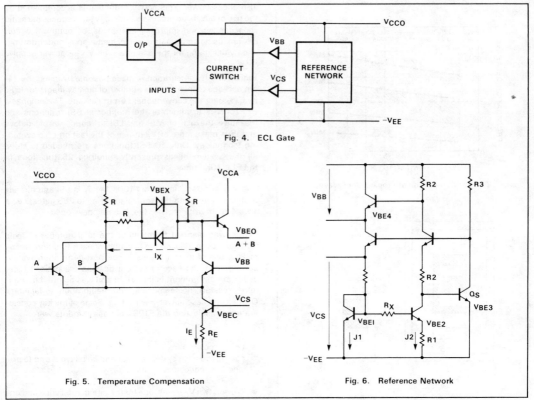

Fig. 4. ECL Gate

Fig. 5. Temperature Compensation

Fig. 6. Reference Network

In the Isoplanar process, a thick oxide is selectively grown between devices instead of the P+ region which is present in the Planar process. Since this oxide needs no separation from the base-collector regions, a substantial reduction in device and chip size can be realized. The base and emitter ends terminate in the oxide wall therefore the masks can overlap the device area into the isolation oxide. This overlap feature means that base and emitter masking does not have to meet the extremely close tolerances that might otherwise be necessary, and standard photolithographic processes can be used.

The "walled emitter" structure allows over a 70% reduction of the transistor silicon area compared to that a conventional Planar transistor. For a given emitter size, the collector-base area is also reduced by more than 60%. The reduced junction areas result in corresponding reductions in collector-base and collector-substrate capacitances.

Since the active transistor area is only under the emitter, all capacitance and resistance values outside this area are reduced. Parasitic values are further reduced by taking advantage of the masking alignment latitude resulting from the self-aligning nature of the structure.

The heart of F100K is fully compensated ECL[2]. The basic gate consists of three blocks – the current switch, the output emitter followers, and the reference or bias network (Figure 4). The current switch allows both conjunctive and disjunctive logic. The output emitter followers provide high drive capability through impedance transformation and allow for increased logic swing. The bias network sets dc thresholds and current-source bias voltages. Temperature compensation at the gate output is achieved by incorporating a cross-connect branch between the complementary collector nodes of the current switch and driving the current source with a temperature insensitive bias network[3] (Figure 5).

As junction temperature increases and the forward base-emitter voltage of the output emitter-follower decreases, the collector node of the current switch must become more negative. Since the current-source bias voltage, V_{CS}, is independent of temperature, the switch current increases with temperature due to the temperature dependence of V_{BEC}. The combination of temperature controlled current, I_e, and the cross-connect branch current, I_x, forces the proper temperature coefficient at the collector node of the current switch to null out the V_{BEO} tracking coefficient.[1]

The schematic for the reference network displays a V_{BE} amplifier in the bottom left corner (Figure 6). Two base-emitter junctions are operated at different current densities, J1 and J2. The resulting voltage difference, V_{BE1} minus V_{BE2}, appears across R1 and is amplified by the ratio R2/R1. Note that R2 is used twice, once to generate V_{CS} and once to generate V_{BB}. The different current densities, J1 and J2, result in a positive temperature tracking coefficient across R2, which cancels the negative diode-tracking coefficient of V_{BE3} and V_{BE4}. The V_{CS} and V_{BB} thus generated are temperature insensitive at the extrapolated bandgap voltage of silicon[2,3] (approximately 1300 nV).[4] RX in the V_{BE} amplifier compensates for process variations of β and $\triangle V_{BE}$[5]. Voltage regulation is achieved through a shunt regulator shown at the right side of the schematic.

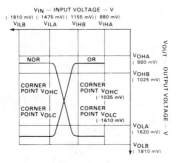

Fig. 7. Transfer Characteristics

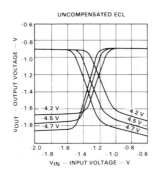

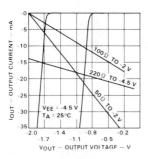

Fig. 8. Output Characteristic vs Output Terminations

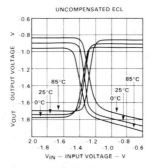

Fig. 9. Transfer Characteristics

REGULATING PERFORMANCE

F100K compatibility with existing ECL logic families and memories permits direct interface with slower logic families and ensures immediate memory availability. The typical logic swing is 800 mV *(Figure 7)* and all voltage levels are specified with a 50 Ω load to −2 V at all outputs to provide transmission line drive capability. However, the inherently low output impedance *(Figure 8)* and maximum specified output current, 50 mA, make 25Ω drive possible at any or all outputs. Alternately, of course, higher termination impedances or other termination schemes are also useful.

F100K exhibits constant output levels and thresholds over the 0°C to 85°C specified temperature range and −4.2 V to −5.7 V specified voltage range *(Figure 9)*. V_{EE} power supply current is also constant over the specified voltage range *(Figure 10)*; therefore:

- Propagation delay is constant versus power supply voltage variations thus tightening the ac window.

- Power dissipation is a linear function of the supply voltage, reducing worst-case power consumption.

The typical propagation delay of an SSI gate function driving a 50Ω transmission line is 0.75 ns, including package, with a power dissipation of 40 mW resulting in a speed-power product of 30 pJ. For optimized MSI functions, the internal gates can dissipate < 10 mW with average propagation delay of < 0.5 ns, giving a power-speed product of < 5 pJ.

F100K has a tighter ac window over the wide range of environmental conditions; thus, the system timing requirements are eased and maximum system clock rates are increased. At the sacrifice of ac performance, the small signal input impedance was conservatively designed to be positive-real over the frequency range encountered by any circuit input. This provides adequate damping to insure ac stability within the system.

SYSTEM ASPECTS

F100K provides high density digital functions that outperform all other families on the market today. How does this increased circuit performance and higher on-chip density improve system performance?

Propagation delay and transition times vary (ac windows) when functions are operated at the extremes of the specified environmental ranges. With F100K, these variations are reduced and more predictable system timing is achieved. For synchronous machines and very high speed asynchronous systems, timing and its predictability are of utmost importance. Due to F100K constant supply current versus power supply voltage and because of constant levels and thresholds with respect to temperature, voltage variations and gradients, speed skews are minimized.

Not only timing but also maximum system clock rate is affected by the tighter ac window. Thus, with F100K the system designer can use a higher speed value in his worst-case calculations. This can be translated into higher pos-

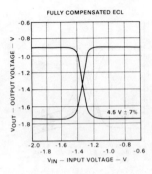

FULLY COMPENSATED ECL

4.5 V ± 7%

V_{OUT} — OUTPUT VOLTAGE — V

V_{IN} — INPUT VOLTAGE — V

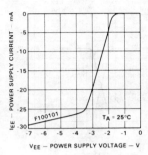

Fig. 10. Change in I_{EE} vs Change in V_{EE}

F100101 T_A = 25°C

I_{EE} — POWER SUPPLY CURRENT — mA

V_{EE} — POWER SUPPLY VOLTAGE — V

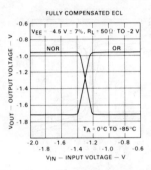

FULLY COMPENSATED ECL

V_{EE} = 4.5 V ± 7%, R_L = 50 Ω TO -2 V

NOR   OR

T_A = 0°C TO +85°C

V_{OUT} — OUTPUT VOLTAGE — V

V_{IN} — INPUT VOLTAGE — V

Fig. 9. Transfer Characteristics (cont'd)

sible system clock rates. Therefore, a machine can perform at up to twice the frequency, solely due to the F100K compensation features. Noise immunity will be of utmost importance in next-generation computers, since much of the noise generated within the system is inversely proportional to the switching transition time of the circuits. The F100K transition time is typically 0.7 ns as compared to 2.0 ns in other ECL families and should therefore increase system crosstalk by the same ratio.

F100K combats the increased system noise by maintaining a virtually invariant noise immunity with variations and gradients in power supply voltage, ambient and junction temperatures. The variation in junction temperatures is much larger than in earlier computer systems because of the mixture of LSI and SSI functions on the same boards.

The initial package selected for the F100K is a 24-pin Flatpak, 0.375 inches square, with leads on 50-mil centers, 6 leads per side. This package was chosen because it offers minimum performance degradations of circuit and system and uses a somewhat conventional packaging technology. More common packaging such as the dual in-line packages do not provide optimum performance due to the loss in speed entering and leaving the package as well as a decrease in system density. With the F100K packaging technique and higher chip complexities within the family, the system density is two to three times higher than that possible with other available ECL families. The various circuits in the F100K family, are listed in the table.

REFERENCES

1   V. A. Dhaka, J. E. Muschinske, and W. K. Owens, "Subnanosecond Emitter-Coupled Logic Gate Circuit Using Isoplanar II", IEEE Journal of Solid-State Circuits, October 1973, pp 368–372.

2   H. H. Muller, W. K. Owens, and P. W. J. Verhofstadt, "Fully Compensated Emitter Coupled Logic: Eliminating the Drawbacks of Conventional ECL", IEEE Journal of Solid-State Circuits, October 1973, pp 362–367.

3   R. R. Marley, "On-chip Temperature Compensation for ECL", Electron Products, March 1, 1971.

4   R. J. Widlar, "New Developments in IC Voltage Regulators", ISSSCC Digital Technical Papers, February 1970, pp 157–159.

5   W. K. Owens, "Temperature Compensated Voltage Regulator Having Beta Compensating Means", United States Patent, No. 3,731,648, December 25, 1973.

SAVES TIME, EFFORT, MONEY

by Peter Alfke

Over the past five years, the art of digital system and logic design has undergone dramatic changes. Integrated circuits of increasing complexity have become available offering substantial cost savings for overall system design. This has changed the classical rules of logic design. No longer is it essential to minimize the number of gates and flip-flops for optimum design; emphasis is now on the total system cost. Before the advent of medium scale integrated circuits, there was a strict design hierarchy. A system design was done first and then converted into a logic design. The logic designer minimized his equations, using all the mathematical tools available, completed the logic design, then went shopping for components *(Figure 1a)*. With MSI—mainly TTL MSI circuits more complex than the quad Exclusive-OR and having less than 150 gates—system design, logic design and component selection are strongly interrelated *(Figure 1b)*.

Treating MSI only as a means to implement a given logic design will usually not result in a cost optimized system. The designer must consider the features of the many available MSI elements at an early stage and be willing to restructure his system and logic design to take advantage of MSI cost saving features. This may, at first, appear demeaning to a pure logician, but it has proven to be the only way to design modern cost-competitive systems.

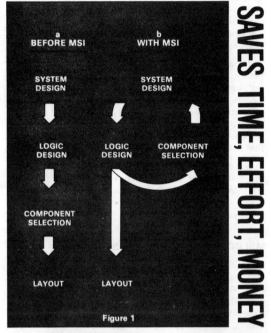

a
BEFORE MSI

b
WITH MSI

SYSTEM DESIGN

SYSTEM DESIGN

LOGIC DESIGN

LOGIC DESIGN

COMPONENT SELECTION

COMPONENT SELECTION

LAYOUT

LAYOUT

Figure 1

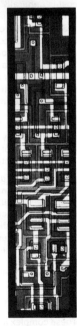

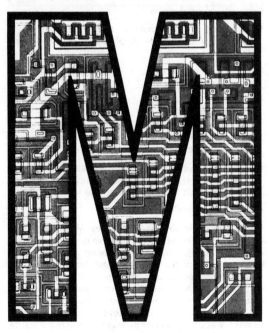

There are some 100 standard MSI circuits in the TTL product area, not counting equivalent low power and Schottky circuits. These provide the logic and system designer with the largest collection of building blocks of any logic family, thus radically expanding his design sphere. Like the brick layer who can put up a wall faster if he uses large concrete blocks, today's designer using MSI building blocks can design complex systems in a fraction of the time it would have taken five or ten years ago.

Imaginative application of these MSI building blocks reduces the role of gates and flip-flops to that of "mortar" between the blocks. The result is an optimized system with more MSI than SSI, with 80 to 90% of the logic implemented with MSI. By keeping MSI in mind when designing his original block diagram, the system designer can frequently accomplish, in one day, work that used to take him a week.

Speed of design is only one consideration. Lower cost, reliability, better performance are some of the other advantages. In addition, because MSI circuits are functional subsystems, debugging and servicing costs are greatly reduced.

MSI COST CONSIDERATIONS

MSI/SSI cost comparisons must consider true total cost, not only the purchase price of the integrated circuits. An unavoidable overhead cost is associated with each IC, attributed to testing, handling, insertion, and soldering plus the appropriate share of connectors, PC boards, power supplies, cabinets, etc. This overhead cost is generally estimated to be $.50 to $1.50 per circuit. When this cost is added to semiconductor cost, MSI offers more economical solutions even in cases when the MSI components are more expensive *(Figure 2)*. The cost comparison is such that MSI is usually more economical even though a number of the gates in the circuit are not used. For example, an IC with 32 gate functions may cost four times as much as an IC with four gate functions. Taking into account the additional overhead costs, the ratio of actual system costs is reduced to only 1.5 to 1. In this very simplified example, it would pay the system designer to use a 32-gate circuit in place of two 4-gate circuits. Whether he needs all 32-gate functions or not is immaterial.

Cost per gate function levels off rapidly and remains steady until manufacturing difficulty causes a relatively sharp rise. Actual system cost per gate function drops sharply with increasing circuit complexity and, as the dashed curve shows in *Figure 2b*, it is economical to use the maximum complexity available with MSI. As the ability of the semiconductor manufacturer to build more complex circuits improves, the minima of these curves will move farther to the right.

MSI SUPERIORITY

These complex MSI devices offer many advantages over SSI gates and flip-flops, both in design and manufacturing.

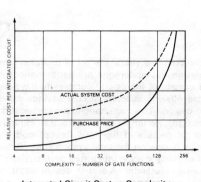

a. Integrated Circuit Cost vs Complexity

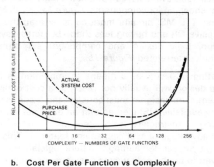

b. Cost Per Gate Function vs Complexity

Fig. 2. Costs vs Complexity

- Increased packing density—more functions on a printed circuit board—simplified mechanical construction.

- Reduced interconnections—solder joints, backplane wiring, and connectors.

- Improved system reliability. Mean time between failure of an MSI is roughly the same as MTBF of an SSI device, so a reduction in package count increases system MTBF. Moreover, the reduced interconnections improve reliability.

- Reduced power consumption and total heat generation. However, the increased density possible with MSI can result in higher power and heat densities.

- Lower final product cost.

Because of these obvious advantages, MSI is generally accepted in the regular and repetitive portions of digital designs. Today, no one would build a synchronous counter with dual flip-flops or a latch array with NAND gates. In less regular and less repetitive areas, notably control circuits, MSI has not yet found such acceptance. Instead, the old gate-minimized approach using SSI devices prevails. To a large extent this is only because designers are not sufficiently aware of the more subtle features of good MSI circuits and the logic manipulations possible. MSI devices can be used to advantage

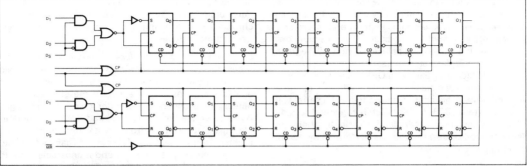

Fig. 3. Logic Diagram of 9328 Dual 8-bit Shift Register

even in very irregular and very specialized design areas. Moreover, the control features of synchronous counters and registers can significantly reduce specialized control logic.

The less visible advantages of MSI are the user-oriented design features frequently provided in a package by the manufacturer. They are not obvious unless one looks at the device logic diagram or notes the features of that particular manufacturer's device. The Fairchild 9328 dual 8-bit shift register in *Figure 3* is a good example. It does not require the use of all 16 leads; in fact, in its most basic form this shift register could have been built using only eight leads. So, with several leads left over, the device designers added extra features to the circuit to fully utilize the leads and space available on the chip. These features include:

● A two-input multiplexer at the data input of each register so that the input can be easily multiplexed either for selection between two sources or between recirculation and input. (pins 4,5,6,11,12 and 13)

● Gated clock input circuitry so that the two registers can have a common clock and separate enables or separate clocks with a common enable. (Pins 7,9 and 10)

● Both True and Complementary outputs for each register. (Pins 2 and 3, 14 and 15)

● Asynchronous master reset so that both registers may be cleared from a common input. (Pin 1)

Also, from the device logic diagrams, it is apparent that many MSI devices are designed to provide for expansion into larger subsystems with little or no external gating. For example, four 4-bit counters may have internal gating to permit the easy formation of a 16-bit counter; four 8-input multiplexers will form a 32-input multiplexer. Such features as enable inputs, decoded terminal count output, group signal outputs, etc., are the type of circuitry added by the device designer at practically no cost to the user.

External devices, such as inverters, can also be eliminated by providing compatible clock and control polarities between various members of a TTL/MSI family. Decoder outputs are made active LOW to reduce power consumption. Therefore enable inputs are also made active LOW because they are often driven by decoders or NAND gates. Flip-flops, registers and counters change output states following the same clock transition (LOW to HIGH) to avoid clock skew problems that can arise with mixed clock polarities.

Since inputs to MSI devices, particularly control and clock inputs, often are used for several internal functions, they are buffered to reduce fan-in requirements and to decrease the number of SSI buffers required in a system. On-chip buffers add little to the chip size and can be designed to drive a known load at reduced voltage swing, thus saving power and increasing speed. Similarly, complete decoders can be placed on the chip inputs adding relatively little to the chip size. Placing decoders on the chip substantially increases the logic capabilities of the circuits and improves logic flexibility.

MSI SYSTEM DESIGN RULES

To avoid problems when using MSI circuits, follow these basic system design rules.

Adapt system architecture to performance required and components used. Use *parallel* architecture and *fast* components for highest speed. Use *serial* architecture and *slow* components for slow systems to reduce cost and power consumption. Use *parallel* architecture with *slow* components or *serial* architecture with *fast* components for intermediate speed requirements.

Modern low cost TTL MSI circuits are fairly fast, capable of operating at clock rates > 10 MHz. Often this speed is not required, but the designer must keep it in mind and adopt the layout, decoupling and clock distribution to the speed capabilities of the components, not to the system clock rate actually used. Therefore it may be expedient to use serial architecture that takes the best advantage of the "free" speed offered by TTL.

Most high speed counter systems will naturally use 4-bit MSI counters in a straightforward system design. However, when the maximum counting speed is slow, < 500 kHz, and the contents of the counter must be continuously displayed, it may be advantageous to change the basic architecture and separate the arithmetic capability (increment/decrement) from the data storage to achieve a better, simpler, less expensive and less power consuming system.

The system shown in *Figure 4* uses only half the number of integrated circuits required by a conventional solution, reduces the power consumption and is easier to lay out on a printed circuit board. In this up/down counter with a display multiplexer driving a 7-segment LED array, the data storage (serial shift register) and arithmetic (adder or Exclusive OR) functions are separate. The result is a class of counters which is economical, but slow. This approach uses four 8-bit serial shift registers (two 9328 dual 8-bit shift registers) to store BCD data four bits in parallel but serial by character. Incrementing or decrementing is performed by a 9383 4-bit ripple/carry adder.

This counter counts (up or down) asynchronous input signals at a maximum rate of 1/8 the clock frequency, which is defined and limited by the timing requirements of the display elements and their decoder drivers ($\approx$500 kHz for the LED scheme shown, only $\approx$10 kHz for neon discharge displays). The clock rate can be increased by using a separate scan counter and holding register and by using full power MSI devices.

Minimize the use of monostables and avoid RC elements in any signal path. Monostables are often used as a "quick and dirty" fix for an improperly designed system. Monostables are inherently linear circuits with limited noise immunity; this is a major disadvantage in noisy digital environments. A carefully designed synchronous system using edge triggered devices *rarely* needs a monostable.

Use extra care with all clock signals to counters and registers and with trigger inputs to monostables. Avoid clock gating as much as possible; use the synchronous enable inputs instead. Beware of the glitches on the outputs of decoders and similar combinatorial logic. Avoid slow rise times ($>$50 ns) and watch out for double pulses (overtones) from crystal oscillators. Most problems with inherently slow systems can be traced to double triggering of registers and monostables due to poor clock and trigger signals. The designer of slow systems must be constantly aware that TTL circuits are capable of speeds from 10 to 50 MHz and that they react to trigger spikes invisible on an oscilloscope used for displaying slow events. A 100 to 150 MHz oscilloscope is required to see these spikes.

Avoid asynchronous systems; convert them to synchronous. Synchronous systems are easier to design, debug and service. They are more reliable than asynchronous systems. A simple, inexpensive clock generator using less than one gate package may be sufficient to solve an inherently asynchronous problem in a synchronous manner.

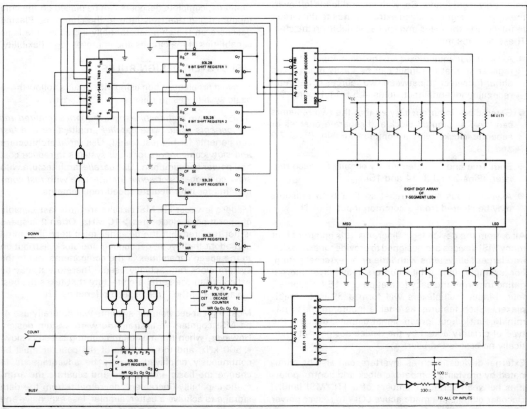

Fig. 4. Serial Counting with Shift Registers

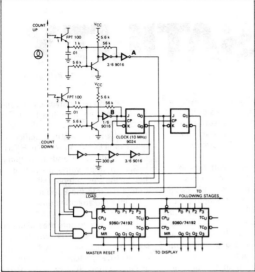

Fig. 5. Light-Controlled Up/Down Counting

TABLE 1

MSI CIRCUITS

DEVICE TYPE	TYPICAL FUNCTIONS AND APPLICATIONS
Multiplexer	Selects one data source Scans over many data sources Reduces number of ROM outputs Generates arbitrary logic functions Generates arbitrary sequential patterns
Decoder	Activates one of a group Routes data to one of many outputs Generates logic functions Scanning keyboard encoding
Encoder	Priority encoding Switch encoding Analog-to-digital and D/A conversion
Operator	Arithmetic functions Logic functions Identity comparison Magnitude comparison Parity error detection and correction Code conversion
Latch	Data storage Memories Holding register Contact bounce eliminators Successive approximation in A/D conversion Data demultiplexing with storage
Memory	Large arrays of latches (RAMs) ROMs (decoder/encoder)
Register	Data storage, shift registers Serial-to-parallel and parallel-to-serial conversion Serial memory Shift register counter Random sequence generator
Counter	Counting events, frequency, time Frequency division Rate multiplication Frequency synthesis D/A conversion
Gates	Logic Clock oscillator
Flip-flop	Counter Switch bounce eliminator Synchronizer

For example, an industrial application *(Figure 5)* requires a precise count of objects moving in one direction. However, starting and stopping of the conveyor can cause objects to reverse direction, thereby giving a false count. A direct logic manipulation of the input signals is complicated and prone to unreliable operation, since some logic states may occasionally last a shorter time than can be resolved by the digital circuitry. It is therefore advisable to synchronize these input signals as early as possible and manipulate only synchronous signals, which do not have timing irregularities.

This circuit illustrates how the two photocell inputs that detect the direction of moving objects are synchronized with only one dual flip-flop and less than two gate packages. The up/down counter operates reliably under all possible conditions, even when the objects move forward and backward in the most irregular fashion.

Explore MSI functional capabilities. Modern MSI circuits are far more versatile than their names imply. These circuits are usually named after their first or most obvious applications; unfortunately, these labels alone do not reveal their versatility.

Table 1 lists the typical functions for various MSI devices along with many applications not immediately obvious by circuit name alone. A synchronous counter can also be used as a shift register; a multiplexer can be a Boolean function generator; a decoder can be a demultiplexer or a data router. Next month's Progress will present detailed illustrations of several of these concepts. However, these examples only scratch the surface of MSI versatility; the experienced designer will find many more unusual ways to use these powerful and cost saving circuits.

Excerpted from "A Logical Approach to MSI",
Electronic Products Magazine, June 17, 1974.

MSI VERSATILITY

by Peter Alfke

Last month's Progress feature discussed the many advantages of designing with MSI. It concluded with a set of helpful system design rules emphasizing the versatility of modern MSI circuits.

Remember, an MSI circuit has many more uses than its name implies. Its functional capabilities, in many cases, go well beyond its obvious application. For example, a synchronous counter can also be used as a shift register; a multiplexer can be a Boolean function generator; a decoder makes a good demultiplexer or a data router. A couple of examples were given in the previous article with the promise of more detailed illustrations to come. So here are just a few concepts to encourage the designer to pursue new and better ways to build more efficient, cost saving systems with MSI.

Decoders as Data Routers

MSI decoders are often used for data routing. For example, the 9321 dual 1-of-4 decoder with common addressing can be used to route two data streams, each into one of four possible outputs as shown in *Figure 1a*. This can be done with any active LOW output decoder that has an active LOW Enable input. When $\bar{E}$ is LOW, the circuit is enabled and the output specified by the address is LOW. When $\bar{E}$ is HIGH, the circuit is disabled and all outputs are HIGH. In other words, the output specified by the Select input follows the data that is fed into the $\bar{E}$ input, routing this data into the specified direction.

It is interesting to note that all unselected outputs are HIGH, which may be confusing to designers who associate an electrically HIGH signal with a True or One signal. In fact, a HIGH signal can be considered True or False, One or Zero, positive or negative logic, depending upon what the designer wishes to make it.

Figure 1b shows how the 9301 1-of-10 decoder can be used as a 1-of-8 decoder with Inhibit by using the A_3 input as a control line, active LOW Enable. It can also be used as an 8-output demultiplexer by using A_3 as a data input. All non-addressed outputs are HIGH.

Multiplexers as Function Generators

In most digital systems there are areas, usually in the control section, where a number of inputs generate an output in a highly irregular way. In other words,

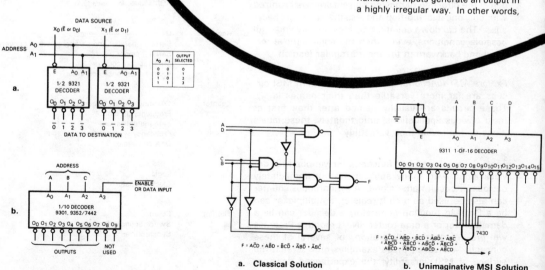

a.

DATA SOURCE

X_0 ($\bar{E}$ or D_0) X_1 ($\bar{E}$ or D_1)

ADDRESS A_0 A_1

A_0	A_1	OUTPUT SELECTED
0	0	0
0	1	1
1	0	2
1	1	3

E A_0 A_1 1/2 9321 DECODER O_0 O_1 O_2 O_3

E A_0 A_1 1/2 9321 DECODER O_0 O_1 O_2 O_3

0 1 2 3   0 1 2 3

DATA TO DESTINATION

b.

ADDRESS

A   B   C

A_0 A_1 A_2 A_3 1/10 DECODER 9301, 9352/7442

ENABLE OR DATA INPUT

O_0 O_1 O_2 O_3 O_4 O_5 O_6 O_7 O_8 O_9

OUTPUTS   NOT USED

Fig. 1. Decoders Used as Data Routers

a. Classical Solution

$F = A\bar{C}D \cdot A\bar{B}D \cdot \bar{B}C\bar{D} \cdot \bar{A}B\bar{D} \cdot \bar{A}B\bar{C}$

b. Unimaginative MSI Solution

A   B   C   D

E A_0 A_1 A_2 A_3 9311 1-OF-16 DECODER

O_0 O_1 O_2 O_3 O_4 O_5 O_6 O_7 O_8 O_9 O_{10} O_{11} O_{12} O_{13} O_{14} O_{15}

7430

$F = A\bar{C}D \cdot A\bar{B}D \cdot \bar{B}C\bar{D} \cdot \bar{A}B\bar{D} \cdot \bar{A}B\bar{C}$
$A\bar{B}\bar{C}D \cdot \bar{A}\bar{B}\bar{C}\bar{D} \cdot A\bar{B}\bar{C}\bar{D} \cdot \bar{A}\bar{B}\bar{C}$
$\bar{A}\bar{B}CD \cdot \bar{A}\bar{B}\bar{C}\bar{D} \cdot A\bar{B}C\bar{D} \cdot \bar{A}BC\bar{D}$

F

Fig. 2. Random Function of Four Variables, A, B, C, D

an unusual function must be generated which is apparently not available as an MSI building block.

In such cases, many designers tend to return to classical methods of logic design with NAND and NOR gates, using Boolean algebra, Karnaugh maps and Veitch diagrams for logic minimization. Figure 2a is the result of using this classical technique to develop a circuit to produce the random function of four variables, A, B, C, D. It requires 1–2/3 3-input NAND gates and 3/6 of a hex inverter. This solution is not only inefficient and expensive, but difficult to design and modify.

The most obvious solution using MSI is shown in Figure 2b. This brute force method uses one 24-pin MSI package and one gate package. It is easy to design and modify, but very expensive and inefficient.

The imaginative MSI approach, using a multiplexer as a function generator, is shown in Figure 2c. This method, using one 16-pin MSI and 1/6 of a hex-inverter package is efficient, easy to design and modify, and inexpensive.

One of the features of multiplexers used as function generators is that, in addition to feeding input variables to the Select inputs, an additional variable can be fed to the appropriate data inputs. Thus, an 8-input multiplexer such as the 9312 shown in Figure 2c, can be operated with four variables in each half.

If a function has a certain regularity, adders or a few NAND, NOR, AND, OR, Exclusive-OR and inverter gates are possibly more economical than a multiplexer. However, for a completely random function, the multiplexer approach is more economical, certainly more compact and flexible, and easier to design.

- The 9322 quad 2-input multiplexer can generate any four of the 16 different functions of two variables.

- The 9309 and 93153 dual 4-input multiplexers can generate any two

of the 256 different functions of three variables.

- The 9312, 93151, and 93152 8-input multiplexers can generate any one of the 65,536 different functions of four variables.

- The 93150 16-input multiplexer can generate any one of over 4 billion different functions of five variables.

The x of y pattern detectors in Figure 3 are practical examples where a straight-forward gate-minimized design would be very complex and usually inefficient. While the use of multiplexers or adders would simplify these designs, the most cost-efficient approach uses a combination of both to reduce package count to less than half of the equivalent conventional design. These circuits are easily programmable for the detection of different patterns.

The detection of a specific number (or a specific set) of Ones among many inputs is a common design problem, particularly with error correcting codes and when reading parallel data from multi-track digital tape decks and discs. Both

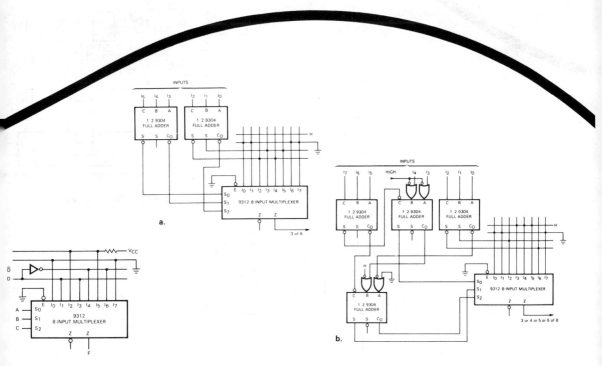

a.

b.

c. Simple, Least Expensive Solution

Fig. 3. X of Y Pattern Detectors

designs use full adders to reduce the number of inputs to four variables; an 8-input multiplexer then generates any desired function of these four variables. The result is an output that is HIGH for a specified number (or specified set) of HIGH inputs.

In the first example, two MSI packages (9304 + 9312) generate a HIGH output when three (and only three) of the six inputs are HIGH. In the second example, three MSI circuits generate a HIGH output when three, four, five or six of the eight inputs are HIGH.

Combination Counter/Decade Register

The 9310 synchronous decimal counter is a good example of the functional versatility of well defined MSI. The decade counter illustrated in *Figure 4* shifts data out of each counter in parallel by decade, with the most significant decade shifted first. To shift the least significant decade first, each output would

be connected to the next less significant decade parallel inputs.

Shifting decades in this manner can be used for:

- Loading or unloading a counter
- Display multiplexing
- Multiplication or division by 10.

The 9310 counts synchronously, activated by a clock and controlled by two Count Enable inputs (CET and CEP). It can also be loaded synchronously, activated by the same clock, and controlled by the Parallel Enable input ($\overline{PE}$).

Since the parallel data inputs ($P_0 \ldots P_3$) feed into four synchronous flip-flops, the outputs can be fed back to the inputs without any danger of race conditions. The counter can thus be used as a shift register.

Light-Controlled Up/Down Counter

The circuit shown in *Figure 5* counts objects as they move between a light source and two phototransistors. This permits a count of objects passing in either direction and allows for *reversals in movement or non-uniform* movement. Each object passing from bottom to top increments the counter. Each

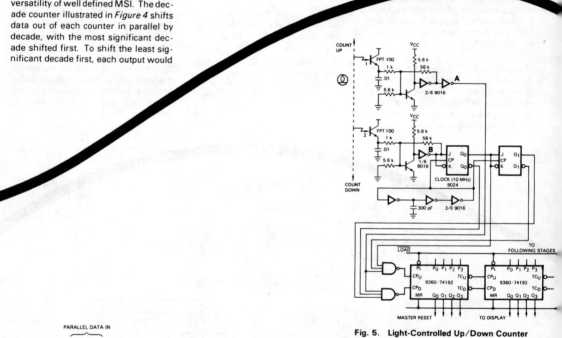

Fig. 5. Light-Controlled Up/Down Counter

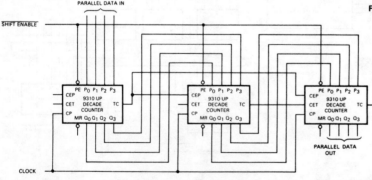

Fig. 4. Counter/Decade Register

44

object passing from top to bottom decrements the counter. Any object passing between the light source and the two phototransistors is counted as long as the object is large enough to cover both transistors simultaneously. Hex inverters serve as a clock generator and as phototransistor amplifiers. The dual flip-flop and 3-input NAND gates are used to synchronize and route the phototransistor signals to the up/down counters.

When an object moves from bottom to top, it covers phototransistor 2 first, bringing line B LOW. This stores a Zero in the 2-bit shift register. As the object continues, phototransistor 1 is then covered and brings line A HIGH. As the object moves even farther, it uncovers phototransistor 2, bringing line B HIGH

again. The next clock pulse loads a One into the first bit of the shift register. This One-Zero combination in the shift register and HIGH level on line A are decoded and gated with the clock to increment the counter. For an object moving from top to bottom, the sequence is reversed and the counter decremented. Even the most erratic forward-backward oscillating motion cannot cause a wrong count.

Scanning Interrupt Encoder
The circuit in *Figure 6* uses only four MSI and two SSI packages to monitor HIGH-to-LOW transitions on eight input lines. It generates and stores the address of the active input together with a Flag output, telling the rest of the system (computer) which input has made a transition. The address outputs are stable until the Flag has been reset (acknowledged) by the computer, but the detection of input transitions continues independent of any delay incurred in this reset.

A free-running counter addresses a multiplexer and thus scans the eight inputs continuously. To avoid timing ambiguities, the multiplexer output is synchronized by an edge-triggered

D-type flip-flop (FF1). The output of FF1 is shifted into an 8-bit shift register (1/2 9328) and is also compared with the output of this shift register, *i.e.,* with the level found on the corresponding input during the previous scan (digital differentiation). When the previous level was a LOW and the present level is a HIGH, a One is inserted into the recirculating second shift register (1/2 9328). This register keeps track of the detected transitions. Whenever the Flag is reset and there is a One in this shift register, three things happen—the One clears itself, the contents of the counter are transferred into a holding register (9316), and the Flag is set ($\overline{Q}$ output of FF2 goes HIGH). The Flag output remains HIGH and the address outputs remain stable until the Flag has been reset by the first rising clock edge following a HIGH level on the Reset Flag input.

This circuit will detect any rising edge on any input, provided the HIGH level lasts at least eight clock cycles, *e.g.,* 1 us at an 8 MHz clock rate. This design can be expanded to cover 16, 32 or 64 inputs by using additional multiplexers and more or longer shift registers. However, with 32 or more inputs, it is more economical to substitute the shift registers with a RAM, *e.g.,* the 93403 16 by 4-bit RAM.

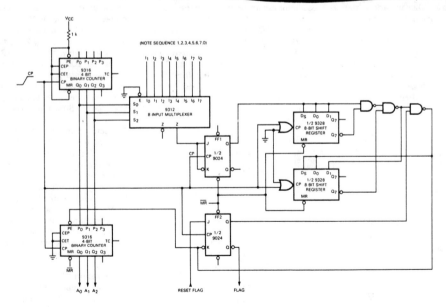

Fig. 6. Scanning Interrupt Encoder

Programmable Bit-Rate Generator

by Krishna Rallapalli

The industry standard Universal Asynchronous Receiver/Transmitter (UART), an MOS/LSI subsystem, has had a considerable impact on data-communication system design. Not only has the UART dramatically reduced chip counts and increased reliability, etc., but it has also provided an incentive to integrate the remaining support functions.

One such subsystem is the 34702 programmable bit-rate generator, designed to provide the necessary clocking signals to operate asynchronous transmitter and receiver circuits. Several standardized signaling rates are used for start-stop communication depending on the transmission medium and other system requirements. The equipment must be capable of generating all the necessary frequencies and provide a way to select the desired one. In the past, this required several SSI/MSI circuits. Now, the 34702 can perform the task more easily and economically.

The 34702 provides any one of the 13 common bit rates on a selectable basis using an on-board oscillator and an external crystal; it also is expandable for multichannel applications. In its most general form, multichannel clocking requires that any of the possible fre-

quencies must be available on any channel. Expansion up to eight channels is accomplished without device duplication. In multiple-device systems, there is no need to use a crystal with every device. *Figure 1* shows the block diagram of the 34702 which consists of the following major parts:

Oscillator and associated gating
Scan counter
Count chains
Initialization circuit
Multiplexer and output storage

Oscillator and Associated Gating

The oscillator circuit together with an external crystal generates the master timing. A 2.4576 MHz crystal provides 16 times the frequency of the baud values marked; for example, 9600 baud corresponds to 153.6 kHz. If the External Clock Enable ($\overline{E}_{CP}$) is HIGH, the oscillator output signal drives the count chain. On the other hand, if it is LOW, the External Clock (CP) signal is enabled and is then the timing source. The External Clock input also participates in the device initialization scheme. The master timing signal, either from the external source or the local oscillator, is available on the Clock Output pin (CO). This signal can be used to drive

other 34702s in a multiple device system, thus eliminating the need to provide more than one crystal.

Scan Counter

The master timing drives a 3-bit binary Scan Counter which, in turn, drives the remaining counter chains on the chip. The Scan Counter allows expansion to eight channels as described later. The prescaling feature of this counter provides another benefit, *i.e.,* it moves the input frequency to 2.4576 MHz which is ideal for low-cost crystals. If it were not for the scan counter, the 34702 would require a more expensive crystal of about 300 kHz.

Count Chains

The Scan Counter output drives an 8-bit binary counter which provides the frequencies corresponding to 9600, 4800, 2400, 1200, 600, 300, 150 and 75 baud. The 1800-baud signal is generated by dividing 9600 by 16/3. The 110 and 134.5 baud signals are approximated by dividing 2400 by 22 and 18 respectively. Dividing 1200 by 6 gives the 200 baud signal, while 50 baud is generated by dividing 200 baud by 4. All division factors except 16/3 are even; thus, all outputs except 1800 baud have a 50% duty cycle.

The actual division by 16/3 is achieved by using a sequence of integers 5 and 6 such that cumulative error after every three cycles is zero. This scheme, in conjunction with the divide by 16 performed in the UART, achieves good timing accuracy demanded by high speed communication equipment. Calculations indicate that the maximum distortion introduced does not exceed 0.78% regardless of the number of elements in a character.

Initialization Circuit

This circuit generates a Master Reset signal to initialize the flip-flops on the 34702 to a known state. If the External Clock Enable ($\overline{E}_{CP}$) is LOW, the local oscillator output is inhibited and timing is derived from the External Clock (CP). The first positive half cycle of the Ex-

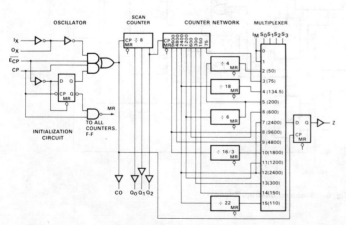

Fig. 1   Block Diagram

ternal Clock is used to generate the Master Reset and all succeeding clock signals are used for timing. This initialization scheme allows software-controlled diagnosis for fault isolation.

The External Clock can be a software generated signal, *e.g.,* setting and resetting a flip-flop. This provides an effective "single-clock" operation mode. Since the reset forces all counters of the 34702 into a known state, simple software can analyze the system behavior after a given number of clock pulses. In general, if the clock were free running, software has meaningful control only at the character boundaries.

Table 1
Truth Table For Rate Select Inputs

S_3	S_2	S_1	S_0	OUTPUT RATE (Z)
L	L	L	L	MULTIPLEXED INPUT (I_M)
L	L	L	H	MULTIPLEXED INPUT (I_M)
L	L	H	L	50 BAUD
L	L	H	H	75 BAUD
L	H	L	L	134.5 BAUD
L	H	L	H	200 BAUD
L	H	H	L	600 BAUD
L	H	H	H	2400 BAUD
H	L	L	L	9600 BAUD
H	L	L	H	4800 BAUD
H	L	H	L	1800 BAUD
H	L	H	H	1200 BAUD
H	H	L	L	2400 BAUD
H	H	L	H	300 BAUD
H	H	H	L	150 BAUD
H	H	H	H	110 BAUD

Multiplexer and Output Storage

All the desired outputs from the count chains are fed as data inputs to a multiplexer. The select inputs for this multiplexer are brought out as Rate Select inputs ($S_0 - S_3$). *Table 1* shows the correspondence between this code and the resulting frequency. The multiplexer output is fed as data input to a resynchronizing flip-flop that is clocked by the leading edge of the master timing.

If only single-channel applications of the 34702 were considered, the output flip-flop would be unnecessary. In multichannel applications, however, the Rate Select inputs change as a function of the Scan Counter outputs ($Q_0 - Q_2$). The resynchronizing flip-flop assures a fixed timing relationship between $Q_0 - Q_2$ and the Bit Rate output (Z).

Three important features should be noted from *Table 1*. First, two of the select codes specify Multiplexed Input (I_M) signal as the data source to the multiplexer. The user can feed a signal into this input, however, the primary intent was to feed a static logic level to achieve a "zero baud" situation. Secondly, the codes corresponding to 110, 150, 300, 1200 and 2400 baud each have a maximum of only one LOW level. These are the most commonly used rates in contemporary data terminals. Thus the rate select mechanism on these terminals need only be a single-pole 5-position switch with the common terminal grounded. Thirdly, 2400 baud is selected by two different codes so that the whole spectrum of modern communication rates will have a HIGH code in the most significant bit position.

TYPICAL APPLICATIONS

In those applications where the Rate Select inputs are static levels, operation of the 34702 is rather straightforward. The multiplexer connects the specified counter output to the data input of the output flip-flop. Because the flip-flop is clocked by the master timing, its output reflects the selected frequency.

Single-Channel Bit-Rate Generator

Figure 2 shows the simplest of all 34702 applications. This circuit provides one of five possible bit rates as determined by the setting of the 5-position switch. The generated frequencies correspond to 110, 150, 300, 1200 and 2400 baud depending on the switch setting. For many low cost terminal applications, these five selectable bit rates are adequate. The 34702 is not only intended for single-channel but also for multichannel operation, as illustrated in the following applications.

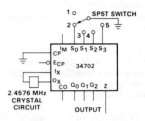

Fig. 2 Switch Selectable Bit-Rate
Generator Configuration
Providing 5 Bit Rates

Multichannel Bit-Rate Generation

Figure 3 illustrates a fully programmable 8-channel bit-rate generator system. Two 4 x 4 register file devices (9LS170) can be loaded with information (rate select codes from *Table 1*) relating to the desired frequency on a per-channel basis. For clarity, circuits for writing into the files are not shown.

The least significant Scan Counter outputs (Q_0, Q_1) control the Read Address of the 9LS170s while the most significant output (Q_2) controls the Read Enable (RE) inputs. Thus, as the counter advances, file locations are read out

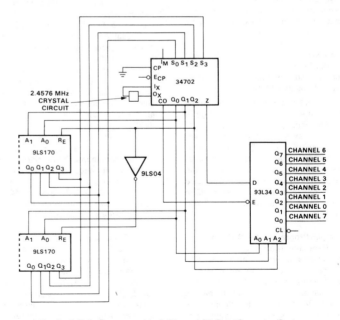

Fig. 3 A Fully Programmable 8-Channel Bit-Rate Generator System

sequentially. The Scan Counter outputs are also the Address inputs for the 93L34 addressable latch. The Bit Rate output (Z) of the 34702 is the Data input to the 93L34 while the Clock Output is the Enable input.

To understand the operation, consider the instant when the Scan Counter outputs become Zero ($Q_0 - Q_2$ = LOW). The same clock that incremented this counter to Zero also

   clocked the counter output, corresponding to the selected frequency for channel 7 into the output flip-flop, and

   disabled the 93L34 latch via the Clock Output (CO), thus preventing any change in the latch outputs while the Scan Counter outputs and the Bit Rate output (Z) are changing.

During the second half of the clock cycle, when the Clock Output (CO) is LOW, the counter output representing the selected frequency for channel 7 is loaded into the 93L34 latch and is locked up on the Q_0 output.

The Scan Counter outputs ($Q_0 - Q_2$), which represent the selected channel, are used to interrogate the register file to determine the assigned bit rate for channel 0. The stored code for channel 0 is routed to the Rate Select inputs ($S_0 - S_3$) to select the appropriate internal frequency, so that during the next LOW-to-HIGH clock transition, the state of this internal signal is clocked into the output flip-flop. Thus, each channel is sequentially interrogated and the 93L34 latch is updated at least once during each half cycle of the highest output frequency (9600 baud).

By connecting the Scan Counter output Q_2 to the Multiplexed input (I_M) a similar technique can be used to implement a system with a maximum output frequency of 19,200 baud, however, the number of channels must be limited to four. This ensures that the output will be interrogated and updated at least once during each half cycle of the highest output frequency (19,200 baud).

Jumper Programmable 8-Channel Bit-Rate Generator
In systems where channel-speed assignments remain relatively fixed, software-controlled channel assignment is not necessary or practical. It may be simpler to program with "jumpers" at appropriate places in the system. See *Figure 4*.

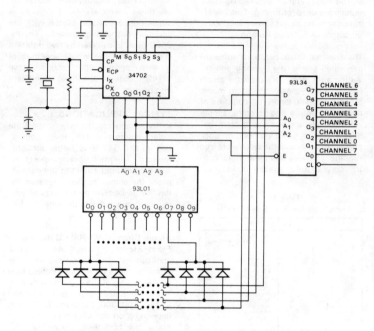

Fig. 4   Jumper Programmable 8-Channel Bit-Rate Generator

In the jumper programmable 8-channel bit-rate generator, the scan counter outputs ($Q_0 - Q_2$) are fed as Address inputs to a 93L01 decoder and a 93L34 addressable latch. The decoder outputs drive the diode clusters which contain four diodes for each channel. All four diode cathodes in a cluster are connected together to a decoder output; the anodes of corresponding diodes in every cluster are connected together to the appropriate Rate Select inputs of the 34702. Presence of a diode results in a LOW on the particular 34702 input; when a diode is absent, a HIGH results. As the scan counter advances, the decoder outputs activate the desired bit-rate code for that channel. The 93L34 synchronously demultiplexes the 34702 output (Z) and reconstructs the specified bit rates at its output.

Clock Expansion
The basic 34702 can be expanded to a maximum of eight channels. In applications where more than eight channels are needed, the 34702 must be duplicated. The device is designed with a clock-expansion feature; therefore only one crystal is required to operate all the channels.

The most economical expansion scheme provides one 34702 with a crystal and all other devices derive their timing from this master. The device wiring is such that the External Clock Enable input and I_x input of all but the master device feeds into the External Clock input of all the other devices. The Clock output of each device is connected to its associated 93L34 Enable input as before. An alternative scheme is shown in *Figure 5*.

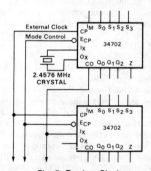

Fig. 5 Tandem Clock Expansion Scheme

The advantage of this scheme is that it can be conveniently used to implement the software external clock feature mentioned previously. Imagine that the External Clock Enable ($\overline{E}_{CP}$) inputs of all the 34702s in the system are controlled by the output of a flip-flop (mode) and the External Clock inputs (CP) of all the devices are tied together and software driven, possibly by operating another flip-flop. During normal operation, the mode control is HIGH, thus selecting the crystal oscillator for timing. Also, the external Clock input of each device is held LOW. When the External Clock Enable goes LOW, in preparation for the diagnostic mode, all devices receive their timing from the External Clock input. When this input goes HIGH for the first time, all devices generate an internal Master Reset signal clearing their counter chains. The next HIGH-to-LOW transition sets the internal control flip-flop and thus terminates the Reset; all counters are free to start counting in response to the External Clock signal.

Pulse Swallowing Revisited

by Charles Alford

Recent developments have aroused greater interest in VHF and UHF counters for applications such as mobile communications and digitally tuned FM and TV receivers. Along with such new applications, of course, comes the need for suitable test instruments and signal generators. Although these applications differ in many ways, they have one thing in common —the need for high speed programmable counters. However, it seems inevitable that for some applications the available programmable counters are not fast enough; or, the counters that are fast enough lack the programming capability. One way of getting around this dilemma is to combine the talents of a high speed counter with those of a programmable counter. *Figure 1* shows such a combination, with a UHF prescaler and a programmable counter (the "units" decade) cooperating in a pulse swallowing* scheme to simulate a programmable UHF decade.

Pulse swallowing has been described as a way of combining a counter that is very fast, but rather dumb, with a counter that is very smart, but rather slow, to make the rest of the logic think that there is a very fast, very smart counter up front. For purposes of discussion, a smart counter is defined as one that is fully programmable and directly or indirectly satisfies a few other requirements. Examples are the 10010/16 and 95010/16 ECL circuits and the 93S10/16 TTL elements illustrated in *Figure 2*. Each circuit has a Terminal Count (TC) output which is normally in the inactive state and goes to the active state (LOW for ECL, HIGH for TTL) when the circuit reaches its maximum count, and stays active as long as the circuit retains the maximum count. Each circuit has an active-LOW Parallel Enable ($\overline{PE}$) input and individual Preset data (P_n) inputs for the four flip-flops. A LOW signal on $\overline{PE}$ inhibits counting and enables synchronous presetting. A Count Enable (CE) input can prevent counting but cannot prevent presetting. Thus the synchronous operating modes of these circuits are Count Up, Hold and Preset, all of which are utilized in either a straightforward programmable counter or

in a pulse swallowing counter. The built-in flexibility of these circuits is at the expense of speed, due to the auxiliary gating, the full synchronism, and the time required to do the housekeeping.

Figure 3 illustrates a conventional divider using the fully programmable circuits. The TC output of the first decade is designated f_2 and gates the f_1 pulses into the second stage. The TC of the second stage is the final output f_3 and also the PE signal for both stages. Following a Preset, the first stage produces an f_2 pulse (one f_1 period wide) after the first K pulses of f_1 and thereafter produces one f_2 pulse for every 10 f_1 pulses. The second stage, which could as easily be two or more decades, produces an output pulse for every 10 pulses of f_2. Treated as a system building block, the overall divide ratio N can be expressed as follows.

$$N = K + 10(M) \qquad (1)$$

For changing the overall divide ratio, K can be considered a fine adjustment and M a course adjustment; therefore, the change in N due to changes in K and M is

$$\Delta N = \Delta K + 10(\Delta M) \qquad (2)$$

The fixed ratio counter or prescaler is at the high end of the speed scale, but at the low end of the intelligence scale. *Figure 4* illustrates a fixed prescaler driving a programmable counter. The fixed prescaler takes away some of the flexibility in choosing the overall divide ratio N and in the fine adjustment of N, as shown in *Equations 3* and *4*.

$$N = P \cdot M \qquad (3)$$

$$\Delta P = 0$$

$$\therefore \Delta N = P(\Delta M) \qquad (4)$$

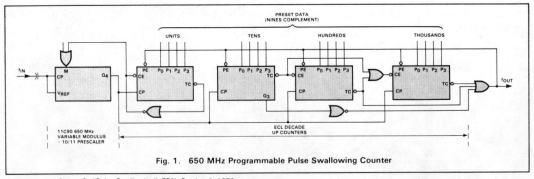

Fig. 1. 650 MHz Programmable Pulse Swallowing Counter

*Nichols, J. and Shinn, C., "Pulse Swallowing", EDN, October 1, 1970.

While fully programmable counters offer a choice of 9 or 15 different divide ratios, the fixed prescaler offers only one choice. In between these two extremes is the variable modulus prescaler, in which a little bit of speed is sacrificed in favor of a little freedom in choosing divide ratios. A prescaler of this type plays a leading role in a pulse swallowing counter. An example is the 650 MHz 11C90 ÷ 10/11 prescaler shown symbolically in *Figure 5*.

The 11C90 contains three ECL flip-flops operating as a synchronous shift counter, driving a fourth ECL flip-flop operating as an asynchronous toggle. A shift counter is used because it is the fastest configuration in the synchronous menagerie. As a concession to speed, there are no preset inputs and only the outputs of the fourth flip-flop are brought out of the package. A third output repeats the Q waveform via an internal converter and a high speed totem-pole TTL buffer. The internal feedback logic is such that the output is HIGH for six cycles and LOW for five cycles of the input clock. An auxiliary input can modify the feedback so that the output is HIGH for five cycles and LOW for five cycles. In either case, at the instant the output goes HIGH, the circuit is already committed as to whether the output period will be 10 or 11 clock cycles long. Further, the decision as to the length of the next output period need not be made until just before the final (10th or 11th) clock of the current period. This feature means that any external logic operating with the 11C90 has almost 10 (or 11) clock periods in which to decide what the divide ratio of the next output period will be and apply the appropriate signal to the auxiliary control input.

A highly simplified block diagram of a pulse swallowing counter is shown in *Figure 6*. The variable modulus prescaler is shown as two fixed prescalers with a switch to select the output of either one. A swallow counter controls the position of the switch, while a program counter provides the net output f_3, which also serves as a Preset control. At the beginning of a cycle, the switch selects the upper prescaler. After S pulses of f_2, the swallow counter throws the switch to the lower prescaler output. Still later, the program counter reaches maximum and causes a Preset. This in turn causes the swallow counter to throw the switch back to the upper prescaler output and start a new cycle.

A slightly more sophisticated block diagram of a pulse swallowing counter is shown in *Figure 7*. The prescaler and the swallow counter are each one stage, while the program counter is normally two or more stages. As a starting point, assume that a parallel enable signal has just occurred and the preset data has been synchronously entered into all the counter flip-flops. This action returns the two TC outputs to the inactive state, ending the Preset mode. The TC signal of the swallow counter enables its CE input and changes the prescaler to the upper (numerically larger) divide ratio. Both counters start counting up, and after S pulses of f_2 the swallow counter reaches maximum. Its TC output becomes active, locking it into the maximum state and simultaneously changing the prescaler to the lower divide ratio. The program counter continues counting up to its maximum, whereupon its TC output goes to the active state to enable the Preset mode and start a new operation cycle.

It is important to note that the divide ratio M of the program counter determines how many f_2 pulses there are in a complete program cycle; the swallow counter isn't involved. The role of the swallow counter is to modify, within limits, the number of f_1 pulses into the prescaler that are required to produce the M pulses of f_2.

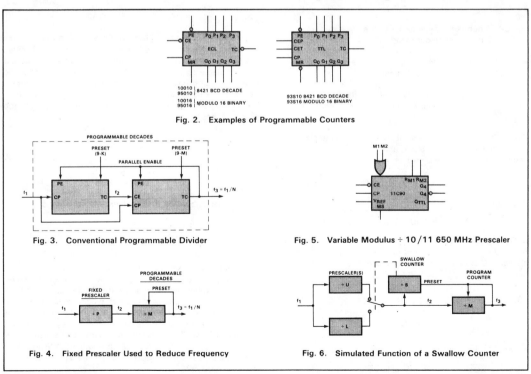

Fig. 2.   Examples of Programmable Counters

Fig. 3.   Conventional Programmable Divider

Fig. 5.   Variable Modulus ÷ 10/11 650 MHz Prescaler

Fig. 4.   Fixed Prescaler Used to Reduce Frequency

Fig. 6.   Simulated Function of a Swallow Counter

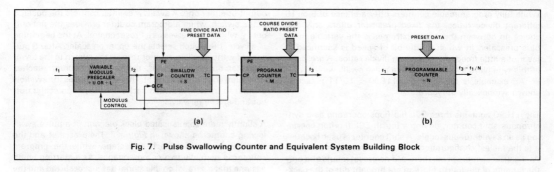

Fig. 7. Pulse Swallowing Counter and Equivalent System Building Block

The divide ratios are summarized as follows:

U = upper (larger) divide ratio of the prescaler
L = lower divide ratio of the prescaler
S = divide ratio of the swallow counter
  = number of times the prescaler divides by U
    in a complete program cycle
M = divide ratio of the program counter
  = total number of prescaler cycles in a
    complete program cycle

From these definitions, the number of times the prescaler divides by its lower ratio in one program cycle can be determined.

M-S = number of times the prescaler divides by L
      in a complete program cycle

The number of f_1 pulses that occur in each of the prescaler modes during a complete program cycle can be stated as follows:

U•S = number of f_1 pulses into the prescaler
      during its upper mode

L(M-S) = number of f_1 pulses into the prescaler
         during its lower mode

U•S + L(M-S) = total number of f_1 pulses into the prescaler during a complete program cycle

Figure 7b shows the pulse swallowing programmable counter as a single functional block, and the overall divide ratio N can be stated from the above definitions.

$$N = f_1 / f_3 = U•S + L(M-S) \qquad (5)$$

Alternatively:

$$N = (U-L)S + LM \qquad (6)$$

In *Figure 7a*, the preset data inputs suggest that S and M are fine and course program controls respectively. The effect of changing S can be determined by letting S increase by one and the subtracting *Equation 6*.

$$N' = (U-L) (S+1) + LM$$
$$= (U-L)S + LM + (U-L)$$
$$\Delta N = N' - N = U-L$$

And in the general case:

$$\Delta N = (U-L) (\Delta S) \qquad (7)$$

Equation 7 offers some insight into why the most popular variable modulus prescalers have divide ratios such as 10/11 and 5/6. U and L differ only by one and changing S by a certain amount changes N by the same amount. Thus the combination of the prescaler and the swallow counter acts like a single, very fast, fully programmable divider. A similar analysis with M as the variable shows that the smallest adjustment afforded by the program counter is L.

$$N' = (U-L)S + L(M + 1)$$
$$= (U-L)S + LM + L$$
$$\Delta N = N' - N = L$$

And in the general case:

$$\Delta N = L(\Delta M) \qquad (8)$$

Combining *Equations 7* and *8* gives an expression for the effects of changing either or both S and M.

$$\Delta N = (U-L)(\Delta S) + L(\Delta M) \qquad (9)$$

Notice that if U is 11 and L is 10, *Equation 9* is the same as *Equation 2* and *Equation 6* is the same as *Equation 1*, since the swallow counter of *Figure 7* and the first stage of *Figure 3* are the same type of circuit; thus S and K have the same meaning. Using 10 for L also means that the program counter can be made up of cascaded decade counters, with each decade corresponding to a decimal digit of the total divide ratio N. This is best shown by a numerical example.

To get N = 4367
with U = 11
and L = 10,
make S = 7
and M = 436

As a check, substitute these values into *Equation 5*.

$$N = U•S + L (M-S)$$
$$= (11) 7 + 10 (436-7) = 77 + 4290$$
$$= 4367.$$

Thus, the pulse swallowing counter is programmed in the same way as the divider of *Figure 3*. A practical limitation on the pulse swallowing technique is that M cannot be less than S; otherwise the program counter would reach maximum count before the swallow counter, and the latter would not have a chance to change the divide ratio of the prescaler before being preset. The prescaler would then operate the same as the fixed prescaler of *Figure 4*. Thus with decade programming, the practical minimum divide ratio for a pulse swallowing counter is 90.

KEY BOARD ENCODERS

by Peter Alfke

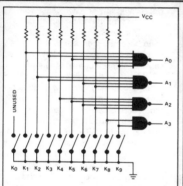

Fig. 1. Keyboard Encoder with Gates

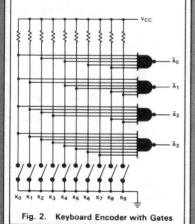

Fig. 2. Keyboard Encoder with Gates

Keyboards are becoming increasingly popular as input devices for digital systems, often as substitutes for banks of rotary switches or push-buttons. Usually only one key is activated at a time. The address of the active key can then be encoded and transmitted to the digital system on fewer wires.

The design of an encoder for a full ASCII keyboard is fairly well known, since several semiconductor manufacturers sell complete MOS/LSI keyboard encoders that are tailored to the ASCII keyboard requirements. For smaller keyboards, however, these LSI chips represent an expensive overkill and may also be too inflexible. Therefore, it seems worthwhile to explore several cost-effective designs for small keyboards with 10 to 64 keys that encode the key strokes in a binary code and provide the proper interface to a digital system.

The design of a keyboard encoder must cope with the following problems:

- Inherently asynchronous key depressions that occur at a very limited rate (< 10 per second) but can change at any moment.

- Mechanical contact bounce whenever contact is made.

- Two-key rollover which results when the second entry key is depressed before the previous one has been released.

10-Key Encoding Using Gates

The simplest, but not the best approach to keyboard encoding is to use TTL NAND gates that require contact closures to ground. This leads to the most straightforward design in *Figure 1* which is not recommended for the following reasons:

- It does not distinguish between "all keys up" and "key zero down".

- It generates erroneous output codes if more than one key is depressed.

- It is difficult to debounce.

- It requires many input pull-up resistors.

- Its parts count becomes prohibitive for more than 16 contacts.

The design in *Figure 2* eliminates the first of these disadvantages by generating an active LOW output signal (address). Thus, the "all keys up" condition generates an "all LOW" output equivalent to a binary 15, and therefore different from "zero". All the other disadvantages remain and obviously this design is only meaningful for up to 15 keys.

Condensed version of this article appeared in Electronic Design, Jan. 18, 1975.

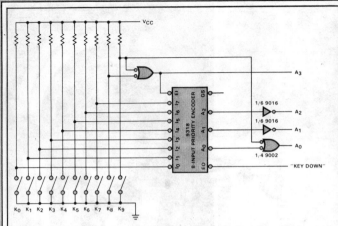

Fig. 3. Keyboard Encoder with Priority Encoder

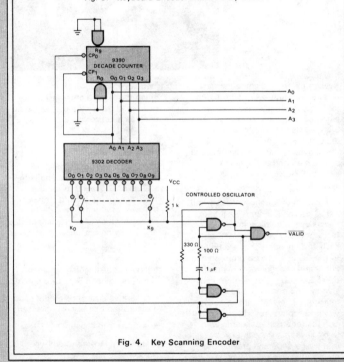

Fig. 4. Key Scanning Encoder

10-Key Encoding Using a Priority Encoder

Figure 3 shows how 10 keys can be encoded with a 9318 priority encoder plus one gate package. A 2-input NAND gate disables the 9318 when inputs $\bar{I}_8$ or $\bar{I}_9$ are LOW and is used to produce the A_3 output code. When $\bar{I}_8$ or $\bar{I}_9$ are not LOW, the encoder is enabled and encodes input $\bar{I}_0 - \bar{I}_7$ normally. This decimal encoder has active HIGH outputs representing the highest order input. However, just inserting the two

inverters in the A_0 and A_3 lines instead of the A_1 and A_2 lines provides active LOW outputs.

The Enable Output (EO) is LOW if no key is activated. If more than one key is depressed, only the key with the highest number is encoded. This is not as desirable as two-key rollover, but it prevents the generating of erroneous codes. Note, however, that wrong output codes can be generated for a few nanoseconds following any key depression. This

circuit is better than the gate configurations, but it is still difficult to debounce, requires pull-up resistors on all inputs, and becomes prohibitively expensive for more than 16 keys.

To solve these problems both economically and reliably, a better approach is to abandon these combinatorial ideas and use a sequential scanning method instead. This increases the response time from nanoseconds to milliseconds which is generally acceptable.

A Simple 10-Key Scanning Encoder

A scanning encoder consists of a counter, decoder, contacts, and a controlled oscillator *(Figure 4)*. When all keys are up, the oscillator free runs at $\approx$ 1 kHz causing the counter to count modulo 10 and activate the open-collector outputs, one after the other, of the 9302 1-of-10 decoder. The 10-key contacts are connected to the decoder outputs and their common terminal is pulled to V_{CC} through a 1 kΩ resistor.

Depressing any key will cause this common terminal to be pulled close to ground as soon as the counter state becomes identical to the number of the depressed key. This causes the oscillator to stop with a LOW level on the clock input to the 9390 decade counter. The oscillator time constant provides some bounce protection; however, under unfavorable circumstances the counter might make one additional complete scan before settling. A LOW output signal on the Valid Code line indicates that the counter output corresponds to the number of the depressed key.

Two-key rollover protection is inherent in this design. If a second key is depressed while the counter is still locked onto the first one, the second key is ignored until the first one is released, and the counter searches for the other key depression. If two or more keys are depressed simultaneously within 10 ms, or if two additional keys are depressed while the first one is still down, the system cannot resolve the entry sequence but still produces valid codes.

This simple scanning circuit has only a couple of remaining drawbacks—lack of perfect bounce suppression and difficulty in distinguishing between key bounce and repetitive entry of the same key. To solve these problems, a retriggerable monostable can be

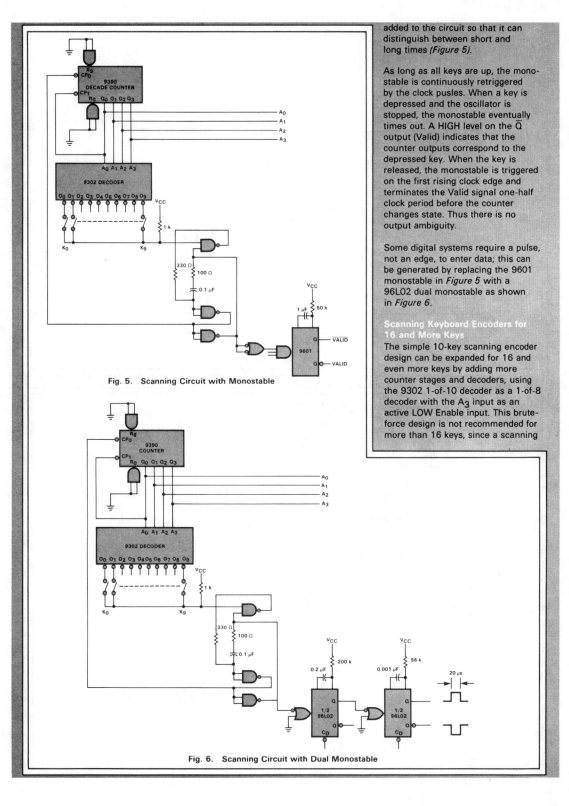

added to the circuit so that it can distinguish between short and long times *(Figure 5)*.

As long as all keys are up, the monostable is continuously retriggered by the clock pusles. When a key is depressed and the oscillator is stopped, the monostable eventually times out. A HIGH level on the $\overline{Q}$ output (Valid) indicates that the counter outputs correspond to the depressed key. When the key is released, the monostable is triggered on the first rising clock edge and terminates the Valid signal one-half clock period before the counter changes state. Thus there is no output ambiguity.

Some digital systems require a pulse, not an edge, to enter data; this can be generated by replacing the 9601 monostable in *Figure 5* with a 96L02 dual monostable as shown in *Figure 6*.

Scanning Keyboard Encoders for 16 and More Keys

The simple 10-key scanning encoder design can be expanded for 16 and even more keys by adding more counter stages and decoders, using the 9302 1-of-10 decoder as a 1-of-8 decoder with the A_3 input as an active LOW Enable input. This brute-force design is not recommended for more than 16 keys, since a scanning

Fig. 5. Scanning Circuit with Monostable

Fig. 6. Scanning Circuit with Dual Monostable

55

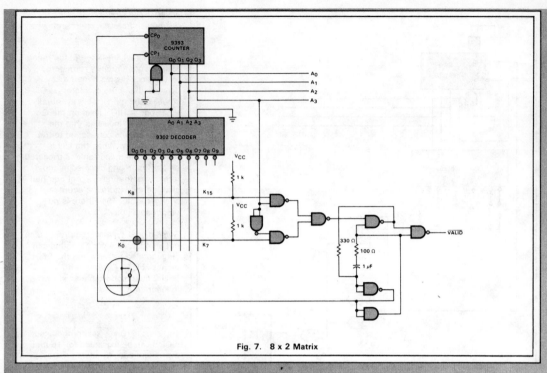

Fig. 7.   8 x 2 Matrix

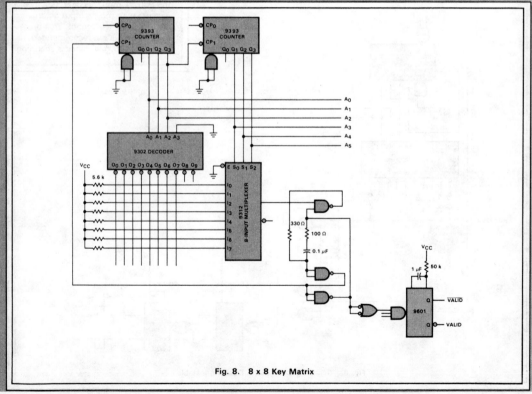

Fig. 8.   8 x 8 Key Matrix

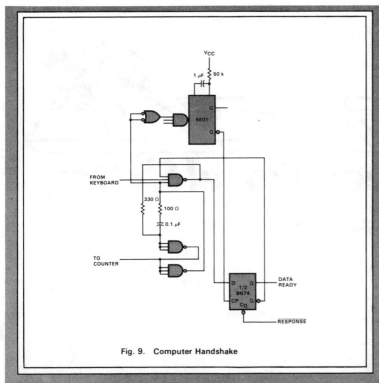

matrix encoder requires fewer parts and significantly fewer wires. An 8 x 2 matrix encoder for 16 keys and an 8 x 8 matrix encoder for 64 keys are shown in *Figures 7* and *8* respectively. Note that these circuits require no diodes at the matrix intersections, since no more than one or two keys should be depressed simultaneously. If three or more keys are depressed, a wrong code could be generated; however, this is no real drawback since the system cannot even resolve the sequence in which these keys were depressed.

Computer Handshake

Some digital systems (computers) require a more sophisticated inter-face between the keyboard encoder (peripheral) and the receiving logic (processor); *Figure 9* shows one possible design. When a key is detected and the bounce has settled, the monostable times out and sets the edge-triggered flip-flop. This generates a Ready signal to the computer and also prevents the scanner from advancing, even if the key is released, until the computer has acknowledged the received data with a strobe pulse which resets the Ready flip-flop.

Fig. 9. Computer Handshake

SYNC BURST DETECTION
IN DISK CONTROLLERS . . . USE THE 9401

by Krishna Rallapalli

The 9401 monolithic CRC generator / checker provides a choice of eight generator poly-nomials selected by appropriate logic levels on three lines, S_0, S_1 and S_2*. Although its use in disk controllers for error checking is well known, the utilization of the 9401 for sync pattern detection is less obvious. A scheme is presented here for using the 9401 for both data validation and sync pattern detection in disk controllers.

"All Zero" preamble followed by a known length of "all Ones" sync burst is commonly used in disk formats. For discussion, assume that a 16-bit sync burst is used. Since it consists of two bytes, the second byte can be considered as check bits for the first byte using a $x^8 + 1$ as the generator polynomial.

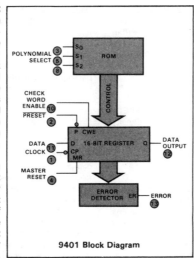

9401 Block Diagram

The 9401 is reset, the CWE input is HIGH and $x^8 + 1$ is declared as the polynomial before the read gate is enabled. The 9401 remains cleared during the preamble and therefore the Error output is LOW. As soon as the first sync bit is entered, this output goes HIGH, not going LOW again until the 16th sync bit is entered. If the 9401 does not indicate a LOW level on its Error output after the 16th bit has been entered, then a sync error has occurred. After successful sync detection, the polynomial select code can be changed from $x^8 + 1$ to the desired polynomial for data validation. This simple scheme, using the 9401, can be investigated for use with more complex and larger sync bursts.

*"Cyclic Redundancy Check Circuit on a Single Chip," PROGRESS; Vol. 3, No. 1; Jan. / Feb. 1975.

High-Speed Barrel Shifter

Expansion Technique Uses ECL Shift Matrix

by Jim Hively

High-speed ECL logic is replacing TTL in many new computer systems now being manufactured or designed. In the past, designers of ECL-based computer systems were forced to resort to smaller, less cost-effective SSI and MSI circuits to implement their designs. Today, with the introduction of the F100K series of MSI/LSI subnanosecond ECL circuits, high-speed computer system design is considerably more cost effective.

Until recently, barrel shifting — a data formatting process found in most large computers — had been implemented in ECL-based systems using a few SSI gates and many 8-input MSI multiplexers. The result was fast but bulky circuitry. With the expansion of the F100K series of ultra-high-speed ECL circuits, an alternative is now available. The F100158 8-bit shift matrix, designed for barrel shifting, bus multiplexing and word masking/merging applications, replaces eight 8 input ECL MSI multiplexers to achieve ultra high speed while occupying minimum pc-board real estate. Other advantages include cost savings and lower power consumption.

In barrel shifting applications, a few F100158s can replace a great many other circuits for a considerably more cost-effective circuit design. Prior to the F100158, more than 200 8-input multiplexers and gates were required for the 0-63 place barrel shift. With the F100158, only 25 chips are needed — a net savings of approximately 175 packages with no sacrifice in speed or efficiency.

DEVICE DESCRIPTION

The F100158 is typical of the F100K subnanosecond ECL family of 24-pin circuits designed for ultra-fast high-density logic applications. The F100158 contains a combinatorial circuit capable of shifting an 8-bit word from 0-7 places with a typical throughput delay of 1.8 ns. Three internally decoded control lines (S_0, S_1, S_2) define the number of places that an 8-bit word, present at the inputs ($D_0 - D_7$), is shifted to the left. A mode control input (M) selects either the "LOW-backfill" or "end-around" shift modes. When M is LOW, all the outputs to the right of the one that contains D_7 are forced LOW. If M is HIGH, an end-around shift causes D_0 to appear at the output to the right of the one that contains D_7 — the operation commonly referred to as barrel shifting. The truth table for the F100158 *(Table 1)* illustrates both LOW-backfill and end-around shifting.

INPUTS				OUTPUTS							
M	S_0	S_1	S_2	Z_0	Z_1	Z_2	Z_3	Z_4	Z_4	Z_6	Z_7
X	L	L	L	D_0	D_1	D_2	D_3	D_4	D_5	D_6	D_7
L	H	L	L	D_1	D_2	D_3	D_4	D_5	D_6	D_7	L
L	L	H	L	D_2	D_3	D_4	D_5	D_6	D_7	L	L
L	H	H	L	D_3	D_4	D_5	D_6	D_7	L	L	L
L	L	L	H	D_4	D_5	D_6	D_7	L	L	L	L
L	H	L	H	D_5	D_6	D_7	L	L	L	L	L
L	L	H	H	D_6	D_7	L	L	L	L	L	L
L	H	H	H	D_7	L	L	L	L	L	L	L
H	H	L	L	D_1	D_2	D_3	D_4	D_5	D_6	D_7	D_0
H	L	H	L	D_2	D_3	D_4	D_5	D_6	D_7	D_0	D_1
H	H	H	L	D_3	D_4	D_5	D_6	D_7	D_0	D_1	D_2
H	L	L	H	D_4	D_5	D_6	D_7	D_0	D_1	D_2	D_3
H	H	L	H	D_5	D_6	D_7	D_0	D_1	D_2	D_3	D_4
H	L	H	H	D_6	D_7	D_0	D_1	D_2	D_3	D_4	D_5
H	H	H	H	D_7	D_0	D_1	D_2	D_3	D_4	D_5	D_6

H = HIGH voltage level
L = LOW voltage level
X = Immaterial

Table 1

Used purely as an 8-bit shifter, however, the F100158 has a limited number of applications since most computer systems use a longer word and the F100158 is not directly expandable. An initial 24-pin limitation placed on the design of the F100K family precluded direct expansion for longer word length (direct expansion capability would require a 40-pin package). If cleverly used, however, several F100158 8-bit shifters can be combined to accommodate any word length with a minimum of external logic. For example, a 64-bit word can be shifted up to 63 places using 24 F100158s and only a single package of OR gates.

The following technique uses two ranks of F100158s to shift a 64-bit word from 0 to 63 places. Although two stage delays are required (one for each rank), the total shift only takes about 4 ns. This technique performs a bit shift on each 8-bit byte in the first rank and then a modulo-8 byte shift on the 64-bit word in the second rank.

BASIC 16-BIT 0 − 7 PLACE SHIFTER

Figure 1 shows the basic 0 − 7 place shift technique which can be expanded to accommodate any word length. Each 8-bit byte requires a pair of F100158s operating in the LOW backfill mode. The address lines for each pair of ICs are driven

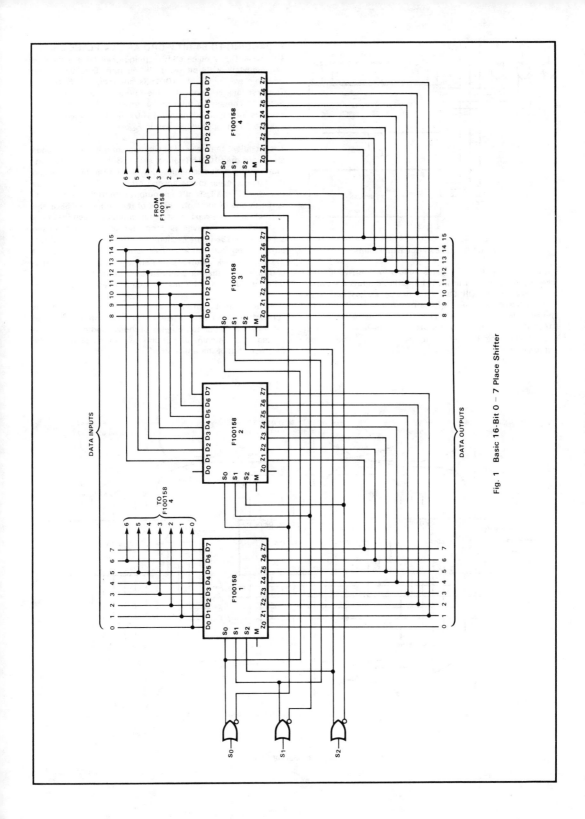

Fig. 1   Basic 16-Bit 0 – 7 Place Shifter

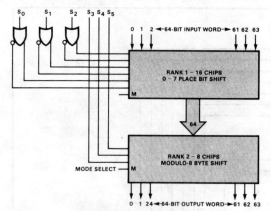

Fig. 2 64-Bit 0 – 63 Place Barrel Shifter

EXPANDING TO 64-BIT WORD AND 64-PLACE SHIFT

This basic 0 – 7 place shift technique can be expanded to accommodate a 64-bit word shifted from 0 to 63 places, however two ranks of F100158s are required *(Figure 2)*. The first rank is identical to the one illustrated in *Figure 1* except it contains a total of 16 devices. The second rank consists of eight additional F100158s connected in the modulo-8 configuration shown in *Figure 3*.

The modulo-8 rank is used to simulate an 8-bit simultaneous shift since the F100158 cannot shift in 8-bit jumps. The modulo-8 configuration is achieved by wiring the first rank and the output device to the second rank as illustrated in blue in *Figure 3*. The LSB of each output byte in the first rank is wired to one of the eight inputs of the first F100158 in the second rank. The next least significant bit of each first-rank F100158 pair, however, is connected to the inputs of the second F100158 in the second rank. The other first-rank outputs are connected in a similar fashion to the remainder of the second-rank inputs. Ultimately, the outputs of the second rank must then be connected to reform the final usable 64-bit word so that the bits are again ordered from 0 – 63.

The effect is that each single-location shift in the second rank appears to be an eight place shift in the final word due to the way the inputs and outputs of the second rank are connected. The combination of the two ranks produces the 64-place shift of the entire word.

out of phase by three OR gates. Inputs for the two ICs are taken from two bytes transposed in order; outputs are transposed and emitter-OR tied. One device shifts right from location 0 and the other shifts left from location 7. The bits shifted off one pair are picked up by the next pair of F100158s or – in the case of the last one in the rank – returned to the first device. The net result is a 0 – 7 place shift of the entire word.

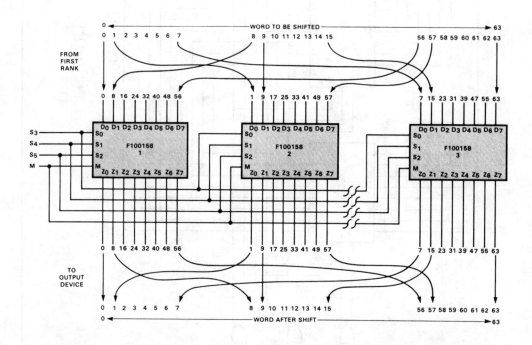

Fig. 3 Modulo-8 Shift

CIRCUIT IDEAS Digital

by Charles Alford

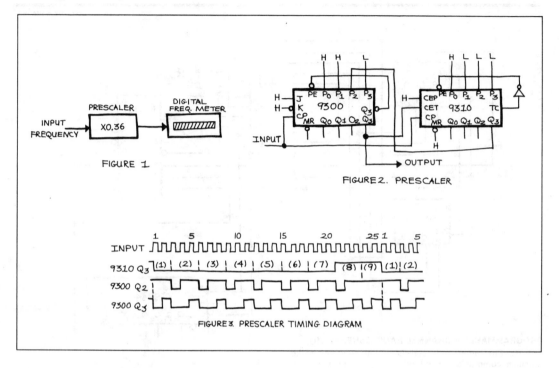

FIGURE 1

FIGURE 2. PRESCALER

FIGURE 3. PRESCALER TIMING DIAGRAM

DIGITAL RATE CONVERTER

Sometimes it is necessary to convert pulses per second (or, more elegantly, "events" per second) into pulses per hour. For simple record keeping, this can be done by accumulating pulses in one-hour intervals to obtain average hourly rates. It can also be done using analog techniques to effectively multiply by 3600. However, when the conversion must be done digitally and in relatively short sampling periods, the scheme presented in Figure 1 can be used.

In this scheme, a digital divider – acting as a prescaler for a digital counter type of frequency meter – in effect multiplies the input frequency by 0.36. Multiplying the result by 10,000, to achieve a total multiplier of 3600, is accomplished in the frequency meter by shifting the decimal point four places to the right in the digital display.

The prescaler consists of a 9300 4-bit shift register and a 9310 synchronous decade counter connected as shown in Figure 2. Both circuits are clocked by the LOW-to-HIGH transitions of the input pulses. The 9300 shifts right until Q_3 goes HIGH, whereupon its complement $\overline{Q}_3$ activates the Parallel Enable input. The next clock pulse executes a parallel load and Q_3 returns to the LOW state in accordance with the LOW state of its parallel input P_3. Simultaneously, $\overline{Q}_3$ goes HIGH to deactivate the Parallel Enable and the register returns to the shift right mode. Q_3 goes HIGH after one or two

shifts, depending on whether Q_2 was parallel loaded HIGH or LOW. Thus, the output pulses from Q_3 occur at either one-half or one-third the rate of the input pulses.

The decade counter, which can change state only when register output Q_3 is HIGH, is synchronously preset to 1 and then counts up to 9 making a total of nine states in a complete cycle. The Q_3 output of the counter is LOW in states 1 through 7 and HIGH in states 8 and 9. Since this output controls register input P_2, it follows that the register divides the input frequency by 3 a total of seven times and by 2 a total of two times and then repeats (Figure 3).

Family	Register	Counter
TTL	9300	9310
LP-TTL	93L00	93L10
S-TTL	93S00	93S10
LS-TTL	74LS195	74LS160
CMOS	40195	40160

Table 1.

A cycle of nine output pulses requires 25 input pulses, therefore the prescaler divides by 25/9. On a continuous basis, this is equivalent to multiplying by 0.36. The prescaler can be implemented by a variety of other circuits that are patterned after the 9300 and 9310 as shown in Table 1.

CIRCUIT IDEAS Digital

by Kris Rallapalli

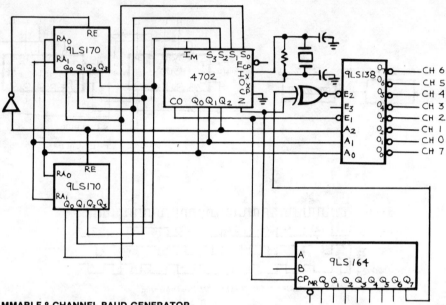

PROGRAMMABLE 8-CHANNEL BAUD GENERATOR

The 4702 Programmable Bit Rate Generator generates all the common communication bit rates using a "time division multiplexed cross point switch" principle. With a very economical 2.4576 MHz crystal, a single 4702 can service up to eight fully programmable channels. The actual frequency of any channel is 16 times the selected bit rate — a frequency sufficient to operate UARTs. However, some recent LSI devices intended as UART replacements require a clock input with 32 times the frequency. The scheme illustrated in the figure achieves this without a corresponding increase of the crystal frequency.

The two 9LS170 register files store the channel frequency selection information and are loaded with information on a per channel basis. For clarity, the write circuitry for these devices is not shown. The least significant 4702 scan-counter outputs (Q_0 and Q_1) are the Read Address inputs of the 9LS170s. The most significant bit (Q_2) controls the 9LS170 Read Enable ($\overline{RE}$) inputs. The 4702 Q_0 - Q_2 outputs are also the inputs to the 9LS138 decoder. The 4702 Clock output (CO) controls one enable input ($\overline{E_1}$) of the 9LS138 and is also the Clock input (CP) for the 9LS164 shift register. The 4702 Bit Rate output (Z) is the Data input (A) to the 9LS164 and is also one input of the exclusive NOR. The second exclusive-NOR input comes from the 9LS164 Q_7 output; the output of this gate controls the second 9LS138 Enable input ($\overline{E_2}$). The 9LS138 outputs are the desired output clock signals.

An example is helpful in understanding the operation of this circuit. Consider the LOW-to-HIGH transition of the 4702 CO

output when the scan-counter outputs change from 7 (HHH) to 0 (LLL). The 4702 Z output reflects the channel-7 output state from the transition to the next LOW-to-HIGH transition of the CO. The 4702 Q_0 - Q_2 outputs are LOW, hence information for channel 0 is available at the 9LS170 outputs. The 4702 S_0 - S_3 inputs are connected to the 9LS170 outputs. On the LOW-to-HIGH transition of the CO output, the channel-0 counter is clocked to the Z output. This transition also clocks the 9LS164 and increments the scan counter so it points to channel 1. Thus, as the clocking continues, 9LS170 locations are read out sequentially and information is shifted into the 9LS164. After eight clock transitions, the previous channel-7 output is at the Q_7 output of the 9LS164 and the present channel-7 output is at the Z output of the 4702.

The output of the exclusive-NOR gate is LOW if the inputs differ. For example, whenever the channel-7 output is to make a transition, the output of the exclusive NOR is LOW. The CO output is connected to the $\overline{E_1}$ input and, during the negative half cycle of the clock, the O_0 output of the 9LS138 is LOW. The 4702 internal counters generate 16 times the selected bit rate. The exclusive NOR generates a signal whenever the selected counter makes a transition, hence this scheme results in 32 times the selected bit rate. As clocking continues, each channel appears serially at the 9LS164 Q_7 output and is compared with the corresponding current channel output. The 9LS138 then corresponds to the appropriate frequency at its output as marked. □

CIRCUIT IDEAS Digital

by Charles Alford

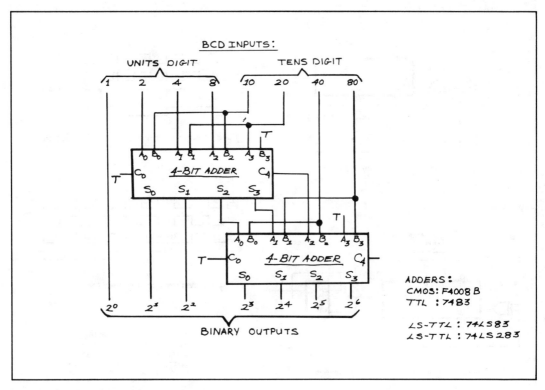

2-DIGIT BCD TO 7-BIT BINARY CONVERTER

Converting a 2-digit BCD number into a 7-bit binary number is accomplished simply and economically with two 4-bit adders. The necessary interconnections are determined by first expressing each of the weighted BCD bits in terms of numbers that are powers of two.

$$80 = 64 + 16 = 2^6 + 2^4$$
$$40 = 32 + 8 = 2^5 + 2^3$$
$$\text{etc.}$$

Arranging the BCD and binary numbers in an orderly array, as shown in the table, makes it easy to see which of the BCD inputs must be summed into the various binary outputs. For example, the 2^0 output is just the least significant bit of the units BCD digit, while inputs 2 and 10 must be summed to produce the 2^1 output. Notice that the 2^3 sum has more than two inputs (8, 10 and 40) and therefore cannot be formed in a single adder stage. Thus, for the 2^3 output, the sum is partially formed in the first adder package and completed in the second, as shown in the connection diagram. Inputs marked with a T must be terminated LOW for active-HIGH inputs and terminated HIGH for active-LOW inputs.

BCD INPUTS

	1	2	4	8	10	20	40	80
2^0	X							
2^1		X			X			
2^2			X			X		
2^3				X	X		X	
2^4						X		X
2^5							X	
2^6								X

BINARY OUTPUTS

TABLE

CIRCUIT IDEAS Digital

by Charles Alford

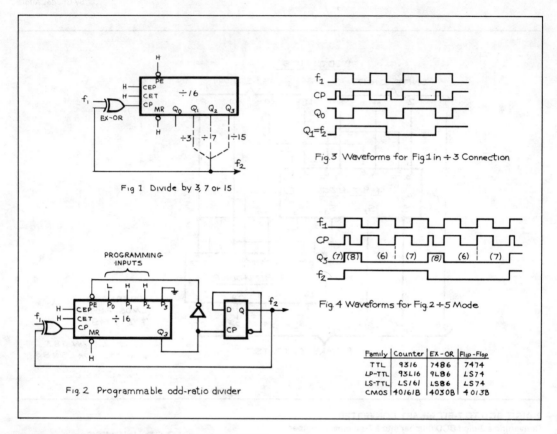

Fig 1 Divide by 3, 7 or 15

Fig. 3 Waveforms for Fig 1 in ÷ 3 Connection

PROGRAMMING INPUTS

Fig. 2 Programmable odd-ratio divider

Fig. 4 Waveforms for Fig. 2 ÷ 5 Mode

Family	Counter	EX-OR	Flip-Flop
TTL	9316	7486	7474
LP-TTL	93L16	9L86	LS74
LS-TTL	LS161	LS86	LS74
CMOS	40161B	4030B	4013B

ODD RATIO DIVIDERS WITH 50% DUTY CYCLE OUTPUT

A design task that arises occasionally involves dividing an incoming frequency by an odd number, yet producing an output that has a 50% duty cycle. The circuit of *Figure 1* will perform such a function, provided that the input frequency f_1 has a 50% duty cycle. When the feedback signal to the Exclusive-OR gate is LOW, the gate output has the same phase as f_1, and thus the counter advances on the rising edge of f_1. When the feedback signal goes HIGH, however, the gate output becomes the complement of f_1, and the counter thenceforth advances on the falling edge of f_1. In this transition from rising-edge to falling-edge sensitivity, the counter effectively gains a clock. The feedback signal will have a 50% duty cycle (minus small differences in rising and falling propagation delays) only if there is uniform spacing between the rising and falling edges of f_1. Waveforms for the divide-by-3 connection are shown in *Figure 3*.

A broader selection of divide ratios is obtained by using a little more logic, as shown in *Figure 2*. The counter operates in a programmable mode, with the rising edge of Q3 clocking the flip-flop and enabling the parallel loading into the counter, which occurs on the next rising edge of CP. The flip-flop is necessary because, in the programmable mode, none of the counter outputs are symmetrical. The overall divide ratio is expressed as follows.

divide ratio $N = f_1/f_2 = 2M - 1$
where M is the divide ratio of Q3 of the counter with respect to its CP input rising edges.

To obtain a particular divide ratio M, the parallel inputs are set to nine minus M. For example, to obtain an overall divide ratio of 5, M must be 3 and the preset data must be 6, which is the value indicted in *Figure 2*. Waveforms for this divide ratio are shown in *Figure 4*. Once again, a 50% duty cycle at f_2 is dependent on equal spacing between the rising and falling edges of f_1. □

CIRCUIT IDEAS Digital

by Charles Alford

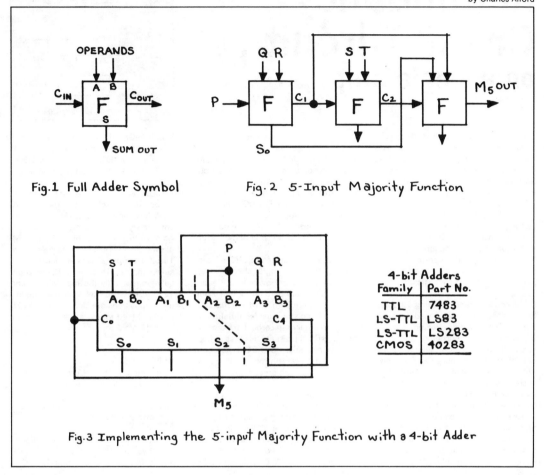

Fig.1 Full Adder Symbol

Fig. 2 5-Input Majority Function

4-bit Adders	
Family	Part No.
TTL	7483
LS-TTL	LS83
LS-TTL	LS283
CMOS	40283

Fig.3 Implementing the 5-input Majority Function with a 4-bit Adder

4-BIT ADDER SERVES AS 5-INPUT MAJORITY GATE

A majority gate is one whose output is True if a majority of its inputs are True, a function also known as voting logic. A full adder *(Figure 1)* acts as a 3-input majority gate since the C_{OUT} is True if any two or all three of the inputs are True.

To obtain a 5-input majority function, as shown in *Figure 2*, inputs P, Q and R are combined in the first adder. Inputs S and T are applied to the second adder, along with the carry C_1 from the first adder. Note that the carry C_2 from the second adder is not sufficient indication that a majority of the inputs are True, since it will be True if only S and T are True but will be False if only P, Q and R are True. But if any two or all three of S_0, C_1 and C_2 are True, then it must be that three or more of the inputs are True. Thus the third adder is used a majority gate for S_0, C_1 and C_2.

A slight dilemma occurs in trying to implement *Figure 2* with one MSI package since there is no triple adder available, and in the 4-bit adder only one carry is brought out of the package whereas access to two carries is needed. The dilemma is solved by using one adder of the 4-bit circuit as an input and an output that are effectively independent of each other, as shown in *Figure 3*. Input function P connects to both operand inputs of the third adder, which means that its C_{OUT} is always equal to P and is independent of its C_{IN}. Thus the function of the first adder in *Figure 2* is performed by the fourth adder in *Figure 3*, whose C_{OUT} is available. The functions of the second and third adders of *Figure 2* are performed by the first and second adders of *Figure 3*. The C_{OUT} of this second adder passes through to the Sum output of the third adder to provide the final output. □

Cyclic Redundancy Check Circuit . . .
on a single chip

by Krishna Rallapalli and Rob Walker

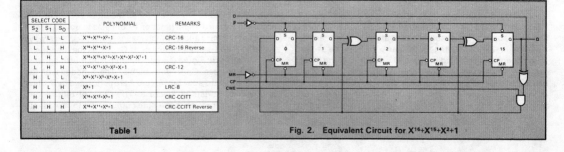

Fig. 1. 9401 Block Diagram

Error detection schemes based on cyclic codes are widely used with serial data handling systems such as floppy disk, digital cassette and data communication systems. The mathematical theory of cyclic code techniques was covered in "Cyclic Checks for Error Detection" (Progress, February 1974) while "Circuit Implementation of Cyclic Checks" (Progress, March 1974) discussed MSI techniques for the function realization. A new one-chip CRC generator/checker, the 9401, has been developed to simplify design and reduce costs.

Cyclic encoding and decoding schemes for error detection are based on polynomial manipulations using modulo arithmetic. For encoding, the data stream is divided by a selected polynomial known as the *generator polynomial*. The remainder resulting from such a division is appended to the data as check bits. For error checking, the bit stream containing both data and check bits is divided by the same generator polynomial. If there are no detectable errors, this division results in a zero remainder. The 9401 has provisions to use any one of eight generator polynomials listed in *Table 1*, selected by appropriate logic levels on three select lines S_0, S_1 and S_2.

The 9401 consists of a 16-bit register, a ROM and associated circuits as shown in *Figure 1*. The polynomial select code presented to S_0, S_1 and S_2 inputs is decoded by the internal ROM. The ROM outputs establish shift mode operation on the register with Exclusive OR gates at appropriate inputs as illustrated in *Figure 2*. The ROM also performs right justification, *i.e.*, the exponents of those polynomials which are less than 16 are appropriately scaled up.

It is possible to clear the CRC register prior to the beginning of check character accumulation. However, this practice results in all Zero check bits when all data bits are Zero. To avoid this situation, the register must be initialized to a pattern other than Zeros. For example, the register is preset to all Ones in floppy disk systems. The 9401 has both Reset and Preset control lines to simplify the initialization procedures.

To generate the check bits, data is entered via the D input using the HIGH to LOW transition of the clock (CP). The Check Word Enable (CWE) input controls the feedback path; it is held HIGH while data is entered. After entering the last data bit, CWE is brought LOW and check bits are shifted out of the register on the Q output.

To check an incoming message for errors, both the data and check bits are entered through the D input while CWE is held HIGH. If there are no detectable errors after receiving the last check bit, the Error (ER) output will be LOW. A HIGH level on ER indicates an error.

A HIGH level on the Master Reset (MR) asynchronously clears the register. A LOW level on the Preset ($\overline{P}$) input asynchronously sets the register. Automatic right justification control from the ROM allows the entire register to be set if a 16-bit polynomial is specified by the select inputs. In case of 12- or 8-bit polynomials, only the most significant 12 or 8 bits will be set while the remaining bit positions are cleared. The 9401 is guaranteed to operate at clock rates up to 12 MHz.

REFERENCES

Peterson, W.W., Error Correcting Codes, MIT Press & John Wiley and Sons.

Martin, James, Teleprocessing Network Organization, Prentice-Hall, Inc.

Binary Synchronous Communications, IBM Systems Reference Library, File No. TP-09, Form GA27-3004-1.

Specifications for Magnetic Tape Cassette for Information Interchange, ANSI x381/579, American National Standards Institute, New York, September 14, 1972.

SELECT CODE			POLYNOMIAL	REMARKS
S_2	S_1	S_0		
L	L	L	$X^{16}+X^{15}+X^2+1$	CRC-16
L	L	H	$X^{16}+X^{14}+X+1$	CRC-16 Reverse
L	H	L	$X^{16}+X^{15}+X^{13}+X^7+X^4+X^2+X^1+1$	
L	H	H	$X^{12}+X^{11}+X^3+X^2+X+1$	CRC-12
H	L	L	$X^8+X^7+X^5+X^4+X+1$	
H	L	H	X^8+1	LRC-8
H	H	L	$X^{16}+X^{12}+X^5+1$	CRC-CCITT
H	H	H	$X^{16}+X^{11}+X^4+1$	CRC-CCITT Reverse

Table 1

Fig. 2. Equivalent Circuit for $X^{16}+X^{15}+X^2+1$

MICROPROCESSORS

The Impact of MICROPROCESSORS on Logic Design

by Peter Alfke

Microprocessors have had a strong impact on logic and system design. From the semiconductor technology point of view, they represent only an evolution of the packing density and processing sophistication achieved on calculator and memory chips. All microprocessors use well-established semiconductor processes. From the user's point of view, however, microprocessors represent a revolutionary step, a total change in design philosophy.

WHAT IS A MICROPROCESSOR?

Microprocessors were born out of a desire in various semiconductor houses to offer the advantages of LSI (Large Scale Integration) without the many problems of custom logic design. Microprocessors require a chip architecture that can efficiently implement a large variety of digital systems. Not surprisingly, such an architecture bears a close resemblance to a minicomputer in that it executes logic and arithmetic functions in a sequence of steps controlled by instructions contained in memory.

This sequential mode of instruction execution results in slow computer operation even when high-speed components are used. Microprocessors implement this architecture on a small number of chips with a limited number of pins which restricted the performance of the first microprocessors, i.e., the 4004 and the 8008, even beyond the natural limitations of MOS circuit speed.

Since 1971, a large number of different microprocessors have been introduced, but it is interesting to note that the rapid introduction of new microprocessors culminated in 1974; '75 and '76 saw fewer totally new microprocessor architectures. A number of factors are responsible for this. There are more than enough different microprocessors around to confuse the potential user; any new architecture would have to represent a significant improvement, or cost reduction, compared to existing products. Also, every broad-based semiconductor company already has one or more microprocessors and is therefore more interested in expanding the sale of existing products to help offset the enormous costs of development. Moreover, all manufacturers realize the tremendous cost of software support and the difficulty in recouping it at the present low component prices.

Instead of totally new architecture and instruction sets, the industry will see microprocessors that emulate established minicomputers, or improvements on existing designs like the Z80 which is a substantial improvement of the 8080.

Microprocessor systems can be divided into two groups:

High performance, computation or data processing microprocessor systems using larger amounts (greater than 4K bytes) of program and data storage memory, implemented in a large variety of designs and manufactured in small production runs (generally less than 10,000 systems and often less than 100). The designer is familiar with minicomputer architecture and programming. The total component cost usually exceeds $100, however the alternative to the microprocessor is an even more expensive naked minicomputer or about 100 TTL or CMOS packages.

System design and software cost is significant. Use of sophisticated development systems (Formulator, Exorciser, Intellec) is mandatory; high level languages are very useful.

Software strategy is similar to that used in larger computers in that programming should be modular, easily modifiable and maintainable but need not be extremely efficient.

Some important considerations in choosing a higher performance microprocessor are

- Speed
- Memory addressing capability
- Interrupt handling
- Subroutine nesting
- DMA capability
- Arithmetic instructions
- Software support

Low performance controllers used in high volume, cost sensitive, I/O oriented applications with smaller amounts of memory (less than 2K bytes). The designer usually has very little computer experience, is more hardware oriented, and sometimes has only electromechanical experience. The total component cost for these systems is substantially below $100. The alternatives are 30 TTL or CMOS packages or motors, gears and relays.

Although system design and software costs may be high, they can usually be amortized over a larger production volume. Code must be efficient to save memory and I/O hardware,

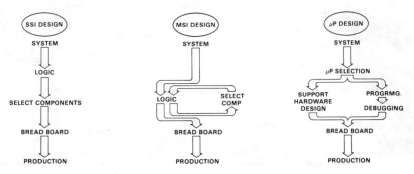

COMPARISON OF DESIGN PROCEDURES

hence the programming may very well be tricky and difficult to understand and modify. There is a limited need for compilers and no place for high level languages that incur higher memory overhead.

When choosing a controller, the following factors should be taken into consideration.

- Chip count and cost
- Total number of pins
- Number of I/O lines
- Clock generation
- On-board timer
- Supply voltages and power

During the next few years, high-performance microprocessors will become even more sophisticated, faster and more like minicomputers whereas controller-oriented microprocessors will evolve into more practical, powerful one-chip microcomputers and thus become even cheaper.

DESIGNING WITH MICROPROCESSORS

During the past fifteen years, digital design has evolved through three generations of increasing chip density and sophistication. Originally, the designer was limited to discrete components such as vacuum tubes, transistors, diodes and RTL, DTL, TTL and CMOS gates. The design approach was very straightforward – little interaction between the phases of system design, logic design and component selection was necessary.

Beginning about ten years ago, MSI components became available offering up to 100 gates in a 16-pin DIP. The efficient use of these MSI devices required a willingness to adapt the logic design to the available components, an upsetting and demanding approach but one that brought about considerable savings in cost and design time.

During the last few years, however, microprocessors have become a more attractive alternative for many digital designs, providing lower cost, faster design, easier modification, smaller size and better reliability. The problem now facing the system designer is that he must decide on a specific microprocessor before he begins a detailed hardware and software design. The choice is made more difficult by the fact that any well defined microprocessor can perform any function given enough memory, support circuitry and execution time. The question is not whether the XYZ microprocessor can be used, but rather whether it is the best – or almost best – choice from a cost/performance point of view.

SELECTING THE BEST MICROPROCESSOR SOLUTION

First, begin with a basic understanding of microprocessors, keeping in mind these main points: they are digital devices, consequently analog inputs and outputs must be treated digitally; they operate like computers, executing a serial stream of instructions stored in memory; fixed program is stored in ROM, but data and varying program are stored in RAM; and in spite of a MHz clock rate, milliseconds are often required to execute a program.

Then, temporarily ignore the features and differences of the possible microprocessor choices and define your application parameters in general terms. Define all inputs and outputs, whether they are keyboards, displays, sensors or drivers. Develop a functional specification describing which process must occur as a function of which input. Determine the response speed required but be careful not to require unnecessary speed – it may be surprisingly expensive. Finally, estimate the amount of data storage area needed.

After determining the application, define the environment in which the microprocessor is to be used. Stringent requirements in this area may drastically narrow the field of potential microprocessors, so be careful not to create unnecessary restraints. Some typical enviromental considerations include critical supply voltages and power, temperature range, space availability and effect of memory volatility.

After all this is done, don't forget about design and production schedules, volume requirements and required pricing. While these factors may not seem design oriented, they may have great influence on the final choice. On small production runs, the development costs can overshadow the parts and assembly costs.

SUMMARY

Microprocessors pose both an opportunity and a challenge to the digital designer. Once the capabilities of microprocessors are understood and appreciated and the designer is willing to adapt his thinking to their idiosyncracies, he will find microprocessors make the design job easier and more interesting. The support systems offered by all serious microprocessor manufacturers simplify the design and programming tasks and the inherent flexibility of microprocessing allows fast reaction to varying demands.

Microprocessors are a reality. They offer a better solution in most digital systems except the fastest or most trivial. The application of microprocessors is limited only by the creative imagination of their potential users.

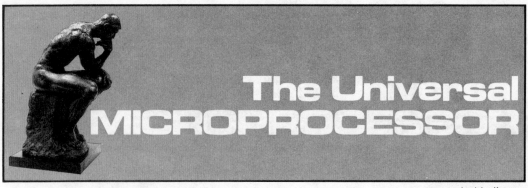

The Universal MICROPROCESSOR

by John Katsaros

Microprocessors, representing an order of magnitude improvement over available LSI chips in terms of versatility, generally fall into two categories—low cost minimum performance minicomputers or replacements for calculator chips in high end calculators and similar equipment such as cash registers, word processors, etc. They are versatile logic boxes with inputs and outputs, consisting of organized register arrays, arithmetic units and instruction sets to implement computer-oriented operations within a system. Microprocessors are certainly more cost effective than LSI chips since they are standard chips manufactured in volume rather than custom designed for limited production.

The one-chip central processing unit seems like the system designer's salvation since it replaces dozens of MSI chips or hundreds of SSI circuits. In reality, however, the designer soon becomes disenchanted when he finds that a workable system may require the addition of six logic circuits, nine memory circuits and two clocks before it has a minimum capability, not to mention address and data buffering to be used for peripherals. Also clock generation and timing, memories and I/O control, multiplexing, and interrupt capability must be considered. What the system designer really needs is a few compatible chips capable of handling all these functions.

During the development of the F8 Microprocessor system, ample opportunity was taken to evaluate not only the problems inherent in previous approaches, but also the requirements of a truly *universal*, cost-effective, standard part with all of the cost savings, time savings, system capabilities required to live up to the *universal* name. The following five main objectives became the F8 design charter.

Minimum parts count for a useful system. A minimum system includes the following functions: RAM, ROM, I/O circuits, computing electronics, interrupt structure, timer, clock generators and power-on reset. The ideal system would have all of these functions on one chip. However, even by using the Isoplanar isolation process, which reduces chip size about 40% when compared to the conventional MOS chips, it still became necessary to have a separate chip for the ROM.

Direct interface with a wide range of devices without additional interface circuits. Sufficient hardware is incorporated on the CPU chip so that the idiosyncrasies of a majority of I/O devices can be handled by the software. This hardware includes an interrupt structure, timer, encoding and decoding, and bidirectional ports, so that each port can be used as an input or output line at different times. Some 95% of the I/O devices including keyboards, printers, readers, displays, modems, and magnetic devices, can be handled directly by this chip.

Simplified programming and debugging. Carefully thought-out software systems should alleviate many of the difficulties facing users today. Although a low cost, non-volatile RAM is yet to be invented, a variety of prototyping units using PROMs are available to provide an easy and inexpensive way of developing and verifying F-8 microprocessor systems, even for small quantity users. Two software packages, an assembler and a simulator, are accessible on national timesharing networks; also, a specially developed terminal built around the F8 microprocessor set will be available.

Modular architecture to handle increasingly complex problems with no theoretical upper limit. Four basic modules were developed—the Central Processing Unit (CPU). the Program Storage Unit (PSU), Memory Interface (MI), and Direct Memory Acces (DMA)—that can be used in any number to implement, in a piecemeal fashion, the most complex system requirements. The key characteristic of this approach is that a minimum system may be built with just two circuits, the CPU and PSU, while larger systems may be realized by adding other modules. To achieve this flexible modularity, there were some architectural tradeoffs. Considering the frequency with which certain operations are normally performed, I/O speed and reduced parts count received the major emphasis with some sacrifice in memory versatility. The majority of microprocessor instructions are I/O oriented and reduced parts count is vital, especially since repetitive memory reference can be eliminated by efficient programming.

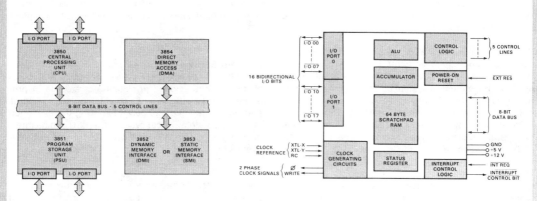

Fig. 1. F8 System Organization

Fig. 2. CPU Block Diagram

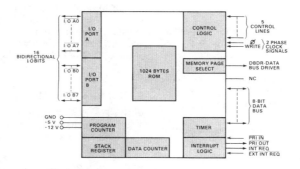

Fig. 3. PSU Block Diagram

Cost effectiveness for any system. The F8 was not developed to handle the jobs requiring a minicomputer, but rather to serve as a universal part that would be cost-effective in a variety of markets—high end or specialized calculators, consumer market (appliances, automobiles), industrial markets such as numerical control systems, etc., and other areas which might consider going to a custom chip design. To make the microprocessor cost effective in these sockets, a system must be realized with a minimum number of circuits.

To keep user costs down, minimum chip size was accomplished by using the Isoplanar isolation process, and by carefully planning the architecture on each chip *(Figure 1)*. Although the CPU chip contains many important functions, it is only 181 x 155 mils, a size that insures high yields and low manufacturing costs. Also, the need for external chips and other components is eliminated because the F8 chips are I/O compatible with TTL logic.

Since much of the equipment manufacturing cost is eliminated—large printed circuit boards, assembly, test-

ing, etc.—the universal F8 can be used in the same way as low cost MSI chips are being used today. The ease in changing a design by simply altering the program eliminates the bugaboo of circuit-design changes that frequently cost four or five times the original estimate.

MICROPROCESSOR DESCRIPTION

The F8 universal microprocessor set is a family of only five individual modules, each containing a single n-channel Isoplanar MOS chip—Central Processing Unit (CPU), Program Storage Unit (PSU), Static Memory Interface (SMI), Dynamic Memory Interface (DMI), and Direct Memory Access (DMA). The distribution of system functions throughout the set is totally unlike any other microprocessor. For example, the program counter is not located on the CPU chip; rather, each memory module (PSU and MI circuits) has a program counter. In addition, the stack register and data counter are also on the memory modules. Thus, the need for a 16-bit address bus between devices is eliminated. An incre-

71

mentor/adder is also located on these chips, so that address modification may be performed "locally". Without an address bus, the CPU and PSU each has 16 pins available for another function, I/O.

For many applications such as small data terminals, calculators and appliance controllers, a two-chip system consisting of the CPU and the PSU is all that is needed. This minimum system performs computational functions and drives a peripheral device directly without an external controller or interface. Bidirectional I/O lines are fully buffered and completely controllable by software. More complex systems can be implemented by simply adding more PSUs.

The SMI and DMI modules are available for expanding the F8 capabilities to include applications that require more RAM than the 64 bytes located on the CPU. Also, PROM devices may be added to the system using these interfaces. The DMA provides a high speed data link to peripheral components.

Central Processing Unit

The 3850 CPU is the central processor for controlling F8 system functions. Communicating to other F8 circuits via an 8-bit bidirectional data bus, the CPU has five control lines to set the state of the other chips. Despite being the smallest microprocessor CPU chip available, the 3850 contains a tremendous amount of logic. As shown in *Figure 2*, the CPU consists of the following:

- Arithmetic Logic Unit, an 8-bit parallel logic network used in binary or decimal functions and to handle many of the F8 instructions.

- Accumulator, an 8-bit storage register for storing the results of arithemtic operations and transferring information into or out of the scratchpad memory.

- Scratchpad RAM, consisting of 64 8-bit registers serving as read/write memories which may be used as a workspace by the programmer.

- Status Register, to store the status indications from an arithmetic or logical operation.

- Two Bidirectional Input/Output Ports, for either gathering data from external circuits or for outputting data to other circuitry.

- Clock Generating Circuits, for generating the necessary two-phase clock signals used by all circuits in the system. Operating frequency can be set by an external RC network, an external crystal when a precise operating frequency is required, or by a connection to an external clock.

- Interrupt Control Logic, whose operation can be interrupted by an internal system timer or by an external source. It permits the microprocessor to operate on a real time basis as well as to generate efficient control signals. The combination of timers, priority interrupts and buffered outputs allows the F8 to serve as a peripheral controller.

- Power-On Reset, causes the CPU to disable the interrupt system and insures that processing starts out from an address zero when power is first applied.

Program Storage Unit

The 3851 PSU, shown in *Figure 3*, has 1024 8-bit bytes of storage and is used principally for storage of programmed instructions and non-volatile data constants that will be fetched as operands during the execution of a program. In a typical system, the PSU can be interfaced directly with the CPU without the use of buffer circuits.

The PSU architecture differs from common microprocessor construction in that each PSU contains a 16-bit program counter, a 16-bit stack register, a local interrupt control which can be set and reset independently under program control, two fully bidirectional I/O ports, a timer for real time delays, and a 16-bit address pointer for referencing memory. The addition of a timer, local interrupt control, program counter and stack register provides another interrupt level to the system and also adds more processing capability independent of the CPU. The PSU functions are briefly outlined.

- 1024 Bytes of ROM Program Storage

- The Program Counter contains the address of the next instruction byte to be fetched from memory and is automatically incremented after a fetch cycle is executed.

- The Stack Register receives the contents of the program counter whenever an interrupt is generated or when the program counter is pushed to the stack register. It also aids in developing a multi-level program function.

- The Data Counter is used for referencing memory addresses. Because it is 16-bits long, it can address up to 65K bytes of memory.

- I/O Ports are fully bidirectional and contain storage latches thus eliminating the need for external latches.

- The Interrupt Address Generator provides the next instruction address when interrupt occurs.

- The Timer greatly increases the versatility of the system. When the CPU is conducting normal routine tasks, it can be interrupted by the timer to service real-time equipment. The timer can also keep track of the elapsed time as data is transmitted to an external device, and automatically initiate the next operation at the end of transmission without the usual wait loop delay caused by interrogation steps from the CPU. In addition to generating real-time interrupts during program execution, the timer is useful for generating waveforms for control functions which may be easily changed with a program modification.

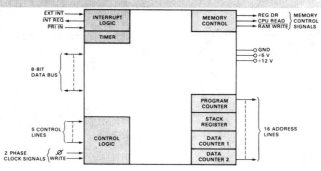

Fig. 4. SMI Block Diagram

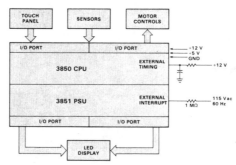

Fig. 5. Appliance Controller

Memory Interfaces

The memory interfaces allow standard memory elements to be incorporated into the F8 system by providing 16 address lines and signals necessary to interface with up to 65K bytes of RAM, ROM or PROM. The SMI *(Figure 4)* contains a full level of interrupt capability and a programmable timer. The DMI contains all of the logic necessary to refresh MOS dynamic memories without degrading the system throughput time. It can also interface with static memories.

Direct Memory Access

The DMA is used to set up a high speed data path between the F8 memory and a high speed peripheral, such as a magnetic tape unit, a FIFO memory or another F8. This circuit must be used in conjunction with a DMI. It does not require overhead electronics to keep track of memory addresses, bytes transferred and handshaking signals. The data transfer is initiated by the CPU under program control; once started, the DMA transfer continues without CPU intervention. The CPU can sense the flag line of the DMA to determine the completion of transfer.

TWO-CHIP SYSTEM

The two-chip F8 system is suitable for small data terminals, controllers and specialty calculators. External devices may be connected directly to the I/O ports without any special interface; the control function becomes a programming task. With a keyboard, for instance, switch-bounce protection, rollover and key encoding are all implemented under software control. Software also performs the decoding function for LED readouts.

The two-chip system can be used as an appliance controller to perform all the input, output-sensing, actuating, timing and computation operations *(Figure 5)*. A similar system using other microprocessor chip sets requies 265 components while the F8 system uses only 55 including 28 LEDs. An alternate design, using a custom MOS circuit, would not only involve heavy initial engineering expense but also severe penalties if changes were required. A considerable amount of time would elapse before production could begin. With the F8 system, changes could be made by merely changing the program. There are no chip development expenses or risk, the system is easily changed or expanded and yet the cost, regardless of the volume used, is based on standard chips that are produced in volume. Other applications that would benefit from the cost effectiveness of a two-chip system include cash registers, word processors, controllers, communication multiplexers, adult games, vending machines, etc.

MEDIUM COMPLEXITY SYSTEM

A more complex system can be designed by merely adding more PSUs. With the 16-bit addressing, a system may contain up to 65,536 bytes of ROM storage.

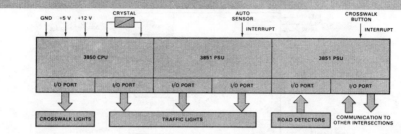

Fig. 6. Traffic Light Controller

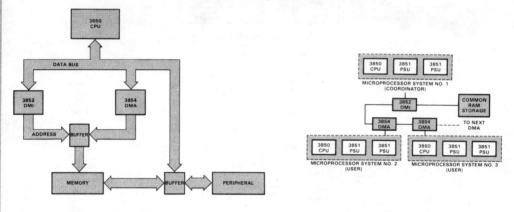

Fig. 7. DMA System

Fig. 8. Common RAM Storage

Each additional PSU adds not only another 1K x 8 ROM storage, but also an additional interrupt level, a system timer and two more 8-bit I/O ports. A good example of this type of system is a traffic-light controller that requies only one CPU and two PSUs. These circuits provide two timers, two interrupts, an onboard clock, onboard power on, onboard switch decoding and 48 bidirectional I/O bits *(Figure 6)*. Vehicle detectors, pedestrian control buttons and traffic lights can be controlled by this system. In addition to controlling vehicle and pedestrian traffic as well as left-turn vehicle traffic, the 48 I/O bits may be used to communicate with neighboring intersections. They also permit the system to be operated manually.

One of the interrupts eliminates the need for external circuits such as a comparator to match the number of cars with a predetermined value to cause a light change. It also eliminates the need for continuous polling of traffic count by the microprocessor. The second interrupt is ideal for permitting pedestrian control to override the automatic system. The internal clock, with an external crystal, is used to count vehicles and to control light routines. The two timers permit simultaneous counting of delay for vehicle signals and flashing warning lights for pedestrians. In case of power failure, the onboard power-on reset automatically starts up when power is renewed. The system bidirectional I/Os have built-in latches that eliminate the need for external latches to "hold" light commands as well as the momentary commands provided by timers and sensors.

MEMORY INTENSIVE SYSTEMS

With the memory interfaces (SMI, DMI) and the direct memory access (DMA), even more complex requirements can be broken down and handled by multiple processors. Using these additional modules, independent F8 microprocessor systems can be connected into a synergistic multiprocessing complex in which each system can operate independently yet can be controlled by one CPU coordinator.

The system in *Figure 7* is a good example of the simple use of a CPU, a DMI and a DMA. The CPU sets up a DMA channel between a peripheral and a memory. Once initiated by the CPU, the DMA coordinates all the elements during the data transfer. Passing data to and from the CPU is accomplished without stopping or even slowing down the CPU; thus a DMA transfer is performed simultaneously with CPU execution. This feature increases system throughput without degrading system performance.

In *Figure 8*, three microprocessor systems, each having a CPU and two PSUs, are connected into a common RAM storage by using a DMI and two DMAs. In this system, all three microprocessor systems operate independently at all times, with no waiting for the operation of another microprocessor. The RAM storage, which all three systems share, serves as an efficient three-way exchange. Although only three microprocessors are shown, more can be added to handle more

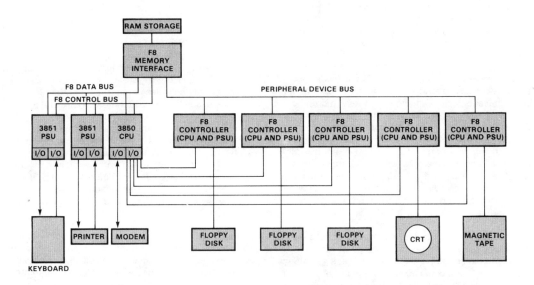

Fig. 9.   Key-to-Floppy-Disk System

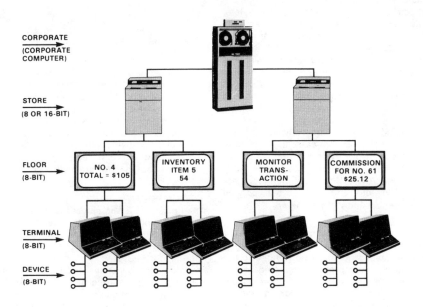

Fig. 10.   POS System Hierarchy

complex subjects. The only limit to the number of microprocessors is the bandwidth limitation of the common RAM storage, which is set at one byte per microsecond. The coordinator microprocessor has priority access to the common RAM storage. Its maximum access time is 0.5 μs/byte; the remainder of the bandwidth, 0.5 μs, is available for the other (user) microprocessors.

A multiprocessor system can be set up to divide specific tasks—secondary storage, diagnostic, computation, communications, etc.—among the various microprocessors. This arrangement exploits the "mailbox" concept to achieve data communication between the coordinator CPU and other microprocessors in an orderly fashion with minimal hardware. The "mailbox" is simply a set of locations in the common RAM storage set aside specifically to serve as an address for each microprocessor or peripheral device. After the coordinator writes in the "mailbox", it uses the interrupt line to get the attention of the selected unit.

Another technique is to assign each microprocessor to handle "subtasks" rather than complete functions. A subtask could be complete subsystem, such as a floppy disk or a CRT, or it could be an assignment of an algorithm and variables. In this modular system, all subtasks are carried out as part of a total program which is controlled by the coordinator.

The key-to-floppy-disk system shown in *Figure 9* is a good example of the multiprocessing concept. It is the most cost-effective way of implementing this system, conservatively costing less than 50% of a conventional design. This system involves concurrent operation of two floppy disks, the magnetic tape, the CRT, the keyboard, the printer, and the modem. While the low speed devices, the keyboard, the printer, and the modem, can be adequately handled by the programmed I/O structure, the high speed devices, the disks, the magnetic tape, and the CRT, require separate F8 controllers.

This scheme provides control simplicity, modularity, and system expandability. In this case, the maximum concurrent operation involves one magnetic-tape unit (25 μs/byte), two floppy-disk units (32 μs/byte each), and a CRT unit (71 μs/byte). This combination requires an aggregate bandwidth of 0.1478 bytes/μs, well within the 0.5 byte/μs bandwidth of the F8.

Point-of-Sale System
F8 microprocessor applications are not limited to the common RAM-storage type system but include many other multiprocessing systems such as point of sale *(Figure 10)*. The peripheral devices—magnetic wands, optical wands, label readers, printers, etc.—are at the lowest level in the system hierarchy. These sophisticated devices require controllers that can be provided with the F8 two-chip system. The POS terminal itself can also be produced with a medium-size F8 system

and at the floor-concentrator level, an F8 multiprocessor system is required. With the exception of the corporate EDP system, the F8 is cost effective for the entire POS system.

DESIGN ASSISTANCE
Software packages—an assembler and a simulator—plus several hardware items are available to expedite design and debugging of an F8 system. Often these procedures can be completed in less than three months. Since the F8 Cross Assembler is written in FORTRAN IV, the programmer can create a source file in assembly language rather than in the more difficult machine language. The assembler checks this file for errors, generates diagnostic information and creates two files—a text file for use by the simulator and an object file in machine language. The F8 Cross Simulator simulates the instructions, I/O and interrupt actions of an F8 system and thereby helps check out and debug the system.

For small quantity users, an F8 Development Module on a 9 x 11" pc board provides a low cost method of developing and verifying a prototype microprocessor system. It contains the necessary F8 devices and interfaces so that the test masks can quickly be burned in on a PROM. This method can save six to eight weeks and permits quick field changes by merely changing PROMs.

The F8 Microcomputer is a complete unit for developing prototypes. It is a more expensive and versatile test system in a desk-top cabinet with built-in power supplies and a control and display panel for manual access to memory data. I/O ports are brought out to connectors for convenient attachment to peripheral devices.

For very large users, an F8 conversational terminal, built around an F8 microprocessor chip set, will be available including a RAM, two floppy disks, alphanumeric keyboard, CRT display, paper tape reader, PROM programmer, etc. With this sophisitcated design aid, the user can write and assemble the program at the terminal, make his own prototype PROM and field test it prior to sending the stored program to Fairchild over the telephone lines for production of the ROM masks.

CONCLUSION
The universal F8 Microprocessor offers the system designer a family of circuits that can be considered separate components. The user no longer has to contend with the expense of adding overhead circuitry to make the microprocessor work. A two-chip system provides a multitude of functions and a larger, more powerful system may be realized by adding more F8 modules. Use of the F8 cuts minimum system requirements from as many as 30 devices down to two by eliminating the need for interface circuits. Cost effectiveness is further enhanced by smaller chip size, sophisticated partitioning of the architecture, and well thought-out design aids for prototype development and debugging.

Condensed version of this article appeared in Electronics, March 6, 1975, McGraw-Hill.

The Ideal Microprocessor

by Peter Alfke

In only twenty years, semiconductor technology has come around full circle. It started with the transistor, an extremely versatile non-specialized device that performs a myriad of functions, limited only by the designer's imagination. The first integrated circuits, op amps and gates, soon developed into more complex MSI and LSI specialized building blocks to implement predetermined functions. Now, the microprocessor has made the full swing back to the universal component, a device that can perform any digital function, given enough time and memory. This raises the question — why are there so many different microprocessors? Is this the result of avid competition or a ploy to confuse the potential user? While the number of incompatible microprocessors differing in architecture, instruction set, technology and I/O capability seems larger than necessary, there is a good reason for diversity. A market exists for a spectrum of microprocessors, each geared to a specific kind of application, offering different performance tradeoffs between the following conflicting requirements.

- Low hardware cost — low parts price, small number of pins, ease of interconnection, adequate drive capability, simple supply and clock requirements.

- Low development cost — ease of programming, similarity to well-known minicomputer architectures and instruction sets, availability of applications software, simplicity of system design.

- High performance — high execution speed, large memory address range, sophisticated interrupt structure, powerful instruction set.

Since these three requirements can never be optimized in one design, it is fortunate they need not all be optimized for any given application.

Extremely cost-sensitive applications — consumer goods, appliances — that demand a working system in the $10 to $50 range must minimize hardware costs. They usually do not require very high performance and are not particularly sensitive to development costs since these costs can be spread over a production run of several thousand systems.

Sophisticated lower-volume applications — data processing, industrial control, word processing — require efficient development including inexpensive software. On the other hand,

....a continuing search

the cost of the microprocessor, excluding memory, is less critical since it tends to be below 1% of the total system cost. The performance of modern 8-bit n-channel microprocessors is usually more than adequate. The user that requires ultimate performance, at or beyond the speed and sophistication of a minicomputer, also does not care about lowest component count and cost. He is generally experienced enough to provide his own software; in fact, he may even want to microcode his design for maximum performance.

TODAYS MICROPROCESSORS

When comparing microprocessors from the simplest appliance controller to the most intricate 8-bit processor, it is surprising that there is little difference in size and complexity of the chips, package size and number of pins. Almost all microprocessor chips are about 200 mils on an edge, i.e., roughly 6 nanoacres of silicon. The really significant differences lie in the size and complexity of the system for which the microprocessors are intended.

Semiconductor technology has not advanced, as yet, to the point where a complete 370 system can be built on a single chip. With today's technological constraints, the device designer must choose between functional completeness and complexity of the intended device application. Indeed, a complete computer can be built on one chip — CPU, RAM for data storage, ROM for program storage, I/O circuits with practical drive capability to interface directly with LEDs and relays. Mundane functions can be included like on-chip clock generation, power-on reset and direct-display drive, but this computer-on-a-chip is very limited in instruction set, memory size, word length, and speed. The Fairchild FPC Programmable Controller is a good example of a stand-alone single-chip microcomputer aimed at relatively simple, cost-sensitive control applications.

The other extreme is the sophisticated microprocessor that does not even attempt to be a computer-on-a-chip, but rather the central processing element of a far more complex multi-chip system. This microprocessor has an extensive instruction decoder, multiple accumulators, fast interrupt, efficient subroutine capabilities, a 16-bit program counter, and 16-bit address-bus drivers. Trivial features like simple clock generation, single power supply and power-on reset are not always provided. This microprocessor forms the foundation for a powerful computer with up to 64K bytes of ROM or RAM, multilevel prioritized interrupt structure, and almost unlimited I/O capability. The F6800 is one of the "cleanest" examples of this approach. In between these extremes, there is room for compromise. The F8™ microprocessor, for example, can implement a complete microcomputer on only two chips and can also be easily expanded to a much larger system.

The most striking difference between simple one- or two-chip design and complicated multi-chip architecture is in memory addressing. A large microcomputer should have homogeneous architecture with instruction storage, data memory and I/O ports residing externally to the CPU chip,

FPC PROGRAMMABLE CONTROLLER
4-Bit Microcomputer with Direct LED Drive

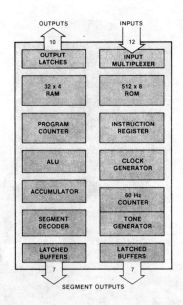

F3870 MICROMACHINE 2
8-Bit Microcomputer with
32 I/O Lines, Interrupt and Timer

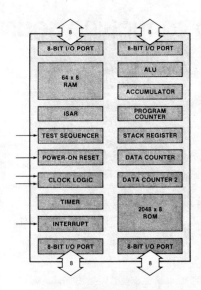

addressed as if they were memory locations. Minicomputers are organized this way and the F6800 best exemplifies this approach. Anyone who has programmed the PDP 11 will immediately feel at home with the F6800 architecture.

This architecture would, however, be very inefficient in a small system. When RAM and I/O are limited to less than a few hundred locations and actually reside on the CPU chip, it would be wasteful in both execution time and program storage to address the busy RAM and I/O ports as if they were part of a 64K-byte memory field. Addressing them with separate instructions and using an indirect scratchpad address register (ISAR) for RAM access is far more efficient; the RAM and I/O ports can be manipulated in single-byte instructions, executed in 2 μs.

When evaluating microprocessors, it is therefore very important to consider the application complexity. Small controllers are dominated by hardware cost considerations and require a microprocessor that emphasizes hardware simplicity, operation efficiency and functional completeness. Large data processing systems, on the other hand, tend to be dominated by software cost and development time. Here, a more regular minicomputer-like architecture is preferable. Fairchild manufactures several microprocessors, one for any kind of application from the simplest to the most complex.

FPC PROGRAMMABLE CONTROLLER

The FPC Programmable Controller is the simplest and least expensive but most self-contained Fairchild microprocessor. It can be considered either as a very advanced timer or a very basic and surprisingly practical single-chip microcomputer. Designed to minimize system cost, the microprocessor chip includes 14 output buffers for direct LED-segment drive of two digits or line-duplexed four digits.

The FPC, a 4-bit microcomputer with only 16 basic instructions, contains 512 bytes of program storage and 32 nibbles (BCD digits) of data storage. Several instructions use indirect data addressing and a read/modify/write cycle automatically places the result of an operation back into memory. Both these features enhance the versatility of the instruction set and save program storage.

Considerably slower than the F8 and F6800, the FPC is not easily expandable and has no subroutine capability or interrupt input. The FPC runs on a self-contained oscillator, thus saving two more pins. Polling the 60 or 50 Hz input for timing reference in many applications eliminates the need for a crystal oscillator.

The FPC is a basic, but surprisingly versatile and flexible, controller with many practical cost-saving hardware features. It is especially well suited for line-operated controllers with keyboard entry and up to four digits of LED display. This basic computer is much more difficult to program than full-fledged microprocessors; therefore the programming is best done by Fairchild specialists. Development costs will nor-

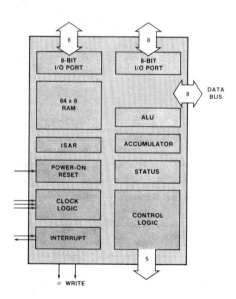

F3850 CPU
8-Bit Central Processing Unit
with 64-Byte RAM and 16 I/O Lines

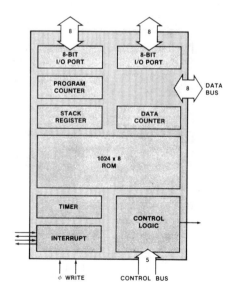

F3851 PSU
1K-Byte Program Storage Unit
with 16 I/O Lines, Interrupt and Timer

mally mandate the use of this device only in very high volume applications (10K or preferably 100K systems per year).

F3870 MICROMACHINE™2 ONE-CHIP MICROCOMPUTER
The F3870 single-chip 8-bit microcomputer, the MicroMachine 2, executes the same instruction set of over 70 commands and is supported by the same development aids as the F8. Several practical features — 32 bidirectional I/O lines, simple and versatile clock generation (crystal, LC, RC or free-running), single power supply voltage (5V ± 10%), and built-in power-on reset — make it attractive for low-cost controller applications.

In addition, advanced features — high speed, an extensive instruction set, a programmable binary timer, vectored interrupt, a large scratchpad RAM with very efficient access, and a 2K-byte ROM for program storage — provide performance unequaled by any other single-chip microcomputer and equal to far more expensive multi-chip microcomputers. The F3870 is an ideal low-cost solution for applications that require up to 64 bytes, or 128 decimal digits, of RAM and up to 2048 bytes of ROM.

THE F8 MICROPROCESSOR FAMILY
The F8 family of microprocessor building blocks combines the hardware efficiency required in low-end controllers with the structural versatility of a high-speed 8-bit n-channel microprocessor. In its most basic form, a complete F8 microcomputer consists of only two chips: the 3850 Central Processing Unit (CPU) and the 3851 Program Storage Unit (PSU). The partitioning between these two chips is very unusual — the address registers are on the PSU chip, which frees many pins normally needed for address bussing for use as I/O and provides room for a 64-byte scratchpad on the CPU chip. This complete two-chip microcomputer contains:

- 64 bytes of RAM for variable data
- 1K or 2K of ROM for program storage and fixed data
- 32 bidirectional I/O lines
- A versatile timer and vectored interrupt
- On-chip power-on reset and clock generator (crystal or LC controlled)

The F8 is not restricted to this simple configuration, but can be expanded in many ways to implement highly sophisticated microcomputers. Additional chips provide for I/O and memory expansion. Each 3861 Peripheral I/O device (PIO) adds 16 more I/O lines and the 3852 Dynamic Memory Interface (DMI) chip drives the 16-bit address bus and contains the counter and control logic for automatic refresh of dynamic RAMs. A 3854 Direct Memory Access chip provides DMA without interfering with the processing speed of the CPU (no cycle stealing or Halt mode).

The architecture and the instruction set of the F8 are very efficient, but somewhat unconventional. The on-chip scratchpad has its own address register for direct and indirect addressing of the 64-byte RAM, providing fast and

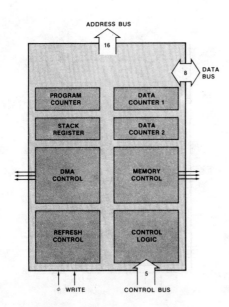

F3852 DMI
Dynamic Memory Interface with
16 Address-Line Drivers and Automatic Refresh Logic

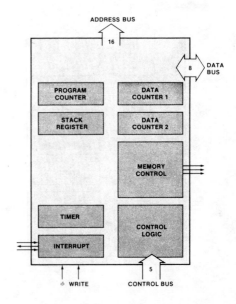

F3853 SMI
Static Memory Interface with
16 Address-Line Drivers, Interrupt and Timer

flexible access with single byte instructions (2 μs). The address counter, located on the PSU chip, is backed up by a second stack register and there is also a pair of memory address counters (data counters 0 and 1) that make table indexing very easy. The F8 has very flexible branching instructions and relative addressing across page boundaries unlike the 8080.

The timer, a function pioneered by the F8 and recently copied by some newer microprocessors, keeps track of time without burdening the program. The timer is presettable and generates an interrupt whenever it times out. Both the external interrupt and the timer-initiated interrupt are vectored and a daisy-chain connection establishes interrupt priority in a multichip system. But, since each interrupt input has its own vector, there is no need for polling.

The F8 is well suited for controller applications that call for minimum hardware and efficient interfacing. For example, a system that requires up to 64 bytes of RAM, up to 4K bytes of program, and up to 48 I/O pins all fits on only three chips. Much larger systems can be built, using the memory interface chips, but the advantages of the F8 then become less dramatic and some of the idiosyncrasies in the architecture and instruction set may make it less convenient to use.

The unorthodox instruction set is not as regular as that of a minicomputer or the F6800; therefore it is difficult for a beginner or a designer with minicomputer programming experience to appreciate and use the F8 instruction set efficiently. Most objections can be put to rest with a few clever applications examples that overcome apparent drawbacks in multibyte arithmetic and in table indexing (look-up tables). The most basic limitation is the inability to nest subroutines in a hardware stack beyond the second level. Software nesting in scratchpad can be used instead but the overhead in time and program storage may be prohibitive.

F6800 MICROPROCESSOR FAMILY

The F6800 microprocessor family is aimed at medium-to-high complexity controller and data-processing applications. The F6800 Microprocessing Unit (MPU) is a "pure" CPU with an extensive, but conventional, instruction set that is easy to learn and apply. It contains three 16-bit registers (program counter, index register and stack pointer), two 8-bit accumulators and an 8-bit status register plus bus drivers for the 8-bit data bus and the 16-bit address bus. The F6800 contains no data or program memory and no I/O; these functions must be provided by additional devices connected to the data and address busses. The F6800 family consists of several compatible devices — the F6810, a 128 x 8 RAM; the F68316, a 2K x 8 ROM; the F6820, a Peripheral Interface Adapter (PIA) with two bidirectional I/O ports and two interrupts; and the F6850 Asynchronous Communications Interface Adapter (ACIA) for asynchronous serial I/O. Other support chips will soon be available; in addition the straightforward architecture of the F6800 allows the use of many other industry-standard devices.

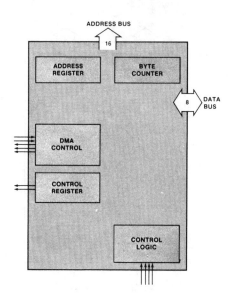

F3854 DMA
Direct Memory Access Controller

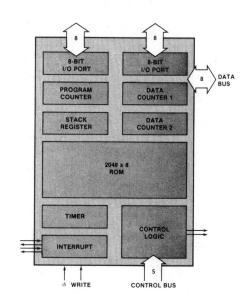

F3856 PSU
2K-Byte Program Storage Unit
with 16 I/O Lines, Interrupt and Timer

The specialized "a la carte" nature of the components in an F6800 system means that even an absolute minimum system must consist of four LSI devices plus a clock driver and reset logic. At this level, it is not competitive with a two-chip F8 or single-chip F3870; but in larger systems, this architecture has many merits. It is easy to design and simple to program.

The F6800 has the appropriate architecture and an extensive instruction set for efficient performance of the different routines, corresponding to the operating system of a larger computer, that monitor and control the execution of the various parts of the program. Orderly transfer of control among these system routines requires efficient stacking of data and status during interrupts. This is done automatically by the F6800. Subroutine return adresses are also stacked automatically. Furthermore, stacking and unstacking can also be performed under program control, when such complexity is warranted.

Another set of features is important for transferring data through the system. The F6800 addressing modes include indexed addressing with a 16-bit index register that enables the program to compute data addresses and to operate efficiently on lengthy data fields such as I/O buffers, translation tables, and the like.

The third kind of activity important in data processing applications is arithmetic. Simple algorithms can be implemented very efficiently with the twin accumulators and the complete

set of conditional branches on signed numbers. When the operation calls for more complex manipulations, such as multiplication and division of multiple-precision data, all microprocessors require elaborate software routines. The rotate and shift instructions of the F6800 help make these routines both efficient and straightforward.

MICROCOMPUTER DEVELOPMENT TOOLS

The development of a microprocessor based system involves four activities.

- Choice of microprocessor devices
- Interconnection of these devices
- Peripheral hardware design
- Programming (software development)

The choice of the appropriate microprocessor devices involves an educated guess of program size and execution speed, especially crucial with the non-expandable single-chip microcomputers. Interconnection of microprocessor components is usually quite straightforward, and well explained by the manufacturer's applications literature.

Peripheral hardware design uses classical electronic and electrical engineering methods. External hardware is used to increase the drive capability, to expand I/O, to perform analog functions or to perform functions that are too fast for the microprocessor. However, the designer must keep in mind the fact that any external hardware increases the manu-

F3857 PSU
2K-Byte Program Storage Unit
with 16 Address-Line Drivers, Interrupt and Timer

F3861 PIO
Programmable I/O Device
with 16 I/O Lines, Interrupt and Timer

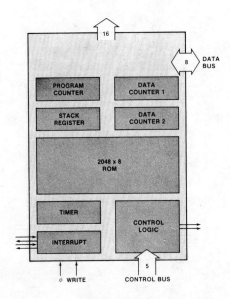

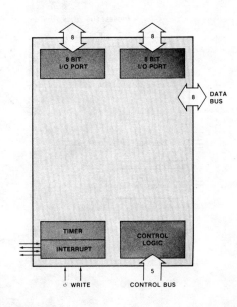

facturing cost. Conventionally, the designer minimizes hardware costs through clever design; with the microprocessor, he often has the option of performing the same functions in software and omitting the external hardware. Whether or not the designer chooses this option depends upon a number of engineering tradeoffs. On the one hand, hardware design is usually considered easier and more straightforward, but adding hardware inevitably increases manufacturing cost. On the other hand, to the designer with a hardware background, programming is a new and unfamiliar activity that takes time. While simple jobs seem to take unwarranted amounts of program, it is important to remember that additional software usually adds little or nothing to the cost of manufacturing.

Software development means programming, but there is one important difference compared to conventional computer programming: microcomputers usually store the program in mask-programmed ROMs, where even a slight change costs over $1000 and takes several weeks. There are no "yellow wires" on silicon, unless the designer chooses the more expensive EPROM for program storage. Since every program of more than trivial complexity begins with several mistakes or oversights, affectionately called "bugs", there must be a way to simulate or emulate the program and debug it before it is committed to ROMs or PROMs.

Moreover, coding a program of more than a few hundred lines in machine code — binary, octal, or hexadecimal —

involves many trivial, tedious and repetitive steps that are performed faster and more reliably by a computer program, called an assembler. The assembler allows the designer to write in a more natural way and produces a printed documentation of the program.

For the F8 and F3870, Fairchild offers the powerful Formulator™ line of development tools, modular microcomputer systems that serve two different purposes. First, the operating system software provides practical support programs which the designer uses in writing and debugging his programs. Second, it is a real-time hardware test bed which can simulate any F8 or F3870 configuration. The user can choose a minimal Formulator configuration with simple peripherals at low cost, or more elaborate versions with convenience features and more sophisticated peripherals as a substantially higher cost.

CONCLUSION

In a world increasingly concerned about growth limitations, inflation, lack of energy and raw materials, the microprocessor stands out as an example of good old-fashioned progress. From a designer's dream and a lab curiosity, it grew in only six years to a family of products that affect nearly everyone's daily life. The alarm clock that starts the day is controlled by a simple microcomputer; the microwave oven, the solar heating system, the automatic telephone dialer, the car engine, the traffic light and the gas pump are microprocessor controlled. The security system and the air condi-

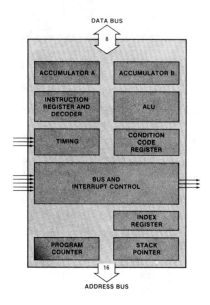

F6800 MPU
8-Bit Microprocessing Unit

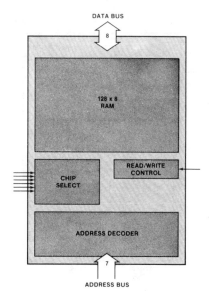

F6810 RAM
128 x 8-Bit Static Random Access Memory

tioning at work, the PABX telephone system and the cash registers in the cafeteria and the supermarket use microprocessors, so do the lawn sprinkling system and the sewing machine at home. A basic microprocessor controls the record player and another remotely controls and tunes the TV and turns the set on at a pre-programmed time. With a microprocessor, the TV can be used to play games. Microprocessors are used in navigation, transportation, education, medicine, forestry and mining. Lumber mills optimize the sawing operation and sailboat skippers figure out the best course with the help of microcomputers. No other major invention has permeated modern life so quickly. The fast growth and immediate acceptance of the microprocessor are the result of the following important factors.

- Industrial and private consumers *expect* increased product sophistication and reliability at a reasonable cost. Only semiconductor LSI can achieve this combination.

- The semiconductor industry must look for a broader market base beyond computers, communications and entertainment. By improving device designs and enhancing fabrication techniques, the industry is reducing component prices at a rate of up to 30% a year. Under these circumstances, traditional markets alone cannot provide any growth in dollar sales.

- Microprocessor fabrication requires no new technologies or innovative mass production techniques; these are already developed for memory and calculator chips.

The intense competition among semiconductor manufacturers will result in dramatically increased chip complexity at reduced prices. The enormous breadth of applications and the large potential volumes — appliance, automotive, personal computers — will lead to even wider product diversification. There will be more practical low-end microcontrollers, eliminating many of the interface components required today. At the other extreme, more powerful microprocessors will take over functions that today need full-fledged minicomputers. They will take advantage of newer and faster semiconductor technologies like I^2L; *and*, they will also be software compatible with established minicomputers. A good example is the Fairchild 9440 16-bit CPU, manufactured using the Isoplanar I^2L process, that executes the Data General Nova instruction set.

The fast-growing market for personal and small-business computers will generate low-cost peripherals and a large variety of inexpensive software written in high-level languages like BASIC. The reduced cost of hardware will stimulate a new approach to software, since memory efficiency is becoming less and less important. The result — more performance at lower cost, for there is no scarcity of either silicon or ingenuity in the world of microprocessors. □

F6820 PIA
Peripheral Interface Adapter with
Two Bidirectional I/O Ports and Two Interrupts

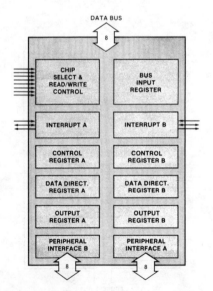

F6850 ACIA
Asynchronous Communications Interface Adapter

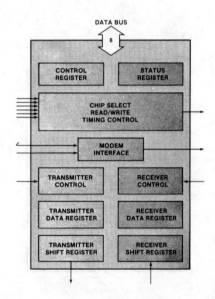

Macrologic

by Peter Alfke

Two basic digital integrated circuit technologies have become dominant in the past decade, MOS and bipolar. Each represents a compromise between complexity, speed and cost. While MOS can easily achieve high functional density and thus complexity at low cost per function, its speed is limited to a few megahertz. Bipolar (TTL and ECL) technology, on the other hand, offers much higher speed but cannot yet compete with MOS density and functional complexity.

Over the last few years, the inherent strong points of both technologies have been significantly improved, but little has been done to overcome their weaknesses. (These remarks do not apply to the very well defined, tightly populated and very competitive world of memories.) Thus MOS functional complexity has increased to the level of a single chip pocket calculator and the two-chip microprocessor, but the processing speed of these elements is quite slow, ≈0.5 MHz.

Bipolar circuits have increased in speed—individual TTL devices can be run at clock rates of 100 MHz; an ECL prescaler can be clocked at up to 1.2 GHz — but their functional complexity has barely increased over the last four years. SSI and MSI with less than 100 gates per chip dominate this field. Therefore, the designer of 5 to 10 MHz systems (mini-computers, process control, communications) has not been able to benefit from the rapid progress made in semiconductor technology.

Recent advances in bipolar processing, specifically LS-TTL, have reduced the power consumption of high performance TTL by a factor of four and decreased component size by a factor of two without

requiring expensive manufacuring methods. Simultaneously, Isoplanar processing has substantially improved the performance of CMOS circuits. Complexities beyond 250 gates per chip are now possible in both technologies and are the basis of a new family of digital integrated circuits called MACROLOGIC™.

These circuits are attractive to the system designer because they reduce cost and design time while maintaining flexibility and performance traditionally offered by TTL SSI/MSI circuits. To the semiconductor manufacturer, these circuits are attractive because a limited number of off-the-shelf components can serve a large number of markets, customers and applications. This means high volume production and low prices, the classical strength of the semiconductor industry.

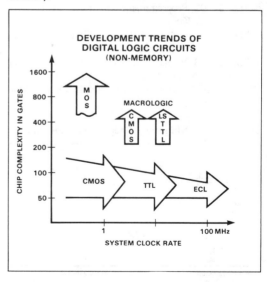

DEVELOPMENT TRENDS OF DIGITAL LOGIC CIRCUITS (NON-MEMORY)

MACROLOGIC circuits are offered in two different technologies:

Advanced Schottky TTL, fully compatible with other TTL logic families, for high performance (9400 series).

- 4 ns delay per gate
- <8 pJ delay power product
- >10 MHz clock rate
- 3-state TTL bus drive capability

Isoplanar CMOS for ultra-low power consumption and high noise margin (34700 series).

- Zero stand-by power
- 20 mW per device at 2 MHz
- 3 to 15 V supply
- >2 MHz clock rate at 5 V

The MACROLOGIC family consists of two groups of circuits—dedicated on-chip subsystems for computer peripherals, communications, and instrumentation applications and functional building blocks for microprogrammed systems.

DEDICATED SUBSYSTEMS

These devices perform complex but well defined and widely used functions offering the designer lower cost, smaller size, reduced power consumption, better reliability, faster design and, if necessary, improved performance over the established MSI/SSI designs. Three devices in this group are presently available:

- The 9401 Cyclic Redundancy Check Generator/Checker—advanced Schottky TTL.
- The 34702 Programmable Bit Rate Generator—Isoplanar CMOS.
- The 9403 16x4 Parallel/Serial First-In First-Out Buffer—advanced Schottky TTL.
- The 34703 Isoplanar CMOS FIFO, functionally identical to the 9403 and offering much lower power consumption and wider supply voltage range, will be available soon.

9401 Cyclic Redundancy Check Generator/Checker

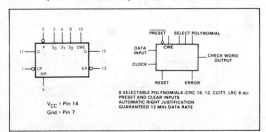

V_{CC} = Pin 14
Gnd = Pin 7

8 SELECTABLE POLYNOMIALS (CRC 16, 12, CCITT, LRC 8 dc)
PRESET AND CLEAR INPUTS
AUTOMATIC RIGHT JUSTIFICATION
GUARANTEED 12 MHz DATA RATE

*For a more detailed description see PROGRESS Jan/Feb 75, page 22.

The 9401 Cyclic Redundancy Check Generator/Checker* is an advanced tool for the implementation of the most widely used error-detection scheme in serial digital data handling systems. A 3-bit control input selects from eight different generator polynomials, including CRC-16 and CRC-CCITT, as well as their reciprocals (reverse polynomials). Polynomials shorter than 16 are automatically right justified. Separate Clear and Preset inputs are provided to simplify floppy disk and similar applications and another control input inhibits the internal feedback during check-word transmission. The Error output indicates whether or not a transmission error has occurred.

The 9401 is guaranteed for a data rate >12 MHz. Fully compatible with all other TTL logic families, it is also pin compatible with the older, slower, less versatile and more expensive MC8503.

34702 Programmable Bit Rate Generator

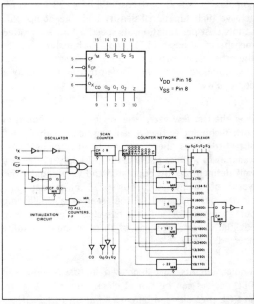

The 34702 Programmable Bit Rate Generator generates any one of the 14 popular bit rates from 50 to 19200 baud used in digital data communications. To operate, it requires only one clock input frequency or a crystal connected across two inputs. Together with a 93L34 8-bit addressable latch, the 34702 can provide eight output frequencies simultaneously; it can also be used in a fully computer-controlled system where the output channel frequency assignments are software controlled. See page 10 of this issue for a detailed description and applications of this circuit.

9403/34703 16x4 Parallel/Serial First-In First-Out (FIFO) Buffer Memory

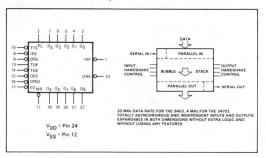

The 9403 is an expandable fall-through type high-speed FIFO Buffer Memory with totally independent and asynchronous inputs and outputs. It is intended for disk and tape controllers and high-speed communications applications with data rates of up to 20 MHz.

Organized as a 4-bit wide by 16-word deep "bubble stack", the 9403 has parallel (four bits) and bit-serial data inputs and outputs. Complete "handshake" control signals are provided for unambiguous operation in asynchronous systems.

The 9403 can be expanded, without any auxiliary parts, to any width (parallel number of bits in multiples of 4) and/or to any depth (number of serial words in multiples of 16). The expanded system retains all the characteristics of a single FIFO, *i.e.* asynchronous handshake control, parallel or serial input and output. The 3-state buffered outputs provide additional system flexibility.

Asynchronous FIFO Buffering

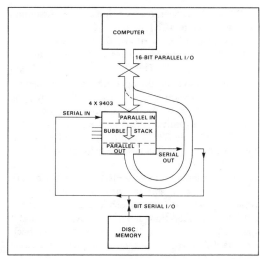

The parallel-serial I/O feature of the 9403 can be used to simplify asynchronous FIFO buffering between a computer and its disk memory. Note that one set of FIFOs (4x9403) buffers both computer-to-disk as well as disk-to-computer transfers without requiring any external multiplexing.

The 9403 FIFO using advanced Schottky technology is available now. The functionally and pin-out identical CMOS device, called 34703, featuring very low power consumption, wider range of supply voltage (3–15 V) and a maximum data rate of 4 MHz will be available soon.

FUNCTIONAL BUILDING BLOCKS

The second group of MACROLOGIC circuits consists of five functional building blocks for microprogrammed systems. These include the following Schottky TTL (9400 series) and CMOS (34700 series) circuits.

- The 9405 and 34705 Arithmetic Logic Register Stacks.
- The 9404 and 34704 Data Path Switches.
- The 9407 and 34707 Data Access Registers.
- The 9406 and 34706 Program Stacks.
- The 9410 and 34710 16x4 RAMs with output registers.

Their common features include
- 4-bit slices, expandable to any word length without auxiliary components.
- Bus-oriented designs: "Output Enable" activates any device as a source (3-state outputs). "Execute" activates any device as a destination.
- Synchronous, single clock operation: TTL devices (9400 series) can operate at a guaranteed 10 MHz clock rate; CMOS devices (34700 series) can operate at a guaranteed 2 MHz clock rate at 5 V supply.
- New slim 24-pin package (400 mil row spacing) saves PC board area.

The advanced Schottky versions combine the high performance and versatility of Schottky MSI/SSI with the advantages of LSI—lower cost, smaller size, reduced power consumption, better reliability, and, last but not least, significantly easier and faster design and debugging. The Isoplanar CMOS circuits, functionally and pin identical to their Schottky TTL counterparts, offer very low power consumption (20 mW at 2 MHz) and a wide range of supply voltage (3–15 V). At 5 V, all delays are roughly five times longer than in the Schottky TTL part and the maximum microinstruction rate is 2 MHz rather than 10 MHz.

Each of these MACROLOGIC circuits performs the function of a well defined section of a typical microprogrammed system that has an instruction set stored in a memory (ROM, PROM, RAM). Unlike the MOS microprocessor on a chip, these MACROLOGIC building blocks do not dictate the system architecture. The designer has full control over the system design and can make a choice between many trade-offs—word length vs instruction and addressing flexibility, single bus vs multiple bus organization, hardware program stack for subroutine nesting vs software controlled RAM-resident stack etc.

MACROLOGIC is the third step in the evolution from transistors to gates and flip-flops (SSI) and then from SSI to functionally defined MSI elements. At each of these steps, there was widespread suspicion that the new higher integration level would sacrifice versatility. But, as designers became accustomed to the new devices, they learned that the higher level of integration not only eliminated the tedious and unimaginative portions of the design task, but opened new possibilities for creative and imaginative system design.

MACROLOGIC does not compete directly with MOS microprocessors. When speed and architectural constraints are acceptable, MOS microprocessors, e.g. 8080, 6800, and Fairchild's new F8, offer the more economical solution. However, when these constraints cannot be tolerated and higher performance or a more specialized architecture is required, then MACROLOGIC is a better choice.

9405/34705 Arithmetic Logic Register Stack (ALRS)

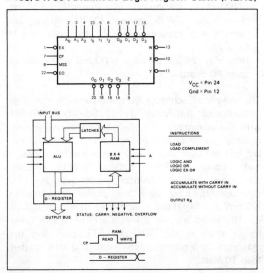

- 8-instruction ALU
- 8-word RAM supplying one operand and storing result.
- Additional edge-triggered output register.
- 3-state output buffers.
- Carry Generate and Propagate outputs for high speed arithmetic over 8, 12, 16 or more bits.
- Status outputs: Zero, Negative, Overflow.
- 9405, 10 MHz instruction rate.
- 34705, 2 MHz instruction rate.

The Arithmetic Logic Register Stack (ALRS, also called a RALU) contains a 4-bit arithmetic logic unit (ALU), an 8-word by 4-bit RAM, an edge-triggered output register, and associated control logic. The ALU implements eight different arithmetic or logic functions where one of the two 4-bit operands is supplied from the input data bus (external source) and the other is supplied from one of the eight RAM words selected by the Address inputs A_0-A_2. The result of the operation is loaded back into the same RAM location and is also loaded into the edge-triggered output register and becomes available on the 3-state output data bus.

The 9405/34705 is a 4-bit slice of a multi-accumulator index-register structure. Carry Propagate and Generate outputs are provided for high-speed expansion through external look-ahead; ripple carry expansion can be used for slower systems. Three Status outputs which qualify the result of an operation, are available—Zero, Negative, and Overflow.

The 9405/34705 operates on a single clock. Assuming that the Execute ($\overline{EX}$) input is LOW, a microcyle starts as the clock goes HIGH. Data is read from the RAM through enabled latches and applied as one operand to the ALU. The Data inputs ($\overline{D}_0$-$\overline{D}_3$) are the other operand and the operation is determined by the Instruction inputs I_0-I_2. When CP is LOW, the latches on the RAM output are disabled, *i.e.*, held stable, and the result of the ALU operation is written back into the same RAM location, provided $\overline{EX}$ is still LOW; A_0-A_2 must obviously be held stable.

On the subsequent LOW-to-HIGH transition of CP, the result is also shifted into the edge-triggered output register and a new microcycle can start. If $\overline{EX}$ is HIGH, the operation determined by the A and I inputs is performed, but the result is not written back into the RAM and is not clocked into the output register.

INSTRUCTION SET FOR THE DPS

I_4	I_3	I_2	I_1	I_0	$\overline{O}_3$	$\overline{O}_2$	$\overline{O}_1$	$\overline{O}_0$	FUNCTION
L	L	L	L	L	L	L	L	L	Byte Mask
L	L	L	L	H	H	H	H	H	Byte Mask
L	L	L	H	L	L	L	L	H	Minus "2" in 2s Comp[1]
L	L	L	H	H	L	L	L	L	Minus "1" in 2s Comp[1]
L	L	H	L	L	$\overline{D}_3$	$\overline{D}_2$	$\overline{D}_1$	$\overline{D}_0$	Byte Mask D-Bus
L	L	H	L	H	H	H	H	H	Byte Mask D-Bus
L	L	H	H	L	$\overline{D}_3$	$\overline{D}_2$	$\overline{D}_1$	$\overline{D}_0$	Byte Mask D-Bus
L	L	H	H	H	L	L	L	L	Byte Mask D-Bus
L	H	L	L	L	L	H	H	H	Negative Byte Sign Mask
L	H	L	L	H	H	H	H	H	Positive Byte Sign Mask
L	H	L	H	L	$\overline{K}_3$	$\overline{K}_2$	$\overline{K}_1$	$\overline{K}_0$	Byte Mask K-Bus
L	H	L	H	H	L	L	L	L	Byte Mask K-Bus
L	H	H	L	L	$\overline{D}_3$	$\overline{D}_2$	$\overline{D}_1$	$\overline{D}_0$	Load Byte
L	H	H	L	H	$\overline{K}_3$	$\overline{K}_2$	$\overline{K}_1$	$\overline{K}_0$	Load Byte
L	H	H	H	L	H	H	H	L	Plus "1"
L	H	H	H	H	H	H	H	H	Zero

I_4	I_3	I_2	I_1	I_0	LO	$\overline{O}_3$	$\overline{O}_2$	$\overline{O}_1$	$\overline{O}_0$	RO	FUNCTION
H	L	L	L	L	$\overline{R}I$	$\overline{R}I$	$\overline{R}I$	$\overline{R}I$	$\overline{R}I$		K-Bus Sign Extend
H	L	L	L	H	$\overline{K}_3$	$\overline{K}_3$	$\overline{K}_2$	$\overline{K}_1$	$\overline{K}_0$		K-Bus Sign Extend
H	L	L	H	L	$\overline{R}I$	$\overline{R}I$	$\overline{R}I$	$\overline{R}I$	$\overline{R}I$		D-Bus Sign Extend
H	L	L	H	H	$\overline{D}_3$	$\overline{D}_3$	$\overline{D}_2$	$\overline{D}_1$	$\overline{D}_0$		D-Bus Sign Extend
H	L	H	L	L	$\overline{D}_3$	$\overline{D}_2$	$\overline{D}_1$	$\overline{D}_0$	$\overline{R}I$		D-Bus Shift Left
H	L	H	L	H	$\overline{K}_3$	$\overline{K}_2$	$\overline{K}_1$	$\overline{K}_0$	$\overline{R}I$		K-Bus Shift Left
H	L	H	H	L		$\overline{L}I$	$\overline{D}_3$	$\overline{D}_2$	$\overline{D}_1$	$\overline{D}_0$	D-Bus Shift Right
H	L	H	H	H		$\overline{D}_3$	$\overline{D}_3$	$\overline{D}_2$	$\overline{D}_1$	$\overline{D}_0$	D-Bus Shift Right Arith[2]
H	H	L	L	L		$\overline{L}I$	$\overline{K}_3$	$\overline{K}_2$	$\overline{K}_1$	$\overline{K}_0$	K-Bus Shift Right
H	H	L	L	H		$\overline{K}_3$	$\overline{K}_3$	$\overline{K}_2$	$\overline{K}_1$	$\overline{K}_0$	K-Bus Shift Right Arith[2]
H	H	L	H	L		$\overline{K}_3$	$\overline{K}_2$	$\overline{K}_1$	$\overline{K}_0$		Byte Mask K-Bus
H	H	L	H	H		H	H	H	H		Byte Mask K-Bus
H	H	H	L	L		D_3	D_2	D_1	D_0		Complement D-Bus
H	H	H	L	H		K_3	K_2	K_1	K_0		Complement K-Bus
H	H	H	H	L							Undefined
H	H	H	H	H							Undefined

H = HIGH Level
L = LOW Level
(1) Comp = Complement
(2) Arith = Arithmetic

9404/34704 Data Path Switch (DPS)

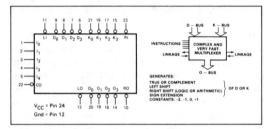

- Very fast combinatorial data router.
- Two 4-bit input busses, one 3-state 4-bit output bus.
- Passes, inverts or shifts either of the two inputs to the output.
- Byte masking, sign extension, and arithmetic shift capability.
- Generates several constants.
- 9404, < 30 ns delay over 16 bits.
- 34704, <150 ns delay over 16 bits.

The 9404/34704 Data Path Switch (DPS) is a very fast combinatorial array for closing data path loops around arithmetic logic networks like the 9405 ALRS. A 5-bit instruction word (I_0-I_4) selects one of the 32 instructions operating on two sets of 4-bit data inputs ($\overline{D}_0$-$\overline{D}_3$, $\overline{K}_0$-$\overline{K}_3$). Four linkage lines (Left Input, Left Output, Right Input, Right Output) are available for expansion in 4-bit increments. An active LOW Output Enable input ($\overline{EO}$) provides 3-state control of the Data Outputs ($\overline{D}_0$-$\overline{D}_3$) for bus oriented applications.

The 9404/34704 combines the functions of a dual 4-input multiplexer, a True/Complement-One/Zero generator, and a shift-left/shift-right array. As shown in the Table, there are two shift-right modes. The arithmetic right shift preserves the sign bit in the most significant position while the logic shift moves all positions. Right shift is defined as a 1-bit shift toward the least significant position.

For half-word arithmetic, the 9404 provides instructions which extend the sign bit left through the more significant slices. Shift linkages are available as individual inputs and outputs for complete flexibility. The 9404/34704 may be used to generate constants +1, 0, −1 and −2 in two's complement notation.

9406/34706 Program Stack (P-Stack)

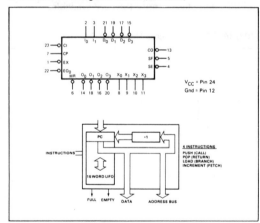

- 16-word deep LIFO for 15-level subroutine nesting.
- On-chip program count incrementer.
- Two output busses to facilitate external address manipulation.
- Four instructions: Load (Branch)
  Push and Load (Call)
  Pop (Return)
  Increment top stack contents (Fetch)
- Stack Full and Empty status outputs.
- 9406, 10 MHz instruction rate.
- 34706, 2 MHz instruction rate.

The 9406/34706 16-word by 4-bit "Push Down-Pop Up" Program Stack stores program counters (PC) and return addresses for nested subroutines in programmable digital systems. It executes four instructions—Return, Branch, Call, and Fetch as specified by a 2-bit instruction. When the device is initialized, PC is in the top stack location. As a new PC value is "pushed" into the stack (Call operation), all previous PC values effectively move down one level. The top location of the stack is the current PC. Up to 16 PC values can be stored, which gives the 9406/34706 a 15-level nesting capability. "Popping" the stack (Return operation) brings the most recent PC to the top. The remaining two instructions affect only the top location of the stack. During Branch operation, a new PC value is loaded into the top stack location from the $\overline{D}_0$-$\overline{D}_3$ inputs. In the Fetch operation, the content of the top stack location (current PC value) is put on the X_0-X_3 bus and the current PC value is incremented.

The 9406/34706 may be expanded to any word length without additional logic. Three-state output drivers are provided on the 4-bit Address outputs (X_0-X_3) and data outputs, ($\overline{O}_0$-$\overline{O}_3$); the X-bus outputs are enabled internally during the Fetch instruction while the O-bus outputs are controlled by an Output Enable ($\overline{EO}_O$). Two status outputs, Stack Full ($\overline{SF}$) and Stack Empty ($\overline{SE}$) are available.

9407/34707 Data Access Register (DAR)

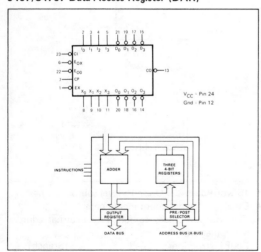

- Contains three registers.
- $\overline{D}$ inputs can be loaded into or accumulated in either register.
- Limited register-to-register transfer capability.
- Edge-triggered output register with 3-state buffers on the 0-bus.

- Pre/post arithmetic selector with 3-state buffers on the X-bus.
- 9407, 10 MHz instruction rate.
- 34707, 2 MHz instruction rate.

The 9407/34707 Data Access Register (DAR) performs a memory address arithmetic for RAM resident stack applications. It contains three 4-bit registers—program counter (R_0), stack pointer (R_1) and operand address (R_2)—a 4-bit adder, a 3-state address output buffer (X_0-X_3), and a separate output register with 3-state buffers ($\overline{O}_0$-$\overline{O}_3$) for providing the register output on the data bus. The DAR performs 16 instructions, selected by I_0-I_3, as listed in the table.

Assuming that $\overline{EX}$ is LOW, a microcyle starts as CP goes HIGH. Data inputs ($\overline{D}_0$-$\overline{D}_3$) are applied to the adder as one of the operands. Three of the four instruction lines (I_1, I_2, I_3) select which of the three registers, if any, is to be used as the other operand. The LOW-to-HIGH CP transition writes the result from the adder into a register (R_0-R_2) and into the output register. If the I_0 instruction input is HIGH, the multiplexer routes the result from the adder to the 3-state buffer controlling the address bus (X_0-X_3), independent of $\overline{EX}$ and CP. If I_0 is LOW, the multiplexer routes the output of the selected register directly into the 3-state buffer controlling the address bus (X_0-X_3), independent of $\overline{EX}$ and CP.

The 9407/34707 is organized as a 4-bit register slice. The active LOW $\overline{CE}$ and $\overline{CO}$ lines allow ripple-carry expansion over longer word lengths. For a Fetch instruction, PC can be gated on the X-bus while it is being incremented, i.e., D-bus = 1. If the instruction calls for an effective address for execution, which is displaced from the PC, the displacement can be added to the PC and loaded into R_2 during the next microcycle.

INSTRUCTION SET FOR THE DAR

INSTRUCTION				COMBINATORIAL FUNCTION AVAILABLE ON THE X-BUS	SEQUENTIAL FUNCTION OCCURRING ON THE NEXT RISING CP EDGE
I_3	I_2	I_1	I_0		
L	L	L	L	R_0	
L	L	L	H	R_0 plus D plus CI	R_0 plus D plus CI · R_0 and 0-register
L	L	H	L	R_0	
L	L	H	H	R_0 plus D plus CI	R_0 plus D plus CI · R_1 and 0-register
L	H	L	L	R_0	
L	H	L	H	R_0 plus D plus CI	R_0 plus D plus CI · R_2 and 0-register
L	H	H	L	R_1	
L	H	H	H	R_1 plus D plus CI	R_1 plus D plus CI · R_1 and 0-register
H	L	L	L	R_2	
H	L	L	H	D plus CI	D plus CI · R_2 and 0-register
H	L	H	L	R_0	
H	L	H	H	D plus CI	D plus CI · R_0 and 0-register
H	H	L	L	R_2	
H	H	L	H	R_2 plus D plus CI	R_2 plus D plus CI · R_2 and 0-register
H	H	H	L	R_1	
H	H	H	H	D plus CI	D plus CI · R_1 and 0-register

L = LOW Level   H = HIGH Level

9410/34710 16x4 RAM with Output Register (R-Stack)

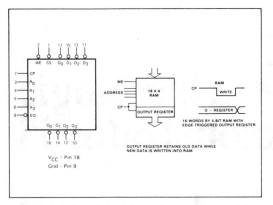

V_{CC} - Pin 18
Gnd - Pin 9

16-WORDS BY 4-BIT RAM WITH
EDGE-TRIGGERED OUTPUT REGISTER

OUTPUT REGISTER RETAINS OLD DATA WHILE
NEW DATA IS WRITTEN INTO RAM

- 16x4 RAM optimized for register stack operation.
- Edge-triggered output register with 3-state buffers.
- 18-pin package.
- 9410, 10 MHz clock rate.
- 34710, 2 MHz clock rate.

The 9410/34710 is a register-oriented high-speed 64-bit Read/Write Memory organized as 16 words by four bits. An edge-triggered 4-bit output register allows new input data to be written while previous data is held. Three-state outputs are provided for maximum versatility.

When the three Control inputs—Write Enable ($\overline{WE}$), Chip Select ($\overline{CS}$), and Clock (CP)—are LOW, the information on the Data inputs ($\overline{D_0}$-$\overline{D_3}$) is written into the memory location selected by the Address inputs (A_0-A_3). If the input data changes while $\overline{WE}$, $\overline{CS}$, and CP are LOW, the content of the selected memory location follows these changes provided set-up time criteria are met.

Whenever $\overline{CS}$ is LOW and CP goes from LOW to HIGH, the contents of the memory location selected by the Address inputs (A_0-A_3) is edge-triggered into the output register. A 3-state Output Enable ($\overline{EO}$) controls the output buffers. When $\overline{EO}$ is HIGH, the four outputs ($\overline{Q_0}$-$\overline{Q_3}$) are in a high-impedance or OFF state; when $\overline{EO}$ is LOW, the outputs are determined by the state of the output register.

Memories for Microprogram Storage.

All microprogrammed systems require a high speed microprogram storage of considerable width (number of parallel bits) but with a limited number of addresses (64 to 256 typically). For high volume production of established designs, mask-programmed read-only memories (ROMs) offer the lowest cost,

but require a volume commitment (usually >1000 devices) and a turnaround time of several weeks.

Field-programmable read-only memories (PROMs) can be programmed by the user, thus avoiding the ROM drawbacks, but they are slightly more expensive and require either significant programming time for each device or sophisticated programming equipment.

Random-access read-write memories (RAMs) offer the ultimate in flexibility since the microprogram can be changed at any time, but they cost more per bit and they are volatile, *i.e.* they lose their information whenever the supply voltage disappears. Therefore they require either battery back-up or they must be reloaded from another non-volatile memory (magnetic disk or tape or paper tape).

A large number of bipolar ROMs, PROMs and RAMs are now, or will soon be available as indicated in the following chart.

FAIRCHILD MEMORIES FOR MICROPROGRAM STORAGE			
BIPOLAR ROMs (High Speed TTL)			
93434	32 x 8	Open Collector	NOW
93406	256 x 4	Open Collector	NOW
93431	512 x 4	Open Collector	2nd Q 75
93441	512 x 4	3-state	2nd Q 75
93432	512 x 8	Open Collector	3rd Q 75
93442	512 x 8	3-state	3rd Q 75
93454	1024 x 8	Open Collector	3rd Q 75
93464	1024 x 8	3-state	3rd Q 75
BIPOLAR PROMS (High Speed TTL)			
93416	256 x 4	Open Collector	NOW
93426	256 x 4	3-state	NOW
93436	512 x 4	Open Collector	NOW
93446	512 x 4	3-state	NOW
93438	512 x 8	Open Collector	2nd Q 75
93448	512 x 8	3-state	2nd Q 75
BIPOLAR RAMs (High Speed TTL)			
93410	256 x 1	Open Collector	NOW
93411	256 x 1	Open Collector	NOW
93421	256 x 1	3-state	NOW
93415	1024 x 1	Open Collector	NOW
93425	1024 x 1	3-state	NOW
93412	256 x 4	Open Collector	2nd Q 75
93422	256 x 4	3-state	2nd Q 75
93419	64 x 9	Open Collector	3rd Q 75
93429	64 x 9	3-state	3rd Q 75
CMOS RAMs			
34720	256 x 1	3-state	NOW
34721	256 x 4	3-state	4th Q 75
34725	16 x 4	3-state	2nd Q 75

CMOS ROMs and PROMs are not yet available from any manufacturer, and the number of CMOS RAMs is still quite limited. It should be noted that the volatility of CMOS RAMs can be overcome with a very small battery.

Macrologic Demonstrator II

By Paul Chu

Macrologic devices are LSI components designed for micro-programming applications. They are available in bipolar and CMOS versions, accommodating both high-speed and low-power design considerations. Earlier this year, PROGRESS carried an article about the Macrologic Demonstrator, a learning aid designed with processor-oriented Macrologic devices and used to demonstrate microprogramming concepts. In the earlier article, the architecture of the Macrologic Demonstrator was described. This article describes some microprogramming examples and system operation.

Before discussing microprogramming examples, however, it is necessary to mention a few changes that have been made to the demonstrator itself since this Spring. The updated demonstrator is now designated the Macrologic Demonstrator II. It has been consolidated on a single printed-circuit board (it was on two), and the microprogram control word width has been expanded from 28 bits to 32 bits.

Organization of the new demonstrator is shown in *Figure 1*. Included are a *data path* section, a *microprogram control* section, an *operator control display* section, and an *S-100 bus interface* section. The *data path* section has the following components: two 9404 Data Path Switches, two 9405A Arithmetic Logic Register Stacks, two 9406 Program Stacks, two 9407 Data Access Registers, and two 9410 Register Stacks. The *microprogram control* section has a 9408 Microprogram Sequencer and eight 93L422 Static RAMs providing a 256-word by 32-bit microprogram memory (known as a control store). Human interface is provided through the *operator control and display* section, which contains switches and LED displays that allow the operator to load and modify the control memory, run or single-step the program, and monitor system status and the contents of the various system busses. The *S-100 bus interface* and a compatible edge connector allow the demonstrator to plug directly into an S-100 bus. This provides the capability of programming the control store with an 8080-based system instead of through the operator panel switches.

MICROPROGRAMMED SYSTEMS

Basically, a microprogrammed machine involves two levels utilizing macro and micro-instructions. Machine commands are the macro-instructions, and the sequence of steps that execute these commands are the micro-instructions. Machine commands or macro-instructions reside in the main memory. With each macro-instruction Fetch, a sequence of

micro-instructions is executed. Each micro-instruction controls the unit for one clock cycle (one microcycle). A group of micro-instructions is called a microprogram and is generally stored in the microprogram memory. The microprogram memory generally uses PROMs. The Demonstrator II, however, uses RAMs to facilitate alterations of the control store.

Microprogram memory storage is in the form of 32-bit words with each word grouped into fields. These fields can be one bit or several bits long. Defining the various fields of the microprogram word is known as *formatting*. There are two areas of information that must be included in each micro-instruction. First, there must be some definition and control of the operations that are to be performed by the data path section or other system logic. This area includes such items as the ALU function, sources of data, destination registers, shift or rotate functions, stack control, and data in or data out functions. Second, the address of the next micro-instruction to be performed must be provided. This may be done with an actual address field value, or it may be accomplished implicitly. An example of an implicit address is the case when the next address is always the current address plus one.

The control word format for the Macrologic II Demonstrator II is shown in the accompanying table. Data path organization is shown in *Figure 2* and serves to illustrate the highly bus-organized configurations possible with Macrologic sys-

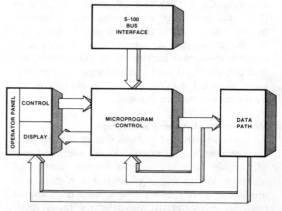

Fig. 1   Demonstrator II Organization

CONTROL WORD FORMAT	
BITS	**FUNCTION**
C0 - C1	0 bus source. These bits select the device driving the input bus of the DPS by activating the proper Output Enable ($\overline{EO}$) input. 00 - ALRS 01 - DAR 10 - P-stack 11 - R-stack
C2 - C3	D-bus destination. These bits specify device to be activated and respond to C4 - C7 by enabling the proper Execute ($\overline{EX}$) input. 00 - EXT* 01 - DAR 10 - P-stack 11 - R-stack
C4 - C7	Shared between P-stack, DAR and R-stack, these bits are Instruction inputs to the P-stack and DAR and Address inputs to the R-stack.
C8 - C13	Instruction inputs to the DPS.
C14	Rotate control. Specifies source of carry in (external or rotate) during DPS shifts.
C15 - C23	Shared between the 9408 Sequencer and ALRS. When the 9408 instruction (C24 - C27) is neither a Fetch or a Return, these bits are the Branch Address. Otherwise, C15 - C17 select one ALRS register for destination of ALU operations, C21 - C23 become ALRS Instruction inputs.
C24 - C27	9408 Sequencer Instruction inputs.
C28	9407 X-Bus enable input.
C29	9406 and 9407 Carry in input.
C30	9404 Carry in input for shift function.
C31	Spare

*External, non-selected

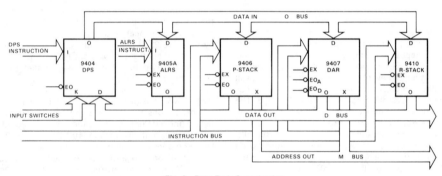

Fig. 2   Data Path Organization

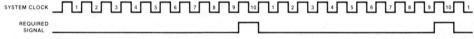

Fig. 3   Desired Timing Signal

tems. Instruction inputs of the P-stack, DAR, and R-stack units are bussed together to provide instruction field sharing. The same 4-bit field (C4 — C7) controls all devices, but only one of the devices can execute a micro-instruction in a given microcycle. The K-bus inputs of the DPS units are connected to the eight Data input switches on the operator panel so that external information can be placed on the data path. Three additional busses are available: a D-bus, an O-bus, and an M-bus. The D-bus is formed by connecting the DPS D inputs to the corresponding O outputs of the ALRS, P-stack, DAR, and R-stack units. The O-bus is a result of connecting the DPS O outputs to the corresponding D inputs of the ALRS, P-stack, DAR, and R-stack units. The M-bus is created by wiring the X outputs of the P-stack units to the X outputs of the DAR units. All devices other than the DPS have an Execute input ($\overline{EX}$), and these devices do not respond to the system clock unless this input is LOW. Also, since the devices have 3-state outputs, the outputs remain in the high-impedance state unless Output Enable is LOW. As a result, during any single microcycle, data can be routed to and from any device on the data path (including itself) through proper control of the $\overline{EX}$ and $\overline{EO}$ inputs.

PROGRAMMING EXAMPLES
Perhaps the best approach to explaining the programming of the system is through examples. The first example involves generating timing signals, which are often necessary in microprogrammed systems for control functions.

Generating A Timing Signal
For this example, assume that it is necessary to generate a timing signal that is required to go HIGH for one clock period out of 10 and be LOW for the remaining nine clock periods, see *Figure 3*. There is an unused control bit (from the control word format table, bit C31), that can be used to generate this timing signal. The strategy behind generating the program is outlined in the flow-chart, *Figure 4*. Register 0 of the ALRS is used as a shift register which is loaded with the binary constant 00001000. This pattern is shifted left one place and the resulting pattern returned to register 0. A test is then initiated to determine if the most significant bit of this result is set. If it is not, the shift left and test procedures are repeated until it is. When the most significant bit is set, control bit 31 is marked HIGH, and the original binary pattern is loaded into ALRS register 0 again.

93

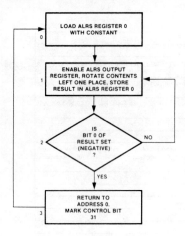

Fig. 4 Timing Signal Flowchart

Flowchart labels:
- 0: LOAD ALRS REGISTER 0 WITH CONSTANT
- 1: ENABLE ALRS OUTPUT REGISTER, ROTATE CONTENTS LEFT ONE PLACE, STORE RESULT IN ALRS REGISTER 0
- 2: IS BIT 0 OF RESULT SET (NEGATIVE) ? — NO / YES
- 3: RETURN TO ADDRESS 0, MARK CONTROL BIT 31

Because of the location of the '1' in the original binary pattern, the system must perform four left shifts of the data before a '1' will appear in the most significant position. This requires nine clock pulses, with a HIGH appearing on the timing signal at bit C31 every tenth pulse, exactly the result intended. A binary representation of this program, which has four instructions (control words) is shown in *Figure 5*. The fields include data in the form of zeros and ones; the blank bit positions indicate a "Don't Care" condition. The first instruction is at location 0 and loads the binary constant on the DPS output bus. Control bits 8 — 13 cause a negative sign mask on the least significant nibble and a positive sign mask on the most significant nibble, resulting in 00001000 on the output bus. Control bits 15 — 23 load the data into register 0 of the ALRS. Control bits 24 — 27 instruct the sequencer to initiate a Fetch, which causes the next instruction (control word) to be read. Execution of the first instruction sets control bit 31 to 0 and the result of the operation is strobed into the output register of the ALRS during the rising edge of the clock.

The second instruction (location 1) effects the shift left of the binary pattern. Control bits 0 and 1 enable the ALRS output register to drive the D-bus of the DPS. Control bits 8 — 13 instruct the DPS to shift left; bit 14 specifies a rotate, and the combination causes a rotate left by one place. Bits 16 — 23 cause the ALRS to load the data that is on the DPS output into

register 0 of the ALRS. Bits 24 — 27 are again used to initiate a Fetch, loading the next instruction or command word for execution. Bit 31 is set to '0' since the most significant bit of the binary pattern is still a '0'.

The third instruction (location 2) causes one of two actions based on the status of the ALRS negative flag. This is accomplished by a conditional branch instruction provided by bits 24 — 27 that indicates a branch if the negative flag is not set. The branch address is specified by bits 16 — 23, and in this case, is location 1 which contains the second instruction. Because all of the ALRS status flags (carry, negative, overflow, and zero) are strobed into the sequencer's internal test registers at the end of the cycle that activates the ALRS, the flags can be examined and further action can be initiated depending on the status of these flags. If the negative flag is not set, the sequencer will cause execution of location 1, which means a repeat of the second instruction. If the negative flag is set, the sequencer will initiate another Fetch and proceed to location 3 which contains the fourth and final instruction or command word.

The fourth instruction (location 3) contains an unconditional branch specified by control bits 24 — 27. The branch address, which is location 0 (the first instruction), is specified by bits 16 — 23 of this instruction. Upon completion of this instruction, control bit 31 is set HIGH since the '1' of the original binary pattern has now been shifted into the most-significant-bit position.

By following this program step-by-step, it can be seen that the instructions at locations 1 and 2 are executed four times before the instruction at location 3 is executed. The sequence of execution is locations 0,1,2,1,2,1,2,1,2,3, causing a HIGH on control bit 31 every tenth clock pulse, (every time the instruction at location 3 is executed). The unconditional branch included in the instruction at location 3 causes a jump to location 0, starting the sequence over.

Accurate timing control can be generated with this type of programming, providing that the durations of the HIGH and LOW portions of the desired waveform are coincident with the multiples of the clock period. The same end result can be accomplished using hardware, e.g., a divide-by-10 counter, in cases involving such simple timing requirements. However, with more complicated timing requirements, hardware approaches would require substantial numbers of SSI or MSI components and are not as structured or as well-organized. Moreover, changes would require hardware alterations instead of simple program modifications.

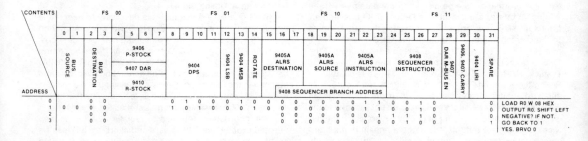

Fig. 5 Timing Signal Program

Using The Timing Signal

Once such a program is generated, it is loaded into the microprogram memory or control store. To accomplish this, the memory address is set to '0' by depressing the demonstrator Reset switch. By using the eight Data switches, the information for the first field of the first location, (from *Figure 5*) is entered by depressing the Deposit switch. The corresponding LED indicators illuminate, indicating which data has been entered so it can be verified. Subsequent data for the following fields is coded with the Data switches and entered via the Deposit Next switch. Once the program is loaded, the single-step mode can be used to step the demonstrator through the program, which can be verified by observing the LED address indicators as the unit steps through the instructions. An LED indicator also illuminates to indicate that the negative status flag is set. In the single-step mode, the various states of the system can be observed one microcycle at a time. The system can be placed in the run mode to observe and evaluate its dynamic behavior. The run mode is also used to evaluate devices under operating conditions and provides the capability of measuring some switching characteristics on an oscilloscope.

If the demonstrator is placed in the run mode and connected to an oscilloscope, the waveforms for this timing signal program appear as illustrated in *Figure 6*. There is a slight delay between the rising edge of the tenth clock pulse and the time that control bit 31 becomes HIGH. This is attributable to a propagation delay caused by a delay between the clock and

the sequencer address output added to the memory access time (t_{AA}), *see Figure 7*. According to Macrologic data sheets, these delays are typically 52 ns and 30 ns, respectively. The address synchronization function of the demonstrator can be used to verify these delays. Referring again to *Figure 6*, the address synchronization signal can be used as a reference on the oscilloscope screen. Since the fourth instruction in the program is the only one that causes a significant transition during execution of the sequence, it is appropriate to use the resulting signal trace for synchronization. This is accomplished by setting the Data input switches to three (the location of the fourth instruction) and placing the system in the run mode. Thus, each time that this instruction is executed, a HIGH pulse appears on the Address Sync output.

The combination of the system clock (CP) and the address synchronization traces can be used to determine the execution sequence. To measure the actual delays encountered, the trace for the least significant address line (A_0) of the sequencer must be considered also. During execution of the fourth program instruction, A_0 goes HIGH some time after CP goes HIGH. Similarly, control bit 31 (C31) goes HIGH during execution of this instruction. Actual control store access time (t_{AA}) can be determined by measuring the interval between the rising edge of A_0 and the rising edge of C31. In this particular example, the actual clock-to-address delay (t_{pd}) is 50 ns and the actual address access time of the control store (t_{AA}) is 25 ns.

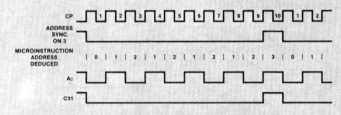

Fig. 6 Timing Signal Program Waveforms

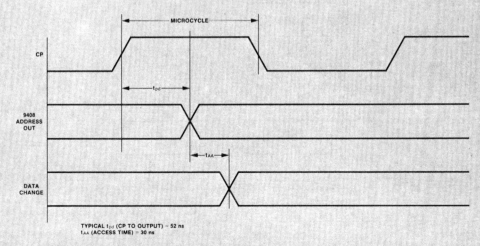

TYPICAL t_{pd} (CP TO OUTPUT) = 52 ns
t_{AA} (ACCESS TIME) = 30 ns

Fig. 7 Typical Delays

Binary Multiplication

Another programming example involves writing a sequence of instructions for performing binary multiplication. This example involves multiplication of two 4-bit binary numbers and provides an 8-bit binary result. A flow chart delineating the necessary actions is shown in *Figure 8*. The program performs the following basic operations. First, a count register is selected and loaded with eight. This count register is used to determine when the multiplication is complete (after eight counts). A result register is selected and cleared by loading it with 0. After loading the multiplicand and the multiplier registers, the most significant bit is examined. If it is set, the multiplicand is added in to form a partial product, and if it is not set, nothing is done. Then, the multiplier and the partial product are shifted left one place and the pro-

cedure repeated until a total product is obtained (the count register is 0). At this time, the result register contains the product and the multiplication program is complete.

The program may be coded by hand with the switches on the demonstrator, as was done in the timing signal example, or it may be prepared by a microprogram assembler. An assembler is a program that allows the user to enter instructions and addresses with mnemonics and symbols that are familiar to the user and that are recognized by the system as machine codes represented by binary bit patterns. The assembler accepts the mnemonic instructions and arranges them as bit patterns in the appropriate fields for each program step. Obviously, this is much easier when coding large programs.

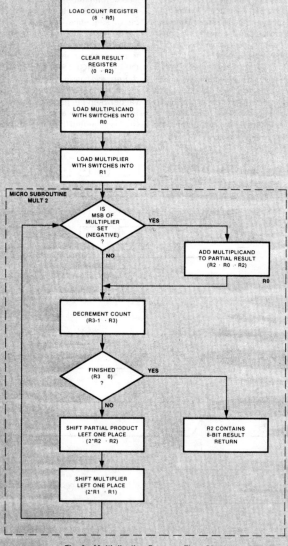

Fig. 8   Multiplication Program Flow Chart

The multiplication program of this example was prepared with an assembler, and the results are shown in *Figure 9*. Each micro-instruction is coded using mnemonics such as "SIGNMASK" or "LOAD", and the assembler produces outputs corresponding to the location and content of the micro-instruction in hexadecimal format. The statements shown on the right-hand side of the program listing are known as comments, and are generated by the user to help identify just what the adjacent mnemonic instruction states. In this example the actual multiplication portion of the program is treated separately as a subroutine. This provides the advantage of listing it in the program only once and calling it to perform multiplication when needed. It also reduces the total amount of memory needed to store the program, since the subroutine is stored once regardless of the number of times it is called in the program.

SUMMARY

Microprogramming for the Macrologic Demonstrator II can be accomplished by using the switches provided on the unit or by connecting the unit to the popular S-100 system bus and entering programs through an 8080-based system. Either way, the resulting program can replace hardware, significantly reducing the effort required when modifications are required. By using programmed logic, memory can be incorporated as a functional building block for system design. In this particular case, utilizing Macrologic circuits that are designed for processor systems and simple programming, a highly structured yet flexible design approach is possible. The Macrologic Demonstrator II is not organized along the lines of typical CPU systems, but it is representative of their functions and provides a valuable learning tool for examining both Macrologic and microprogramming concepts. □

```
MULTI       SIGNMASK,MS1,D3,LOAD                            LOAD 8
      5D 0A44C326

            ZERO,D2,LOAD                                    CLR RESULT REG
      5E 0A7C8326

            DAREX,D->R0,KMASK0,MS1,D0,LOAD                  LOAD NIBBLE
      5F 1AD40326

            PSTKEX,BRANCH,KMASK0,MS1,D1,LOAD                FROM SWITCHES
      60 29D04326

            MULT2,BSR                                       MULTIPLY
      61 0A606316

MULFIN      BRVO,MULFIN
      62 0A606246

MULT2       MULT1,BNNEG
      63 0A6065E6

            DAROE,PASS,D2,S2,ADD
      64 4A609126

MULT1       MINUS-ONE,D3,S3,ADD                             DECREMENT COUNT

      65 0A1CD926

            MULTEXIT,BZERO                                  FINISHED ?
      66 0A606BC6

            D2,S2,OUTPUT                                    SET UP PARTIAL RESULT
      67 0A609426

            DSHL,D2,LOAD                                    CONTINUE
      68 0AA08326

            PSTKOE,PSTKEX,BRANCH,DSHL,D1,LOAD
      69 A9A04326

            BRVO,MULT2
      6A 0A606346

MULTEXIT    D2,S2,OUTPUT,RTS                                DISPLAY RESULT AND RETURN
      6B 0A609406
```

Fig. 9 Assembled Multiplication Program Listing

Single-Board Microcomputer

by Juan Monico

Labels: XTAL, PROM, RAM

*FAIRBUG INCLUDED

SINGLE-BOARD MICROCOMPUTER

Based on the F8 and completely supported by Formulator™ program development aids, this microcomputer is built on a 7 1/2" x 10 1/2" printed circuit board with room left over for a pre-drilled 8-square-inch breadboard area for customizing by the user. Features such as truly bidirectional I/O lines and sockets that can be used for different functions provide completeness and flexibility that mean you can use this microcomputer the way you get it. Just hook up a power supply and teletypewriter...

WHAT YOU GET

An OCM-1 single-board microcomputer system provides the following features.

- Complete F8 Instruction Set Execution

- Complete Fairbug Resident Monitor

- Up to 64 Individually Programmable, Bidirectional Latched, and Decoded I/O Lines

- User-Defined Breadboard Area

- TTY or RS-232C Interface

- Static Memory Interface

- Two or Four Programmable Interrupts

- 64 Bytes of High-Speed Scratch-Pad Memory

- 1K Bytes of RAM for Permanent Storage

- Up to 6K Bytes of ROM

- Up to 4K Bytes of PROM

- Up to 2K Bytes of EPROM

- 2 MHz Crystal-Controlled Clock

- Simple Access to Address and Data Busses

At this time, the OCM-1 is the only single-board microcomputer to offer this much capability. The amount and variety of storage available, the number of bidirectional I/O lines, the interfaces provided, and the functions possible have generally required more than one board, often several.

HOW YOU GET IT

The system is based on the 8-bit F8 CPU and also includes an F8 Program Storage Unit, a static memory interface circuit, 1K byte of RAM, a TTY RS-232C interface, a clock, and supporting circuitry. These basic units provide a portion of the total capability. Two 8-bit I/O ports and the high-speed 64-byte scratch-pad memory are included in the CPU. The Program Storage Unit (PSU) contains the Fairbug™ Resident Monitor and also provides 1K of ROM and two more 8-bit I/O ports. This unit plugs into a socket and can be replaced by other circuits if it is not required.

Sockets are provided for the other circuits used in the OCM-1, and they provide for the expansion capabilities and versatility possible with this microcomputer board. Four sockets are available for 1K PROMs. Two sockets are available for 1K Erasable PROMs. Two other sockets are provided that can accept either F8 PIO circuits or F8 PSU circuits. In either case, four additional 8-bit I/O ports are provided, bringing the total to 64 bidirectional I/O lines. Also, either the PIO or PSU circuit can be used in place of the Fairbug circuit if this monitor is not required for a particular application. This

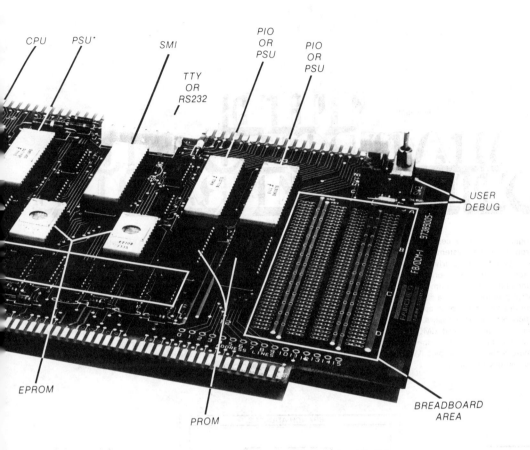

CPU PSU* SMI TTY OR RS232 PIO OR PSU PIO OR PSU USER DEBUG

EPROM PROM BREADBOARD AREA

provides another 1K byte of ROM. This same socket can also accept the K-D Bug system in place of the Fairbug. The K-D Bug system contains all of the functions of the Fairbug and also includes the capability of operating with a calculator-style keyboard and an LED display. OCM-1 microcomputers are normally furnished with the Fairbug. K-D Bug is an optional monitor.

BIDIRECTIONAL I/O
Each of the possible 64 I/O lines on the OCM-1 is truly bidirectional and fully decoded on the board, offering direct TTL compatibility. These lines are programmable for either input or output functions with single-byte instructions. Each line can be used for both input and output at the same time. A line can be providing an input from a key-closure on a keyboard matrix and also be providing an output to drive a display segment. Simultaneous use of these I/O lines greatly expands the capability and versatility of the system.

TERMINAL INTERFACE
A circuit is included on the board for interface to a standard teletypewriter or other 20 mA current loop terminal. Simple jumper connections convert this circuit for RS-232C interface applications.

SOME NICE TOUCHES
In addition to the flexibility offered by the interchangable nature of using sockets for storage and I/O functions, there are other advantages incorporated in the OCM-1 board. A Formulator-compatible 100-pin edge connector is included as well as two 44-pin edge connectors for I/O connections. A large pre-drilled breadboard area is available for user-defined functions. Switches allow simple selection of either the system or user-defined starting address.

In its standard configuration, the OCM-1 has two interrupts and two timers - one each in the PSU and one each in the static memory interface. If two more PIO circuits are used, two additional interrupts and timers are provided. A "daisy chain" priorty systems determines the order of servicing simultaneous interrupt requests.

All of the lines of the Data Bus and the Address Bus are brought out on the board for simple user access.

Included with each OCM-1 microcomputer are a user's manual, a Fairbug user's guide, an F8 programming guide, an F8 microprocessor user's reference card and technical data sheets on the circuits. □

by Paul Chu

THE MACROLOGIC DEMONSTRATOR

Macrologic is a family of cost-effective LSI circuits designed for microprogrammed systems. Bit-slice design makes Macrologic components particularly suitable as functional building blocks for microprocessor-oriented applications, processor emulation and microprogrammed replacements of hard-wired logic. Microprogramming is a capability that gives Macrologic a greater flexibility for special applications not found in fixed-instruction-set microprocessors. As an added bonus to the designer, both bipolar and CMOS Macrologic circuits are available. For faster system operation, high-speed bipolar Macrologic is the logical choice. Where power is at a premium, use low-power CMOS.

The Macrologic Demonstrator is an educational tool designed to familiarize the engineer with the processor-oriented devices in the Macrologic family and demonstrate concepts used in microprogramming. The system consists of three main functional blocks *(Figure 1)*. The 8-bit wide *data path* contains an ALU, a register file, LIFO stack and miscellaneous logic. The *microprogram controller* contains the control memory as well as microprogram addressing and sequencing logic. The operator *control and display panel* provides the human interface and allows the operator to load and modify the control memory, run or single step the microprogram, and monitor system status and contents of the various system busses.

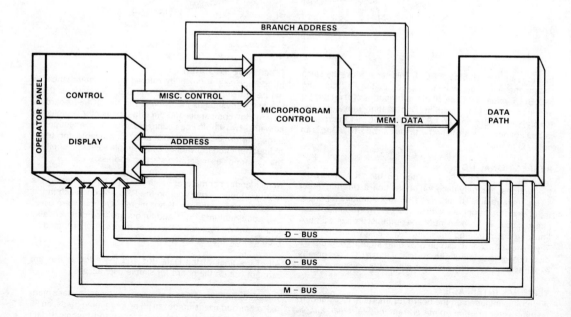

Fig. 1 System Block Diagram

THE DATA PATH

Two 4-bit slices of the following Macrologic devices form the 8-bit wide data path *(Figure 2)*.

- The Data Path Switch (9404 DPS) allows shifting, constant generation and other operations.
- An Arithmetic Logic Register Stack (9405A ALRS) performs eight arithmetic and logic functions and includes eight data registers.
- The Program Stack (9406 P-stack) contains a 16-level stack used for last-in, first-out storage.
- The Data Access Register (9407 DAR) includes three general purpose registers and an adder network which can be used for RAM-resident stack-type functions.
- A Register Stack (9410 R-stack) provides 16 words of high-speed read/write memory for scratch pad area.

The instruction inputs of the P-stacks, DARs and R-stacks are bussed together to allow instruction-field sharing. The K-bus inputs of the DPSs are tied to the eight data input switches on the operator panel so external information can be introduced into the data path. Three other busses are also available – the D-bus, O-bus and M-bus. The D-bus is created by connecting the D-inputs of the DPSs to the corresponding O-outputs of the ALRSs, P-stacks, DARs and R-stacks. The O-bus is the result of connecting the O-outputs of the DPSs to the corresponding D-inputs of the ALRs, P-stacks, DARs and R-stacks. The M-bus is created by wiring the X-outputs of the P-stacks to the X-outputs of the DARs.

Except for the DPS, all Macrologic devices in the data path are clocked by a common system clock. Each of these devices has an Execute input ($\overline{EX}$) and the device will not respond to the clock unless $\overline{EX}$ is LOW. In addition, the tri-state outputs of the devices remain in the high impedance state except when the Output Enable ($\overline{EO}$) is LOW. Thus, during a single clock cycle, information can be routed from any device in the data path to any other device (including itself) by controlling the proper $\overline{EX}$ and $\overline{EO}$ inputs.

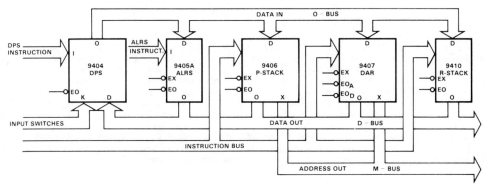

Fig. 2   Data Path

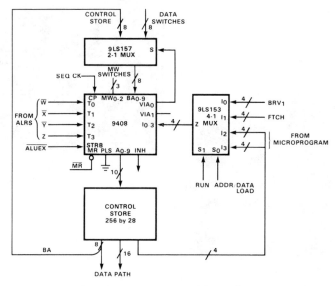

Fig. 3   Microprogram Memory and Sequencing Logic.

Microprogram Control

The control memory is constructed using seven 1K 93L422 fully decoded RAMs organized as 256 words by 28 bits. A 9408 Microprogram Sequencer provides address inputs to the control memory in one of two ways *(Figure 3)*.

During the Run or Single Step mode, the 9408 is clocked by the system clock (CP) and its address controls the order in which microinstructions are fetched from the control memory. The Instruction ($I_0 - I_3$) and Branch Address ($BA_0 - BA_7$) inputs are entered into the 9408 via the microprogram control memory outputs. The multiway switches (MW) on the control panel feed the $MW_0 - MW_2$ inputs for multiway branching. The four ALRS status flags (zero, overflow, carry and negative) are strobed into the 9408 internal test register at the end of the previous microcycle for conditional testing during the current microcycle. The PLS (Pipeline Select) input is grounded for non-pipeline operation.

In the Halt mode, the 9408 increments the microprogram address by one or loads the microprogram address from the control panel input switches. Normally, the clock input of the 9408 is disabled and the Fetch instruction is forced on the Instruction inputs. When Field Select (FS1 and FS0) is 11 (described later) and either the Examine Next or Deposit Next switch is activated, the 9408 is clocked once. This increments the address by one, allowing the next control word to be examined or loaded. Operation of the Load Address switch forces the BRV_1 instruction on the 9408 Instruction inputs and selects the input switches as the Branch Address (BA) input. The 9408 is again clocked once to match its address outputs to the input switch data.

OPERATOR PANEL

The operator panel consists of two sections — control and display. The control section provides the operator interface to the control memory and data path. The display allows the operator to monitor the microprogram address and data, ALU status flags and the various system busses.

Display

The display consists of two rows of eight LEDs that read the microprogram address and data, a row of eight bus status LEDs, four ALU status LEDs and two Field Select LEDs. Since the microprogram control word is 28 bits wide, two control inputs (FS1 and FS0) select four separate fields to be displayed by a single set of eight LEDs. Setting FS1 and FS0 to 00 produces the rightmost (least significant) eight bits, of a control word. A setting of 01 produces the next eight bits, 10 the next and 11 the leftmost (most significant) 4-bit field. The ALRS flags are latched into the four status LEDs during the end of each microinstruction so the ALU status can be continuously monitored.

Control

The panel control section contains a group of eight toggle switches for data input to the system as well as a number of miscellaneous control switches. *The Clock Select* switch selects between an internal 2 MHz oscillator or an external clock provided by the user. A group of three *Multiway* switches ($MW_0 - MW_2$) provides the Multiway inputs to the 9408 for 8-way branching. Two *Data Bus Select* switches select either a lamp test or the contents of one of three data busses (O, D, M) for display by the eight data-bus LEDs. The *Master Reset* switch halts the system and clears the microprogram address and field to zero.

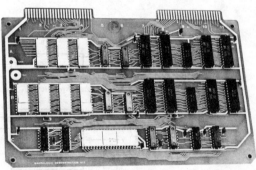

Microprogram Control and Data Path

Operator Panel

The *Run/Halt* switch is a two-function momentary toggle that selects either the Run or Halt mode. If the processor is halted, pressing this switch returns the processor to the Run mode. The processor then executes the microprogram beginning with the instruction contained in the memory location pointed to by the microprogram address. It continues in this fashion until the Run/Halt switch is pressed again; however the processor halts only after completion of the current microinstruction.

During the Run mode, Address Sync outputs a HIGH pulse whenever the microprogram address matches the input switch word. Address Sync is useful for program debug. An oscilloscope can be used to examine signals in the vicinity of the synchronized instruction by placing the microprogram in a loop while triggering on Address Sync.

While the processor is in the Halt mode, a number of other switch functions can be activated. The Load Address switch loads input switch data as the microprogram address. The *Deposit* switch writes the 8-bit word, at the input switches, into the field of the memory location addressed by the 9408 address and Field Select (FS1 and FS0) outputs. The *Deposit Next* switch operates similarly to Deposit, however the field is incremented by one before the input switch data is written into memory. Moreover, if Field Select is 11, the field is recirculated to 00 and the 9408 address outputs are incremented by one before the input switch data is written into memory. Thus, the user can load a microprogram eight bits at a time — without laboriously loading addresses — by repeatedly setting up data switches and then pressing the Deposit Next switch.

The *Examine Next* switch displays the data in the next field by lighting the appropriate LEDs and allows the operator to examine memory data field by field and location by location. The microprogram address LEDs display the memory location of the next processor instruction. Pressing the *Single Step* switch executes that instruction and then halts the processor. The Single Step switch is especially useful in program debug.

CONTROL WORD FORMAT

The Macrologic Demonstrator uses a 28-bit control word *(Table 1 and Figure 4)*. The format is only one of many possibilities and is by no means unique. The width of the control word has been minimized using the following overlapping and encoding techniques. System performance is not greatly degraded by minimization. For example, in a single microcycle, an operand from the ALRS can be shifted, added to one of the DAR registers and the system branched to another address.

The control inputs for the ALRS and the Branch Address inputs of the 9408 are overlapped since most program structures consist of more fetches than branches. The address for the 9408 Microprogram Sequencer is implicit during FTCH and RET, which suggests that the branch address field of the 9408 can be overlapped with the instruction input field of another Macrologic element in the system. In this case, the 8-bit branch address field can be conveniently shared with the instruction and register fields of the ALRS. The 9408 INH output simplifies field overlap; the $\overline{EX}$ input of the ALRS is simply disabled except during a FTCH or RET.

Since the O-bus is tri-state, only one of the four Macrologic elements can drive this bus at any time. Thus the four O-bus sources can be encoded by two bits. Since the likelihood is small that more than one Macrologic element in the system will need to operate on the same input during the same microcycle, the four D-bus destinations can also be encoded by two bits. Actually, there are only three Macrologic destinations and four possible permutations of two bits, which leaves a "free" state — 00. This state can be used to select an external device or to deactivate all three Macrologic elements. Note that the ALRS execution is controlled by the INH output of the 9408 and is unaffected by this field.

The final technique used in minimizing the control word length involves overlapping the P-stack, DAR and R-stack instruction fields. Since only one of these elements can be activated during a microcycle, the instruction fields can be shared without degrading system performance.

CONTROL WORD FORMAT	
BITS	**FUNCTION**
C0 – C1	O-bus source. These bits select the device driving the input bus of the DPS by activatiing the proper Output Enable ($\overline{EO}$) input. 00 – ALRS 01 – DAR 10 – P-stack 11 – R-stack
C2 – C3	D-bus destination. These bits specify device to be activated and respond to C4 – C7 by enabling the proper Execute ($\overline{EX}$) input. 00 – EXT* 01 – DAR 10 – P-stack 11 – R-stack
C4 – C7	Shared between P-stack, DAR and R-stack, these bits are Instruction inputs to the P-stack and DAR and Address inputs to the R-stack.
C8 – C13	Instruction inputs to the DPS.
C14	Rotate control. Specifies source of carry in (external or rotate) during DPS shifts.
C15 – C23	Shared between the 9408 Sequencer and ALRS. When the 9408 instruction (C24 – C27) is neither a Fetch or a Return, these bits are the Branch Address. Otherwise, C15 – C17 select one ALRS register for destination of ALU operations, C18 – C20 select one ALRS register as source of ALU operations, C21 – C23 become ALRS Instruction inputs.
C24 – C27	9408 Sequencer Instruction inputs
	*External, non-selected

Table 1.

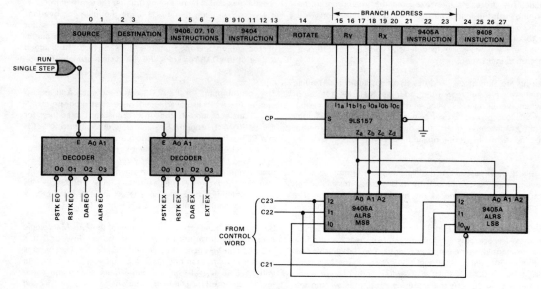

Fig. 4   Address Multiplexing and Sharing of Instruction and Carry Bit in ALRS.

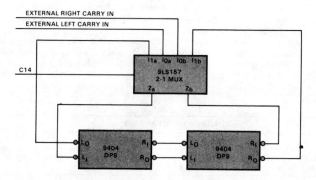

Fig. 5   Rotate Control.

The ALRSs are operated in the general register mode (see blue area of *Figure 4*). A 2-1 multiplexer routes the A field inputs of the 9405s to the source or destination registers during the HIGH or LOW periods of the clock respectively. The I_0 input of the most significant ALRS slice is used both to pass instructions and carry information from the least significant ALRS slice.

To provide a rotate capability in the data path, a 2-1 multiplexer selects data, originating from either external sources or the right and left serial DPS outputs, and enters it into the left and right serial inputs of the DPSs *(Figure 5)*. If the rotate

select bit (C14) is HIGH during a left shift, the right serial output is shifted into the most signicant DPS position which — in effect — makes the instruction a left rotation.

CONCLUSION

The Macrologic Demonstrator requires approximately 60 ICs, 30 for the data control path and another 30 for operator panel control and display. In the non-pipeline mode, the Demonstrator can be operated at speeds up to 5 MHz. System speed can be improved by adding a pipeline register between the control memory and the data path.

Part one of a two-part series on learning to use and microprogram Macrologic, this article describes the architecture of a learning aid known as the Macrologic Demonstrator. A future article will describe microprogram examples and system operation. A full set of schematics is available for building the demonstrator. See PROGRESS Vol. 4, No. 1, September/October 1976 for more information on the 9408 Microprogram Sequencer.

Microprogram Sequencer

the newest member of the Bipolar Microprocessor Family

by Kris Rallapalli
and Dan Wilnai

Macrologic* is an LSI bit-slice family of versatile building blocks for use in computer peripherals and microprocessor-oriented applications. The main goal in its development was to provide the system designer with a set of compact ICs for implementing the important system functions he frequently had to design with SSI/MSI in the past. The newest member of this family is the all important controller or microprogram sequencer, the 9408, that controls the order in which microinstructions are fetched from the control memory.

The 9408 microprogram sequencer is manufactured using the I³L™ (Isoplanar Integrated Injection Logic) process that combines the low power and high packing density of I²L and the high speed and high packing density of the Fairchild Isoplanar technology. The result is a process that gives the speed of low power Schottky and the packing density of MOS. Die size is a mere 11,000 square mils; a comparable low power Schottky version would have been immense.

The 9408 is a 40-pin device containing a 10-bit microprogram – address register. There are seven test inputs, four of which participate in conditional branches, and three in multiway branches. The conditional test lines are flip-flop buffered and these flip-flops can be tested individually by appropriate branch instructions. The three Multiway test inputs are used to form the least significant three bits of the branch address for an 8-way branch, depending on the bit pattern present on these three inputs.

This sequencer contains several features that make it easy and inexpensive to use. For example, the user can select pipeline or non-pipeline mode of operation. A pair of VIA outputs allow the sequencer to control an external multiplexer when choosing the source of a branch address. An Inhibit output facilitates sharing the microprocessor control fields with the next address field, thereby reducing the width of the associated control store.

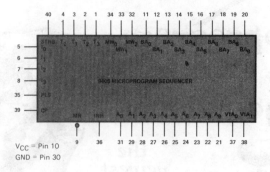

Figure 1

V_{CC} = Pin 10
GND = Pin 30

FUNCTIONAL DESCRIPTION

The 9408 Microprogram Sequencer, shown in the block diagram (*Figure 1*), consists of a 10-bit Program Counter (PC), a 4-word by 10-bit Last-In First-Out (LIFO) Stack with associated control, an Input Multiplexer, a Pipeline Multiplexer, an Instruction Decoder, a 10-bit Incrementer, and a 4-bit Test Register comprised of four edge-triggered D flip-flops.

The Pipeline Multiplexer has two ports — the PC output provides the input port for the non-pipeline mode and the Input Multiplexer output provides the input port for the pipeline mode. Port selection is controlled by the Pipeline Select (PLS) and Master Reset ($\overline{MR}$) inputs. A LOW level on the $\overline{MR}$ input forces the non-pipeline mode of operation and clears the PC. Thus when the 9408 is initialized by the $\overline{MR}$ input, the A_0 through A_9 outputs are LOW regardless of the state of the PLS input. A LOW level on the PLS input specifies non-pipeline mode and a HIGH specifies pipeline mode.

The Program Counter is a 10-bit edge-triggered register. The LOW-to-HIGH transition on the Clock (CP) input loads the Input Multiplexer output into the PC. Because of the edge-triggered nature of the PC register, the PC output remains static for a full clock cycle. Thus, in the non-pipeline mode, the PC output can be used to address a control memory built with static devices without storing the memory output in an external microinstruction register. However, in the pipeline mode, the 9408 provides the next address information as soon as available; therefore, execution of a microinstruction can be overlapped with the fetching of the next microinstruction. To ensure microinstruction stability for a full clock cycle, the control-memory output should be buffered with an external microinstruction register.

The Input Multiplexer receives data from four different sources. One port is the output of the LIFO Stack; a second is the output of the 10-bit Incrementer. The Incrementer always adds one to the PC contents. The third and fourth ports are the branch and multiway-branch ports, the latter comprised of the seven most significant Branch Address inputs (BA_3 through BA_9) and the three Multiway inputs, (MW_0 through MW_2).

The 4-word by 10-bit LIFO Stack is a RAM and receives data from the Incrementer output. The stack control logic generates the appropriate control signals, while stack pointers in the Stack Control generate the read and write addresses.

The 4-bit Test Register consists of four type-D flip-flops. The data inputs, which are the four Test inputs (T_0 through T_3), are loaded on the LOW-to-HIGH transition of the Strobe input (STRB).

The Instruction Decoder receives the 4-bit Instruction input (I_0 through I_3) and the Test Register output and generates the VIA_0, VIA_1 and Inhibit (INH) outputs of the 9408. In addition, it generates appropriate logic signals for the Stack Control and Input Multiplexer.

9408 INSTRUCTIONS

The 9408 instruction set has 16 instructions (*Table 1*). These instructions can be divided into three groups — unconditional branches, conditional branches and miscellaneous — and are specified by appropriate logic levels on the $I_0 - I_3$ inputs.

The unconditional branch group consists of four Branch VIA instructions ($BRV_0 - BRV_3$), Branch Multiway (BMW) and Branch to Subroutine (BSR). This group requires that the next address be explicitly specified on the BA inputs.

The conditional branch group consists of eight instructions, Branch Test HIGH ($BTH_0 - BTH_3$) and Branch Test LOW ($BTL_0 - BTL_3$), for interrogating the four test flip-flops of the 9408 individually. The $BTH_0 - BTH_3$ instructions test flip-flops $T_0 - T_3$ respectively for a HIGH on the Q output (see block diagram). Similarly $BTL_0 - BTL_3$ test for a LOW on the corresponding Q output. If the test condition is satisfied, the next address is taken from the Branch Address ($BA_0 - BA_9$) inputs. If the test condition is not satisfied, the 9408 performs a Fetch operation.

The miscellaneous group consists of two instructions — Fetch (FTCH) and Return from Subroutine (RTS). These instructions do not require explicit specification of the

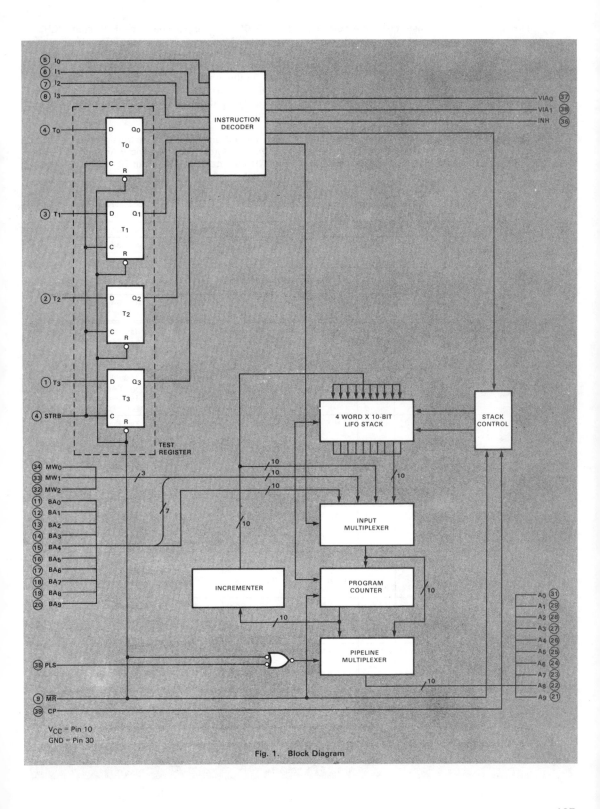

Fig. 1. Block Diagram

next address. For the FTCH instruction, the next address is the address of the current microinstruction + 1. For RTS, the next address is taken from the Stack.

Unconditional Branches

$BRV_0 - BRV_3$. Whenever a Branch VIA instruction code is present on the $I_0 - I_3$ inputs, the Instruction Decoder (see block diagram) establishes the appropriate HIGH/LOW pattern on the VIA_0 and VIA_1 outputs per *Table 1*. The Instruction Decoder also forces the INH output HIGH. Moreover, the $BA_0 - BA_9$ inputs are selected as the source of the next address by the Input Multiplexer.

If the 9408 is in the pipeline mode (PLS input HIGH), the Pipeline Multiplexer transfers the $BA_0 - BA_9$ inputs to the $A_0 - A_9$ outputs. The $BA_0 - BA_9$ inputs are loaded into the PC on the LOW-to-HIGH transition of the CP input. On the other hand, if the non-pipeline mode of operation is selected, the $BA_0 - BA_9$ inputs appear on the output only after the LOW-to-HIGH transition of the CP input.

BMW. For a Branch Multiway instruction, the Instruction Decoder forces the VIA_0 and VIA_1 outputs LOW and INH output HIGH. The Input Multiplexer selects

	MNEMONIC	DEFINITION	$I_3I_2I_1I_0$	$T_3T_2T_1T_0$	$O_9O_8O_7--O_2O_1O_0$	$VIA_1 \, VIA_0$	INH	DESCRIPTION OF OPERATION
Unconditional	BRV_0	Branch VIA_0	L H L L	X X X X	$BA_9 \, BA_8--BA_1 \, BA_0$	L L	H	$BA_0 - BA_9 \rightarrow PC$
	BRV_1	Branch VIA_1	L H L H	X X X X	$BA_9 \, BA_8--BA_1 \, BA_0$	L H	H	$BA_0 - BA_9 \rightarrow PC$
Branch	BRV_2	Branch VIA_2	L H H L	X X X X	$BA_9 \, BA_8--BA_1 \, BA_0$	H L	H	$BA_0 - BA_9 \rightarrow PC$
	BRV_3	Branch VIA_3	L H H H	X X X X	$BA_9 \, BA_8--BA_1 \, BA_0$	H H	H	$BA_0 - BA_9 \rightarrow PC$
Instructions	BMW	Branch Multiway	L L H H	X X X X	$BA_9 \, BA_3--MW_2 \, MW_0$	L L	H	$MW_0 - MW_2,$ $BA_3 - BA_9 \rightarrow PC$
	BSR	Branch to Subroutine	L L L H	X X X X	$BA_9 \, BA_8--BA_1 \, BA_0$	L L	H	$BA_0 - BA_9 \rightarrow PC$ & Push the Stack
	BTH_0	Branch on T_0 HIGH	H H L L	X X X H / X X X L	$BA_9 \, BA_8--BA_1 \, BA_0$ / PC+1	L L	H	If Test Register 0 is HIGH: $BA_0 - BA_9 \rightarrow PC$ If Test Register 0 is LOW: PC+1 $\rightarrow$ PC
	BTH_1	Branch on T_1 HIGH	H H L H	X X H X / X X L X	$BA_9 \, BA_8--BA_1 \, BA_0$ / PC+1	L L	H	If Test Register 1 is HIGH: $BA_0 - BA_9 \rightarrow PC$ If Test Register 1 is LOW: PC+1 $\rightarrow$ PC
	BTH_2	Branch on T_2 HIGH	H H H L	X H X X / X L X X	$BA_9 \, BA_8--BA_1 \, BA_0$ / PC+1	L L	H	If Test Register 2 is HIGH: $BA_0 - BA_9 \rightarrow PC$ If Test Register 2 is LOW: PC+1 $\rightarrow$ PC
	BTH_3	Branch on T_3 HIGH	H H H	H X X X / L X X X	$BA_9 \, BA_8--BA_1 \, BA_0$ / PC+1	L L	H	If Test Register 3 is HIGH: $BA_0 - BA_9 \rightarrow PC$ If Test Register 3 is LOW: PC+1 $\rightarrow$ PC
Conditional	BTL_0	Branch on T_0 LOW	H L L L	X X X L / X X X H	$BA_9 \, BA_8--BA_1 \, BA_0$ / PC+1	L L	H	If Test Register 0 is LOW: $BA_0 - BA_9 \rightarrow PC$ If Test Register 0 is HIGH: PC+1 $\rightarrow$ PC
Branch	BTL_1	Branch on T_1 LOW	H L L H	X X L X / X X H X	$BA_9 \, BA_8--BA_1 \, BA_0$ / PC+1	L L	H	If Test Register 1 is LOW: $BA_0 - BA_9 \rightarrow PC$ If Test Register 1 is HIGH: PC+1 $\rightarrow$ PC
Instructions	BTL_2	Branch on T_2 LOW	H L H L	X L X X / X H X X	$BA_9 \, BA_8--BA_1 \, BA_0$ / PC+1	L L	H	If Test Register 2 is LOW: $BA_0 - BA_9 \rightarrow PC$ If Test Register 2 is HIGH: PC+1 $\rightarrow$ PC
	BTL_3	Branch on T_3 LOW	H L H H	L X X X / H X X X	$BA_9 \, BA_8--BA_1 \, BA_0$ / PC+1	L L	H	If Test Register 3 is LOW: $BA_0 - BA_9 \rightarrow PC$ If Test Register 3 is HIGH: PC+1 $\rightarrow$ PC
Miscellaneous	RTS	Return from Subroutine	L L L L	X X X X	Contents of the Stack Addressed by Read Pointer	L L	L	Pop the Stack
Instructions	FTCH	FETCH	L L H L	X X X X	PC+1	L L	L	PC+1 $\rightarrow$ PC

L = LOW Level
H = HIGH Level
X = Don't Care

Table 1. 9408 Instruction Set

the $BA_3 - BA_9$ inputs as the most significant seven bits and $MW_0 - MW_2$ inputs as the least significant three bits of the next address. If the pipeline mode of operation is selected, the next address formed by the Input Multiplexer ($BA_3 - BA_9$ and $MW_0 - MW_2$ inputs) is transferred to the $A_0 - A_9$ outputs. On the LOW-to-HIGH transition of the CP input, this next address is also loaded into the PC. For non-pipeline mode, the next address is available on the $A_0 - A_9$ output only after the CP transition.

BSR. During a Branch-to-Subroutine instruction, the Instruction Decoder forces a LOW on the VIA_0 and VIA_1 outputs and a HIGH on the INH output. The Input Multiplexer selects the $BA_0 - BA_9$ inputs as the source for the next address. If the pipeline mode is selected, this next address is transferred to the $A_0 - A_9$ outputs by the Pipeline Multiplexer. As usual, the PC is updated with this next address on the LOW-to-HIGH transition of the CP input. During non-pipeline operation, the next address appears on the output only after the CP transition.

The PC holds the address of the current microinstruction. For the BSR instruction, the return address must be stored in the Stack, which is fed by the PC through an Incrementer (see block diagram). When the CP input is LOW, the incremented value is written into the Stack as a return address. The LOW-to-HIGH transition of the CP input not only loads the PC with the next address, *i.e.*, $BA_0 - BA_9$ inputs, but also increments the Stack Pointer.

Conditional Branches
$BTH_0 - BTH_3$. For a Branch Test HIGH instruction, the Instruction Decoder establishes a LOW on VIA_0 and VIA_1 outputs and HIGH on the INH output. It then tests for a HIGH on the Q output of the corresponding flip-flop in the test register. If a HIGH level is found, the Input Multiplexer selects the $BA_0 - BA_9$ inputs as the source for the next address.

On the other hand, if the tested Q output of the flip-flop is LOW, the Incrementer output is selected as the source of the next address by the Input Multiplexer. In either case, the PC is loaded with the next address on the LOW-to-HIGH transition of the CP input. As usual, if the pipeline mode is selected, the next address is transferred to the $A_0 - A_9$ outputs. For non-pipeline mode, the next address appears on the output after the clock transition.

$BTL_0 - BTL_3$. Operation of the Branch Test LOW instructions is identical to $BTH_0 - BTH_3$ except that Q outputs of the test register flip-flops are tested for a LOW. If the tested output is LOW, a branch occurs. If tested output is HIGH the Incrementer output is the next address.

Miscellaneous
FTCH. For a Fetch Instruction, the Instruction Decoder establishes a LOW on the VIA_0 and VIA_1 outputs. In addition, the INH output is also LOW. The Input Multiplexer selects the Incrementer output as the next address. If pipeline mode is selected, the Incrementer output is transferred to the $A_0 - A_9$ outputs. For non-pipeline mode, the incremented address appears at the output only after the clock transition.

RTS. For a Return-from-Subroutine instruction, the Instruction Decoder establishes a LOW on the VIA_0, VIA_1 and INH outputs. The Input Multiplexer selects the Stack output as the source of the next address. As usual, for the pipeline mode, the next address is transferred to the output by the Pipeline Multiplexer. For non-pipeline operation, the next address appears on the output only after the clock transition. In addition, this instruction also decrements the Stack Pointer.

SHARING THE CONTROL FIELDS FOR NEXT ADDRESS
A straightforward microinstruction consists of fields for specifying data-path control and an explicit specification of the next address. An explicit next-address specification is mandatory in many microprogram sequencer architectures. However, in the 9408, a Fetch instruction is provided to facilitate writing a microprogram where a large number of instructions fit naturally into sequential memory locations. The next address for a Fetch instruction need not be explicit; it is always implied to be PC + 1. In general, the total number of bits required for the data-path control (total control-field width) is more than the number of bits needed to explicitly specify the next address. Thus, if there is an easy way to use the control fields, or part of them, to specify the address, significant reduction of the microinstruction width can be achieved. The Inhibit output of the 9408 is provided to facilitate sharing of microinstruction fields.

There are two 9408 instructions that do not require next-address specification, FTCH and RTS. The remaining 14 instructions fall into a branch class requiring an external next address. The Inhibit output is LOW for FTCH and RTS only and HIGH for all other instructions. Thus, if the system clock can be inhibited from operating the data path whenever the Inhibit output is HIGH, then the microinstruction field that normally operates on the data path can be fed into the 9408 as the next address. Inhibiting the data path operation is extremely simple with the Macrologic processor elements. In some Macrologic systems, the devices are connected as a bussed system; an example is shown in *Figure 2*. Although the 9405A and 9406 devices derive their instructions from the same microinstruction field, either the 9405A or the 9406 can be individually selected to respond to an instruction by controlling the $\overline{EX}$ inputs. Macrologic systems can employ an encoded field in the microinstruction, called destination field, for this purpose. A decoder is commonly used to drive the individual $\overline{EX}$ inputs. Now, if the Inhibit output of the 9408 is connected to the Enable input of the decoder, all $\overline{EX}$ inputs are HIGH for branch-class instructions. Thus

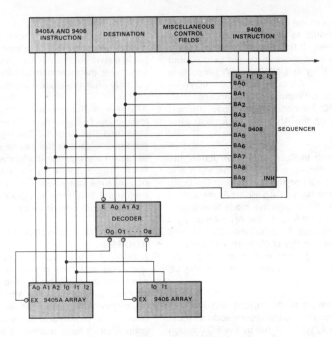

Fig. 2. Sharing the Control Fields

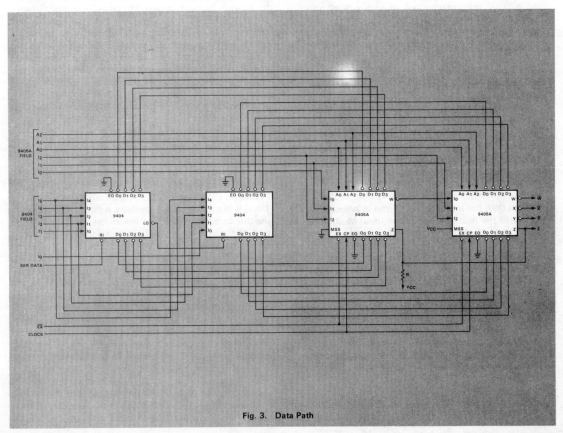

Fig. 3. Data Path

clocking would not affect the devices. This technique of sharing fields is beneficial only if a large percentage of the operations is from sequential memory locations with an occasional random branch. If a microprogram has many branch instructions, the extra clock cycle needed for branch operation may affect the system speed.

USING THE VIA OUTPUTS

Since a microinstruction contains information relating to the address of the next microinstruction, it would seem that the $BA_0 - BA_9$ inputs of the 9408 are derived from the next address field. However, in most practical systems, the $BA_0 - BA_9$ inputs must be obtained from other sources in addition to the microinstruction next-address field.

For example, a system designed to emulate the instruction set of a target computer contains a "macroinstruction register" to hold the bit patterns corresponding to the target instruction that currently requires execution. There is a routine in the control store starting at a certain address which corresponds to the current macroinstruction. It is simple to connect an address mapper, consisting of PROMs or PLAs, to the macroinstruction register. The address inputs, or input variables to the mapper, are the outputs of the macroinstruction regis-

ter and the mapper outputs is the starting address of the microsequence for the current target instruction. Thus, if the mapper outputs is used as another source of next address, a very fast macroinstruction decoding can be accomplished. This source selection could easily be accomplished by feeding the addresses from different sources into a 4-input multiplexer and using the VIA outputs of the 9408 to select the appropriate set of inputs.

A MICROPROGRAM EXAMPLE

The simple microprogram example shown in *Figures 3*, *4* and *Table 2*, is an assembly of a 7-bit word from a serial data stream (SER DATA) using the associated clock (SER CLK). *Figure 5* illustrates the assumed timing relationship between SER DATA and SER CLK signals. Consider an 8-bit wide data path using two 9405A and two 9404 devices as shown in *Figure 3*. A 6-bit instruction bus is obtained (9405A field) by appropriate connections of the 9405A instruction inputs. These six bits are controlled by an appropriate field in the microinstruction, bit 4 through bit 9 of the control store (see *Figure 4*). The 6-bit 9404 field is obtained by connecting I_1 through I_4 of the 9404 devices using I_0 of each device separately. These six bits are also controlled by an appropriate field in the microinstruction, bit 10 through bit 15 of the control store. In this illustration,

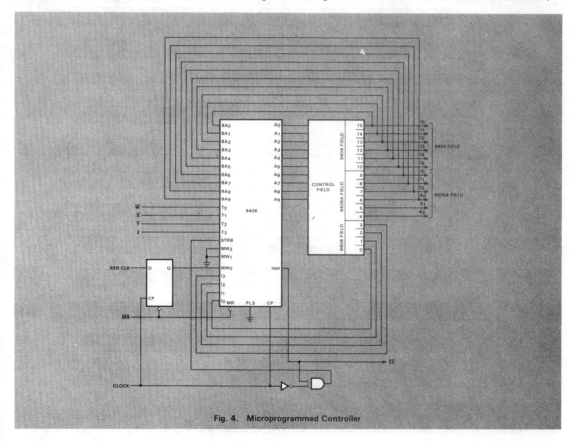

Fig. 4. Microprogrammed Controller

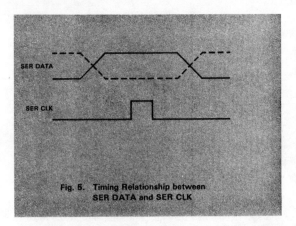

Fig. 5. Timing Relationship between SER DATA and SER CLK

The status outputs from the most significant 9405A, $\overline{W}$, $\overline{X}$, $\overline{Y}$ and Z, are connected to the $T_0 - T_3$ inputs of the 9408 although only the $\overline{X}$ output is used in this example. The $\overline{EX}$ inputs of both 9405As are connected to the INH output of the 9408. The Clock signal operates the 9405As and the 9408. In addition, the Clock is gated with the INH output to operate the STRB input of the 9408.

The SER CLK input is synchronized to the Clock input by using a synchronizing flip-flop with the Q output connected to the MW_0 input of the 9408 while MW_1 and MW_2 inputs are grounded. The $A_0 - A_9$ outputs of the 9408 are used to address the control store. The SER DATA is fed into the right shift input of the least significant 9404.

the 9404 and 9405A control fields of the microinstruction are also used to provide the 10-bit branch address for the 9408. The instruction inputs for the 9408 are provided by the appropriate microinstruction field, bit 0 through bit 3 of the control store.

The flow chart in *Figure 6* shows the sequence of operations assuming the sequence is a subroutine starting at location (10)8 in the control store. The program for implementing this flow chart is shown in *Table 2*. Note that register R_0, the first of the eight general purpose

ADDRESS (Octal)	9408 FIELD				9405A FIELD						9404 FIELD					
	0	1	2	3	4	5	6	7	8	9	10	11	12	13	14	15
10	FTCH				RO		LOAD				PLUS 1					
	L	H	L	L	L	L	L	L	H	H	L	H	H	H	L	H
11	BMW				X	X	2X									
	H	H	L	L	X	X	L	L	L	L	L	H	L	X	X	X
12	FTCH				RO		LOAD				SHIFT LEFT D-BUS					
	L	H	L	L	L	L	L	L	H	H	H	L	H	L	L	L
13	BMW				X	X	3X									
	H	H	L	L	X	X	L	L	L	L	L	H	H	X	X	X
14	BTL1				X	X	16									
	H	L	H	H	X	X	L	L	L	L	L	L	H	H	H	L
15	BRV0				X	X	11									
	L	L	H	L	X	X	L	L	L	L	L	L	H	L	L	H
16	RTS				RO		EXCLUSIVE-OR				BYTE SIGN MASK					
	L	L	L	L	L	L	L	H	H	L	L	H	L	L	H	L
20	BRV0				X	X	11									
	L	L	H	L	X	X	L	L	L	L	L	L	H	L	L	H
21	BRV0				X	X	12									
	L	L	H	L	X	X	L	L	L	L	L	L	H	L	H	L
30	BRV0				X	X	14									
	L	L	H	L	X	X	L	L	L	L	L	L	H	H	L	L
31	BRV0				X	X	13									
	L	L	H	L	X	X	L	L	L	L	L	L	H	L	H	H

X = Don't Care

Table 2. Control Store Listing

registers of the 9405A, is used for the serial-to-parallel conversion. Thus bit 4 through bit 6 (address bits of the 9405A field) are L L L. To indicate that a load operation into R_O is desired, bit 7 through bit 9 (9405A instruction field) is L H H.

Bit 10 through bit 15 of the microinstruction (9404 instruction field) is L H H H L H so that bit pattern 0 0 0 0 0 0 0 1 is present at the inputs of the 9405A. This becomes apparent when the 9404 truth table in the data sheet is consulted (the 9405A treats a LOW level data input as logic "1"). Bit 0 through bit 3 (9408 instruction field) require the 9408 to perform a Fetch for the next instruction.

Location $(11)_8$ contains a Branch Multiway, BMW, instruction to determine whether or not the synchronization flip-flop is set. Bit 6 through bit 15 of the microinstruction is specified as L L L L L H L X X X where X indicates "don't care". Thus, if the synchronization flip-flop is not set, the 9408 generates L L L L L H L L L L as the next address $(20)_8$. At location $(20)_8$, there is a Branch VIA, BRV_O, to location $(11)_8$ instruction. Thus, the microprogram loops between locations $(11)_8$ and $(20)_8$ testing for a HIGH on the SER CLK input. When the synchronization flip-flop is set, the BMW instruction at location $(11)_8$ results in $(21)_8$ as the next address instead of $(20)_8$. Location $(21)_8$ contains the instruction "BRV_O to location $(12)_8$".

The instruction in $(12)_8$ shifts the contents of the 9405A to the left and loads the shifted value back into R_O. Because the SER DATA input is connected to the shift input of the 9404, the information present as the SER DATA input is loaded into R_O. Thus after taking the first data bit, R_O reads 0 0 0 0 0 0 1 B_1, where B_1 is the first bit assembled. The instruction in location $(12)_8$ specifies a Fetch for the 9408, thus the INH output is LOW. This activates the $\overline{EX}$ inputs of the 9405As. Moreover, the LOW level also enables the gate so that the Clock activates the STRB input of the 9408; thus, the 9405A status outputs can be loaded into the 9408 test register. As long as the result of an ALU operation is positive, *i.e.,* most significant bit HIGH, the negative status ($\overline{X}$ output of the 9405A) is HIGH.

Location $(13)_8$ contains BMW with $(3X)_8$ as the next address. Thus if MW_O input is HIGH, the next address is $(31)_8$; if MW_O is LOW, the next address is $(30)_8$. Location $(30)_8$ contains "BRV_O to location $(13)_8$" and $(31)_8$ contains "BRV_O to $(14)_8$." Thus, as long as the SER CLK input is HIGH, the program loops between locations $(13)_8$ and $(31)_8$. When the synchronizing flip-flop is cleared, the program goes to location $(14)_8$ due to the instruction in location $(30)_8$.

At location $(14)_8$, the "Branch Test LOW, BTL_1, to location $(16)_8$" is used to determine when the T_1 input of 9408 is LOW. It will not be LOW until seven SER DATA bits have been shifted. Instead of branching to $(16)_8$, the program goes to location $(15)_8$, which contains "BRV_O to location $(11)_8$." The program loops around

until seven data bits have been shifted in. At this time, the 9405A has indicated a LOW on its $\overline{X}$ output and the BTL results in a branch to location $(16)_8$.

At location $(16)_8$, the 9404 provides 1 0 0 0 0 0 0 0 as a mask and an exclusive OR is performed in R_O of the 9405A to eliminate the marker bit that was previously loaded into R_O. R_O then contains seven data bits assembled from the SER DATA bit stream. It has been assumed that this small program is a subroutine. Therefore, by specifying RTS to the 9408 in location $(16)_8$, a return to the main program is effected.

This simple example is only an illustration of the versatility of the microprogram sequencer. It is important to realize that the Macrologic LSI bit-slice family can be used to implement highly sophisticated microprogrammed digital systems. Future articles will describe different approaches and trade-offs in Macrologic system design.

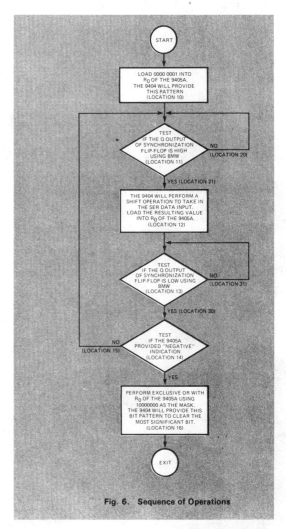

Fig. 6. Sequence of Operations

multi-level nesting of subroutines
in a one-level microprocessor

by Philippe de Marchin

While investigating potential microprocessor applications, engineers must often execute familiar hardware functions with less familiar software. Although the logical design process is essentially the same, the software details are sometimes baffling. One such detail is the use of subroutines that can perform the same task at different points in a program with a single short sequence of instructions. Nested subroutines, in which one subroutine calls for another, perhaps another, and still another may seem perplexing.

Subroutines can be extremely valuable when using microprocessors. However, when one subroutine must call another in a microprocessor that is designed to handle only one at a time, a special sequence of instructions is necessary. Each subroutine requires temporary storage of the contents of the program counter, so that at the conclusion of the subroutine, the processor "remembers" where to resume the main routine. In general, multiple-nested subroutines require as many temporary storage locations as there are levels of nesting.

Thus multiple-nested subroutines in a microprocessor having only a 1-level stack register might seem difficult, if not impossible, to implement. Such is not the case, however, since under software control, nesting is quite simple. The stack register contained in the Fairchild F8 microprocessor (*Figure 1*) readily handles nested subroutines with the aid of the microprocessor's 64-byte scratchpad memory that is used as an automatically expandable stack register.

Where to Use Nesting

Nested subroutines are useful, for example, in square-root computation and in transferring data to a serial printer

such as a teletypewriter. As part of its execution, a square-root subroutine requires a division process that is executed by another subroutine. This, in turn, requires a subtraction process that may be performed by yet another subroutine. Thus, computing a square root requires 3-level subroutine nesting, in which three subroutines are called in sequence from the main program.

In serial printing, a line of 8-bit characters is printed one at a time. The task requires the main program to call one subroutine, SEND. As the microprocessor leaves the main program and begins executing this subroutine, its first step is to locate the beginning of the data to be printed. It loads the first character in a preassigned scratchpad register and calls a second-level subroutine, designated PRINT. At this level, two calls are made to two third-level subroutines, PARC and TTYO. PARC is a parity check routine that verifies the validity of the character, or, if it detects an error, replaces it with a special character, such as @. TTYO, which stands for Teletype® Output, transmits the bits of the character, one at a time, preceding and following them with start and stop bits, according to the standard code for such printers. After the character is transmitted, TTYO returnes to PRINT, which then returns to SEND, which fetches the next character if the last one in the line has not already been printed.

Under different circumstances, the same routines can be called for use in other ways. For example, PARC can be used independently of any printing operation—perhaps in connection with another type of output or input, or where an error following an internal operation is suspected. This independence of operation is what makes a subroutine a

114

subroutine, as opposed to inline code. Executing a subroutine as part of another subroutine is nesting.

Multiple Nesting with One Pointer

In the F8, the program counter is 16 bits wide; each address thus requires two scratchpad registers, each of which holds one byte (eight bits). The coding shown here is good for up to 31 levels of nesting, limited only by the number of available scratchpad registers. In most programs, the scratchpad will contain other data, and for most applications only a few levels of nesting are necessary.

Any subroutine can call another subroutine, provided the calling routine contains certain preparatory instructions, and that the called routine sets up a capability for lower levels of nesting before it does anything else. To execute a subroutine, certain preparatory instructions in the main routine are required, together with a special 11-byte

sequence of 10 instructions, called Service (SERV), which stores the previous contents of the program counter in the scratchpad (*Figure 2*). Following the subroutine, another sequence of 1-byte instructions, called Go Back (GOBA), reloads this stored address in the program counter. Each subroutine must begin and end with the two specific instructions that call these two sequences, which are themselves, in fact, short subroutines.

At the moment a jump to a subroutine occurs, whether from the main routine or a higher-level subroutine, scratchpad location 0 must contain an address into which the stack register contents will be moved after the jump. Location 0 is a working register for use with the indirect scratchpad address register (ISAR), a 6-bit register that points to one of the 64 locations in the scratchpad.

The two preparatory instructions in the main program establish the address for

the stack register contents. Load Immediate Hex (LI H'40') (see Table) places the hexadecimal number 40 in the accumulator, and Load Register 0 from Accumulator (LR 0,A) transfers it to scratchpad location 0. Then, the jump itself, which is the execution of a Push Immediate (PI) instruction, automatically moves the contents of the program counter into the stack register and puts the address of the start of the subroutine—operand SUBN—into the program counter. SUBN, of course, will be a number assigned when this symbolic-language program is assembled into machine code.

What the Subroutine Must Do

To permit nesting, the first instruction in the subroutine must save the contents of the stack register. It does this with a Load Register instruction (LR K,P) that moves the stack register contents to the K register (actually scratchpad locations 11 and 12). This number, which is the return address in the main pro-

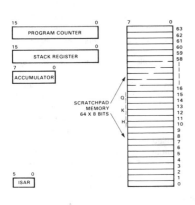

Fig. 1. F-8 registers.

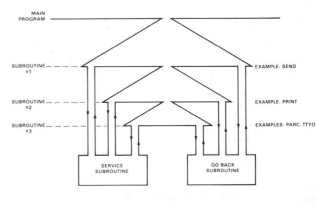

Fig. 2. Nesting.

gram once the subroutine is completed, cannot stay in K because, if a lower-level subroutine is called in, it will also clear the stack register in the same way. Therefore, the second instruction in the subroutine calls on the special sequence SERV to transfer this number to the high end of the scratchpad, in a location defined by the contents of scratchpad 0. The number in scratchpad 0 was placed there by the main routine or by SERV itself at the start of the previous-level subroutine.

This sequence first loads the accumulator with the contents of scratchpad location 0, decrements it by 1 to make the address point to the next empty location in the scratchpad, then moves the result to ISAR (LR IS,A). If the jump to the subroutine is from the main routine, location 0 will contain the hex number 40. The decrementing instruction is Add Immediate Hex FF (AI H'FF'), which adds the binary number 1111 1111 to the contents of the accumulator. This is equivalent to subtracting 1. Thus, at the first level, ISAR contains the hex number 3F, which is the address of the last scratchpad register. Now, with a series of four Load Register instructions, the original contents of the stack register, that were temporarily moved into scratchpad registers 12 and 13, are steered by ISAR via the accumulator into scratchpad registers 63 and 62. In these instructions, KU and KL refer to the high- and low-order bytes of K, while designations D and S are codes that, respectively, cause ISAR to be decremented and remain unchanged. Thus instruction LR-D,A transfers a byte from the accumulator to the scratchpad location specified by ISAR, and then decrements the contents of ISAR. Two steps later, instruction LR S,A again transfers a byte in the same way but leaves ISAR unchanged. Thus, after the transfer, ISAR contains hexadecimal digits 3E, having been decremented twice. Two more Load Register instructions restore the address to location 0, again via the accumulator. Finally, the POP instruction restores the contents of the stack register to the program counter so that the subroutine can begin in earnest.

Executing its assigned task, this subroutine can jump to a lower subroutine, if necessary, without taking the preliminary steps required of the main routine because the Service sequence has already modified the contents of scratchpad register 0. However, every lower-order subroutine must begin with the same two instructions—LR K,P and PI

Two-Level Nesting

MAIN	SERV	GOBA	SUB1	SUB2
INSTR	LR A,0	LR A,0	LR K,P	LR K,P
INSTR	AI H'FF'	LR IS,A	PI SERV	PI SERV
LI H'40'	LR IS,A	LR A,I		
LR 0,A	LR A,KL	LR KU,A	INSTR	INSTR
PI SUB1	LR D,A	LR A,S	INSTR	INSTR
	LR A,KU	LR KL,A	INSTR	INSTR
INSTR	LR S,A	LR A,IS	PI SUB2	JMP GOBA
INSTR	LR A,IS	INC		
INSTR	LR 0,A	LR 0,A	INSTR	
	POP	PK	INSTR	
			INSTR	
			JMP GOBA	

Gaps in listing indicate where each routine stops to wait for a subroutine execution; actual instructions at these points are consecutive.

SERV. Again, these temporarily store the stack register in scratchpad locations 11 and 12, and again, the Service sequence first decrements the contents of location 0 and puts the result in ISAR. However, because this is a lower-level routine, the decrementing changes 3E to 3D and moves the stack register contents into scratchpad registers 61 and 60.

Going Back to the Main Routine
Every subroutine, at whatever level, ends with PI GOBA. GOBA is essentially the reverse of the Service sequence. It obtains the most recent program address from the high end of the scratchpad, places it in register K and increments the pointer in scratchpad 0. Two Load Register instructions transfer the contents of scratchpad location 0 into ISAR via the accumulator. This identifies the location of the address, which, in turn, is the point in the main routine or the higher-level subroutine to which the machine is now returning. Four more LR instructions make the transfer into K; one of them—LR A,I—automatically increments ISAR. Then ISAR is moved into the accumulator and incremented. This new scratchpad address, having been incremented twice, is returned to location 0, and PK takes the machine back to the main routine or the higher subroutine. Note that the actual return from the subroutine is executed directly from GOBA.

Both Service and Go Back sequences utilize automatic decrementation or incrementation of ISAR, with the respective instructions LR D,A in SERV and LR A,I in GOBA. These instructions, as

designed in the F8, affect only the three lower bits of ISAR, which operates as an up/down counter. However, in this application, the updating is always even-to-odd when incrementing and odd-to-even when decrementing. This means that these instructions affect only the least significant bit of ISAR. The real updating, which can include carries through all six bits of ISAR, is executed by instructions AI 'FF' and INC. These actually update the accumulator but, at the moment they are being executed, the contents of ISAR are passing through the accumulator en route to or from temporary storage.

For example, suppose a fourth-level subroutine is being executed and a call is made to a fifth level. At the beginning of SERV, register 0 contains H'38' which is binary 0011 1000. This is decremented by AI'FF' to H'37', or binary 0011 0111. Part way through SERV, it is decremented again by LR D,A to H'36', or binary 0011 0110. The second change affects only the last bits; the first one affects the last four bits. A similar process applies in GOBA.

Regardless of the number of nested levels, the amount of added software is minimal. Service and Go Back sequences, including call and return, are executed in 45 and 37 μs, respectively, provided that the clock frequency is 2 MHz. The same technique can be applied to store in the scratchpad any additional information, such as the contents of the status register, special counters, or other processor data, along with the return address.

Revised and republished, with permission, from Computer Design, February 1976.
© Computer Design Publishing Corp.

Calculating an Error Checking Character in Software

CRC characters, which follow the blocks of data to be transmitted, although usually generated in a hardware shift register with feedback loops, can be created quickly by software in microprocessor-based system.

Suresh Vasa

A software approach is used in the F8 microprocessor to generate a cyclic redundancy check (CRC) character for a block of data. The character provides a means of detecting the occurrence of bursts of errors in the block that it follows. The technique can be used for any cyclic code, including that used for the IBM synchronous data link control (SDLC) communication protocol.

To form the CRC, the binary value is premultiplied by x^{16} and is divided by an appropriate polynomial, which for SDLC is

$$x^{16} + x^{12} + x^5 + 1$$

In many digital systems these operations are performed in a feedback shift register. *Figure 1* shows how the CRC characters are generated for IBM SDLC protocol. Assume that the initial content of this register is represented by A15, A14, A13, . . . , A0, and that an 8-bit character is received, represented by

B7, B6, B5, . . . , B0 (A15 and B7 are the most significant bits). The CRC generation process is performed by these eight bits, one at a time as they arrive serially at the shift register shown in *Figure 2*. The last line of the figure indicates the result, after the last bit of character B has been received.

To generate the CRC with software would require more instructions and more time than is usually available, unless the system instruction set includes

	CRC Generation Routine		
XS 1	Exclusive-OR scratchpad 1 and accumulator	SR 1	
LR 2,A	Store result in scratchpad 2	SR 1	
SR 4	Shift accumulator right four places; (accumulator contains 0000IJKL)	SR 1	Shift accumulator right three places; contains 000IJKLM
		XS 1	Exclusive-OR scratchpad 1 with accumulator
XS 2	Exclusive-OR scratchpad 2 and accumulator	LR 1,A	Store results in scratchpad 1
LR 2,A	Result is IJKLMNOP, store in scratchpad 2	LR A,2	Again bring back IJKLMNOP to accumulator
SL 4	Shift accumulator left four places; contains MNOP0000	SL 4	
XS 0	Exclusive-OR scratchpad 0 and accumulator	SL 1	Shift left five places; contains NOP00000
LR 1,A	Store result in scratchpad 1	XS 2	Exclusive-OR scratchpad 2 with accumulator
LR A,2	Bring back IJKLMNOP to accumulator	LR 0,A	Store in scratchpad 0

commands such as exclusive-OR and 4-bit left and right shifts that can be executed in one machine cycle. The F8 includes such instructions.

To use these instructions, assume that scratchpad registers 0 and 1 together contain a 16-bit remainder (A15 − A0), and that character B is in the accumulator register. Scratchpad register 2 is available for temporary storage.

A routine that generates the CRC (see listing) consists of five exclusive-OR instructions interspersed with various shifting steps that align the bits for the successive exclusive-ORs, corresponding to the shifting and feedback steps in the hardware generation of the CRC. The exclusive-OR is performed bit-for-bit on the contents of the accumulator and a specified register; the F8 contains 64. The result of the operation replaces the input bits in the accumulator. A shift in either direction leaves 0s in its wake; a subsequent exclusive-OR, of course, simply moves the bits from the other register into the positions containing 0 in the accumulator, and inverts the remaining bits.

At the end of the sequence, scratchpad registers 1 and 0 (in that order) contain the same data as the feedback shift register after receipt of character B; the lower eight bits of this result are also found in the accumulator. Register 2 contains an intermediate result that is no longer needed.

The sequence contains 19 instructions, each of which occupies one byte of memory; its total execution time is 38 µs.

Reprinted, with permission, from Computer Design, May 1976, ©Computer Design Publishing Corp.

X15	X14	X13	X12	X11	X10	X9	X8	X7	X6	X5	X4	X3	X2	X1	X0	
A15	A14	A13	A12	A11	A10	A9	A8	A7	A6	A5	A4	A3	A2	A1	A0	INITIAL VALUE
A14	A13	A12	A11⊕I	A10	A9	A8	A7	A6	A5	A4⊕I	A3	A2	A1	A0	I	B7 RECEIVED
A13	A12	A11⊕I	A10⊕J	A9	A8	A7	A6	A5	A4⊕I	A3⊕J	A2	A1	A0	I	J	B6 RECEIVED
A12	A11⊕I	A10⊕J	A9⊕K	A8	A7	A6	A5	A4⊕I	A3⊕J	A2⊕K	A1	A0	I	J	K	B5 RECEIVED
A11⊕I	A10⊕J	A9⊕K	A8⊕L	A7	A6	A5	A4⊕I	A3⊕J	A2⊕K	A1⊕L	A0	I	J	K	L	B4 RECEIVED
A10⊕J	A9⊕K	A8⊕L	A7⊕M	A6	A5	A4⊕I	A3⊕J	A2⊕K	A1⊕L	A0⊕M	I	J	K	L	M	B3 RECEIVED
A9⊕K	A8⊕L	A7⊕M	A6⊕N	A5	A4⊕I	A3⊕J	A2⊕K	A1⊕L	A0⊕M	I⊕N	J	K	L	M	N	B2 RECEIVED
A8⊕L	A7⊕M	A6⊕N	A5⊕O	A4⊕I	A3⊕J	A2⊕K	A1⊕L	A0⊕M	I⊕N	J⊕O	K	L	M	N	O	B1 RECEIVED
A7⊕M	A6⊕N	A5⊕O	A4⊕I⊕P	A3⊕J	A2⊕K	A1⊕L	A0⊕M	I⊕N	J⊕O	K⊕P	L	M	N	O	P	B0 RECEIVED

I = A15⊕B7   M = A11⊕B3⊕I
J = A14⊕B6   N = A10⊕B2⊕J
K = A13⊕B5   O = A9⊕B1⊕K
L = A12⊕B4   P = A8⊕B0⊕L

Fig. 1. Feedback Shift Register

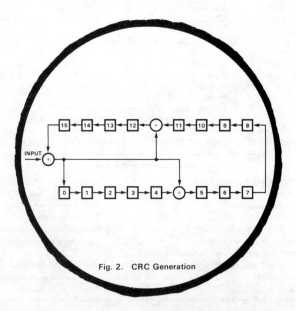

Fig. 2. CRC Generation

Mini-Computer CPU packed on One Chip

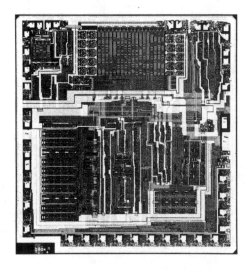

by Dan Wilnai

There is no doubt that integrated injection logic, I2L, is the fastest growing technology in the industry today. It offers the ideal combination of the high speed inherent in bipolar devices and the low power and high density usually associated with MOS. Fairchild I3L™ technology combines this innovative technique with the advanced Isoplanar process to realize high speed and complex LSI devices featuring low-power Schottky TTL characteristics. I3L has extended LSI horizons beyond bit slices, conventional memories and microprocessors into the more complex realm of minicomputers.

The 9440 16-bit bipolar processor, compactly packaged in a 40-pin DIP, is a minicomputer CPU (central processing unit). Data as well as instructions are stored in an external memory and a 16-bit wide, 3-state information bus carries both data and addresses between the CPU and other computer circuits. Although the processor handles 16 bits of information, only 15 bits are used for addressing the memory. Thus, the intrinsic memory capacity of the 9440 system is 32,768 sixteen-bit words.

The input/output ports can serve up to 63 peripheral devices using programmed I/O, interrupt-driver I/O or direct memory access (DMA). Under program control, the 9440 can transfer a 16-bit data word to or from a peripheral device while controlling its operation at the same time. The interrupt system allows any peripheral device to interrupt the normal program flow on a priority basis. The processor responds to an interrupt request by saving the current program-counter (PC) content and executing a jump to master-interrupt service routine. High-speed devices, such as a magnetic tape or disc, can gain direct access to the main memory through a data channel without requiring the execution of any instructions. The DMA rate is limited only by memory speed.

Though structurally different from the Data General Nova line of minicomputers, the 9440 offers comparable performance and executes the same instruction set. To fully utilize this instruction set, the Fairchild Integrated Real-Time Executive (FIRE™) software package is provided. It consists of all the required program development aids such as editors, assemblers, loaders, debuggers plus a full set of diagnostic programs and high-level language processors including Basic and Fortran.

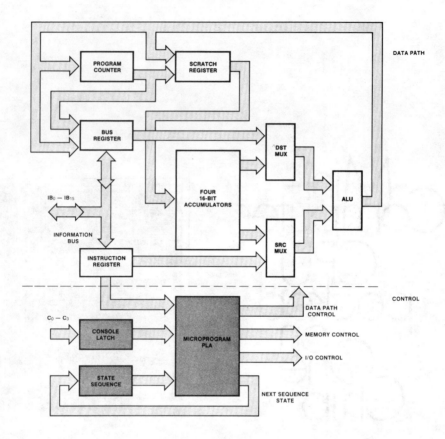

Fig. 1 9440 Block Diagram

ARCHITECTURE *(Figure 1)*

The 9440 consists of a collection of data paths and all the necessary control circuitry. It governs peripheral I/O equipment, performs the arithmetic, logical and data handling operations and sequences the program.

Data Paths

The data-path portion includes a bank of four 16-bit general-purpose registers (accumulators AC0 - AC3), two multiplexers, an ALU, and four 16-bit special registers — scratch register, bus register, instruction register and program counter. Internal data flows between the various registers via 4-bit wide data paths.

The accumulators store the operands required for all arithmetic/logic operations. Accumulators AC2 and AC3 are also used as index registers and AC3 serves as the subroutine linkage register as well. All input-output data transfers take place through the accumulators; however, a word in a memory location may be incremented or decremented without accumulator participation. Data can be moved in either direction between the memory and any accumulator.

The destination and source multiplexers are connected to all four accumulators and select source and destination registers for each operation. The multiplexers also receive other

inputs from the bus and instruction registers, which permit the ALU to be used for effective-address calculations and other purposes.

The ALU is four bits wide and operates on two 16-bit words in four consecutive steps, taking one 4-bit nibble per step. By adding the associated Carry bit to the 16-bit result from the ALU, a 17-bit word is formed which may be rotated either left or right.

Data from the ALU to the destination accumulator is held in the scratch register for one cycle. The bus register is connected to the bidirectional information bus and can either supply or receive 16 bits of data in parallel. The instruction register is loaded with 16 bits in parallel, directly from the information bus during an instruction-fetch operation. The 15-bit program counter determines the sequence in which instructions are executed. It is incremented to take instructions from consecutive locations and the instruction sequence can be altered at any time by changing the PC contents (jump-class instruction) or by incrementing PC twice (skip-class instruction).

Control

Control signals are supplied to the data path by the internal mask-programmed logic array (PLA). For each of 72 different data-path operations, there is a 24-bit output word in the PLA selected according to the combination of 19 input lines. These are defined in *Figure 2*.

The 9440 operates with an on-chip oscillator when a crystal is tied between CP and XTL or it can be driven by an external oscillator via the CP input. The on-chip clock logic circuit generates the internal clock signal, a synchronization signal $\overline{\text{SYN}}$, and several other timing pulses.

A macro-instruction in the 9440 consists of several micro-cycles, each with a corresponding one of 16 sequence-control states. Each microcycle consists of several phases, or nanocycles, four devoted to controlling the data-path circuitry. During each of these phases, the data path circuitry operates on a 4-bit nibble out of the 16 bits of the operands and clocks its various registers on the falling edges of the internal clock pulse. Another phase provides the time delay required for a new output word of the PLA to become valid after the PLA inputs are changed.

The bus register and the instruction register are loaded from the information bus at different times during the execution cycle. Bus-register parallel clock (BRPCL) and instruction-register parallel clock (IRPCL) are the timing pulses, shown in the Read and Write memory cycles in *Figures 4 and 5*.

SIGNAL DESCRIPTIONS *(Figure 3)*
Information Bus — $\overline{\text{IB}}_0$-$\overline{\text{IB}}_{15}$ — The 16-bit bidirectional 3-state information bus is used to transfer address, data, and instruction information between the processor and main memory, and to transfer data and control information to and from I/O devices. A LOW level defines a binary '1'.

Status Lines — RUN, CARRY, INT ON — These lines are used to convey the status information of the processor mainly for display on an operator console.

Operator Console Control — C_0-C_3, $\overline{\text{MR}}$ — These lines are used by the operator to control 9440 operation.

Input/Output Control — O_0, O_1, $\overline{\text{INT REQ}}$, $\overline{\text{DCH REQ}}$ — O_0 and O_1 outputs control the I/O devices. The I/O devices can interrupt normal program flow by activating the Interrupt-Request input ($\overline{\text{INT REQ}}$) and can gain direct access to the main memory by activating the Data-Channel-Request input.

Memory Control — $\overline{\text{M}}_0$-$\overline{\text{M}}_2$, $\overline{\text{MBSY}}$ — The processor controls the main memory via the three open-collector control lines ($\overline{\text{M}}_0$-$\overline{\text{M}}_2$) and synchronizes itself to the memory cycle time indicated by the memory-busy ($\overline{\text{MBSY}}$) signal.

Timing — CP, XTL, CLK OUT, $\overline{\text{SYN}}$ — The 9440 can operate with an on-chip oscillator when a crystal is tied between CP and XTL or it can operate from an external clock (CP). The internal oscillator is available to the outside world on CLK OUT. $\overline{\text{SYN}}$ is an active LOW synchronization signal for memory and I/O devices.

Power Supplies — V_{CC}, I INJ, GND — V_{CC} requires 5V, I INJ requires 180 mA current source at about 1 V.

MODES OF ADDRESSING
The flexible addressing structure of the 9440 consists of four types of addressing — one is absolute addressing of page

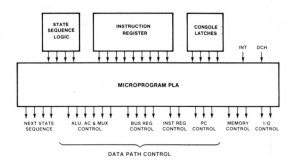

Fig. 2   Programmed Logic Array

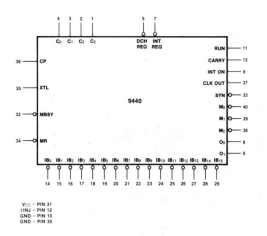

V_{CC} = PIN 31
I INJ = PIN 12
GND = PIN 10
GND = PIN 30

Fig. 3   Logic Symbol

zero, i.e. the first 256 locations in the memory; the other three are relative addressing where an 8-bit displacement in the memory reference instruction is treated as a signed number and added to a 15-bit base address in an index register, either AC2, AC3, or PC. Each type may be either direct or indirect for a total of eight modes. Relative addressing using accumulator AC2 or AC3 is useful for accessing consecutive entries from a table in the memory, e.g., where a displacement is added to the incremented index in the accumulator. Relative addressing utilizing the program counter is used for jumping to nearby locations when a relocatable program is executed.

In direct addressing, the 15-bit computed value is the actual address used to read or store the operand. In the case of indirect addressing, the computed value is the address of an address. The data read from an indirectly addressed location can be the final effective address or another nested indirect address depending on the most significant bit in that word. When locations $(20)_8$ through $(27)_8$ are indirectly adressed, the auto-increment feature takes over and the contents of the selected location are first incremented and then the new value is treated as the new address, which can be either direct or indirect. Locations $(30)_8$ through $(37)_8$ are used as auto-decrement locations in a similar fashion

121

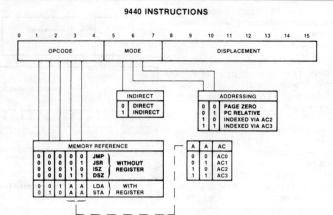

Memory Reference Instructions:

0	1	2	3	4	5	6	7	8	9	10	11	12	13	14	15
OPCODE					MODE			DISPLACEMENT							

INDIRECT

0	DIRECT
1	INDIRECT

ADDRESSING

0	0	PAGE ZERO
0	1	PC RELATIVE
1	0	INDEXED VIA AC2
1	1	INDEXED VIA AC3

MEMORY REFERENCE

0	0	0	0	0	JMP	WITHOUT REGISTER
0	0	0	0	1	JSR	
0	0	0	1	0	ISZ	
0	0	0	1	1	DSZ	
0	0	1	A	A	LDA	WITH REGISTER
0	1	0	A	A	STA	

A	A	AC
0	0	AC0
0	1	AC1
1	0	AC2
1	1	AC3

Memory Reference instructions without register are used for branching (JMP, JSR) without involving accumulators. These instructions are also used for modifying memory (ISZ, DSZ). Memory Reference instructions with register are used to move 16-bit words between the memory and the accumulators.

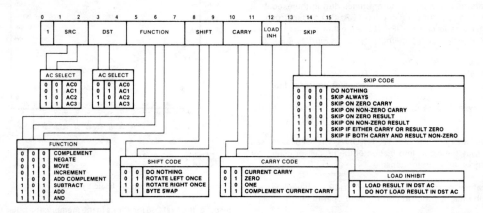

0	1	2	3	4	5	6	7	8	9	10	11	12	13	14	15
1	SRC		DST		FUNCTION			SHIFT		CARRY		LOAD INH	SKIP		

AC SELECT

0	0	AC0
0	1	AC1
1	0	AC2
1	1	AC3

AC SELECT

0	0	AC0
0	1	AC1
1	0	AC2
1	1	AC3

SKIP CODE

0	0	0	DO NOTHING
0	0	1	SKIP ALWAYS
0	1	0	SKIP ON ZERO CARRY
0	1	1	SKIP ON NON-ZERO CARRY
1	0	0	SKIP ON ZERO RESULT
1	0	1	SKIP ON NON-ZERO RESULT
1	1	0	SKIP IF EITHER CARRY OR RESULT ZERO
1	1	1	SKIP IF BOTH CARRY AND RESULT NON-ZERO

FUNCTION

0	0	0	COMPLEMENT
0	0	1	NEGATE
0	1	0	MOVE
0	1	1	INCREMENT
1	0	0	ADD COMPLEMENT
1	0	1	SUBTRACT
1	1	0	ADD
1	1	1	AND

SHIFT CODE

0	0	DO NOTHING
0	1	ROTATE LEFT ONCE
1	0	ROTATE RIGHT ONCE
1	1	BYTE SWAP

CARRY CODE

0	0	CURRENT CARRY
0	1	ZERO
1	0	ONE
1	1	COMPLEMENT CURRENT CARRY

LOAD INHIBIT

0	LOAD RESULT IN DST AC
1	DO NOT LOAD RESULT IN DST AC

Arithmetic/Logic instructions perform arithmetic (ADD, ADC, INC, NEG, SUB) or Boolean (AND, COM, MOV) operations on the contents of two registers. The result of each operation together with the Carry bit can be rotated and tested for skip conditions as part of the same arithmetic/logic instruction; loading in the destination register is optional.

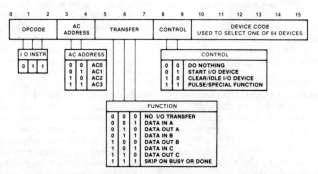

0	1	2	3	4	5	6	7	8	9	10	11	12	13	14	15
OPCODE			AC ADDRESS		TRANSFER			CONTROL		DEVICE CODE USED TO SELECT ONE OF 64 DEVICES					

I O INSTR

0	1	1

AC ADDRESS

0	0	AC0
0	1	AC1
1	0	AC2
1	1	AC3

CONTROL

0	0	DO NOTHING
0	1	START I/O DEVICE
1	0	CLEAR/IDLE I/O DEVICE
1	1	PULSE/SPECIAL FUNCTION

FUNCTION

0	0	0	NO I/O TRANSFER
0	0	1	DATA IN A
0	1	0	DATA OUT A
0	1	1	DATA IN B
1	0	0	DATA OUT B
1	0	1	DATA IN C
1	1	0	DATA OUT C
1	1	1	SKIP ON BUSY OR DONE

Input/Output instructions move data between the 9440 accumulators and three buffers in the peripheral device interface. These instructions also perform control functions in the I/O device and test the status flags in both the peripheral circuitry and the central processor.

MAIN MEMORY

In addition to a 16-bit wide memory array, the memory system consists of a memory address register (MAR) to define a memory address, a data-in register to hold the data to be written into the memory, and output buffers to store the data read from the memory. Memory operations are controlled by the $\overline{M}_0$ - $\overline{M}_2$ open-collector lines, common to the 9440 and to all I/O devices having DMA capability.

A LOW on $\overline{M}_0$ indicates memory Read, LOW on $\overline{M}_1$ memory Write and LOW on $\overline{M}_2$ means Load MAR. During data-channel operations, the $\overline{M}$ lines are not driven by the 9440 and an external device can control the memory by driving the appropriate $\overline{M}$ line LOW. When the Memory-Busy input ($\overline{MBSY}$) is LOW memory operation is in process.

Memory Operation

Since the 9440 information bus is shared by both addresses and data, data on the bus during each memory operation, and the location in the memory array to be affected must be clearly defined.

Read Operation (Figure 4)

For a Read cycle, the 9440 activates $\overline{M}_0$ and $\overline{M}_2$ after the first nibble ($\overline{M}_1$ remains HIGH) and puts the address on the information bus at the end of the fourth nibble. After a deskewing delay, $\overline{SYN}$ goes LOW. The memory then latches the information into the MAR, responds with the $\overline{MBSY}$ signal and begins the Read cycle.

When the 9440 receives the $\overline{MBSY}$ signal, it removes the address from the information bus. When the Read operation is completed, the memory enables the output buffers and terminates the $\overline{MBSY}$ signal. Data from the memory is loaded from the information bus into the bus register or the instruction register and $\overline{SYN}$ is terminated. The memory disables the output buffers on the trailing edge of $\overline{SYN}$.

Write Operation (Figure 5)

The Write operation requires two cycles. At the beginning of the first, the 9440 activates $\overline{M}_2$. At the end of the fourth nibble, the 9440 puts the address on the information bus and, after a deskewing delay, generates $\overline{SYN}$. The information is latched into the MAR and the memory responds with a $\overline{MBSY}$ signal. At the beginning of the second cycle, the 9440 activates M_1 and, at the end of the fourth nibble, puts the data to be written into the memory onto the information bus. Again, $\overline{SYN}$ is activated after a deskewing delay. The memory latches the data into the data-in register, responds with the $\overline{MBSY}$ signal and begins the Write operation. Upon completion, the memory terminates the $\overline{MBSY}$ signal.

As indicated in Figure 5, for a Write operation as well as for a LD MAR operation, the 9440 does not wait for the memory to complete its operation. $\overline{MBSY}$ going LOW is the indication to the 9440 that the memory has started operation; it triggers the termination of the SYN state of the internal clock and the beginning of the PLA state.

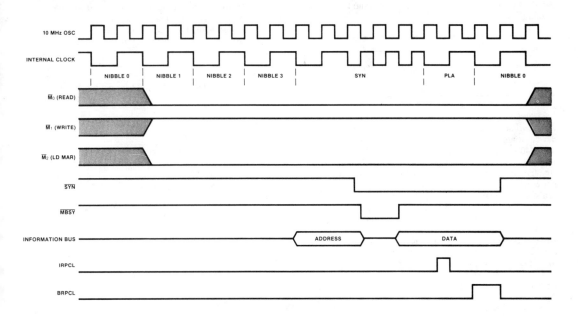

Fig. 4 Memory Read Cycle

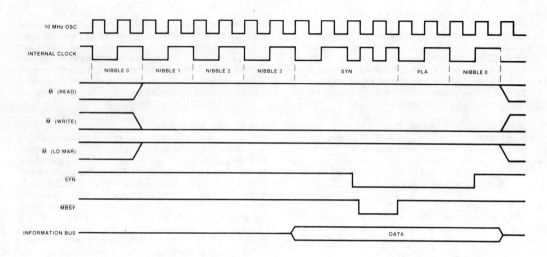

Fig. 5 Memory Write Cycle

INPUT/OUTPUT CONTROL

I/O devices communicate with the 9440 through the common information bus under either program or interrupt control. Also, high-speed devices can gain access to main memory via the data channel. To avoid conflicts on the information bus, the I/O devices are sent sychronization signals. A code, defining one of four functions, is conveyed to each I/O device over O_0 and O_1, which are valid before and during $\overline{SYN}$.

O_1	O_0	FUNCTION
0	0	Instruction Fetch
0	1	Data Channel Acknowledge
1	0	I/O Execute
1	1	No Operation

For interfacing under program control, each I/O device provides two status signals, one for device-busy, the other for device-done. These signals are provided, upon request from the 9440, on the $\overline{IB}_0$ and $\overline{IB}_1$ lines of the information bus. Since there may be several devices requesting interrupt simultaneously, a serially propagated interrupt-priority signal, connected to each device, establishes device priority in a "daisy-chain" fashion. The first device requesting an interrupt, with a LOW on its interrupt-priority input, blocks the propagation of the interrupt-priority signal with a HIGH on its interrupt-priority output; it then answers the interrupt-acknowledge instruction from the 9440. The processor, however, can disable the interrupt system in any I/O device by executing a mask-out instruction.

For operation under direct memory access, three control lines similar to the interrupt-control lines are available. The data-channel-request ($\overline{DCH\ REQ}$) line, like the interrupt-request ($\overline{INT\ REQ}$), is common to all I/O devices. Priority is set in the same way it is established under interrupt control by connecting the data-channel-priority input and output lines between I/O devices.

OPERATOR CONSOLE

Using the operator console, a special I/O device, the operator controls 9440 operation via the four C lines and the reset line. The three status lines from the 9440 communicate directly with the operator console.

The console can transfer data to any one of the four accumulators, as well as to the program counter, and can examine their contents. It can either read from or write into a memory location addressed by the program counter. In addition, the console can command the 9440 to start execution or halt the program.

The various console operations are coded on the C lines as shown below. These control lines must be active long enough for the 9440 to respond to the command and should be disabled immediately thereafter.

C_3	C_2	C_1	C_0	OPERATION
0	0	0	0	Examine AC0
0	0	0	1	Examine AC1
0	0	1	0	Examine AC2
0	0	1	1	Examine AC3
0	1	0	0	Load PC
0	1	0	1	Examine Memory
0	1	1	0	Not Used
0	1	1	1	Halt
1	0	0	0	Deposit AC0
1	0	0	1	Deposit AC1
1	0	1	0	Deposit AC2
1	0	1	1	Deposit AC3
1	1	0	0	Load PC
1	1	0	1	Deposit Memory
1	1	1	0	Continue/Run
1	1	1	1	No Operation

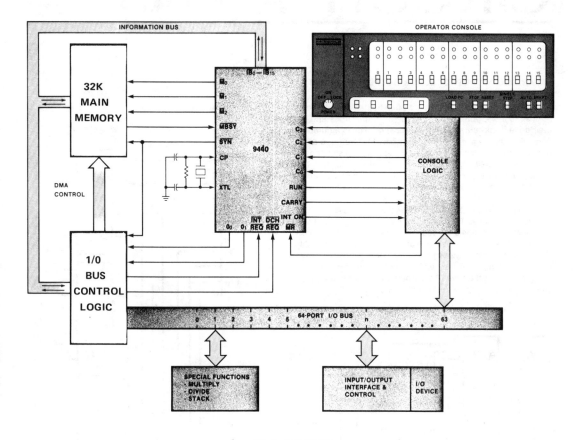

Fig. 6 9440 System

9440 SYSTEM

A typical system configuration is shown in *Figure 6*. The 9440 processor is the central element of this computer system. It is connected to the 32K-word main memory and to I/O bus control logic as well as to operator console logic. Sixty-two of the 64 ports on the I/O bus can be used for operating peripheral devices under program, interrupt, or DMA control. Port 1 is reserved for special functions such as hardware multiply/ divide instructions, memory-stack instructions, etc. Port 63 is saved for special CPU instructions such as Mask Out or Read switches from the front panel.

The invention of I2L and the obvious need for high-density bipolar logic prompted Fairchild to launch a broad development program — the 9440 project. A multidisciplinary task force was headed by Peter Verhofstadt, manager of the Advanced Products operation. I3L development was achieved by R & D under Drs. Thomas Longo, James Early and Madhu Vora. Bob Moeckel and Chuck Erickson of the Processor Development group, lead by Dan Wilnai, provided system architecture and logic design. The 9440 circuit was designed by Hemraj Hingarh of the I3L Circuit Design group headed by Dick Crippen. The Software Engineering group led by Dr. Ashok Suri was responsible for software support. The successful completion of the 9440 project is the result of a well coordinated effort by everyone involved, backed by a strong commitment from Fairchild management.

CIRCUIT IDEAS μP

by Peter Alfke

EXPANDING MICROPROCESSOR OUTPUT CAPABILITY

Small microprocessor systems are often limited by their output capabilities, both in the number of output lines and in their drive (sink) current. The classical remedy is a number of quad-latches, e.g. eight 7475s driven by four buffered data outputs and selected by a decoder (Figure 1). This expands one microprocessor output port (eight lines) to 32 TTL outputs at the expense of 10 TTL packages. Obviously, only one set of four TTL outputs can be changed at a time.

A cheaper and more compact solution that achieves the same results with only five TTL packages is shown in Figure 2. This circuit uses four 9334 8-bit addressable latches and one hex inverter. The 74LS259 low-power Schottky and the 4724 CMOS addressable latches are equivalent devices. They eliminate the need for the hex inverter but offer less output drive. Note that the four TTL outputs that can be changed simultaneously are now on different packages.

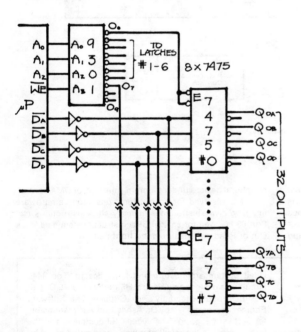

FIGURE 1·

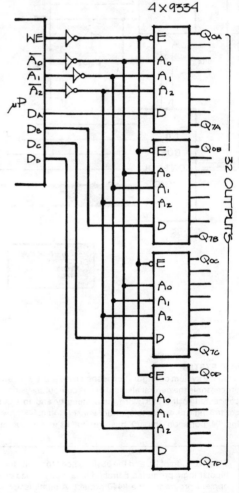

FIGURE 2·

MEMORIES

Bipolar Memory comes of Age

by Gene Miles and Rex Rice

Designers have traditionally considered cost per bit the dominant parameter when choosing between bipolar and MOS memories; consequently MOS has been selected for most memory systems except those requiring bipolar high speed. Now, due to improved processing techniques, volume production and economical packaging, bipolar RAM costs on a system basis are rapidly approaching those of MOS. The time has come to take a new look at the choice of memory components*.

Since the introduction of the 1024-bit bipolar RAM (93415) in 1972, die size has been reduced by approximately 45%. This was accomplished by shrinking cell size as opposed to changing layout rules. The smaller die can now be packaged in the low-cost 16-pin ceramic or plastic DIP. At the same time, speed has been improved about 40% at no increase in power. With the 93L415, a 75-ns RAM at 175 mW typical power, bipolar speeds are available at MOS power levels without the constraints of charge pumping or refreshing, multiple power supplies, and the larger 18 or 22-pin packages.

The combination of high volume production and economical packaging has sliced the high volume cost per bit of the 1024-bit RAMs to under a penny; projected high volume cost in 1976 for commercial devices is less than 0.5 cent per bit *(Figure 1)*.

Now that the price differential on a system basis between bipolar and high speed MOS is disappearing, the designer can give a higher priority to the inherent characteristics of the two memory types. The following considerations are essential in any design choice.

The rapid decrease in the cost of fast static bipolar RAMs has opened up a broad range of applications heretofore reserved for MOS. With the recent cost reductions in bipolar components and when contemplating complete memory-system lifetime costs, the designer should consider bipolar memories in the following applications.

- Memories of any speed where a prototype and a small number of units, or a low production rate, is anticipated. Here, design and development costs outweigh the cost-per-bit differences.

- Memories where rapid development of a complete computing system is important. Assembling the memory first allows easy debugging of the rest of the system. This technique was used for the ILLIAC IV system.

- Memories for systems where dynamic refresh requirements would create interrupt and software management difficulties. Eliminating refresh saves both calculate time and memory space which may outweigh raw component cost-per-bit considerations.

- Production memory systems where field diagnosis and maintenance are important. Fault analysis and troubleshooting in a static one-voltage unclocked system place fewer demands on the quality and quantity of field-support personnel.

- Memories in systems where hierarchies of buffers, queuing, etc., are used to boost performance. Simpler less-expensive systems can result by taking advantage of the higher speeds of bipolar RAMs to save software and calculate time costs and to eliminate hardware.

ITEM	MOS	BIPOLAR
System Power	Same or lower	Same or higher
Read and Write Cycle times	Slower	Faster to much faster
Dynamic	Yes — Less expensive than static	No
Static	Yes — Slower than bipolar	Yes — Faster
Ease of design	Dynamic — Difficult	NA
	Static — Easier than dynamic	Easiest — Same rules as for TTL (or ECL logic)
Ease of service	Dynamic — Difficult	NA
	Static — Easier than dynamic	Easiest
Ease of use	Dynamic causes interrupt, software and compute time problems	Simple and direct

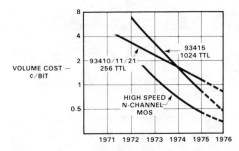

Fig. 1. Decrease in Volume Cost of Commercial Bipolar Memory Devices

*For details on available Fairchild bipolar memories, including cost, see "Bipolar Memories Update", Progress Vol. 2, No. 10, October, November, December 1974.

BIPOLAR RAM DESIGN EXAMPLE

The best way to illustrate the ease of design and other advantages of bipolar static RAMs is to give a design example. It is assumed that the designer needs a modular rack-mounted system to cover a broad range of applications. Since all parts of the system—components, architecture, packaging, modularity, testing, etc.,—are closely interrelated, they have equal importance and must all be considered. Consequently, for this design, the packaging for example assumes the same importance as the circuit considerations. No part of the design should be treated separately.

Memory Modularity

Basic Memory Cards: *(Figure 2)*

One with 8K words and 8 or 9 bits, *i.e.,* one design with last row not inserted, for 8 bits.

One with 4K words and 8 or 9 bits, *i.e.,* one 8K design may be used with 93L415s for 4K words not inserted and for 8 bits; one row is not inserted.

Basic Memory Module: *(Figure 3)*

One memory card (basic)
One address drive card
One base
Power
Card cage (rack mount)

Expanded Memory Module: *(Figure 3)*

Modular from one to eight memory cards
One address drive card
One base
Power
Cables
Card cage (rack mount)

Memory size range using multiple cards in one module:

WORDS/BYTES	WORDS/BITS	CARDS/MODULE
4K x 8/9	4K x 8/9	1/2
-----	4K x 16/18	1
8K x 8/9	8K x 8/9	1
16K x 8/9	8K x 16/18	2
24K x 8/9	8K x 24/27	3
32K x 8/9	8K x 32/36	4
40K x 8/9	8K x 40/45	5
48K x 8/9	8K x 48/54	6
56K x 8/9	8K x 56/63	7
64K x 8/9	8K x 64/72	8

Memory size range using multiple modules:

WORDS/BYTES	WORDS/BITS	NO. MODULES
64K x 8/9	8K x 16/72	1
128K x 8/9	16K x 16/72	2
192K x 8/9	24K x 16/72	3
256K x 8/9	32K x 16/72	4
320K x 8/9	40K x 16/72	5
384K x 8/9	48K x 16/72	6
448K x 8/9	56K x 16/72	7
512K x 8/9	64K x 16/72	8

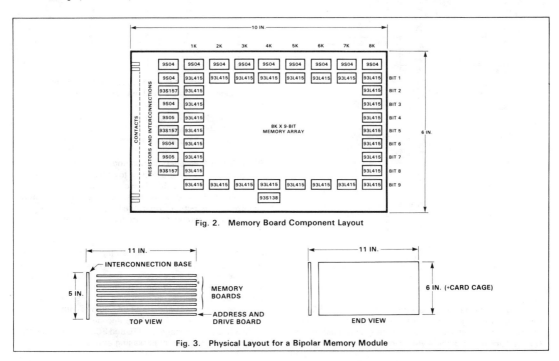

Fig. 2.   Memory Board Component Layout

Fig. 3.   Physical Layout for a Bipolar Memory Module

Packaging System

Memory and Address Boards:

Two-sided printed circuit boards with plated holes.

Base:

A two-sided printed circuit board.

Memory Board Connectors:

Conventional pc board connectors which permit wire wrap on the back side. All memory address and control interconnections are directly on the base.

Byte-oriented systems:

All wiring on the base; no wire wrap needed.

Word-oriented systems:

The address and control lines remain on the base.

The data input and data output cables to the computer are brought directly to the pins on the respective memory cards.

Power Distribution:

Power conducted along the base and distributed to pins on each pc card. Power distribution bars for ground and the one voltage, +5 V, augment the copper on the base pc board.

Cooling:

Forced air cooling, 400 or more feet per minute flowing between the cards. Stacks of memories up to four deep require about 500 feet per minute.

Card Cage:

Available standard catalog-item card guides.

The Basic Memory Card

Figure 2 shows the layout of the components on the basic memory card. The contact pins are located on the left. The resistors terminating the input data cables from the computer are in the first component column. Next is a column of ICs with the following functions.

ITEM	NO. PACKAGES	SIGNALS	FIGURE	FUNCTION
9S04	2	A_0	4	Drive In
		A_1	4	
		A_2	4	
		A_3	4	
		A_4	4	
		A_5	4	
		A_6	4	
		A_7	4	
		A_8	4	
		A_9	4	
		WE	6	
93S157	1	$D_{OUT}1$	8	Output Latches
		$D_{OUT}2$	8	
		$D_{OUT}3$	8	
9S04	1	Data Strobe	8	Drive In
		$D_{IN}1$	7	
		$D_{IN}2$	7	
		$D_{IN}3$	7	
9S05	1	$D_{OUT}1$	8	Drive Out
		$D_{OUT}2$	8	
		$D_{OUT}3$	8	
93S157	1	$D_{OUT}4$	8	Output Latches
		$D_{OUT}5$	8	
		$D_{OUT}6$	8	
9S04	1	$D_{IN}4$	7	Drive In
		$D_{IN}5$	7	
		$D_{IN}6$	7	
		$D_{IN}7$	7	
		$D_{IN}8$	7	
		$D_{IN}9$	7	
9S05	1	$D_{OUT}4$	8	Drive Out
		$D_{OUT}5$	8	
		$D_{OUT}6$	8	
		$D_{OUT}7$	8	
		$D_{OUT}8$	8	
		$D_{OUT}9$	8	
93S157	1	$D_{OUT}7$	8	Output Latches
		$D_{OUT}8$	8	
		$D_{OUT}9$	8	

The memory columns are organized in pairs. The 9S04 inverters are used at the top to give fan-out drive to each pair of columns. The schematic of this drive/fan-out is illustrated in *Figures 4* and *6*. Since there are six inverters per package and

eleven lines to be driven, *i.e.*, A_0 through A_9 plus WE, two 9S04 hex inverter packages are sufficient. The input characteristics of the 93L415 1024-bit RAM are such that two columns represent only 4.1 unit loads for the 18 inputs. The four inverters represent 5 unit loads to the driver.

		IC COLUMNS 2 AND 3		
ROW	ITEM	SIGNAL COL. 2	SIGNAL COL. 3	FIGURE
Top	9S04	WE	A_1	
		A_0	A_3	4
		A_2	A_5	6
		A_4	A_7	9
		A_6	A_9	
		A_8	--	
Bit 1	93L415	0–1K	1K–2K	9
Bit 2	93L415	0–1K	1K–2K	
Bit 3	93L415	0–1K	1K–2K	
Bit 4	93L415	0–1K	1K–2K	
Bit 5	93L415	0–1K	1K–2K	
Bit 6	93L415	0–1K	1K–2K	
Bit 7	93L415	0–1K	1K–2K	
Bit 8	93L415	0–1K	1K–2K	
Bit 9	93L415	0–1K	1K–2K	

The same arrangement is used to provide four column pairs. The additional pairs implement memory words as follows:

Pair #2: 2K–3K and 3K–4K
Pair #3: 4K–5K and 5K–6K
Pair #4: 6K–7K and 7K–8K

A 93S138 1-of-8 decoder, located under column 4 of the array, performs the address selection to choose the column representing 1K of the possible 8K words of memory. As illustrated in *Figure 5*, the decoder drives each column separately to control chip selection. Addresses A_{10}, A_{11}, and A_{12} as well as E_1, *i.e.*, memory select, are the inputs controlling the decoder.

When arranged this way, all lines on the memory board are short enough so that terminating resistors and controlled impedance lines are unnecessary. The longest line running from the address drive to the last column is approximately eight inches. The vertical lines driving the array start at row 1, split into a "U" shape and drive two columns with branches about five inches long. The 1-of-8 decoder drive lines vary from five to eight inches long. TTL and ECL systems operate satisfactorily in this type of packaging environment.

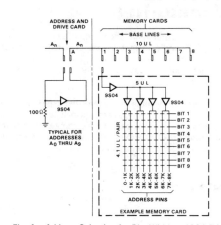

Fig. 4. Address Selection for Bits Within a 1024 RAM

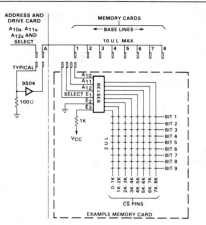

Fig. 5. Address Selection Groups of 1024 RAMs

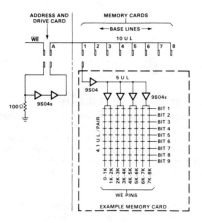

Fig. 6. Read/Write Selection

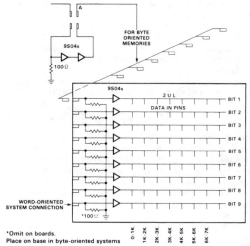

*Omit on boards.
Place on base in byte-oriented systems

Fig. 7. Data Input System

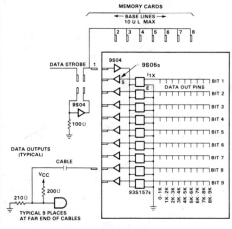

Fig. 8. Data Output System

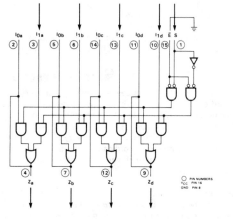

Fig. 9. 93S157 as a Pass Through Latch for Data Output System

Memory Module Packaging

Figure 3 shows one possible layout for a memory module. The base on the left is used to connect the address card with one to eight memory cards. For byte-oriented systems, the cables to other equipment are connected to the base at one end. The cable termination and fan-out drive circuits are contained on the address and drive board. For word-oriented systems, the address and control lines are routed to one end of the base and through the address board to drive the memory cards. However, due to the large number of cables involved, the data input and data output lines should be attached, i.e., wire wrap or other means, directly to the data input and output pins of each memory card. The cards are

designed so that termination for data input is on the memory board (Figure 7) and sufficient drive is provided on the output (Figure 8). A pair of resistors to $+V_{CC}$ and ground should be used to terminate the data output lines within the receiving equipment.

For tightly packaged systems where the other logic is adjacent to the memory, omit the address card and include the required signal drive and inverters as part of the computer. The memory card design provides great flexibility for integration into other systems. Normal TTL circuit rules apply.

Address Board

The address board is a very simple two-layer pc board. It receives the address and control signals from the equipment attached to the memory and provides the necessary fan-out drive. The inversion function is also performed if required. There are few components and pin connections on the address board. In tightly coupled systems, it may be omitted and the required circuits can be part of the other equipment. In this case, it may be necessary to provide circuits that can drive 10 unit loads plus a terminating resistor mounted on the base opposite the input cable end. When using an address board, the longest output line is less than nine inches so no terminating resistors are needed within the memory for a TTL design.

ADDRESS BOARD COMPONENTS		
ITEM	*SIGNAL	FIGURE
9S04	A_0 A_1 A_2 A_3 A_4 A_5	4
9S04	A_6 A_7 A_8 A_9	4
	WE WE	6
9S04	A_{10} A_{11} A_{12} E_1	5
	DS	8

*100 Ω terminating resistors to ground are assumed on each input

Memory Board Circuits & Layouts

Figures 4 through 8 are combination circuit and pseudo-physical routing schematics. Figure 4 through 6 illustrate (on the upper left side) the circuits that can be either on an address board or in attached equipment. The base lines for plugging in the eight memory boards are illustrated across the top. An example memory board circuit/routing schematic is shown in each figure along with the relationships of bits and words in the rows and columns. Refer to Figure 2 for the memory board layout. The ICs include Schottky TTL types 9S04, 9S05, 93S138, and 93S157, and the TTL 1K RAM 93L415. The faster higher powered 93415 or 93415A can be substituted without any electrical design or layout changes. The power supply must be increased and more cooling provided; also memory timing pulses must be adjusted to take advantage of these faster parts.

Figure 7 illustrates the data input system. If the cables for word-oriented systems come directly to the memory card, the

100 Ω terminating resistors are used. In byte-oriented systems, these resistors are omitted. The drive circuits for byte-oriented systems may be located either on the address drive board or in the attached equipment. If sufficient fan-out drive is supplied from the attached equipment and long cables are used, a terminating resistor is placed at the far end of the base.

The data output system is shown in Figure 8. The 93L415 outputs for each bit are connected together and run to the I_{1x} pin of a 93S157 multiplexer. The multiplexer is connected to provide a pass through latch as shown in Figure 9 to permit rapid data access, long data hold time, and to minimize strobe skew. 9S05 drivers with open collectors are provided for output drive so the various bits in a byte-oriented memory can be OR-tied together. A resistor network as illustrated in Figure 8 is placed at the receiving end of the output data cables.

Some Interconnection Hints

The dual-in-line package is designed with space to run one pc board conductor between pins. Two-layer printed circuit boards provide for running horizontal connections on the back and vertical connections on the front. This and the regularity of connections in a memory array allow very tight packaging. IC spacing on the memory board can be on a pitch of one inch horizontally and one-half inch vertically, which is a common industry practice.

Interconnections are made using straightforward simple wire routings on two-layer boards. Figure 10 presents part of the actual layout showing three columns of the array. The connections to the 9S04 address drive are at the top. Ground and $+V_{CC}$ trees are also illustrated; note that one ground and

one $+V_{CC}$ line go between each column. It is important that the designer run one line horizontally across the board and attach it through plated holes to $+V_{CC}$ at every other package row. This forms a screen or mesh for power distribution. A similar arrangement should be used for ground.

The vertical lines are routed to pin rows of the DIPs. This provides address, read/write and chip selection on the front side of the pc board. The data input and output lines are on the back side along with the V_{CC} and ground cross connections. Appropriate capacitors should be placed between V_{CC} and ground for about every four packages. Normal TTL design rules apply.

Performance Characteristics

The chart below and *Figure 11* summarize the performance that can be expected from a system using Schottky TTL parts and 90-ns 93L415 1K RAMs. The power dissipation is calculated for worst-case conditions for the Schottky parts and for typical dissipation on the memory parts. This is reasonable, since so many memory parts are used, the averages apply. The timing calculations are made using 2 ns/foot delays for signals on conductors and worst-case Schottky values. The read and write cycle times for the 93L415 are assumed to be 90 ns for the example calculations; however the user may specify shorter access times at added cost. To adjust the times shown, a designer may add the nanosecond differences for maximum RAM times or subtract the differences if he uses faster parts. Pipelining effect through the memory system logic is not included; if it is, the cycle times can be reduced a few nanoseconds.

Minor adjustments in timing may have to be made to accommodate a specific design. Layout dimensions and the minimum and maximum times established for all components will affect the system delays. The time values used in this example take line-length delays and circuit skews into account with appropriate allowance for margins.

MEMORY PERFORMANCE SUMMARY

USING 93L415 RAMs AND SCHOTTKY TTL PARTS

ITEM	SINGLE 8K x 9 CARD	MODULE 8 CARDS	SYSTEM *8 MODULES
Size: Words/Bits	8K/9	8K/72 or 64K/9	64K/72 or 512K/9
Total Bits	73,728	589,824	4,718,592
Read Access	120 ns typ	125 ns typ	135 ns typ
Data Window	80 ns typ	80 ns typ	80 ns typ
Read Cycle	120 ns typ	125 ns typ	135 ns typ
Write Cycle	120 ns typ	125 ns typ	135 ns typ
Inputs & Outputs	TTL	TTL	TTL
Supply Voltage (one)	+5.0 V	+5.0 V	+5.0 V
Supply Current	3.11 A	24.9 A	199 A
Power	15.6 W	125 W	998 W
Inlet Air	0°C to 55°C	0°C to 55°C	0°C to 55°C
Cooling Air	400 fpm	400 fpm	500 fpm

*Two rows of four modules.

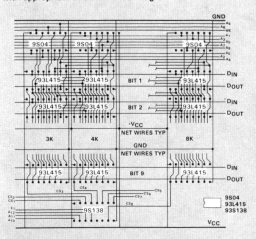

Fig. 10. Memory Column Interconnection System

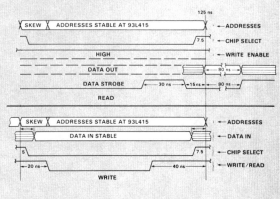

Fig. 11. Timing Example for 93L415 Memory

Conclusion

Smaller die size, increased yields and economical packaging have reduced bipolar 1K RAM costs to the point where bipolar memories have become attractive for some applications reserved, in the past, for slower, lower cost MOS memories. Instead of emphasizing the cost per bit, the designer should look at the total memory system cost and inherent device characteristics when choosing a RAM for a specific application. The chief advantages of bipolar RAMs are outlined below.

● Simple design, construction, testing and field maintenance features of static bipolar TTL memories mean lower total system-lifetime hardware costs.

● Fast static memories greatly ease system interrupt and software storage and access problems as well as enhance system throughput, thus providing system lifetime savings.

References

R. Rice, F. Greene, and W. Sander, "Design Considerations Leading to the ILLIAC IV Process Element Memory," IEEE Solid-State Circuits Journal, October 1970.

TTL Data Book, Supplement Number One, Schottky, Mountain View: Fairchild Semiconductor, 1973.

"TTL Isoplanar Memory 93L415, 1024-Bit Fully Decoded Random Access Memory," Preliminary Data Sheet, Mountain View: Fairchild Semiconductor, 1974.

Acknowledgements

The authors wish to express thanks to Brooks Cowart and Wendell Sander for their help in preparing this article.

Bipolar RAM Goes Dynamic

by Wendell B. Sander
and James M. Early

The 93481 dynamic random access memory (RAM), utilizing Isoplanar Integrated Injection Logic (I³L™), is the first bipolar memory to intrude upon MOS RAM territory, in particular, main memory. This 4096 x 1-bit dynamic RAM offers the best of two worlds – the high packing density and low cost of dynamic MOS and the high speed and applications ease of bipolar 4K RAMs. Die size is only 11,700 square mils, the smallest 4K RAM available. With a typical access time (90 ns) twice as fast as most 4K MOS memories, the 93481 has an active power dissipation of 400 mW and 70 mW stand-by power. The application-oriented features associated with bipolar RAMs include high speed, single 5 V supply (MOS dynamic RAMs require three) and TTL-compatible inputs and outputs. Other features include 240 ns cycle time, two Chip Selects, controllable data latching and 65 ns access and cycle times when using the paging mode. Also, the 93481 offers lower input capacitance and a higher drive capability than its MOS counterpart.

A time multiplexing scheme is utilized for five of the seven address inputs, reducing the required number of address lines from 12 to seven to fit the device in a 16-pin DIP. Address multiplexing provides an added speed bonus during the paging mode. There are effectively two levels of memory hierarchy on the same chip — a large cell array for storage and a set of latches that behave like a 128-bit static memory. A selected page in the memory array is transferred into the latches in which any read/write operation may be performed on any number of bits. This cuts the access time nearly in half since the page need not be returned to the memory array between each bit selection in the same page.

The dynamic I^{3}L RAM cell is beautifully simple, merely a single pair of complementary transistors merged in silicon taking up little more space than a single device. The design eliminates the 6-component flip-flops required to store charge in static memory cells and the separate space-consuming charge-storage capacitors used in MOS cells. In the 2-transistor cell, charge is stored on the capacitance in the shared collector-base junction of the merged transistors. This junction is reverse biased during cell storage. The cell amplifies the stored charge at read out, providing a larger signal than an MOS cell. Both the cell and the peripheral circuitry are designed to use single layer metal, which reduces processing costs and increases yields.

BIPOLAR RAM ARCHITECTURE (Figure 1)
The 93481 RAM is organized as a linear select array of 32 rows by 128 columns. The seven input-address lines are precoded to drive the row-address decoder, the column-address decoder and the sense/latch/drive circuits. A single timing input (Address Enable AE) is used to power up from standby and to initiate the on-chip timing circuits. Address lines A_0–A_4 are fed to the row-address decoder and transferred to the address latch to select one of the thirty-two 128-bit rows. The 128 sense/latch/drive circuits are then activated to latch the data for each bit stored in that row. Once latched, these circuits behave like memory elements; the column-address decoder, the sense/latch/drive circuits and the output circuits form a 128 x 1 static RAM.

For column (bit) selection, all seven address lines are used to select one of the 128 sense/latch/drive circuits; the data can then be fed through a transparent latch to an output buffer. Any normal read/write operation can be performed in this 128-bit static RAM. Every bit in the selected row can be randomly accessed by changing the column address and waiting the appropriate page access time with no further timing strobes required. When AE is activated (LOW), the 128 bits are written back into the original row in the memory array. Over all, it's like having 32 fast 128-bit static RAMs on a single chip.

The read/write logic is more sophisticated than is usual for high-density RAMs. The Write Enable (WE) and Data input (D$_{IN}$) behave in an edge-triggered fashion where D$_{IN}$ timing is specified relative to the trailing (rising) edge of WE only. When the Latch Enable (LE) is HIGH, data simply passes through the data latch. When

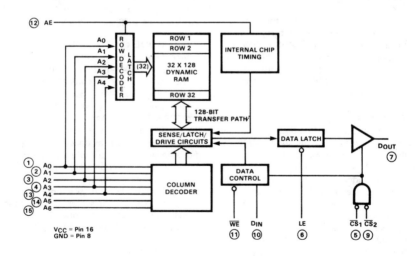

Fig. 1 Bipolar Dynamic RAM

135

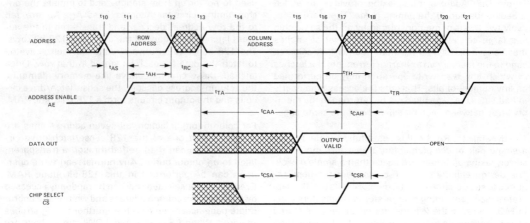

Fig. 2 Standard Read Cycle

LE is made LOW, the data is latched and held indefinitely in the data latch; it is subsequently read out via the Chip-Select lines even while the chip is performing a write or refresh cycle. The two active LOW Chip Selects force the output into a high impedance state (tri-state) and are placed after the data latch so that data can be latched without an active Chip Select.

The 93481 architecture, combined with the inherent speed of bipolar, offers several novel features and significant advantages over multiplexed MOS RAMs. The many applications for bipolar dynamic RAMs, from large computer systems to microprocessors, can be appreciated by looking at the 93481 operating cycles and how they may be used.

STANDARD READ CYCLE
Figure 2 shows a 93481 standard read cycle. The five row-address lines, A_0-A_4, must be stable for 5 ns (t_{AS}) before the AE signal rises (t_{11}) and remain stable for time t_{AH}. At t_{12}, all seven address lines are changed to column-address lines. The memory can tolerate an instantaneous change; however, the user's circuitry will require some time (t_{RC}) to accomplish this change. When the change is complete (t_{13}), the device now acts like a 128-bit static RAM. The data output becomes valid at t_{15}, t_{CAA} after the column address is stable. The access time is then $t_{AS} + t_{AH} + t_{CAA} + t_{RC}$. The Chip Select line must be active LOW at t_{14} (t_{CA} before t_{15}) for the output to be read at t_{15}.

The on-chip data latch may be used by making LE LOW any time after t_{CAA} (t_{15}), whether or not the Chip

Select is active. A convenient way to use the data latch is to connect LE to AE which latches the data into the next cycle with simplified latch timing. By contrast, the data latch in MOS RAMs is usually non-existent or tied to the Column Address Strobe input ($\overline{CAS}$). The latter requires a $\overline{CAS}$ cycle for positive deactivation, but the latch is not static so data-out eventually becomes invalid. Data is available in the static latch of the 93481 as long as LE is held LOW.

PAGE-MODE OPERATION
Figure 3 illustrates successive page mode cycles. Once the t_{AS} of the AE-to-row address has been satisfied (t_{11}), the memory is considered to be in the page mode. Block transfers, write cycles, or read/modify/write cycles can be thought of as page operations in the 128 x 1 static RAM. As previously discussed, data from a page read may be latched and held during succeeding cycles to provide the latching for read/modify/write or for data transfers to another address. The page-cycle time is equivalent to page access time (65 ns) and is limited by data set-up and hold times. With the on-chip data latch, read-cycle time may approach read-access time in a real system environment. This contrasts with dynamic n-channel memories where page-cycle time is nearly double the page-access time.

Read/Modify/Write
One application of the data-latch page-mode operation is for read/modify/write cycles. Data set-up-and-hold time is defined relative to the trailing edge of $\overline{WE}$ so the $\overline{WE}$ may be active LOW before D_{IN} is stable. One way to exploit this property is to connect $\overline{WE}$ to LE so that a single edge will latch data and prepare for write.

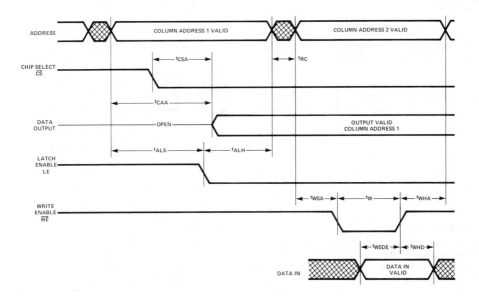

Fig. 3 Page Mode Cycles

When the modified D$_{IN}$ is settled, a HIGH level on the $\overline{WE}$-LE line executes an edge-triggered write. Functionally the RAM looks like a positive edge-triggered D-type flip-flop when used in this mode.

Block Transfers
A second application of page mode is for block-oriented read/write cycles, particularly in systems that require fast direct memory access (DMA) to peripherals such as CRT displays or frame storage for image sensors. Since the 93481 can handle transfer rates in excess of 10 MHz, eight or more bytes can be transferred in a 1 μs microprocessor cycle. When combined with a bipolar FIFO, such as the 9403, a constant output rate can be maintained.

Cache-Like Systems
Another page-mode application is a cache-like memory store in which individual RAMs on the same data lines can be at different row addresses at the same time. This can easily be accomplished by proper decoding of the AE signals. Compared to conventional cache memory storage, multiple 128-word pages can be more rapidly accessible with shorter transitions to new pages when using the 93481 in the page mode.

Chip-Select Read
Read cycles faster than page-cycle time can be achieved using the Chip Selects. Multiple RAMs on common data lines may be successively read by sequencing the Chip Select access time. If valid data has been latched, the data is available through Chip Select even though the Chip is powered down. Thus data words can be latched in several RAMs and successively read out while the RAMs are cycling into the next address.

SYSTEMS APPLICATIONS
Main Memory
The 93481 has a number of advantages in performance-oriented main-frame memory. The low capacitance, high output drive, and sharp thresholds permit use of fewer and less expensive overhead circuits. The single +5 V power supply simplifies power distribution and the low dI/dt with sharp thresholds minimizes noise problems while permitting low-power operation. The controlled data latch and simple timing minimize system overhead.

For minimum system power dissipation, the AE signals for multiple RAMs on common data lines may be decoded so that only the RAMs containing addressed data are powered up. When using this mode, care must be taken to assure that refresh can take place on all RAMs. The data latch permits reading previous data from any RAM during refresh or write cycles.

Microprocessor

For micoroprocessor-based systems using any 5 V microprocessor, the single +5 V power supply of the 93481 is a very attractive feature. The cost advantage of dynamic RAMs can be exploited without expending the savings on extra power supplies.

The speed, including fast page mode, and single supply are also attractive for use with the Macrologic bipolar bit-slice microprocessor series. The fast page-cycle time permits 10 MHz operation; therefore the 93481 can be used for both main memory and microprogram store in these systems. In some microprocessor systems, the short main cycle time of the 93481 can be used to conceal refresh activity. In this mode, two or more memory cycles appear in each machine cycle. One of these can be used for scheduled refresh and need not interrupt the microprocessor.

REFRESH PROPERTIES

A common misconception is that a bipolar cell cannot provide dynamic storage because of the required transistor base current. However, in the 93481, storage takes place on back-biased junctions only, so junction leakage is the only concern. In this respect, the bipolar junction has a significant advantage over the junction in the MOS cell. Since the bipolar junction has a high doping concentration, it has both low leakage current and high capacitance per unit area. In fact, the bipolar junction capacitor is theoretically capable of longer storage time than the MOS cell capacitor even though the stored voltage is lower.

Figure 4 shows the percentage of devices in which all 4096 bits of the 93481 have refresh time greater than a given value at different junction temperatures. Significantly, 60% of these devices could operate at 100°C (125°C T_J) with 2 ms refresh and over 40% could operate at 125°C (150°C T_J) with 1 ms refresh, even though they are rated for the 0 to 70°C temperature range. Since storage time limits are somewhat wafer oriented, further process evolution will substantially improve these refresh times. Operation at temperatures as low as −55°C is no problem, therefore bipolar dynamic 4K RAMs are imminent for the full military temperature range.

BIPOLAR SYSTEM COMPATIBILITY

The 93481 is fully TTL compatible. The inputs have standard TTL threshold and temperature properties and the output is a TTL tri-state totem pole with a conventional unit load of 10. The small I³L device used for the input limits input capacitance to less than 1 pF plus pad and package capacitance. A standard low-power Schottky buffer (9LS365) driving thirty-two 93481 inputs on a memory board produces the waveform in

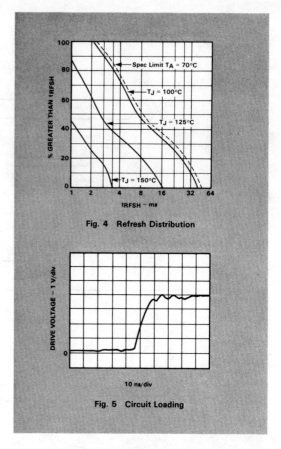

Fig. 4 Refresh Distribution

Fig. 5 Circuit Loading

Figure 5. Since an LS buffer is comparable to a full Schottky gate, the choice of memory board circuits covers a wide range. All 93481 inputs including the AE are equivalent in line loading.

In comparison, MOS inputs, particularly the clock lines, are significantly more capacitive and require higher voltages to satisfy the input thresholds. Thus, an MOS RAM needs more memory-board support circuitry or special clock drivers, which affects system performance. In addition, the bipolar output circuit has a high transient-drive capability, permitting many more RAMs on a common data line without hindering performance. This reduces the support-circuit requirements, therefore cuts costs and improves system reliability.

POWER SUPPLY CURRENT TRANSIENTS

It is always beneficial to retain data in a memory at reduced power. Dynamic RAMs have a fundamental advantage in this respect since the cell dissipates no power while storing. MOS RAMs have extended the dynamic properties to the address-decoder logic on the chip; therefore, often the only power dissipated is that required to charge or discharge the capacitors. This results in excellent standby power but creates very large

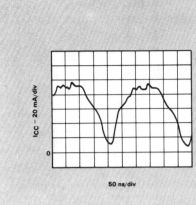

Fig. 6   Power Supply Transient

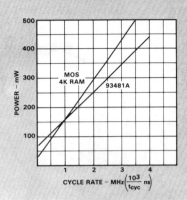

Fig. 7   Power vs. Cycle Rate

current transients in the power supply when the circuit is activated. This produces ground and supply transients which cause noise problems, especially since MOS circuits do not have a sharp signal threshold.

The peripheral circuitry in the 93481 is static but is powered down when not activated. The current-transient waveform is shown in *Figure 6*. The key concern is not the current itself but its rate of change (dI/dt), which introduces voltage noise on the supply. The 93481 has a small dI/dt and a sharp V_{BE} threshold of two diode drops on all inputs to provide optimum system performance. As shown in *Figure 7*, at short cycle times (high cycle rates), the 93481A has lower power dissipation than a fast n-channel RAM but dissipates more power at long cycle times (low cycle rates).

FULLY COMPATIBLE 16K

A major goal in Fairchild's development of the dynamic I³L RAM has been to design both a 4096 x 1 and a 16,384 x 1 RAM. As a result, a 16K memory will be available in late 1977 that is fully compatible with the 93481 using the same circuits and the same process. This new device will use single-layer surface interconnection like the 93481 as opposed to the three layers of surface interconnection (two poly and one metal)

required for the 16K MOS RAM. The process complexity of the 16K MOS and bipolar RAMs is comparable, yet the bipolar RAM will be faster and have significantly smaller chip size.

Remarkably, the 16K bipolar RAM will have *exactly* the functions, pin connections, and speed of the 4K device; thus, the 16K will work in a board designed for the 4K memory. This happens by design. Each RAM has the same seven address pins, but in the 4K 93481, only five are multiplexed and, in the 16K 93483, all seven are multiplexed. The architecture, features, and applications potential are the same for both the 4K and 16K; the only difference is memory size. Knowledge and experience gained with the 4K bipolar dynamic RAM is directly applicable to the 16K.

REFERENCES

1. Wendell B. Sander, James M. Early, Thomas A. Longo, "Applications-Oriented Fast Low-Cost I³L Dynamic Rams," Electro-77, Session 5 Technical Paper, April 19, 1977.

2. Wendell B. Sander, James M. Early, Thomas A. Longo, "A 4096 x 1 (I³L) Bipolar Dynamic RAM," ISSCC Digest of Technical Papers, pp. 182-183, Feb., 1976.

3. Wendell B. Sander, William H. Shepherd, and Richard D. Schinella, "Dynamic I²L Random-Access Memory Compares with MOS Designs," Electronics, pp. 99-102, August 19, 1976.

MUNCH

CHIPS

Static Bipolar Memory Chips Keep Shrinking

by William Herndon, Wally Ho & Roger Ramirez

The dramatic reduction in static bipolar-memory chip size, and corresponding price decrease, during the 70's can be directly attributed to advanced processing techniques such as Fairchild's Isoplanar process. The Isoplanar oxide isolation technique, introduced in 1971, reduced the static bipolar-RAM cell size from 30 sq mils to 11 sq mils. The walled-emitter Isoplanar process, developed in 1975 *(Figure 1)*, eliminates emitter-base spacing which further reduces cell size to the 3 sq mils *(Figure 2)* used in the 23,650 mil^2 93470/71 4K 4096 x 1 static-RAM die *(Figure 3)*. Furthermore, parasitic capacitances are reduced, thus improving memory performance. The 3 sq-mil cell has emitter-base capacitance of 0.05 pF, collector-base capacitance of 0.09 pF and collector-substrate capacitance of 0.255 pF.

Die-size reduction of the 1024-bit RAM from 19,500 mil^2 in 1972 to 9,000 mil^2 in 1976 *(Figure 4)* was achieved through pattern-size and alignment-tolerance reductions and better layout strategies. These advances represent a learning curve that each year shrinks the die to 0.82 of its former size. A similar die-size reduction can be predicted for the 4096 x 1 RAM. By 1978, cell layouts incorporating near-term refinements in manufacturing tolerances will reduce the die size to 16,000 mil^2. Applying the learning curve demonstrated on the 1024-bit RAM to the 4096-bit RAM, the die size can be reduced to less than 11,000 mil^2 by 1981.

The internal circuitry of the 93470/71 4096-bit static TTL RAM is very similar to that used in earlier 1024-bit devices and can be modified for ECL designs by simply altering the input/output buffers. Two important internal circuit modifications have been made to enhance performance — a word-line discharge circuit amortizes the discharge current over 64 word drivers and each bit-line current sink is shared with four bit-line pairs to reduce power consumption and word-driver loading. The 93470 and 93471 are organized 4096 words by one bit and are identical except for the output stage *(Figures 5 & 6)*. The 93470 has an uncommitted collector output while the 93471 has a 3-state output. Selection is accomplished using a 12-bit address, A0 through A11. The Chip Select input $\overline{CS}$ is provided for logic flexibility. For large memories, fast chip-select access time permits $\overline{CS}$ decoding from the address without increasing address access time.

In many applications, such as memory expansion, the outputs of several 93470s can be tied together. In other applications, the wired-OR is not used. In either case an external pull-up resistor must be used to provide a HIGH at the output when it is off. The 3-state outputs of the 93471 provide drive capability for higher speeds with high capacitive-load systems. The third state (high impedance) allows bus-organized systems with multiple outputs connected to a common bus.

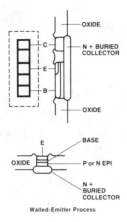

Walled-Emitter Process   Standard Process

Fig. 1   Isoplanar Devices

Fig. 2   4K x 1 RAM Cell

Fig. 3   The 4K x 1 RAM Chip

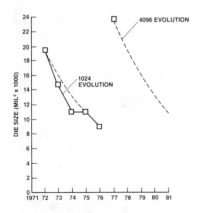

Fig. 4   Die Size Evolution

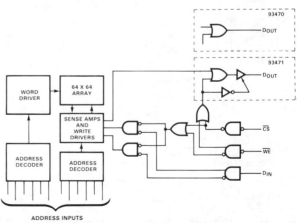

Fig. 5   4K TTL RAM Block Diagram

141

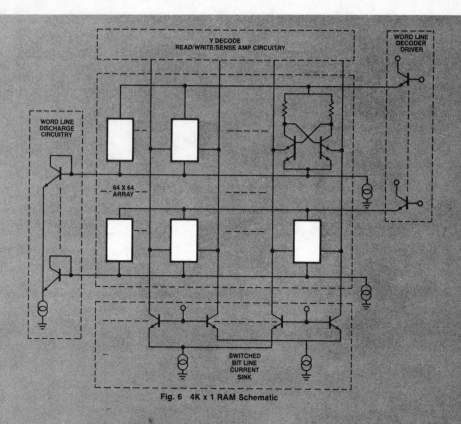

Fig. 6   4K x 1 RAM Schematic

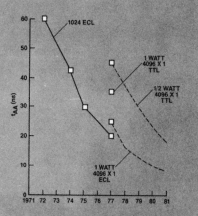

Fig. 7   Performance Evolution

The typical address access time of the 93470/71 TTL RAM is 30 ns. Because the ECL/TTL output translator carries a 10 ns overhead, the ECL 4K RAM, available in the near future, will have 20 ns typical access time. The 500-mW 1024-bit ECL RAM, introduced in 1972, had a maximum address access time that was reduced in five years from 60 ns to 20 ns *(Figure 7)*. Directly related to die-size reduction, this decrease preci-

pitated improved configurations and parasitic-capacitance reduction. Applying this learning curve (0.8 of the former value per year), TTL RAMs in 1981 will have a typical access time of 12 ns, while ECL will be a mere 7.5 ns.

Advanced processing techniques have been used to produce very high performance (7.5 ns access time) 1024-bit ECL RAMs at the 500-mW power level. Historically, at the same power level, increasing the RAM complexity by a factor of four doubles the delay. Again, future address access times for the 4096-bit ECL RAMs can be extrapolated — 15 ns for the 500-mW device and 7.5 for the 1-W device.

The 4K static bipolar RAM — TTL today and ECL soon — replaces four 1K devices thus greatly reducing memory-system component count and simplifying design. Since both versions are fully static, there is no need for special clocking, refresh circuits or multiple power supplies. It is apparent that static bipolar RAMs are on learning curves that will result in enhanced performance and significant cost reductions. By 1981, sub-10 nanosecond, 1-W 4096-bit ECL RAMs on silicon chips smaller than 11,000 mil² should be available. TTL RAMs will sacrifice some speed to remain below the half-watt level; 12 ns access times will be available by 1981. The combination of high volume production and economical packaging will push the high-volume cost per bit down to less than 0.4 cents by 1978 and 0.2 cents in 1979. □

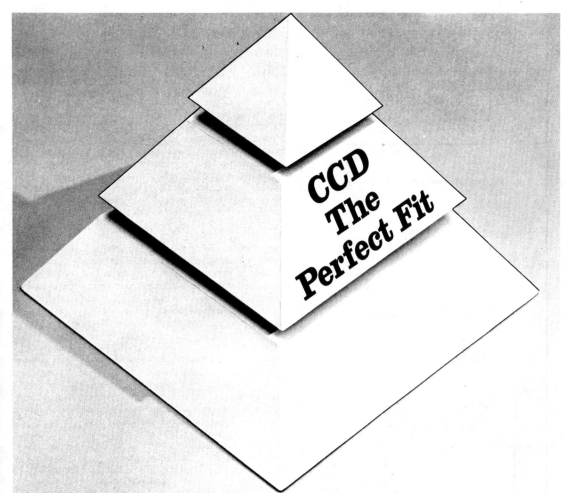

CCD
The
Perfect Fit

by Bruce Threewitt

MOS processing, with its inherent capability of producing a large number of transistors in an extremely small area, is a natural for building LSI component-intensive logic families that require relatively few interconnects. Patterned logic is component intensive − a memory is a good example* in which memory cells are repeated many times on a given circuit, and decoders, read/write and clock overhead circuitry are added to provide an easy interface to the system.

As the complexity of a given LSI logic block increases (*Figure 1*), the number of general applications for that block decreases. At the same time, the number of different kinds of logic blocks required to service the market increases. Qualitatively, the declining curve represents return on investment for the IC supplier while the rising curve indicates relative engineering and manufacturing costs. Clearly, more complexity eventually results in an untenable economic position. For these reasons, MOS/LSI producers tend to concentrate on patterned logic, i.e., memories. Obviously, there are exceptions such as random logic circuits that generate

*See "Memories Come of Age." PROGRESS Vol. 4, No. 1 Sept/Oct. 1976

sufficient volume in one application to warrant interest. Calculators and watch circuits are good examples.

The remarkable progress in charge-coupled device (CCD) technology has contributed significantly to recent improvements in LSI memory techniques. Since charge coupling is the movement of the mobile electric charge in the substrate by applying a potential above the surface, a serial memory can be implemented without contact to the substrate. This feature reduces memory cell size by as much as a factor of three, simplifies the manufacturing process, and improves yields (*Figure 2*). Also, CCD and MOS manufacturing techniques are essentially the same, therefore NMOS logic circuitry can be incorporated in the periphery of the same chip to provide control logic functions. This technique results in optimum architectural flexibility.

Since no dc power is dissipated by the CCD memory function, power dissipation is reduced to a frequency dependent component − $P_D = 1/2 \ CV^2 \ f$. This power savings results in lower chip temperature which favorably impacts reliability.

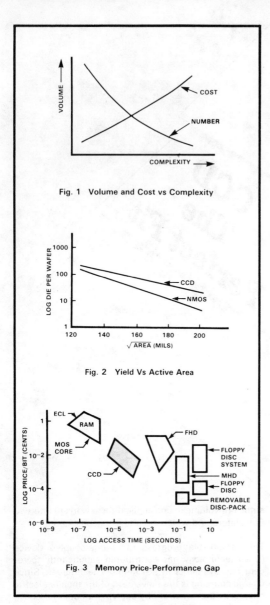

Fig. 1 Volume and Cost vs Complexity

Fig. 2 Yield Vs Active Area

Fig. 3 Memory Price-Performance Gap

conductor RAMs into which low-cost CCD serial memories fit perfectly.

The existence of low-speed low-cost memories presupposes an applications niche for these devices. The pyramidal shape in *Figure 4*, used to illustrate the memory performance spectrum in typical computers, qualitatively indicates the relative number of bits consumed by each group. Note that the least expensive memories are the largest. Utilizing a cache function allows slower, lower cost memories to serve as bulk storage. Caching data takes advantage of the fact that data used by the computer is seldom required in a random order; in other words, the CPU tends to use data in a block fashion. In such cases, the data rate (reciprocal of memory cycle time) is more crucial than random access time; therefore, simpler serial access memories can be used in place of higher cost RAMs.

Another feature of existing magnetic bulk store memories is non-volatility. In other words, data is not lost if power is removed. Semiconductor memories can accomplish the same feature by resorting to battery back-up if power levels are low enough. It is doubtful that semiconductor memories could replace removable media moving head disc memories.

The shaded area in *Figure 4* (head-per-track or HPT), however, is vulnerable to replacement by solid state memories, especially if additional architectural advantages are utilized. For example, so called "hybrid" systems are becoming more popular. Here, HPT disc memory is incorporated in the same mechanical structure as a moving head disc (MHD) so that the mechanics of the MHD are shared with the higher performance HPT disc. The result is a lower cost HPT disc. This approach is useful for extending the cache concept to the bulk store where large blocks of data are moved from the MHD to the HPT disc on the assumption that the mainframe memory, usually RAM, requires the entire block.

This function is the most likely to be replaced by CCD memories. Not only are CCDs 10-to 50-times faster than HPT discs, but they offer other architectural features. For example, current hybrid structures are organized as a single track for the fixed-head portion while CCD structures provide multiple tracks for improved performance.

The cost-per-bit projections of CCD memories, shown in *Figure 5*, are consistent with HPT disc replacement. This equivalent cost is for vastly improved performance and reliability. The rapid growth of semiconductor technology promises continued improvements in performance and reductions in cost.

In addition to replacing HPT discs at the lower end of the price-performance spectrum *(Figure 3)*, CCD memories have cost/density advantages that will soon see a CCD invasion into the lower performance areas of RAM at the higher speed end of the spectrum. In particular,

THE PRICE-PERFORMANCE GAP

Figure 3 illustrates the inherent compromise between price and performance in memories. The familiar bipolar and MOS RAM devices occupy the high-speed end since they typically have access times in the range of 10^{-8} to 10^{-6} seconds. In addition, RAMs are available today with up to 16K bits on one chip. The low cost end of the spectrum is comprised of magnetic bulk storage devices such as discs and drums. Bit cost is low and storage densities high. Latency, coupled with the large minimum size of these memories, causes a capacity and speed gap between the magnetic bulk storage and semi-

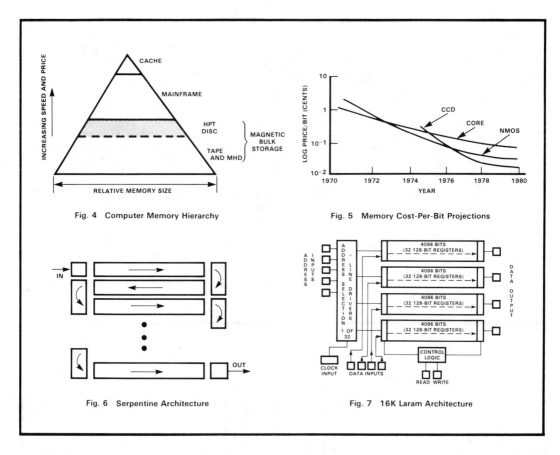

Fig. 4 Computer Memory Hierarchy

Fig. 5 Memory Cost-Per-Bit Projections

Fig. 6 Serpentine Architecture

Fig. 7 16K Laram Architecture

CCDs will be used in applications, such as video processing, where RAMs are over-qualified and too expensive and fixed head discs (FHD) are too large to be practical and are not cost effective.

ARCHITECTURAL PARAMETERS
Because MOS logic elements can be incorporated on the same chip with CCD memory cells, architectural options are available to optimize device performance. Architectural parameters affect density, speed (latency), power, and interface characteristics.

The simplest approach, called a serpentine structure due to the winding nature of the data path, is illustrated in *Figure 6*. Data is entered at frequency f and shifted synchronously through n bits. It is then refreshed and sent back through a similar structure. This structure has several basic characteristics. First, since the refresh amplifiers require little space, the architecture is very dense. In fact, high density and simplicity were the primary reasons for using this structure in early memories. However, other performance parameters are less than optimum. For example, since all bits are shifted synchronously, the clock capacitance is larger than that in other CCD structures. So, special interface

circuits are required to provide the large transient current to charge the load capacitance. Since most of the power dissipated on chip is related to charging capacitances, this synchronous structure uses a relatively large amount of power ($P_D = 1/2CV^2f$). Also, unless taps are used or logic is added to provide access to smaller blocks, the latency (random access to a bit) becomes very long (1/f times the number of bits). Taps cost pins, and the added logic reduces the density advantage of the serpentine approach.

A Line Addressable Random Access Memory (LARAM) architecture, shown in *Figure 7*, enhances the performance of CCD memories. A 16,384-bit memory, namely the CCD460, is a good example. It consists of 32 sectors, called lines, each of which is 128 bits long and four bits wide. NMOS circuitry is added to perform peripheral functions. A 1-of-32 decoder selects one line as a function of the 5-bit address input and determines which line is connected to the I/O circuitry and which line is clocked. In other words, a non-selected line is not shifted. Interruption of the access to one line, for example, to refresh another line, does not necessitate recirculating the original line to re-access the data − a plus feature of the LARAM.

145

A LARAM, when compared to a serpentine device, has a lower density because of the added NMOS overhead circuitry. However, this is more than compensated by several improvements. First, since the clock is only connected to the addressed line, the clock capacitance is drastically lower. In fact, a serpentine device with the same number of bits has ten times the clock capacitance. Second, the power dissipation, dominated by the CV^2f term, is reduced since non-selected lines are not shifting. Third, the latency (random access time) is based on a 128-byte block length. Thus, LARAM latency is $1/f$ times 128 in the worst case or $1/f$ times 64 on the average. LARAM refresh characteristics are a combination of RAM and shift register characteristics, i.e., refresh is accomplished by accessing lines and shifting at some minimum frequency.

In keeping with the goal to replace magnetic bulk-storage memories with semiconductor memories, the next step in CCD memory evolution emphasizes increased density. The architecture shown in *Figure 8* is called Serial-Parallel-Serial (SPS). Data is entered into a serial register at frequency f. When this register is filled, a series-to-parallel conversion occurs, and data is shifted in parallel at frequency f/n where n is the length of the serial register. At the other end of the parallel register, a parallel-to-series conversion takes place, and data is shifted out at frequency f.

The SPS structure is extremely dense since the series-to-parallel and parallel-to-series conversions require essentially no logic. Rather, these conversions involve clocking the cells in a different direction. Four clocks are required to accomplish this function. Two phases are used for the serial registers, and two phases are used for the parallel registers. Since the high-frequency clocks only drive 2n bits per block, the clock capacitance for these clocks is relatively small. Also, the two parallel transfer phases are much lower frequency (f/n; typically n = 64). At this much lower rate, these clocks can be buffered on the CCD memory chip without dissipating significant power; hence the resulting clock capacitance at the input pins is significantly reduced. The low capacitance of all four phases makes interfacing to TTL logic much simpler with standard low-cost drivers.

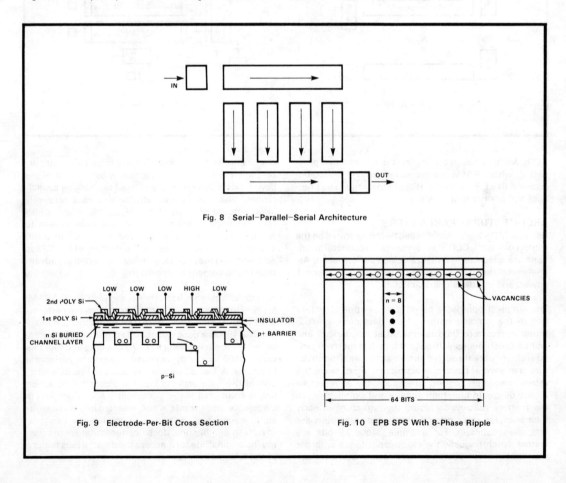

Fig. 8 Serial–Parallel–Serial Architecture

Fig. 9 Electrode-Per-Bit Cross Section

Fig. 10 EPB SPS With 8-Phase Ripple

Furthermore, since most of the cell capacitance is shifted at f/n, the power dissipation (related to CV^2f) is very low. A reduction in power dissipation can mean significantly lower junction temperature, thereby increasing reliability and improving switching performance. Relative to other CCD approaches, the SPS device latency is long, $1/f$ times the number of bits per block. For a 64K device based on 4K-bit clocks, the average latency is 500 μs at a 4 MHz shift rate, which is 10-to-50 times better than FHDs. The density/price levels for the 64K SPS memory and the FHD are comparable, however, the SPS device has superior performance.

The SPS architecture combines all of the performance and density benefits found in other architectures with a slight sacrifice in latency. To further enhance the density of SPS devices, a ripple clock technique can be used to provide an electrode-per-bit structure. *Figure 9* illustrates this concept. Rather than requiring 2n electrodes, only $n + 1$ electrodes are used. Obviously, these bits cannot be shifted synchronously. A vacancy must first be created in the last bit location; it then ripples

back toward the first bit location under the influence of an n-phase clock. Clearly, a large value for n results in a complex clocking scheme.

To minimize the clock complexity and still utilize an electrode-per-bit (EPB) approach, a compromise architecture like that shown in *Figure 10* can be used. In this case $n = 8$, and nine electrodes serve eight bits — a dramatic increase in density. For $n = 8$, the clock generator becomes an 8-phase ripple counter, easily achievable with current design techniques.

CONCLUSION

The improved performance and comparable FHD costs of CCD memories have filled the price-performance gap in computer memories. The on-chip NMOS support logic permits several architectural choices, each offering improved performance parameters for serial memories. Since a CCD memory with optimum density has cells 1/3 the size of those in RAMs at 1/4 the price per bit, there is no question that CCD memory will penetrate several other application areas in memory systems.

64K CCD Memory
First Low-Cost
Solid-State Bulk Memory

by Bruce Threewitt

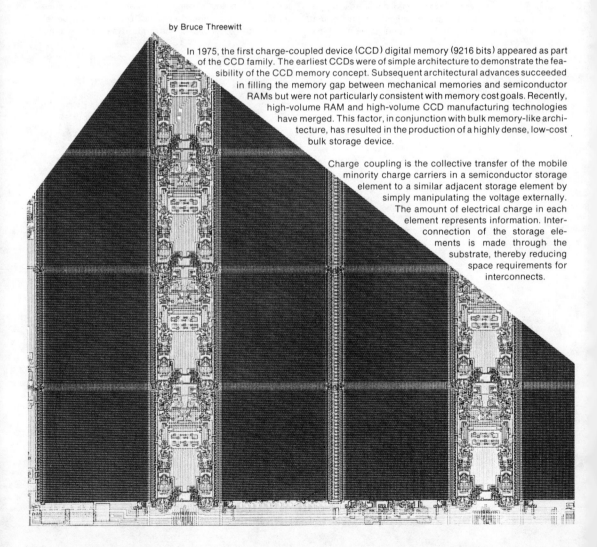

In 1975, the first charge-coupled device (CCD) digital memory (9216 bits) appeared as part of the CCD family. The earliest CCDs were of simple architecture to demonstrate the feasibility of the CCD memory concept. Subsequent architectural advances succeeded in filling the memory gap between mechanical memories and semiconductor RAMs but were not particularly consistent with memory cost goals. Recently, high-volume RAM and high-volume CCD manufacturing technologies have merged. This factor, in conjunction with bulk memory-like architecture, has resulted in the production of a highly dense, low-cost bulk storage device.

Charge coupling is the collective transfer of the mobile minority charge carriers in a semiconductor storage element to a similar adjacent storage element by simply manipulating the voltage externally. The amount of electrical charge in each element represents information. Interconnection of the storage elements is made through the substrate, thereby reducing space requirements for interconnects.

These features reduce memory cell size by as much as a factor of three *(Figure 1)*, simplify the manufacturing process, and improve yield. Also, NMOS logic circuitry can be incorporated in the periphery of the memory chip to provide control logic functions, resulting in optimum architectural flexibility. Furthermore, little peripheral circuitry is required for a CCD memory, resulting in efficient use of chip area.

In less than three years, CCD memory chip capacity has increased sevenfold, from 9K to 64K bits. This rapid growth, nearly double that of MOS dynamic RAM *(Figure 2)*, can be attributed to several factors:

- Compatibility with MOS process technology

- High packing density, resulting in low cost

- Low power dissipation, giving higher reliability

- Improved yield due to dark (leakage) current averaging*

- Fewer contacts per bit, resulting in better yield*

- Low testing cost

- Faster access time (latency) than magnetic storage memories and higher data rate than large MOS RAMs.

Perhaps the single most important reason for CCD success is that the fabrication technique is the same as that used to manufacture high-volume, n-channel MOS RAMs. Consequently, the years of experience with a familiar manufacturing process can be put into practice immediately.

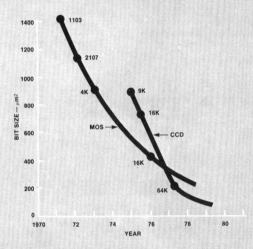

Fig. 1   CCD and MOS Memory Bit (Cell) Size Improvement

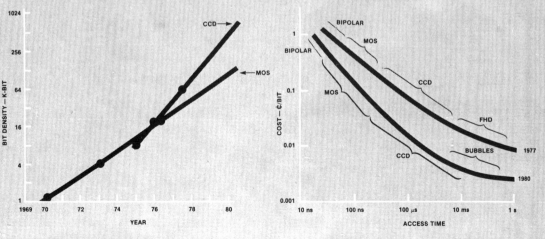

Fig. 2   CCD and MOS Dynamic Memory Growth

*Not applicable to LARAMs

Fig. 3   Memory Cost Versus Performance

CCD memory is a low-cost alternative for bulk memory and is not intended as a replacement for high-speed RAM. In general computer architectures, a memory can be utilized as a cache for storing data in block form, which need not be accessed randomly. Since a computer usually performs operations sequentially, it is well suited to CCD serial organization. In this case, data rate (reciprocal of memory cycle time) is more crucial than random access time, thus making the simpler, cost-effective serial-access memory more practical for bulk storage than RAM. As shown in *Figure 3*, CCDs fill the void between magnetic memories and RAMs and at a cost 3.5 to 5 times less per bit than RAMs.

CCD MEMORY COMPONENT ARCHITECTURES

To produce a CCD memory for bulk-storage applications, it is imperative to select the appropriate architecture, process and clocking schemes to optimize device characteristics. There are three major architectures *(Figure 4)*, offering various cost-performance trade-offs.

- Serpentine or synchronous — the simplest organization featuring a wide operating-frequency range.

- Line Addressable Random Access Memory (LARAM) — a combination of CCD and RAM architectures. This memory offers high performance (low power dissipation, low clock capacitance, excellent latency) but lacks the high density required for low-cost memory.

- Serial Parallel Serial (SPS) — the best organization for high-density, cost-effective memory. Combines the performance and density benefits found in other architectures with significant latency improvements when compared to magnetic media.

Development of the SPS architecture is in keeping with the goal of replacing magnetic bulk-storage memories with semiconductor memories. Briefly, SPS works like this. Data is entered into a serial input register at frequency f. When the register is full, a serial-to-parallel conversion occurs, and data is shifted in parallel at frequency f/n, where n is the length of the serial register. At the other end of the parallel register, a parallel-to-serial conversion takes place, and data is shifted out at frequency f.

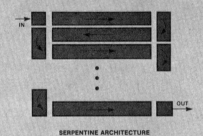

SERPENTINE ARCHITECTURE

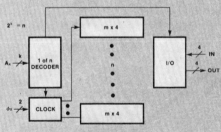

LINE ADDRESSABLE RANDOM ACCESS MEMORY (LARAM)

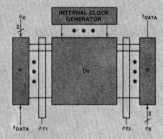

SERIAL-PARALLEL-SERIAL ARCHITECTURE

PARAMETERS	SERPENTINE	LARAM	SPS
DENSITY	GOOD	POOR	EXCELLENT
POWER	HIGH	LOW	LOWER
FREQUENCY RANGE	WIDE	LIMITED	LIMITED
LATENCY	AVERAGE	EXCELLENT	POOR
CLOCK LOADING	HIGH	LOW	LOW

Fig. 4 CCD Memory Architecture

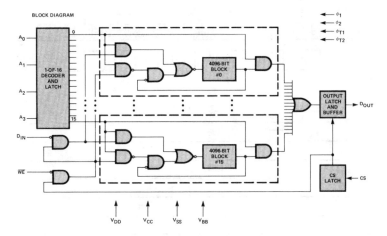

Fig. 5   F464 Block Diagram

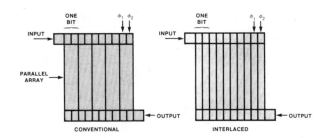

Fig. 6   SPS Structures

The SPS structure is extremely dense since the serial-to-parallel and parallel-to-serial conversions require little overhead logic. Rather, these conversions involve clocking the cells in a different direction. Four external clocks are required to accomplish these functions, two phases for the serial registers and two for the parallel conversion. The two parallel-conversion clocks are only connected to the interface between the serial and parallel registers.

Since parallel conversion is a low capacitance function, the external input capacitance of these two phases is very low. The serial-register clocks only drive 2n bits per block; therefore, the clock capacitance for these clocks is also relatively small. The low capacitance of all four external phases makes interfacing to TTL logic much simpler with standard low-cost drivers. The internal parallel phases are much lower frequency (f/n; typically n = 64) than the serial-register clocks and can be buffered on the CCD memory chip without dissipating significant power.

The best process approach for SPS architecture is buried channel. It is preferred, at 64K-bit densities, over surface channel because of higher transfer efficiency with no "fat zero" requirement and a higher maximum frequency. "Fat zero," a small (non-zero) amount of charge representing a

"0", is required in surface-channel devices to compensate for surface state losses. Therefore, a "0" is represented by a partially full, rather than an empty, storage well that decreases the amount of charge available for storage.

THE F464 64K-BIT CCD MEMORY

The F464 dynamic CCD memory *(Figure 5)* is the first economically feasible semiconductor bulk-storage device. Bits are organized 65,536 x 1 in 16 randomly accessible SPS shift registers (blocks) of 4096 bits each. Four TTL- compatible address inputs are provided for selecting one of the 16 blocks for Read and Write or Read-only operations. Each shift-register block is implemented using an *interlaced* SPS structure in which each bit (two electrodes) of the 2-phase serial input register serves two parallel shift registers *(Figure 6)*. The input serial register transfers data to the odd-numbered parallel registers and then, on a second scan, transfers the next 32 bits of data to the even-numbered parallel registers. As a result, each serial input register stores 32 bits using 64 electrodes that service 64 parallel shift registers. In a conventional SPS structure, each bit of the serial shift register serves only one parallel shift register.

In the usual SPS structure, the minimum width of the parallel shift register is limited to the width of two electrodes of the serial shift register. Using the interlaced scheme, this width is

151

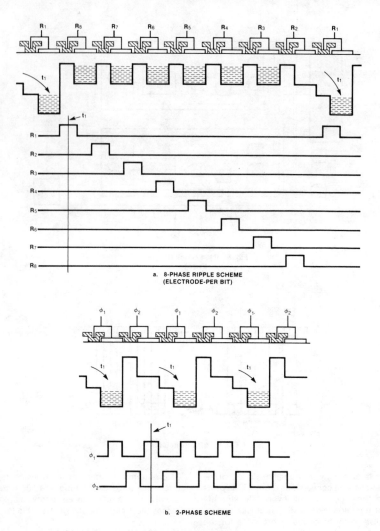

a. 8-PHASE RIPPLE SCHEME
(ELECTRODE-PER BIT)

b. 2-PHASE SCHEME

Fig. 7 CCD Clocking Schemes

limited to that of only one electrode; hence, the packing density is doubled. To further enhance the packing density, an 8-phase ripple technique is used in the F464 to shift the data in the parallel shift registers *(Figure 7a)*. Normally, in a synchronous 2-phase clocking system *(Figure 7b)*, two CCD electrodes are required to store one bit of information, while in a ripple system, a little more than one electrode is needed for storing one bit. In general, the number of electrodes, n_b, required to store one bit is given by

$$n_b = \frac{N}{N-1}$$

where N is the number of ripple clocks.

As the number of ripple phases is increased from two to eight, the number of electrodes required to store one bit is reduced from two to 1.14. Thus, by using the 8-phase ripple system,

packing density is almost twice that of a 2-phase system. In addition, the ripple technique reduces the number of transfers required to move a packet from a shift-register input to output. In an M-bit shift register, the number of required transfers is M x n_b. Thus, a 63-bit shift register needs only 72 transfers in an 8-phase ripple system, compared to 126 transfers in a standard 2-phase system. This obviously minimizes signal degradation. Another advantage is the reduction of average leakage current per bit since the charge collected is reduced in proportion to the number of electrodes required to store a bit.

F464 OPERATION

The 16 blocks, each consisting of a 4096-bit SPS shift register for data storage, are randomly accessible using four Address inputs (A_0-A_3). The data in all 16 blocks advances simultaneously at the rate of one bit per cycle. Each block has its own reference charge generator, sense amplifier, input/output

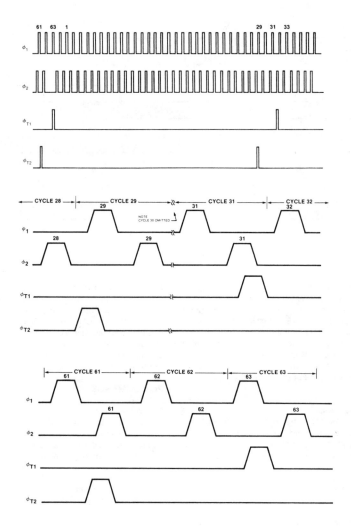

Fig. 8 MOS-Level Clocks

logic, and CCD input circuit. The Data In (D_{IN}), Data Out (D_{OUT}), and Write Enable ($\overline{WE}$) circuits are common to all blocks and are activated by the Chip Select (CS) signal to minimize standby power.

The memory requires four MOS-level clocks *(Figure 8)*. The two high-frequency clocks, ϕ_1 and ϕ_2, run at a frequency equal to the data rate and control the movement of data within the input and output series registers of each 4096-bit block. These clocks also control all the peripheral MOS circuits. The two low-frequency transfer clocks, ϕ_{T1} and ϕ_{T2}, are used to transfer charge from the serial-to-parallel and parallel-to-serial registers of each block.

Interlacing of the data is achieved by first transferring data from the input serial register into the parallel registers when the charge packets are under the ϕ_1 gates, then reloading the input register with the next 32 bits and transferring this data

when the charge packets are under the ϕ_2 gates. Parallel-to-serial transfer is accomplished in a similar manner. To achieve proper transfer phasing, the two transfer clocks must be asymmetrical around a 32-cycle interval, but symmetrical around a 64-cycle interval. The ϕ_{T1} and ϕ_{T2} clocks are skewed to achieve correct bit storage in each block. When ϕ_{T1} occurs during ϕ_1 time, ϕ_{T2} occurs during ϕ_2 time, 1.5 cycles prior to ϕ_{T1}. When ϕ_{T1} occurs during ϕ_2 time, ϕ_{T2} occurs during ϕ_1 time, 2.5 cycles prior to ϕ_{T1}. *Figure 8* illustrates the clock phase relationships, which are generated only once in a memory system using simple logic at minimum cost.

The functional timing diagram for a Read cycle is shown in *Figure 9*. The four Addresses (A_0-A_3) and Chip Select (CS) are buffered when ϕ_1 is HIGH. The trailing edge of ϕ_1 latches the information and disables the addresses and chip-select buffers to prevent changes that occur on these pins from entering the internal circuitry when ϕ_1 is LOW.

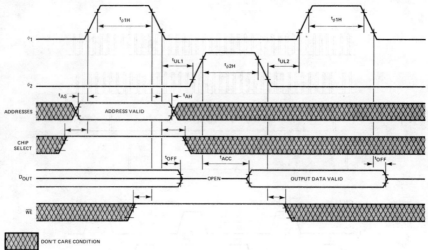

Fig. 9 Read-Recirculate Cycle

The $\overline{\text{WE}}$ dynamic buffer is unconditionally preset during ϕ_1 time. In the Read-only mode, $\overline{\text{WE}}$ remains HIGH, disabling the buffer. In the Write mode, $\overline{\text{WE}}$ may go LOW before or after the trailing edge of ϕ_1, and the $\overline{\text{WE}}$ buffer is activated by ϕ_1 going LOW or $\overline{\text{WE}}$ going LOW, whichever occurs later. The D_{IN} buffer, which is disabled during ϕ_1 HIGH time, is enabled when the $\overline{\text{WE}}$ buffer is activated. Therefore, in the Write mode, the data must be valid before ϕ_1 goes LOW or $\overline{\text{WE}}$ goes LOW, whichever occurs later. Following are the four modes of operation.

Standby (Recirculate) Mode

In the standby mode (CS LOW), the contents of all 16 blocks are recirculated automatically, and the device disregards the $\overline{\text{WE}}$, Address, and D_{IN} inputs. The output latch goes into the high-impedance state after the trailing edge of the ϕ_1 clock. Minimum power dissipation occurs when the device is operated in the recirculate mode with minimum ϕ_1 and ϕ_2 pulse widths at the lowest allowed frequency.

Read-Recirculate Mode

In this mode ($\overline{\text{WE}}$ HIGH and CS HIGH), the data from the selected block is presented to the output buffer immediately following the leading edge of ϕ_2 and appears at the output (D_{OUT}) after a delay equal to the access time t_{ACC}. Thus, the access time is referenced from the leading edge of the ϕ_2 pulse and is independent of the duration of ϕ_2. The output buffer is latched by the trailing edge of ϕ_2 and output data remains valid at the D_{OUT} pin until the end of the ϕ_1 clock pulse in the next cycle. D_{OUT} then goes into the high-impedance state until the next bit is accessed. The data in all 16 blocks recirculates automatically.

Read and Write Mode

In the Read and Write mode ($\overline{\text{WE}}$ LOW and CS HIGH), the output data from the selected block is available at the output pin as in the Read-recirculate mode; however, the recirculate path of that particular block is disabled. Input data present at the D_{IN} pin during ϕ_2 is written into the selected block by the falling edge of ϕ_2, while the other 15 blocks automatically recirculate their contents.

Read-Modify-Write Mode

The Read-Modify-Write mode (CS HIGH, $\overline{\text{WE}}$ HIGH goes LOW) is simple because the memory is always in the Read mode whenever CS is HIGH. Since the access time is referenced to the leading edge of ϕ_2 and the setup times of $\overline{\text{WE}}$ and D_{IN} are referenced to the trailing edge of ϕ_2, this mode of operation requires only an extended ϕ_2 HIGH time to provide the required modify time.

PERFORMANCE

The F464 dynamic serial CCD memory operates over a 1- to 5-MHz frequency range with power dissipation of less than 3.5 μW per bit in the active mode at 5 MHz and less than 1 μW per bit in the standby (recirculate) mode at 1 MHz. Typical capacitance on the TTL-compatible inputs — Addresses, CS, $\overline{\text{WE}}$, and D_{IN} — is only 5 pF and, on the 12 V clocks, capacitance is 100 pF (ϕ_1 and ϕ_2) and 30 pF (ϕ_{T1} and ϕ_{T2}). Use of CCD techniques, interlaced SPS architecture and electrode-per-bit design results in a chip of less than 40K mil^2 that fits in a standard 16-pin DIP (300 mils wide).

CONCLUSION

The buried-channel CCD process using SPS architecture, coupled with proven Isoplanar n-channel silicon-gate technology, successfully fulfills bulk memory requirements for high density and low cost. The 64K CCD serial memory is made to order for bulk storage. It should be emphasized that CCD memories are not intended to replace high-speed RAMs. In serial applications, cost/performance trade-offs make 64K-bit CCD more cost effective. Interfacing the F464 with microcomputers is simple due to the solid-state nature of CCD memories. At the system level, peripheral logic requirements are extremely small.

The 64K CCD memory is an excellent vehicle for demonstrating workable techniques that can be used in larger memories such as 256K and 1 megabit. All indications point to 256K CCD memory availability by late 1979 or early 1980 at costs under 10 millicents per bit. Solid-state replacement of mechanical memories will be well under way at that time. □

The author wishes to acknowledge the assistance of Ramesh C. Varshney and K. Venkateswaran in preparation of this article. These two gentlemen, along with their design team, on their first attempt, designed a high-volume low-cost 64K CCD bulk memory.

Anatomy of a FIFO

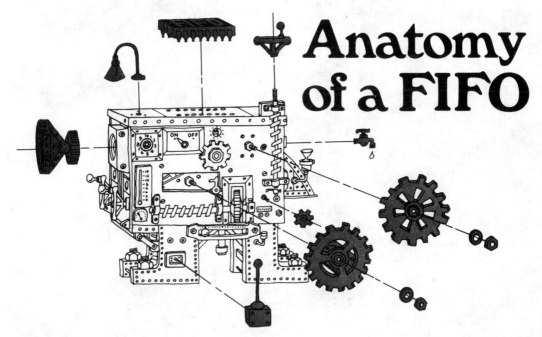

by Kris Rallapalli

The First-In First-Out (FIFO) memory is rapidly becoming a standard LSI building block. Widely used in computer peripherals and digital communication equipment, the device acts as an "elastic" memory between two or more subsystems that operate at different speeds. One of the most popular FIFOs is the 9403 16-word by 4-bit FIFO, a member of the Macrologic bipolar-microprocessor family of advanced Schottky TTL building blocks. Knowledge of the internal operation of the 9403 is vital to the component engineer for generating test patterns — to the test engineer for devising a gate-level simulator for automatic printed-circuit-board testing — and to the design engineer for a better understanding of device operation.

The 9403 input register consists of five edge-triggered flip-flops, F1 through F5. Serial data from the D_S input enters the register through F1, while parallel data is loaded by activating the appropriate Set or Reset inputs of the flip-flops. When the D_3 input is LOW, a HIGH on the Parallel Load (PL) input activates the F1 Reset (R) input LOW, thereby clearing it. A HIGH on the D_0, D_1 or D_2 input activates the Set (S) input of the corresponding flip-flop when PL is HIGH. The input register is initialized by the gate K output. Since the Master Reset ($\overline{MR}$) of the 9403 is one of the inputs to this gate, whenever the $\overline{MR}$ is LOW, the gate K output is LOW. Thus, F2, F3 and F4 and F5 flip-flops are reset and F1 is set.

If the PL input is HIGH, the Set input of F5 is activated LOW. The Q output of F5 generates the Input Register Full ($\overline{IRF}$) output of the 9403, while the $\overline{Q}$ output is connected to the Set input of the J flip-flop. A HIGH on the Set or Reset input of J sets or resets the flip-flop accordingly. Thus, when the input register is initialized, J remains set and its $\overline{Q}$ is LOW.

Serial data entry occurs on the HIGH-to-LOW transition of the Serial Input Clock ($\overline{CPSI}$). The input register operates as a "clock-metering" shift register, i.e., it not only assembles serial data bits but also indicates when the desired number of bits has been received. This is achieved by setting F1 (marker) and clearing F2 through F5. As data is shifted into F1, the marker shifts towards F5. After the fourth $\overline{CPSI}$ transition, the marker is in F5 and the $\overline{IRF}$ output goes LOW to indicate that four bits of data are in the input register. The $\overline{CPSI}$ does not operate the flip-flops directly; it is merely an input to gate N. The actual clock is obtained from the gate N output. Gate N has three inputs — $\overline{CPSI}$, $\overline{Q}$ of F5 and the 9403 Input Serial Enable ($\overline{IES}$). Thus if F5 is set or there is a HIGH on $\overline{IES}$, the gate is disabled.

Two cross-coupled gates, L and M, constitute a latch. If the $\overline{IES}$ input is LOW, a LOW on $\overline{MR}$ results in a HIGH at the M output. This establishes the row master. When $\overline{MR}$ goes HIGH, the latch holds this condition. In the row master, one of the AND clusters (C1) of gate K is enabled. C1 is disabled for slave mode and C2, activated by $\overline{IES}$, controls gate K. Note that as long as PL is HIGH, both C1 and C2 are disabled to prevent internal initialization of the input register.

The 9403 contains a 14-level fall-through stack. Each stack level consists of a control flip-flop and four data flip-flops. K1 is the control flip-flop at stack level 1, K2 controls stack level 2 etc., through stack level 14. Flip-flop S10 corresponds to data bit 0 at stack level 1, S20 corresponds to data bit 0 at stack level 2 etc., through S140 at level 14. A NOR gate is associated with each control flip-flop, H1 with K1, H2 with K2 etc. A LOW on the $\overline{MR}$ input resets all control flip-flops.

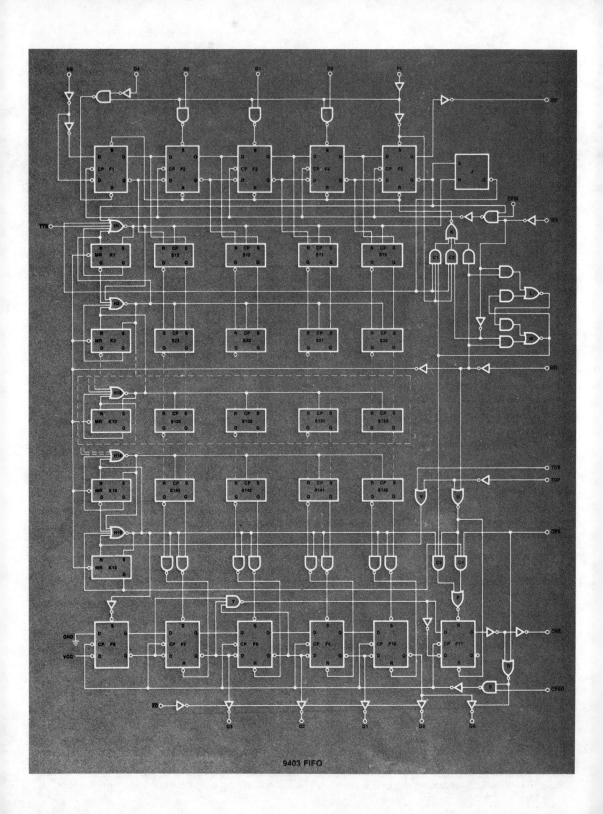

9403 FIFO

PIN NAME	DESCRIPTION	LOADING (Note a)		COMMENTS
		HIGH	LOW	
$D_0 - D_3$	Parallel Data Inputs	1.0 U.L.	0.23 U.L.	
D_S	Serial Data Input	1.0 U.L.	0.23 U.L.	
PL	Parallel Load Input	1.0 U.L.	0.23 U.L.	HIGH on PL enables $D_0 - D_3$. Not edge triggered. Ones catching.
$\overline{CPSI}$	Serial Input Clock	1.0 U.L.	0.23 U.L.	Edge triggered. Activates on falling edge.
$\overline{IES}$	Serial Input Enable	1.0 U.L.	0.23 U.L.	Enables serial and parallel input when LOW.
$\overline{TTS}$	Transfer to Stack Input	1.0 U.L.	0.23 U.L.	A LOW on this pin initiates fall through.
$\overline{OES}$	Serial Output Enable Input	1.0 U.L.	0.6 U.L.	Enables serial and parallel output when LOW.
$\overline{TOS}$	Transfer Out Serial Input	1.0 U.L.	0.23 U.L.	A LOW on this pin enables a word to be transferred from the stack to the output register. (TOP must be HIGH also for the transfer to occur. Not edge triggered.
TOP	Transfer Out Parallel Input	1.0 U.L.	0.23 U.L.	A HIGH on this pin enables a word to be transferred from the stack to the output register. ($\overline{TOS}$ must be LOW for the transfer to occur). Not edge triggered.
$\overline{MR}$	Master Reset	1.0 U.L.	0.23 U.L.	Active LOW.
$\overline{EO}$	Output Enable	1.0 U.L.	0.23 U.L.	Active LOW.
$\overline{CPSO}$	Serial Output Clock Input	1.0 U.L.	0.23 U.L.	Edge triggered. Activates on falling edge.
$Q_0 - Q_3$	Parallel Data Outputs	130 U.L.	10 U.L.	(Note b)
Q_S	Serial Data Output	10 U.L.	10 U.L.	(Note b)
$\overline{IRF}$	Input Register Full Output	10 U.L.	5 U.L.	LOW when input register is full (Note b).
$\overline{ORE}$	Output Register Empty Output	10 U.L.	5 U.L.	HIGH when output register contains valid data.

NOTE: a. 1 Unit Load (U.L.) = 40 μA HIGH, 1.6 mA LOW.
b. Output fan-out with $V_{OL} \leqslant 0.5$ V.   **9403 Pin Names**

Gate H1 has five inputs — the 9403 Transfer-to-Stack ($\overline{TTS}$), the $\overline{Q}$ output of F5, $\overline{Q}$ of J, the Q output of K1 and the output of gate H2. The H1 output is the clock input to the data flip-flops at stack level 1. A HIGH on this clock input transfers data from the input register into stack level 1 and activates the Reset input of J and the Set input of K1. The $\overline{Q}$ output of J is connected to the AND clusters C1 and C2 of gate K.

When the 9403 is initialized by the $\overline{MR}$ input, the first data word is loaded into the input register, either serially or in parallel, and all inputs to gate H1 are LOW exept $\overline{TTS}$. When $\overline{TTS}$ is LOW, the output of H1 goes HIGH and sets flip-flop K1; the HIGH from the $\overline{Q}$ output of K1 disables H1. The circuit is designed so that the resulting pulse width at the H1 output is suitable for operation of the 9403.

Data from the input register is clocked into stack level 1 and flip-flop J is reset while the $\overline{Q}$ output of J enables the C1 and C2 clusters of gate K. If PL is LOW, initialization occurs through C1 in a row master.

For a slave, initialization is through C2 when PL is LOW and IES is HIGH. When the HIGH at the H1 output is terminated, all H2 inputs are LOW and the H2 output goes HIGH. This clears the K1 flip-flop and K2 is set, and data from stack level 1 is transferred to stack level 2. The action continues through all of the stack levels until data arrives at stack level 14.

Data from level 14 is jammed into the output register, consisting of flip-flops F6 through F11, by activating the appropriate Set or Reset inputs of the output flip-flops. Flip-flops F7 through F10 provide the 9403 data outputs via 3-state buffers controlled by the Output Enable ($\overline{EO}$). Flip-flop F10 supplies the serial data output to D_S, also through a 3-state buffer. The Output Register Empty ($\overline{ORE}$) signal is obtained from F11. Control flip-flop K15 and gate H15 are associated

with the output register. If there is no valid data in the output register, K15 is clear. When the Transfer-Out Serial ($\overline{TOS}$) input is LOW and the Transfer-Out Parallel (TOP) input is HIGH and when K14 is set, H15 is enabled and data from stack level 14 is loaded into the output register. The H15 output also sets K15. In the case of a row master, the AND cluster C3 of gate P is enabled by the HIGH output from gate M; this activates the set input of F11 LOW, hence $\overline{ORE}$ goes HIGH. If the Serial Output Enable ($\overline{OES}$) is LOW and F11 is set, gate R is enabled. The output of R enables the 3-state buffer associated with Q_S. When data is transferred from the stack into output register, F6 is also set.

The HIGH-to-LOW transition on the Serial Output Clock ($\overline{CPSO}$) input clocks the output register. Gate R not only enables the Q_S 3-state buffer but also enables gate S. The output register is also a clock-metering shift register. On the first $\overline{CPSO}$ transition, a LOW is shifted into F6. Thus after the third clock transition, flip-flops F6, F7 and F8 are clear. The output of gate T goes LOW and F11 is cleared on the fourth clock transition. As a result, ORE goes LOW and Q_S is disabled into a high impedance state. Clearing F11 also disables gate S and $\overline{CPSO}$ can no longer shift the output register. A HIGH on the $\overline{TOS}$ input or a LOW on TOP resets K15 through gate V and disables H15. Under these conditions, no transfer can take place from the stack into the output register. Moreover, a LOW on TOP or $\overline{MR}$ clears F11 through gate U. Also, note that cluster C4 controls the setting of F11 for the slave mode.

In actual operation, the 9403 FIFO performs several internal activities simultaneously. If any of the intricate details of this complex operation have inadvertently been omitted, the answer is in the logic diagram. Indeed, a picture can be worth 1000 words.

PROGRAMMABLE READ ONLY MEMORIES

A read only memory (ROM) is a random access memory in which the data is fixed (mask programmed) during the manufacturing process. In a sense, a ROM is a code converter that accepts input codes and generates arbitrarily assigned output patterns. Programmable ROMs (PROMs) can be selectively programmed after manufacturing thus providing flexibility and cost savings for the user. He can program devices to his own specifications and make system changes quickly, when necessary, while avoiding mask charges, manufacturing turn-around and inventories of different patterns. Certain types of MOS PROMs (EPROMs) can be erased and reprogrammed but bipolar (TTL) PROMs can be programmed only once.

Bipolar-TTL PROMs offer access times in the 25–50 ns range; ECL devices are available with access times in the 15–20 ns range, while MOS is over ten times slower than either type. MOS has historically been available in larger bit configurations than bipolar, but advances in bipolar memory technology are narrowing the gap. The Isoplanar Schottky PROMs, for example, offer densitites between those of PMOS and silicon-gate NMOS. They are also cost and performance competitive not only with ROMs, but also with standard TTL on a per function basis. Now selling for under 0.3¢ per bit, bipolar PROMs are replacing random logic at a rapid rate.

In the past, PROMs have been used primarily for program and microprogram storage in the computer industry. Currently, much attention is being focussed on their use as replacements for combinatorial logic where they can replace from two to twenty TTL packages[1]. This is possible because the PROM is logically equivalent to a truth table having as many input variables as the PROM has address inputs and as many functions as the PROM has outputs. For example, a 4K PROM organized 512 x 8 bits implements the truth table for eight functions of nine variables. Some examples of the use of PROMs as replacements for combinatorial logic are discussed in the applications section.

Several methods are used to provide the programmable links within bipolar PROMs. The nichrome fuse link is the most popular because of flexibility, high speed, programming yield and reliability. Nichrome has a long history of use as a thin film resistor and a great deal of experience has been obtained with this material[2-5]. In the Fairchild PROMs, the fuse consists of a thin film nichrome link with a small square notch to concentrate the fusing energy and assure a wide clean break.

The increased use of PROMs has been accompanied by considerable progress in the area of reliability. Programming yields of 95% or higher are common and reliability in use is excellent. A reliability report available from Fairchild indicates an extrapolated failure rate of less than .001% per 1000 hours at a maximum junction temperature of 100°C.

Isoplanar Schottky TTL PROMs in various sizes and configurations are available with high performance guaranteed across both commercial and military temperature ranges. These include the 93417/93427 256 x 4-bit, the 93436/93446 512 x 4-bit, the 93438/93448 512 x 8-bit and the 93452/93453 1024 x 4-bit* PROMs (*Figure 1*). They are completely TTL compatible, include fully decoded addressing and are available with open-collector or 3-state outputs. A 256 x 4-bit Isoplanar ECL PROM with a typical access time of 15 ns is also available.

On older data sheets, the PROM outputs have been called $\overline{O}_n$ and were drawn with bubbles to show that the open-collector output pulls LOW and to indicate that the unprogrammed PROM has HIGH outputs. Since the bars and bubbles are not normally used to convey such a meaning, this Application Note and all future data sheets describe the outputs as active HIGH, call them O_n and, therefore, show no bubbles. When the terms "0" and "1" are used in coding or describing PROMs, positive logic is assumed, *i.e.*, a "0" is a LOW and a "1" is a HIGH signal.

APPLICATIONS

PROMs are widely used today in microprogrammed computers ranging from the largest mainframe systems to microcomputers. They are also finding increased use as a replacement for random logic in peripheral controllers, digital controls of all kinds, instruments, and terminals. Circuit applications include fixed data and instruction storage in computers, microprogrammed system control storage, look-up and decision tables of all kinds, and address and priority mapping. Other applications include character/vector generation, encoding/decoding, sequential controllers and other applications traditionally implemented by combinatorial logic.

4-Bit Comparator

The 93417/93427 1K (256 x 4-bit) memory can readily be used as a 4-bit comparator (*Figure 2*). In this example, four of eight address lines are assigned to each of the input vari-

*To be announced 3rd quarter 1976.

FAIRCHILD

SEMICONDUCTOR

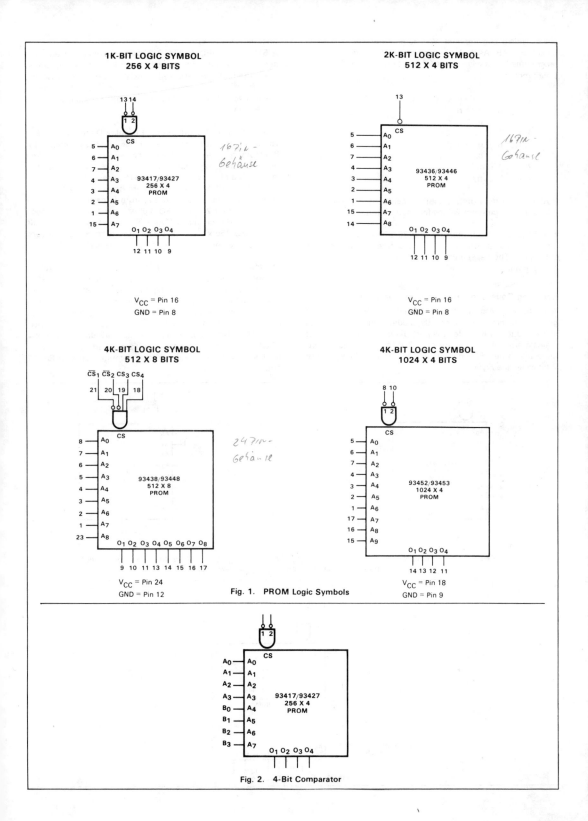

1K-BIT LOGIC SYMBOL
256 X 4 BITS

13 14

1 2

CS

5 — A0
6 — A1
7 — A2
4 — A3   93417/93427
3 — A4   256 X 4
2 — A5   PROM
1 — A6
15 — A7

O1 O2 O3 O4

12 11 10 9

16Pin-
Gehäuse

V_{CC} = Pin 16
GND = Pin 8

2K-BIT LOGIC SYMBOL
512 X 4 BITS

13

CS

5 — A0
6 — A1
7 — A2
4 — A3
3 — A4   93436/93446
2 — A5   512 X 4
1 — A6   PROM
15 — A7
14 — A8

O1 O2 O3 O4

12 11 10 9

16Pin-
Gehäuse

V_{CC} = Pin 16
GND = Pin 8

4K-BIT LOGIC SYMBOL
512 X 8 BITS

$\overline{CS}_1$ $\overline{CS}_2$ CS₃ CS₄

21 20 19 18

CS

8 — A0
7 — A1
6 — A2
5 — A3
4 — A4   93438/93448
3 — A5   512 X 8
2 — A6   PROM
1 — A7
23 — A8

O1 O2 O3 O4 O5 O6 O7 O8

9 10 11 13 14 15 16 17

24Pin-
Gehäuse

V_{CC} = Pin 24
GND = Pin 12

4K-BIT LOGIC SYMBOL
1024 X 4 BITS

8 10

1 2

CS

5 — A0
6 — A1
7 — A2
4 — A3
3 — A4   93452/93453
2 — A5   1024 X 4
1 — A6   PROM
17 — A7
16 — A8
15 — A9

O1 O2 O3 O4

14 13 12 11

V_{CC} = Pin 18
GND = Pin 9

Fig. 1. PROM Logic Symbols

1 2

CS

A0 — A0
A1 — A1
A2 — A2
A3 — A3   93417/93427
B0 — A4   256 X 4
B1 — A5   PROM
B2 — A6
B3 — A7

O1 O2 O3 O4

Fig. 2. 4-Bit Comparator

ables. Unlike conventional MSI comparators with outputs limited to A=B, A<B, A>B, the four PROM outputs can be programmed for a wide variety of functions. Some of the possible functions are:

1. $A + B: = n, > n, < n$
2. $A - B: = n, > n, < n$
3. $B - A: = n, > n, < n$
4. $A \times B: = n, > n, < n$
5. $A \div B: = n, > n, < n$
6. $B \div A: = n, > n, < n$
7. $n < A < m$
8. $n < B < m$

where n and m can be any number or set of numbers and can be assigned different values for each output.

If a 2K (512 x 4-bit) memory (93436/93446) is used, the function can be programmed for two different values or sets of n and m. The desired value or set can then be selected by the A_8 input.

Hamming Code Generator/Checker/Corrector

A PROM can also be efficiently used as a Hamming code generator/checker/corrector. By adding three additional check bits to a 4-bit code, it is possible to detect and correct a single error. A 1K (256 x 4-bit) PROM can be used to generate the three additional bits and to check and correct the 7-bit code (see Figure 3).

Encoder/Decoder

A 512 x 8-bit PROM (93438/93448) is used as an encoder/decoder in another simple application illustrated in Figure 4. Since the ninth address (A_8) is the Decoder/Encoder Select, both functions can be implemented in a single package. Specific applications include emulation, mapping and code conversion.

8-Bit Binary to 3-Digit Decimal Display Decoder

The popular 8-bit microprocessor has created a demand for 8-bit binary-to-decimal display converters, since a 3-digit number is not only easier to read, interpret, and remember than an 8-bit binary word, but also requires less panel space for read-out. ROMs and PROMs are particularly well suited for such code conversion, but a brute-force textbook design would require a 256 x 10 ROM plus three 7-segment decoder/drivers. The circuit in Figure 5 achieves the same result with only a 256 x 4 PROM, three 7-segment decoder/drivers with input latches (9374) and two gate packages.

The total number of required PROM bits is reduced by excluding the least significant bit from the code conversion ($LSB_{in} \equiv LSB_{out}$) and by generating the three possible values of 'hundreds' information (0,1,2), according to the small truth table, by combining the I_7 input with one PROM output. This reduces the PROM requirement to 128 x (3+4+1) bits. Since a PROM of this size is not commercially available, a 256 x 4 PROM can be used in a time multiplexed arrangement with the latches at the decoder inputs for demultiplexing the PROM output information.

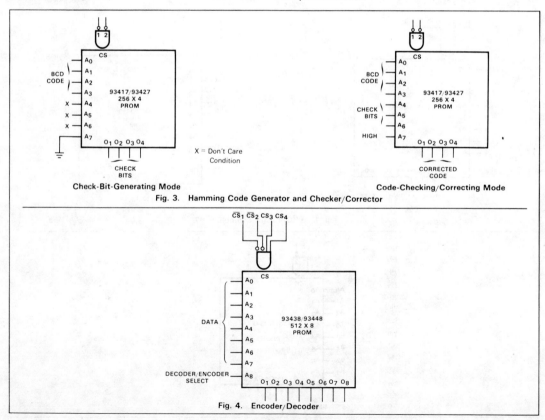

Check-Bit-Generating Mode
X = Don't Care Condition
Code-Checking/Correcting Mode

Fig. 3. Hamming Code Generator and Checker/Corrector

Fig. 4. Encoder/Decoder

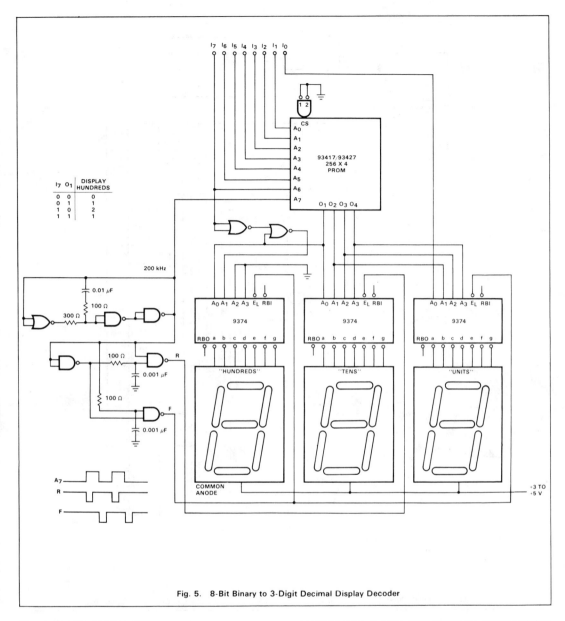

I_7	O_1	DISPLAY HUNDREDS
0	0	0
0	1	1
1	0	2
1	1	1

Fig. 5.   8-Bit Binary to 3-Digit Decimal Display Decoder

Programmed Logic Controller

This easy-to-understand TTL/MSI oriented design for a small dedicated controller is applicable where a minicomputer would be too expensive and a microcomputer would be too slow, too cumbersome to program or too complicated to understand. This concept uses one or two dozen inexpensive TTL/MSI circuits plus one or two PROMs and can implement practically any control function with up to 16 inputs and up to 50 outputs.

A simple open loop controller, as found in every washing machine, is a good beginning. Here a synchronous motor drives a reduction gear, which in turn drives a drum with pro-

gramming pins or cams that activate the output switches (*Figure 6*). The electronic equivalent of this pin-drum controller is shown in *Figure 7* where an oscillator (motor) drives a ÷ 256 counter (gearbox) addressing a PROM (drum) with eight outputs. If the objective were to generate eight arbitrarily changing, completely random outputs, the design would stop here. Fortunately the real world does not usually require outputs that change in a completely random fashion. Rather, the requirement is to be able to activate and hold certain outputs (solenoids, valves, lights, etc.) starting at a certain position in the program, and deactivate them later at a different position. For this purpose the PROM represents an over-design. It is simple to reduce the number of PROM outputs

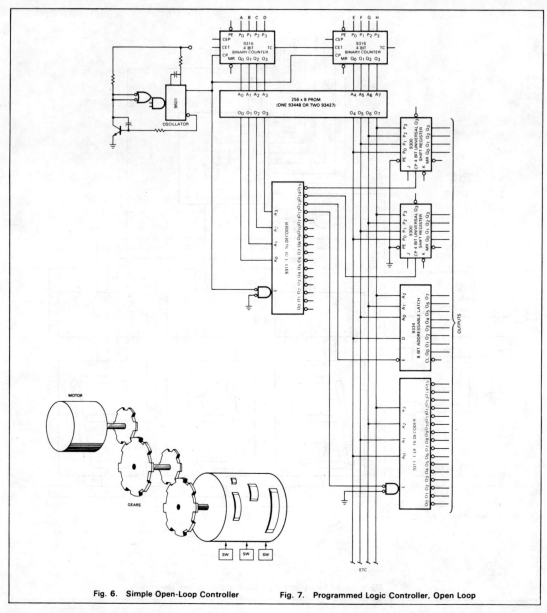

Fig. 6.   Simple Open-Loop Controller   Fig. 7.   Programmed Logic Controller, Open Loop

and/or increase the number of system outputs by using additional inexpensive MSI components.

The PROM outputs can be interpreted as addresses and instructions. As shown in the example of *Figure 7*, the first four outputs are an address activating, through a 9311 1-of-16 decoder, any one of up to 16 MSI circuits. The remaining four PROM outputs are used as instructions to the selected MSI circuit. Address 15 activates the first 4-bit register, changing its four outputs to the associated 4-bit instruction code coming out of the PROM. Address 14 selects another 4-bit register while address 13 selects a 9334 8-bit addressable latch. The 4-bit instruction determines which output is

to be changed and to what level it is to be changed. For an insignificant increase in cost, the number of outputs has been increased from eight to over 64, with the constraint that only one group can be changed simultaneously.

This is still a very unsophisticated open-loop controller. It can be improved by adding a controlled speed reduction, consisting of a presettable counter (*Figure 8*). One instruction can change the instruction rate to any one of 16 values, maintaining it there until it is changed again. The real power of this design is shown, however, when a conditional feedback, or − in programming terms − a conditional jump capability is included (*Figure 9*). One of the 16 addresses is used

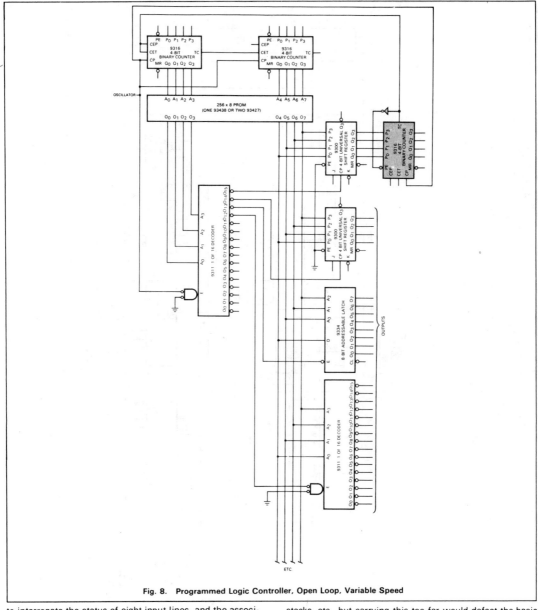

Fig. 8. Programmed Logic Controller, Open Loop, Variable Speed

to interrogate the status of eight input lines, and the associated instruction defines which input is to be interrogated and which level is the desired one. The subsequent PROM output is then not interpreted as an address/instruction pair, but rather as a program jump address. If the input under test has the expected level (HIGH or LOW), this jump address is loaded into the program counter and the program continues from this new address. If the input under test does not have the expected level, the jump address is ignored and the program continues without a jump.

Obviously this design can be made even more sophisticated by adding arithmetic capabilities, data memory, address

stacks, etc., but carrying this too far would defeat the basic advantage of this design, its simplicity and economy. The advantage of this approach over conventional logic implementation lies in the flexibility that it gives to the circuit designer.

The design of a small control system usually starts with a clear knowledge of the number of outputs and inputs required and their electrical characteristics. But, the exact definition of how the control inputs affect the outputs (under all normal and abnormal circumstances) takes most of the time and leads to most of the usual errors. The classical logic design can only start when the system design is finished, and

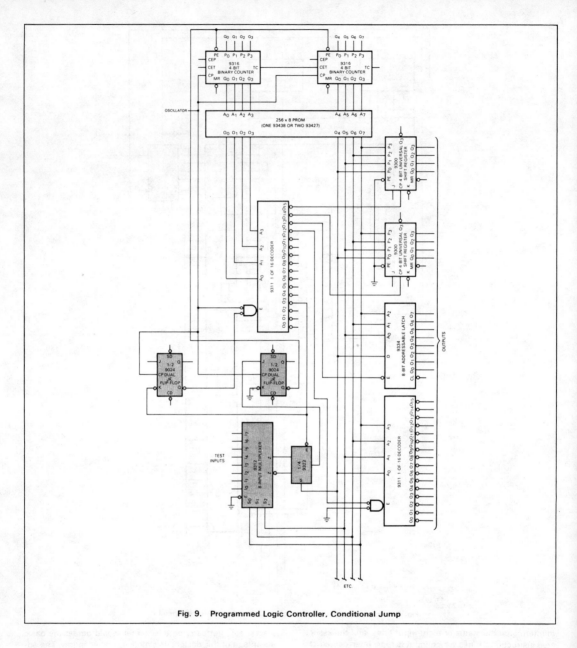

Fig. 9. Programmed Logic Controller, Conditional Jump

will require extensive changes if the system design is changed due to mistakes or new requirements.

The programmed controller, however, can be designed, constructed and tested as soon as the required inputs and outputs are defined, essentially simultaneous with the detailed systems design. System design, programming, and circuit design can be done in parallel, significantly reducing turnaround time. System changes can be implemented by changing the PROM, and can be tested and verified in hours instead of weeks.

ADDRESS AND WORD EXPANSION

Many PROM applications require expansion of the word length or the number of words. *Figure 10* shows the interconnection of two 256 x 4-bit memories to develop a 256 x 8-bit array. Address expansion is shown in *Figure 11*, which illustrates the use of two 256 x 4-bit memories to form a 512 x 4-bit array. A 512 x 6-bit array utilizing three 256 x 4-bit devices is shown in *Figure 12*. As a final example of the expansion versatility of PROMs, *Figure 13* shows how sixteen 512 x 4-bit memories are interconnected to form a 2048 x 16-bit array.

164

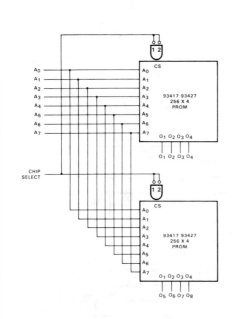

Fig. 10.   Word-Size Expansion, 256 x 8-Bit Array

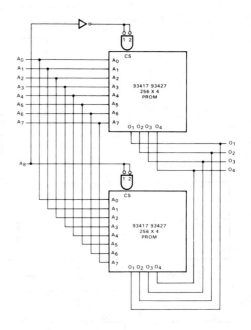

Fig. 11.   Address Expansion, 512 x 4-Bit Array

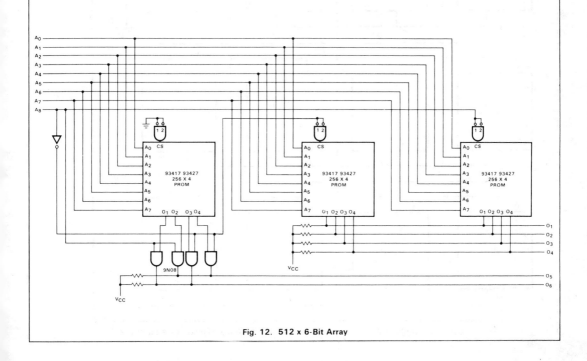

Fig. 12.   512 x 6-Bit Array

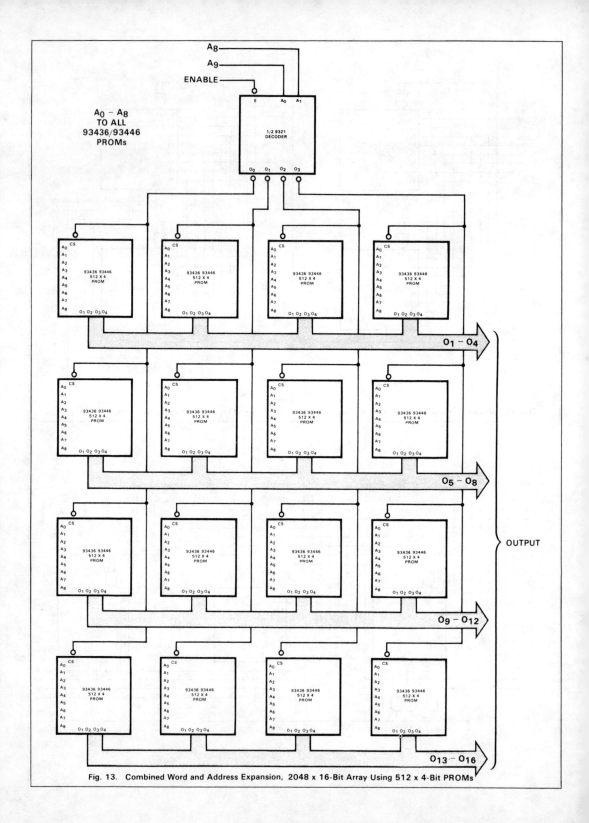

Fig. 13. Combined Word and Address Expansion, 2048 x 16-Bit Array Using 512 x 4-Bit PROMs

PRODUCT DATA

Fairchild's family of Isoplanar Schottky TTL PROMs are fully decoded, very high speed (typically 25 to 35 ns) nichrome fused memories (*Figure 1*). 1K-bit, 2K-bit and 4K-bit devices are available with either uncommitted-collector outputs or 3-state outputs. All are supplied with bits in the HIGH state which can be programmed to the LOW state by following a simple field programming procedure. These PROMs are, depending on size, packaged in industry standard 16, 18 or 24-pin DIPs. The Fairchild PROM family includes:

The 93417 and 93427 are 1024-bit PROMs, organized 256 words by four bits per word. The 93417 has uncommitted-collector outputs, the 93427 has 3-state outputs. In both cases, the outputs are disabled when either Chip Select input is HIGH.

The 93436 and 93446 are 2048-bit PROMs, organized 512 words by four bits per word. The 93436 is an open-collector device and the 93446 is a 3-state device. Outputs are disabled when the Chip Select input is HIGH.

The 93438 and 93448 are 4096-bit PROMs, organized 512 words by eight bits per word. The 93438 is the open-collector version and the 93448 provides 3-state outputs. Outputs are disabled when either active LOW Chip Select input is HIGH or when either active HIGH Chip Select is LOW.

The 93452 and 93453 4096-bit PROMs, organized 1024 words by four bits per word, are scheduled for availability in 3rd quarter 1976. The 93452 is the open-collector device and the 93453 is the 3-state-output version. In both cases, the outputs are disabled when either Chip Select input is HIGH.

AC CHARACTERISTICS

DEVICE	Address to Output Access Time, t_{AA} – ns			Chip Select Access Time, t_{ACS} – ns		
	TYP	MAX 0 to +75°C	MAX −55 to +125°C	TYP	MAX 0 to +75°C	MAX −55 to +125°C
93417/27	25	45	60	12	20	30
93436/46	30	50	60	15	25	30
93438/48	35	55	70	15	25	30
93452/53	35	55	70	15	25	30

AC WAVEFORMS

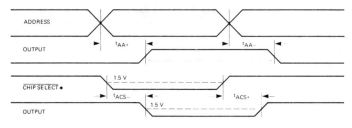

*93436/46, CS = CS
93417/27 and 93452/53, CS = $CS_1 \bullet CS_2$
93438/48, CS = $CS_1 \bullet CS_2 \bullet CS_3 \bullet CS_4$

AC TEST OUTPUT LOAD

5.0 V
R_{L1} 300 Ω
OUTPUT
15 pF R_{L2} 600 Ω

5.0 V
R_{L1} 300 Ω
OUTPUT
30 pF R_{L2} 600 Ω

**15 mA Load
Applies to O.C. Only**

**15 mA Load
Applies to 3-State Only**

DC CHARACTERISTICS: Over guaranteed operating ranges unless otherwise noted.

SYMBOL	CHARACTERISTIC	MIN	TYP (Note)	MAX	UNITS	CONDITIONS
I_{CEX}	Output Leakage Current (O.C. only)			50	μA	V_{CC} = MAX, V_{CEX} = 4.0 V, 0°C to +75°C Address any HIGH Output
I_{CEX}	Output Leakage Current (O.C. only)			100	μA	V_{CC} = MAX, V_{CEX} = 4.0 V, −55°C to +125°C Address any HIGH Output
V_{OL}	Output LOW Voltage		0.30	0.45	V	V_{CC} = MIN, I_{OL} = 16 mA A_0 = +10.8 V, $A_1 - A_8$ = HIGH
V_{OH}	Output HIGH Voltage (3-state only)	2.4			V	V_{CC} = MIN, I_{OH} = −2.0 mA
I_{off}	Output Leakage Current for HIGH Impedance State (3-state only)			50 −50	μA μA	V_{OH} = 2.4 V V_{OL} = 0.4 V $\quad$ 0°C to +75°C
I_{off}	Output Leakage Current for HIGH Impedance State (3-state only)			100 −50	μA μA	V_{OH} = 2.4 V V_{OL} = 0.4 V $\quad$ −55°C to +125°C
V_{IH}	Input HIGH Voltage	2.0			V	Guaranteed Input HIGH Voltage for All Inputs
V_{IL}	Input LOW Voltage			0.8	V	Guaranteed Input LOW Voltage for All Inputs
I_F	Input LOW Current $\quad I_{FA}$ (Address Inputs) $\quad I_{FCS}$ (Chip Select Inputs)		−160 −160	−250 −250	μA μA	V_{CC} = MAX, V_F = 0.45 V
I_R	Input HIGH Current $\quad I_{RA}$ (Address Inputs) $\quad I_{RCS}$ (Chip Select Input)			40 40	μA μA	V_{CC} = MAX, V_R = 2.4 V
C_O	Output Capacitance		7		pF	V_{CC} = 5.0 V, V_O = 4.0 V, f = 1.0 MHz
C_{IN}	Input Capacitance		4		pF	V_{CC} = 5.0 V, V_O = 4.0 V, f = 1.0 MHz
V_C	Input Clamp Diode Voltage			−1.2	V	V_{CC} = MIN, I_A = −18 mA

NOTE: Typical limits are at V_{CC} = 5.0 V, +25°C and Max loading.

DC CHARACTERISTICS

Power Supply Current − mA

	TYP	MAX	CONDITIONS
93417/27	85	110	V_{CC} = Max
93436/46	95	130	Outputs Open
93438/48	130	175	Inputs Grounded
93452/53	120	160	Chip Selected

PROGRAMMING

Fairchild Isoplanar Schottky TTL PROMs are manufactured with all bits in the HIGH state. Any bit can be programmed LOW by following the procedure below and referring to the specifications in *Table 1.* When a programming pulse is applied to a bit (output), current is driven into the circuit as shown in *Figure 14.* Due to careful device design, almost all of the energy is delivered to the fuse consisting of a notched nichrome link. Minimal losses to leakage paths and intermediate circuits permit the link to open rapidly with a low-energy programming pulse. This in turn improves reliability. These nichrome fuses actually program on the rise time of the programming pulse which permits reduction in programming pulse width for high-speed low-energy programming.

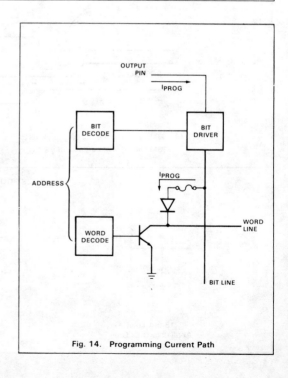

Fig. 14. Programming Current Path

TABLE 1
PROGRAMMING SPECIFICATIONS

PARAMETER	SYMBOL	MIN	RECOMMENDED VALUE	MAX	UNITS	COMMENTS
Address Input	V_{IH}	2.4	5.0	5.0	V	Do not leave inputs open
	V_{IL}	0	0	0.4	V	
Chip Select	$\overline{CS}_1, \overline{CS}_2$	2.4	5.0	5.0	V	Either or both
	CS_3, CS_4	0	0	0.4	V	
Programming Voltage Pulse	V_{OP}	20	21	21	V	Applied to output to be programmed
Programming Pulse Width	t_{pw}	0.05	0.18	50	ms	
Duty Cycle Programming Pulse			20	20	%	Maximum duty cycle to maintain $T_C < 85°C$
Programming Pulse Rise Time	t_r	0.5	1.0	3.0	μs	
Number of Required Pulses		1		4		
Power Supply Voltage	V_{CC}	4.75	5.0	5.25	V	
Case Temperature	t_c		25	85	°C	
Programming Pulse Current	I_{OP}			100	mA	If pulse generator is used, set current limit to this max value.

Programming Procedure (refer to *Table 1*)

1. Apply the proper power, V_{CC} = 5.0 V, and ground.

2. Select the word to be programmed by applying the appropriate levels to the Address pins.

3. Select the chip for programming by deselecting it; apply logic "1" (input HIGH) to the active LOW Chip Select input(s) **or** logic "0" (LOW) to the active HIGH input(s) if present. All PROMs have active LOW CS inputs; only the 93438/93448 have active HIGH CS inputs as well.

4. Apply a 21 V programming pulse to the output associated with the bit to be programmed. The other outputs may be left open or tied to any logic "1" (output HIGH), *i.e.*, 2.4 V to 4.0 V. Note that only one output at a time may be programmed.

5. To verify a LOW in the bit just programmed, remove the programming pulse from the output and sense it after applying a logic LOW to the active LOW Chip Select(s) and a logic HIGH to any active HIGH Chip Select(s).

6. Repeat steps 1–5 as necessary for each bit that requires programming.

Although, for convenience, most programming is done by commercially available programmers, the circuit shown in *Figure 15* can be used to sequentially program all bits of a given word for up to an 8-output PROM. Selection of the bit patterns to be programmed is made by the bit switches while the address of the word to be selected is selected by the address switches. The contents of the PROM at the address, defined by the address switches, are displayed on the eight FLV117 LEDs until the program switch is depressed. If a bit is a logic HIGH or the chip is deselected, the associated LED is turned on with current supplied by the 390 Ω resistors. If

the content of the PROM is a logic LOW and the PROM is enabled, the output is logic LOW turning the LEDs off. The 1N4002s isolate the LEDs from the 21 V programming pulse. One-half of a 9024 JK flip-flop is used as a switch debouncer while the other half is the "run" flip-flop. The 9601 is a 10 kHz oscillator. When the program is initiated by depressing the program switch, the first half of the 9024 (switch debouncer) is set and clocks the other half of the 9024 ("run" flip-flop) to the "run" state. This enables the pulse and bit counters to operate and enables the PROM for programming. The pulse counter is preset to 5 to provide the 20% duty factor and the bit counter is preset to 8. To avoid overlap problems between the programming pulse, the chip enable and the scan, the bit counter advances when the pulse counter goes from state 3 to state 4. The bit to be programmed is decoded by the 9301 and wired-OR with the bit switch. The OR gate is a high-voltage driver supplying the drive to the programming transistors. When the last bit has been programmed, the counter presets itself and resets the "run" flip-flop. The programming sequence is now complete for the selected word.

It is often convenient to program PROMs mounted on a circuit board in wired-OR configurations such as the one shown in *Figure 13*. The Fairchild devices are particularly convenient for board programming in that only the Chip Select and Output pins need to be accessed to program the part. *Figure 16* shows the circuit and procedure for board programming. The programmer is connected to the output bus as shown, while the Chip Selects are driven by a decoder with elevated voltage levels. Thus, all that is required for board programming is the ability to raise V_{CC}, V_{EE} and the Device Select inputs on the decoder 7.6 V above their normal operational levels. The standard 21 V programming pulse will now program bits in the PROM having an active LOW Chip Select input of approximately 7.8 V.

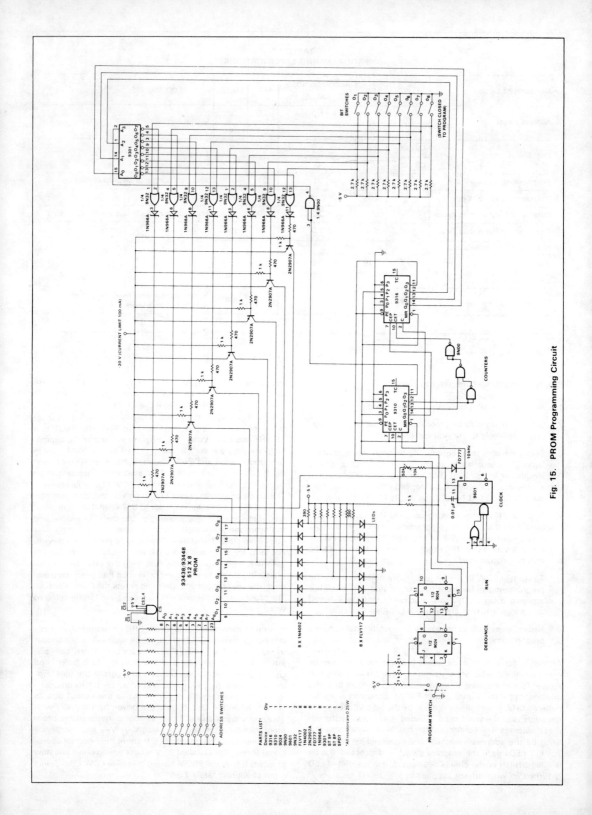

Fig. 15. PROM Programming Circuit

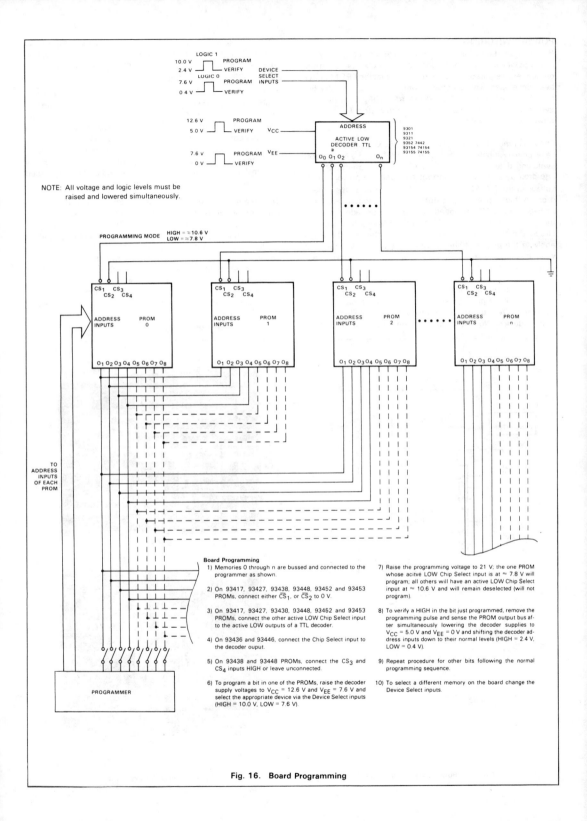

Fig. 16. Board Programming

171

POWER SWITCHING

Power dissipation in a bipolar PROM can be reduced by applying power only when the PROM is selected or when the outputs are required to be valid. Some bipolar PROMs have been developed with on-chip power switching circuitry but they are much slower than standard PROMs. An external switching circuit, such as that shown in *Figure 17*, provides power switching with little loss in speed.

The switching circuit must be capable of switching the worst-case power supply current of the PROM, have very short switching delays and have a small collector-to-emitter voltage drop V_{CE}. This is important because the power supply voltage at the PROM is reduced by the amount of this voltage drop. A high-speed pnp saturated logic switch, *e.g.*, the 2N5455, and a 100 pF speed-up capacitor provide a switching delay of approximately 10 ns at the V_{CC} pin. Using this circuit, the effective access time, which is the delay between applying the power strobe to the V_{CC} pin and availability of valid data, is approximately 10% greater than the normal address access time t_{AA}.

Conditions during power switching, both on and off, must also be considered. *Figure 18* shows the power strobe, V_{CC} and HIGH and LOW output waveforms for an open-collector and a 3-state device. Note the glitch in the HIGH output of both

parts during power-up and the exponential rise of the LOW output during power-down. Care should be taken in system design to ensure that transient conditions do not adversely affect other parts of the system.

It is also important to consider the effect of the collector-emitter voltage drop V_{CE} across the switching transistor on PROM performance. Fairchild Isoplanar PROMs are capable of operating over the full commercial range (0° to 75°C) with the standard 5 V ± 5% power supply reduced by a V_{CE} of 300 mV. Military grade devices operate from 0° to 125°C with the standard 5 V ± 10% power supply reduced by 300 mV. For operating to −55°C, screened parts or tightened power supply specs are recommended.

The steady state condition must also be considered. In a typical memory array, inputs and/or outputs of several devices are bussed together (see *Figure 12*). Therefore, PROMs that are to be used in power-switched arrays should be specified for input and output leakage under power-down conditions, since any leakage in the powered-down devices loads the powered device(s). The allowable leakage is a function of the number of devices bussed together and the drive requirements of the bus. Since manufacturers do not normally specify devices under power-down conditions, customer specifications should reflect the actual system requirements under power-down operation.

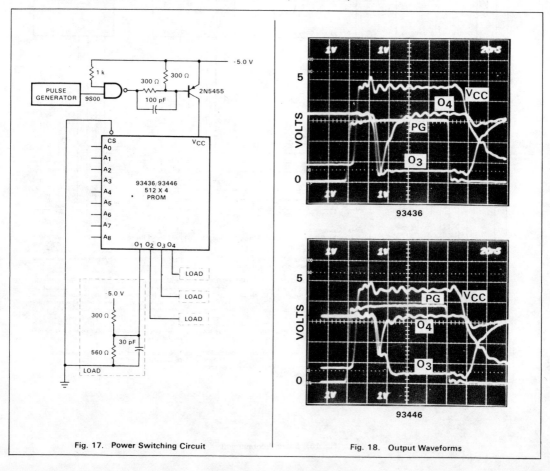

Fig. 17. **Power Switching Circuit**

Fig. 18. **Output Waveforms**

MARKING

Since PROMs come marked with a device type for the unprogrammed part, it is usually necessary for the user to mark the parts after programming so that he can identify individual patterns. An ordinary pencil works well on the common white ceramic packages but any convenient marking method can be used as long as it is relatively permanent. Fairchild PROMs are marked with device type and date code on the lower 2/3 of the top surface. This leaves the upper 1/3 available for customer marking, which can be performed using a thermosetting ink such as Markem*. The ink can be applied with a stick stamp readily available from many suppliers. Acetone removes illegible or incorrect marks and isopropyl alcohol can be used for clean up. After marking, the packages should be baked for one hour at 150°C to fix the ink.

RELIABILITY

The reliability of the programmable read-only memories has long been of concern to potential users. Failures, in addition to those associated with any integrated circuit, result from the spontaneous programming of bits in normal operation and the restoration of programmed bits to the unprogrammed state.

Spontaneous programming of bits in normal operation is governed by an Arrhenius model relationship which indicates a lifetime of tens of thousands of hours at normal operating temperatures[4]. Restoration of programmed bits, often referred to as "regrowth" when associated with nichrome fuse

---

*Markem Corporation, 150 Congress Street, Keen, NH 03431. Stock numbers 8055521 for cerdip, 8058791 for solderseal (white) ceramic or 805933 for plastic.

links, was a problem with early designs. Although processes which avoid the use of nichrome fuses are available, they have other drawbacks such as the etching of silicon by aluminum[5] and high programming energy. Research indicates that regrowth is associated with interdigitated fuse structures. Fairchild's circuits are designed to produce wide clean breaks which accounts for the high reliability of Fairchild's Isoplanar PROMs.

REFERENCES

1. "The New LSI," Electronics, (July 10, 1975)

2. Barnes, D.E., and Thomas, J.E., "Reliability Assessment of a Semiconductor Memory by Design Analysis," IEEE 12th Annual Proceedings on Reliability Physics, (1974)

3. Eisenberg, P.H., and Nalder, R., "Nichrome Resistors in Programmable Read Only Integrated Circuits," IEEE 12th Annual Proceedings on Reliability Physics, (1974)

4. Mo, R.S., and Gilbert, D.M., "Reliability of NiCr 'fusible link' used in Proms," Journal of Electrochemical Society, Vol 120, No. 7 (1973), p. 1001

5. Franklin, P., and Burgess, D., "Reliability Aspects of Nichrome Fusible Link PROMs," IEEE 12th Annual Proceedings on Reliability Physics, (1974)

6. Devaney, J.R., and Sheble III, A.M., "Plasma Etching and Other Problems," IEEE 12th Annual Proceedings on Reliability Physics, (1974)

4096 SERIES DYNAMIC MOS RAMs

Bruce Threewitt

INTRODUCTION

There is a tremendous amount of misinformation floating about concerning memories in general, and dynamic MOS RAMs in particular. As memory size continues to increase, so-called disadvantages as well as honest advantages tend to become confusing. In order to fully understand and utilize today's larger, denser, more versatile memory devices, some knowledge of their design and development considerations is very helpful. Consequently, this application note devotes the first few pages to a review of the circumstances that have influenced memory development. The balance of this note is devoted to particulars concerning 4K dynamic MOS RAMs.

BACKGROUND

Continuing development of MOS technology, coupled with growth that has brought about economic manufacturing processes, have provided a present-day capability to efficiently build component-intensive digital circuits with large scale integration (LSI). The term "component-intensive" refers to devices with an active chip area for logic functions significantly greater than the chip area required to interconnect these logic functions. Memories are prime examples of component-intensive integrated circuits.

Because memories use cells arranged in highly regular arrays to minimize interconnections and simplify circuit design, MOS processing techniques can be used to produce very dense memory devices. As a result, the cost per memory bit for MOS memories has been reduced to the point where it is possible to replace magnetic core memories with solid state devices. The use of semiconductor memories has become particularly attractive since the introduction of 4K dynamic Read/Write memories. This is due not only to the cost-per-bit reductions brought about by circuit density, but also to the fact that 4K RAMs require significantly less peripheral support circuitry than that required by core memories or even earlier dynamic semiconductor memories.

To make 4K (4096 bit) densities possible, MOS technology has utilized n-channel silicon gate circuits for better yields and improved speed-power performance. Also, n-channel circuits are much simpler to interface with standard logic families such as TTL and CMOS. Prior to these n-channel circuits, MOS memories had generally been considered for highly dense but relatively slow memory system applications. Improved n-channel memory performance, however, has prompted the use of MOS memories in higher speed memory

applications. A case in point is the Fairchild 4096-bit dynamic RAM, capable of 200 ns access times and 300 ns cycle times. This provides a 3.3 MHz data rate and power dissipation significantly less than with other memory approaches. In this instance, active power dissipation is less than 430 mW, or less than 110 μW/bit. Without dynamic logic circuit techniques, until recently confined to MOS technology, sufficient speed-power performance in a 4K memory would not have been attainable.

THE HOWs AND WHYs

Dynamic memories store data as a capacitive charge and periodically refresh this charge before it can leak away, as opposed to static memories that store data in a bistable multivibrator and do not require periodic refresh. A comparison of typical static and dynamic memory cells (*Figure A*) illustrates that a dynamic cell requires only a fraction of the transistors needed by a static cell and also does not require a dc power component. Obviously, density is greatly improved with a dynamic memory cell and power requirements are potentially much less. The dynamic cell shown is the 1-transistor dynamic memory cell used in Fairchild's 4096 Series RAMs.

All memory cells have at least a storage element and two access dimensions; in this case, these access dimensions are called Row Select and Bit Line. The Bit Line (to the sense amplifier) is selected by a column decoder, and the appropriate Row Select line is selected by a row decoder, determined by address inputs (*Figure B*).

The operation of both static and dynamic memory cells is fairly straightforward. A static memory cell is merely an RS flip-flop. When set to a state, the cell remains in that state as long as power is supplied to the cell. For a read operation, the bit line reflects a "1" or "0" logic level provided by the appropriate half of the cell and determined by the data stored in the cell. Such read operations are non-destructive. Note that there is always one dc current path between V_{DD} and ground. This means that the static RAM standby current is relatively large. It also means that the sense amplifier (driven by the cell) can be a simple switched buffer, because the data remains in a static cell and does not require restoration by the sense amplifier.

A dynamic memory cell stores data momentarily and loses the data unless it is restored somehow. It has a switching transistor, activated by a row select line that turns on all the

©1976 Fairchild Camera and Instrument Corporation   Printed in U.S.A.   204-21-0002-096   20M

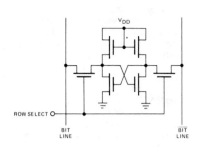

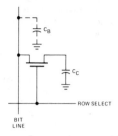

* Assumes enhancement mode load devices.

a) Static RAM Cell   b) Dynamic RAM Cell

Fig. A. Static and Dynamic RAM Cell Comparison

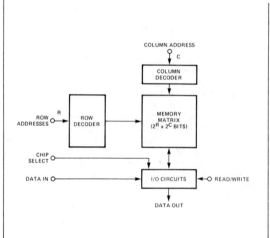

Fig. B. General RAM Block Diagram

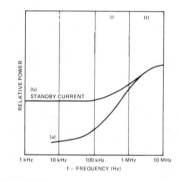

(a) - DYNAMIC
(b) - STATIC

REGION I: POWER REQUIRED BY STATIC BUFFERS DOMINATES.
REGION II: 1/2 CV²f POWER DOMINATES.
REGION III: DECREASED ON CHIP GAIN CAUSED BY INCREASED
JUNCTION TEMPERATURE REDUCES SLOPE OF CURVE.

Fig. C. Power Versus Frequency for MOS RAMs

cells in a given row. Once each cell transistor is on, each cell capacitor shares its charge with a parasitic capacitance on the bit line. The bit-line voltage, a function of the ratio $C_C{:}C_B$, is sensed by the sense amplifier. Because the charge is shared, each cell capacitor charge is restored by a sense amplifier whenever a cycle is executed, providing non-destructive readout. The sense amplifier is also a latch. When the cell contains a charge, the sense amplifier rewrites this charge to its *original level* each time the cell is read. This feature is important, because successive read operations at a given cell location do not diminish the stored charge. Consequently, certain pattern sensitivities are significantly reduced.

A dynamic memory cell itself does not dissipate significant dc power. The sense amplifier may or may not dissipate dc power depending on the particular design. The ac power dissipation is a function of the rate at which the memory is cycled. The power vs. frequency curve in *Figure C* shows memory power dissipation variations relative to frequency (inverse of cycle time) for static and dynamic memory cells. The lower curve (a) represents dynamic cell dissipation; the upper curve (b) represents static cell dissipation. The static memory cell dissipates power more or less evenly over the cycle, so as a result, power does not vary with time. Bypassing is less important for the static device, but on the other hand, standby power is nearly as high as active power.

As illustrated by the dynamic cell curve (a), reducing the cycle rate can reduce the power required to a small standby level. Coupled with the very small dc power requirements of dynamic cells, this characteristic allows the design of non-volatile memory boards by simply incorporating a small power supply (battery) to provide standby power. Dynamic memories do, however, require heavy peak currents over short intervals during the precharge and discharge portions of a cycle.

COSTS AND OTHER CONSIDERATIONS

Magnetic memories such as core were really the only economical mainframe memories until reduced price-per-bit levels and reduced overhead circuit requirements for semiconductor memories made dynamic RAMs attractive for the replacement of magnetic core memories in computer mainframes.

The dynamic nature of these semiconductor RAMs, however, as well as the increased speed performance, make noise considerations in the memory system design significantly important. Noise can arise from several sources, one being the edge-related I_{DD} current spike. This RAM induced noise can be largely eliminated with appropriate bypassing techniques. Another noise source is related to the current required to drive the RAM clock line(s). The clock in many 4K RAM designs represents the largest capacitive load of any of the device inputs. This load is the sum of all the dynamic nodes that the clock must charge during the percharge time. The clock is typically a high voltage input (not TTL compatible) to increase the speed of the RAM and is commonly driven by a low-impedance source such as a TTL/MOS converter. The converter is used to boost the TTL voltage level to the +12 V required by the dynamic MOS RAM. The current required to charge this load can be very large over a short period of time. Assuming a 20 ns rise time, the current required to charge an 800 pF load (32 devices) through a 12 V swing can be derived as follows.

$$ i = C \frac{dv}{dt} = \frac{(8 \times 10^{-10}F)\,(12\,V)}{(2 \times 10^{-8}\,s)} = 480\,mA \qquad (1) $$

This current spike is supplied by a 12 V supply and represents a healthy noise voltage. However, circuit design itself can improve the noise characteristics of a dynamic RAM. For example, the 1-transistor cell greatly improves dynamic-RAM noise rejection. Because each RAM cycle involves restoring not only the addressed cell but also all other cells in the same row, crosstalk between cells and from cells to power lines can only occur during one cycle. The charge-sharing action of the 1-transistor cell in conjunction with the on-chip differential sense amplifier provides some common-mode noise rejection. In addition, the bit line is precharged to a fixed voltage to prevent noise coupling from the bit line to cells in a given column.

Further improvements can be realized by reducing the input clock capacitance and voltage swing. Any resulting speed loss due to such buffering can be offset in other portions of the circuit design. This approach was used in the Fairchild 16-pin 4K RAM design. The power savings in just the clock driver alone represent a factor of about 60 compared to the high voltage clock approach, reducing clock driving power requirements to levels comparable to static RAM address driver requirements.

Another consideration when designing systems with dynamic RAMs is charge restoration, or memory refresh. With static devices, of course, no refresh is required. Although dynamic memories do require refresh, fortunately the additional logic is minimal and its cost can generally be amortized over the system in large or even medium size memories. Naturally, it is more significant for smaller memories (4K to 8K words). As an offsetting advantage, the Fairchild 4096 Series address, control, and clock signals are all TTL compatible, making the cost and complexity of this overhead logic relatively minor.

It can be concluded from the above considerations that static RAMs are at present slightly easier to use, but they do require more power and cost more per bit than dynamic RAMs. Further, present 4K dynamic RAMs are much easier to use than previously available dynamic RAMs, and are approaching the simplicity of static RAMs. Specifically, in systems with a word depth of 4096 bits and up, the dynamic approach is the most cost effective, since the support logic costs so little relative to the memories.

DEVELOPMENT

Continuing in a general vein, today's high speed dense 4096-bit RAMs are the result of the evolution of the static 6-transistor cell into the dynamic 1-transistor cell, (refer to *Figure D*). The first step in this sequence involved simplifying and shrinking the static cell by eliminating the load resistors and relying on parasitic capacitors to store a charge. The resulting memory cell had four transistors and three and one-half interconnections. (The half interconnect refers to the substrate connection.) Next came the 1103 cell, the first dynamic 1024-bit RAM to be volume produced. Considering present-day RAMs, it had several drawbacks.

● High Voltage Address Lines (relative to TTL)
● Complex Timing (multi-phase with critical phasing)
● Bare Drain Output (sense amplifiers required)

The next step resulted in still smaller 3-transistor inverting cells, requiring only three and one-half interconnects (one less than the 1103 cell). This cell was used in a 2048-bit RAM circuit, but it still required 3-phase high level clocks. Although timing was simplified, and the address and control inputs were TTL compatible, this 2K RAM was not enthusiastically accepted. (4K RAMs were imminent.) Also, it must be recalled that "learning curves" dictated that memories should evolve according to a "4X" rule. In other words, new RAMs were expected to have four times the capacity of their predecessors. There have been exceptions to the rule involving word-wide architectures — witness the Fairchild 3539, a 2048-bit (256 x 8) static RAM.

Then came the first 4096-bit dynamic RAM, utilizing a 3-transistor cell very similar to the 1103. It was a very slow device with excessive power dissipation. Shortly thereafter, another 4K RAM was introduced using a single transistor cell with only two and one-half interconnects, promising a significant size reduction. As mentioned earlier, a 1-transistor cell approach offers better noise immunity and potentially lower power requirements. In addition, to make further expansions possible (following the "4X" rule, a 16K RAM is next) a 1-transistor approach is almost essential. The 1-transistor cell 4K RAM became the first high volume dynamic RAM produced with n-channel silicon gate technology. Obviously, it was a combination of circuit design techniques and process development refinements that led to a practical 4K RAM. A similar set of circumstances will make 16K RAMs economically feasible . . . it is only a matter of time and dollar considerations.

Right now, though, a novel design approach, time multiplexing of address lines, has further reduced memory size by 50%, and cut the number of address lines by 50%. With time multiplexing, a pair of addresses can be supplied on each address input, reducing the number of address inputs from 12 to 6. Since the cell matrix is organized in 64 rows and 64 columns, supplying the row addresses first and the column address next is easily implemented with on-chip latches and simple

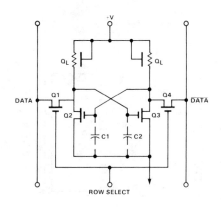

a) 6-Transistor Static Cell
with 4 1/2 Interconnects

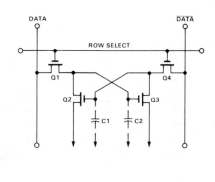

b) 4-Transistor Dynamic Cell
with 3 1/2 Interconnects

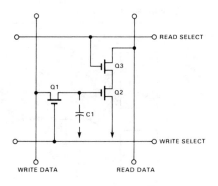

c) 3-Transistor Dynamic Cell
with 4 1/2 Interconnects

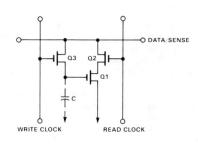

d) 3-Transistor Dynamic Cell
with 3 1/2 Interconnects

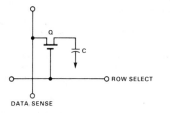

NOTE: ⊥ = SUBSTRATE

e) 1-Transistor Dynamic Cell

Fig. D. RAM Cell Evolution

177

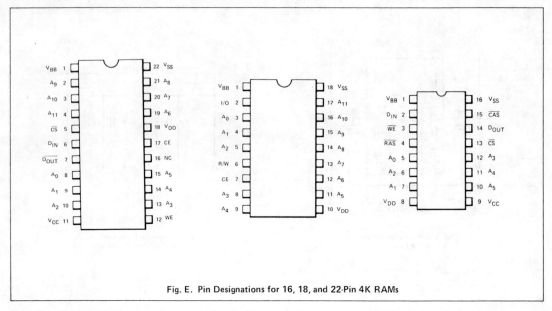

Fig. E. Pin Designations for 16, 18, and 22-Pin 4K RAMs

logic. This multiplexing does not reduce access time, because the row address path is considerably slower than the column address path. Thus, while row addresses are propagating toward the cell matrix, the column addresses are entered and used to select a particular sense amplifier and prepare the output latch for data. So the brand new 1-transistor cell dynamic RAM now has a new density, a new price, and an old industry-standard 16-pin package.

The advent of the 16-pin 4K RAM caused a mild panic amongst the 22-pin device manufacturers. They looked for reasons why address multiplexing would cost more money, or consume more power, or cause a major performance penalty. Of course, there were no valid reasons to claim drawbacks about address multiplexing, but nevertheless, the myth against multiplexing was born.

One attempt to combat the inroads that the 16-pin 4K RAM was making was to modify the 22-pin RAM to fit into an 18-pin package. The 18-pin package did offer some of the same board-space savings as the 16-pin package; actually, it is only about 10% larger than a 16-pin package. However, significant system performance sacrifices were made. By checking the package comparison drawing, *Figure E* it is evident that three connections were eliminated or altered in the conversion from 22-pin to 18-pin packages (one pin was not used on the 22-pin-package). The connections eliminated were $\overline{CS}$ (TTL Chip Select), and V_{CC} (+5 V power supply). Also, Data In and Data Out were altered to form a single I/O structure.

These changes caused several problems. The elimination of V_{CC}, used to provide an active pull-up, implied a bare drain output structure with an external passive pull-up. This external resistor reduced the load driving capability of the 18-pin RAM. Then, chip selection was altered, requiring the manipulation of the Chip Enable clock input. This input required a 12 V swing, and was not TTL compatible. Also, Read and Write operations required careful timing to avoid data overlap problems on the

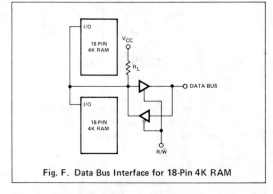

Fig. F. Data Bus Interface for 18-Pin 4K RAM

I/O pin. This was usually overcome by using an external bi-directional 3-state buffer to control the data interface to the RAM. This circuit is illustrated in *Figure F*.

One additional less apparent difficulty hinges on compatibility of the 18-pin RAM with the expected 16K RAM in 16-pin packages. Also, the 12 address lines used in the 18-pin design must be distributed throughout the memory matrix just as with the 22-pin design. This not only affects pin count and board space, but is also not compatible with 16-pin 16K devices that use address multiplexing.

A 16-pin 4K RAM offers the most Read/Write memory per connection presently available. And reducing the address lines by 50% means that only half the address drivers are required. Then, consider the reduction in peripheral components, power, and interconnects, meaning lower cost and higher reliability . . . not to mention the noise reduction resulting from having only half as many signals change state at any given time. Then, as a result of the "4X" rule, 16K RAMs are here in the same 16-pin package with the same connections.

It is difficult to condemn address multiplexing, but to be fair, there is a matter of timing to consider. Since the addresses are entered in two sections, there must be two address strobes or clocks to properly synchronize these inputs. However, the 2-phase timing is made easier by the input voltage and timing characteristics of the two clocks. First, the clock inputs are low capacitance, actually 1/5 the capacitance of the non-multiplexed designs. Second, input voltages are TTL compatible. These two factors reduce peripheral clock power to 1/60 of the amount required by non-multiplexed designs. Additionally, the 2-phase timing is interrelated in such a way that it looks like single-phase timing. In actual fact, the logic required to implement this 2-phase timing is no more complex or costly than that required for single-phase timing.

Since the introduction of the 4096-bit Read/Write RAM, semiconductor and core memory costs have been very competitive. The transition from core memory to semiconductor memory, however painful, has been inevitable. True, some of the pain was caused by the lack of standard semiconductor RAMs. In addition, new technology doesn't help any transition, and in this case, magnetic core was well known for dense, high capacity computer memories, and semiconductors were new and esoteric. However, users have applied sufficient pressure, the semiconductor industry has done sufficient homework, and a standard definition of a 4K RAM is converging on a multiplexed address approach and one particular non-multiplexed approach. The 4K dynamic RAM, in a 16-pin package, with a multiplexed addressing approach, presently offers improved noise immunity, lower power, lower cost, and improved system reliability without increasing system complexity. It also provides for a simple and easy transition to 16K RAM devices when they become practical.

THE FAIRCHILD 4096 SERIES DYNAMIC MOS RAMS

Fairchild 4K MOS RAMs are designated the 4096 Series, 4,096-bit dynamic Read/Write Random Access Memories organized as 4,096 1-bit words. These memory circuits utilize the single transistor dynamic memory cell. The series is offered in a standard 16-pin Dual In-line Package allowing construction of very dense memory systems utilizing widely available automatic testing and insertion equipment. Worst-case access times range from 200 ns to 350 ns, depending on the particular versions selected. *Table 1* lists the available versions with

Access times, Read/Write cycle times, Read/Modify/Write cycles times, and worst-case average I_{DD}. The Fairchild n-channel Isoplanar process is used to manufacture the 4096 Series RAMs.

A 4096 Series block diagram, logic symbol, and connection diagram are shown in *Figure 1*. The following discussion covers the electrical specifications of the 4096 Series in detail. The first part of the discussion deals with dc parametric specifications. The second part explains the nature of the forcing function timing requirements necessary for proper operation of 4096 Series devices.

ADDRESS, CHIP SELECT AND DATA IN INPUTS

Individual access to 4,096 bits requires 12 address inputs ($2^{12} = 4,096$). However, judicious cycle timing can supply 12 address inputs while using only six address lines. Since the memory array is a binary square (64 rows x 64 columns), two 6-bit address bytes can be time-multiplexed on six address lines. Synchronization is accomplished with two signals — Row Address Strobe ($\overline{RAS}$) and Column Address Strobe ($\overline{CAS}$). Contrary to expectations, this approach does not necessarily reduce RAM speed in a memory system. In actual operation, the two 6-bit address bytes are latched on the chip, releasing the address lines for the next address bytes. The Chip Select input ($\overline{CS}$), used as a column address in this case, strobes its latch with the falling edge of $\overline{CAS}$. Because $\overline{CS}$ is not required until this point in the cycle, $\overline{CS}$ decoding time does not affect system access or cycle times. Also, Data In signals are latched on the chip, and they are strobed by a combination of the $\overline{CAS}$ and $\overline{WE}$ signals. The specific details concerning Data In timing are discussed in a later section covering Write and Read/Modify/Write cycles.

Address, Chip Select, and Data In inputs are standard MOS inputs with built-in static protection networks (*Figure 2*). D1 is a parasitic diode resulting from the diffusion of R1. R1 and C1 form a low-pass filter to slow down fast-rising static electricity inputs. The nominal values of R1 and C1 are 1 kΩ and 5 pF, respectively. D2 can be modeled as a Zener diode, and depending on the particular process, its breakdown voltage can range from 7 V to 30 V. Breakdown voltage for the 4096 Series is roughly 30 V. Since the dielectric structure of Q1 can withstand 100 — 150 V, D2 causes accumulated static charge

PART NUMBER	RANDOM ACCESS TIME (ns)	READ OR WRITE CYCLE TIME (ns)	READ/MODIFY/WRITE* CYCLE TIME (ns)	MAX I_{DD} (AVG — mA)
40962DC **	200	300	440	35
40963DC	250	365	535	30
40964DC **	300	425	620	27
40965DC	350	500	720	25
40964DL	300	425	620	27
40965DL	350	500	720	25
40964FL **	300	425	620	27
40965FL	350	500	720	25

* $t_{RMW} = t_{RCL} + t_{CAC} + t_{MOD} + t_{CWL} + t_{RP} + t_{CRL} + 4t_T$

**D = CERDIP, F = FLATPAK, C: $T_A = 0°C$ to $+70°C$, L: $T_A = -55°C$ to $+85°C$

Table 1. 4096 Series Selection Matrix

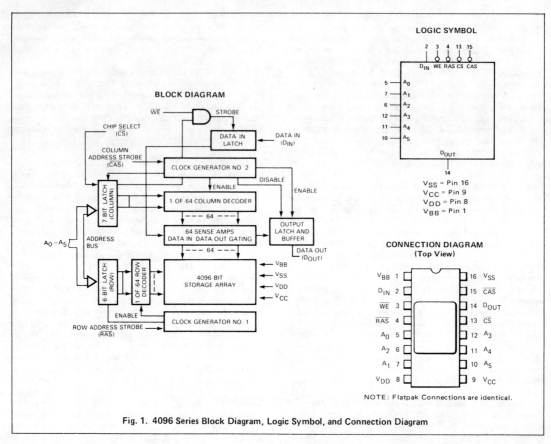

Fig. 1. 4096 Series Block Diagram, Logic Symbol, and Connection Diagram

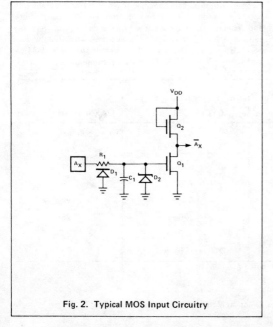

Fig. 2. Typical MOS Input Circuitry

to be shunted to the substrate long before the gate of Q1 is damaged. However, it is still possible to damage the metalization around R1 if sufficient voltage is applied too quickly.

For example, a production worker can accumulate a static charge as high as 50 kV. Such a voltage applied to an MOS input with V_{SS} grounded causes a current spike of approximately 50 Amps, sufficient to destroy the input. Obviously, careful handling is necessary. Usually, the maintenance of a conductive environment around the MOS device is sufficient.

MOS devices are generally shipped in conductive foam or anti-static tubes or shunts, and these materials should be left in place until the MOS devices are inserted in the printed circuit board. Once boards are loaded, MOS inputs should not leave the board without a termination to insure low impedance. Popular board terminations are TTL buffers, 10 or 20 kΩ resistors between the inputs and V_{DD} or V_{SS} — any approach that reduces the input impedance seen by a static charge voltage source. Buffers and other logic isolate the MOS inputs effectively because they enter junction breakdown at a sufficiently low voltage to protect the MOS inputs. But, board termination can be as simple as wrapping aluminum foil around the edge connectors, adequately protecting the MOS devices by shorting all pins together. Shipping and careless handling of unterminated boards can damage MOS inputs, so the boards should be treated as carefully as the individual MOS devices.

PIN NUMBER	PIN NAME	FUNCTION	MINIMUM V_{IH} (V)
1	V_{BB}	POWER SUPPLY	—
2	DATA IN	INPUT TYPE A	2.4
3	WRITE ENABLE	INPUT TYPE B	2.7
4	ROW ADDRESS STROBE	INPUT TYPE B	2.7
5	ADDRESS 0	INPUT TYPE A	2.4
6	ADDRESS 2	INPUT TYPE A	2.4
7	ADDRESS 1	INPUT TYPE A	2.4
8	V_{DD}	POWER SUPPLY	—
9	V_{CC}	POWER SUPPLY	—
10	ADDRESS 5	INPUT TYPE A	2.4
11	ADDRESS 4	INPUT TYPE A	2.4
12	ADDRESS 3	INPUT TYPE A	2.4
13	CHIP SELECT	INPUT TYPE A	2.4
14	DATA OUT	OUTPUT	—
15	COLUMN ADDRESS STROBE	INPUT TYPE B	2.7
16	V_{SS}	POWER SUPPLY	—

Table 2. 4096 Connections — by Function

Table 2 characterizes the 4096 Series connections by function (inputs, outputs, and power supplies) and by minimum input voltage required to establish a logic HIGH (V_{IH}). The Address, Chip Select, and Data In inputs are Type A inputs, with a minimum Input HIGH Voltage of 2.4 V. In other words, the input voltage must be at least 2.4 V to be recognized as a logic "1." The maximum input voltage recognized as a logic "0" (V_{IL}) is 0.8 V. This parameter, V_{IL}, is of concern because Schottky TTL circuits, with superior speed and drive current, are often used to drive the addresses in MOS RAM systems. Fully-loaded Schottky drivers guarantee a maximum Output LOW Voltage (V_{OL}) of 0.5 V, with the resulting noise margin at the TTL/MOS interface of a paltry 300 mV. A system design rule can be derived from this consideration; address drivers should not be loaded with a significant dc load current. In other words, the drivers should be connected to MOS inputs only, not to a mixture of MOS and TTL circuits. The resulting unloaded V_{OL} is about 0.2 V, allowing a 600 mV noise margin, consistent with TTL system levels.

Ringing is an important input consideration. It is oscillation caused by an impedance mismatch. Undershoot is unimportant as long as it is more positive than V_{SS} − 5 V. However, the positive portion of this ringing is a function of the undershoot, and if it is not limited, V_{IL} specifications will not be met. A simple clamp diode termination at the output of each address and clock driver will do the job. (The same techniques are used on TTL inputs for noise suppression.)

In large memory arrays, the effects of ringing become more important because the high speed driving of address inputs causes some transmission-line behavior. With the 4096 Series, as long as input voltages remain more positive than V_{BB}, the substrate remains reverse biased. This is a necessity for continued isolation of the MOS transistors from each other.

ROW/COLUMN ADDRESS STROBES AND WRITE ENABLE

As indicated in *Table 2*, the Row Address Strobe ($\overline{RAS}$) and Column Address Strobe ($\overline{CAS}$) are Type B inputs, requiring a minimum Input HIGH Voltage of 2.7 V. The input protection circuitry and leakage current characteristics of Type B inputs are identical to those of Type A inputs. Type B inputs employ a bootstrapping technique to enhance their speed/power product, shown in *Figure 3*, and this is the reason why the Input HIGH Voltage requirement is greater than the minimum V_{IH} requirement of Type A circuits. The bootstrapping technique follows.

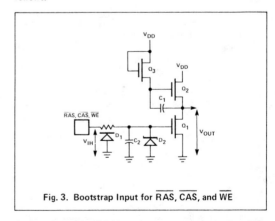

Fig. 3. Bootstrap Input for $\overline{RAS}$, $\overline{CAS}$, and $\overline{WE}$

At first glance, the 2.7 V requirement precludes a direct TTL interface. Fortunately, the physical aspects of the situation allow direct interface of 4096 Series devices with both standard and Schottky TTL circuits. The output structure of a standard 7400 Series logic gate, shown in *Figure 4a*, and the accompanying charts illustrate a common misconception about using

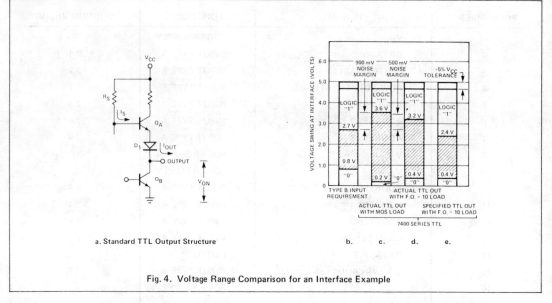

Fig. 4. Voltage Range Comparison for an Interface Example

MOS devices with standard TTL circuits. TTL specifications (*Figure 4e*) apparently indicate that normal TTL logic "1" output levels are insufficient to drive MOS devices directly. Close examination of TTL specifications and the TTL device output structure shows that this is not a valid conclusion. The TTL logic "1" output level, V_{OH}, is derived from the following equation.

$$V_{OH} = V_{CC} - I_B R_B - V_{BE(Q1)} \Big|_{I_{OUT}} - V_{D1} \Big|_{I_{OUT}} \quad (1)$$

The value of $I_B R_B$ is negligibly small. The other two values are the voltage drops across the two diodes in the TTL output structure with a forward current equal to I_{OUT}. When a TTL device is loaded by an MOS device, I_{OUT} is extremely low (10 μA max). At this current level, V_{D1} and $V_{BE(Q1)}$ are about 540 mV each at an ambient temperature of 25°C. Thus, V_{OH} is 3.67 V.

$$V_{OH} = 4.75\,V - I_B R_B^{\;\;0} - 1.08\,V = 3.67\,V \quad (2)$$

Temperature correcting for each diode at 2 mV/°C, worst-case V_{OH} at an ambient temperature of 0°C is derived as follows.

$$V_{OH} \Big|_{T_A = 0°C} = V_{OH} \Big|_{T_A = 25°C} - (0.002 \times 25 \times 2) =$$

$$3.67\,V - 0.100\,V = 3.57\,V \quad (3)$$

Measurements of V_{OH} without load current verify this result. The noise margin, then, for a logic "1" level at $T_A = 0°C$ is approximately 900 mV. When the TTL gate is loaded with a fanout of 10 and an MOS input, V_{OH} is 3.31 V.

$$V_{OH} = 4.75\,V - 1.44\,V = 3.31\,V \quad (4)$$

Again, temperature correcting for each diode to an ambient temperature of 0°C, V_{OH} becomes 3.21 V.

$$V_{OH} \Big|_{T_A = 0°C} = V_{OH} \Big|_{T_A = 25°C} - 100\,mV =$$

$$3.31\,V - 0.10\,V = 3.21\,V \quad (5)$$

For this situation, then, the noise margin at $T_A = 0°C$ is still about 500 mV. The original TTL specifications, now taken as industry standards, evolved from the input voltage requirements. Specifying TTL $V_{IH(min)}$ at 2 V and allowing for a 400 mV noise margin implies a $V_{OH(min)} = 2.4$ V, even though physically, device V_{OH} is considerable higher. Consequently, input pull-up resistors are not actually required on 4096 Series device inputs for a proper TTL/MOS interface.

POWER SUPPLIES

A simplified cross section of Q1 is shown in *Figure 5*. Since the 4096 Series is n-channel silicon gate, a positive gate voltage relative to the source causes a conducting channel to be induced between the drain and source. The gate-to-source voltage required to initiate conduction is known as the enhancement mode threshold voltage, or V_{TE}. For most n-channel silicon gate processes, V_{TE} is about 1 V.

There are four power supply connections for the 4096 Series RAMs, V_{BB} (−5 V ±10%), V_{SS} (Ground), V_{CC} (+5 V ±5%), and V_{DD} (+12 V ±5%).

The −5 V Supply − V_{BB}

The V_{BB} supply is a substrate bias voltage that establishes the enhancement and field threshold voltages. The voltage required to cause Q1 to conduct can be determined with the following equation (refer to *Figure 5*).

$$V_{TE} = V_{TEO} + \Delta V_{TE} \quad (6)$$

where V_{TEO} = enhancement mode threshold without a substrate bias voltage,

and ΔV_{TE} = additional threshold voltage occuring when source-to-substrate voltage $\neq$ 0. Refer to *Figure 6*.

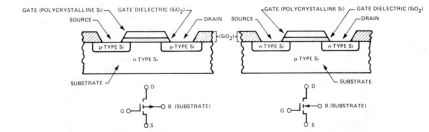

a) Simplified Cross Section and Circuit Symbol of
   P-Channel Enhancement Mode MOSFET

b) Simplified Cross Section and Circuit Symbol of
   N-Channel Enhancement Mode MOSFET

c) Simplified Circuit Symbol for
   N- and P-Channel Devices

Fig. 5. Basic MOSFET Transistor Structure (Enhancement Mode)

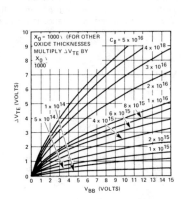

**Fig. 6. Change in Gate-to-Source Threshold Voltage
Versus Substrate Bias — MOS Transistor**

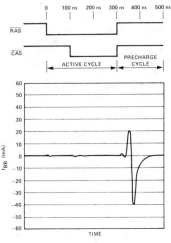

CONDITIONS: t_{CRL} = 0, MEMORY
CONTAINS ALL LOGIC
"0" LEVELS.

Fig. 7. I_{BB} Versus Time

There are many considerations related to V_{BB}. Some MOS processes result in an enhancement mode threshold less than zero with no substrate bias. In other words, Q1 of *Figure 3* is a depletion mode device if V_{BB} = 0 V. Depletion mode devices conduct current unless a negative gate-to-source voltage is applied. Fairchild 4096 Series devices are not in this category; the process used for the 4096 Series produces enhancement mode devices at V_{BB} = 0 V. As a result, the power supplies can be switched on in any order. Unfortunately, other processes may require V_{BB} to be switched on prior to or at least coincident with the other supplies.

Dynamic logic techniques usually result in current spikes that occur in conjunction with the clock signals. An I_{BB} versus time curve for 4096 Series devices is shown in *Figure 7*. Al-

though the average I_{BB} value is less than 75 μA, some large transients occur that can cause significant variations in V_{BB} unless sufficient bypassing is employed. Maximum I_{BB} transients occur with an all "0" data pattern. It is often incorrectly assumed that because of the low V_{BB} supply current levels, bypassing is not required, but this is not so. Adequate bypassing can be accomplished by using a 0.01 μF ceramic disc capacitor every few devices. The ceramic disc structure is recommended because of the high frequency response required to respond to narrow I_{BB} spikes. A stable V_{BB} supply is essential because it affects V_{TE} and field threshold, and as a result, it also affects RAM noise margins. Worst-case noise margins occur at the most positive value for V_{BB}. The critical effect that V_{BB} has on "soft" failures is perhaps illustrated best with a "schmoo" plot, *Figure 8*. A "soft" failure occurs when

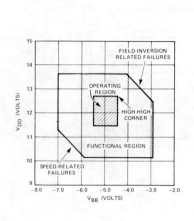

Fig. 8. Typical V_{BB}/V_{DD} Schmoo Plot

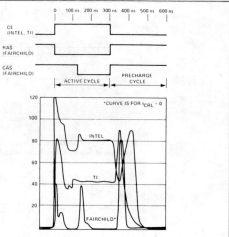

Fig. 9. Comparison of I_{DD} for Various 4K RAMs

one or more bit locations in the RAM temporarily malfunction, even though data can be rewritten into the cell correctly. A schmoo plot is a functionality representation plotting the operating region of the device as a function of variations in operation conditions — in this case V_{BB} and V_{DD}. Operating functionality is checked with worst-case patterns, timing, and input voltage levels. To some extent, the operating region margin around the specified voltage range determines the device's immunity to soft failures.

Some device characteristics can be inferred from the shape of the schmoo plot. For example, the high-high corner (V_{BB} most positive, V_{DD} most positive) functionality is jeopardized by field inversions caused by V_{DD} values in excess of the field threshold voltage, V_{TM}. V_{TM} is minimized at the most positive value for V_{BB}. The schmoo plot indicates this. The cross-hatched area represents the specified V_{BB}/V_{DD} operating range. All unshaded areas represent non-functional conditions.

Notice that functionality is also jeopardized at minimum values for V_{DD} with maximum (most negative) values for V_{BB}. In this region, speed is the limiting parameter. As V_{BB} is decreased toward zero and on-chip thresholds are reduced, the device can tolerate less V_{DD} and still be able to operate at the required speed. Thus, the schmoo plot provides the user with an indication of margins and to some extent, indication of failure modes.

The +12 V Supply — V_{DD}
The V_{DD} supply is the main power component for 4096 Series devices. TTL level inputs are converted to approximately 12 V by the first buffer stages. From that point, signals are at MOS levels.

There are two I_{DD} current levels of concern. Dynamic logic generally executes a precharge portion of a cycle followed by an active portion. As a result, the majority of the power dissipation is an average of the I_{DD} current transients over the entire memory cycle multiplied by V_{DD}. *Figure 9* is a comparison of I_{DD} variations with time for various 4K RAMs presently available.

Since the amplitude of I_{DD} is large for a short period of time, power supply bypassing is essential. The bypass capacitors must supply the current for the devices during this short interval because the power supplies cannot react quickly enough. The capacitance required is readily determined. The current that a capacitor can supply over a given time with a given voltage change is derived and capacitance is then calculated.

$$i = \frac{C\Delta V}{\Delta t} \tag{7}$$

$$\text{or} \quad C = \frac{i\Delta t}{\Delta V} \tag{8}$$

For example, a 100 mA peak current over a 50 ns interval requires a 0.008 μF capacitance to restrict the voltage change to 0.6 V (5% of +12 V).

$$C = \frac{(100 \text{ mA}) (50 \text{ ns})}{0.6 \text{ V}} = 0.008 \,\mu\text{F} \tag{9}$$

This means that a 0.01 μF ceramic disc capacitor should be used at each RAM location.

Power Reduction
Minimum active power requirements in a memory system can be realized utilizing a logic feature of the 4096 Series. The $\overline{RAS}$ input can be used instead of the $\overline{CS}$ input to select a chip and power it down. This approach is useful in memory systems of 8K words or more. Whenever the 4096 Series device receives a $\overline{CAS}$ input without having first received an $\overline{RAS}$ input, the output goes to a high impedance state and stays there regardless of the $\overline{CS}$ input. At the same time, the chip begins powering down toward standby levels, the second I_{DD} level of concern ($I_{DD(max)}$ = 2 mA). *Figure 10* illustrates this behavior. The first cycle is a full power cycle in which the RAM has been selected; it has received both $\overline{RAS}$ and $\overline{CAS}$ signals. During the second cycle, $\overline{RAS}$ is gated out, and the RAM is

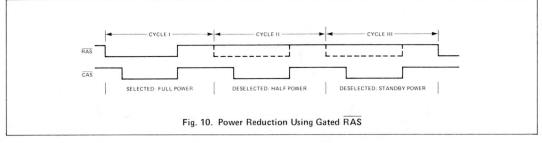

Fig. 10. Power Reduction Using Gated $\overline{RAS}$

deselected. However, it still dissipates about one half of the power of Cycle I. This power component is used by the circuitry that turns off the output. During Cycle III ($\overline{RAS}$ is still gated out), the RAM dissipates standby power only, about one-tenth of full power. So in the worst case, when a new 4K-word block is selected every cycle, the overall system power is determined as follows.

$$P \text{ (System)} = (1.5) \text{ (Active Power)} + (n - 2) \text{ (Standby Power)} \qquad (10)$$

where n = number of 4K-word blocks in the system

Minimum power dissipation occurs when a given 4K-word block is addressed for three or more successive cycles. In this case, power drops to active power plus (n − 1) times standby power.

There is an additional benefit derived by using $\overline{RAS}$ as a Chip Select input. New 16K RAMs are expected in the same 16-pin packages used for the 4096 Series, except that the present $\overline{CS}$ input becomes an additional Address input, A_6. Without $\overline{CS}$, $\overline{RAS}$ will be used as a Chip Select input for these 16K RAMs, and systems using this approach now for 4K RAM memory systems will be easier to convert to 16K RAM devices.

The +5 V Supply — V_{CC}

The V_{CC} supply serves only one purpose, providing power to the output buffer. V_{CC} does affect the source current of the 4096 Series output buffer, but since V_{CC} does not provide reference levels internally as with some 18 and 22-pin designs, V_{CC} supply regulation is less critical when using 4096 Series devices. However, since V_{CC} is the TTL supply, bypassing should be consistent with normal TTL design rules.

The decoded $\overline{RAS}$ approach for chip selection can cause data bus conflicts during a refresh cycle, because the $\overline{RAS}$ signal is supplied to all RAMs in parallel to accomplish refresh. The discussion of the output circuitry later explains why this possible conflict does not harm the RAMs. However, a large current transient could result on the V_{CC} line unless appropriate steps are taken to prevent it. One approach simply switches off the V_{CC} supply to the RAMs during refresh operations (*Figure 11*). V'_{CC} is then less than V_{CC} as determined by the voltage drop across Q1. This approach leaves the V_{CC} pin open, rather than shunted to ground to conserve power. Because V'_{CC} is used only by the output buffers, it does not need to be stable until late in the cycle after the refresh cycle. Q1 is selected to drive the relatively small capacitance of the 4096 Series V_{CC} lines, typically about 10 pF per device. Another approach is to use a $\overline{RAS}$ only refresh cycle to leave the outputs disconnected at the expense of some extra logic to account for a special refresh cycle.

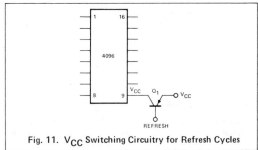

Fig. 11. V_{CC} Switching Circuitry for Refresh Cycles

Ground — V_{SS}

The ground line (V_{SS} supply) connection serves as a return for the large V_{DD} current spikes. As such, V_{SS} lines should be arranged as carefully as V_{DD} lines to prevent ground spikes from causing spurious inputs. Since 4096 Series device thresholds are referenced to ground, transients on V_{SS} relative to input signal voltage levels can cause erroneous inputs. The most noise-resistant systems result from using 4-layer printed circuit boards with V_{DD} and V_{SS} as solid internal planes and with signal traces on the outside planes. Power distribution is probably the most critical printed circuit board design parameter in dynamic memory systems, and 2-layer boards are the most difficult to design with proper power distribution.

OUTPUT CIRCUITRY

The 4096 Series device Data Out is logic true; in other words, the Data Input signal is not inverted by the RAM. The output circuitry is shown in *Figure 12*. The output buffer is a push/pull amplifier driven by the True and Complement outputs of the data latch. Output drive current is specified for two cases, logic "0" and logic "1." For a logic "0" output signal, output sink current I_{OL} is guaranteed to be greater than 2 mA with $V_{OL} = 0.4$ V. Even in the worst case, this current can supply the 1.6 mA required to drive a standard TTL input plus 400 μA of bus leakage current. Alternatively, the 4096 Series device output can drive four low power Schottky TTL inputs plus 400 μA. Substitution of low power Schottky TTL is a convenient method for increasing MOS device fanout without compromising system performance. Typical values of I_{OL} are around 5 mA with $V_{DD} = 12$ V. Minimum I_{OL} (2 mA) occurs at an ambient temperature of 70°C with $V_{DD} = 11.4$ V, $V_{BB} = -5.5$ V.

For a logic "1" output signal, output source current I_{OH} is always greater than 5 mA with $V_{OH} = 2.4$ V. The dc current required to drive TTL circuitry is much lower (40 μA max). However, to drive line capacitance, the output requires some edge current. Again, the worst case occurs at an ambient temperature of 70°C with $V_{DD} = 11.4$ V, $V_{CC} = 4.5$ V.

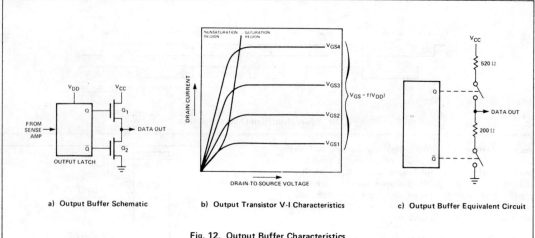

a) Output Buffer Schematic   b) Output Transistor V-I Characteristics   c) Output Buffer Equivalent Circuit

Fig. 12. Output Buffer Characteristics

The capacitive fanout can be determined by subtracting the dc current from the current capability of the output buffer and computing the amount of capacitance that can be driven at the required voltage slew rate. Keep in mind that for a High-to-Low output transition (effected by I_{OL}), the 4096 Series output is not significantly dc loaded until the TTL input switching threshold has been reached. So essentially all of the output sink current can be used to discharge line capacitance until V_{OL} equals approximately 1.5 V. The output impedance characteristics of Q1 in *Figure 12* are similar to those of switched resistors. Their V-I characteristics are shown in *Figure 12b*, and switching characteristics can be calculated based on the model circuit shown in *Figure 12c*. Resistance values are determined by the following equations.

$$R_{Sink} = \frac{V_{OL}}{I_{OL}} = \frac{0.4\ V}{2\ mA} = 200\ \Omega \qquad (11)$$

$$R_{Source} = \frac{V_{CC} - V_{OH}}{I_{OH}} = \frac{5.0 - 2.4}{5.0\ mA} = 520\ \Omega \qquad (12)$$

Output capacitance is specified at 8 pF maximum for each output. Considering the circuit of *Figure 12*, the short-circuit characteristics of the output buffer can be predicted. This short-circuit characteristic is important in memory systems using a decoded $\overline{RAS}$ technique for chip selection. When a refresh cycle occurs in these systems, all of the 4096 Series device outputs that are OR-tied on a given bit line are active. If these devices happen to be in opposing data states, a large V_{CC} transient results, (discussed earlier under Power Supplies). In a worst-case situation, all OR-tied outputs but one could be in a logic "1" state while the one device in the logic "0" state attempts to pull the data bus low. In a system containing enough words to make R_{Source} significantly lower than R_{Sink}, short-circuit current is 5 V divided by 200 Ω, or 25 mA. This current level does not harm device outputs if only present for the time required for a refresh cycle.

Conversely, if all but one of the outputs are in a logic "0" state, the one device in the logic "1" state experiences a current of 5 V divided by 520 Ω, or about 10 mA. Again this current does not harm 4096 Series outputs.

TIMING CONSIDERATIONS

Timing parameters have various effects on dynamic RAM operation. This section covers important timing characteristics of the 4096 Series devices. Typical 4096 Series timing for Read, Write, and Read/Modify/Write cycles is illustrated by the waveforms in *Figure 13*. A Read cycle allows information stored in the RAM to be retrieved. The data can be read from the RAM in any order desired. A Write cycle accommodates the storage of data in the RAM for future use. As with the Read operation, data can be written into the RAM in any order desired. During a Write cycle, the output is blanked (a logic "1"). A combination of these two cycles results in a Read/Write or Read/Modify/Write cycle, allowing data to be read from the memory, modified by external logic, and then rewritten into the memory. This type of cycle is useful for error correction.

Timing parameters of major interest are listed in *Table 3* and are characterized as to type (forcing functions and device responses). The timing values listed are for the 4096-4 device with an access time of 300 ns. The first parameter listed is Random Read or Write Cycle Time, t_{RC}. Strictly speaking, it is not a forcing function; it is a computed parameter based on other forcing functions. It is calculated with the following equation.

$$t_{RC} = t_{RCL} + t_{CPW} + t_{CRL} + t_{RP} + 3t_T \qquad (13)$$

Clearly, most timing specifications relate to forcing functions. The first three forcing functions in the table, t_{RP}, t_{RCL}, and t_{CPW}, are related to the 2-phase clock timing of 4096 devices. The function t_{RP} is the time required to precharge the dynamic logic on the chip.

Due to an additional feature of 4096 Series devices, gated $\overline{CAS}$, $t_{RCL}(min)$ has been reduced to $t_{AH}(min)$. However, in order to meet the column Address Set-up Time, t_{AS}, $\overline{CAS}$ must be held HIGH until the address multiplexer has stabilized the column addresses. So, $t_{RCL}(min)$ is $t_{AH}(min)$, plus the switching time through the multiplexer, plus the rise or fall time of the address drivers. This rise or fall time depends on the number of addresses driven by one driver (the capacitive load) and the current driving capability of the particular

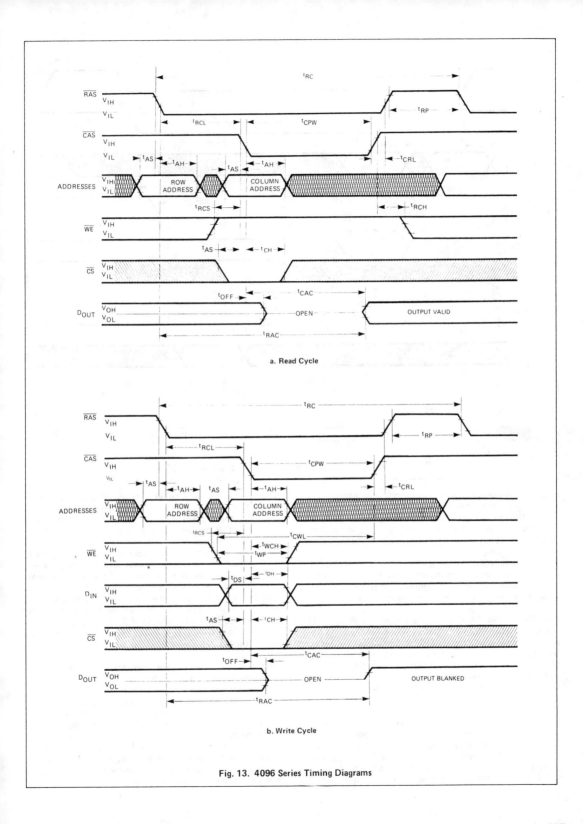

a. Read Cycle

b. Write Cycle

Fig. 13. 4096 Series Timing Diagrams

187

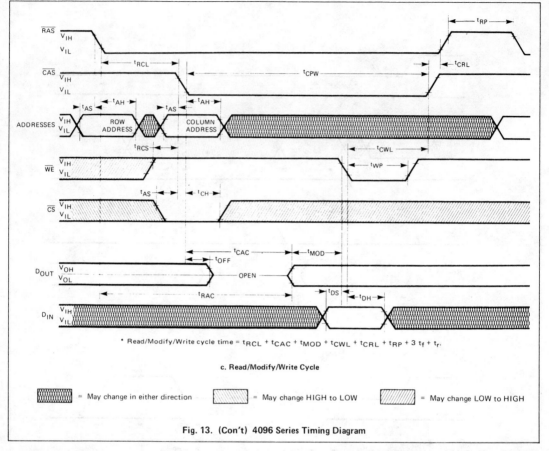

$$* \text{ Read/Modify/Write cycle time} = t_{RCL} + t_{CAC} + t_{MOD} + t_{CWL} + t_{CRL} + t_{RP} + 3\,t_f + t_r.$$

c. Read/Modify/Write Cycle

▨ = May change in either direction   ▧ = May change HIGH to LOW   ▨ = May change LOW to HIGH

Fig. 13. (Con't) 4096 Series Timing Diagram

address driver selected. Allowing for 20 ns to stabilize addresses, 5 ns for each clock transition, and 20 ns delay from the rising edge of $\overline{CS}$ to the rising edge of $\overline{RAS}$, total cycle time for the 4096-4 is 425 ns. The 20 ns value for t_{CRL} is based on noise considerations explained later.

The $\overline{CAS}$ pulse width, t_{CPW}, is a key factor in the minimum logic configuration that accomplishes the 2-phase timing for the 4096 Series. Its role in the timing chain is discussed after some of the more straightforward timing considerations.

Chip Select Hold Time, or t_{CH}, is similar to Address Hold Time, t_{AH}, but Chip Select Hold Time is slightly longer because the chip select latch is slightly slower. The discussion on timing logic illustrates that this difference is immaterial. Chip Select need not be present until the falling edge of $\overline{CAS}$, and this feature allows adequate time for decoding Chip Select from high order addresses without affecting system cycle time or access time.

The next four parameters, t_{RCS}, t_{RCH}, t_{WCH}, and t_{WP}, all deal with the write circuitry. If the present cycle is to be a Read, and the previous cycle was a Write, $\overline{WE}$ must go HIGH no later than the HIGH-to-LOW transition of $\overline{CAS}$ ($t_{RCS} = 0$). Since the write pulse generated internally is the combination of $\overline{WE}$ and $\overline{CAS}$, the Read Command Hold Time specification

prevents spurious write pulses from occurring when changing from a Read cycle to a Write cycle. The Write Command Hold Time guarantees sufficient overlap of $\overline{WE}$ in a LOW state and $\overline{CAS}$ in a LOW state to provide a minimum required internal write pulse. In Read/Write or Read/Modify/Write cycles, the Write Pulse Width, t_{WP}, is the limiting factor. $\overline{WE}$ can be a level; it need not be a pulse. Several successive Write cycles can be performed without changing the $\overline{WE}$ level. Notice that when $\overline{WE}$ goes LOW after the falling edge of $\overline{CAS}$, as in a Read/Modify/Write cycle, the output is not blanked but rather represents data from the addressed cell. The Write Command to Column Strobe Lead Time, t_{CWL}, is another parameter that results from internal generation of the write pulse. Note that it is the same as t_{WP}.

Column to Row Strobe Lead Time, t_{CRL}, is a controversial parameter in that its value is strongly a function of the output latch design. The several versions of the 16-pin 4K RAM differ in this parameter. The output latch is intended to hold data valid until after the falling edge of $\overline{CAS}$ in the next cycle. If a particular application does not use this feature, t_{CRL} becomes less important. Ignoring this specification causes the output latch to be precharged, erasing data. The selected cell, however, is not affected, so violation of the t_{CRL} limit does not cause the RAM to lose data. The timing logic discussion explains how to meet this specification easily.

SYMBOL	PARAMETER	TYPE *	4096-4 MIN	4096-4 MAX	4096-4 TYP **	UNITS
t_{RC}	Random Read or Write Cycle Time	F.F.	425		—	ns
t_{RAC}	Access Time from Row Address Strobe	RESP		300	—	ns
t_{CAC}	Access Time from Column Address Strobe	RESP		175	150	ns
t_{OFF}	Output Buffer Turn-off Delay	RESP	0	90	—	ns
t_{RP}	Row Address Strobe Precharge Time	F.F.	125		75	ns
t_{RCL}	Row to Column Strobe Lead Time	F.F.	70		—	ns
t_{CPW}	Column Address Strobe Pulse Width	F.F.	175		110	ns
t_{AS}	Address Set-up Time	F.F.	0		−15	ns
t_{AH}	Address Hold Time	F.F.	70		30	ns
t_{CH}	Chip Select Hold Time	F.F.	90		30	ns
t_{RCS}	Read Command Set-up Time	F.F.	0		−20	ns
t_{RCH}	Read Command Hold Time	F.F.	40		10	ns
t_{WCH}	Write Command Hold Time	F.F.	140		—	ns
t_{WP}	Write Command Pulse Width	F.F.	175		75	ns
t_{CRL}	Column to Row Strobe Lead Time	F.F.	−20		−50	ns
t_{CWL}	Write Command to Column Strobe Lead Time	F.F.	175		110	ns
t_{DS}	Data In Set-up Time	F.F.	0		−20	ns
t_{DH}	Data in Hold Time	F.F.	130		75	ns
t_{RFSH}	Refresh Period	RESP		2	10	ms
t_{MOD}	Modify Time	F.F.		10	—	μs

* F.F. = Forcing Function, RESP = Device Response

** Typical values indicate the approximate margin between the specified values and actual performance determined by device characterization.

Table 3. Timing Parameters

The largest I_{DD} current spikes occur at the trailing edge of $\overline{RAS}$ and $\overline{CAS}$ (*Figure 8*). The area under the curve of I_{DD} versus time represents the charge required to precharge the dynamic logic. By carefully timing the trailing edges of $\overline{RAS}$ and $\overline{CAS}$, the amplitude of this current spike can be minimized. The optimum value for t_{CRL} is roughly one TTL gate delay (10 − 15 ns). Since the charge required is constant, reducing the amplitude of the I_{DD} spike increases its width, and by-passing requirements are unchanged. However, inductive system noise is a function of the amplitude of the current spike.

$$V_{Noise} = L \frac{di}{dt} \qquad (14)$$

Reducing the I_{DD} spike and increasing its width causes V_{Noise} to vary as the square of t_{CRL} up to the optimum t_{CRL} value. The timing logic discussion shows how an optimum t_{CRL} can be provided.

The Data Set-up and Hold Times define the phase relationship between Data In and the Column Address Strobe and Write Enable signals. During a Write cycle, the Data In latch is strobed by a combination of $\overline{CAS}$ and $\overline{WE}$. During a Read/Modify/Write cycle, the data is set up and held relative to the Write Enable pulse. In interleaved systems where 4K memories are

multiplexed for higher data rates, the theoretical upper limit on the data rate is determined by the minimum data pulse width ($t_{DS} + t_{DH}$).

The refresh interval, t_{RFSH}, is the parameter which dynamic memory systems must meet that static memory systems do not require. This interval is the time during which each cell in the memory must be accessed. The 4096 Series refresh is accomplished 64 cells (one row) at a time. As a result, 64 refresh cycles must be executed in 2 ms to meet the refresh requirement. This requirement implies a 1.6% refresh duty cycle if a refresh cycle is approximately 500 ns.

$$\text{Duty Cycle} = \frac{500 \text{ ns Refresh Cycle}}{2 \text{ ms/64 Refresh Cycles}} = 1.6\% \qquad (15)$$

The refresh interval is a function of cell leakage currents and sense amplifier sensitivity. Worst-case refresh intervals occur, then, at maximum temperature with minimum V_{BB} (−4.5 V) and maximum V_{DD}. Maximum V_{DD} causes worst-case refresh behavior due to a field inversion phenomenon. During normal operation, the MOS transistors on the chip are isolated from each other because the source and drain junctions are reverse biased relative to the substrate. Interconnects are routed over thicker oxide field areas so that parasitic conduction paths are not induced. However, if parasitic conduction paths do occur,

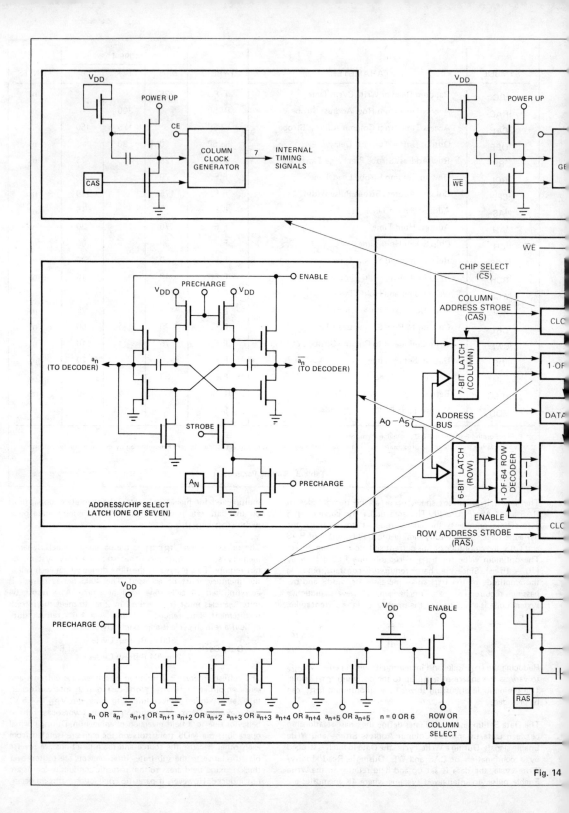

Fig. 14

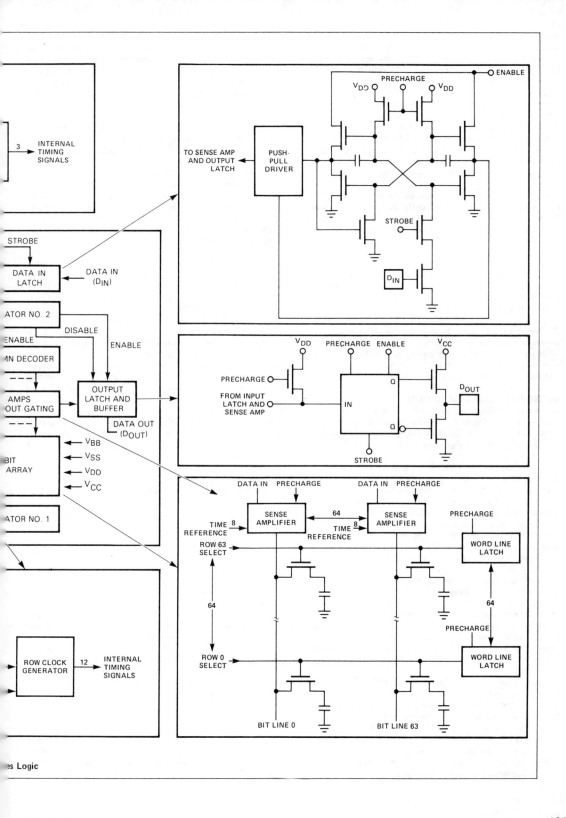

they occur at maximum V_{DD}. This field threshold parameter is at a minimum (worst case) at the minimum V_{BB} in the same manner as V_{TE} is minimized at the minimum V_{BB}. Factors related to leakage current in the refresh interval are worst case at maximum temperature.

Refresh for the 4096 Series can be accomplished in several ways. For example, to minimize timing logic, a normal Read cycle should be used to perform a Refresh cycle. This approach is usually used in systems that use $\overline{CS}$ for selecting chips since all the RAMs can be disabled during a Refresh cycle by leaving $\overline{CS}$ High. The disadvantage of this approach is that all 4K-word pages are dissipating full active power whether selected or not.

Using the decoded $\overline{RAS}$ technique described earlier results in bus contention during a Refresh cycle. Switching V_{CC} to the RAMs, as indicated earlier, prevents this problem. The decoded $\overline{RAS}$ approach results in a slight addition in logic to account for a Refresh cycle that is not exactly the same as a regular memory cycle.

For systems where a refresh duty cycle is critical, using a shortened $\overline{RAS}$-only Refresh cycle can reduce the percentage of time spend refreshing. As mentioned earlier, extra logic is required to accomplish this approach.

The two most common techniques for refreshing the memory involve interleaving Refresh cycles (one Refresh cycle every 31.25 μs) with memory cycles and burst refreshing (64 cycles in a burst every 2 ms). Refer to the Applications Pointers section for some concrete suggestions.

4096 SERIES LOGIC DESCRIPTION

This section describes the various logic blocks in the general block diagram of *Figure 1*. An expanded version of this block diagram including examples of the circuitry used to implement each section is shown in *Figure 14*.

It is obvious that the 4096 Series makes extensive use of dynamic logic techniques in areas other than the memory cells. Using dynamic logic in the periphery of the memory allows a reduction in power consumption without a corresponding reduction in speed. Decoders, latches, sense amplifiers, and cell matrices all use dynamic logic. In fact, the only area that does not use dynamic logic is the TTL/MOS converter used to buffer the clocks, and this circuitry is responsible for a majority of the standby power required (25 mW maximum).

The 4096 Series timing uses dynamic logic techniques extensively, also. In some cases, the precharging sequence of the on-chip logic is critical. Consequently, a significant portion of the timing logic is used for generating precharge signals in the proper order. The 4096 Series uses dynamic MOS buffers to introduce delays producing the proper sequence of signals. *Figure 15* shows the logic structure of the 4096 Series timing chain.

Separate delay chains are used for the $\overline{RAS}$, $\overline{CAS}$, and $\overline{WE}$ signals. The $\overline{RAS}$ delay chain initiates row access to the cell array, and the $\overline{CAS}$ network controls the column access. The $\overline{WE}$ chain is used during Write or Read/Modify/Write cycles only. The Chip Select input ($\overline{CS}$) controls the output latch enable and column address decoder enable signals. The "FX" signal, derived from the $\overline{RAS}$ chain, gates the column decoder enable signal (this is the gated $\overline{CAS}$ feature that reduces the Row to Column Strobe Lead Time, t_{RCL}).

The timing logic generates a complex set of signals with interactions requiring close scrutiny when testing the 4096 Series devices. To guarantee operation over a worst-case temperature range, 4096 Series memories are tested at low as well as high temperatures, because race conditions are most common at low temperatures where MOS gate delays are shortest.

Most of the peripheral circuits in the 4096 Series are driven from the $\overline{RAS}$ clock circuitry. Note, however, that the output and chip select latches are controlled by the $\overline{CAS}$ clock circuitry.

TESTING 4096 SERIES DEVICES

Figure 16 represents the actual layout of a 4096 Series device. The decoder is connected linearly, allowing adjacent cells to have adjacent addresses. This feature eliminates many testing problems that plagued earlier dynamic RAMs; with the decoder connected linearly, 4096 Series access times do not vary significantly with address patterns.

In the past, dynamic RAM design did not consider potential testing problems. No doubt, this was at least partially due to the fact that there was a relatively small number of cells per device. The testing time required for thorough functional testing of devices with 1024 cells or less was small relative to the time required for parametric testing. (Parametric testing time depends on the number of pins per memory package and the number of dc current levels to be measured, and can be lengthy.) As a result, circuit designs were not optimized for minimum functional test times. The expansion of devices to 4096-bit and denser memories has made functional testing time a significant consideration for both the manufacturer and the user.

Recall that the 4096 Series devices have a decoder with a linear structure, reducing access-time related pattern sensitivities. As a result, thorough functional testing is possible without parabolic test patterns.

Because the number of memory cycles required to complete a parabolic pattern depends upon the square of the number of bits, it can become significantly large.

$$\text{Number of Cycles} = an^2 + bn + c \qquad (16)$$
where a, b, and c = pattern-dependent constants,
and n = number of memory bits.

With a 4096-bit memory, more than 16 million cycles are required to perform just one parabolic functional test. Assuming a 2 MHz cycle rate, such a test requires a minimum of eight seconds. Considering the large volume of 4096-bit devices being manufactured and used, parabolic test patterns are prohibitive. Fairchild 4096 Series devices can be thoroughly functionally tested with linear test patterns, a significant time and money saving aspect resulting from considering testing at the design stage. Naturally, this testing-time problem is greatly compounded with larger memory devices, such as 16K RAMs. In fact, testing considerations most likely will delay general use and acceptance of 16K RAMs.

No matter what the size of the RAM, testing is of great importance because the denser semiconductor RAMs are being used to replace core memories, and a great deal of user confidence must be developed. Because of this fact, Fairchild 4096 Series devices are probably the most thoroughly tested commercial grade products presently on the market. Each 4096 Series

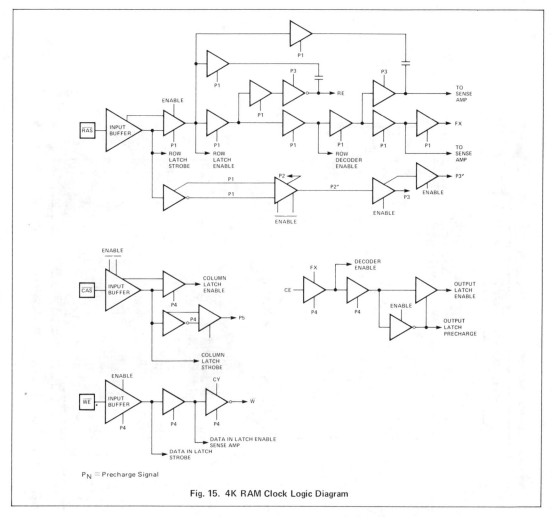

$P_N \equiv$ Precharge Signal

Fig. 15. 4K RAM Clock Logic Diagram

device undergoes 640 functional and parametric tests, plus a functional burn in, before it leaves a Fairchild plant.

Such exhaustive testing requires sophisticated, expensive test equipment. A user desiring to verify the quality of a manufacturer's product by duplicating the manufacturer's testing sequence would have to invest considerable capital.

Obviously, this is not possible, but incoming inspection is necessary. To be effective, incoming inspection should really concentrate on those areas where a device might have been damaged in transit. For example, a simple opens and shorts test on MOS inputs relative to V_{SS} is an effective screen for static damage. This test, combined with an application-oriented functional test should be sufficient. After damaged parts have been eliminated, a system run-in test can be used to insure proper operation at the system level. System run-in testing is the same as system burn-in, except that the temperature used (say 70°C) is less than burn-in temperatures. Also, the address patterns usually more closely match actual system address patterns; often they are identical.

4096 SERIES APPLICATIONS POINTERS

This section describes some basic design techniques for various system design considerations associated with 4K dynamic RAMs. The following topics are covered.

- Refresh Logic
- Address Multiplexing
- Timing Logic
- Power Supply Layout
- Clock Drivers

A typical memory system utilizing 4K dynamic RAMs is illustrated in the block diagram in *Figure 17.*

Refresh Logic

As mentioned earlier, memory refresh represents a major difference between dynamic and static RAMs. In this discussion, a refresh interval of 2 ms for a 4096 Series device using a 64-cycle refresh scheme is assumed. A simplified example of the refresh logic usually required for a dynamic RAM system is shown in *Figure 18.*

193

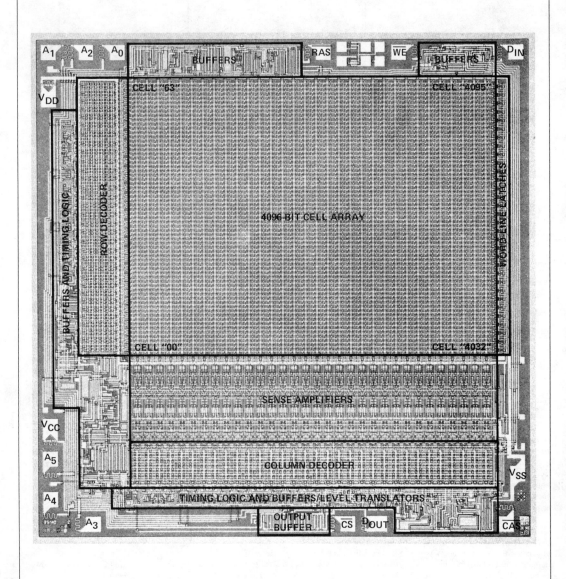

Fig. 16. 4096 Series Chip Layout

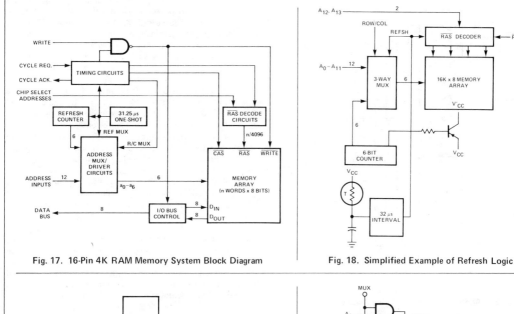

Fig. 17. 16-Pin 4K RAM Memory System Block Diagram

Fig. 18. Simplified Example of Refresh Logic

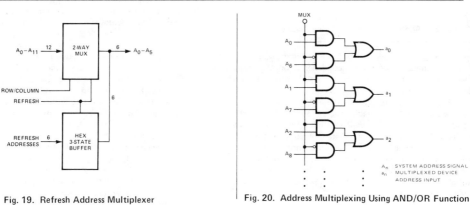

Fig. 19. Refresh Address Multiplexer

Fig. 20. Address Multiplexing Using AND/OR Function

In this case, an interleaved refresh is used. In other words, every 31.25 μs (2 ms ÷ 64 cycles), a Refresh cycle is executed at a specified row address. This timing interval need not be overly precise, so a one-shot can be used to trigger this interval. A thermistor could be used to vary the interval based on local operating temperatures. This approach takes advantage of the exponential relationship between the refresh interval and temperature. Room temperature refresh intervals are roughly 32 times longer than the intervals at 70°C. At 25°C, the refresh duty cycle is reduced to 0.016 ÷ 32, or 0.05%. In order to take full advantage of this approach, a handshaking interface between the control unit and the memory is required. Whenever a Refresh cycle is required, a Busy Flag signals that normal memory cycles have been prevented.

Refresh cycles require address multiplexing. For the 4096 Series, this simply means expanding the address multiplexer to a 3-wide configuration as shown in *Figure 19*.

An alternative to interleaved refreshing is called burst refreshing. As the name implies, burst refreshing executes 64 consecutive Refresh cycles at 2 ms intervals. In applications where a

gap in the data flow occurs, this refresh approach is ideal. If the gap is 32 μs or longer, the RAM refresh can be made transparent to the system.

Refresh transparency is also possible when the address pattern is inherently sequential as in CRT refresh applications. In such cases, if the row addresses are made the lowest order bits in the address word, refresh is automatically accomplished as the data is accessed. Refresh considerations for dynamic memories actually represent a minor expense in most memory systems. As a result, full advantage of the cost benefits of dynamic RAMs is possible without any significant sacrifices at the system level.

Address Multiplexing

Earlier, some common misconceptions concerning the complexity and speed factors of address multiplexing were mentioned. It's time to dispel these notions. One approach to address multiplexing is illustrated in *Figure 20*. The Multiplex signal (MUX) is derived from the clock timing to coincide with minimum Address Hold Time (t_{AH}). Sufficient time must be allowed to drive the address lines with their associated

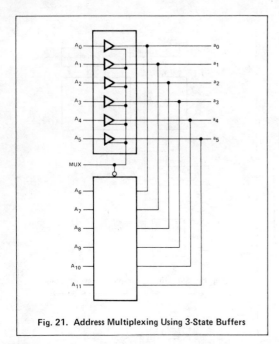

Fig. 21. Address Multiplexing Using 3-State Buffers

capacitance (worst case is 10 pF per Address input). The amount of time actually required depends on the address driver used and the number of 4K RAMs driven by each address driver. *Figure 21* illustrates an alternate approach using 3-state hex buffer circuits. The buffers used have inverted and non-inverted Enable inputs (Fairchild 9647). From a logic standpoint, the AND/OR multiplex function is equivalent to OR-tied buffers with 3-state enable controls. The same number of circuits are required for this buffering/multiplexing operation as are required to simply buffer the 12 address lines for 18 or 22-pin RAM approaches. Address multiplexing, then, is clearly not the problem that the uninitiated have claimed.

Figure 22 is a timing diagram for a typical 4096 Series memory system. The 18 and 22-pin designs require a 2-way multiplex to refresh the memory. The lowest order six memory address lines are switched to refresh once every 31.25 μs (64 rows x 31.25 μs = 2 ms, the refresh period). The same scheme is used in the 16-pin 4K RAM system except that the additional multiplex operation switches between the row and column addresses and back at the times shown in *Figure 22*. If timing is done in this manner, there is no speed penalty for address multiplexing. The next section specifically explains the timing logic required.

Timing Logic
Certain aspects of system timing logic are peculiar to the 2-phase 16-pin 4K RAM and are discussed in this section. Detailed timing information is presented in *Figure 23*. This diagram shows the timing required and the cause/effect relationship between the clock edges and the MUX (multiplex) signal. Two cases are considered.

- Case A — the memory cycle request is a pulse repeated every cycle
- Case B — the cycle request is a dc level.

In Case A, there are only two critical times, t_{AH} (Address Hold Time for the Row Address) and t_{CPW} ($\overline{CAS}$ Pulse Width). A memory cycle request initiates the falling edge of $\overline{RAS}$. At the end of t_{AH}, the timing logic generates the MUX signal to switch the address multiplexer and begins a delay interval for generating the falling edge of $\overline{CAS}$. This delay is equal to the propagation delay through the multiplexer plus the time required for the address to settle. One or two gates could be used to establish this delay. This rise and fall time factor is a function of the number of addresses driven by one driver and the current drive capability of the driver used. After t_{AH}, the next interval is t_{CPW} plus the previously mentioned delay to establish the rising edge of $\overline{CAS}$. This event causes $\overline{CAS}$ to rise, returns the MUX signal to the row address state for the next cycle (since t_{AH} for the column addresses is shorter than t_{CPW}), and causes $\overline{RAS}$ to rise through one or two TTL gate delays. With this approach, the I_{DD} spike is minimized, the t_{CRL} condition is met automatically, and an independent $\overline{RAS}$ pulse width term is not needed, simplifying the timing logic.

Since a new memory cycle request is generated for each cycle, including refresh, a row precharge time signal need not be generated. Notice that this timing logic for a 2-phase 16-pin 4K RAM system is no more complex than the logic required for a single phase 18 or 22-pin approach which requires a Chip Enable pulse width and an Address Hold Time.

In Case B, the only additional timing factor to consider is t_{RP}, because memory cycle request signals are not generated after the first memory cycle. Since the precharge time is required is the same for all speed grades of the 4096 Series ($t_{RP} \cong 2t_{AH}$), generating t_{RP} becomes simple. This precharge time consideration is necessary with 18 or 22-pin approaches in this situation since the $\overline{CE}$ Low time must be generated.

A digital approach to a Case B system is shown in *Figure 24*. This simple circuitry generates all of the 2-phase timing factors required for a 16-pin 4K RAM. An inexpensive Johnson Counter (9319) is used to decode a high frequency clock — in this case — 20 MHz (50 ns resolution). The $\overline{RAS}$, $\overline{CAS}$, and MUX signals are decoded at appropriate intervals. If tighter resolution is required, a higher frequency clock or a one-shot approach can be used. This example is based on a 4096-5 device with a 350 ns Access Time and a 500 ns Cycle Time. The gate delays are structured so $t_{CRL} > 0$, minimizing I_{DD} transients.

The approach illustrated requires a Cycle Request signal to be present through state six of the counter to prevent premature termination of $\overline{RAS}$ or $\overline{CAS}$. If this is not possible, a lockout circuit (*Figure 25*) can be used to maintain the $\overline{RAS}$ and $\overline{CAS}$ signals independent of Cycle Request. In this lockout circuit example, Cycle Request is an active LOW signal.

The 2-phase timing circuitry costs about $2 at the present time and is capable of driving about $100 worth of memory. Clearly, the overhead circuitry is a small cost consideration when using the 16-pin 4K RAM. There are other 4K RAM approaches, however, that require special interface circuits for clock driving that add significantly to the cost.

Power Supplies and Signal Distribution
The dynamic logic circuitry of 4K MOS RAMs places fairly heavy peak current requirements on the +12 V (V_{DD}) power supply. To minimize transient effects, V_{DD} traces on the

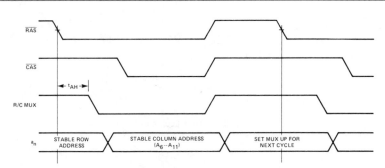

Fig. 22. 4096 Series Address Timing

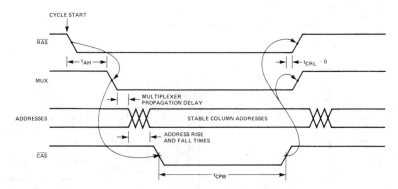

Fig. 23. 4096 Series 2-Phase Timing

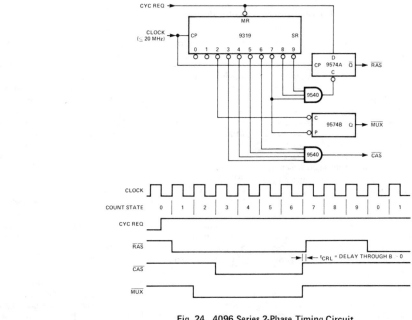

Fig. 24. 4096 Series 2-Phase Timing Circuit

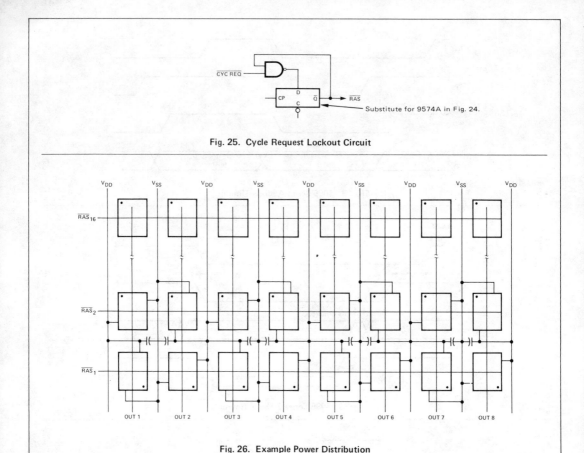

Fig. 25. Cycle Request Lockout Circuit

Fig. 26. Example Power Distribution

printed circuit board should be as large as possible. In multi-layer boards, an entire plane should be devoted to V_{DD}. For 2-layer boards, layout constraints are placed on V_{DD} traces relative to the device selection dimension. For example, if a decoded $\overline{RAS}$ scheme is used to reduce power, the $\overline{RAS}$ line should be perpendicular to the V_{DD} traces. This approach places a minimum current load on each V_{DD} trace, since only two devices on each trace are dissipating full power. The other devices on that trace are either at standby power, or one-half active power. *Figure 26* illustrates such a power distribution structure. For a 64K x 8-bit memory, each V_{DD} trace is required to supply full current to only one of the eight selected devices. For this illustration, it is assumed that a different group of eight 4K RAMs was selected during the previous cycle, and that the remaining 14 devices were in a standby mode (powered down).

Bypass capacitors can be shared by staggering the layout as shown. A 0.02 μF capacitor for every other device provides sufficient V_{DD} bypassing, since the transmission line distances can be kept short.

Clock Signals
Clock signals should also be perpendicular to the address traces to avoid noise coupling. This factor is less important for the 16-pin 4096 Series devices than for the 18 and 22-pin

approaches, because the 4096 Series devices have TTL level clocks. In general, design rules developed for TTL logic systems should be observed when using the 4096 Series. Since the input impedance to the clock lines is extremely high, the clock inputs could be modeled as pure capacitances. Clock drivers must be capable of driving a capacitive load with reasonably fast rise and fall times (0.5 – 1 V/ns). Special clock drivers are not required for the 4096 Series. Standard 7400 series or 74S00 series devices perform quite well for clock and address driving in systems using 4096 Series devices.

SUMMARY
Fairchild 4096 Series devices provide all of the user-oriented features and cost savings required to make them the industry standard 4K RAM. This application note has discussed this device type, its features, characteristics, and made comparisons with other approaches to bulk memory. Hopefully, the mis-givings of users who have not been exposed to the simplicity of using the 4096 Series devices have been removed.

Some specific application suggestions were included to illus-trate the simplicity of using 4K dynamic MOS RAMs. The 4096 Series 4K RAM is paving the way for using the 16,384-bit RAM. Experience gained in using these 16-pin devices will make the transition to the 16K RAMs that much easier.

OPTO-IMAGING

OPTICALLY COUPLED ISOLATORS ISOLATORS COUPLED OPTICALLY

Stu Harris

About three years ago, a semiconductor device known variously as a solid state relay, an opto-isolator, a photon coupler, an optical coupler, or an optically coupled isolator became commercially available. Whatever it is called, this device provides information coupling without physical or electrical contact between the input and the output—through optics. The principal is not new. Simply use a lamp and some form of light detector; that's an optical coupler.

However, a present-day solid state optical coupler in a sealed package, with electrical isolation, almost completely impervious to outside influence, utilizing advanced semiconductor technology, provides designers with a long list of advantages and applications, and open-ended versatility.

Present optically coupled isolators use many combinations of source and sense elements, but basically today's unit employs a light emitting diode (GaAs, GaP, or GaAsP), as the light source and a photo sensitive silicon device such as a diode, transistor, Darlington transistor, or an SCR as the light sensor.

The most appropriate device for a given use must be selected based on the following considerations.

- Switching Time
- Coupling Efficiency
- Current Transfer Ratio
- Voltage Isolation
- Input/Output Capacitance
- Phototransistor Breakdown Voltage
- Cost

In high speed logic systems where the optical coupler is a link to the outside world, switching time is the most important consideration. In applications such as ac power control systems, voltage isolation and the current transfer ratio (CTR) are most significant. CTR is the ratio of input current to output current and is generally less than 20% due to a combination of optical/electrical inefficiencies.

200

WHAT IS AN OPTICAL COUPLER, OR OPTO-ISOLATOR?

Using today's technology, an efficient optically coupled isolator is an infrared LED source placed strategically opposite a photo sensitive silicon detector, in a single, small package. Most opto-isolators come in a DIP, the LED on one side, the detector on the other, with clear, light-transmitting material between them, and a neutral, opaque material around them, providing electrical isolation and protection from ambient light.

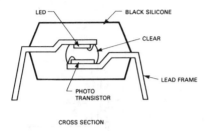

CROSS SECTION

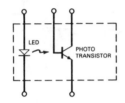

WHAT CAN AN OPTICAL COUPLER DO?

It can obviously perform the function of a relay, the isolation of a transformer, and in some cases provide the coupling of a capacitor. IC optical couplers can provide electrical isolation of up to 4,000 V. However, by separating the light source from the light detector and increasing the distance between them, using fiber optics for light conveyance, there is almost no limit to the amount of voltage isolation possible.

Optical couplers can eliminate feedback, and crosstalk. They can handle dc to MHz frequencies. Generally, they have two modes of operation, digital and linear, i.e., stereo volume control. Used to replace a relay in an explosive atmosphere such as in mining operation, they are the ultimate device because there is no possibility of explosion due to contact spark.

These couplers are fast, with positive action, no interference, have no mechanical action to wear, operate reliably over wide temperature ranges, are compatible with almost all logic, are small, and their cost/performance ratio, already good, is steadily improving. An IC optical coupler can be purchased today for less than one dollar.

Not only can optically coupled isolators improve performance by replacing existing products such as mechanical relays, but they can provide functions previously marginal, such as driving high voltage displays with guaranteed safety for the drive logic, or in medical applications where it is essential to monitor a surgery patient yet eliminate even minute ground-loop current, which could prove fatal.

IT CAN DRIVE SOLENOIDS OR RELAYS

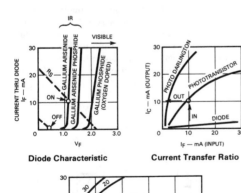

Diode Characteristic

Current Transfer Ratio

Photo Transistor Characteristic

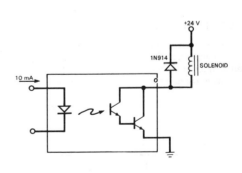

IT CAN TURN OFF AN SCR

Active turn-off gives high dV/dt capability for the SCR, and allows very low LED current to turn on the SCR. Other methods sacrifice one or the other . . . high dV/dt or low turn-on current.

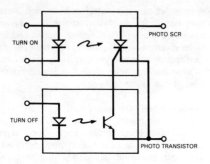

IT CAN SAVE INPUT POWER

An optically coupled isolator replacing a reed relay between the control circuitry and a TRIAC or SCR output of a solid state relay uses only 2 mA @ 3 V to trip the relay. Digital logic is isolated from the ac power line.

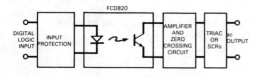

IT CAN ELIMINATE NOISE

As a line receiver, with NO ground return path, an optically coupled isolator *eliminates* ground-loop noise between a remote terminal and a central processor. As of now, maximum frequency is approximately 10 MHz.

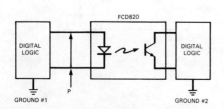

IT CAN DETECT ac/dc SIGNALS

A telephone exchange, for example, can insert a light emitting source in the line to monitor dc current levels. Lifting a handset closes the circuit, drawing power from the telephone 48 V supply, and signaling digital logic elsewhere in the system. Because the LED source has a lower voltage drop than standard relay coils, it can respond to millisecond current interruptions.

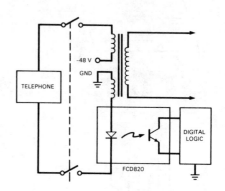

IT CAN CONTROL OUTPUT POWER

A 60 Hz switching power supply is much heavier and much less efficient than, say, a 20 kHz supply. An optically coupled isolator in a linear circuit can regulate output power by simply controlling the pulse width of the chopper transistors. In a given system, more than one optically coupled isolator can be used to feed back data to the chopper circuit.

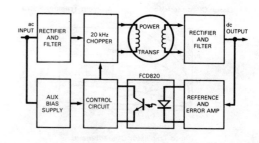

IT CAN LISTEN

Provide audio remote gain control without danger of shock. A log potentiometer allows wide dynamic range; the phototransistor defines the amplifier gain. Low Beta transistors have minimal noise problems, offering "clickless" audio switching.

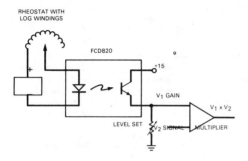

IT CAN READ

Reflective optically coupled isolators can detect either holes in or marks on paper . . . or any similar medium. The limitation is the lens used, and marks or holes as small as 1/16" x 1/16" can be identified.

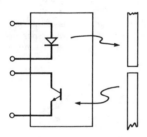

IT CAN TUNE YOUR CAR

Picture an optically coupled slotted isolator and a rotating blade. With conventional high rpm engines, fast optical detectors stand a better chance for accuracy than mechanical or even magnetic systems. Provide temperature protection for approximately 135°C.

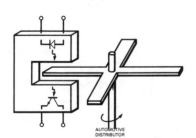

BEWARE

Protect an LED source with a bypass diode if any possibility of reverse current in excess of 1 mA, or reverse voltage in excess of 3 V, exists.

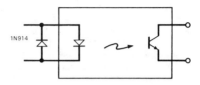

Prevent false triggering of outputs by tying down the base of the phototransistor/detector.

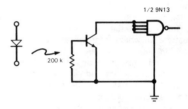

Use a high value base-emitter resistor (10 to 100 M Ω) to measure I_{CEO} with automatic testing because the transistor Beta is very high, at very low current.

Bring voltage up slowly when testing isolation voltage to avoid excessive voltage spikes at turn-on. Once a coupler breaks down, the part is worthless.

Isolated couplers are not the answer to every design problem, but in the areas of speed, reliability, control, noise, testing, and safety, they are easy to use, versatile and quite effective. Optically coupled isolators offer these advantages.

- Easy to use
- Mount readily on PC boards
- Size is compatible with other PC board components
- Impervious to shock and vibration
- High speed
- Long life (no wear)
- Broad temperature and frequency ranges
- Compatible with all existing IC technology
- Low cost

look into them

THE AIR-FILLED LIGHT

by Jeff Griffith

The primary considerations in manufacturing discrete LED digits are reliability, ease of construction, quality of appearance, light intensity and viewing angle. Over the last few years, several techniques have been developed for manufacturing discrete LED digits; each technique optimizes a different set of parameters. As with any process where a number of approaches are possible, discrete digit production presents its own share of trade-offs.

The area of digit production that shows the greatest similarity from one manufacturer to another is the fabrication of the LED dice. LED dice are produced on III-V wafer material using photolithographic and diffusion techniques similar to those used in silicon processing (Figure 1). The III-V material starts with a gallium arsenide (GaAs) substrate on which is grown an epitaxial layer of gallium arsenide phosphide (GaAsP) tailored to give the desired color and light-emission characteristics. After epitaxy, diode junctions are diffused in and aluminum patterns deposited to make electrical contact with the diffused regions. Each die is tested for electrical and brightness characteristics and the entire wafer is scribed and then broken into individual dice.

Although there are some minor differences in LED fabrication methods from one manufacturer to another, it is the assembly technique and material selection used in completing the digit that gives each manufacturer's device a distinctive appearance. Over the last few years, three major techniques have been developed for assembling discrete LED digits.

The oldest technique is the *filled digit*, in which the LEDs are wire bonded to a lead frame. A plastic cover with seven rectangular slots is placed over the lead frame and the entire assembly back-filled with a red translucent diffused-plastic encapsulant. Another technique uses a *pc board* instead of a lead frame to hold the LEDs, segment cover and lens cap.

The third approach is Fairchild's advanced *air-filled light pipe process (Figure 2)*, a newer technique that combines the advantages of substantially lowered manufacturing costs with improved display intensity and appearance. A lead frame provides mechanical support for, and makes electrical contact with, the LEDs. Lead frames are a silver-plated steel alloy that offers excellent die-attach and lead-bond characteristics along with rigid support. The silver protects the frame and improves solderability. After die attach, the entire frame is placed in a mold and encapsulated with a clear optical grade plastic. Magnifying lenses for the LEDs are cast in indentations in the mold surface (Figures 3 and 4).

After encapsulation, a reflector assembly (light pipe) is placed over the die platform. Light pipes are injection molded from an ABS (Acryonitrile Styrene) plastic that

Fig. 1   LED Dice

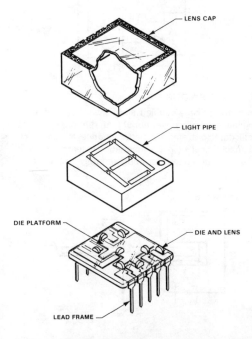

Fig. 2   Light Pipe Digit Construction

PIPE DIGIT

Fig. 4 Magnifying Lens

Fig. 3 Die Platform

contains a reflective compound to increase the brightness of the display. The light pipe contains trapezoidal cavities and is positioned so that the small ends of the cavities are situated directly over the LEDs and lenses. The larger top ends of the cavities have many times the surface area of the LEDs at the bottom. Finally, a lens cap is mounted over the die platform/light pipe assembly and the entire unit sealed. When an LED illuminates, light—in addition to that passing directly from the die to the viewer—is reflected off the sidewalls of the cavities. The light is diffused by a diffusing agent in the lens cap and the reflecting action of the light pipe. The net effect is that much more light reaches the viewer than would be emitted by a digit without a light pipe.

Regardless of the manufacturing technique, all digits need a light-diffusing system to give each segment an evenly lighted appearance. In filled digits, a diffusing chemical is mixed into the encapsulation which then acts as the diffusing surface. PC-board digits have a thin diffusing film mounted in back of the lens cap. The light pipe digit, however incorporates a diffusing agent into the polycarbonate plastic of the lens cap itself. Furthermore, the light pipe acts as a diffuser since it breaks up and scatters the light by reflection. This scattering of the reflected light, combined with the diffusing agent in the lens cap, results in digits that emit light evenly and pleasantly over the entire segment viewing area.

Although the diffusing encapsulant in filled digits is an inexpensive technique, it does cause greater light loss, hence less light reaches the viewer. The diffusing film used in the pc-board technique has better light transmission

qualities, however it is more expensive to assemble. The light-diffusing lens-cap light-pipe combination provides optimum light transmission while simplifying assembly. Polycarbonate was selected as the lens cap material because it offers excellent light transmission along with a high heat-deflection point, chemical resistance and compatibility with the diffusing agent.

Segment-brightness uniformity and digit-brightness levels are an important part of digit manufacturing since even the slightest variation in brightness between segments of a digit or digits in an array is discernable. Therefore, a great deal of attention is given to matching the light output between individual segments of a digit and between one digit and another. Fortunately LED dice in any given area of a wafer all tend to have a very tight light-intensity distribution. Thus, eight adjacent dice can be selected and die attached with a high degree of confidence that they will be of the same brightness level.

After the digits are assembled, they are sent to a test area where each is measured for brightness and placed in one of several closely spaced bins corresponding to its brightness level. Therefore, a tube of digits can be purchased with assurance that all digits in the tube and all segments in each digit are of equal brightness.

Fairchild discrete light pipe digits are available in red, orange and green. For high brightness applications, a special digit is available that has a silver-plated light pipe to maximize the amount of reflected light reaching the viewer.

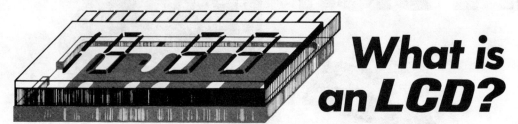

What is an *LCD?*

by Keith Riordan

Liquid crystal displays (LCDs) differ from other types of displays in that they scatter, rather than generate, light. Two basic types are available: reflective, which require front illumination, and transmissive, which require rear illumination. Both types use a field-effect cell that is filled with liquid crystal material.

A liquid crystal material is an organic compound — that is, a compound containing carbon, hydrogen, oxygen, and nitrogen — that has the optical properties of solids and the fluidity of liquids. In the liquid crystal state, which is exhibited over a specific temperature range, the compound has a milky, yellow appearance. At the high end of the temperature range, the milky appearance gives way to a clear liquid. At the low end of the range, the compound turns to a crystalline solid.

The molecules of a liquid crystal compound are in the form of long, cigar-shaped rods. Because of the special grouping of the atoms that form these molecules, the rods act as dipoles in the presence of an electrical field. This characteristic enables the molecules to be aligned in the direction of the electrical field and provides the basis for operation of a liquid crystal display.

FIELD-EFFECT CELL STRUCTURE

A field-effect liquid crystal cell consists of two glass plates, each with a transparent conductive coating, between which the liquid crystal material is sandwiched (*Figure 1*). A thin film of indium oxide — a transparent electrical conductor — is deposited on the top, or front, glass plate. This oxide is patterned to produce a series of 7-segment characters. Each segment has a lead that extends to the long edge of the glass. The bottom, or back, glass plate also has an indium oxide coating, but the pattern is designed as a common electrode that, when the plates are fused, registers to the top glass pattern. The oxide-coated side of both the top and bottom glass plates is entirely covered by an evaporated layer of silicon monoxide dielectric, which produces the desired alignment of the liquid crystal molecules.

After the conductive and dielectric coatings have been applied, the top and bottom plates are fused to within 0.0005 inch by a glass ring that has a 0.05-inch opening on one side. Both plates have a strip of solderable metal — gold over copper over chrome — on the side with the opening. This opening is used to introduce the liquid crystal material into the display envelope, after which the metal strips are soldered to seal the opening.

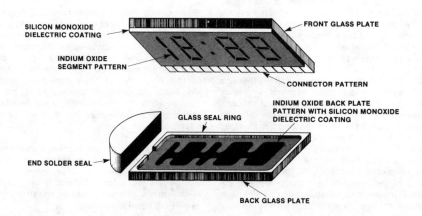

SILICON MONOXIDE
DIELECTRIC COATING

FRONT GLASS PLATE

INDIUM OXIDE
SEGMENT PATTERN

CONNECTOR PATTERN

INDIUM OXIDE BACK PLATE
PATTERN WITH SILICON MONOXIDE
DIELECTRIC COATING

GLASS SEAL RING

END SOLDER SEAL

BACK GLASS PLATE

Fig. 1 Field-Effect Cell Structure

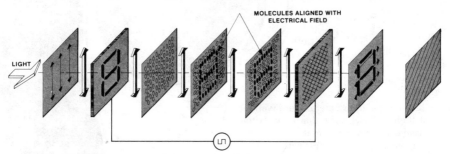

Fig. 2 Unenergized Reflective LCD

(Figure 2 labels: FIELD-EFFECT CELL; INDIUM OXIDE CHARACTER SEGMENTS; INDIUM OXIDE COMMON ELECTRODE PATTERN; LIGHT; A; B; C; D; E; VERTICAL POLARIZER; FRONT GLASS PLATE; LIQUID CRYSTAL MATERIAL; BACK GLASS PLATE; HORIZONTAL POLARIZER; REFLECTOR)

(Figure 3 labels: MOLECULES ALIGNED WITH ELECTRICAL FIELD; LIGHT)

Fig. 3 Energized Reflective LCD

REFLECTIVE LCD OPERATION

A reflective LCD consists of a vertical polarizer, liquid crystal field-effect cell, horizontal polarizer, and reflector (Figure 2). With no voltage applied, the treatment of the liquid crystal cell plates produces a uniform alignment of the crystal molecules. If the front and back plates are mounted at right angles to one another — according to the way in which the crystal molecules line up — a 90-degree rotation, or twist, of the alignment occurs. Vertically polarized light entering the front of the cell (A) follows the rotation of the crystal alignment as it passes through the cell (B, C, D). Having been rotated 90 degrees, the polarized light passes through the horizontal polarizer to the reflector (E). The light is then returned through the cell, again rotating 90 degrees, and passes out of the LCD through the vertical polarizer.

When voltage is applied across one or more of the character segments (Figure 3), the crystal molecules in the area of the segments align themselves with the electrical field. Rotation therefore does not occur in the region of the energized pattern elements. The vertically polarized light conforming to the image produced by these elements cannot pass through the horizontal polarizer but is, rather, absorbed by it. The energized display elements therefore appear as black images against a light background.

TRANSMISSIVE LCD OPERATION

A transmissive LCD consists of a vertical polarizer, field-effect cell, horizontal polarizer, and light source. The light source, which may be of any suitable type, is in the same position as the reflector in a reflective display.

With no voltage applied to the cell, light from the source passes through the horizontal polarizer, is twisted by the cell, and passes out of the LCD through the vertical polarizer at the front of the display. When voltage is applied to the cell, the twist is destroyed in the region of the energized pattern segments. The horizontally polarized light emitted by the source is absorbed by the vertical polarizer, forming the black-on-white image of the energized pattern segments.

A white-on-black effect can be achieved by using two horizontal (or two vertical) polarizers. In this case, light in the area of the energized pattern elements passes through both polarizers while light in the surrounding area is absorbed.

FAIRCHILD LCDs

Fairchild has entered the LCD market with a line of 3 1/2-, 5 1/2-, and 6-digit watch and 8-digit calculator displays. Supported by a major investment in production capacity, the LCD product range will continue to expand as customer needs and desires are identified. □

Device No.	Description	Digit Height (mm)	
		Hour and Minute	Second
FLC3503-1	Lady's 3-1/2 digit	3.3	
FLC3505-1	Man's 3-1/2 digit	4.6	
FLC3505-2	Man's 3-1/2 digit	5.1	
FLC3507-1	Man's 3-1/2 digit	6.7	
FLC5505-1	Man's 5-1/2 digit	5.1	3.6
FLC5505-3	Man's 5-1/2 digit	5.3	3.8
FLC6005-2	Man's 6-digit	4.6	3.1
FLC6005-3	Man's 6-digit	4.5	3.1
FLC8004-1	8-digit calculator	3.5	
FLC8006-1	8-digit calculator	6.0	

picture this camera...

1024-Element Resolution

CCD Sensitivity

Compact Size

Interchangeable Lenses

Computer-Compatible

Low Voltage Requirements

Exposure and Gain Control

Simplicity of Operation

by Dennis Stoscher

Want to know how far it is from here to there without going here and there? Easy! Easy, that is, with the CCD1300 line-scan camera subsystem that includes a small lightweight camera and a sophisticated control unit. Systems using the CCD1300 can measure distances, detect objects and control processes automatically, thus saving labor and reducing errors in repetitive or continuous precision monitoring applications.

Two small units – a camera with timing and signal processing capability and a control unit with video output/data rate control as well as exposure control – do the work for you. And power supplies are included.

HOW?

The camera, not too much larger than half a carton of cigarettes, covers the entire visible range and the near-infrared with a dynamic range of up to 200:1. The control unit provides both analog and digital video output control, video data rate control ranging from 150 kHz to 10 MHz, and automatic exposure control independent of power fluctuations and interference.

The camera, which weighs less than 1.7 pounds, contains a 1024-element CCD linear image sensor, a timing control module, a signal processing module, and can be fitted with a variety of standard lenses. It connects to the control unit by cable, allowing remote placement of the camera. Lenses available include 13, 25, 50, and 75 mm interchangeable C-mount types and a 15 to 150 mm zoom lens. Precise measurement and sensing of optical data make the unit ideal for accurate non-contact measurement, facsimile sensing, velocity measurement, surface flaw detection, shape recognition sorting, and similar optical sensing functions.

SENSING

In operation, the 1024-element line-scan array in the camera senses a line of optical information and produces an analog waveform proportional to the brightness of the optical image. When the application involves motion, a series of line scans can be generated, producing a complete picture.

Because the unit has ultra-low light-level sensitivity, almost any light source can be used – incandescent, fluorescent, LED, or even sunlight. In many applications, standard fluorescent lighting is perfectly adequate if high intensity is not required. With moving objects, intensity requirements increase as the speed of the object increases.

CONTROL

Three principal functions are provided by the camera control unit – video-output control, video data-rate control and exposure control. In addition, the control unit can accept input from a microprocessor or computer, thus permitting external control of the camera system. Fixed or automatic gain is selected by a front-panel switch and an automatic gain control voltage terminal is provided for further signal processing. Automatic gain control is useful for signal compensation in situations such as aging of the light source or variations in object color (as when scanning facsimile documents). Digital quantizing of the video output signal over the complete signal range is accomplished by a binary

LINE SCAN CAMERA, MODEL CCD1310

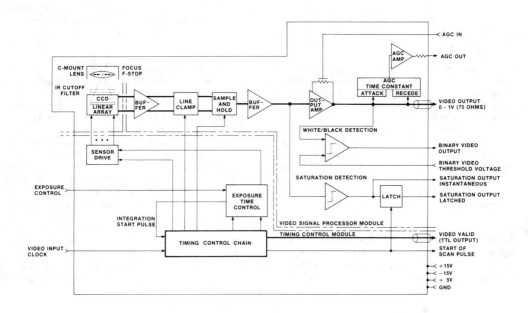

CONTROL UNIT, MODEL CCD1320

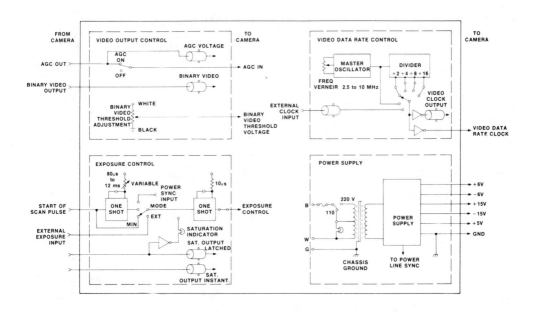

video threshold-adjustment potentiometer. Also, a TTL-level binary video-output signal is conveniently provided at the front panel.

Video data rate is controlled by a clock oscillator. Continuous frequency adjustment from 150 kHz to 10 MHz is accomplished with a 6-position switch and a Vernier potentiometer. The camera can be synchronized with an external system via a TTL-level external-clock input on the front panel.

Two exposure modes are possible — synchronous and asynchronous. In the synchronous mode, the exposure is controlled by the camera-control unit or by a computer. In the asynchronous mode, exposure is controlled by the camera. In addition, the camera-sensing subsystem can be synchronized with the power line. This means that when the light source is ac powered, no amplitude modulation by the light source appears on the video output signal. Many exposure-time selections are possible in the "variable" mode, with the minimum exposure time set by the video line rate and a maximum exposure time of 12 ms.

Power to the camera is provided by an internal power supply in the control unit. The control unit itself operates on 110 or 220 V ac, 50–440 Hz power. Selection of the power option is by a switch on the unit.

PUTTING IT TO WORK

Whether the application is document scanning, industrial inspection, surveillance, spectroscopy, microscopy or precision measurement, the line-scan camera subsystem is a powerful scanning and recognition tool. Coupled with a computer or microprocessor, it becomes even more powerful. An example of this capability is a currency sorter that not only recognizes the denomination but also determines the quality of the bills.

As each back-lighted bill is sensed by the camera, it is compared to a digital representation of the desired bill that has been stored in the microprocessor memory. The digital representation is synchronized with the image of the unknown bill on the transport. When the camera video output and the microprocessor output match, the appropriate binning control is activated to place the currency in the proper sorting bin. If for any reason a match cannot be determined, the binning control simply selects a reject category. With the software flexibility of a microcomputer, it is simply a matter of proper programming to recognize currency quality as well as denomination. This approach is readily adaptable to search for defects in a large population of objects. By implementing object viewing masks in the microprocessor, selection of certain fields of optical information on the object is possible and only these fields are processed. Other areas of the object are ignored.

CURRENCY SORTER

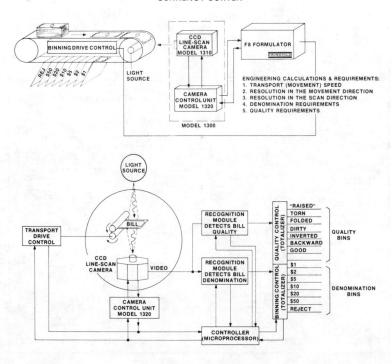

Another interesting application for the line-scan camera subsystem, precision object measurement, uses standard fluorescent lighting, is easy to align and maintain, and is self calibrating for both length measurement and light level. Two line-scan cameras are used. They are positioned farther apart than the length of the longest object to be measured, and the distance between the cameras is measured. A known reference length is established in the viewing range of the cameras. In this particular set up, the bottom edge of the object is sensed to eliminate the effects of varying diameters or thicknesses. A good black/white transition is required between the background and the object. Each camera senses the edge in its viewing area and the video output of each camera is sent to a counter with BCD output. Because there is a known reference length (LT), the distance from each reference edge to the black/white transition can be determined by the cameras. By subtracting these distances (L1 and L2) from LT, the length of the object is known. A programmable calculator may be used to make corrections for lens magnification. This approach can be adapted to make area or volume measurements in addition to length measurements. Systems that determine gap, thickness, or position as well as correction systems can be developed in a similar fashion by using the camera(s) as a feedback sensor to some type of system controller. Write for data on the new CCD1300 line-scan camera subsystem.

LENGTH MEASUREMENT

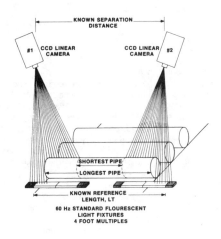

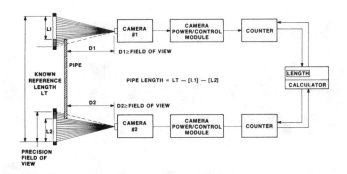

Fast Sorting with CCD

by Howard Murphy and Joe Rothstein

Charge-coupled imaging devices, introduced in the early 1970's, have been designed into a myriad of industrial applications. These range from sophisticated scientific optical instruments for use in research laboratories to rugged industrial inspection systems for steel, lumber, and glass mills; from facsimile and OCR scanning systems to miniaturized low-light-level television cameras; and from precision geometric instrumentation to simple object counting systems. In many of these applications, the CCD image sensor is used as a functional replacement for components manufactured using older technologies, e.g., the Vidicon tube in a TV camera. CCD sensors offer significant advantages — wider dynamic range, broadened spectral response, low voltage and low power operation, monolithic solid-state reliability, high operating speeds and precise geometric accuracy.

On the other hand, CCD technology is creating solutions to engineering problems that seemed almost impossible to solve economically in the past. Camera systems using CCD line-scan image sensors are being used for non-contact measurement, inspection, defect detection, shape and pattern recognition, color sorting, and for a wide variety of quality process-control industrial applications. The self-scanning feture makes this system ideal in a large variety of industrial applications in which the object or material to be inspected is in motion or is being moved by a conveyor belt or other mechanism. The sensor provides scanning along one axis of the object while object motion provides scanning in the other. The use of fully automatic optical inspection systems enhances productivity by improving quality control in automated manufacturing processes.

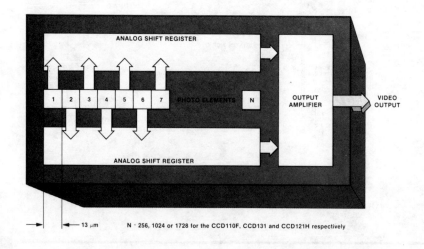

N · 256, 1024 or 1728 for the CCD110F, CCD131 and CCD121H respectively

Fig. 1   Linear Image Sensor Block Diagram

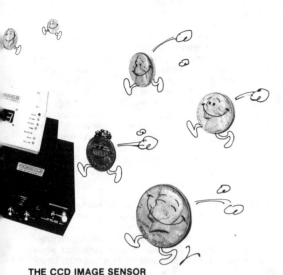

THE CCD IMAGE SENSOR

The essence of a line-scan system is, of course, a line-scan sensor. In a typical CCD sensor *(Figure 1)*, a row of 13 μm-square photosites is formed within a monolithic silicon chip, at present, either 256, 1024, or 1728 photosites in a row. The photosites detect light from the object and accumulate charge packets of electrons that are directly proportional to the light intensity. The packets, representing information, are periodically transferred to the adjacent analog shift registers, and are then transported out of the CCD as a serial analog-video data stream, controlled by external clock signals.

CCD LINE-SCAN CAMERA SUBSYSTEMS

There are presently three models of line-scan camera subsystems—the 256-element CCD1100, the 1024-element

CCD1300, and the 1728-element CCD1400. The choice among them is determined primarily by resolution requirements, since each camera model offers essentially equivalent performance in other respects. The line-scan camera can be ordered equipped with a C-mount lens with a focal length to meet the specific application.

Each camera subsystem includes a line-scan camera, a camera-control unit and interconnecting cables. Within the camera is a CCD image sensor, a logic board to provide clock signals for controlling sensor operation, and a video processing assembly to generate an analog-video and a binary-video output signal. The analog-video signal is a continuous analog representation of the spatial distribution of image brightness, obtained by sample-and-hold processing of the raw sensor output. The binary-video output, provided by a comparator, is a digital version of the analog video waveform and corresponds to black-to-white and white-to-black transitions of the analog-video signal across the threshold. The threshold adjustment can be varied across the full dynamic range of the camera.

The camera-control unit provides the power supply voltages and interface connections for the subsystem input and output signals. It also contains the adjustment controls for camera exposure time, video data rate, the threshold voltage for the binary-video comparator, and an AGC off-on switch.

AN APPLICATION EXAMPLE—COIN SORTER

When a CCD camera subsystem is combined with the versatile microprocessor, the result is a powerful metrology system that includes an internal decision-making capability. This dynamic combination can best be illustrated by describing a simple system such as a coin sorter; the concepts can readily be extended to solve more complex industrial problems. The basic operating principle of the coin sorter *(Figure 2)* is the optical measurement of the diameter of an unknown object, and comparison of the measured diameter to a diameter-limit table for six denominations of U.S. coins.

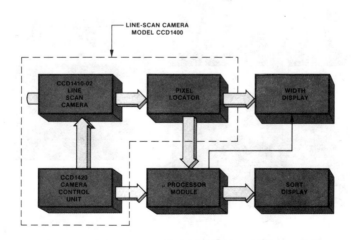

Fig. 2 Optical Sorting System

A CCD1400 line-scan camera subsystem measures the back-lighted opaque objects which are transported past the camera by a conveyor mechanism — a gravity-powered slide. The image sensor within the camera has 1728 photosites spaced along an active channel length of 0.884". The camera is equipped with a 50-mm focal-length lens and provides a scanned line length of 1.728" across the coin slide at a lens-to-object working distance of 5.8". Each sensor photosite, or pixel, thus senses the brightness of a 0.001"-square area in the object plane; the total image sensing array detects the spatial distribution of brightness across a 1.728"-long scan line which is 0.001" wide in the axis of object motion. The length of the scan line covered by the camera could, of course, be set to any desired width by selecting different lens focal length and working distance; the available resolution in this particular camera would remain 1728 pixels per scan line under any condition.

The maximum velocity of objects moving past the camera is assumed to be 20 ips. The smallest object of significant interest to the coin-sorter system is a U.S. dime with a diameter of 0.7". Hence a dime will travel by the camera in approximately 35 ms. It seems reasonable to ask that the system check the width of each object at least 100 times as it passes the inspection station, thus requiring the camera to provide 100 scan-line readouts in 35 ms. This defines a $350 \mu s$ exposure time which, in turn, requires a video data rate of about 5 MHz per pixel. These conditions are comfortably within the normal operating range for the CCD line-scan camera, although they are considerably faster than can be achieved by other technologies. Exposure-time and data-rate adjustments can be made by front panel controls on the camera-control unit.

The binary video output of the camera is a HIGH TTL-compatible signal for a readout of pixels that detect an image brightness above an adjustable threshold level; it is a LOW signal during the readout of pixels detecting less than the threshold brightness value. Therefore, the binary video output for this system is HIGH for scan-line locations that are not shadowed by coins and LOW when coins interrupt light transmission.

A counter in the pixel-locator accessory (Figure 3) provides a bit-parallel data stream to indicate which of the 1728 sensor pixels in the camera are supplying data at the moment. As video transitions from white to black and black to white occur, the edge detector, driven by the binary video output, strobes the pixel addresses into a FIFO buffer memory. These addresses then become available at the FIFO output as latched parallel 15-bit words to be used by the microprocessor portion of the system for dimensional analysis. When an object enters the camera's field of view, two address words are stored in the FIFO during each scan line; the first indicates the pixel address of the left edge of the object and the second word indicates the address for the right edge.

A FIFO buffer memory used as a data interface between the camera and data processor permits asynchronous operation of the two portions of the system. The camera is running at a 5-MHz data rate with a $350 \mu s$ exposure time to achieve a high density of scan lines across the smallest object, while microprocessors are typically restricted to clock rates below 1 MHz and require two-to-six clock cycles per arithmetic operation. The pixel-locator accessory, designed for use in camera-microprocessor interface applications, is equipped with an optional hand-shake I/O capability for ease of system design and control.

The 8-bit microprocessor hardware used for the coin-sorter camera system (Figure 4) includes an F6800 MPU, a 256-byte RAM, and a PROM that stores a development program called JBUG. Capability for audio tape I/O is included in the JBUG

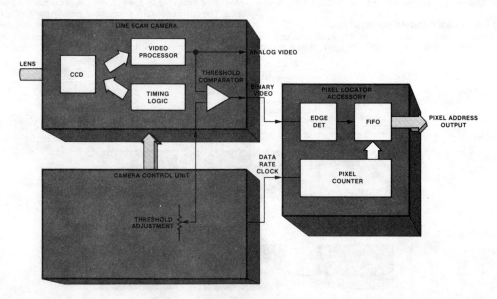

Fig. 3   CCD1400 Camera Configuration Using Pixel Locator Accessory

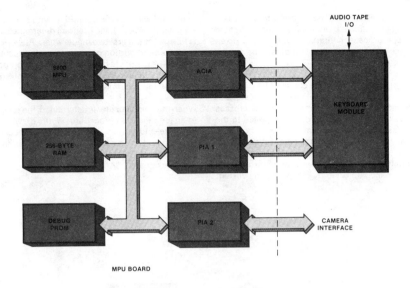

Fig. 4   Microprocessor Hardware

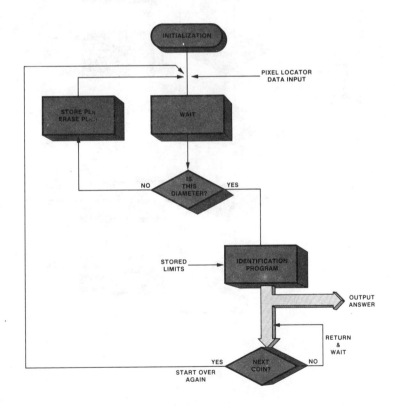

Fig. 5   Microprocessor Software

program and hardware. An F6820 peripheral interface adaptor with two 8-bit bidirectional I/O ports is also used. Eight of the lines are microprocessor inputs, driven by the pixel-locator output; the other eight lines are outputs to the display from the coin-sorter program.

As a coin (or slug) moves through the camera's field of view, the measured dimension is a chord with a width that starts at zero pixels and increase until the camera scan line crosses the center of the coin. Dimensional data is supplied to the microprocessor as 8-bit address words at the end of each camera scan-line readout. After system initialization (Figure 5), the microprocessor follows a compare-and-branch procedure to determine when the camera scan is through the coin center. This is accomplished by comparing the current measured width of the coin (PL_N) with the preceding measured width (PL_{N-1}); the program determines that a diameter is PL_{N-1} for the first two inputs where $PL_N < PL_{N-1}$. The first measurement portion of the program is executed faster than the 350-μs exposure time, hence, the microprocessor spends most of its time in a loop waiting for an interrupt indicating that new input data is ready.

When the coin diameter is determined, the program branches to an identification procedure (Figure 6), which is a series of compare-and-branch instructions. The measured diameter is compared to low and high specification limits that were supplied to the microprocessor during initialization and stored in designated RAM addresses.

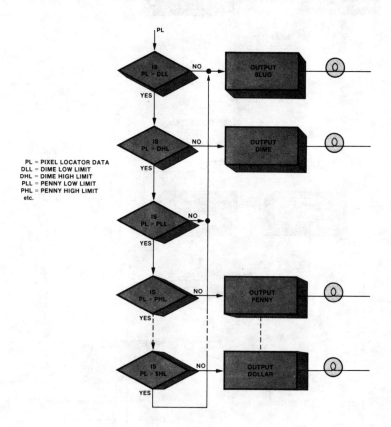

PL = PIXEL LOCATOR DATA
DLL = DIME LOW LIMIT
DHL = DIME HIGH LIMIT
PLL = PENNY LOW LIMIT
PHL = PENNY HIGH LIMIT
etc.

Fig. 6   Identification Program

If the measured diameter (PL) is less than the low limit specified for a dime (DLL), the program outputs a "1" on a bit line which drives the SLUG indicator light. If DLL < PL < DHL (high limit for dime), the program outputs a bit on another line to illuminate a DIME indicator. If DHL > PL > PHL (high limit for penny), the system signals the SLUG indicator. This procedure is repeated through the high spec for a silver dollar ($HL). The program then enters another wait loop until PL goes to zero, which indicates that the analyzed object has moved completely past the camera inspection line.

The microprocessor is dealing with 8-bit pixel addresses which provide adequate resolution for coin identification. The 1728-element camera resolution is represented in the pixel locator as 13-bit BCD numbers. A full-resolution digital display of measured-object diameters *(Figure 7)* is driven by the pixel-address output. The strobe input to the display-circuit latches is controlled by the microprocessor so that the display continuously shows the measured diameter of the last object analyzed.

CONCLUSION
The coin-sorter system is a simple example of the broad potential of the line-scan camera/microprocessor combination. Actually, modern vending machines require considerably more complex analytical ability to foil users of washers, slugs and counterfeit coins. However, these simple principles of system design and operation can be adapted for sorting rapidly moving items, e.g., oranges, apples, and other fruit and vegetables, by size, in a food-processing plant. With a little more microprocessor programming, nuts, washers, and other mechanical components could be sorted in a hardware manufacturing plant.

The system can be generalized into a two-dimensional inspection capability by using a more complex set of microprocessor software and a larger RAM storage capacity. Also, the system can be made "self-educated", i.e., the high and low limits of the diameter widths could be derived by measuring a statistical sample as it passes the inspection station, as opposed to having the limits supplied by the operator.

The coin-sorter system design exploits the high-speed capability and excellent optical sensitivity of the CCD image sensor combined with the flexibility of the CCD-camera subsystem. A key requirement for all non-contact inspection-system designs is the precise dimensional accuracy inherent in CCD image sensors. In addition, CCD imaging devices offer wide dynamic range, linearity, and low light-level operation.

The relatively detailed consideration given to the overall design of this simple system should provide an appreciation of the exciting potential that optical inspection systems have in modern manufacturing operations.□

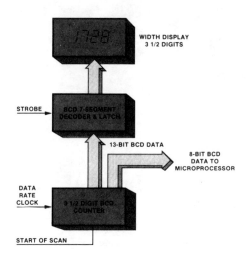

Fig. 7 Measured-Width Display System

LINEAR

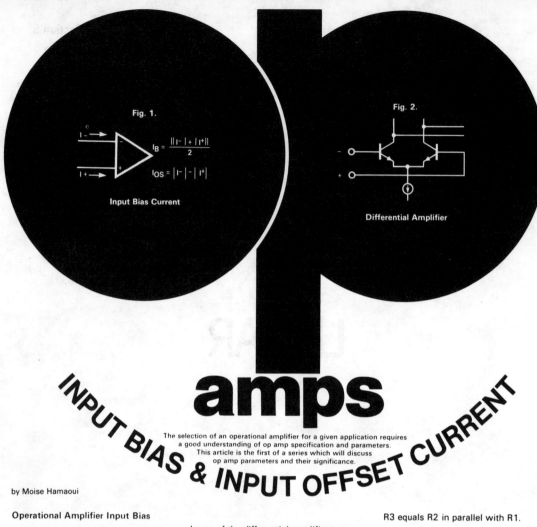

Fig. 1.

$$I_B = \frac{\|I^-\| + \|I^+\|}{2}$$

$$I_{OS} = |I^-| - |I^+|$$

Input Bias Current

Fig. 2.

Differential Amplifier

amps

The selection of an operational amplifier for a given application requires a good understanding of op amp specification and parameters. This article is the first of a series which will discuss op amp parameters and their significance.

INPUT BIAS & INPUT OFFSET CURRENT

by Moise Hamaoui

Operational Amplifier Input Bias

Input bias current probably affects all applications of operation amplifiers. All applications are not included here, of course, but the problems caused by input bias current are usually the same, and the same derivations (hopefully) should apply.

In order for op amps to operate properly, it is necessary to supply a certain dc current (typically from pA to µA) at each input. Input bias current is the *average* of the two input currents *(Figure 1)*. Input offset current (I_{OS}) is the *difference between* the two input currents *(Figure 1)*.

What Causes Input Bias Current?

The input stage of an op amp is ordinarily some type of differential amplifier with a dc current source which sinks current from the emitters *(Figure 2)*. The inputs to the op amp which feed the

bases of the differential amplifier transistors must supply the base current. This base current is the input bias current. It is primarily a function of the large signal current gain of the input stage (B). Input offset current is usually caused by mismatch of the differential amplifier, which results in different input bias currents for the two inputs.

How Does Input Bias Current Affect Applications?

The output offset voltage due to bias current for both inverting and non-inverting amplifiers is the same *(Figure 3)*. *Equation 1* shows derivation (also see *Figure 4*).

$$V_{offset} = I_{B1}R2 - I_{B2}R3 \left(1 + \frac{R2}{R1}\right) \quad (1)$$

For inverting and non-inverting operation, R3 is selected to minimize output offset without affecting gain.

R3 equals R2 in parallel with R1.

$$R3 = \frac{R1\,R2}{R1 + R2} \quad (2)$$

Substituting *Equation 2* for *Equation 1*

$$V_{offset} = (I_{B1} - I_{B2})\,(R2) \quad (3)$$

$$V_{offset} = I_{OS}\,R2 \quad (4)$$

For R3 = 0

$$V_{offset} = I_B R2 \quad (5)$$

NOTES:

(a) For the inverting configuration it is usually simple to make R3 equal to R1 in parallel with R2, which reduces the output offset voltage to only $I_{OS}R2$. If, however, the application doesn't require very low output offset voltage, or if the input bias current I_B is very low, make R3 = 0 and the output offset is simply $I_B R2$. Therefore, it is wise to

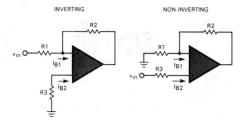

Fig. 3. Output Offset Voltage

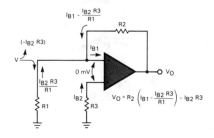

$$V_O = R_2 \left(I_{B1} - \frac{I_{B2}\ R3}{R1} \right) - I_{B2}\ R3$$

Fig. 4. Output Offset Voltage

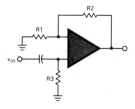

Fig. 5. AC Amplifier

first calculate the output offset voltage produced by the op amp assuming R3 = 0 (I_BR2). If this offset is low enough for the application, the use of one resistor is saved. If the offset is too high, add R3 to the circuit and then calculate offset (I_{OS} R2) to see if it meets your specification.

(b) In the non-inverting configuration, R3 is part of the signal source impedance and, in some cases, that source impedance is not well known and this complicates the minimizing of the output offset. If the source impedance is known to be very low, then a known series resistor can be added to make R3 = R1/R2. The limiting factor for increasing the value of this resistor is the op amp input impedance. If a high value of resistor is used, say 1 MΩ , and the amplifier input impedance is around 9 MΩ in the frequency range of interest, the result is a 10% drop in signal gain.

(c) Never forget the need for a dc current path to the op amp inputs. If the op amp is used in an ac amplifier as shown in *Figure 5*, notice that R3 is required to provide a dc current path to the non-inverting input. Without R3, the circuit just doesn't work! R3 is also necessary if the source can't supply the bias current.

(d) A fixed offset is not usually much of a problem and extra input circuitry may be added to cancel it. It is usually the *drift* of the offset with temperature, time, etc., which causes problems. Therefore, once an op amp with acceptable output offset voltage is found, it is necessary to investigate the offset change as a function of temperature voltage, supply, time, etc., and assure that it won't cause problems in a particular application. Most data sheets give input bias current and offset current as functions of temperature, supply voltage, and time, and also provide temperature dependance curves.

Where Does Input Bias Current Affect Applications?

Input bias current comes into effect in circuits where op amps act as buffers or amplifiers with a charged capacitor as a source. Because of input bias current, the charge across the capacitor starts draining even if the op amp input impedance is very high. Two examples are shown in *Figures 6* and *7*.

The sample and hold circuit shown in *Figure 6* consists of a voltage v_{in} which charges a holding capacitor C. When the electronic switch opens, the capacitor is expected to hold the voltage v_{in}, and the op amp simply acts as a buffer. The output of the op amp, therefore, should hold the value of v_{in} at the level it was when the switch opened for as long as the switch remains open. Because of bias current and other leakage, however, the held voltage gradually changes. This voltage changes at the following rate.

$$\frac{\Delta V}{\Delta t} = \frac{I}{C} \qquad (6)$$

where I is input bias current plus other leakages

Equation 6 determines how long a held voltage remains within specified accuracy of its original value. In this sample and hold application, the effect of input bias current shows in the holding time. For example, if the capacitor C = 1 μF, and the maximum permissible change of voltage ΔV is 10 mV, using a μA741 (I_B = 0.5 μA) and neglecting other leakages, the holding time is expressed as follows.

$$\Delta t = \frac{C \Delta V}{I} = \frac{1 \times 10^{-6} \times 10 \times 10^{-3}}{0.5 \times 10^{-6}} = 20 \text{ ms} \qquad (7)$$

With a μA740, (I_B = 300 pA) a better holding time results.

$$\Delta t = \frac{C \Delta V}{I} = \frac{10^{-6} \times 10 \times 10^{-3}}{300 \times 10^{-12}} = 33.3 \text{ s} \qquad (8)$$

Low input bias current is not the only criterion for sample and hold buffers, offset voltage drift is another important parameter.

Equation 6 also applies in circuits where the voltage held is across a capacitor in a feedback loop, *(Figure 7)*.

Another application where input bias current plays a role is in current-to-voltage conversion, *(Figure 8)*.

The causes and effects of input bias current have been briefly discussed. A few examples of applications where input bias current is important have been illustrated. Input offset voltage, also a factor, will be discussed in a future article.

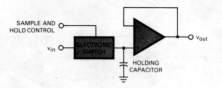

Fig. 6. Sample and Hold

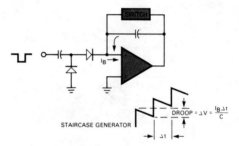

Fig. 7. Staircase Generator

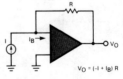

$$V_O = (-I + I_B) R$$

Fig. 8. Current-to-Voltage Conversion

op amps

INPUT OFFSET VOLTAGE

This is the second in a series of articles discussing op amp parameters and their significance. Last month the cause and effects of input bias and input offset current was the subject. Input offset voltage is a natural continuation of the series

by Moise Hamaoui

What is Input Offset Voltage?

Input offset voltage is the magnitude of the voltage that, when applied between the inputs of the op amp, gives zero output voltage. This means that, even without applying a signal across the inputs of the op amp, a dc voltage difference exists between the inputs which is amplified and causes the output to be at a non-zero value. When a voltage is applied across the inputs of the op amp such that it gives zero output voltage, the initial input offset is cancelled. Therefore, the applied voltage is of the same magnitude as the initial input offset but of opposite polarity.

What Causes Input Offset Voltage?

Well, essentially every mismatch between the signal flow of the inverting input and the non-inverting input contributes to input offset voltage, V_{OS}.

The major contributor, however, is the V_{BE} mismatch of the differential input stage. V_{OS} is generally in the 1 to 10 mV range for non-FET input op amps.

How Does Offset Voltage Affect Applications?

For inverting and non-inverting amplifier applications (Figures 1 and 2), the output voltage has a dc output level due to V_{OS}. Output voltage offset is given by

$$V_O = V_{OS} \left(1 + \frac{R2}{R1}\right) \qquad (1)$$

and derived from the following (See Figure 3).

Input bias current = 0

$$I_1 = \frac{V_{OS}}{R1} \qquad I_2 = I_1 \ (I_{Bias} = 0)$$

$$V_O = I_2 R2 + I_1 R1$$

$$V_O = I_1 (R2 + R1)$$

$$V_O = \frac{V_{OS}}{R1} (R2 + R1)$$

Remember that the output offset voltage given in *Equation 1* is caused only by the input offset voltage, V_{OS}. The last article explained the output offset voltage caused by the input bias and offset current. The total output offset voltage is thus given by the sum of the two offsets.

Total dc output offset, $\qquad$ (2)

$$V_O = \left(1 + \frac{R2}{R1}\right) V_{OS} + I_{B1} R2 - I_{B2} R3 \left(1 + \frac{R2}{R1}\right)$$

For $R3 = \dfrac{R1 \ R2}{R1 + R2}$

$$V_O = V_{OS} \left(1 + \frac{R2}{R1}\right) + I_{OS} R2$$

where I_{OS} is the input offset current.

For R3 = 0
$$V_O = V_{OS} \left(1 + \frac{R2}{R1}\right) + I_{Bias}\, R2$$

Here are some examples that will give an idea of the range of values discussed.

For a gain of 10 in an inverting configuration,
R2 = 100 kΩ R1 = 10 kΩ R3 = 9 kΩ

Using µA741C,
$V_{OS(max)}$ = 6 mV
$I_{OS(max)}$ = 200 nA
Output Offset = 86 mV max

Using µA777,
$V_{OS(max)}$ = 2 mV
$I_{OS(max)}$ = 3 nA
Output Offset = 22 mV max

Using µA740C,
$V_{OS(max)}$ = 110 mV
$I_{OS(max)}$ = 0.3 nA
Output Offset = 1.2 V max

Keep in mind, however, that the input offset voltage and current vary with temperature and this is usually the most objectionable factor of those offsets. Most op amp data sheets give input offset voltage values and temperature dependance curves.

Offset Voltage Nulling

In some op amps, offset voltage may be nulled with only an external potentiometer to two device leads *(Figure 4)*. Usually what is happening internally is that one side of the input stage differential amplifier gets more or less current than the other side and thus causes a V_{BE} difference to null the initial V_{BE} mismatch.

Where Else Does Input Offset Voltage Affect Applications?

If V_{OS} is considered as a small dc voltage source connected to an ideal op amp *(Figure 5)*, its effect can be analyzed in almost every application. From *Figure 5*, it is apparent that in comparator applications, the output does not vary state until the inverting input is at least a V_{OS} different than the non-inverting input. That is, if a zero crossing detector is being designed and the non-inverting input is connected to ground, the output would change states at a V_{OS} voltage different than ground.

Hopefully, this discussion will help the designer choose the best op amp for a given application. Future articles will discuss such important parameters as open loop voltage gain, slew rate, input resistance, etc.

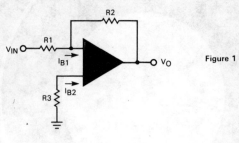

INVERTING

Figure 1

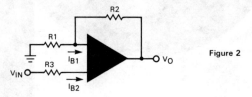

NON-INVERTING

Figure 2

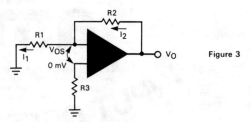

Figure 3

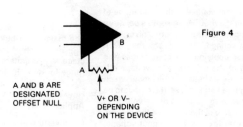

Figure 4

A AND B ARE DESIGNATED OFFSET NULL

V+ OR V– DEPENDING ON THE DEVICE

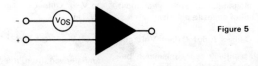

Figure 5

op amps

Our discussion series of op amp parameters and their significance in particular applications continues with a look at open loop voltage gain as a function of frequency.

OPEN LOOP VOLTAGE GAIN

by Moise Hamaoui

AS A FUNCTION OF FREQUENCY

What is Open Loop Voltage Gain?

Open loop voltage gain, A_{VOL}, is defined as the ratio of the change in output voltage to the change in input voltage causing it *(Figure 1)*.

How Does Open Loop Voltage Gain Affect Applications?

In a typical application *(Figure 2)*,

$$\frac{V_{OUT}}{V_{IN}} = -\frac{R2}{R1}$$

This is true *only* if the op amp has infinite or very high open loop gain. However, in practical op amps, the A_{VOL} decreases with frequency until it becomes even less than one. The question

is, then, to what frequency does *Equation 1* hold true for a particular op amp? Simple derivations show that if

$$V_{OUT} = -\frac{R2}{R1}\ V_{IN}$$

is assumed, an error arises due to neglecting A_{VOL} given by the following equation.

$$\text{(1)}$$

$$\text{Closed loop gain error} = \frac{100}{1 + \dfrac{A_{VOL}\ R1}{R1 + R2}}\ \%$$

For instance, if the op amp is a µA741 with R2/R1 = 100, $A_{VOL} = 10^4$ at 100 Hz, as determined from the curve of *Figure 3*. From *Equation 1*, there is an

error in assuming $V_{OUT}/V_{IN} = 100$ at 100 Hz given by

$$\frac{100}{1 + \dfrac{10^4 \times 1}{101}}\ =\ 1\% \qquad (2)$$

The A_{VOL} of the µA741 is equal to 100 at 10 kHz and the 1% error in *Equation 2* becomes substantial.

$$\frac{100}{1 + \dfrac{100}{101}}\ =\ 50\%\ !$$

Note that when the open loop voltage gain is equal to the feedback ratio, (R2 + R1)/R1, the amplifier gain drops by 6 dB.

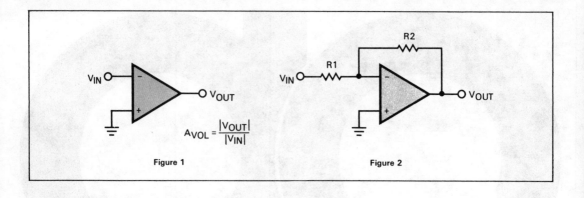

Figure 1

Figure 2

$$A_{VOL} = \frac{|V_{OUT}|}{|V_{IN}|}$$

It's Easy to Choose the Right Op Amp.

Use the following simple rule. For a dc closed loop gain y and a decrease in gain of no more than x percent at a given maximum signal frequency f_{max}, an op amp is needed with an A_{VOL} at f_{max} given by

$$A_{VOL} \geq \frac{100(1 + y)}{x} - y + 1$$

For example, to achieve a dc closed loop gain of 100 with a decrease in gain of only 10% at 10 kHz, an operational amplifier is required with an A_{VOL} at 10 kHz of at least

$$\frac{100(1 + 100)}{10} - 100 + 1 = 911$$

One possibility is the µA725 which has an A_{VOL} of 1000 at 10 kHz with the proper compensation.

The graph in *Figure 4* is also helpful when choosing the right op amp. The horizontal axis is the feedback ratio (R2 + R1)/R1 in dB. The vertical axis is the minimum A_{VOL} required to be within 1, 3, 6 or 10 dB of the dc closed loop gain, V_{OUT}/V_{IN}.

For example, if R2 = 9 kΩ and R1 = 1 kΩ, the feedback ratio is 20 dB. At the frequency where the A_{VOL} of the op amp will be 28 dB, the closed loop gain will be 3 dB down from its dc value R2/R1. Therefore, to insure that amplifier gain does not fall off by more than 3 dB at f_{max}, choose an op amp with $A_{VOL} > 28$ dB at f_{max}.

Open loop voltage gain is not the only parameter that affects high frequency operation. Slew rate must be considered. Next month's article will cover this important subject.

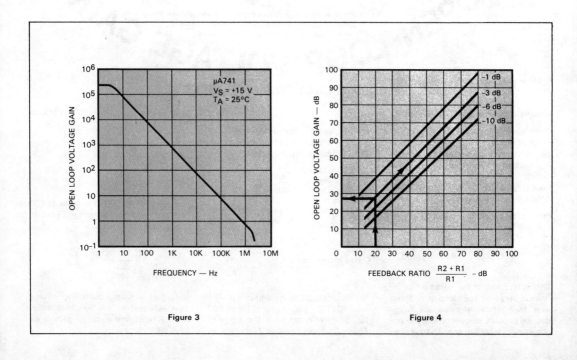

Figure 3

Figure 4

op amps

amps

Fourth in the series of helpful suggestions on how
to select the right op amp for your
particular application

SLEW RATE-WHAT IS IT?

by Moise Hamaoui

Slew rate is the maximum rate of change of output voltage with respect to time, usually specified in volts per microsecond. For example, a 0.5 V/µs slew rate means that the output rises or falls no faster than 0.5 V every microsecond. Slew rate is also sometimes specified indirectly in data sheets as *output voltage swing as a function of frequency* or as *voltage follower large signal pulse response.*

What Causes Slew Rate?

Slew rate is caused by current limiting and saturation of an op amp internal stage. That limited current is the maximum current available to charge the compensation capacitance network.

The voltage across the capacitor rises at a rate,

$$\frac{dV}{dt} = \frac{I}{C}$$

This capacitor charging rate is reflected at the output and causes slew rate limiting. Slew rate limiting therefore occurs with large input signals which saturate the internal stages. Remember that for small signals, *i.e.,* when the op amp is operated in its linear region, the step

227

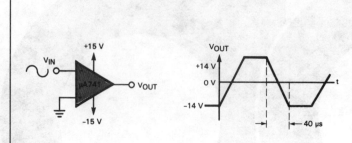

Figure 1

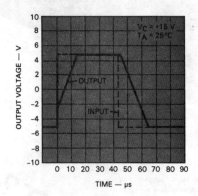

Figure 2

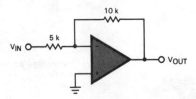

Figure 3

response of the op amp is an exponential of time constant

$$\tau = \frac{1}{2\pi\ f_{CL}}$$

where f_{CL} is the closed loop bandwidth of the circuit.

How Does Slew Rate Affect Applications?

In a simple application using a µA741 as a comparator *(Figure 1)*, the output will go to about –14 V and then to +14 V each time the input signal crosses zero volts. The µA741 has a typical slew rate of 0.7 V/µs, determined under electrical specifications or calculated from the slope of the output curve in *Figure 2*. Therefore, the µA741 output will go to +14 V from –14 V in

$$\frac{28\ V}{0.7\ V/\mu s} = 40\ \mu s$$

If the full 28 V output swing is desired, the input signal must have at least 40 µs between zero crossings. That is, the maximum input signal frequency should be 1/(2 x 40 µs) or 12.5 kHz assuming 50% duty cycle. Even at that frequency, the output is triangular instead of square wave. For higher frequencies or a more square wave output, an op amp with a faster slew rate is needed.

As another example of the effect of slew rate, consider the simple amplifier with a gain of two in *Figure 3*. Again, the µA741 is used. Its open loop voltage gain as a function of frequency curve *(Figure 4)* indicates that the amplifier circuit will operate with a gain of two up to about 80 kHz.

Now, what is the maximum input signal voltage that may be used up to 80 kHz? If the output is to be an undistorted sine wave, A sin ωt, then the rate of change of the output is

$$\frac{d}{dt}A \sin \omega t = A\omega \cos \omega t$$

and the maximum rate of change of the output is Aω. The minimum slew rate of the operational amplifier, therefore, must be equal to Aω. Thus, with ω = 2π (80 x 10³) = 503000 and the slew rate of the µA741 typically 0.7 V/µs, the maximum output swing A of the sine wave without distortion is

$$\frac{\text{slew rate}}{\omega} \text{ or } \frac{0.7 \text{ V/}\mu\text{s}}{503000} = 1.4 \text{ V}_{pk}$$

or 2.8 $V_{pk\text{-}pk}$

The maximum input signal should, therefore, be less than 2.8/2 $V_{pk\text{-}pk}$. The maximum output swing can also be easily read from the output voltage swing as a function of frequency curve on the data sheet (Figure 5). From this curve, the maximum output swing without distortion can be determined for different frequencies.

To Sum Up

In applications where square wave outputs (comparators, oscillators, limiters, etc.) are expected, it is important to remember that the op amp output takes some time to change from one value to another. That time, which usually limits the maximum frequency of operation, is determined by the change of output voltage divided by the slew rate.

In applications where the output should be free of distortion, the slew rate determines the maximum frequency of operation for a desired output swing. The required slew rate can be determined by a simple formula. For a desired undistorted output voltage swing V_{pk} at a maximum frequency f_{max}, an op amp is needed with a slew rate given by

$$\text{slew rate} > 2 \pi f_{max} V_{pk}$$

Figure 6 gives the slew rate required for different output swings at different frequencies. Another easy way to choose the right op amp is to check the data sheet curves of output voltage swing as a function of frequency (Figure 5).

Remember, however, that these curves are typical and slew rate varies as a function of supply. Slew rates at different supply voltages are usually shown on the data sheet.

In some applications such as D/A or A/D, slew rate is not the only criterion for fast response. The settling time is another parameter to consider. High slew rate op amps sometimes have associated overshoot and ringing which may cause the output to reach a steady state after a longer period of time than maybe a slower slew rate op amp.

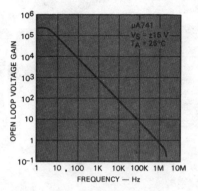

Figure 4

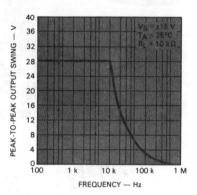

Figure 5

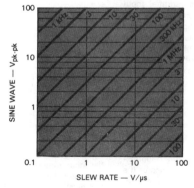

Figure 6

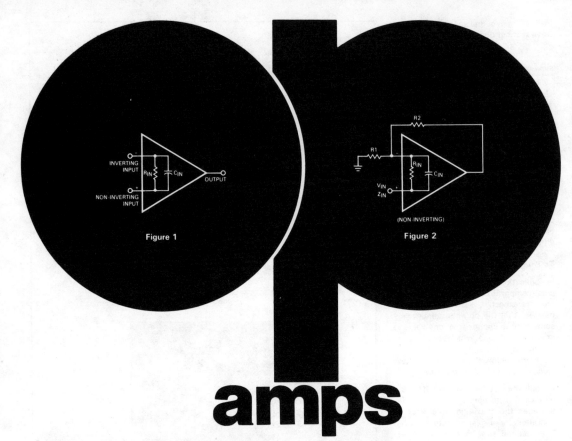

Figure 1

Figure 2

(NON-INVERTING)

amps

Number five in our series — the importance
of input impedance when designing
with op amps.

INPUT IMPEDANCE

by Moise Hamaoui

Input Resistance and Input Capacitance—Major Factors of Op Amp Input Impedance

Input resistance, or differential input resistance usually specified in the data sheets, is the small signal resistance measured between the inverting and non-inverting inputs of the op amp. Input capacitance is the capacitance seen between the same two inputs. See *Figure 1*.

How Does Input Impedance Affect Applications?

The input impedance of an amplifier circuit with feedback is not only dependent on the op amp, but also on the circuit configuration. First order approximation for the input impedance of the non-inverting and inverting configurations is discussed.

Non-inverting Configuration (Figure 2)
Input impedance of an amplifier in the non-inverting configuration is expressed as follows.

$$Z_{IN} = Z + \frac{A_{VOL} \, Z}{1 + \frac{R2}{R1}} \qquad (1)$$

$$Z_{IN} = Z\left(1 + \frac{A_{VOL}}{1 + \frac{R2}{R1}}\right)$$

where $A_{VOL}\,(\omega)$ is the open loop gain of the op amp and Z is the op amp input impedance.

As indicated in *Equation 1*, the amplifier input impedance is equal to at least the op amp impedance and can go much higher at low frequencies due to high open loop gain. For example, if the μA741 is used with R2 = 9 kΩ and R1 = 1 kΩ, the open loop gain at dc is 10^5

and the input impedance of the op amp is 2 MΩ at low frequencies *(Figures 3 and 4)*. Therefore the low frequency input impedance of the amplifier, according to *Equation 1* is

$$Z_{IN} = 2 \text{ M}\Omega + \frac{10^5 \times 2 \text{ M}\Omega}{10} = 20002 \text{ M}\Omega$$

At 100 kHz, the op amp open loop gain is 10 *(Figure 3)* and R_{IN} = 1.8 MΩ *(Figure 4)*. Since the input capacitance is 2 pF, op amp input impedance is

$$Z = 1.8 \text{ M}\Omega // \frac{1}{2\pi \, (100 \text{ kHz}) \, 2 \times 10^{-12}} = 0.55 \text{ M}\Omega$$

From *Equation 1*,

$$Z_{IN} = 0.55 + \frac{10 \, (0.55)}{1 + 9} = 1.10 \text{ M}\Omega$$

Obviously, it is important to consider the input impedance both at the minimum and maximum frequencies of operation. It is safe to assume that in the non-inverting configuration, the input impedance is *at least* equal to the *input impedance* of the op amp.

For op amps to operate properly, it is necessary to supply a certain dc current at their inputs. That current is given in the data sheets as input bias current and ranges in value from picoamps to microamps depending on the op amp. In the non-inverting configuration of *Figure 2*, if V_{IN} has a series resistance of 1 MΩ and the input bias current of the op amp is 0.5 µA, there is a dc drop across the 1 MΩ series resistance of 0.5 µA x 1 MΩ = 0.5 V. This is independent of the signal (V_{IN}) amplitude. If V_{IN} is 1 V, there is 1 – 0.5 = 0.5 V at the non-inverting input. However, it is erroneous to assume that the op amp input impedance is 1 MΩ just because there is a straight voltage division. The drop is caused by input bias current and not by input impedance. If an ac signal is riding on the 1 V dc value of V_{IN}, the ac amplitude is not halved and only a 0.5 V offset is constantly there due to bias current. The signal amplitude is affected by the 1MΩ series resistance and the op amp input impedance.

Inverting Configuration (Figure 5)

Input impedance of an amplifier in the inverting configuration is

$$Z_{IN} = R1 + \frac{R2\,(Z+R)}{A_{VOL}Z} \qquad (2)$$

$$Z_{IN} \approx R1$$

In this configuration, the effect of the op amp input impedance is minimal. The input impedance is at least R1; at high frequencies, as A_{VOL} decreases, the input impedance increases and the value of $[R2\,(Z+R)]/A_{VOL}\,Z$ becomes comparable to that of R1.

For all practical applications, however, it is safe to assume that the input impedance is just R1. Again, remember that a constant dc bias current is required at the inverting input to operate the op amp. The dc bias current limits the increase in value of R1. The higher the value of R1, the greater the magnitude of the dc offset voltage occurring at the output.

Another interesting point concerning *Equation 2* is that the effect of increased input impedance at higher frequencies (A_{VOL} decreases in the denominator) is very similar to an inductance effect, usually referred to as Miller inductance. See Fairchild Application Note 321, "Operational Amplifiers as Inductors," for more detail.

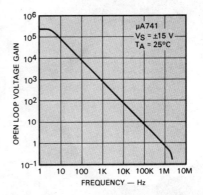

Figure 3

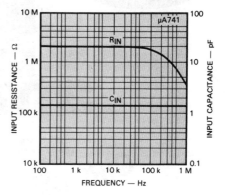

Figure 4

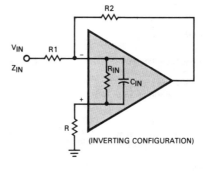

Figure 5

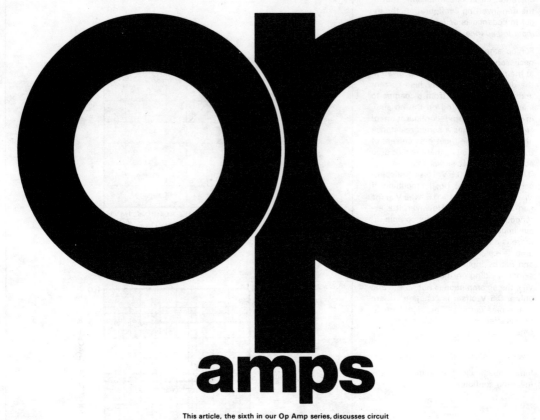

op

amps

This article, the sixth in our Op Amp series, discusses circuit stability criteria and implementation along with a look at some basic applications.

CIRCUIT STABILITY

by Moise Hamaoui

How Can Circuit Stability Be Assured?

Circuit stability can easily be determined by following one simple rule and referring to the phase response and open loop voltage gain curves on the op amp data sheets.

Open loop voltage gain, $A_{VOL}(\omega)$, of the op amp is one consideration when determining circuit stability. It is defined as the ratio of the change in output voltage to the change in input voltage*. Open loop voltage gain versus frequency, readily available from the data sheets, may be written as:

*See PROGRESS, Vol. 2, No. 5, May 1974, pg. 8.

$$A_{VOL}(\omega) = \frac{120 \times 10^3}{\left(1 + j\,\dfrac{f}{5}\right)\left(1 + j\,\dfrac{f}{3\,MHz}\right)}$$

(From *Figure 1*)

Next, it is necessary to consider the transfer functions for the inverting and non-inverting configurations shown in *Figures 2* and *3*. They can be expressed by the following equations.

Inverting:

$$\frac{V_{OUT}}{V_{IN}} = \left(\frac{Z2}{Z2 + Z1}\right)\left(\frac{-A_{VOL}(\omega)}{1 + \dfrac{A_{VOL}(\omega)}{1 + \dfrac{Z2}{Z1}}}\right)$$

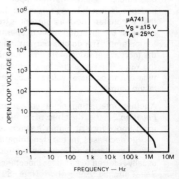

Fig. 1

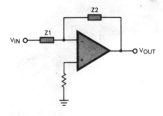

Fig. 2

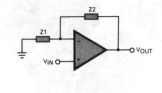

Fig. 3

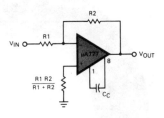

Fig. 4

Non-Inverting:

$$\frac{V_{OUT}}{V_{IN}} = \frac{A_{VOL}(\omega)}{1 + \dfrac{A_{VOL}(\omega)}{1 + \dfrac{Z2}{Z1}}}$$

From these transfer functions, as well as from feedback theory, the stability of the inverting and non-inverting configurations can be determined by following this simple rule. The circuits will be stable if the magnitude of the term

$$\frac{A_{VOL}(\omega)}{1 + \dfrac{Z2}{Z1}}$$

is less than unity when its phase angle reaches 180°. Stated another way, the phase angle of the above term must be less than 180° when its magnitude reaches unity. The simplicity of this rule is illustrated in the following example.

Amplifier and Voltage Follower Stability

In amplifiers where Z2 and Z1 are resistive, the circuit stability depends mainly on $A_{VOL}(\omega)$ because there is no phase shift in 1 + Z2/Z1. For example, in the circuit of *Figure 4,*

for R2 = R1,

$$1 + \frac{Z2}{Z1} = 2 \angle 0°$$

Now, when $A_{VOL}(\omega) = 2$, the term

$$\frac{A_{VOL}(\omega)}{1 + \dfrac{Z2}{Z1}} = 1$$

From the open loop voltage gain curve *(Figure 5)*, it is apparent that $A_{VOL}(\omega)$ = 2 at about 500 kHz with C_C = 30 pF or at about 5 MHz with C_C = 3 pF. In *Figure 6*, note that the phase shift of the $A_{VOL}(\omega)$ is close to 180° at 5 MHz; therefore the circuit is potentially unstable or oscillatory. The phase is close to 110° at 500 kHz. Therefore the compensation, C_C = 30 pF, should be used instead of C_C = 3 pF since with C_C = 3 pF

$$\frac{A_{VOL}(\omega)\ (5\ MHz)}{1 + 1} = 1 \angle 180° \quad \text{(unstable)}$$

and with C_C = 30 pF

$$\frac{A_{VOL}(\omega)\ (500\ kHz)}{1 + 1} = 1 \angle 110° \quad \text{(stable)}$$

Summary

To determine stability for a resistive feedback circuit, the frequency at which $A_{VOL}(\omega)$ is equal to 1 + R2/R1 is found on the open loop voltage gain curve. At that frequency, the ratio

$$\frac{A_{VOL}(\omega)}{1 + \dfrac{Z2}{Z1}} = 1$$

The phase shift at that frequency is then read on the op amp phase response curve. If the phase shift is less than 180°, the configuration is stable; if it is more than 180°, the configuration is unstable. Often the results of these computations are given in the data sheet as frequency response for various closed loop gains using recommended compensation networks *(Figure 7)*.

When Z2/Z1 is non-resistive as in integrators and differentiators, the same rule holds but the phase response of both $A_{VOL}(\omega)$ and 1 + Z2/Z1 must be considered. For more information on stability rules for integrators and differentiators, see Fairchild Application Note 289, "Applications of the μA741 Operational Amplifier".

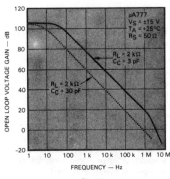

Fig. 5

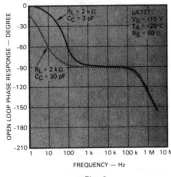

Fig. 6

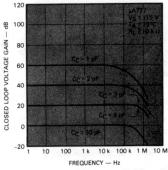

Fig. 7

233

op
amps

The last two articles in this series will explain how to check
op amp parameters to find the most efficient
and cost-saving device to meet operational
amplifier specifications.

DESIGN STEPS FOR INVERTING AMPLIFIERS

by Moise Hamaoui

This series to date has discussed the most important op amp parameters and offered guidelines for choosing the right op amp for a particular application. Now, how do these guidelines translate into practical amplifier design? The final two articles will present some simple steps leading to four basic requirements for designing op amp amplifier circuits—inverting this month, non-inverting next month. Reference is made to the previous issue(s) of Progress that contains the discussion of the parameter considered in each step.

Inverting Amplifier Specifications

First, of course, is to establish circuit specifications that are necessary for the application. For this discussion, the following specs were assumed.

Gain = A = –9

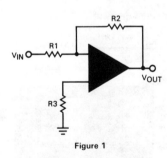

Figure 1

Minimum 3 dB down frequency, f_c = 10 kHz

Maximum input signal amplitude,
V_1 = 2 V_{pk-pk}

Maximum dc output offset voltage,
$V_{O(max)}$ = ±25 mV

Input resistance, R_{IN} = 10 kΩ

DC drift from 0 to 70°, $\Delta V_{O(max)} \leq$ 15 mV

Step 1—Circuit Configuration

Using the circuit of *Figure 1*,

$$\frac{V_{OUT}}{V_{IN}} = \frac{-R2}{R1} = A = -9; \quad \frac{R2}{R1} = 9 \qquad (1)$$

Step 2—Frequency Response (Progress, May 1974)

The first op amp specification to check is the minimum open loop voltage gain, A_{VOL}, needed to meet the amplifier frequency response requirement. This is easy to do by using the graph in *Figure 2*. Since R2/R1 = 9 then (R2 + R1)/R1 = 10, locate the 10 ratio (20 dB) on the (R2 + R1)/R1 axis. Go up to the 3 dB line and read, on the vertical axis, the minimum A_{VOL} required, 28 dB. Therefore, to insure that amplifier gain

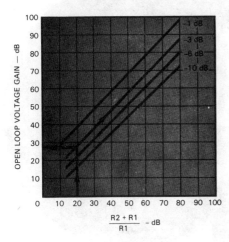

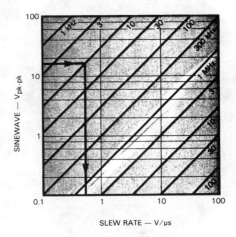

Figure 2

Figure 3

does not fall off by more than 3 dB at f_c, the op amp must have an open loop gain of

Step 3—Output Swing (Progress, June 1974)

Since the maximum input signal amplitude is 2 V_{pk-pk}, the maximum output swing will be 18 V_{pk-pk}. Therefore, an op amp is needed with a slew rate fast enough to give 18 V_{pk-pk} up to 10 kHz. By checking *Figure 3*, it is apparent that an op amp is required with

Step 4—Maximum DC Output Offset Voltage V_O (Progress, March and April 1974)

The dc output offset voltage, V_O, for the circuit in *Figure 1* is given by the following equations.

For R3 = 0

$$V_O = (1 + \frac{R2}{R1}) V_{OS} + I_{Bias} R2 \quad (2)$$

For R3 = R1 in parallel with R2
$$= \frac{R1 \ R2}{R1 + R2}$$

$$V_O = (1 + \frac{R2}{R1}) V_{OS} + R2 \ I_{OS} \quad (3)$$

where V_{OS} = input offset voltage

I_{Bias} = input bias current

I_{OS} = input offset current

Unless the output offset voltage spec is very wide, it is usually more economical to add R3 than use a very low input bias current op amp. For the example in this discussion, R3 = R1 in parallel with R2. From *Equation 3*, it can be seen that the V_O value will be low when R2 is small; therefore the smallest possible value should be chosen for R2.

For the inverting configuration, the input resistance R_{IN} is at least R1 (Progress, July 1974). Therefore, choose R1 so that

$$R1 \geq R_{IN} \geq 10 \ k\Omega \quad (4)$$

From *Equations 1* and *4*, R2/R1 = 9 and R1 ≥ 10 kΩ; therefore when R1 is 10 kΩ, R2 = 90 kΩ and R3 = 9 kΩ. *Equation 3* becomes

$$V_O = (1 + 9) V_{OS} + (90 \times 10^3) I_{OS}$$

Thus, an op amp is needed such that V_{OS} and I_{OS} give

To simplify the search for an op amp to meet this requirement, look first for one that has the following specs.

$$V_{OS} < \frac{V_{O(max)}}{10} \ or < \frac{25}{10} \ mV$$

$$I_{OS} < \frac{V_{O(max)}}{90 \times 10^3} \ or < 270 \ nA$$

Step 5—Drift

Drift is given by

where ΔV_{OS} and ΔI_{OS} are the changes in input offset voltage and input offset current over the 0 to 70° temperature range.

Step 6—Final Hints in Choosing the Right Op Amp

It is usually best to start by finding the op amps that meet the first and second requirements; this will eliminate many. Then check the good ones with the third and fourth requirements starting with the lowest cost op amp. There are usually other specifications such as supply voltage and current, supply rejection, load current, etc., that should be considered. However, the op amps that meet the four requirements will narrow down the field of choice to only a few; they can then be checked further to see if they meet the rest of the specifications.

op

amps

This completes our series on the most important op amp parameters, their significance in applications, and how to put them to use when selecting the best op amp for a particular amplifier design.

DESIGN STEPS FOR NON-INVERTING AMPLIFIERS

by Moïse Hamaoui

The design steps for non-inverting amplifiers are similar to those for inverting amplifiers. As in the discussion last month on inverting amplifier design, reference is made to the previous issue(s) of Progress that contains the explanation of the parameter considered in each step.

Non-Inverting Amplifier Specifications

For this discussion, the following specifications were assumed.

Gain = A = 10
Minimum 3 dB down frequency,
f_c = 10 kHz
Maximum input signal amplitude,
V_1 = 2 V_{pk-pk}

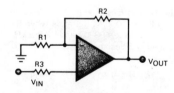

Figure 1

Input resistance, R_{IN} = 5 MΩ min
Maximum dc output offset voltage,

$$V_{O(max)} = \pm 25 \text{ mV}$$

DC drift from 0 to 70°,
$$\Delta V_{O(max)} \leq 15 \text{ mV}$$

Step 1 — Circuit Configuration
In the circuit of *Figure 1*,

$$\frac{V_{OUT}}{V_{IN}} = \frac{R2 + R1}{R1} = A = 10 \qquad (1)$$

Step 2 — Frequency Response
(Progress, May 1974)
As with inverting amplifier design, the first op amp specification to check is the minimum open loop voltage gain,

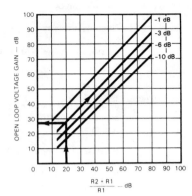

Figure 2

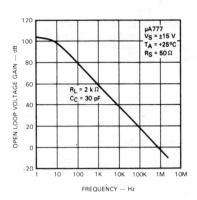

Figure 3

A_{VOL}, needed to meet the amplifier frequency response requirement. This is easy to do by using the graph in *Figure 2.* Since (R2 + R1)/R1 = 10, locate the 10 ratio (20 dB) on the (R2 + R1)/R1 axis. Go up to the 3 dB line and read, on the vertical axis, the minimum A_{VOL} required, 28 dB. Therefore, to insure that amplifier gain does not fall off by more than 3 dB at f_c, the op amp must have an open loop gain of

First Requirement

$$A_{VOL} \geq 28 \text{ dB at } f_c \text{ (10 kHz)}$$

Examination of the open loop voltage gain versus frequency curves on various op amp data sheets will quickly determine which devices will meet this requirement. *Figure 3* is a good example. An op amp with a gain bandwidth product of 25,000 (28 dB x 10 kHz) will do the job, assuming the op amp has just one pole.

Step 3 — Output Swing
(Progress, June 1974)
Since the maximum input signal amplitude is 2 $V_{pk\text{-}pk}$, the maximum output swing will be 20 $V_{pk\text{-}pk}$. Therefore, an op amp is needed with a slew rate fast enough to give 20 $V_{pk\text{-}pk}$ up to 10 kHz. By checking *Figure 4*, it is apparent that an op amp is required with

Second Requirement

$$\text{slew rate} \geq 0.85 \text{ V/}\mu\text{s}$$

Step 4 — Input Resistance
(Progress, July 1974)
The input impedance for the non-inverting configuration is given by

$$Z_{IN} = Z \left(1 + \frac{A_{VOL}}{1 + \frac{R2}{R1}} \right) \quad (2)$$

where Z is the op amp input impedance and R3 $\ll$ Z.

The op amp for this design must satisfy the amplifier input impedance requirement of 5 MΩ up to at least 10 kHz. In step 2, it was determined that the op amp must also have an A_{VOL} of no less than 28 dB (or 25 V/V) at 10 kHz. Therefore, the required op amp must have an input impedance at 10 kHz of at least the following.

Third Requirement

$$Z \geq \frac{Z_{IN}}{1 + \frac{A_{VOL} \text{ (10 kHz)}}{1 + \frac{R2}{R1}}} = \frac{5 \text{ M}\Omega}{1 + \frac{25}{10}} = \frac{5 \text{ M}\Omega}{3.5}$$

$$Z \geq 1.4 \text{ M}\Omega$$

From curves, such as that of *Figure 5*, of input resistance and input capacitance as a function of frequency, it is easy to select an op amp to meet the input impedance requirement.

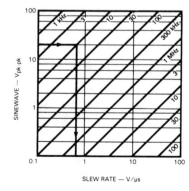

Figure 4

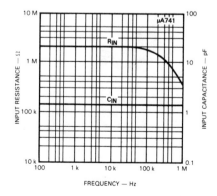

Figure 5

Step 5 — Maximum DC Output Offset Voltage, V_O

(Progress, March and April 1974)

The dc output offset voltage, V_O, for the circuit in *Figure 1* is given by the following equations.

For R3 = 0

$$V_O = (1 + \frac{R2}{R1}) V_{OS} + I_{Bias} R2 \qquad (3)$$

For R3 = R1 in parallel with R2

$$= \frac{R1\,R2}{R1 + R2}$$

$$V_O = (1 + \frac{R2}{R1}) V_{OS} + R2\, I_{OS} \qquad (4)$$

where V_{OS} = input offset voltage
I_{Bias} = input bias current
I_{OS} = input offset current

Unless the output offset voltage spec is very wide, it is usually more economical to add R3 than use a very low input bias current op amp. For the example in this discussion, R3 = R1 in parallel with R2. From *Equation 4*, it can be seen that the V_O value will be low when R2 is small; therefore the smallest possible value should be chosen for R2. From *Equations 1* and *2*,

$$\frac{R1 + R2}{R1} = 10 \text{ and } R3 \ll Z$$

Therefore, choose R1 = 10 kΩ ; then R2 = 90 kΩ and R3 = 9 kΩ and *Equation 4* becomes

$$V_O = (1 + 9) V_{OS} + (100 \times 10^3) I_{OS}$$

Thus, an op amp is needed such that V_{OS} and I_{OS} give

Fourth Requirement

$$10\,V_{OS} + (100 \times 10^3) I_{OS} \leq 25 \text{ mV} \leq V_{O(max)}$$

To simplify the search for an op amp to meet this requirement, look first for one that has the following specs.

$$V_{OS} < \frac{V_{O(max)}}{10} \text{ or } < \frac{25}{10} \text{ mV}$$

$$I_{OS} < \frac{V_{O(max)}}{100 \times 10^3} \text{ or } < 250 \text{ nA}$$

Step 6 — Drift

Drift is given by

Fifth Requirement

$$\Delta V_O = 11\,\Delta V_{OS} + (100 \times 10^3)\,\Delta I_{OS}$$

$$\leq \Delta V_{O(max)}\,(15 \text{ mV})$$

where ΔV_{OS} and ΔI_{OS} are the changes in input offset voltage and input offset current over the 0 to 70° temperature range.

Final Hints in Choosing the Right Op Amp

It is usually best to start by finding the op amps that meet the first and second requirements; this will eliminate many. Then check the good ones with the third, fourth and fifth requirements starting with the lowest cost op amp. There are usually other specifications such as supply voltage and current, supply rejection, load current, etc., that should be considered. However, the op amps that meet the five requirements will narrow down the field of choice to only a few; they can then be checked further to see if they meet the rest of the specifications.

IC Power Op Amps...

versatile and efficient

by Russell Apfel and Donald Smith

Over the last few years, linear integrated circuits have penetrated the power-circuit area, impelled by new power-package developments and improved IC power transistors. Three-terminal IC voltage regulators, supplied in power-transistor packages, led the way in the early 1970s with output currents exceeding 1 A. Audio amplifiers capable of delivering 5 W into a 4 Ω load have been available for several years in multi-terminal plastic power "batwing" packages. In 1974, 4-terminal adjustable regulators were introduced in several new packages including the 4-lead TO-3, mini-batwing, and the 4-lead Power Watt package. Today, monolithic power op amps, that can deliver up to 5 W rms into an 8 Ω load, are available with 1 A current capabilities.

WHY POWER OPERATIONAL AMPLIFIERS?

The operational amplifier is the most versatile and commonly used linear building block. It performs the basic gain and control functions in many analog systems and has become widely used with a never-ending list of applications. Most of the limitations of general purpose op amps are overcome in various special purpose types, but none of these can deliver more than 5 to 10 mA to a load. Specialized power circuits such as voltage regulators and audio amplifiers are basically operational amplifiers with some extra components. Power op amps can be used to give improved performance for regulator and audio applications, as well as providing high current outputs to drive a variety of loads such as ac and dc servometers, high current relays, and 50 Ω cables. The versatility of the power op amp makes it a valuable tool for the system design engineer.

POWER TRANSISTORS AND PACKAGES

Power transistors have limitations which, if exceeded, can lead to device destruction. They can be destroyed if the current exceeds a limit at which the metal interconnections fuse or blow out, or if the safe operating area is exceeded. Also, if the chip temperature becomes too high, the device may go into secondary breakdown. Current-limiting, safe-area-protection and thermal-shutdown circuits have been added to prevent power transistor destruction, thereby making power integrated circuits nearly indestructable.

Power packages have been slower to develop than other integrated-circuit packages due to the difficulty of removing the heat, generated by the power dissipation, from the die in a multi-lead package to the outside environment. The first power integrated circuits were packaged in TO-3s and TO-220s, commonly used for transistors. Recently, several new packages have been developed including the following plastic and metal types.

- A plastic batwing package with a 16-pin copper lead frame for better thermal conductivity and two heat-spreading copper wings in place of the center two leads.

- Two types of 4-lead plastic power packages with copper lead frames. The mini-batwing is a Mini DIP with heat-spreading wings in place of the center two leads on each side. The single-sided Power Watt package has four leads on one side and a tab or wing on the other side.

- A 4-lead TO-3, which is a conventional TO-3 with two extra leads. This is the first low-cost multi-lead TO-3 type available.

THERMAL LAYOUT OF POWER OPERATIONAL AMPLIFIERS

Great care is required in the internal layout of a power operational amplifier to avoid thermal interaction problems between the input and output components. These interactions are more critical for op amps than for other power devices, due to the high gain and low offset drift requirements. *Figure 1* shows a thermal model of an operational amplifier. The thermal feedback voltage, V_{tf}, is caused by a change in the input offset voltage resulting from an overall change in chip temperature and thermal gradients on the die. The thermal feedback factor must be quite small to assure good open loop gain. Therefore, both a low drift input stage and a layout, designed using symmetrical layout techniques to avoid thermal transients, are required as shown in *Figure 2*.

A HIGH POWER OPERATIONAL AMPLIFIER

The μA791 power op amp has been available since 1972 in a rather expensive 10-lead TO-3 package. It is now available in the new 16-lead plastic batwing package that makes it cost effective in new applications. The μA791 is a high gain, high power amplifier with μA741 type input characteristics and an output current capability of 1 A.

The μA791 has a standard 2-stage amplifier circuit with an added power output stage (*Figure 3*). Thermal-shutdown and current-limiting circuits are included to protect the output transistors. An external resistor is selected to set the output current limit. The first two stages are identical in design to the μA741 and offset adjust terminals are provided, using the same kind of null pot as the μA741. A second stage compensation capacitor is not included in the circuit and the compensation terminals are brought out to external pins so that the

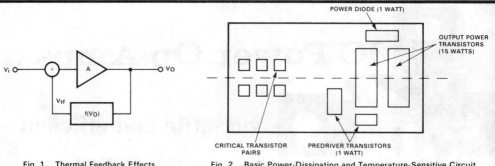

Fig. 1.   Thermal Feedback Effects

Fig. 2.   Basic Power-Dissipating and Temperature-Sensitive Circuit

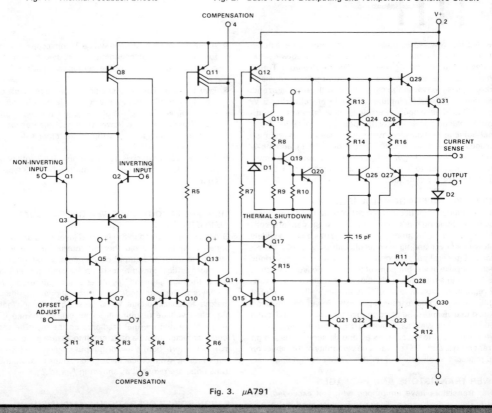

Fig. 3.   μA791

user can select a capacitor value for the required gain, band-width and slew rate. The output stage is an all npn transistor class A-B diode-coupled type. Local shunt feedback, consisting of R11, R15 and a 15 pF capacitor, is used with the following results:

- The open-loop output impedance is minimized so that re-active loads on the amplifier do not strongly affect closed-loop stability.

- The output stage is broad-banded so that the dominant pole of the amplifier can be provided by the second stage.

- The output stage is linearized, which minimizes high-frequency closed-loop distortion.

Thermal shutdown is accomplished using D1, Q18, Q19 and R8 through R10. The thermal shutdown temperature is approximately 160°C. A sense resistor connected in series with the output turns on either Q26 or Q27 to limit the output current when excessive current is drawn.

The μA791 has the same small-signal input specifications as the μA741 with improved output performance and the total supply current is only 12 mA. Each output deivce is rated for 10 W maximum continuous power with a peak power of 15 W. Total dissipation on the die must be limited to 15 W. The device can drive a 10 Ω load with a closed loop gain of 100 and has better than 0.2% gain accuracy. It delivers up to 5 W rms into an 8 Ω load with only 0.4% total harmonic distortion at 1 kHz.

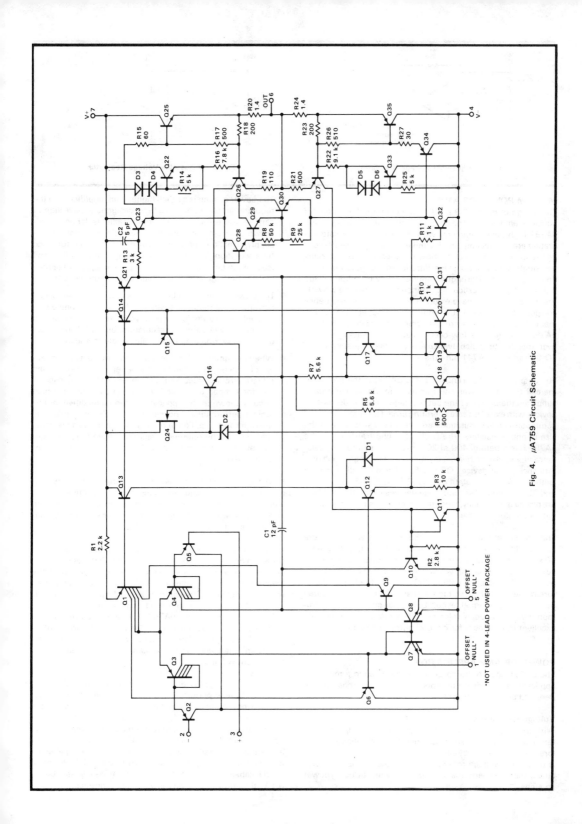

Fig. 4. μA759 Circuit Schematic

*NOT USED IN 4-LEAD POWER PACKAGE

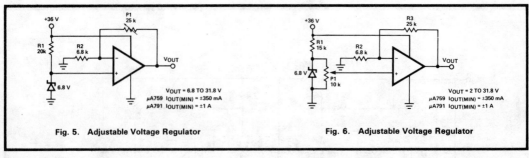

Fig. 5. Adjustable Voltage Regulator

Fig. 6. Adjustable Voltage Regulator

MEDIUM POWER OP AMP

The design of the µA759 exhibits the continued evolution of power op amp design. The circuit has the same features as the µA791 high power amplifier with the addition of a safe operating area protection circuit similar to the type used in voltage regulators. The circuit, shown in *Figure 4*, incorporates the single-supply input stage introduced for quad op amps, and a simplified Darlington emitter-follower output stage that has a power vertical pnp transistor. Unlike the µA791, the µA759 does not have external connections for frequency compensation, short circuit limiting, or offset voltage adjustment. These functions are performed internally so that the µA759 can fit into a low-cost 4-lead power package. However, this device is also available with offset adjustment in a TO-99 can with µA741 pin-outs.

The output vertical Darlington in the µA759 is the first commercial use of a power pnp transistor in ICs, which greatly simplifies the design of the output stage and provides output devices with excellent safe operating area. The beta-rolloff and saturation-voltage limitations are the only restrictions on the size of pnp transistors. The Darlington pnp transistor in the µA759 has a beta of 400 at 200 mA and a saturation resistance of 4 Ω. An isothermal layout is used to insure good performance. Input devices Q2 to Q5, Q7 and Q8 all lie on the isotherm as do the output devices Q23, Q25, Q34, Q35, R20 and R24. Additional second stage devices Q31, Q32 and Q21 are placed isothermally, since their power dissipations change with the output voltage.

The isothermal layout of the µA759 works so well that there is little difference in the transfer characteristics between a 50 kΩ and a 50 Ω load. The safe-area and current-limiting circuitry protect the circuit while allowing a 500 mA peak output at 25°C and a guaranteed 200 mA over the full temperature range. Low offset voltage drift and high gain are assured by the good isothermal layout. Low input current, high common mode and supply rejection ratios make this op amp an excellent replacement for general purpose amplifiers.

POWER OP-AMP APPLICATIONS

The µA791 and µA759 op amps can be used in a myriad of applications in addition to replacing general purpose amplifiers and power transistors.

Voltage Regulators

With the wide variety of fixed 3-terminal and adjustable 4-terminal regulators, use of op amps to build voltage regulators seems questionable. However, since a voltage regulator is basically a voltage reference and a power amplifier combined, improved performance can be obtained by using power op amps.

- The power op amp is a much higher gain amplifier than the regulator amplifier, and has been designed to have significantly lower errors due to thermal gradients. It has typically two orders-of-magnitude higher gain, superior power-supply rejection and lower drift due to temperature and time variation. This results in greatly improved line and load regulation (<1 mV) and improved ripple rejection, making the regulator a very high quality reference.

- The power op amp can both source and sink its rated load current, while regulators can supply current in one direction only. For example, if a positive 5 V regulator must sink 100 mA, it will go out of regulation; but, a 5 V regulator using a power op amp can easily handle this load.

- When designing with power op amps, low-cost high-quality references with significantly better performance than integrated circuit regulator references can be used, especially for temperature stability. The simple reference bias circuits shown in the applications can be modified for improved performance and because the Zener is external, filtering can be applied to reduce the output noise voltage. Additionally, the reference separation from the power device eliminates thermal interaction between them and improves performance.

Power op amp regulators can be used whenever a very high quality regulator is required. Using a low cost reference and amplifier offers a very good cost/performance tradeoff. Some typical ways to use operational power amplifier regulators are as follows.

An adjustable 6.8 to 31.8 V positive regulator/reference is shown in *Figure 5*. The reference is a 6.8 V Zener and the amplifier is used in the non-inverting configuration with the feedback resistor P1 adjusted to obtain the required output voltage. Amplifier drifts add only about 1 ppm/°C to the reference drift, and line and load regulation is better than 0.01%. When using the µA759, full output current is not available with low output voltage due to the safe-area protection circuitry. If only lower voltage values are needed, the supply and the feedback resistor can be reduced and the output current will increase.

An adjustable 2 to 31.8 V regulator/reference is shown in *Figure 6*. Similar performance to the circuit in *Figure 5* is obtained over a wider output range by connecting the adjustable resistor across the Zener. The µA791 can be used down to approximately 2 V at which point it runs out of common-mode range. The µA759 includes ground in its common-mode range and is output limited. When both source and sink capabilities are needed, the output can go down to about 2 V. If only a source capability is needed, the output can be adjusted below 0.1 V, thus providing a very low voltage reference.

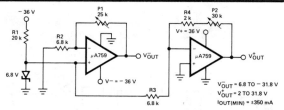

Fig.   Fig. 7.   Dual Adjustable Regulator

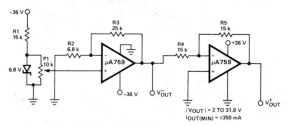

Fig. 8.   Dual Tracking Adjustable Voltage Regulator

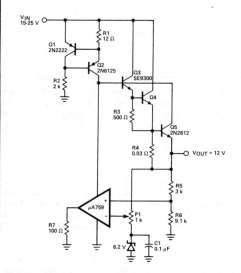

Fig. 9.   10 A, 12 V Regulator

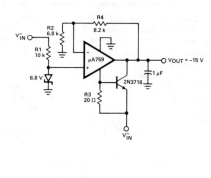

Fig. 10.   5 A, −15 V Regulator

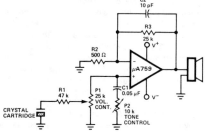

Fig. 11.   Phono Amplifier

SPEAKER IMPEDANCE (Ω)	μA759, $I_{OUT} \geq 350\,mA$			μA791, $I_{OUT} \geq 1\,A$		
	$V_{OUT(p-p)}$ (V)	$V_{S(MIN)}$ (V)	$P_{OUT(MIN)}$ (W)	$V_{OUT(p-p)}$ (V)	$V_{S(MIN)}$ (V)	$P_{OUT(MIN)}$ (W)
4	2.8	9	0.245	8	14	2
8	5.6	12	0.49	16	22	4
16	11.2	17	0.98	32	38	8
32	22.4	29	1.96			

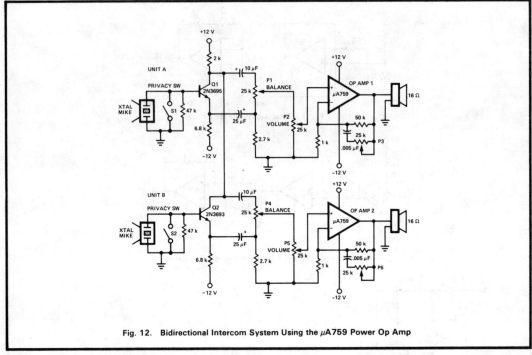

Fig. 12. Bidirectional Intercom System Using the μA759 Power Op Amp

Figure 7 shows a *dual adjustable regulator* with two power op amps. The Zener diode is connected as a negative reference and the negative output circuit is similar to *Figure 5*. The positive output uses an inverting amplifier and therefore has a wider adjustment range. Both outputs are adjustable and completely independent of each other. The positive output amplifier can use ground for the negative supply because of the good common-mode range of the μA759. *Figure 8* shows a dual tracking regulator in which the positive output uses the negative output for its reference. Tracking accuracy is dependent on the ratio of the feedback resistors around the positive amplifier.

A 10 A, 12 V regulator is shown in *Figure 9*. In this circuit, the μA759 operates as an error amplifier and the V+ terminal of the device is the output. The current source Q1, Q2, R1 and R2 provides 50 mA to the SE9300 Darlington and the feedback causes the μA759 to sink any current not used by the Darlington. Using the V+ terminal as the output reduces the dropout voltage.

Figure 10 shows a *5 A, −15 V regulator* circuit that has a single pass transistor connected to a μA759. The minimum beta needed by the pass transistor is only 20, since the μA759 can provide 250 mA minimum base drive. The circuit has an input output differential of approximately 3.5 V.

Audio Amplifiers

As in the case of voltage regulators, there are a variety of good, low cost monolithic audio amplifiers available today. However, power op amps can be used in many applications and require fewer external components than standard audio circuits. The μA791 provides a minimum of 2 W into a 4 Ω load and 4 W into an 8 Ω load. Its single capacitor compensation makes a good audio amplifier. The μA759 does not provide a lot of power, 0.25 W in a 4 Ω load, 0.5 W in an 8 Ω load, and 1 W in 16 Ω; but it can still be useful in a variety of lower powered applications such as headphone amplifier and intercom systems. A few typical audio applications are as follows.

A low cost *phono amplifier* is shown in *Figure 11*. The circuit has a fixed gain of 50 and two potentiometers provide volume and tone control. The μA791 is sensitive enough to be driven directly from a crystal cartridge and, when used as an audio amplifier driving an 8 Ω load, can typically provide a 5 W power output with 0.4% total harmonic distortion at 1 kHz. The chart shows the minimum output power that can be obtained for various speaker loads with several power supply voltages.

A *bidirectional intercom system* is shown in *Figure 12* that uses μA759 power op amps to drive 16 Ω speakers. Audio signals from the crystal microphone in Unit A are fed into the phase-splitter transistor Q1 which produces both in-phase and 180° out-of-phase signals. The 180° signal is coupled through the connecting cable to op amp 2 in Unit B and the resulting amplified audio is heard in the speaker. The balance control P1 is adjusted to prevent local audio feedback between the crystal microphone and the speaker in Unit A by cancelling out the in-phase signal and a portion of the 180° signal in the input circuit of op amp 1. The operation of Unit B is similar to Unit A. Each unit has its own volume control, P2 and P5, and also a tone control, P3 or P6. Switches S1 or S2 may be closed for privacy.

Driver and Other Applications

Power op amps can be used for a variety of gain-control applications, and to generate functions such as sine waves, square waves and triangle waves; some possible applications are shown on the following pages.

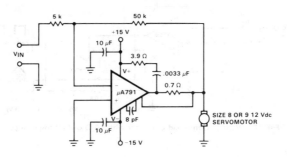

Fig. 13. DC Servo Amplifier

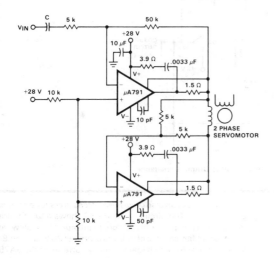

Fig. 14. AC Servo Amplifier Bridge Type

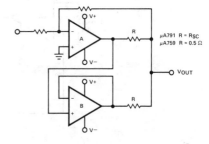

Fig. 16. Parallel Power Amplifier

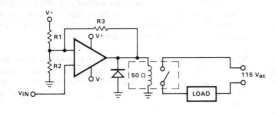

Fig. 15. Comparator with Hysteresis Driving a 50 Ω Relay

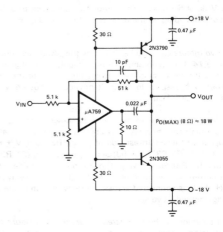

Fig. 17. High Slew Rate, Power Op Amp

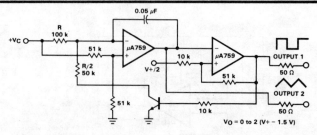

Fig. 18. Voltage Controlled Oscillator with 50 Ω Output Impedance

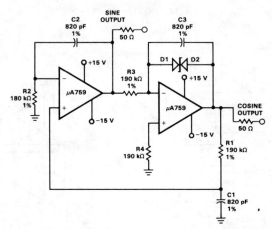

Fig. 19. Quadrature Oscillator with 50 Ω Output Impedance

DC servo motors can be driven with a µA791, *Figure 13* shows the µA791 with a circuit gain of 10, driving a size 8 or 9, 12 V dc servo motor. The motor can be driven in either direction depending on the polarity of the input signal.

AC servo motors can also be driven by the µA791 as shown in *Figure 14*. The upper amplifier is ac coupled with a gain of −10, and the lower amplifier inverts the output of the first amplifier with respect to V+/2. It provides about 44 Vp-p across the motor load.

A *power comparator with hysteresis* is shown in *Figure 15*, driving a high current relay with a 50 Ω coil. The comparator has upper and lower thresholds of (V_{REF} R2 R3 + V + R1 R2)/(R1 R2 + R2 R3 + R1 R3) and (V_{REF} R2 R3)/(R1 R2 + R2 R3 + R1 R3) respectively. The µA759 can provide adequate current to drive one or several high current relays. A flyback diode is connected across the relay to protect the op amp against inductive spikes.

Power op amps can be *connected in parallel* as in *Figure 16*, to provide additional output current. The main amplifier "A" is connected in whatever configuration is desired and the paralled amplifier is connected as a voltage follower. Low-value series-output resistors equalize current loads in the amplifiers. For the µA791, the short-circuit resistor is used, while the µA759 requires a 0.5 Ω series resistor.

Power op amps can also *drive power transistors* for additional power output. The circuit in *Figure 17* shows a µA759 driving npn and pnp power transistors to provide a high slew rate power amplifier capable of delivering almost 20 W into an 8 Ω load. The positive and negative supply currents of the µA759 supply base drive for the external power transistors, and the overall gain is set by the feedback resistors around the operational amplifier.

A *voltage-controlled oscillator* with two µA759s, capable of driving a 50 Ω terminated cable, is shown in *Figure 18*. With the component values shown, the output frequency is equal to 600 V_C/V+, the triangle waveform has an amplitude of V+ −3 V. The control voltage can be varied from 0 to 2 V (V+ −1.5 V) and the circuit will remain functional.

Figure 19 shows a standard *dual op amp quadrature oscillator* for sine and cosine outputs. Using µA759s, this oscillator can drive 50 Ω terminated lines and can also function as a signal source. The component values give a 14 Vp-p output at 1 kHz.

CONCLUSION
The power op amp has evolved into a versatile device, providing a valuable tool for the system design engineer. These op amps, particularly those in the new low-cost power packages, offer great flexibility in a wide range of uses and can provide improved performance over more conventional types.

The world of voltage regulators, particularly IC voltage regulators, is expanding very rapidly even by today's accelerated standards. While certain of these low power devices use external power transistors, there are now several series of power regulators that feature on-chip pass transistors. In the vast majority of cases, these are 3-terminal, fixed output voltage regulators. The monolithic 3-terminal regulator is particularly attractive for providing local on-card regulation with virtually no external components required.

Even though IC voltage regulators are considered to be "universal" circuit building blocks, certain considerations are critical to efficient application designs. The following is intended as an aid in identifying the major design considerations, establishing the optimum application trade-offs, and minimizing the misuse of 3-terminal regulators. Also provided are nomographs and a heat sink chart which allow "customized" circuit design, and useful applications for voltage regulators.

Thermal Considerations

The thermal characteristics of the voltage regulator chips and packages determine that some form of heat sinking is mandatory whenever the power dissipation exceeds 1 W for the TO-39 package, 2 W for the TO-220 package, or 3 W for the TO-3 package. These basic characteristics are listed in *Figure 1*. From the table, maximum permissable dissipation without a heat sink is derived by

$$\frac{T_{J(max)}-T_A}{\theta_{JA}}$$

where T_A is the maximum ambient operating temperature. If the average dissipation of the device in question exceeds this figure, a heat sink will be required. The thermal resistance necessary for the heat sink may be found from

$$\theta_{HS} = \frac{T_{J(max)}-T_A}{P_D} - \theta_{JC}$$

where T_A is the maximum ambient operating temperature and P_D is the maximum average dissipation of the device in no case to exceed $P_{D(max)}$. θ_{HS} is the thermal resistance of the heat sink to ambient, and includes the package/heat sink interface. Commercially available heat sinks are usually well characterized for this information. However, if a chassis or other convenient surface is to be used as the heat sink, use *Figure 2* to estimate the required surface area for a variety of commonly used materials. Surface area refers to both sides of the heat sink material.

As a further aid in determining which package/heat sink combination is best suited to a given application, the nomograph in *Figure 3* solves for θ_{JA} from basic current, input/output voltage differential and ambient temperature information. The package thermal resistances have been superimposed on the θ_{JA} line E. If the required θ_{JA} is less than θ_{JC} for a package, then that package cannot be considered; for even if an infinite heat sink were possible, the junction temperature would exceed 125°C. If the required θ_{JA} is greater than θ_{JA} for a package, that package may be used without a heat sink. In all other cases a package/heat sink combination is necessary. Subtract θ_{JC} for the preferred package from the required θ_{JA} to arrive at the necessary heat sink thermal resistance θ_{HS}.

	1.0 A Regulators			0.5 A Regulators			
SERIES	7800	7800C	7800C	78M00	78M00C	78M00C	
PACKAGE	TO-3	TO-3	TO-220	TO-39	TO-39	TO-220	Units
Maximum Junction Temperature, $T_{J(max)}$	150	125	125	175	175	125	°C
Minimum Ambient Temperature, $T_{J(min)}$	−55	0	0	−55	0	0	°C
Thermal Resistance, Junction-to-Case, θ_{JC}	4	4	4	20	20	5	°C/W
Thermal Resistance, Junction-to-Ambient, θ_{JA}	35	35	50	150	150	50	°C/W
Maximum Allowance Dissipation, $P_{D(max)}$	15	15	15	5	5	5	W

Temperatures shown in the table are operating temperatures. Storage temperatures are −65°C to 150°C for 7800 and 78C.
−65°C to 200°C for 78M00 and 78M00C.

Fig. 1. Basic Characteristics Table

The nomograph of *Figure 3* is based on a maximum junction temperature of 125°C. This will result in conservative figures for θ_{JA} for the 78M00 and 78M00C in the TO-39 package as junction temperatures up to 175°C are permissible in these cases.

To use the nomograph, select the maximum load current on Line A and the maximum input/output voltage differential on Line D. The line joining these points intersects Line B at a point representing the maximum power dissipation. Join this Line B intersection to a point on Line C representing the maximum expected ambient temperature. Extend this line so it intersects Line E. The Line E intersection represents the total junction-to-ambient thermal resistance required for the particular application. If the Line E intersection falls above the junction-to-ambient thermal resistance, θ_{JA}, no heat sink is required.

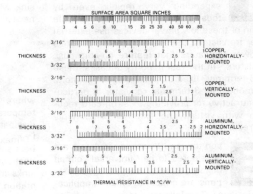

Fig. 2.   Heat Sink Selector Guide

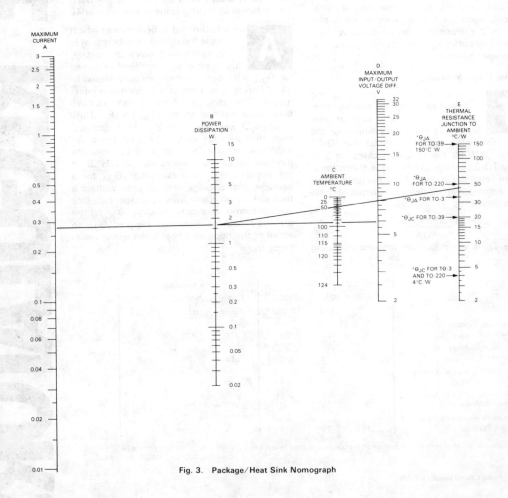

Fig. 3.   Package/Heat Sink Nomograph

o determine the thermal resistance of a heat sink, subtract the junction-to-case thermal resistance, Θ_{JC}, of the selected package from the Line E intersection.

For TO-39, subtract 20°C/W

For TO-3, subtract 4°C/W

For TO-220, subtract 4°C/W

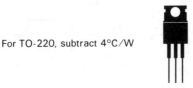

Example

hoose a regulator to supply 275 mA (max) with an input/output voltage differential of 6 V (max) at an ambient temperature of 50°C (max). Join the 275 mA point on Line A to the 6 V point on Line D. The intersection with Line B gives a power dissipation of 1.7 W. Join 1.7 W to the 50°C point on Line C and extrapolate to an intersection with Line E. This gives a total junction-to-ambient thermal resistance requirement of 45°C/W. There are three regulator package choices.

A TO-39 package with a heat sink of 25°C/W thermal resistance (subtract 20°C/W Θ_{JC})

A TO-220 package with a heat sink of 41°C/W thermal resistance (subtract 4°C/W Θ_{JC})

A TO-3 package with no heat sink (45°C/W falls above Θ_{JA} for the TO-3).

Typical Applications

he versatility of these regulator series may be increased beyond the basic 3-terminal uses by the addition of external components. The following applications contain circuits which cover the range of 0.5 V to 30 V output, and output currents in excess of 10 A. Note that apart from power considerations, the 1.0 A and 0.5 A devices are interchangeable in all applications.

Fixed Output Regulator

n this basic application, *Figure 4,* the last two digits of the device code specify the nominal output voltage. The insulating washer normally used when heat-sinking a power transistor may be omitted when mounting the regulator since the case of the device is at ground potential here. This is true unless circulating ground currents are a problem.

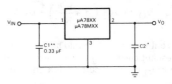

Fig. 4. Fixed Output Regulator

Fig. 5. Current Regulator

Current Regulator

he circuit shown in *Figure 5* supplies a regulator current to a load, its value being determined by an external resistor. The minimum input/output differential in this application is (minimum regulator input/output differential voltage) + (maximum regulator output voltage). For currents up to 1 A, 0°C to 70°C, this voltage is typically 2.2 V + 5.25 V, or 7.45 V.

High Current Voltage Regulators

urrents in excess of the output capabilities of the basic regulator can be obtained with the circuit shown in *Figure 6a.* The value of R1 determines the point at which Q1 begins to conduct and hence bypasses the regulator. This supply can be protected against a short circuit load by adding a short circuit sense resistor, R2, and a pnp transistor Q2, as in *Figure 6b*. In this circuit Q2 must be able to handle the short circuit current of the regulator, since when Q1 is bypassed, the regulator goes into its short-circuit mode. Foldback current limiting may be provided for the external power device by adding R3 and R4 as shown in *Figure 6c*.

Variable Output Voltage Regulators

 n *Figure 7a* a voltage pedestal is developed across R2, which is then added to the normal regulated output V_{XX}, such that

$$V_O = V_{XX}\left(1 + \frac{R2}{R1}\right) + I_Q R2.$$

The current through R1 should be set much higher than the quiescent current I_Q to minimize the effects of the change in I_Q which occurs with a change in V_{IN}.

 modification *(Figure 7b)* provides a continuously variable output in the range of 7 to 30 V. An op amp buffers the pedestal voltage across R2 from the regulator quiescent current. This removes the interaction of I_Q and

$$V_O = V_{XX}\left(1 + \frac{R2}{R1}\right), \text{ i.e. } V_O = 5\left(1 + \frac{R2}{R1}\right) \text{ V.}$$

Supply regulation is the same percentage per parameter change as for the basic 3-terminal device used, and current limiting and thermal shutdown remain operative over the full adjustment range. Maximum input voltage ratings must be observed to protect the regulator.

 or adjustable outputs in the range 0.5 to 7 V the schematic shown in *Figure 7c* may be used. A negative supply, $-V_{IN}$, is required to allow adjustment to the lower output voltages.

$$V_O = V_{XX}\left(\frac{R1 + R2}{11R1}\right) \text{ or } 0.45\left(1 + \frac{R2}{R1}\right) \text{ V}$$

Switching Regulators

A switching regulator may be used in those cases where the dissipation of a linear regulator is excessive. *Figure 8* shows that when power is first applied, current flows through R3 and the 1.0 A device to the output. As soon as the current generates a voltage drop sufficient to forward bias Q1's base emitter junction, Q1 is driven toward saturation. The increase in voltage at the collector applies power through L1 to the load and provides positive feedback through R1 and R2 to assure a full switching action. As the output voltage approaches the sum of the 7800 regulated output plus the voltage developed across R2, current flow through the 7800 decreases.

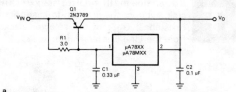

a

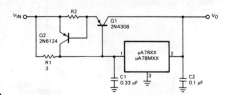

b

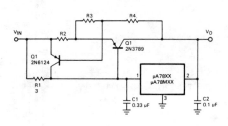

c

Fig. 6. High Current Regulators

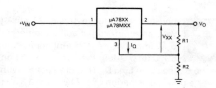

a

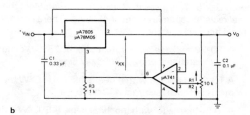

b

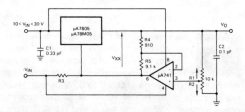

c

Fig. 7. Variable Output Voltage Regulators

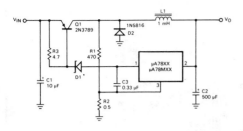

Fig. 8. Switching Regulator

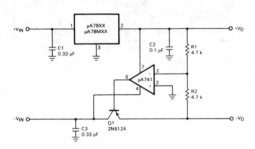

a

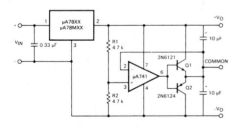

b

Fig. 9. Dual Polarity Regulators

nput voltages in excess of the maximum input voltage rating of the regulator may be accommodated by the inclusion of a voltage dropping Zener (D1). This reduces the voltage appearing across leads 1 and 3 of the 1.0 A regulator to an acceptable level. When the base current drops below the level required to keep Q1 in saturation, the collector voltage starts to decrease and the positive feedback loop completes the switching action.

Dual Polarity Regulators

ual polarity regulators supply positive and negative output voltages from either positive and negative input voltages or from a single floating input voltage. In this application a 1.0 A or 0.5 A regulator establishes the positive output voltage. An operational amplifier is then used as an inverting amplifier to provide the negative output voltage. Bipolar input supplies must be referenced to the common terminal. Since the op amp always drives the negative output to a voltage that maintains the junction of R1 and R2 very close to zero volts,

$$-V_O = -\left(\frac{R2}{R1}\right)\left(+V_O\right)$$

s shown in *Figure 9*, with R1 = R2 = 4.7 kΩ, equal bipolar output voltages are generated. Note that the negative output tracks the positive output (that is, any change occurring on the positive output appears inverted on the negative output), but the positive output does not track changes generated on the negative output. This unidirectional tracking is also common to all monolithic IC tracking regulators.

n improved dual polarity regulator is shown in *circuit b*. A 1.0 A or 0.5 A regulator provides the total output voltage from a single, floating input. An operational amplifier with a complementary emitter follower output stage, connected as a voltage follower, is then used to generate a common output line at a level set by R1 and R2 ($+V_O/-V_O$ = R1/R2). Again, with R1 = R2 = 4.7 kΩ as shown, equal positive and negative outputs are obtained. With this circuit, either output tracks changes occurring on the other. A limitation of this circuit is that the differential output current, i.e., the current that flows into or out of the common terminal, is limited to Q1/Q2 h_{FE} x op amp maximum current, which is typically in excess of 750 mA. This limitation is rarely met using these particular components, and most loads exhibit a considerable degree of balance which minimizes the differential current. Another improvement, as shown in *circuit b*, is the superior line regulation on the negative output due to the op amp being supplied by a well regulated voltage; in *circuit a*, the op amp is supplied directly from $-V_{IN}$.

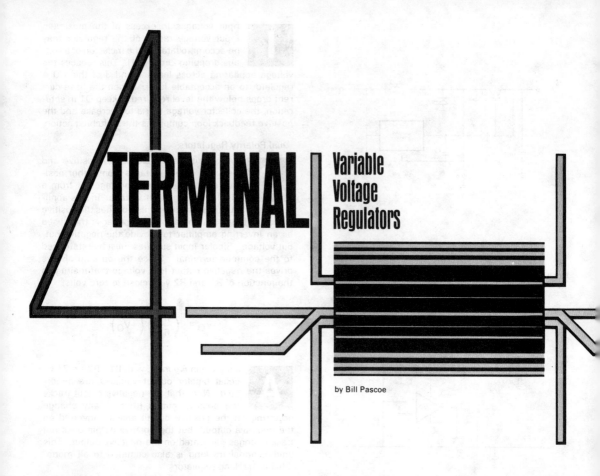

4 TERMINAL Variable Voltage Regulators

by Bill Pascoe

The 3-terminal fixed-output voltage regulator has revolutionized power supply design by making on-card voltage regulation practical and cost-effective. The 7800 series and the 109 devices pioneered this trend. The 7800 series offers a wide range of voltages—from 5 to 24 V in seven ranges—at > 1 A current capability. Soon after, a lower current, more economical version, the 78M-500 mA series was introduced, followed by the 78L-100 mA series. As a result, 3-terminal regulators became available covering the voltage range from 2.6 to 24 V, with current capability from 100 mA to 1.5 A. The only drawback was that variable voltages or non-standard voltage options could only be achieved at a sacrifice in performance or with increased circuit complexity. That is, until recently.

To fill this need for medium-current variable voltage regulators with no performance loss, two new products have been designed—the 78MG 4-terminal positive regulator and the 79MG 4-terminal negative regulator —both rated at 500 mA. Up to 10 A can be achieved with external series-pass transistors. The error amplifier reference (V_{REF}) is 5 V for the 78MG and –2.23 V for the 79MG which set the lowest outputs obtainable with these devices. However, the output can be selected

anywhere between V_{REF} and V_{IN} –2 V simply by the choice of two resistors. In addition, internal current limiting, thermal shutdown and safe-area protection make these regulators virtually indestructible. Construction is similar to the 78M and 79M series regulators, respectively, using the Planar* epitaxial process. The mini-batwing power package configuration allows the designer great flexibility in choosing the most appropriate heat sinking scheme.

THE 78MG POSITIVE VOLTAGE REGULATOR

The 78MG circuit is divided into seven functional blocks as shown in *Figure 1*—start-up, reference, error amplifier, thermal shutdown, safe-area protection, short-circuit protection and series-pass. *Figure 2* shows the equivalent schematic. Transistors Q1 through Q6 and resistors R1, R2 and R3 constitute a 5-volt temperature-compensated internal voltage reference for the regulator. The base-emitter voltages of transistors Q3, Q4, Q5 and Q6 provide the negative temperature-coefficient component of the output voltage. The voltage drop across R2 is the positive temperature-coefficient component. This is derived from the differential base-emitter voltages across transistors Q1 and Q2 operating at a current ratio of > 20 to 1. The output

*Planar is a patented Fairchild process.

252

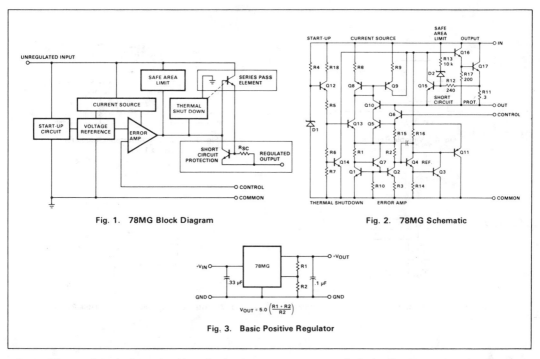

Fig. 1.   78MG Block Diagram

Fig. 2.   78MG Schematic

$$V_{OUT} = 5.0 \left(\frac{R1 + R2}{R2} \right)$$

Fig. 3.   Basic Positive Regulator

voltage of the regulator is determined by selecting two external resistors to multiply the reference voltage. The current required by the load is supplied from the input terminal through the series pass transistor Q17, driven by transistor Q16. Transistor Q3 is the gain stage providing regulation. Its effective gain is increased by the pnp transistor Q11 which acts as a buffer to drive the active collector load formed by the pnp current-source transistor pair Q8 and Q9.

The current from Q8 and Q9 is set by the current through resistor R1. During regulator turn on, the current in R1 flows first through transistor Q13—part of a start-up circuit containing Zener diode D1, transistors Q12 and Q13, and resistors R5, R6 and R7. After the device is in regulation, Q13 is biased off and the regulator takes over setting the current in R1 which now flows through Q5 and Q10. This start-up circuit is required since the current sink is off during initial device turn on.

Thermal limiting is accomplished by transistor Q14. The base of Q14 is clamped to ≈ 0.4 V by the resistive divider string R5, R6 and R7 in the start-up circuit. As the junction temperature rises, the turn-on threshold of Q14 decreases at –2.2 mV/°C. At a junction temperature of 175°C, transistor Q14 turns on and the base current to the driver transistor Q16 is removed. This shuts down the pass transistor Q17 and prevents further increases in chip temperature.

Although this form of thermal protection is effective against persistent overloads that cause excessive chip

temperature, it is ineffective against instantaneous overloads that could result in a secondary breakdown of the pass transistor or damage to metal interconnections due to abnormally high current density. Transistor Q15 and resistor R11 protect against instantaneous overloads by limiting output current. If the output current rises to a high level, the current through R11 turns on Q15, thus shunting base current away from the driver transistor and preventing further increases in output current.

A compensating network is included to limit the instantaneous power in the output transistor Q17 to ensure that it operates within its forward safe area. When the voltage across this transistor exceeds 8 V, current through resistor R13 and diode D2 reduces the limiting threshold on Q15. The higher the voltage across Q17, the lower the limiting threshold.

A 30 pF MOS capacitor is incorporated on the chip to ensure stable operation without the need for a bypass capacitor on the output.

78MG APPLICATIONS
The 78MG voltage regulator is ideal for designing a medium current regulator with excellent performance over wide ranges of output voltage, current level and ambient temperature. The basic configuration is shown in *Figure 3*. Similar to the 78M series of regulators, the 78MG requires an input capacitor (0.33 µF) if the regulator is located more than a few inches from the unregulated supply filter capacitor. This reduces the effect of the connecting line inductance on regulator perform-

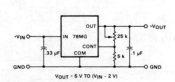

Fig. 4. Variable Regulator

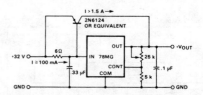

Fig. 5. 5 to 30 V Adjustable Regulator
($I_{OUT} > 1.5$ A)

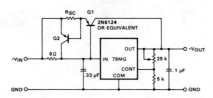

Fig. 6. High Current Short Circuit Protected Regulator

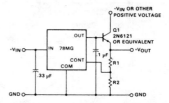

Fig. 7. Alternate Approach to Adjustable Regulator

ance. The output capacitor is used to improve transient response. Any output voltage from 5 V (V_{REF}) to 30 V (V_{IN} – 2) may be obtained by proper selection of R1 and R2 using the following formula.

$$V_{OUT} = V_{REF}\left(\frac{R1 + R2}{R2}\right)$$

where V_{REF} = 5 V

If 1 mA is chosen as the current through the divider (to reduce bias current effects), then R2 = 5 kΩ and the output voltage (V_{OUT}) is simply equal to R1 + R2 where R1 and R2 are in kΩ. It should be noted that V_{OUT} is equal to V_{REF} when the control terminal is tied directly to V_{OUT}. Also, the control terminal should not be returned to ground. Although no damage results from doing so, the regulator is actually out of regulation in this case.

When using the regulator with a variable resistor as shown in *Figure 4*, a resistor must be inserted between the lower end of the potentiometer and ground. This configuration allows a constant current division ratio to set the output voltage giving a linear relationship between output voltage and shaft rotation. A standard potentiometer configuration could be used; however, the output voltage versus shaft rotation would not be linear.

The 78MG may also be used in higher current applications with the use of an external series-pass transistor as shown in *Figure 5*. Here, the output is about 1.5 A.

The value of the series input resistor is selected as follows.

$$R = \frac{V_{BE}}{I_{REG}}$$

In this case the regulator current was selected to be $\approx$ 100 mA. The total output current is calculated by

$$I_O \approx I_{REG} + \beta I_{REG}$$

where β is the gain of the external series-pass transistor.

The circuit of *Figure 5* has one serious drawback. While the regulator is protected against short circuits, the series-pass device is not. This has a disturbing tendency to produce ppp or pip transistors for which there are limited applications. Left in the circuit, this configuration will degrade the regulator performance. This drawback can be corrected by using the circuit in *Figure 6* where a general purpose pnp transistor Q2 and a short circuit sensing resistor, $R_{SC} = V_{BE(Q2)}/I_{SC}$, have been added. As current through R_{SC} increases to the value of $V_{BE(Q2)}$, Q2 begins to conduct and reduces the base current in Q1, which, in turn, reduces the output current, thus protecting Q1 against short circuits.

An alternate approach to the problem of external series-pass devices is shown in *Figure 7*. Here, an npn transistor is used for the external series-pass device. This

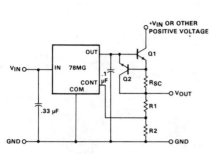

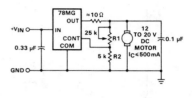

Fig. 8. Alternate Approach to Short-Circuit Protected Regulator

Fig. 9. Motor Speed Control

circuit has two advantages over the circuits of *Figure 5 and* 6. First, the V_{BE} of the series-pass device is included in the feedback loop of the regulator and therefore cancels the V_{BE} drop as well as the temperature-dependent characteristic of V_{BE}. Second, the collector of the external series-pass transistor can be returned to a voltage other than V_{IN} to reduce dissipation. The maximum output current is limited to 0.5 (β_{Q1}) A. The output voltage calculation is now the following.

$$V_{OUT} = V_{REF} \left(\frac{R1 + R2}{R2} \right) + V_{BE(Q1)}$$

This circuit suffers the same drawbacks as that of *Fig-* *ure 5* and can be corrected in the same manner; see *Figure 8* where $R_{SC} = V_{BE(Q2)}/I_{SC}$.

Figure 9 shows another application of the 78MG, a motor speed control that gives excellent line and load regulation. The circuit operates by using the voltage drop across the $10\,\Omega$ resistor to sense increased current demand by the motor when the load on the motor is increased. This slightly raises the voltage across the motor while allowing a greatly increased current to flow in the load. For applications where the current drain by the motor is greater than 0.5 A, an external series-pass device as shown in *Figures 5* through *8* may be used.

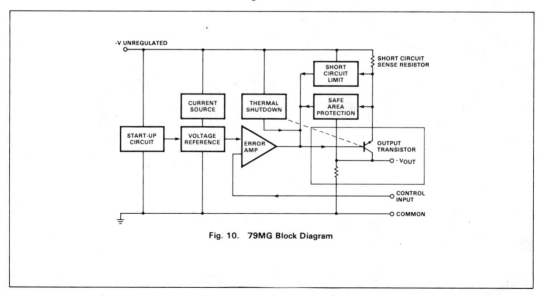

Fig. 10. 79MG Block Diagram

255

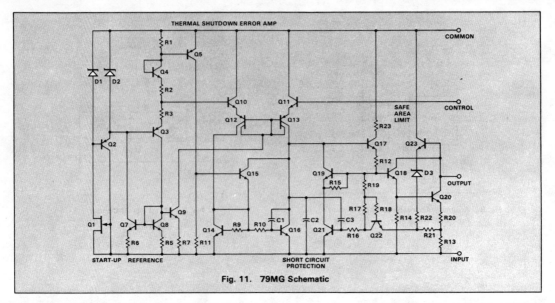

Fig. 11.   79MG Schematic

THE 79MG NEGATIVE VOLTAGE REGULATOR

All of the features of the 78MG are available in the 79MG. From the standpoint of the block diagrams *(Figures 1* and *10)*, the only difference between the two regulators is that the 79MG provides V_{OUT} from the collector of the series-pass transistor instead of the emitter as in the 78MG. From the circuit designer's viewpoint, the devices are very similar except that, in the 79MG, V_{REF} is –2.23 V instead of 5 V and is formed by D2, R1, R2, R3, Q3 and Q4. The circuit, shown in *Figure 11*, is somewhat more complex than that of the 78MG primarily because the integrated power transistors must be npn.

The basic negative regulator, shown in *Figure 12*, is similar to that of the 78MG with the exception of the –2.23 V reference. All 79MG applications are the same as those shown for the 78MG except for larger values of input and output capacitors (to ensure circuit stability) and the polarity of the external transistors. Note that the value of R2 is 2.2 k Ω for negative regulators. *Figure 13* shows an application of both regulators in a dual tracking regulator with ±500 mA capability that can be constructed using two ICs and seven external components.

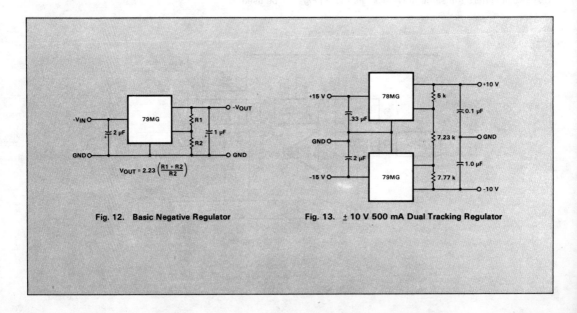

Fig. 12.   Basic Negative Regulator

$$V_{OUT} = 2.23 \left(\frac{R1 + R2}{R2} \right)$$

Fig. 13.   ± 10 V 500 mA Dual Tracking Regulator

256

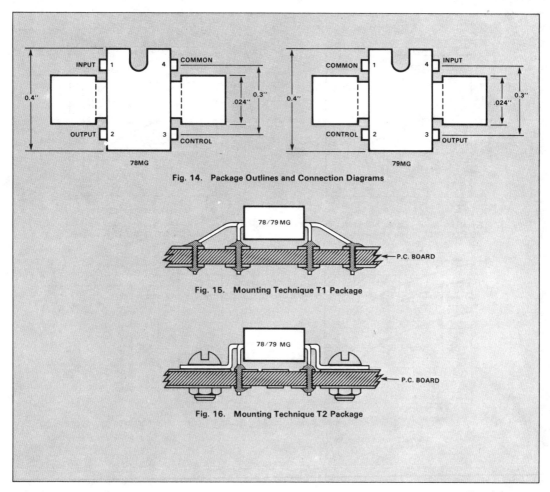

Fig. 14. Package Outlines and Connection Diagrams

Fig. 15. Mounting Technique T1 Package

Fig. 16. Mounting Technique T2 Package

PACKAGING

A 4-terminal package instead of standard 3-terminal transistor packages is now required. *Figure 14* shows the lead connections of the mini-batwing power transistor package; size and pin spacing are compatible with the mini dip configuration. The batwings on each side are internally connected and provide a heat sink for the die. For free air dissipation, the wings can be bent straight or upward. There are two primary heat sinking methods; the wings may be bent downward (T1 package) and soldered through the PC board, or bent parallel to the upper surface of the board and bolted or riveted in place (T2 package). See *Figures 15* and *16*. Other lead bends are possible for external or PC board heat sinking.

What happens if a positive regulator is accidentally inserted into a negative socket or vice versa? The regulator won't work properly but there will be no damage to the regulator or surrounding circuits because the pinouts protect against this possibility. Since pin 1 is the most positive potential and pin 8 and the batwings are the most negative potential on both regulators, accidental mis-insertion will not destroy either the regulator or the circuit. A wrong insertion is "flagged" by the failure of the regulator to operate properly because the output and control pins are reversed (pins 2 and 3).

Thermally, the package performs very well. For the 78MG and 79MG, θ_{JC} = 7.5°C/W typical (11°C/W maximum) and θ_{JA} = 75°C/W. The internal safe area limits are set at 7.5 W and the maximum junction temperature is 150°C. Therefore, derating would begin (with infinite heat sink) at 85°C for both the 78MG and the 79MG. Derating curves showing typical performance and guaranteed limits are shown in *Figures 17* and *18* respectively.

THERMAL DESIGN OF A REGULATOR USING THE 78/79MG

It is quite simple to thermally design the tracking regulator in *Figure 13*. First, the maximum operating temperature, input/output differential voltage, and the output current are selected. For example, assume a

257

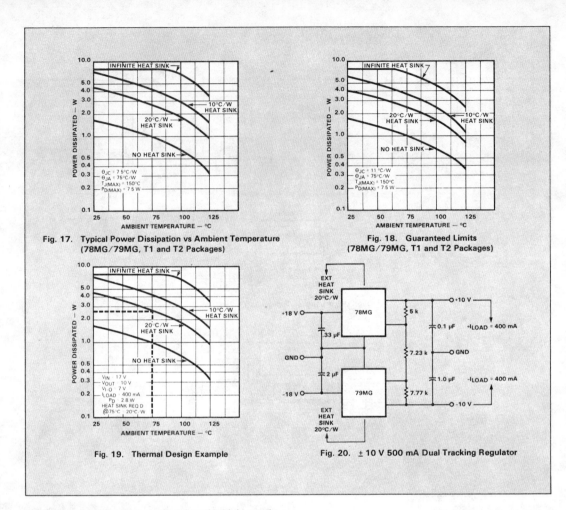

Fig. 17. Typical Power Dissipation vs Ambient Temperature (78MG/79MG, T1 and T2 Packages)

Fig. 18. Guaranteed Limits (78MG/79MG, T1 and T2 Packages)

Fig. 19. Thermal Design Example

Fig. 20. ± 10 V 500 mA Dual Tracking Regulator

75°C maximum temperature, an unregulated dc supply of ± 17 V and a + 400 mA requirement for output current at ± 10 V. Therefore, the input/output differential is 7 V for each regulator and the dissipated power is 2.8 W. Referring back to the thermal graphs, a 20°C/W heat sink is chosen for worst-case design *(Figure 19)*. Using the same resistor values as the circuit in *Figure 13*, the final circuit is shown in *Figure 20*. A PC board heat sink with 9 sq in. area, yields 20°C/W. While this procedure may seem very simple or even trivial, it illustrates the design simplicity achieved with voltage regulators of this type.

CONCLUSION

The 78MG and 79MG 4-terminal regulators fill the industry need for simple to use, minimum component count, variable voltage regulators. Both electrically and thermally, they perform well in all medium current applications and as drivers for higher current regulators. These 4-terminal regulators have definite advantages over 3-terminal devices in the five following situations.

- When a voltage is required which is not in the standard 3-terminal options.

- When a tighter voltage tolerance than the standard ± 5% is required.

- When a variable regulator is required.

- To cut down inventory. Logistically, stocking one device can provide a whole range of voltages which, at present, requires stocking up to six different part numbers.

- To eliminate voltage drop and temperature variation effects from the output. This can be done by including external pass devices, protective diodes, etc., in the error amplifier feedback loop.

CIRCUIT IDEAS Linear

by Andy Adamian

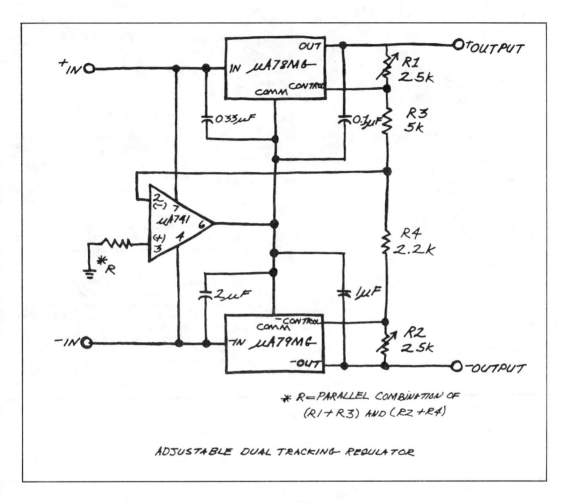

ADJUSTABLE DUAL TRACKING REGULATOR

ADJUSTABLE DUAL TRACKING REGULATOR

This simple combination of two adjustable regulators, a comparator and a few external parts economically achieves true adjustable dual tracking regulation. The circuit illustrated not only tracks, but also has internal short circuit protection, thermal overload protection, safe area limiting and is capable of delivering currents up to 500 mA. Potentiometers R1 and R2 adjust the positive and negative outputs independently.

For the component values shown, the output voltage of the positive μA78MG can be varied from 5 to 30 V while the negative μA79MG output can be adjusted from −2.2 to 27.2 V. Care must be taken not to exceed the maximum voltage ratings of the μA741.

To achieve tracking, the common terminals of the regulators are both tied to the output of a μA741 creating a potential for floating the common terminals of both regulators. A change in one of the outputs produces a corresponding change in the common terminals causing the other output to track in the opposite direction. For example, a decrease due to temperature or load variation in the positive output causes a reduction in the inverting input voltage of the μA741. This reduction forces the potential of the common terminals down and raises the output of the negative regulator towards zero.

Since each regulator is independently referenced, there is no slaving; tracking is true and independent of sides. The output voltages and degree of tracking are proportional to the ratio (R1 + R3)/(R2 + R4).

259

High Power 3-Terminal Voltage Regulator

by Len Arguello

As the trend toward smaller equipment increases and higher volumetric efficiency becomes more important in overall system design, power supply requirements increase accordingly. The monolithic voltage regulator, because of its high performance and reliability, cost effectiveness, and ease of use has become an integral part of most system designs. Three-terminal regulators are available covering the voltage range from 2.6 to 24 V, with current capability from 100 mA to 1.5 A. To meet the demands for variable voltages or non-standard voltage options, two pairs of 4-terminal adjustable regulators rated at 500 mA and 1 A respectively have been introduced.*

But, what about the designer who needs a voltage regulator with higher current capability? He has thus far been forced to add external components to a basic voltage regulator — anywhere from a single series pass device to several components — depending upon his requirements such as thermal protection, current limiting, etc.

Now, the 78H05 *(Figure 1)* is available with a 5 A output current capability. It is a hybrid integrated circuit offering all the inherent characteristics of the monolithic 3-terminal voltage regulator, *i.e.,* full thermal and short circuit protection, and is packaged in a standard TO-3 providing 50 W power dissipa-tion. The 78H05 voltage regulator is intended for a wide range of systems where a regulated 5 V supply is required and can be used for a variety of on-card regulation and circuit isolation applications.

VOLTAGE REFERENCE

Until recently, the normal voltage reference used in a voltage regulator was a temperature-compensated Zener diode, However, it is limited to a breakdown voltage greater than 6 V, thus imposing a lower limit on the input voltage to the regulator. Zeners also require excessively tight process control to maintain a satisfactory tolerance for non-adjustable regulator applications.

A voltage reference that does not use a Zener diode has been developed from the predictable temperature, current and voltage relationships in an emitter-base junction. To obtain a temperature-compensated reference voltage, the positive temperature coefficient of an emitter-base voltage differential between two transistors operated at different current densities is added to the negative temperature coefficient of emitter-base voltage. *Figure 2* shows such a reference. Transistor Q1 operates at a considerably higher current level than Q2 and the emitter-base voltage differential is amplified by the voltage gain of transistor Q2.

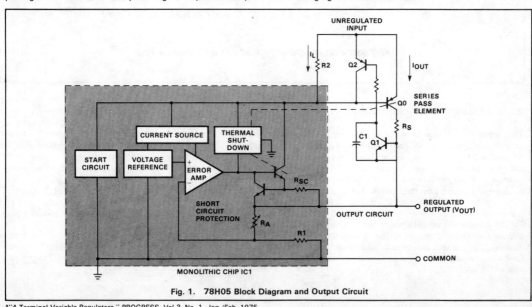

Fig. 1. 78H05 Block Diagram and Output Circuit

*"4-Terminal Variable Regulators," PROGRESS, Vol 3, No. 1, Jan./Feb. 1975

The reference voltage can be expressed as follows.

$$V_{REF} = V_{BE3} + I_{CQ2} \, R2 + I_{BQ3} \, R2$$

$$V_{REF} = V_{BE3} + \frac{R2}{R3} \, (\Delta V_{BE}) + I_{BQ3} \, R2$$

$$V_{REF} = V_{BE3} + \frac{R2}{R3} \left(\frac{KT}{q} \, Ln \, \frac{J1}{J2} \right) + I_{BQ3} \, R2$$

$$V_{REF} \cong V_{BE3} + \frac{R2}{R3} \left(\frac{KT}{q} \, Ln \, \frac{R2}{R1} \right)$$

where J = current density
K = Boltzmann's constant
T = ° Kelvin
q = Electron charge

By selecting the resistor ratios R2:R3 and R2:R1, a low voltage, temperature-compensated reference is obtained.

$$\frac{KT}{q} \approx 0.026 \text{ V at } 300°K$$

Figure 3 shows a simplified schematic of the actual circuit used in the regulator. The base-emitter drops of Q4, Q5 and Q6 have been added to increase the reference level to 5 V. The reference then becomes:

$$V_{REF} = (V_{BE3} + V_{BE4} + V_{BE5} + V_{BE6}) + \frac{R2}{R3} \left(\frac{KT}{q} \, Ln \, \frac{R2}{R1} \right)$$

Resistors R1, R2 and R3 are selected so that the reference voltage is constant over the temperature range and also has a nominal value of 5 V at room temperature.

A very tight reference voltage tolerance is, therefore, obtained without special process controls. This is because base-emitter characteristics are better understood and more predictable than Zener references. Also, monolithic circuits lend themselves more readily to resistor and transistor matching than

to generating absolute values of resistance. An external adjustment to trim output voltage is unneccesary in most applications. An additional benefit is that this reference has low noise output compared to a Zener reference, thus eliminating the need for a large bypass capacitor to remove noise.

ERROR AMPLIFIER

An error amplifier (see Figure 1) compares the output feedback signal with the voltage reference and corrects the output by the amount of the error. The regulator circuit shown in Figure 3 has the error amplifier combined with the voltage reference. The advantage is that noise at the regulator output is minimized since the amplifier and reference are no longer separate sources of noise. In Figure 3, transistor Q3 is used as the error amplifier; and at the same time, its base-emitter voltage is used as part of the reference.

A current source is used as the active load to the error amplifier. A negative feedback path is provided through feedback resistors R4 and R5. If the voltage at the output increases due to a reduction in load current, that voltage change is transmitted to the base of transistor Q3. Transistor Q3 then conducts more, effectively reducing the base drive to the output transistor by current steering. The result is a decrease in output voltage, which tends to correct the change in output voltage due to the load current change. As the loop settles, an equilibrium value at the output is reached. The output voltage is derived using the following formula.

$$\text{Output Voltage} = V_{REF} \left(\frac{R4 + R5}{R5} \right)$$

Varying the resistor ratio (R4 + R5): R5 yields different fixed output voltages.

THERMAL OVERLOAD PROTECTION

One of the benefits of including the series pass transistor on the common substrate is that it is then possible to incorporate both thermal and current overload protection. Low power

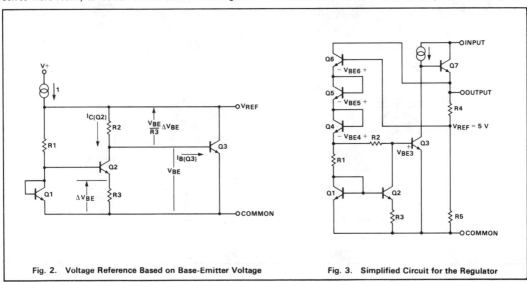

Fig. 2.   Voltage Reference Based on Base-Emitter Voltage

Fig. 3.   Simplified Circuit for the Regulator

IC regulators usually rely on current limiting for overload protection as there is no practical way to sense junction temperature in a separate pass transistor. As a result, excessive heating of the pass transistor is one of the primary failure mechanisms of solid-state regulators. A thermal overload protection circuit in a hybrid regulator with the pass transistor on a common substrate limits the maximum temperature of the transistor junction. This limiting is independent of input voltage, the type of overload or degree of package heat sinking.

The base-emitter junction of a transistor is used to sense the temperature of the series pass device. The temperature limiting transistor normally is biased below its conduction threshold so that it does not affect normal circuit operation. If the pass-device temperature rises to its maximum limit due to a load fault or other condition, the temperature limiting transistor turns on. This removes the base drive to the output transistors and shuts down the regulator, preventing further chip heating.

OUTPUT CIRCUIT (See Figure 1)

Output voltage V_{OUT} is derived from the monolithic chip IC1 which is also a reference as well as a buffer and driver for the output stage. When a load is placed across the output terminals, the load current supplied by IC1 is sensed by resistor R2, which then develops a voltage drop that forward biases the emitter-base junction of Q0. At this time, IC1 begins to supply base current to Q0, which supplies the bulk of the load current ($\approx$95%) during operation. The output circuit is designed so that the worst-case current requirement of the Q0 base added to the current through R2 always remains below the current limit threshold of IC1. Resistor R_S in conjunction with Q1 and Q2 make up a current-sense and limit circuit to

protect the series pass device from excessive current drain. As the output current begins to increase, the voltage drop across R_S starts to forward bias the emitter-base junction of Q1. As Q1 conducts, its collector current flows through the Q2 base; thus Q2 begins to conduct and therefore shunts away some of the current available to the base of Q0. This process continues until a natural state of electrical equilibrium is reached, at which time the 78H05 is in a current-limit mode of operation. Capacitor C1 provides frequency stability by adding a pole in the output-circuit transfer function that lowers the overall loop gain below the critical levels at high frequencies.

78H05 CONSTRUCTION

The 78H05 voltage regulator is constructed using state-of-the-art hybrid circuit technology and is packaged in a hermetically sealed TO-3. A beryllium-oxide substrate is used in conjunction with an isothermal layout to optimize the thermal characteristics of the device and still maintain electrical isolation between the various chips. This ensures nearly ideal thermal transfer between the series pass device and the temperature sensing circuit within IC1, thus providing the thermal-limiting feature. All active chips are gold-eutectic attached to the beryllium-oxide substrate. The substrate is reflow soldered onto a solid copper slug that fits within the cavity of the TO-3 header aluminum base. This process guarantees junction-to-case thermal impedances in the order of 1.5 to 2°C/W, thereby providing package dissipation as high as 50 W at 25°C case temperature. Output voltage sensing is performed at the device output pin, so that the error amplifier can correct for any output voltage errors caused by finite impedances in the output circuit, i.e., lead bonds, metal traces, etc. Some 78H05 typical characteristics and applications are shown in *Figures 4* and *5* respectively.

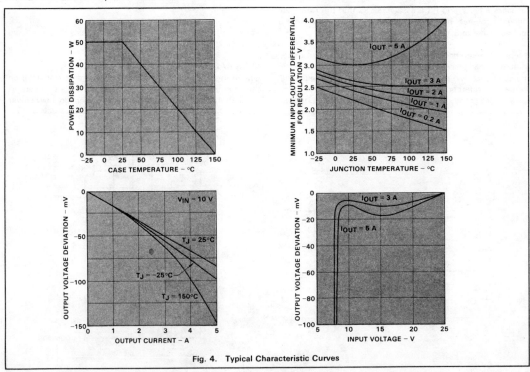

Fig. 4. Typical Characteristic Curves

Fixed Output 5 A Regulator

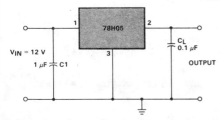

This is the basic application for the 78H05 and can be used when a fixed 5 V output is required with 5 A current capability. The input capacitor C1, as well as C_L, are required for stability when the regulator is placed at some distance from the main power source. C_L and C1 should be attached as close as possible to the 78H05 socket.

10+ A Regulator

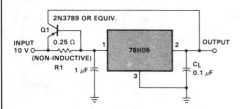

For applications requiring output current in excess of that offered by the basic device (5 A), the circuit shown can be used. The value of R1 determines the point at which Q1 begins to conduct, thus bypassing the regulator. In this circuit, the 78H05 is used as a high current reference device, and the overall circuit does not offer short circuit protection. The maximum current capability of this circuit can be defined as:

$$I_O(MAX) = \left[I_{SC} - \frac{V_{BE1}}{R1} \right] \beta \, Q1(MIN)$$

where:

$$I_{SC} = \text{78H05 short circuit current}$$

Increased Output Voltage

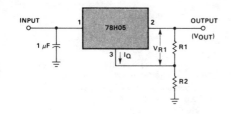

In this circuit, a voltage pedestal developed across R2 is added to the normal regulated output V_{R1} to provide an output voltage that can be described by the following:

$$V_{OUT} = V_{R1} \left(1 + \frac{R2}{R1} \right) + I_Q \, R2$$

0-10 V Adjustable Regulator

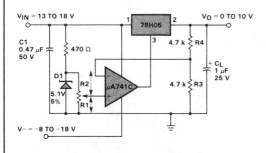

When an application requires a continuously variable voltage, or a voltage that can be adjusted to a given output, this adjustable regulator circuit can be used. The output voltage is given by the expression:

$$V_{OUT} = V_{Z1} \left(\frac{R1}{R1 + R2} \right) \left(1 + \frac{R4}{R3} \right)$$

Care should be taken to insure that the input voltage never exceeds 18 V (ripple included) or damage to the μA741C may occur. For a V_{IN} of more than 18 V, a higher working-voltage op amp must be used. This circuit offers all the 78H05 features plus the capability of adjusting the output above and below the nominal 78H05 output.

Fig. 5. Typical Applications

NOTE: Maximum 50 W power dissipation for the 78H05 must be observed and proper heat sinking must be used when required.

Thermal Considerations ...When Designing with IC Voltage Regulators

by Andy Adamian

Maintaining a well regulated voltage to the various areas of an electronic system has always plagued the system designer. Not long ago, he was confined to using bulky power regulators or regulators consisting of discrete components to do the job. Unfortunately, additional problems were often encountered – spurious signals, degraded local regulation and unwanted coupling between critical parts of the system. Today, these problems can be avoided by using IC voltage regulators in each section of the system. Reliable, versatile and cost effective, both fixed and adjustable IC regulators are available in a wide choice of positive and negative voltages from 2.6 to 30 V with current capabilities from 10 mA to 1.5 A. The variety of available packages (*Table 1*) adds to the versatility of these easy-to-use on-card regulators.

A crucial aspect in the efficient use of the various regulator packages is the removal of unwanted heat caused by the power dissipation level, the means of removing the heat caused by the power dissipation level, and by the temperature of the body, or heat sink, to which the heat is removed. *Figure 1* shows a simplified equivalent circuit for a typical semiconductor device in equilibrium. The power dissipation, which is analogous to current flow in electrical terms, is caused by a heat source similar to a voltage source. Temperature is analogous to voltage potential and thermal resistance to ohmic resistance. Extending the analogy of Ohm's law to *Figure 1*,

$$\theta_{JA(tot)} = \theta_{JC} + \theta_{CS} + \theta_{SA} = \frac{T_J - T_A}{P_D}$$

Thermal resistance, then, is the rise in the temperature of a package above some reference level per unit of power dissipation in that package, usually expressed in degrees centigrade per watt. The reference temperature may be ambient or it may be the temperature of a heat sink to which the package is connected. There are several factors that affect thermal resistance including die size, the size of the heat source on the die (series-pass transistor in an IC regulator), die-attach material and thickness, leadframe material, construction and thickness.

THERMAL EVALUATION OF VOLTAGE REGULATORS

For effective thermal management, the user must rely on important parameters supplied by the manufacturer, such as junction-to-case and junction-to-ambient thermal resistance and maximum operating temperature. To measure thermal resistance, the difference between the junction temperature and the chosen reference temperature, case, sink or ambient, must be determined. Ambient or sink temperature measurement is straightforward. For case-temperature measurement, the device should have a sufficiently large heat sink and the power level should be close to the specified rating of the package-die combination. The case or tab temperature can be measured by an infrared microradiometer or by using a thermocouple soldered to a point in the center of the case or tab at the tab-heat-sink interface as close to the die as practical.

Measurement of the junction temperature, unfortunately, is not as simple and involves some calibrations. There are several methods available for junction-temperature measurement; the two most commonly used are described here.

Thermal Shutdown Method

With this method, the thermal shutdown temperature of each device is used as the thermometer in determining the thermal resistance. The device is first heated externally, with as little internal power dissipation as practical, until it reaches thermal shutdown. Then, with the device mounted on a heat sink, the regulator is powered externally until it reaches thermal shutdown again. With some packages, the ambient of the device and its heat sink may have to be elevated sufficiently to force the regulator into shutdown. The thermal resistance of the device can then be calculated by using

$$\theta_{JC} = \frac{T_J - T_C}{P_D}$$

where

θ_{JC} is the junction-to-case thermal resistance
T_J is the measured thermal shutdown temperature
T_C is the measured case temperature
P_D is the power dissipated to force the device into shutdown and is equal to

$$(V_{IN} - V_{OUT}) I_{OUT} + V_{IN} I_Q$$

I_Q is the quiescent current of the device and can be neglected for low thermal resistance packages such as the TO-3 and TO-220.

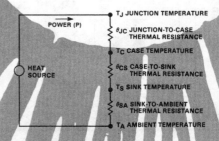

Fig. 1. Simplified Thermal Circuit

Substrate or Isolation Diode Method

The second method of thermal-resistance measurement utilizes the isolation diodes within the integrated circuits as temperature sensing elements*. Under normal operating conditions, the substrate diodes are reverse biased and separate or "isolate" active as well as passive components within an integrated circuit. (See *Figure 2*). When the regulator is reverse biased and a constant current is forced through the device between the input terminal and ground, the substrate diodes become forward biased; naturally, when the forward drop is measured, the diode with the highest temperature (lowest forward drop) is detected. Measurement of the thermal resistance of the regulator then involves two steps:

Calibrating the substrate diode at a fixed I_{SUBS} level in an oven or bath at two temperatures, preferably near the device operating junction temperature. It is assumed that this voltage drop changes linearly with temperature.

Measuring the junction temperature. The device is powered through a switching circuit S1 at a duty cycle greater than 99% (*Figure 3*); thus the device is electrically heated until it reaches equilibrium. During short measuring intervals (< 1% duty cycle), the switching circuit de-energizes the device and the forward drop of the substrate diode is measured at the previously calibrated I_{SUBS} current level. This voltage drop must be measured as soon as possible (several microseconds) after the removal of the power pulse to avoid inaccurate readings due to cooling of the chip. Diode D1 prevents reverse current from flowing through the load resistor R_L during the substrate-diode measuring interval. Since the change in the isolation diode drop is assumed to be linear with temperature, the measured voltage drop can be converted to its corresponding junction temperature by interpolation or extrapolation. Thermal resistance can then be calculated by the same formula used in the thermal-shutdown method.

HEAT SINK REQUIREMENTS

When is a heat sink necessary, and what type of a heat sink should one use? The answers to these questions depend on reliability and cost requirements. Heat sinking is necessary to keep the operating junction temperature T_J of the regulator below the specified maximum value. Since semiconductor reliability improves as operating junction temperature is lowered, a reliability/cost compromise is usually made in the device design.

Table 1 is a tabulation by package of the various regulators available from Fairchild. It also lists the average and maximum values of thermal resistance for the regulator chip-package combinations and can be used as a guide in selecting a suitable package when designing a regulator circuit. Some form of heat sinking is mandatory whenever the power dissipation exceeds the following.

0.67 W for the TO-39 package
0.69 W for the TO-92 package
1.5 W for the power miniDIP and PowerBat packages
1.8 W for the TO-220 package
2.8 W for the TO-3 package

at 25°C ambient or lower power levels at ambients above 25°C.

*For more detailed explanation of this method, see Fairchild Application Note 205, "Thermal Evaluation of Integrated Circuits."

To choose or design a heat sink, the designer must determine the following regulator parameters.

$P_{D(max)}$ — Maximum Power dissipation:
$(V_{IN} - V_{OUT}) I_{OUT} + V_{IN} I_Q$

$T_{A(max)}$ — Maximum ambient temperature required for regulator operation

$T_{J(max)}$ — Maximum operating junction temperature, specified by the manufacturer.

θ_{JC}, θ_{JA} — Junction-to-case and junction-to-ambient thermal resistance values, also specified by the regulator manufacturer.

θ_{CS} — Case-to-heat-sink thermal resistance which, for large packages, can range from about 0.2°C/W to about 1°C/W depending on the quality of the contact between the package and the heat sink.

Maximum permissible dissipation without a heat sink is determined by

$$P_{D(max)} = \frac{T_J - T_A}{\theta_{JA}}$$

Cross-sectional Diagram Showing Two Monolithic Transistors Isolated by Substrate Diodes

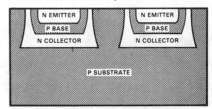

Equivalent Circuit

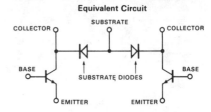

Fig. 2. Monolithic Transistor Isolation

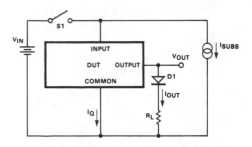

Fig. 3. Thermal Resistance Measurement Circuit Using Substrate Diode Technique

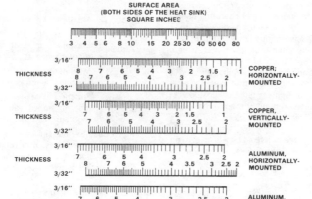

SURFACE AREA
(BOTH SIDES OF THE HEAT SINK)
SQUARE INCHES

THERMAL RESISTANCE IN °C/W

NOTE:
To determine either area required or thermal resistance of a given area, draw a vertical line between the top (or area) line down to the material of interest.

Fig. 4. Heat Sink Material Selection Guide

If the device dissipation P_D exceeds this figure, a heat sink is necessary. The total required thermal resistance may then be calculated.

$$\theta_{JA(tot)} = \theta_{JC} + \theta_{CS} + \theta_{SA} = \frac{T_J - T_A}{P_D}$$

Case-to-sink and sink-to-ambient thermal resistance information on commercially available heat sinks is normally provided by the heat sink manufacturer. If a chassis or other conventional surface is used as a heat sink, *Figure 4* can be used as a guide to estimate the required surface area.

How to Choose a Heat Sink – Example
Determine the heat sink required for a regulator which has the following system requirements:

Operating ambient temperature range: 0°C to 60°C
Maximum junction temperature: 125°C
Maximum output current: 800 mA
Maximum Input-Output Voltage Differential: 10 V

From *Table 1*, the choice is narrowed down to the µA7800 family, available in TO-3 and TO-220 packages. The TO-220 package is sufficient (lower cost, better thermal resistance).

$\theta_{JC} = 5°C/W$ maximum (from data sheet or *Table 1*)

$$\theta_{JA(tot)} = \theta_{JC} + \theta_{CS} + \theta_{SA} = \frac{T_J - T_A}{P_D}$$

$$\theta_{CS} + \theta_{SA} = \frac{125 - 60}{0.8 \times 10} - 5 = 3.13°C/W$$

Assuming $\theta_{CS} = 0.13°C/W$ then $\theta_{SA} = 3°C/W$

This thermal resistance value can be achieved by using either 20 square inches of 3/16 inch thick vertically mounted aluminum (*Figure 4*) or a commercial heat sink.

Tips for Better Regulator Heat Sinking
Avoid placing heat-dissipating components such as power resistors next to regulators.

When using low dissipation packages such as TO-5, TO-39, and TO-92, keep lead lengths to a minimum and use the largest possible area of the printed board traces or mounting hardware to provide a heat dissipation path for the regulator.

When using larger packages, be sure the heat sink surface is flat and free from ridges or high spots. Check the regulator package for burrs or peened-over corners. Regardless of the smoothness and flatness of the package and heat-sink contact, air pockets between them are unavoidable unless a lubricant is used. Therefore, for good thermal conduction, use a thin layer of thermal lubricant such as Dow Corning DC340, General Electric 662 or Thermacote by Thermalloy.

In some applications, especially with negative regulators, it is desirable to electrically insulate the regulator case from the heat sink. Hardware kits for this purpose are commercially available for such packages as the TO-3 and TO-220. They generally consist of a 0.003 to 0.005 inch thick piece of mica or bonded fiberglass to electrically isolate the two surfaces, yet provide a thermal path between them. As expected, the thermal resistance will increase but, as in the direct metal-to-metal joint, some improvement can be realized by using thermal lubricant on each side of the mica.

If the regulator is mounted on a heat sink with fins, the most efficient heat transfer takes place when the fin is in a vertical plane, as this type of mounting forces the heat transfer from fin to air in a combination of radiation and convection.

If it is necessary to bend any of the regulator leads, handle them carefully to avoid straining the package. Furthermore, lead bending should be restricted since repeated bending will fatigue and eventually break the leads.

THERMAL RESISTANCE (θ_{JC}, θ_{JA}) BY DEVICE AND PACKAGE

RESISTANCES LISTED AS FOLLOWS:
$\theta_{JC}(\text{TYP})$ $\theta_{JC}(\text{MAX})$ in °C/W
$\theta_{JA}(\text{TYP})$ $\theta_{JA}(\text{MAX})$

REG. TYPE	DEVICE NO./SERIES	IOUT (A)	TO-3	4-LEAD TO-3	TO-220	POWER MINIDIP	POWER WATT	TO-39	4-LEAD TO-39	TO-92	TO-99 8-LEAD TO-5	TO-100 10-LEAD TO-5	TO-116 14-PIN PLASTIC	TO-116 14-PIN CERAMIC	8 PIN MINIDIP
POS. 3-TERM.	μA78XX	1	3.5 5.5 40 45		3.0 5.0 60 65										
	μA78MXX	0.5			3.0 5.0 62 70			18 25 120 185							
	μA78LXX	0.1						20 40 140 190		— — 160 180					
	78H05, 5V	5	1.5 2.0 37 40												
	SH0323, 5 V	3	1.5 2.0 37 40												
	μA309, 5 V	1	3.5 5.5 40 45												
NEG. 3-TERM.	μA79XX	1	3.5 5.5 40 45		3.0 5.0 60 65										
	μA79MXX	0.5			3.0 5.0 62 70			18 25 120 185							
POS. ADJ.	μA78G 4-TERM.	1		4.0 6.0 44 47			7.5 11 75 80								
	μA78MG 4-TERM.	0.5				7.5 11 75	8 12 75 80		18 25 125 185						
	μA723	0.125									25 40 150 190	25 50 150 190	— — 150 190	— — 125 160	
	μA105/305/376	0.012 to 0.045													— — 160 190
NEG. ADJ.	μA79G 4-TERM.	1		4.0 6.0 44 47			7.5 11 75 80								
	μA79MG 4-TERM.	0.5				7.5 11 75	8 12 75 80		18 25 125 185						
	μA104/304	0.020										25 40 150 190			

Table 1.

POWER SUP

Proper Wiring Avoids Problems

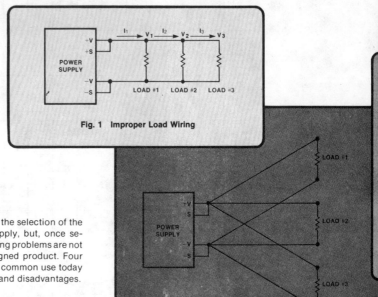

Fig. 1   Improper Load Wiring

Fig. 2   Proper Load Connection

by George Niu

Using a power supply involves not only the selection of the most appropriate and cost-effective supply, but, once selected, hooking it up properly so that wiring problems are not introduced into an otherwise well-designed product. Four major types of regulated supplies are in common use today and each has its own share of features and disadvantages.

Most commercially available power supplies employ either series, switching, SCR or ferroresonant techniques. Of the four, the series supply is the best understood and most popular. Series regulators provide superior regulation, ripple, noise and transient response; disadvantages are large size and weight and low efficiency. More recent in popularity, switching regulation fits well into the current mood for power saving. Because the current is switched at a fast pulse repetition rate, transformers, inductors and filter capacitors can be much smaller than those required for 60 Hz operation. Switching supplies exhibit high power density, low heat dissipation and minimum size and weight; however, they typically produce higher noise, switching spikes and a lower degree of stabilization performance. The "new generation" components used in the latest designs permit a reduction in noise and spikes and cost less. Switching supplies have started to become competitve — especially those rated over 200 W of output — and are now used in many large systems.

Low in cost, the SCR regulator also offers high efficiency and small size. However, relatively poor regulation, high ripple and noise and slow transient response limit their use to systems that can tolerate greater noise and ripple. The ferroresonant regulator is outstanding in its circuit simplicity and offers lower cost, higher reliability and fewer components compared with the other standard regulators. It also has excellent immunity to line-voltage transients. Disadvantages include poor load regulation, high ripple and fixed output voltage as well as higher losses.

Reprinted with permission from EDN, May 5, 1977
©1977 Cahners Publishing Company

There's a Science To Load Wiring

Even the best power supplies can become troublesome unless the basic rules applying to interconnection are carefully followed. In particular, improper wiring connections to the input and output terminals are likely to degrade performance and reliability. If ignored, potential trouble sources such as dc distribution, ground loops, remote-sensing connections and ac inputs usually degrade system performance, especially in large systems.

Multiple loads require specific connection techniques for best results. *Figure 1* shows a common improper load-wiring connection that causes unequal load voltages and interaction between loads. Each load sees a power-supply voltage that depends on the current drawn by the other loads (because of IR drops in the common wiring). Voltages V_1, V_2 and V_3 have increasingly lower potentials.

Since most loads draw a current that varies with time, a time-varying interaction between loads is likely — resulting in noise, cross talk, pulse coupling or a tendency toward interload oscillation. Proper connections for more than one load are shown in *Figure 2*. Here two dc distribution points are

PLIES

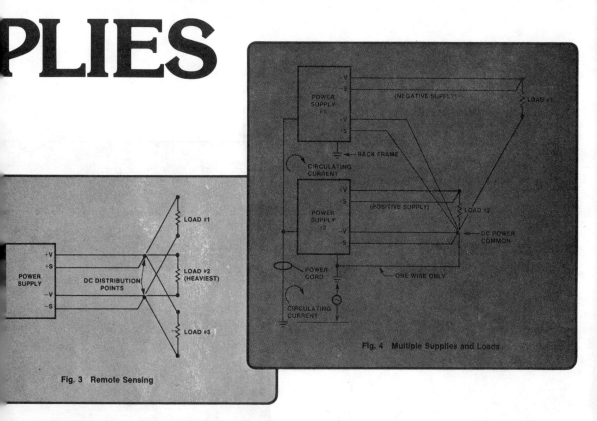

Fig. 3   Remote Sensing

Fig. 4   Multiple Supplies and Loads

established at the output terminals, avoiding improper inter-action between loads so loads receive inputs of equal quality. These points should be located as close as possible to those terminals, except when remote sensing is used.

Remote sensing calls for locating the dc distribution points as close as possible to the terminals of the heaviest load. Sense leads should be connected from the supply sensing terminals to the dc distribution points as shown in *Figure 3*. With remote-sensing connections, the voltage sensed at the heaviest load controls the output, and IR drops from the dc distribution points to the other (lighter) loads are small. Whether connections are made as in *Figure 2* or *Figure 3*, there should be no direct connection from one load to an-other except by way of the dc distribution points.

In a dc distribution system, the wires that carry the dc load must be of sufficient size to tolerate the current that would flow if the associated load terminals were short-circuited. Wire sizes should also be sufficient to hold IR drops between distribution points and loads to an acceptable level.

In Case of Ground Loops — Rewire

Generally, ground loops represent the most troublesome problem connected with power-supply wiring. Ground-loop sources are so subtle and diverse that designers frequently resort to empirical solutions. Looking realistically at the situation, there are no two ground points in a system that

have exactly the same potential. These potential differences, even though small in many cases, cause a large amount of current to flow. This grounding current generates noise, voltage spikes and unequal voltages at different loads, de-grading system performance.

To sidestep ground-loop problems, there should be only one ground return point in a system — including the supply, all its loads and all other supplies connected to the same loads. In a large system, the best dc ground point depends upon the complexity of the loads and dc wiring. Rack-mounted sys-tems that contain separately mounted power supplies and loads generally have multiple ground connections. *Figure 4*, while simplified, shows how to treat such a combination. Each power supply usually has its chassis tied to the "safety ground" lead of the ac power cord, while the rack that holds the supply is connected to the earth ground. Since this arrangement has the power supplies attached to the rack frame, circulating ground currents are inevitable. However, as long as these ground currents are confined to the ground system and do not flow through any of the wiring that distributes the dc output, their effect should be insignificant.

When only one connection path joins the earth ground and dc power common (as in *Figure 4*), ground-loop currents cannot affect the power-supply output and load circuits. Therefore, no matter how complicated the system, there should be only one dc power common point in the system, and it should be connected to ground by only one wire.

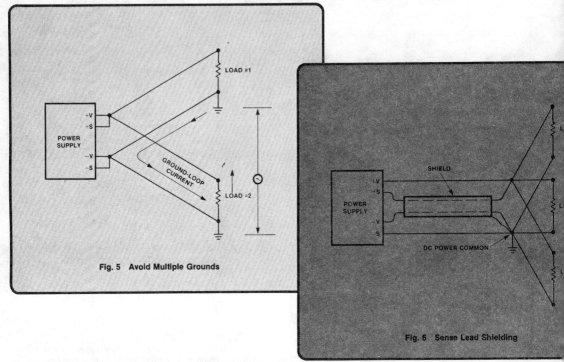

Fig. 5 Avoid Multiple Grounds

Fig. 6 Sense Lead Shielding

To illustrate what can happen when multiple loads have multiple grounds, consider the circuit of *Figure 5*. Trouble is inevitable, for ground-loop currents will circulate through the wiring as long as separate loads connected to the same power supply also have separate ground returns. Connections such as these should be avoided in any system.

Remote Sensing Allows Accurate Voltages

When loads must have accurate voltages across them, the remote-sensing feature should be brought into use. The Kelvin connection is made at the center of the loads, so that the voltage between the connection points can be adjusted to a precise value and maintained in spite of variations of load current (especially with high-current loads). Properly employed, remote sensing improves both transient performance and output impedance of the remote terminals. Noise pickup can be minimized by shielding the sensing leads between the power-supply terminals and remote terminals as shown *Figure 6*.

The sensing-lead shield should be connected to dc power common, and must never be used as one of the sensing leads. In a large system with complicated combinations of leads and wiring, it is wise to verify by experiment where the shields should be grounded to minimize ripple and noise.

If a sensing lead should open, output voltage usually climbs rapidly toward the maximum rectifier voltage — a value signifiantly larger than the power supply's rated output voltage. Such an increased level will probably damage active loads on

the power supply, so any open-circuit conditions between the sensing terminals and dc distribution terminals should be avoided. Many well regulated power supplies include internally wired resistors or diodes between the output and sense terminals *(Figure 7)* to overcome the open-circuit problem.

If the supply application requires long sensing leads, or has sensing paths that include relays, switches or connector contacts, there must be open sensing-lead protection. If not an internal part of the supply circuitry, either resistors or diodes should be added externally.

Most supplies with the sensing-lead provision have a maximum IR-drop limitation (typically 0.5 to 2 V) on the force leads. If the IR drop is allowed to exceed the maximum limitation, proper regulation control will be lost. To prevent this, increase the wire size of the force leads between the power-supply output terminals and the load point where the Kelvin connection is made.

When connected for remote sensing, some supplies oscillate due to phase shift and added time delay. If this occurs, contact the power-supply manufacturer since it is a very difficult problem. In some cases, readjusting the supply's internal "loop-stability" control will do the job, but in other cases the supply may have to be redesigned and tailored for the application.

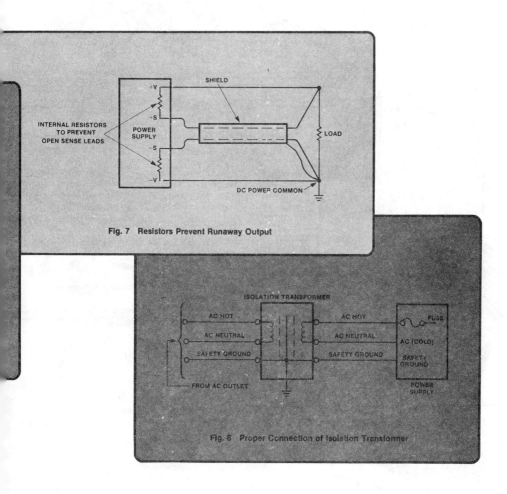

Fig. 7 Resistors Prevent Runaway Output

Fig. 8 Proper Connection of Isolation Transformer

The 3-Wire AC Input: Errors Can Kill

AC input to power supplies is usually obtained from an ac outlet that contains an "ac hot," an "ac neutral" and a "safety ground." It is essential to retain the 3-wire continuity, without interchange, from the ac outlet to the input terminals of the power supply.

If "ac hot" and "safety ground" are accidentally interchanged, the power-supply chassis is elevated to an ac potential equal to the line voltage. A potential hazard occurs if the chassis is floating, and protective fuses or circuit breakers will blow if the chassis is grounded.

Reversal of the "ac hot" and "ac neutral" places power-supply fuses or switches in series with the cold side of the power line (instead of the hot side). If the fuses or circuit breakers open as a result of overload protection, the hot side will still be connected and exposed within the power supply, constituting a hazard.

Interchanging "ac neutral" and "safety ground" leads places the chassis at the neutral potential. The "neutral" generally has a different potential than ground, causing a circulating ground current to flow through the power-supply chassis and other associated ground-return paths. This ground current in turn causes increased output ripple, degrading system performance. For both safety and proper supply operation, it is clearly important to maintain the continuity of ac leads from the ac outlet to the power-supply input terminals.

Some systems use isolation transformers connected between the ac power outlet and power-supply input terminals. Here, the transformer primary common terminal should always be connected to the "ac neutral" of the line, and the secondary common terminal should be connected to the power supply neutral terminal (Figure 8). □

271

IC Timers

by Robert C Frostholm

Conventional timers — motor driven types, dashpot relays, solid sta
hybrid and rack-mounted electronic units — meet the demands f
which they were designed. However, they are too bulky, require t
much power and are too costly for today's applications in portab
and battery-powered products. IC timers, now readily availabl
offer the required miniaturization, operate on less than a watt a
are extremely cost effecti

These ICs are basic building blocks that can be used either alone
time a single machine function, or as part of a complex digital contr
system and provide functions ranging from simple timed cycles
precision clock pulses. Their output power capacity can drive relays, T
circuits and even subminiature moto

For applications requiring more than one timer, dual timers are available
prices considerably below those of single timers. A more sophisticat
programmable timer/counter can extend the time delays from a few micr
seconds to five days and ultra long time delays, up to three years, c
be generated by cascading two of these device

IC timers have internal circuit elements interconnected to provide a variety
operation modes, depending on how the user connects the device terminals. Ir
typical timer circuit, such as the μA555, transistors, diodes and resisto
are internally connected to form a flip-flop, two comparators and an output sta
Figure 1. There are two basic modes of operation — monostable or one-sh
and astable (multivibrator or oscillator) or free-running. In the monostable mode, the delay tir
is precisely controlled by one external resistor and a capacitor; in the astable mo
the frequency and duty cycle are controlled with two external resistors and one capacit

MONOSTABLE OPERATION — Simple Time De

In the monostable configuration, *Figure 2*, the timing function is started by a negative-going pulse appli
to the trigger terminal. A comparator detects when this voltage falls below the threshold which is o
third the power-supply voltage V_{CC}. Since V_{CC} for the μA555 can be any value from 5 to 15

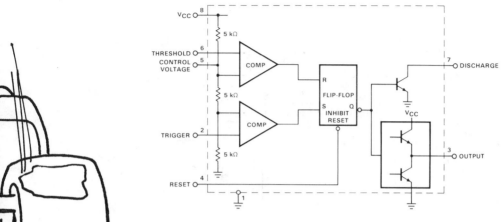

Fig. 1. μA555 Block Diagram

the threshold may be anywhere between 3.3 and 10 V. At this point, the comparator sets a flip-flop which removes a short circuit across the external timing capacitor C and causes the output voltage to go HIGH. Capacitor C then begins to charge exponentially with the time constant (time required to charge to 63% of final voltage or discharge to 37% of initial voltage) determined by internal circuit design and the values of R and C. The μA555 has a time constant of 1.1 RC.

When the voltage on C reaches $2/3$ V_{CC} and is detected at the threshold terminal, a second comparator resets the flip-flop which short circuits C, discharging the timing capacitor through pin 7 and simultaneously forcing the output voltage to decrease at the end of one cycle.

The control-voltage pin 5 can be used for filtering out electrical noise; however, it is intended to vary timing independent of the RC network with a forced voltage at this point. When this connection is not in use, it can act as an antenna, picking up signals and changing the time interval. It should be bypassed to ground with a 0.01 μF capacitor. A reset connection, pin 4, is also provided. When unused, it should be tied to V_{CC}. When used, the voltage should first be dropped to below 0.4 V to reset the timer, then raised to greater than 1 V. Between 0.4 and 1 V, the device is in an indeterminate state.

ASTABLE OPERATION – Multivibrator or Oscillator

Adding a second resistor between the discharge and threshold terminals of the circuit of *Figure 2* changes the device from a one-shot time delay to an oscillator with a programmable duty cycle and frequency. For astable operation, *Figure 3*, continuous retriggering is required. The simplest way to do it is by connecting the trigger to the threshold pin. When power is applied, the capacitor is uncharged, pins 6 and 2 are below $1/3$ V_{CC}, and the device is initially triggered. The timer remains on for time t_1.

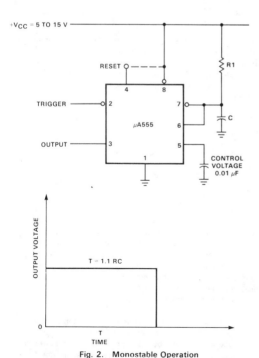

Fig. 2. Monostable Operation

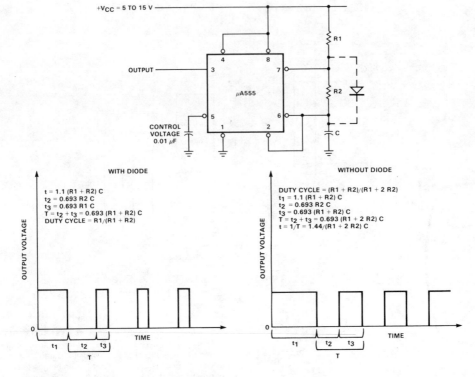

WITH DIODE

$t = 1.1 (R1 + R2) C$
$t_2 = 0.693 R2 C$
$t_3 = 0.693 R1 C$
$T = t_2 + t_3 = 0.693 (R1 + R2) C$
DUTY CYCLE $= R1/(R1 + R2)$

WITHOUT DIODE

DUTY CYCLE $= (R1 + R2)/(R1 + 2 R2)$
$t_1 = 1.1 (R1 + R2) C$
$t_2 = 0.693 R2 C$
$t_3 = 0.693 (R1 + R2) C$
$T = t_2 + t_3 = 0.693 (R1 + 2 R2) C$
$t = 1/T = 1.44/(R1 + 2 R2) C$

Fig. 3. Astable Operation

At the end of this time period, the voltage on C reaches 2/3 V_{CC} and the device shuts off, allowing C to discharge through R2. At the end of discharge time t_2, the voltage on C is 1/3 V_{CC} and the device retriggers. C then begins to charge up to 2/3 V_{CC} to repeat the cycle. The second and subsequent charge times are t_3. So the total time period for an oscillation, not counting the first cycle when on time is slightly longer because C must charge from 0 V to 2/3 V_{CC}, is T, where $T = t_2 + t_3$.

As R2 decreases, the duty cycle (on time/total time) approaches 100% and, as R2 increases, the duty cycle approaches 50%.

$$\text{Duty Cycle} = \frac{R1 + R2}{R1 + 2R2}$$

To obtain duty cycles less than 50%, an additional diode is required to effectively switch out R2 during on time. Diode forward resistance is small enough to be ignored in determining on time. Similarly, the reverse resistance of the diode is large enough that its effect can be ignored in determining off time. As R2 increases, the duty cycle approaches a very low value; and as R2 decreases, the duty cycle approaches 100%.

$$\text{Duty Cycle} = \frac{R1}{R1 + R2}$$

The output of the timer can sink (consume current) or source (supply current) up to 200 mA when operated from a +15 V supply. When using either of these configurations, the total resistance, R1 + R2, should not exceed 20 MΩ to insure that the comparator input current, supplied through R1 + R2, does not affect the timing.

An ac signal on the control-voltage pin 5 can provide an output for pulse-position modulation. When not in use, pin 5 should be bypassed to ground with a 0.01 μF capacitor as in the monostable configuration. When the reset pin 4 is between 0.4 and 1 V, the device is in an indeterminate state; this pin is usually tied to V_{CC}.

SHORT TIMERS

The minimum output time delay of the timer is determined by the propagation delay, which is lot dependent and actually a function of the IC processing. The propagation delay is a combination of two factors — the delay, typically 100 ns, incurred because the trigger must be present for a finite amount of time before the trigger comparator goes into saturation and, more important, the minimum time, typically 1.8 μs, required for the trigger comparator to come out of saturation when the trigger pulse is removed.

In applications where timing is initiated by applying power to the device, there are a couple of hazards to be avoided. First, if power is applied by a switch, noise, such as that due to contact bounce, can cause the device to false trigger. Many

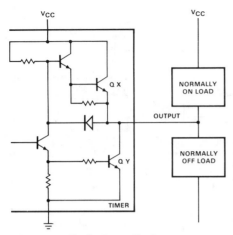

Fig. 4. Output Circuit

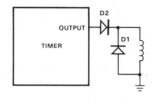

Fig. 5. Protective Diode Scheme

times this can be avoided by using a well regulated supply and bypass capacitors. Second, if the power is applied slowly at the time the device is supposed to trigger, the device may not trigger. In this case, connect the trigger to the timing capacitor. When using this type of circuit, retriggering is accomplished by interrupting the V_{CC} line.

The output of the μA555 timer has a totem pole structure that provides single-pole double-throw action (*Figure 4*). Each transistor is capable of handling 200 mA at 15 V V_{CC}. This timed switch operates on command, measures the time, and resets itself.

When using the timer with TTL logic, the timer must be powered from a 5 V supply to obtain suitable drive levels. With this supply, the timer sinks only a limited amount of current before the output voltage exceeds the TTL threshold level. For fanouts of six or more, a buffer is probably needed. Another problem can arise. Occasionally, a step in the output waveform occurring at the TTL threshold band causes the driven circuit to false trigger. The difficulty can be avoided by adding a 1000 pF capacitor from the output to ground. This lowers the level at which the step appears and removes it from the TTL threshold zone.

In some applicatons, the μA555 can be used as a relay driver; however, care must be taken to connect the circuit properly. While driving the load is no problem, difficulty can occur when the relay is deactivated. The collapsing magnetic field of the coil produces a reverse emf (electromotive force) that can cause the timer to latch up. The solution is to add protection diodes (*Figure 5*). Diode D1 shorts out the reverse emf generated by the collapsing magnetic field. However, a negative voltage equivalent to one diode drop can appear between the timer output and ground; D2 prevents this. If the relay is connected to V_{CC} rather than ground, D2 is omitted.

High Temperature Operation
Operating a μA555 timer at elevated temperatures can be tricky, particularly if appreciable current output is required. For example, will the μA555 operate at 125°C when powered from a 12 V supply driving a 60 mA load? To answer

this, the maximum operating die temperature (150°C) and the thermal resistance θ_{JA} of the 8-lead TO-5 metal can (0.15°C/mW) must be known.

Total device dissipation is then calculated. For 12 V operation, the typical quiescent current is 10 mA; therefore dissipation is 120 mW (12 x 10). For this example, dissipation of the output structure is approximately 1.7 V times the 60 mA load current, or 102 mW. So the total dissipation is 120 + 102 or 222 mW.

To determine the amount of temperature derating, multiply the power dissipation times θ_{JA}.

$$(222 \text{ mW}) (0.150°C/mW) = 33.3°C$$

The maximum temperature, then, is:

$$(150°C) - (33.3°C) = 116.7°C$$

Therefore, the μA555 in a TO-5 package will not operate at 125°C with a 12 V power supply driving a 60 mA load. Some handy maximum temperatures for this TO-5 packaged device at $V_{CC} = 15$ V and $I_{CC} = 10$ mA are: 102°C for 100 mA operation and 52.5°C for 200 mA. The 8-pin plastic package with θ_{JA} of 0.16°C/mW is only rated to 70°C but, within this range, will have slightly lower maximum temperature limits than the TO-5 device.

LONG-PERIOD TIMER AND CLOCK
There are several alternatives for measuring long intervals. One is to connect several units in tandem so that the output of one triggers the input of the second, etc. Time intervals can be increased by a factor of two by using a dual timer (μA556).

In applications requiring extremely long time delays, standard one-shot devices are inadequate. They either require very expensive capacitors (large value and very low leakage types), or they require so much external circuitry that they become economically unfeasible. It is better to use a programmable timer/counter, such as the μA2240, that is capable of producing accurate microsecond-to-five-day time

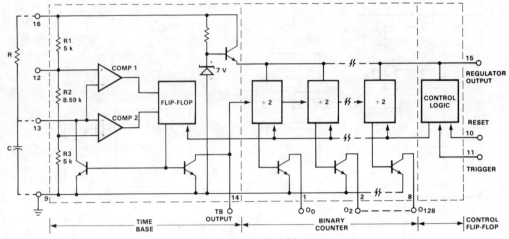

Fig. 6. μA2240 Block Diagram

delays. Even longer delays, up to three years, can be generated by cascading two timers. The μA2240 (Figure 6) consists of a time base oscillator, programmable 8-bit counter and control flip-flop. An external resistor capacitor (RC) network sets the oscillator frequency and provides for selection of delay times from 1 to 255 RC. In the astable mode of operation, 255 frequencies or pulse patterns can also be easily synchronized to an external signal. The trigger, reset and outputs are all TTL and DTL compatible for interfacing with digital systems.

When power is applied to the μA2240 with no trigger or reset inputs, the circuit starts with all outputs HIGH. Application of a positive-going trigger pulse to TRIG, pin 11, initiates the timing cycle. The trigger input activates the time-base oscillator, enables the counter section and sets the counter outputs LOW. The time-base oscillator generates timing pulses with a period $T = 1$ RC. These clock pulses are counted by

the binary counter section. The timing sequence is completed when a positive-going reset pulse is applied to R, pin 10.

Once triggered, the circuit is immune from additional trigger inputs until the timing cycle is completed or a reset input is applied. If both the reset and trigger are activated simultaneously, the trigger takes precedence. When the circuit is in a reset state, both the time-base and the counter sections are disabled and all the counter outputs are HIGH.

In most timing applications, one or more of the counter outputs are connected to the reset terminal with S1 closed (Figure 7). The circuit starts timing when a trigger is applied and automatically resets itself to complete the timing cycle when a programmed count is completed. If none of the counter outputs are connected back to the reset terminal (switch S1 open), the circuit operates in an astable or free-running mode following a trigger input.

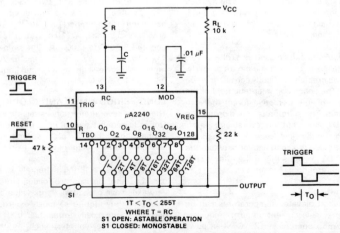

Fig. 7. Basic Circuit Connection for Timing Applications

Operation with External Clock

The μA2240 can be operated with an external clock or time-base by disabling the internal time-base oscillator and applying the external clock input to TBO, pin 14 (*Figure 8*). The internal time-base is deactivated by connecting a 1 kΩ resistor from RC, pin 13, to ground. The counters are triggered on the negative-going edges of the external clock pulse. For proper operation, a minimum clock pulse amplitude of 3 V is required. Minimum external clock pulse width must be $\geqslant 1\,\mu s$.

Ultra Long Time Delay

Two μA2240 devices can be cascaded as shown in *Figure 9* to generate extremely long time delays. Total timing cycle of two cascaded units can be programmed from $T_O = 256\,RC$ to $T_O = 65,536\,RC$ in 256 discrete steps by selectively shorting one or more of the counter outputs from Unit 2 to the output bus. In this application, the reset and the trigger terminals of both units are tied together and the Unit 2 time base is disabled. Normally, the output is HIGH when the system is reset. On triggering, the output goes LOW where it remains for a total of $(256)^2$ or 65,536 cycles of the time-base oscillator. In cascaded operation, the time-base section of Unit 2 can be powered down to reduce power consumption. In this case,

the V_{CC} terminal (pin 16) of Unit 2 is left open, and the second unit is powered from the regulator output of Unit 1 by connecting the V_{REG} (pins 15) of both units together.

OTHER TIMER APPLICATIONS

The flexibility of IC timers has resulted in their use in many other applications. Here are just a few ideas; there are many more. Because of its excellent power-handling capability, the single-shot timer, with the addition of a few external components, can drive relays. Since the operation of the single-shot timer is based on the device detecting the 1/3 V_{CC} point on the discharge pin and the 2/3 V_{CC} point on the threshold pin, it is adaptable to temperature-control applications by adding three external resistors and a thermistor.

The μA2240 timer/counter adapts well as a frequency synthesizer by using the programmable counter section to generate discrete frequencies from a given time-base setting. Interconnected with an external op amp and a precision resistor ladder, the μA2240 becomes a staircase generator. Other useful applications include digital sample-and-hold, analog-to-digital conversion and time-base generation for a digital tachometer.

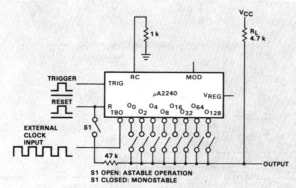

Fig. 8. Operation with External Clock

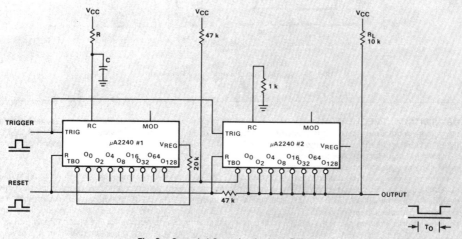

Fig. 9. Cascaded Operation for Long Delays

CIRCUIT IDEAS Linear

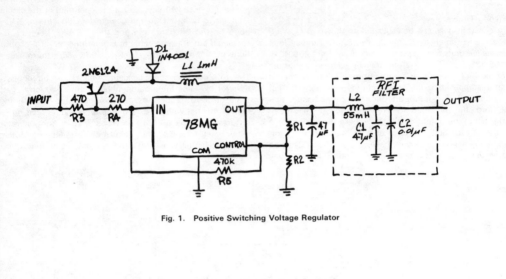

Fig. 1. Positive Switching Voltage Regulator

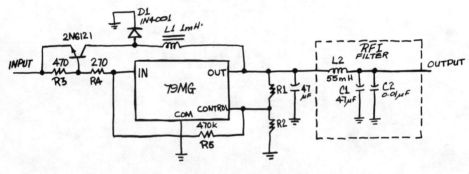

Fig. 2. Negative Switching Voltage Regulator

LOW COST SWITCHING REGULATORS

Adjustable voltage regulators, used in the switching mode, are highly efficient in applications where there is a large difference between the input voltage and the regulated voltage. This is particularly important for battery operated equipment where power dissipation of the regulator must be kept to a minimum. Either a positive or negative switching regulator can be designed using the 78MG (positive) or 79MG (negative) 4-terminal adjustable voltage regulator. The circuits are similar and require only a few components at minimum cost.

In both designs, the voltage regulator is basically used as a voltage comparator; the voltage drop across R3 created by the input current to the regulator turns the series pass transistor on or off. Resistor R5 provides positive feedback to the control input of the regulator, improving the turn-on and turn-off times.

The core material of inductor L1 should be moly-permalloy material with an inductance of approximately 1 mH (Magnetics Inc. P/N 55206 or equivalent). The no-load switching frequency is around 20 kHz. In some applications, an RFI filter composed of inductor L2 and capacitors C1 and C2 may be required to eliminate rf oscillations from the power-supply line. Output voltage is adjustable by modifying the ratio of resistors R1 and R2 (refer to 78MG and 79MG data sheets).

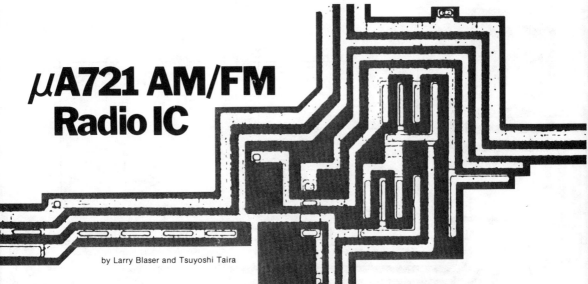

μA721 AM/FM Radio IC

by Larry Blaser and Tsuyoshi Taira

The design of a new AM/FM integrated circuit was prompted by two primary design considerations — cost and space. Cost reductions have always been a strong motivation for IC development; space requirements are becoming increasingly important as more electronics are crammed into consumer equipment. An excellent and relevant example of a space problem is the packing difficulty encountered in designing an AM/FM radio/citizens-band transceiver combination to fit into a car dashboard.

An AM/FM development program, which included guidance from numerous radio manufacturers, has culminated in the introduction of a new device, the μA721, which performs most of the functions needed in an AM/FM radio. A complete AM/FM radio designed around the μA721 requires only a few other active devices — two or three transistors for the FM tuner front end and one audio power IC. The μA721 offers a more cost-effective and space-saving approach to AM/FM radio design than is possible with either discrete or other existing IC devices. Further savings are possible by using the μA721 in a minimum-alignment receiver.

The μA721 is a versatile device that meets the performance requirements of car, hi-fi, clock and portable AM/FM radio systems, but is also attractive for other applications such as FM communications receivers, CB radio receivers, high-gain ultrasonic amplifiers and wireless telephone receivers. It operates over a supply voltage range of 3.5 V to 16 V with low current drain for either battery or line operation. The device is supplied in a standard 16-pin plastic DIP. The IC chip itself, shown in *Figure 1*, is fabricated using a standard, high-yield bipolar process.

DEVICE DESCRIPTION

The μA721 has relatively independent sections that can be used in a variety of ways depending on external circuitry. The versatility of this IC is apparent in the following circuit description. In the μA721 block diagram shown in *Figure 2*, the functions are grouped into five essentially independent sections — bias circuit, AM oscillator-mixer, amplifier I, amplifier II and the FM IF amplifier-limiter/detector.

Bias Circuit (Figure 3)

The bias circuit provides regulated voltages to critical circuits to minimize variations as a function of supply voltage and junction temperature. It contains a 3.5 V reference diode string (D2 through D6) driven by the current-mirror transistors Q16 and Q17 with buffer Q18. Current into the mirror is set by Q19 which ties back into the reference diode string. Resistor R26 provides start up. All the current from Q16 flows into the reference string except for any external loading on the bias terminal and almost negligible internal bias currents that flow through Q16 into the bases of several buffer transistors. For a typical application, the only load on the bias terminal is the oscillator coil during AM operation. The FM quadrature coil also ties to the bias terminal, but its loading is negligible.

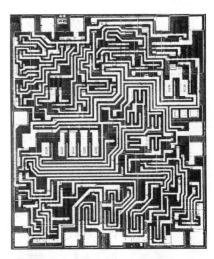

Fig. 1   Die Photo

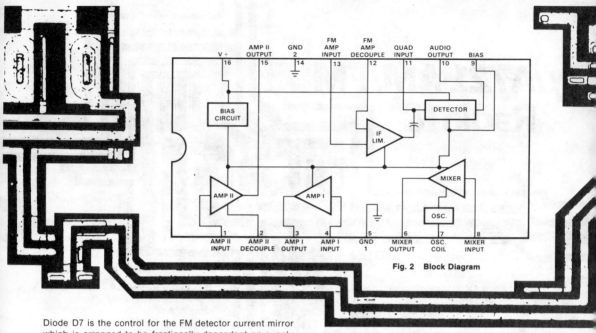

Fig. 2   Block Diagram

Diode D7 is the control for the FM detector current mirror which is arranged to be fractionally dependent on supply voltage. The current through R28 is regulated, whereas the current in R27 varies directly with supply voltage. The purpose of a fractionally tracking detector is discussed in the description of the FM detector. Resistor R23 is included in the reference string to maintain AM operation at the lowest possible supply voltage, an important consideration in portable radio applications.

AM Oscillator-Mixer (Figure 4)
The AM oscillator-mixer section operates as an AM converter or as a single-stage AM or FM IF amplifier when the oscillator is disabled. A negative impedance into the oscillator coil is developed by the differential amplifier, Q1 and Q2, which has positive feedback applied around it via R1 and R2. The oscillator voltage across the tank circuit connected to this terminal is limited to 0.7 peak (1.4 V p-p) by diode D8.

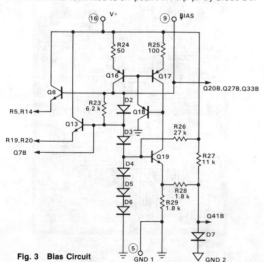

Fig. 3   Bias Circuit

The oscillator signal developed across R3 is buffered and level shifted by Q3 and Q4 and applied through the low-impedance resistive divider R8 and R9 to the emitter of mixer transistor Q5. The input signal to the mixer is fed into the base of Q5 where the non-linear V-I characteristics of the base-emitter junction produce difference (IF) frequencies that are amplified and passed by the frequency-selective network connected externally at the mixer output terminal.

The AM oscillator-mixer is converted to a simple single-stage amplifier by disconnecting the dc path to the oscillator coil terminal which turns off Q1 and turns on D1 and Q2. The voltage dropped across R3 turns Q3 and Q4 off, permitting Q5 to operate as a common-emitter amplifier with degeneration resistor R9. Biasing of Q5 is set by current-mirror transistor Q6 and bias resistor R12.

Amplifiers I and II (Figure 5)
Amplifier I consists of a single common-emitter transistor Q9 that shares current-mirror transistor Q10 with the current supply, Q11, the current source for amplifier II output transistor Q12. Transistor Q9 operates in the reverse-AGC mode so that the control voltage takes the base negative with respect to the emitter. The control voltage is developed external to the IC and applied via the amplifier I input terminal. Amplifier II also has a reverse-AGC input transistor, but is a two-stage amplifier with a higher gain than amplifier I. The amplifier II decouple terminal is normally bypassed with a capacitor, but a resistor may be added in series with a bypass capacitor for lower gain. The dc voltage at this terminal increases when reverse AGC is applied to amplifier II; therefore, the decouple terminal can be used to drive an external antenna shunt AGC diode or a signal strength meter.

Since AGC control voltages for amplifiers I and II often originate from common external circuitry, these amplifiers are designed for equal dc voltages. Under full-gain internally set biasing, no biasing interaction occurs even if there should be an external resistive path between the two inputs.

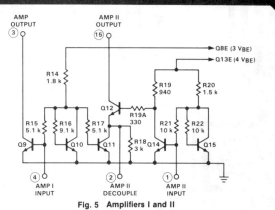

Fig. 5 Amplifiers I and II

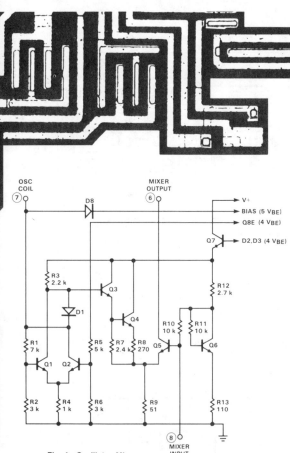

Fig. 4 Oscillator-Mixer

FM IF Amplifier-Limiter and Detector (Figure 6)

The FM If amplifier-limiter contains three stages. DC feed-back is applied around the first two stages (Q21 through Q26) which obtain their supply voltage from the bias circuit through isolation transistor Q20. The third stage is separately isolated through Q27. Transistors Q30 and Q31 provide a dc bias to the detector which tracks the quiescent dc voltage from Q32, the third stage output transistor. A quadrature drive signal for the detector is provided by R40, the collector-load resistor of Q29.

The output from the third stage feeds the bottom differential pair (Q39 and Q40) of the conventional quadrature detector. The upper matched pairs (Q35 through Q38) are driven from the quadrature circuit consisting of an external tuned circuit in conjunction with the on-chip emitter-base junction, phase shift capacitor C1. The output from the detector feeds load resistor R53 through a pnp current mirror (Q42 and Q43). The current mirror allows the detector to operate down to a supply voltage of about 3 V. The audio signal developed across R53 is buffered through the short-circuit-protected output transistor Q44.

The detector current source Q41 is designed to fractionally track the supply voltage, thus making the recovered audio output level a function of the supply voltage. This technique obtains an acceptably large output level at normal supply voltages and reduces the ouput level at minimum supply

voltages to prevent clipping in the output stage. The resulting poor ripple rejection requires that the supply voltage be free of hum.

APPLICATIONS

The independent functional blocks of the μA721 can be arranged for a variety of AM and FM receiver applications. Amplifier I, amplifier II and the AM oscillator-mixer have open-collector output circuits that give complete flexibility for selecting load impedances. The FM IF amplifier-limiter and detector section needs only a few external components. It can be designed to be free of alignment if ceramic filters are used for selectivity and the conventional quadrature coil is replaced by a ceramic resonator. With appropriate external circuit arrangements, the four functional blocks can be combined to cover the FM IF amplification, FM detection and all AM functions in most AM/FM receivers.

Two ground systems are used in the μA721 to minimize the likelihood of high-frequency instability due to common-ground impedances. Nevertheless, to insure stable system operation, care must be taken in the selection and placement of external components and in the layout of the printed-circuit board.

Minimum-Alignment AM/FM Radio (Figure 7)

Reduction of labor costs and component count are mandatory requirements for most new radio designs. While ICs with more functions in the package offer one solution, components that need no alignment are also helpul. With the availability of low-cost 455 kHz ceramic filters and the development of a high-performance ceramic resonator for quadrature FM detection, a minimum-alignment AM/FM radio can be designed around the μA721. Conventional 3-transistor, AM/FM subsystems require nine IF transformers and many associated components. This application reduces the IF transformer count to three.

In this application, amplifier I, which is used as an AM RF amplifier, has a resistive load and is coupled to the converter stage through a capacitor. Amplifier II is used for both AM and FM IF amplification. The AM AGC control voltage for amplifiers I and II is developed in the AM detector and applied through the AGC diode.

281

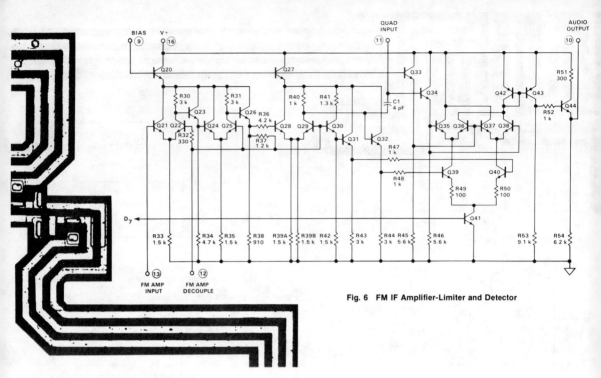

Fig. 6   FM IF Amplifier-Limiter and Detector

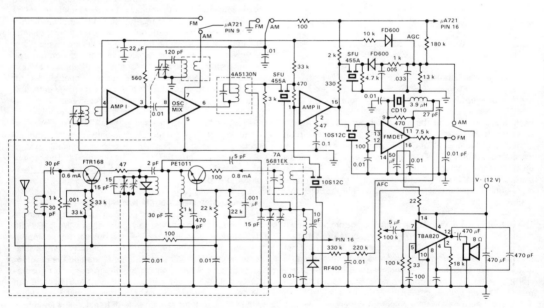

Fig. 7   Minimum-Alignment AM/FM Radio

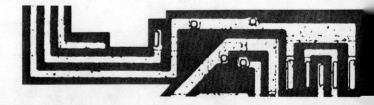

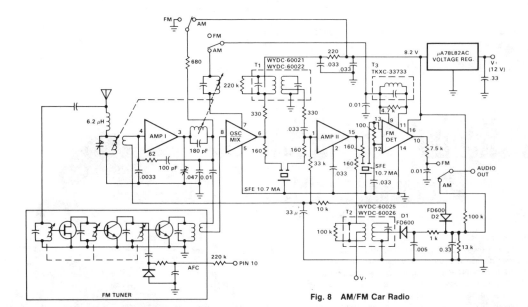

Fig. 8 AM/FM Car Radio

Two 455 kHz ceramic filters are used in the AM IF amplifier stage. A transformer is used with the first filter to reduce feedthrough of RF and local oscillator signals. (The use of higher selectivity ceramic filters eliminates the need for a transformer, but their higher cost must be considered.) Consequently, the AM section of the receiver has only two coils — the AM oscillator and the first IF transformer. This is comparable to an conventional AM radio design that uses one oscillator and three IF transformers.

The FM section design also simplifies alignment. Except for the FM tuner front end, there are no adjustable components. Two 10.7 MHz ceramic filters are used for FM IF stage selectivity. The FM detector uses a ceramic resonator and a fixed coil in place of the conventional quadrature coil. In a conventional FM IF amplifier and detector design using IF transformers and a ratio-detector coil, there are five coils that must be precisely tuned.

Car Radio Application (Figure 8)
This application uses amplifier I as the AM RF amplifier and the AM oscillator-mixer section as the AM converter and also as the first FM IF amplifier when the AM oscillator is disabled by disconnecting the oscillator coil. Amplifier II is used as the AM IF amplifier which drives the separate AM detector diode and also as the second FM IF amplifier. Additional FM IF amplification followed by FM detection is accomplished in the FM IF amplifier-limiter and detector section of the μA721. High selectivity is achieved by using 262.5 kHz double-tuned coils (T1 and T2) in the AM IF amplifier and by the two 10.7 MHz ceramic filters used in the FM IF amplifier.

AGC for AM reception is activated by the negative-going voltage developed in D1, the AM detector, and it is coupled through D2. AGC action begins as D2 conducts, lowering the internally set bias voltage on pins 1 and 4 and thereby lowering the gains in amplifiers I and II. Very large signal conditions are handled by this AGC scheme which supplies a negative-bias voltage to the input of amplifier I, thus operating it in a fully cut-off mode. Distortion is kept at an acceptable level for high input signals by the RC network (62 Ω and 100 pF) connected across amplifier I. The FM tuner front end has a junction-FET input stage and transistors for the oscillator and mixer stages. The AFC control voltage is derived from the FM detector output (pin 10).

The number of alignments required in the car radio application can be reduced by incorporating ideas from the minimum-alignment AM/FM radio application. Standard high-selectivity ceramic filters can be used to replace the double-tuned transformers, however the AM IF stage must be changed from 262.5 kHz to 455 kHz. A ceramic resonator can be used in the FM detector in place of the quadrature coil. In addition, variable-capacitance tuning diodes can be used to replace tuning mechanisms.

CONCLUSIONS
The μA721 contains four relatively independent functional sections that can be used in a variety of ways to meet the demands of a number of different AM/FM radio applications. This radio subsystem IC can produce considerable savings not only in terms of components count, but also in design time. It is a flexible, cost-effective circuit useful for low-cost space-saving AM/FM radio designs.

Switching Regulators
efficient and flexible

by David Jones

THE BACKGROUND

Regulated power supplies are found almost universally in system design. Basically, they consist of some type of network to convert ac input voltages to unregulated dc voltages and a voltage regulator to provide dc voltage regulation. Integrated circuit voltage regulators have been available for about 10 years, evolving from the first industry standard, the μA723. This device had low output currents compared to present devices and required several external components and significant design considerations. It was followed by a series of 3-terminal regulators that provided higher output currents (up to 1 A) with most of the circuitry on the chip but had a limited number of fixed output voltages. The introduction of adjustable 4-terminal regulators solved this output voltage limitation.

Such *series-pass* regulators have dominated the power supply regulator market because they are simple, easy to use, offer high performance, and a wide range of high quality circuits is available from a number of manufacturers. Increasing concern about wasted power has caused designers to seriously consider switching regulators, which are not only much more efficient but also provide output voltages *higher or lower* than the input voltage supplied. In addition, then can provide an output voltage of the *opposite polarity*.

Switching regulators do have some drawbacks. They are complex, require some external components, and should be used with some degree of care. They generate noise and an output ripple, and are slower to respond to transient load conditions. However, these disadvantages can be minimized and are overshadowed by the very high efficiency (up to 90%) of switching regulators. With good control electronics, attention to timing, and some filtering, switching regulators can be used in power supply designs that provide lower operating costs and reduce power dissipation. A new integrated circuit switching regulator subsystem, the μA78S40, makes possible a variety of switching *or* series-pass regulator systems with minimum external parts.

THE CONCEPT

Switching regulators are capable of storing energy and cycling on and off as necessary to supply adequate power to the load. They store energy in inductors and capacitors, which do not dissipate power. (Series-pass regulators apply the input/output differential voltage across a pass transistor, which *does* dissipate power.) Output transistors act as switches with the on/off cycle rate determined by the input/output voltages and the load current. Control circuitry monitors the output voltage and modifies timing to maintain a constant output voltage. While the regulator is off, energy is stored in an output capacitor which averages the current flow to the load. The basic modes of operation provide *increased, decreased, or inverted* voltage at the output from a fixed input voltage.

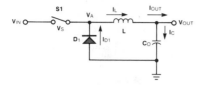

Fig. 1a   Step-Down Voltage Regulator

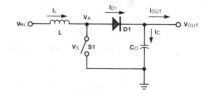

Fig. 1b   Step-Up Voltage Regulator

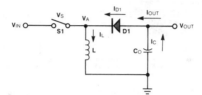

Fig. 1c   Voltage Inverter

Figure 1 illustrates the three basic operating modes of a switching regulator. The same basic components — a switch, a diode to direct current, an inductor and a capacitor to store energy — are used for the step-down, step-up, and inverting modes. In a step-down voltage regulator *(Figure 1a)*, when the switch closes, the applied voltage (V_A) rises toward the input voltage, and voltage V_A - V_{OUT} is applied across the inductor, causing current to increase from zero. This current flows to the load/output capacitor. If the instantaneous inductor current is less than the load current, the output capacitor provides additional current causing a slight decrease in the output voltage. If the instantaneous inductor current exceeds the output (load) current, the excess current flows into the output capacitor, increasing the output voltage. The instantaneous inductor current increases continuously until the switch opens. Because the inductor current cannot change instantaneously, when the switch does open V_A drops to -V_D and the diode supplies the inductor current path. At this time, the voltage across the inductor is -(V_{OUT} + V_D); hence the inductor current falls at the rate of -(V_{OUT} + V_D)/L and continues to fall until zero-current is reached or the switch closes again, starting the cycle over.

The on/off cycling of the switch is governed by a control circuit to maintain an average inductor current equal to the output current. The average capacitor current is zero, and the output voltage remains constant. Such control circuits may have an oscillator with on and off timing set so the inductor current will increase to its maximum and then decrease to zero. There is also some type of a sensing circuit for the output voltage that adjusts the oscillator to increase the off time if the output voltage becomes too high. In this type of a system, the maximum output current is 1/2 of the peak value of the inductor current. When the output current is less than this value, the control circuit increases the off-time by an amount adequate to make the average inductor current equal the output current.

Peak current in a step-down regulator is a function of the input, output, and switch voltages, the inductor size, and the amount of time that the switch is on. Similarly, the amount of time required for the inductor current to drop to zero is related to the output, switch, and diode voltages and is the off-time. The ideal on/off-time ratio is a function of the input, output, switch and diode voltages, with the maximum output current being 1/2 of the peak value of the inductor current. The average input current is a function of 1/2 of the peak inductor current and the percentage of time that the switch is on. Regulator efficiency (excluding control circuit current and switching losses) can be expressed as (V_{OUT}/V_{IN}) (V_{IN} + V_O - V_S/V_{OUT} + V_D) a function of the input, output, switch, and diode voltages. If the switch and diode voltages can be kept small compared to the input and output voltages, extremely high efficiency is possible. (If the switch and diode voltages were zero, the regulator would be 100% efficient.) Ripple on the output is a function of the peak current, the on/off-time cycling, and the output capacitor. It can be reduced by increasing the output capacitance, which does not affect the other portions of the circuit.

Switching regulators operating in a step-up mode, *Figure 1b*, provide an output voltage *greater* than the input voltage. In the case of a step-up regulator, when the switch closes, the applied voltage drops to almost zero (V_A = V_S), and voltage V_{IN} - V_S is applied across the inductor, causing the inductor current to increase linearly. Because the applied voltage is less than the output voltage, the diode is reverse-biased and current cannot flow to the output. Again, when the switch opens, the inductor current cannot change instantly, and the applied voltage changes to the total of the output voltage plus the diode voltage. At this time current can flow through the diode to the load capacitor, and the inductor current decreases at a linear rate, determined by V_{OUT} + V_D - V_{IN}. Timing adjustments control the average diode current (I_{D1}) so it is equal to the load current. The diode current can only

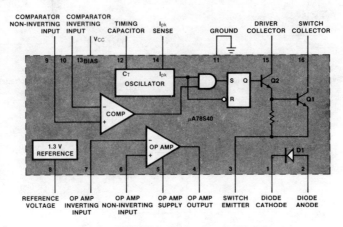

Fig. 2 µA78S40 Universal Regulator Partitioning

flow during off-time, so the maximum output current is $(I_{pk}/2)\,(t_{off}/t_{on} + t_{off})$. If the load current is less than the maximum output current, off-time is increased by a dead time with no current to the output. Input current can flow during both on and off-times, so the average input current is always greater than the maximum output current.

With a step-up regulator, on-time is a function of the input and switch voltages and inductance; off-time is a function of the input, output, and diode voltages, and inductance. The on/off ratio and the maximum output current are also functions of the circuit voltages, as is the efficiency of the regulator. In the step-up mode, efficiency approaches 100% as the switch and diode voltages become small relative to the input and output voltages, the same as in the step-down mode. Output ripple, a function of peak and output currents, the off-time, and the output capacitance, can also be reduced by increasing the output capacitance without affecting overall regulator performance.

Figure 1c illustrates a basic voltage inverter that generates a negative output from a positive input. Upon closing the switch, the applied voltage V_{IN} - V_S is impressed on the inductor and causes inductor current to increase linearly. When the switch opens, the current cannot change instantaneously so the applied voltage decreases to $(V_{OUT} - V_D)$ which forward biases the diode. The current decays linearly, and the diode current flows to the load with its average value equal to the load current. Since input current only flows when the switch is closed, it is equal to $(I_{pk}/2)\,(t_{on}/t_{on} + t_{off})$.

Optimum time-on and time-off values for the inverter mode of operation are functions of the input, output, and switch voltages, and inductance. The ratio of on-time to off-time depends only on the voltages. Maximum output current and average input current are always less than 1/2 of the peak current. In the inverter mode, efficiency depends on the input

and output voltages and is basically independent of current level. As with the step-up and step-down modes, output ripple can be minimized by increasing output capacitance without affecting regulator performance.

THE REGULATOR
In order to operate effectively in step-down, step-up, and inverting modes, a switching regulator should have several functional building blocks common to all of its operational modes, minimizing the need for external parts and maximizing its versatility. The µA78S40 universal regulator meets this goal and allows a wide variety of regulators to be built with minimum external parts. This regulator's functional blocks are illustrated in *Figure 2* and outlined below.

- A Current-Controlled Oscillator
- A Temperature-Compensated Current-Limiting Circuit
- A Temperature-Compensated Voltage Reference
- An Error Amplifier
- A Power-Switching Circuit
- A High-Gain Amplifier

The current-controlled oscillator has drive circuitry for the transistor power switch. Oscillator frequency is set by an external capacitor so it can be varied according to application. The oscillator duty cycle is internally fixed at 8:1. A current-limiting circuit controls oscillator on-time, adjusting the duty cycle for optimum timing. This temperature-compensated current-limiting circuit senses the switching transistor current across an external resistor and modifies the oscillator on-time, limiting the peak current and protecting the switching transistors.

A 1.3 V temperature-compensated voltage reference source can provide up to 10 mA of current without an external pass transistor. A high-gain differential comparator disables the power switch when the output voltage becomes too high. A

286

power Darlington switching transistor handles 1.5 A of current and can withstand up to 40 V. The switch collectors and the emitter drive are externally available to allow optimized connection of the switch. A power-switching diode handles 1.5 A of forward current and 40 V of reverse voltage.

The high-gain independent operational amplifier has 150 mA output current capability and a separate positive voltage supply connection. Its input common mode range *includes* ground. It may be connected to provide series-pass regulation or feedback control for switching regulators.

This switching regulator can operate over a wide range of power conditions, from battery power to high-voltage, high-current supplies. Low voltage requirements with minimum current drain make the regulator very useful in battery or 5 V systems. It typically operates from 2.2 to 40 V dc. At the 5 V level, the regulator draws only 2 mA. A low standby-current drain significantly improves regulator efficiency in low-power applications and greatly increases battery lifetime in battery applications. This high efficiency in low-power applications is *not* typical of other switching systems. Combined with the capability of the µA78S40 to handle up to 40 V input and provide as much as 1.5 A switching current, efficient low power operation makes the regulator performance over a wide operating range unmatched.

Using a versatile circuit such as this requires some care, but the benefits are well worth the attention since this IC subsystem provides the user with the flexibility for optimizing power supply performance. A critical parameter is oscillator timing. Although the on-time/off-time ratio is internally fixed at 8:1, the user can adjust this ratio down through the proper selection of peak current, the oscillator capacitor value, the inductor value, and the input/output voltages. Peak current is determined solely by the current-limiting circuit. Selection of

the timing capacitor is based on the off-time required. The user should establish the off-time and let the current-limiting circuit modify the on-time. This off-time can be set by the user for either intermittent or continuous operation. For intermittent operation, the user should set the off-time equal to the time required for the inductor current to drop to zero. For continuous operation, the off-time should be set at something less than the time required for the inductor current to drop to zero. When operated in the continuous mode, average inductor current exceeds 1/2 of the peak current, making more power available at the output. However, timing is very critical (See Box), and if on-time and off-time periods are too short, switching losses can significantly reduce efficiency. With this regulator, on-time and off-time should be kept greater than 10 µs.

Switching is accomplished by a Darlington pair with the switch emitter as well as both transistor collectors available for external connection. Either the collector inputs or the emitter output can be used. If the emitter output is used, the collector inputs can be shorted, resulting in a switch voltage of 1.6 V typical. If the collector inputs are used with the emitter grounded, the user must consider the performance tradeoffs between shorting both collectors or using the switch output. System performance is affected by the input and output voltages, the output current, and the expected variations of the input voltage. If both collectors are shorted, there is no switching loss due to base current (switch voltage is typically 1.1 V). If the switch output is used, base drive through the driver is provided by connecting an external resistor to the input voltage line (switching voltage is typically 0.5 V). A switching diode in the circuit is capable of handling voltage up to 40 V and current up to 1.5 A for both step-up and step-down modes. To use the regulator for inverting applications, an external diode is required because the diode voltage drops below the circuit common.

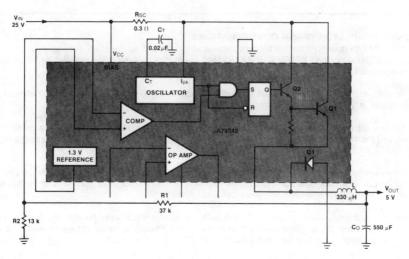

Fig. 3 Step-Down Voltage Regulator

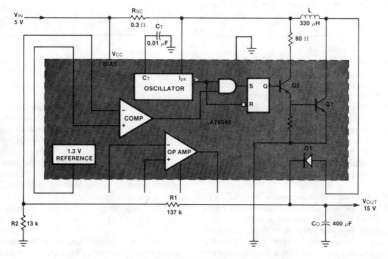

Fig. 4 Step-Up Voltage Regulator

THE APPLICATIONS

Typical applications of the universal regulator include the three switching regulator modes previously discussed; step-down, step-up, and inverting. *Figure 3* illustrates the necessary connections for using the μA78S40 in the step-down mode. This version satisfies a requirement for a 5 V output at 500 mA with output ripple less than 25 mV. In this application, the power switch (Q1 and Q2) is connected between the +25 V supply and the inductor. Switch voltage is determined by the emitter output limit of 1.6 V. For this value, off-time is approximately three times the on-time. Considering that the on-time should be greater than 10 μs, off-time is set by the user at 60 μs ($C_T = 0.02 μF$), and the inductor value is selected at 330 μH. The output voltage is set by resistors R1 and R2. Output capacitance is calculated to be 400 μF. The circuit

standby power is less than 50 mW. Efficiency at full load is 79%; at 10% of full load it is 70%.

For operation as a step-up voltage regulator, the μA78S40 is connected as shown in *Figure 4*. In this case, the objective is to use a 5 V input and get a 15 V output at 150 mA, again with output ripple less than 25 mV. Using $V_S = 0.5$ V and $V_D = 1$ V, on-time is approximately 2 1/2 times the off-time. Timing capacitance is selected at 0.01 μF, setting the off-time at 30 μs. On-time is consequently approximately 73 μs. An 80 Ω resistor on the drive collector provides a 50 mA base drive to the switch. With a peak input current of 1.1 A, R_{SC} is selected at 0.3 Ω. At full load with an average input current of 555 mA, efficiency is 80%. At 10% of full load, regulator efficiency is 78%. Output capacitance is calculated to be 492 μF.

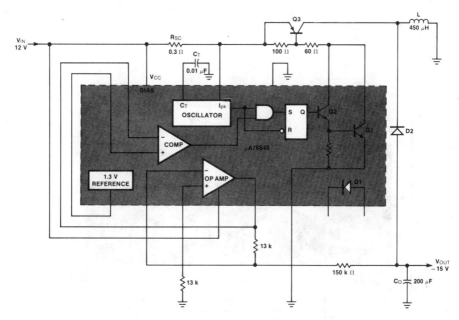

Fig. 5 Inverting Voltage Regulator

A voltage inverter configuration is shown in *Figure 5*. This mode requires an external pnp transistor (Q3) and a catch diode (D2). With a +12 V input, output voltage is -15 V at 200 mA, with output ripple less than 50 mV. With a timing capacitor value of 0.01 μF, off-time is 30 μF. Peak current can be calculated (0.96 A) as can the value of the inductor (500 μH). Average input current for this inverter mode is 275 mA with a regulator efficiency of 93% at full load and 90% at 10% load. Output ripple is held to 50 mV by using an output capacitor with a value of 251 μF. In this inverter mode, the internal operational amplifier inverts the output voltage to compare it to the 1.3 V reference. This is only possible because the common mode range of the op amp includes ground. Circuit breakdown does not limit output voltage, because no portion of the control circuitry sees any negative voltage.

MORE SOPHISTICATED APPLICATIONS

With the addition of a few external parts, the μA78S40 can provide output power up to 100 W and output voltages up to and even exceeding 100 V. Two regulated outputs can be made available by using a switching output and a series-pass output.

One such interesting variation is the use of the universal regulator to provide a constant output for voltage inputs that are both higher and lower than the output, *Figure 6*. In this case, 12 V at 100 mA is provided at the output for input voltages over a 4 V to 24 V range. This is done by using a step-

up mode similar to the version shown in *Figure 4* to provide a 15 V output and then using the internal op amp as a series-pass regulator to reduce the 15 V output to a 12 V output. When the input voltage exceeds 16 V, the step-up regulator circuit follows the input at approximately the input voltage minus 1 V, but the series-pass output remains constant at 12 V. The op amp exhibits excellent noise rejection, so output ripple is virtually non-existent at the 12 V output. Regulator efficiency is about 50% for the upper and lower limits of the input range (4 V and 24 V) and increases to a maximum of about 75% for intermediate voltages.

Another variation involves the addition of an external pnp transistor and an external catch diode to the step-down regulator. *Figure 7*. The transistor (Q3) increases output current capability by a factor of 10 and also improves switching efficiency because the switching voltage drops from 1.6 V to 1 V. The npn Darlington pair switch is connected to provide the base drive for Q3, with a 56 Ω resistor limiting the base drive to 500 mA. A peak input current of 10 A (plus the 0.5 A base drive) with an input voltage of 30 V provides a 5 V, 5 A output. The average input current is 1.1 A. Efficiency of the regulator is approximately 73%, with the control circuit dissipating the base drive power (0.5 A x 30 V). In this case the off-time/on-time ratio is about 4:1, with the off-time at 150 μs and on-time at 38 μs. Output capacitance of 2500 μF keeps output ripple to 100 mV. The external diode (D2) is required to handle the 10 A switching current.

289

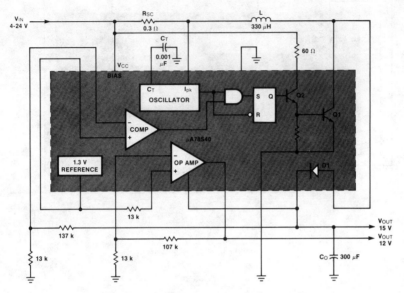

Fig. 6 Constant Output Voltage Regulator Over 4-24 V Input Range

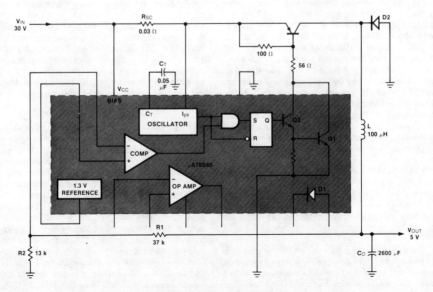

Fig. 7 Modified Step-Down Regulator with 5A, 5 V Output

290

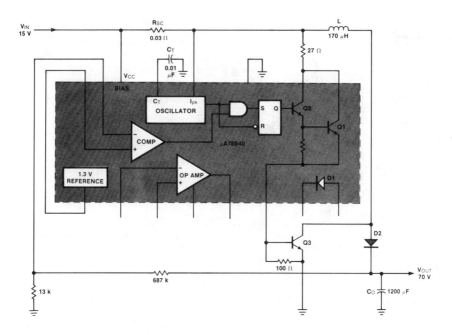

Fig. 8 Switching Regulator with 15 V Input, 70 V Output

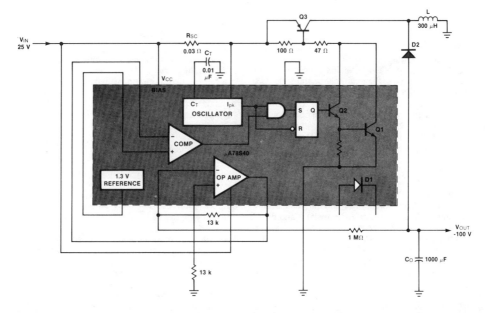

Fig. 9 Switching Regulator with 25 V Input, -100 V Output

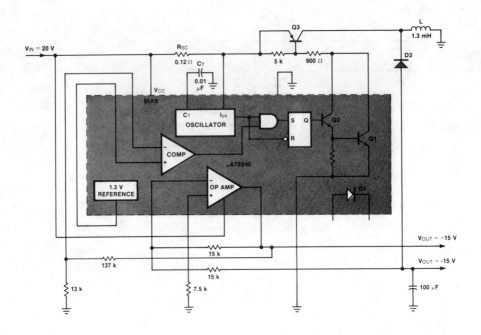

Fig. 10 Dual Tracking Supply

The addition of a boost transistor and a flyback diode to the step-up regulator configuration develops a regulated 70 V, 1 A output, *Figure 8*. The Darlington pair switch emitter output provides base drive to the external npn transistor Q3. Output voltage is limited by this transistor and diode break-down voltages, not by the IC. The base drive to Q3 is limited to 0.5 A by a 27 Ω series resistor on the switch collector. For this situation (15 V in — 70 V, 1 A out) the on/off ratio is 4:1 with on-time at 120 μs and off-time at 30 μs ($C_T = 0.01 \mu F$). Average input current is 5.4 A, (1/2 the peak current plus the 0.5 A base drive). Regulator efficiency is 84%, and output ripple is limited to 100 mV by a 1200 μF output capacitor.

A voltage inverting regulator with an external pnp switch (Q3) and an external diode (D2) can generate almost any negative output voltage, because the external transistor and diode limit the output voltage, *Figure 9*. This particular version provides -100 V at 1A from a +25 V input. The peak current is 10.5 A, average current is 4.44 A, and the regulator efficiency is 83%. The on-time to off-time ratio is a little more than 4:1, resulting in an off-time of 30 μs and an on-time of 126 μs. A 1000 μF output capacitor limits output ripple to 120 mV.

Figure 10 illustrates a dual-tracking regulator that provides both +15 V and -15 V outputs from a single +20 V input. The negative output voltage is generated with an inverter circuit similar to the circuit of *Figure 5*, but the op amp is connected in a gain-of-1 configuration with its output divided down and compared to the 1.3 V reference voltage. As shown, this regulator provides ±15 V at 100 mA with 80% efficiency — 75% postive voltage, 85% negative voltage — with output ripple limited to 30 mV.

A high-output regulator with two outputs is illustrated in *Figure 11*. From a single 5 V input voltage, a 12 V and a 15 V output are provided. Two external npn transistors are used; Q3 boosts the step-up function, and Q4 increases the series-pass output to 1 A. A total of 1.5 A is available from the two outputs, with 80% efficiency on the 15 V output and 64% efficiency on the 12 V output.

The final switching regulator variation shown is a negative input/output regulator, *Figure 12*. This presents a slightly more difficult challenge, since the reference voltage is refer-red to a negative input rather than ground. A ground refer-ence of -2.6 V can be generated by using the op amp as a differential amplifier. Then, using a typical step-down regula-tor configuration, a -48 V input produces a -12 V output at 300 mA with a regulator efficiency of 85%.

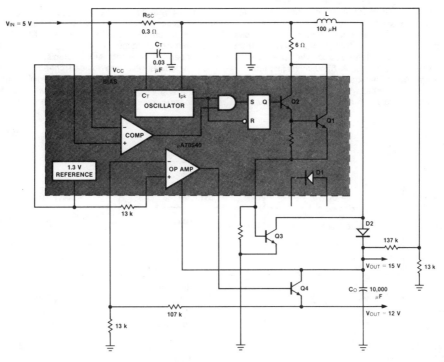

Fig. 11 Step-Up and Series-Pass Regulator

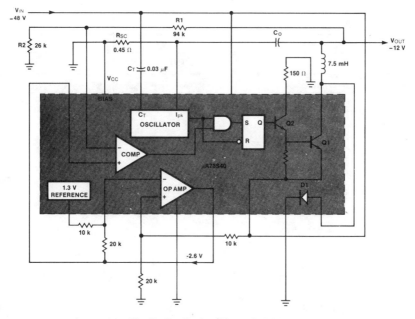

Fig. 12 Negative Input/Output Regulator

THE ANALYSIS

Switching regulators, although somewhat more complex than series-pass regulators, offer power system designers very high efficiency voltage regulators appropriate for a variety of applications. A wide range of power conditions can be met, from battery operation to high-power, high-current applications. Step-down, step-up, and inverter modes of operation are possible with the μA78S40 universal regulator with a minimum number of external parts. Constant output voltages can even be supplied when the input voltages cover a substantial range. The advantages of switching regulators

— low operating cost, high efficiency, low power dissipation — are enhanced by the on-chip circuitry of the μA78S40 universal regulator and the circuit partitioning. This partitioning makes available to the power supply designer the common functions needed for most power supply systems and minimizes the need for external components. There are some inherent disadvantages involving switching regulators such as slower response to load changes, some output ripple, and some noise. However, these disadvantages are often outweighed by the advantages of lower operating cost, high power-conversion efficiency, and versatility. □

78S40 Design Formulae

CHARACTERISTIC	STEP DOWN	STEP UP	INVERTING
I_{pk}	$2\,I_{OUT(max)}$	$2\,I_{OUT(max)} \cdot \dfrac{V_{OUT} + V_D - V_S}{V_{IN} - V_S}$	$2\,I_{OUT(max)} \cdot \dfrac{V_{IN} + \lvert V_{OUT} \rvert + V_D - V_S}{V_{IN} - V_S}$
R_{SC} *	$0.33\ \text{V}/I_{pk}$	$0.33\ \text{V}/I_{pk}$	$0.33\ \text{V}/I_{pk}$
$\dfrac{t_{on}}{t_{off}}$	$\dfrac{V_{OUT} + V_D}{V_{IN} - V_S - V_{OUT}}$	$\dfrac{V_{OUT} + V_D - V_{IN}}{V_{IN} - V_S}$	$\dfrac{\lvert V_{OUT} \rvert + V_D}{V_{IN} - V_S}$
L *	$\dfrac{V_{OUT} + V_D}{I_{pk}} \cdot t_{off}$	$\dfrac{V_{OUT} + V_D - V_{IN}}{I_{pk}} \cdot t_{off}$	$\dfrac{\lvert V_{OUT} \rvert + V_D}{I_{pk}} \cdot t_{off}$
t_{off}	$\dfrac{I_{pk} \cdot L}{V_{OUT} + V_D}$	$\dfrac{I_{pk} \cdot L}{V_{OUT} + V_D - V_{IN}}$	$\dfrac{I_{pk} \cdot L}{\lvert V_{OUT} \rvert + V_D}$
C_T * (μF)	$45 \times 10^{-5}\ t_{off}(\mu s)$	$45 \times 10^{-5}\ t_{off}(\mu s)$	$45 \times 10^{-5}\ t_{off}(\mu s)$
C_O *	$\dfrac{I_{pk} \cdot (t_{on} + t_{off})}{8\,V_{ripple}}$	$\dfrac{(I_{pk} - I_{OUT})^2 \cdot t_{off}}{2\,I_{pk} \cdot V_{ripple}}$	$\dfrac{(I_{pk} - I_{OUT})^2 \cdot t_{off}}{2\,I_{pk} \cdot V_{ripple}}$
Efficiency	$\dfrac{V_{IN} - V_S + V_D}{V_{IN}} \cdot \dfrac{V_{OUT}}{V_{OUT} + V_D}$	$\dfrac{V_{IN} - V_S}{V_{IN}} \cdot \dfrac{V_{OUT}}{V_{OUT} + V_D - V_S}$	$\dfrac{V_{IN} - V_S}{V_{IN}} \cdot \dfrac{\lvert V_{OUT} \rvert}{\lvert V_{OUT} \rvert + V_D}$
$I_{IN(avg)}$ (Max load condition)	$\dfrac{I_{pk}}{2} \cdot \dfrac{V_{OUT} + V_D}{V_{IN} - V_S + V_D}$	$\dfrac{I_{pk}}{2}$	$\dfrac{I_{pk}}{2} \cdot \dfrac{\lvert V_{OUT} \rvert + V_D}{V_{IN} + \lvert V_{OUT} \rvert + V_D - V_S}$

The CCD321 Analog Delay Line

The inherent capability of charge-coupled devices (CCD) to manipulate information in the form of discrete charge packets makes this technology ideal for analog signal processing applications. Electrical information in voltage form is transformed to discrete charge packets by sampling the input; the charge packets are shifted in analog shift registers by applying an external clock. Information is then recovered at the output in discrete levels and, with proper filtering, information representing the input analog data is retrieved.

The CCD321 is a dual 455-bit analog shift register designed for use in analog signal processing systems that require delay and temporary storage of analog information. Fairchild's buried-channel CCD approach provides excellent bandwidth and high-speed capability. The device can be used in applications ranging from the audio band to high-speed video processing due to the wide range of data rate of the CCD321 — 20 kHz to 20 MHz.

DEVICE DESCRIPTION
The CCD321 consists of two independent 455-bit analog shift registers, each with an injection port, transport clock and output port; therefore, the device may be used as two 455-or one 910-bit analog delay line. The CCD321 consists of the following functional elements. See *Figures 1 and 2*.

Two Charge-Injection Ports — The analog information in voltage form is applied to two input ports at V_{IA} (or V_{IB}). Upon the activation of the analog sample clock, ϕ_{SA} (or ϕ_{SB}), a charge packet linearly dependent on the voltage difference between V_{1A} and V_{RA}, (V_{1B} and V_{RB}), is injected into analog shift register A (or B).

Two 455-Bit Analog Shift Registers — Each register transports the charge packets from the charge injection port to the corresponding output amplifier, A or B. Both registers are op-

erated in the 1-1/2 phase mode where one phase (ϕ_{1A} or ϕ_{1B}) is a clock and the other phase (V_2) is an intermediate dc potential. Phases ϕ_{1A} and ϕ_{1B} are completely independent; V_2 is a dc voltage common to both registers.

Two Output Amplifiers — Each output amplifier consists of three source-follower stages with constant-current source bias. A sample-and-hold transistor is located between the second and third stages of the amplifier. When the gate of the sample-and-hold transistor is clocked (ϕ_{RA} or ϕ_{RB}), a continuous output waveform is obtained. The transistor can be defeated by connecting ϕ_{RA} and/or ϕ_{RB} to V_{DD}. In this case the output is a pulse modulated waveform.

MODES OF OPERATION
The CCD321 can be operated in three different modes.

455-Bit Analog Delay — Either 455-bit analog shift register can be operated independently as a 455-bit delay line. The input voltage signal is applied directly to V_{IA}. The input sampling clock ϕ_{SA} samples this input voltage and injects a proportional amount of charge packet into the first bit of register A, which is clocked by ϕ_{1A}. If the sample-and-hold circuit is not used, the output appears as a pulse amplitude modulated waveform; ϕ_{RA} should be connected to V_{DD}. If the sample-and-hold circuit is used, the output appears as a continuous waveform; ϕ_{RA} should occur at the same time as ϕ_{SA} and the two pins should be connected. Analog shift register B can be independently operated in the same manner with V_{IB} as the analog input, ϕ_{1B} as the transport clock, ϕ_{SB} as the input sampling clock and ϕ_{RB} as the output sample-and-hold clock.

910-Bit Analog Delay in Series Mode — The two analog shift registers A and B can be connected in series to provide 910 bits of analog delay as shown in *Figure 3a*. The analog-signal

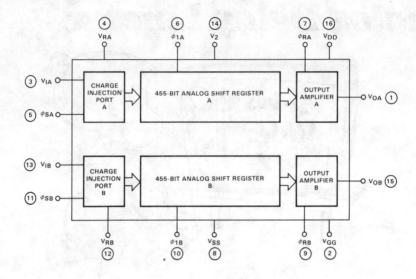

Fig. 1. Block Diagram

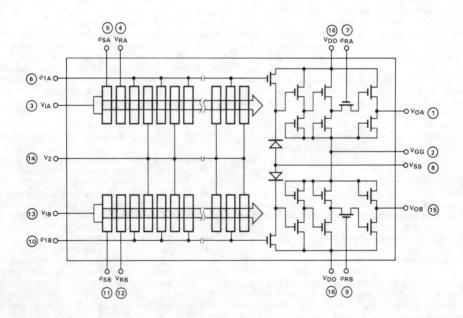

Fig. 2. Circuit Diagram

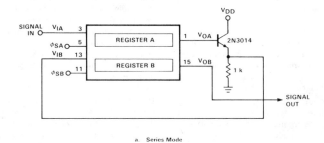

a.   Series Mode

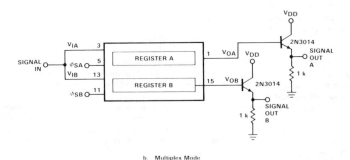

b.   Multiplex Mode

Fig. 3.   Modes of Operation

input voltage is applied to V_{IA}. The output of register A is connected to the input of register B with a simple emitter-follower buffer stage.

910-Bit Analog Delay in Multiplex Mode   The two analog shift registers can be connected in parallel to provide 910 bits of analog delay as shown in *Figure 3b*. The analog-signal input voltage is applied to both V_{IA} and V_{IB}. To recover the analog input information, the outputs at V_{OA} and V_{OB} should be combined. This mode of operation results in an effective sampling rate of twice the rate of ϕ_{1A}, ϕ_{1B}, ϕ_{SA} and ϕ_{SB}.

WHY 910?
The delay τ from input to output for a CCD delay line can be written simply as follows.

$$\tau = \frac{N}{f}$$

where N is the number of bits and f is the shifting clock rate, in this case ϕ_{1A} or ϕ_{1B}.

Due to the basic structure of the CCD input stage and register, the sampling clock rate is equal to the shifting clock rate, but they have different pulse widths. The sampling clock frequency is established by bandwidth considerations. When the input-signal bandwidth (BW) is sampled by the input charge-injection port to recover the analog information, the input must be sampled at a frequency of 2 BW, theoretically. In practice, however, a 3 BW sampling frequency is required.

The number of bits in the CCD321 was specifically selected to be capable of delaying the video information for one horizontal line of a TV signal in the NTSC television system. This line (1 H) is approximately 63.5 μs long; therefore a delay of 3.5 μs is required. The standard TV video bandwidth is 4.2 MHz, thus the sampling rate must be more than 10 MHz.

A second requirement for video sampling systems is that the sampling rate must be a multiple of a fundamental frequency called the color subcarrier frequency which is approximately 3.58 MHz. Therefore, a 3X subcarrier frequency of 3 x 3.58 10.7 MHz could be used for sampling frequency. Using this sampling frequency and a τ of 63.5 μs,

$$\tau = \frac{N}{f}$$

$$N = \tau f$$

$$= (63.5\ \mu s)\ (10.7\ MHz)$$

$$= 680\text{-}1/2\ bits$$

There are three very good reasons why the CCD321 analog delay line is not 680-1/2 bits.

● Even though a simple 1/2-cycle shift on the clock would provide a 1/2-bit delay, it would complicate the clocking requirement.

- A sampling rate of 10.7 MHz for a 4.2 MHz bandwidth is, in practice, not sufficient for proper reconstruction of higher frequency components.

- Since the output of the CCD321 is a pulse amplitude modulated waveform, the analog information is recovered by filtering the output waveform with a low pass filter. Good separation between video and clock components is difficult to achieve with a 10.7 MHz clock and a 4.2 MHz bandwidth unless complex filters are used.

The CCD321 was, therefore, designed to be capable of delaying 63.5 μs at a sampling frequency of 4X subcarrier or $4 \times 3.58 = 14.318$ MHz. Therefore

$$N = \tau f = 63.5 \ \mu s \times 14.3 \ MHz = 910 \ bits$$

The even multiple of subcarriers provides an even number of bits. The higher sampling frequency assures better bandwidth and makes post filtering of the output easier.

WHY DUAL 455?
A key advantage of CCD analog delay lines over glass delay lines is the capability of varying the input-to-output delay by simply varying a clock. With this advantage, the devices can be used in systems that require variable delay of analog data. In most applications, a particular $\Delta\tau$ is obtained by a Δf on the clock.

To simplify the driving requirement of the shifting clock, the CCD321 is organized into two registers that can be operated either in series or in parallel. In applications where fixed delay of analog data is required, the series mode is recommended. For variable delay applications, the multiplexed mode is recommended because a frequency variation, which can be from 10 to 20 MHz, might be required. If the device is used in series in the particular example of a 63.5 μs delay, the ϕ_{1A} clock rate equal to the ϕ_{1B} clock rate is 14.3 MHz. The output of the A register is connected to the input of the B side through a buffer and the delay output is recovered from the B output. In the multiplexed mode, the input is connected to both V_{1A} and V_{1B} and the clocks are all at 14.3 MHz/2 = 7.1 MHz. The input is effectively sampled at 14.318 MHz but all the clocks (ϕ_{1A}, ϕ_{1B}, ϕ_{SA} and ϕ_{SB}) are at 7 MHz. If clock variations are desired, drivers on the main shifting clocks (ϕ_{1A} and ϕ_{1B}) are easier to design if the CCD321 is operated in the multiplex mode.

WHERE IS IT USED?
CCD321 applications vary from fixed delay of analog information to variable delay of data in a continuous mode. In video systems, the CCD321 1 H delay line is very efficient for delaying a full bandwidth NTSC video line in applications such as comb filters for separation of chrominance and luminance information from the composite video waveform. This enhances higher frequency components in the signal output. The device is used in a series mode with a fixed clock rate of 14.318 MHz for a precise 63.5 μs delay.

In video tape recorders, the CCD321 can be used in two distinct applications...first as a fixed-mode 1 H delay for dropout compensation (DOC) to delay the video signal from the tape before display. In the event of a line loss arising from tape discontinuities or other phenomena, the display repeats the previous line stored instead of producing a white or black line on the screen.

In the other VTR application, the CCD321 can be used to eliminate time-base errors introduced with the video signal during the reading process of the heads. Time-base errors are caused by various factors including contraction or expansion of the recording medium and tape-to-head speed variations. They must be eliminated to avoid picture distortion at the TV receiver. By clocking the CCD321 at a rate proportional to the error, a continuous stream of properly timed video lines is provided at the device output.

The CCD321 can be used in other than video applications, e.g., in time-base compression and expansion systems where data is fed to the device at one rate, clocking is stopped, and the data is clocked out at a different rate. The wide range of operating frequencies (20 kHz to 20 MHz) and flexible clocking requirements make the CCD321 a powerful device for systems that require complex manipulation of analog data.

VIDEO DELAY MODULE
To aid the circuit designer in evaluating the CCD321, a complete delay line module, the CCD321M, is available consisting of a printed circuit board containing a CCD321, input and output signal processing circuitry, and the required clocking signal sources and bias voltage controls. A single power supply input of +20 V is required.

The delay time for analog signals through the CCD321M is precisely determined by the frequency of a clock signal which can be provided by an external source or obtained from an internal VCO. The CCD321M can be used as a 910-bit 1 H delay for TV video bandwidths of 5 MHz when operating with $4 \times 3.58 = 14.3$ MHz clock frequency, serve as a temporary analog store for a single full-bandwidth TV line, or can be used as a variable or adjustable delay by controlling either the internal or external clock frequency. Operating as two 455-bit registers, it can delay two independent analog signals.

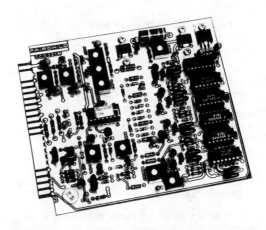

Fig. 4.   Video Delay Module

THE SH1549

✳ U U M
1 2 3

• • • An Electronic Tuner
Memory For Radio and Television Receivers

by Jim Holt

Electronic tuning systems are rapidly replacing their mechanical counterparts in the commercial radio and television receiver markets. Europe was first to convert commercial tuners to electronic (varactor-controlled) circuits, thus making more sophisticated tuner control systems economically feasible. However, many systems today—although electronic—have simply replaced the mechanically variable capacitor with a varactor diode tuned by adjusting a potentiometer resistor divider.

The Fairchild SH1549 hybrid tuner control/memory circuit is a cost-effective solution to the requirements of multi-station

memory for AM, FM and TV tuners. The SH1549 hybrid circuit gives the user the capability of storing and recalling up to 16 stations in additon to conventional varactor tuning. Using the SH1549 system, stations are stored by manually tuning to the appropriate station and pushing a Write button. The SH1549 converts the analog tuning voltage into a 12-bit digital word and stores the information in a memory for later recall. The station is recalled by pushing a Station button that is encoded as an address for a RAM. The RAM then outputs the digital information to a D/A converter, contained in the SH1549, that reproduces the correct analog voltage for the station originally stored.

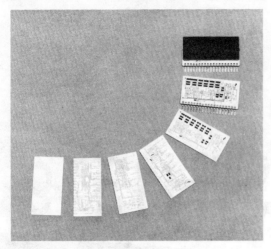

Fig. 1 SH1549 Process Steps

The SH1549 is constructed using thick-film hybrid techniques *(Figure 1)*. The resistors and conductors are printed on a 1″ × 2″ 2-layer ceramic substrate to create the 12-bit R/2R resistor ladder network and circuit interconnections. Next, the components are attached and wire bonded. Finally, the external leads are attached and the active components are sealed under a ceramic lid.

Hybrid construction is well suited to this type of application because it offers rapid conversion of discrete functions into a single package that can be tested and assembled similarly to a monolithic integrated circuit. This construction technique is less expensive than comparable discrete solutions because only one packaging step is involved. Hybrids also offer the advantage of flexibility, since they allow for easy implementation of custom modifications as well as longer term development of more complex functions.

CIRCUIT DESCRIPTION *(Figure 2)*

The SH1549 is constructed from standard CMOS and linear integrated circuits (LIC). The CMOS components provide the clock and memory functions and are connected to a separate reference supply (V_{DD2}). The CMOS logic must be powered at all times to retain the station information. Because CMOS devices have low current drain, battery backup can be used to insure that memory contents are not lost.

The LIC section provides two functions—the comparator and op amp. The comparator provides a "conversion-completed" signal to the flip-flop by sensing the instant when the contents of the memory provide an analog voltage equal to the tuning voltage. The op amp acts as a buffer to isolate the resistor ladder network from the varactor tuner. The inverting output of the op amp is brought out externally to allow for external gain setting. The gain is set to make the system compatible with various reference and varactor systems. For example, although CMOS cannot be operated at 27 V, a 27-V varactor system can be constructed using a 9-V reference supply (V_{DD2}) for the CMOS and a 30-V op amp supply (V_{DD1}) with the op amp gain set to 3.

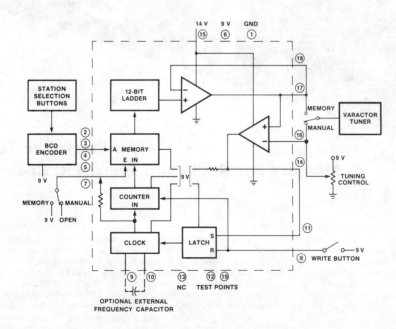

Fig. 2 SH1549 Block Diagram

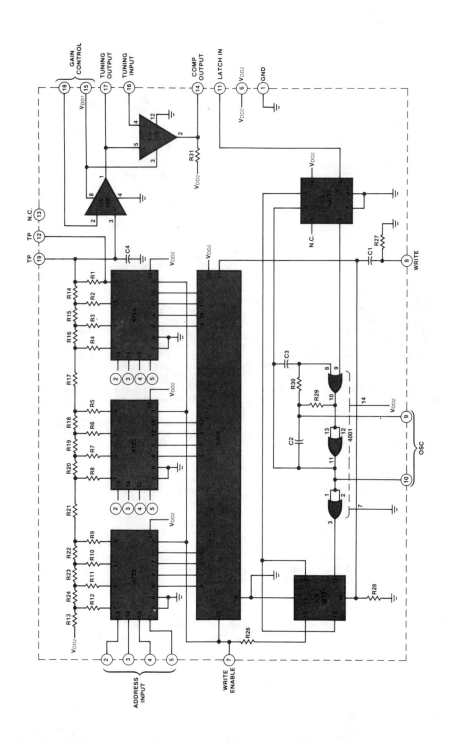

Fig. 3   SH1549 Schematic

301

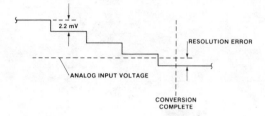

Fig. 4   Ladder Output

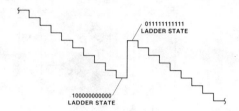

Fig. 5   Characteristics of Most Significant Bit Transition

MODES OF OPERATION

The schematic of the SH1549 is shown in *Figure 3*. The circuit has two modes of operation, manual and memory, controlled by an external switch. In the manual mode, a tuning potentiometer is switched to the tuner for conventional station tuning. Once the station is tuned, it is stored in the SH1549 by pushing the Write button. This action resets a flip-flop and enables a 12 kHz clock oscillator. The clock is fed into the 12-bit counter that drives the 12-bit resistor ladder network. The ladder output *(Figure 4)* is a staircase ramp that begins at V_{DD2} and decrements in steps of $V_{DD2}/4096$. The counter begins at the 1111...1 state and counts down. Thus, at the beginning of the cycle, all '1s' are input to the R/2R ladder which then produces a voltage into the buffer op amp equal to the V_{ref} voltage. The counter continues to decrement until the comparator senses the point at which the ramp voltage from the ladder equals the tuning (input) voltage. As the ladder output steps past the input voltage, the comparator switches. This sets the flip-flop, stops the timer and produces a digital word that accurately represents the tuning voltage. The word, now stored in RAM, can be recalled at any time by addressing the memory.

In the memory mode, the varactor tuner receives the tuning control voltage directly from the SH1549. Stations are selected by addressing the RAM with 4-bit parallel words encoded from the Station switches. The digital output from the RAM drives the resistor ladder network to decode the word into an analog voltage. The output voltage is buffered by an amplifier and fed into the varactor tuner through the manual/memory selector switch.

PERFORMANCE

The resolution of the SH1549, one part in 4096, is limited by the 12-bit thick-film ladder network. An overall system accuracy of one part in 2000 is achieved by placing the 12-bit ladder in a closed-loop configuration so that the analog conversion of each digital ladder code is compared to the input analog voltage before a storage decision is made. Thick-film ladder networks are not generally used for 12-bit D/A converters because the trimming tolerances are too

severe to be cost effective—the most significant bits usually require a trim tolerance of one part in 10,000. The closed-loop technique of the SH1549 corrects for trim errors in excess of 1% as long as the most significant bits are trimmed deliberately high. This produces a non-monotonic staircase ramp *(Figure 5)* which insures that a digital voltage code can be generated to accurately represent any analog input voltage. The fact that two digital codes representing the same voltage may exist is of no consequence to the system.

The present SH1549 is designed for a 9-V (V_{ref}) radio system and is capable of reproducing an input voltage at 25°C to within 8 mV, and maintaining the converted voltage to 12 mV over the 0-70°C range. The circuit is easily converted to a television tuning configuration by the addition of external feedback resistors to raise the op amp gain to accommodate the 30-V varactor tuning range. The maximum error in this configuration is 15 mV at 25°C and 24 mV over 0-70°C.

CONCLUSION

The SH1549 is currently being used in a European car radio and in a television application. The radio application uses eight memory recall switches that are divided into four station buttons and four band buttons. Four stations can be stored on each of four bands for a total of 16 stations. The bands are divided into two FM, and one AM and one long wave. The band switching is done externally to the SH1549 to allow conversion to other switching combinations. In the television application, band switching is done between UHF and VHF. The television tuner uses a 27-V varactor with the SH1549 op amp gain set to 3; otherwise the operation of the SH1549 is identical in both the television and the radio.

In the next generation SH1549, the standard CMOS components will be combined into a single custom array *(Figures 6 and 7)*. This will reduce the cost of the system, improve performance and also provide free ceramic area that can be used to provide additional functions such as station search, address encode, tuner-band switching with memory, and voltage reference. □

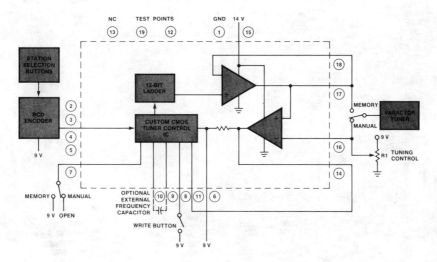

Fig. 6   Schematic of Next Generation SH1549

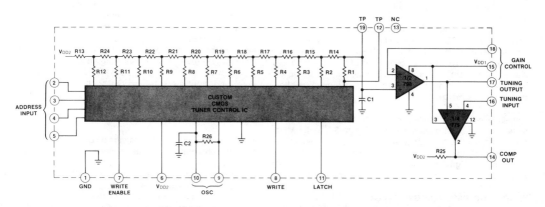

Fig. 7   Block Diagram of Next Generation Electronic Tuner

CCD COMB FILTERS FOR TELEVISION RECEIVERS

by Steve Barton

In an NTSC color television receiver, the method and degree of separation of the luminance (brightness) and chrominance (color) information in the detected video signal have a considerable effect on the quality of the displayed picture.

The standard technique for processing the luminance component of the NTSC video signal *(Figure 1a)* is to place a trap circuit, tuned to the color subcarrier frequency, in the luminance channel. The trap removes most of the chrominance signal components and shapes the frequency response of the luminance channel to produce an overall low-pass filter response *(Figure 1b)*.

Conventional chrominance signal processing circuitry is designed with a band-pass response of from 3.1 to 4.1 MHz *(Figure 1c)* so that luminance signal components below 3.1 MHz are not accepted by the chrominance channel. The chrominance signal is thus treated as a double-sideband signal with a maximum modulating frequency of 500 kHz.

TRAP/BAND-PASS DISADVANTAGES
In the luminance channel, the presence of the 3.58-MHz trap causes a number of problems. For example, luminance signal

frequencies above approximately 3 MHz are lost, reducing the horizontal resolution of the displayed picture. At the same time, the trap has virtually no rejection of the I-signal component of the chrominance signal below 3.1 MHz; the chrominance signal sidebands not rejected by the trap interfere with the luminance in areas of fine color detail. The worst effect produced by the trap circuit is ringing on the vertical edges of the displayed picture, which is partly responsible for dot crawl on the vertical edges. Ringing is worst on a transition between areas of highly saturated colors with different hues and brightness levels. On such a transition, step changes in color subcarrier amplitude and phase, and in luminance signal amplitude, occur and tend to excite the 3.58-MHz trap.

Although it rejects luminance signal components below 3.1 MHz, the chrominance circuitry does accept luminance signals in the 3.1- to 4.1-MHz region of the spectrum, causing a "cross-color" effect in areas of the picture having fine luminance detail. The band-pass nature of this circuitry also keeps the full bandwidth of the I-signal chrominance component from being used, which reduces the amount of horizontal color resolution possible.

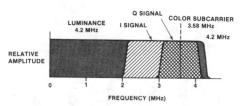

Fig. 1a   Spectrum of NTSC Video Signal

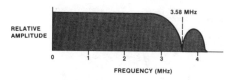

Fig. 1b   Overall Frequency Response of Luminance Channel

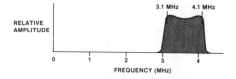

Fig. 1c   Overall Frequency Response of Chrominance Channel

These problems arise largely because the conventional trap/band-pass separation technique processes the luminance and chrominance signals as though they possess continuous spectra and makes no use of the frequency interleaving of these signals in the NTSC system.

FREQUENCY INTERLEAVING

In an NTSC-encoded composite video signal, frequency interleaving is the result of energy distribution characteristics. The spectral energy of the luminance signal in a vertically correlated television picture (no change from line to line) is clustered around harmonics of the horizontal scanning frequency (f_h), with very little energy between the harmonics. The chrominance sidebands are spaced at multiples of f_h away from the color subcarrier frequency, which in the NTSC system is at 227.5 f_h, or midway between two of the harmonics of f_h. The spectra of the luminance and chrominance signals are thus interleaved (Figure 2).

An ideal device for separating the luminance signal from the composite video signal is a filter with a frequency response that matches the spectral distribution of luminance energy across the luminance signal bandwidth. Similarly, the chrominance signal can be separated by a filter with a response that matches the spectral distribution of chrominance sidebands across the chrominance bandwidth. The frequency response of both these filters contains a large number of pass-bands spaced at intervals of f_h, with a stop-band midway between each adjacent pair of pass-bands. Because this response resembles the teeth of a comb, the filters are generally referred to as "comb" filters.

BASIC COMB FILTERS

A basic comb filter to perform luminance and chrominance signal separation consists of a time delay element and two summation networks that combine direct and delayed signals (Figure 3). If the delay time (T) is equal to the horizontal scanning period (1/f_h), the filter transfer function to the luminance output is maximum at multiples of f_h and the transfer function to the chrominance output is minimum at multiples of f_h (Figure 4).

The combed luminance output signal represents the sum of the picture content of successive scanning lines. Since the color subcarrier frequency is an odd harmonic of $f_h/2$, the color subcarrier phase changes by 180 degrees between corresponding points on successive scanning lines. The chrominance signals therefore cancel when the lines are summed, leaving only the luminance signal.

The combed chrominance output signal represents the difference in picture content between successive scanning lines. In a vertically correlated picture, the luminance signal is the same on successive scanning lines, so luminance cancellation occurs when the difference is taken. Because of the 180-degree phase change of the color subcarrier from line to line, the combed chrominance signal remains.

The physical effect of the filter is that each line in the displayed television picture is the average of the corresponding transmitted line and the previously transmitted line in the same field.

A comb filter for luminance and chrominance signal separation can be realized using as a time delay element a device that provides a non-dispersive delay of exactly one horizontal scanning period (1H). A glass block delay, which employs acoustic-wave propagation, has been used in the past for this purpose. The charge-coupled device (CCD) analog shift register, however, lends itself readily to such delay applications and has, in addition, marked advantages over the glass block.

For example, glass-block insertion loss is typically greater than 6 dB, while the CCD has 0 dB insertion loss. Similarly, the CCD has high input and low output impedances, which simplifies matching; the input and output impedances of the glass block, in contrast, change with frequency. The CCD can also handle the full 4.2-MHz NTSC video signal bandwidth, but the glass block cannot pass the full bandwidth unless the signal is modulated onto an rf carrier.

The delay time of the glass is dependent, to some extent, upon temperature, and there is a long-term aging effect on the delay time. The delay time of the CCD shift register is dependent upon the clock frequency, which can be referenced to the color subcarrier by using a phase-locked loop to produce a high degree of accuracy. An additional advantage of the CCD is that it is packaged in a 16-pin DIP and is, therefore, considerably smaller than the glass block.

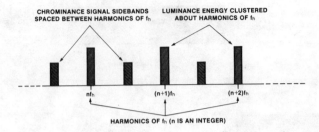

Fig. 2   Interleaving of Luminance and Chrominance Signal Spectra

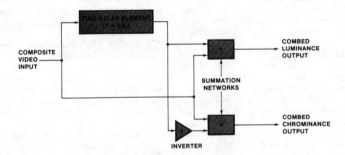

Fig. 3   Basic Comb Filter

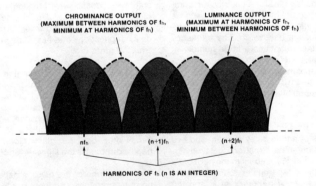

Fig. 4   Transfer Functions for Basic Comb Filter

REALIZATION OF A CCD COMB FILTER

A practical CCD comb filter, intended specifically for NTSC television applications, can be constructed using the CCD-321A shift register as the time delay element. The CCD321A is a 910-bit analog shift register that provides a delay of exactly 1H when driven by a clock signal of four times the color subcarrier frequency.

In this CCD comb filter *(Figure 5)*, a 14.3-MHz (four times the NTSC color subcarrier frequency) crystal-controlled oscillator is the source of clock signals for the clock drivers that supply the CCD shift register with two-phase clock signals. With an NTSC composite video signal at the system input, the input attenuator gives a video signal amplitude of 400 mV peak-to-peak at the input of the CCD321A delay element. The low-pass filter removes the 14.3-MHz clock component from the CCD output signal. The delayed and filtered composite signal is fed to a phase splitter, which supplies anti-phase delayed signals to the two summation networks. Each summation network is also supplied with a direct video signal through the variable attenuators. In practice, the functions of the summation networks and output buffers are performed by two video operational amplifiers, resulting in better combing action over a wider frequency range than is possible with circuits using discrete components.

The upper frequency limit of combing is determined by the frequency response of the low-pass filter and the CCD delay element, the output of which starts to fall off as the signal frequency approaches half the clock frequency. The lower limit of combing is determined by the value of the coupling capacitors used in the system; these are made large enough so that the time constants are equal to several vertical scanning periods.

VERTICAL RESOLUTION IMPROVEMENT

The comb filter provides optimum luminance and chrominance signal separation in a vertically correlated television picture. In practice, however, television pictures are often not vertically correlated. Luminance spectral energy in such a picture is present at frequencies between harmonics of f_h. Removal of this energy by the comb filter results in loss of vertical resolution and its attendant problems. There are two basic techniques for solving these problems.

The first technique removes as little of the luminance information from between harmonics as possible. This is accomplished by restricting combing to those portions of the spectrum in which luminance and chrominance signal interleaving occurs. Addition of a band-pass filter to the comb filter *(Figure 6)* restricts combing to the range of frequencies containing the color subcarrier sidebands. This filter has a pass-band of from approximately 2.1 to 4.1 MHz if the entire chrominance signal bandwidth is used. Its pass-band is from approximately 3.1 to 4.1 MHz if the chrominance signal is treated as a double-sideband signal.

The second technique provides combing across the full video bandwidth, but adds a signal containing some of the luminance information removed by combing. To implement this technique, the combed chrominance of the basic comb filter is passed through a 2-MHz low-pass filter to remove the chrominance information *(Figure 7)*. The resulting signal is added to the combed luminance signal. The net effect for the luminance signal is that combing occurs only above 2 MHz. The low-pass filter output represents changes in picture content in the vertical direction; this is used as a "detail signal" to improve vertical resolution.

The CCD321A can be used as a delay element to construct an efficient, economical comb filter that performs more than adequate separation of luminance and chrominance in an NTSC television receiver. Such a filter is the first that is low enough in cost to be acceptable for receiver, as well as broadcast and professional, applications. The use of the comb filter does produce a loss in vertical color resolution, but the improvements in displayed picture quality — particularly on vertical edges — more than compensate for the degradations on horizontal edges, and vertical resolution correction can be readily provided. □

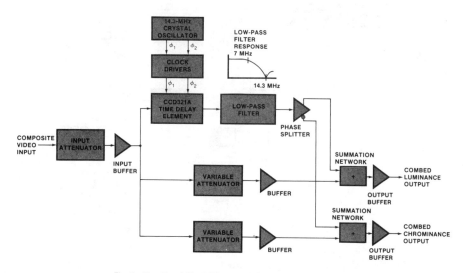

Fig. 5 Functional Block Diagram of Practical CCD Comb Filter

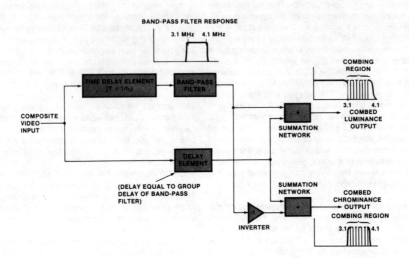

Fig. 6   Comb Filter with Restricted Combing Bandwidth

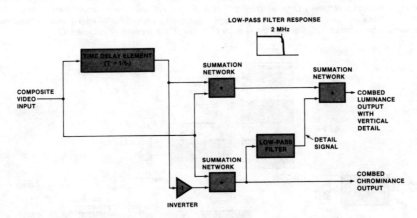

Fig. 7   Comb Filter with Addition of Detail Signal

THE µA715
A VERSATILE HIGH SPEED OPERATIONAL AMPLIFIER

INTRODUCTION

The µA715 is a high speed, high gain (92 dB) monolithic operational amplifier designed to have wide bandwidth and high slew rate and thus, high output voltage capability. It has built in compensation and four points to which lag or lead-lag compensation can be applied. The µA715 is intended for use in A/D and D/A converters, phase locked loops, sample and hold circuits, multiplexed analog gates, or in other applications requiring wide bandwidth or fast signal acquisition.

The five applications described in this note were chosen to illustrate the capabilities and the techniques for using the µA715 as a building block for many amplifier configurations.

● An image orthicon head amplifier with a 4-way distribution amplifier designed to feed 75 Ω cable.

● A general purpose video amplifier with 40 dB gain, 50 Ω input impedance, and 10 V peak-to-peak output capability.

● As above, except 60 dB gain, and 75 Ω input impedance.

● A 40 dB high input impedance amplifier.

● A high speed sample and hold circuit.

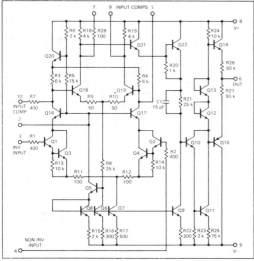

Fig. 1. µA715 Schematic Diagram

MAXIMUM STABLE GAIN AND BANDWIDTH CONSIDERATIONS

The expression for overall gain for a feedback amplifier is:

$$A = \frac{-A_0}{1 + BA_0}$$

A_0 = Gain without feedback
B = Feedback ratio

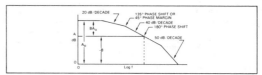

For the amplifier to be stable, $1 + BA_0$ must never go negative. The only way $1 + BA_0$ can go negative is if the phase shift in A_0 exceeds 180°; thus for a stable system, A_0 must fall below 0 dB before the phase shift reaches 180°. These considerations are related to a typical frequency response without feedback, as shown in *Figure 2*. The 180° phase shift point occurs about half way down, between the second and third break points.

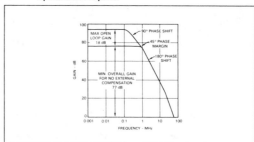

Fig. 2. Typical Open Loop Frequency Response of an Operational Amplifier

Fig. 3. Open Loop Response for µA715 without Compensation

It must also be remembered that this is a limit condition that corresponds to zero phase margin. In practice, a designer requires at least 45° phase margin. Gain with no feedback (and no compensation) for the µA715 is plotted in *Figure 3*. The minimum closed loop gain for a phase margin of 45° is also included. To construct an amplifier with less than this overall gain, the basic amplifier characteristic must be altered so that the second break point coincides with the desired gain as shown in *Figure 4*.

FAIRCHILD
SEMICONDUCTOR

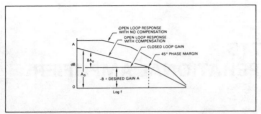

Fig. 4. Change of Open Loop Response when Compensation is Added

This alteration of the basic amplifier ac performance is called compensation and is required to ensure stability. In the example above, only one dominant phase lag is used to compensate the amplifier. The μA715 has four compensation points brought out on leads 1, 7, 9, and 10. Thus many compensation techniques are possible. Internal lead compensation is supplied by the R21, C1 combination. In the amplifier design described, it is possible to empirically optimize frequency performance by observing the square wave response and adjusting the compensation for the best combination of rise time, overshoot and ringing. It is possible to get wider bandwidths on individual units by this method.

A HEAD AMPLIFIER FOR AN IMAGE ORTHICON

There are many problems associated with amplifying the signal generated by an image orthicon. The most relevant of these is the frequency compensation for the frequency roll off due to output capacitance. *Figure 5* shows an approximate equivalent circuit of an image orthicon and the associated input network of an amplifier.

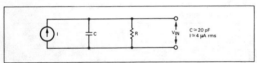

Fig. 5. Equivalent Circuit of a Vidicon

Here, the break frequency occurs at

$$f_B = \frac{1}{2 \pi RC}$$

and roll off is 20 dB per decade for R = 50 kΩ and f_B = 160 kHz. There are two main ways to compensate for this roll off. One is to create a comparative boost in the amplifier characteristic. This is done in a great many head amplifiers today, but it has the inherent disadvantage of requiring a set up control to adjust the boost to start at the break frequency. The other approach, which is preferred, is to use an amplifier with low input impedance and high transresistance (*Figure 6*). The low input resistance swamps the effect of input capacitance, and essentially all the current generated by the image orthicon flows into the amplifier. Input impedance and transresistance are determined as follows:

$$Z_{IN} = \frac{1}{\dfrac{1}{R1} + \dfrac{A_0}{R2}} = R1 \text{ in parallel with } \frac{R2}{A_0}$$

$$\simeq \frac{R2}{A_0} \text{ if } A_0 R1 \gg R2$$

$$\text{Transresistance} = R_T = \frac{V_o}{I_{IN}} = \frac{-A_0 I_{IN} Z_{IN}}{I_{IN}} \simeq R2$$

$$\text{if } A_0 R1 \gg R2$$

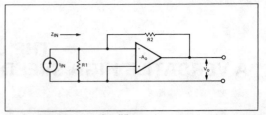

Fig. 6. Transresistance Amplifier

Figure 7 shows both the circuit diagram and the frequency response for a typical device under fixed compensation conditions. The circuit diagram shows the μA715 feeding a complementary emitter follower with overall feedback. The overall feedback resistor establishes the transresistance of the amplifier which is 51 kΩ .

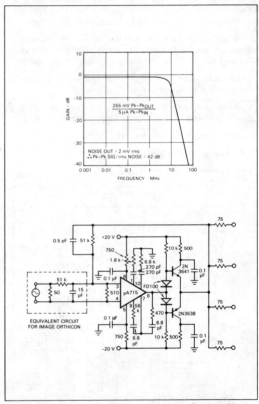

Fig. 7. Typical Frequency Response for Image Orthicon Head Amplifier

Isolation (cross talk) between the outputs is measured by applying a signal back into one of the outputs with zero input to the amplifier and measuring the voltage at another output (see *Figure 8*). Isolation of 40 dB corresponds to an output impedance from the emitter follower of 0.75 Ω . As can be seen from *Figure 8*, the degree of isolation between outputs decreases with the increase of frequency. This is because the output impedance of the emitter follower becomes higher as the degree of feedback lessens, due to the open loop gain characteristic rolling off at higher frequencies.

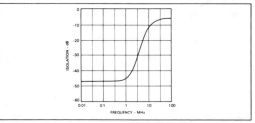

Fig. 8. Typical Isolation Between Outputs for Head Amplifier Shown in Figure 7

For a nominal input signal of 5 µA peak-to-peak, the output is 255 mV peak-to-peak. Noise at the output is about 2.0 mV rms or a peak-to-peak signal to rms noise ratio of 42 dB under nominal conditions.

The following three amplifier applications demonstrate the ability of the µA715 to handle large voltage swings at the output.

A 40 dB AMPLIFIER—LARGE SIGNAL HANDLING CAPABILITY

The first of these is a 40 dB amplifier with 50 Ω input impedance. The schematic, together with the frequency response for three levels of output, is shown in *Figure 9*. As can be seen from the graph, the frequency response at various levels of output is dependent on the overload capability of the µA715. A plot of maximum voltage output versus frequency, given in *Figure 10*, was obtained by monitoring the voltage output so that a 2 dB change in voltage input produced a 1 dB change in the voltage output. In essence, for large signals the bandwidth of the amplifier is limited by the overload characteristic rather than RC roll off. For 10 V peak-to-peak output, the signal to noise ratio is about 63 dB.

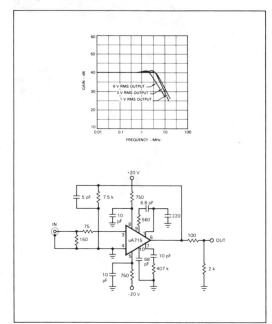

Fig. 9. A High Voltage Output, 40 dB Amplifier with 50 Ω Input Impedance

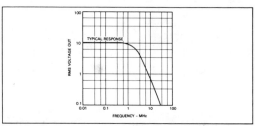

Fig. 10. Maximum Output Voltage vs Frequency for the Amplifier in Figure 9

A 75 Ω INPUT IMPEDANCE WIDEBAND 60 dB AMPLIFIER

Figure 11 demonstrates a similar amplifier with 60 dB of gain. The higher gain results in a slightly lower bandwidth because the high frequency roll off characteristic is governed by the open loop roll off.

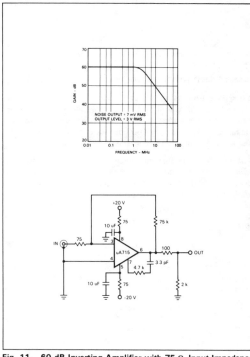

Fig. 11. 60 dB Inverting Amplifier with 75 Ω Input Impedance

A 40 dB HIGH INPUT IMPEDANCE AMPLIFIER

Wideband amplifiers with high input impedances are particularly useful in sonar, crystal strain guage, and biomedical applications. An amplifier with 40 dB gain is shown with frequency response in *Figure 12*. This configuration has a very high input impedance at dc, but it falls with increase in frequency due to the input capacitance of the µA715. This restricts the available bandwidth to about 500 kHz with a 100 kΩ source resistance. Also, the high input impedance configuration needs an input offset control because of the presence of input offset current flowing through the input resistance, causing an input offset voltage. Thus, the higher the input resistance, the higher the offset.

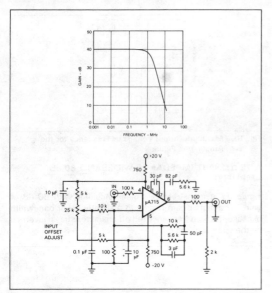

Fig. 12. 40 dB Non Inverting High Input Impedance Amplifier

SAMPLE AND HOLD CIRCUIT

Many data processing systems require that analog input signals be sampled and that the sample value be held constant for the time necessary to perform an analog-to-digital conversion. This sample and hold function may be accomplished using the μA715 high speed operational amplifier.

A schematic of the basic sample and hold circuit is shown in *Figure 13*. In the sample mode, the sampling switch Q1 is turned on and the circuit functions as an inverting operational amplifier with voltage gain given by the negative of the resistor ratio R2/R1. If R1 is equal to R2, the circuit is a unity gain inverting amplifier and the output is an inverted replica of the input.

When Q1 is switched off, the circuit enters the hold mode. The output voltage value at the instant Q1 is switched off is retained across the holding capacitor C1. In the hold mode the circuit functions as an operational integrator. With Q1 off, there is no input to the integrator and the output remains constant.

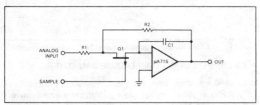

Fig. 13. Basic Operational Sample and Hold Circuit

The acquisition time when going from the hold mode to the sample mode is a function of the time constant R2C1 and the required accuracy. The time required to reach the input level when switching from hold to sample is given by:

$$t_a = R2C1 \ln\left(\frac{100}{\% \text{ accuracy}}\right) \qquad (1)$$

A practical sample and hold circuit, shown in *Figure 14*, includes the components necessary to compensate for the dc and ac errors inherent to the basic circuit of *Figure 13*. The dc offset is adjusted to zero by connecting a 50 kΩ potentiometer R4 across the input frequency compensation terminals of the μA715 and returning the wiper of R4 through an 82 kΩ resistor to V+. The μA715 is frequency compensated for unity gain operation by C3, C4 and C5. A junction field effect transistor Q1 is used as the sampling switch. Because there is some capacitance from the gate to the source of Q1, a portion of the gate signal is coupled through the device to the holding capacitor C1. Thus, a slight offset voltage is added to the output when switching from sample to hold.

A definite advantage of the operational sample and hold is that the ac offset is independent of the analog signal level. The offset can be compensated by removing a fixed amount of charge from the holding capacitor when switching to the hold mode. In *Figure 14*, the offset is removed by an opposing signal, coupled by C2 from the sample pulse input to the holding capacitor.

During the hold time, the output voltage will tend to drift as the holding capacitor integrates the μA715 input bias current. This drift can be compensated by supplying bias current from a separate source so there is no current flow through the holding capacitor. In *Figure 14*, this compensation is provided by R5, R6, R7 and D1. D1 acts as a temperature dependent voltage source causing the bias current through R5 to decrease with increasing temperature. This provides partial temperature compensation of bias current because the μA715 bipolar input stage causes a negative temperature coefficient of input bias current.

With a 10 V step input (±5 V to ∓5 V) the settling time to ±0.05% is 10 μs. This is slightly longer than that given by *Equation 1* due to the finite ON resistance of the sampling switch Q1. If C1 is decreased to 100 pF, the settling time is about 1 μs. Temperature drift of the output in the hold mode is approximately 0.001%/°C for a hold time of 100 μs.

The sample and hold circuit described can be used with a sequential approximation A/D converter. If 9-bit accuracy is required (0.2%) and 0.1% of the overall error is assigned to the sample and hold, the acquisition time for a full scale input change is 10 μs. This corresponds to the amount of time that must be allowed before the most significant bit can be converted. If subsequent bits are converted at the same rate, the required holding time is 90 μs to complete conversion of the nine bits.

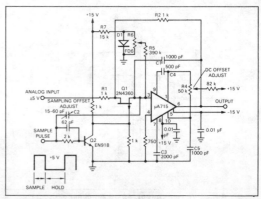

Fig. 14. μA715 Sample and Hold Circuit

A LOW DRIFT, LOW NOISE MONOLITHIC OPERATIONAL AMPLIFIER FOR LOW LEVEL SIGNAL PROCESSING

INTRODUCTION

The field of low level signal processing and precision analog computation has been the exclusive domain of high-priced, discrete, chopper-stabilized operational amplifiers. A new monolithic amplifier, designated the μA725, with superior input characteristics, has been designed to compete with these discrete devices. It features low offset voltage and low current drift with temperature and time, low noise, high power-supply rejection, high common-mode rejection and range and extremely high open-loop gain. A closed-loop gain of 1000 ±.03% is possible.

A new process has been developed which offers transistors with high β (for both NPN s and lateral PNP s), low noise, excellent β linearity at low currents, and low output conductance. The combination of new process and circuit techniques makes the μA725 ideal for the instrumentation and low level signal processing fields. Additional attributes of the μA725 are: output and input short circuit protection, offset voltage nulling capability, no latch-up when common mode range is exceeded, operation over a wide range of supply voltages (±3 V to ±20 V, with a gain of 250,000 at ±3 V).

CIRCUIT DESCRIPTION

Input Stage

The circuit diagram of Figure 1 illustrates the main design philosophy of the input stage: *There is no substitute for simplicity where matching of devices is a primary criterion.* The number of transistor junctions in the input signal path must be kept at a minimum for best input offset voltage and current matching and for lowest input noise figure. PNP-NPN input stage configurations as well as "punch-through" or cascade configurations must be avoided since they increase the number of sources of input error. In addition, active collector loads must be avoided since they do not exhibit the matching or temperature tracking of resistive loads and may be subject to g_m modulation from substrate current variations.

The μA725 utilizes the simplest input configuration: two differentially connected transistors with well-matched resistor loads. The two input transistors shown in Figure 1 are each physically two parallel connected devices, Q_{1A}, Q_{1B}, Q_{2A}, Q_{2B}. They are biased by current source Q_3 and loaded by

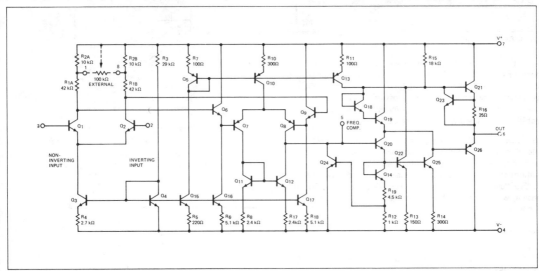

Fig. 1.   Schematic diagram of the μA725.

FAIRCHILD
SEMICONDUCTOR

464 ELLIS STREET, MOUNTAIN VIEW, CALIFORNIA 94040 (415) 962-5011/TWX 910-379-6435

matched resistors R_1 and R_2. The placement of the input quad is in a criss-cross fashion as shown in Figure 2. This configuration substantially reduces thermal gradient effects. The importance of this configuration is obvious if one considers that variations occuring in output stage power dissipation or in the location of the heat generating components can cause thermally induced input errors.

As an example, for a heat source at point P in Figure 2, the effective temperature differential between the cross-connected input pairs is 2a/b (or 16 times less for the μA725) than between two input devices (say Q_{1A}, Q_{2B}) only. Although the Q_{1A}-Q_{2B} temperature differential is minute, it should be remembered that even a $.01^\circ$C difference is equivalent to a 25 μV change in offset voltage because $\Delta V_{BE}/\Delta T \cong -2.5$ mV/$^\circ$C for silicon transistors. Since the aforementioned $\pm.03\%$ closed-loop gain stability is achieved by keeping the open-loop gain over one million under all conditions (i.e. less than 10 μV produces a 10 V output), a 25 μV change in input would be disastrous. This temperature gradient effect is practically eliminated by the unique geometrics employed in the μA725.

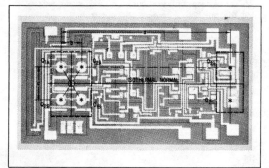

Fig. 2.   Overlay of μA725 die.

An additional bonus of the large area input quad arrangement is that the matching of input devices is significantly improved. Therefore, the performance of matching dependent parameters such as input offset voltage, input offset current, common-mode rejection, and power-supply rejection are superior to that hitherto obtainable.

The presence of the input quad introduces the concept of three dimensional matching. Just as first order thermal gradients are eliminated by the quad pair, first order diffusion variations (the third dimension) are also removed because the effective "centers of gravity" of Q_{1A}, Q_{1B} and Q_{2A}, Q_{2B} coincide, while centers of neighboring pairs are separated by six mils or more.

Second Stage

The major consideration in the design of the second stage is to diminish its influence on input noise, offset, and drift. Although the gain of the first stage attenuates second stage effects, careless layout and high second stage current levels can result in considerable error contributions at the input. Therefore, the current levels are low and emitter followers Q_6 and Q_9 are used to limit the loading of the first stage; Q_7, Q_8, and Q_6, Q_9 are carefully matched. Current sources Q_{10}, Q_{16}, and Q_{17} maintain constant V_{BE} match in the second stage and provide constant impedance load to the first stage. The combination of Q_{11} and Q_{12} retains the full differential gain

of the second stage, while converting from differential to single-ended output. The high impedance load in the second stage provides high gain and allows frequency stabilization at a single compensation point (lead 5).

Driver and Output Stage

The minimum current in the driver transistor Q_{22} is fixed by current source Q_{13} and results in a highly linear output swing. Transistors Q_{18} and Q_{19} provide the proper bias for class AB operation of the output power transistors Q_{21} and Q_{26} and prevent cross-over distortion in the output. In addition Q_{19} is connected in an emitter follower configuration providing low output resistance even with h_{FE} variations in Q_{26}.

Short Circuit Protection

The output current limiting is provided by Q_{23} which prevents overload of Q_{21} and current source Q_{25} limiting the base current drive of Q_{26}. The currents in Q_{22} and Q_{25} are limited by the normally off transistor Q_{24}, which becomes active when the output is overdriven and removes the base drive.

FREQUENCY COMPENSATION

The open-loop and closed-loop frequency response curves are shown in Figures 3 and 4 for the various gain configurations. Note that the μA725 does not require compensation at the input. The advantages are the reduction in the number of external components required for frequency stability and the elimination of noise pickup and stray feedback from the output to the collectors of the input quad.

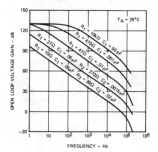

Fig. 3.   Open loop response for various values of compensation.

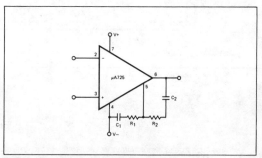

Fig. 4.   Frequency compensation connection diagram.

The requirement for low current levels in the second stage and the capacitance required for single terminal compensation reduce unity gain slew rate. However, this is not a disadvantage since this amplifier is designed for low level signal processing applications where high closed-loop gain configurations are used. At high gains the μA725 slew rate is over 5 V/μs as shown in Figure 5, better than other general purpose operational amplifiers available today.

PERFORMANCE

Typical electrical performance is summarized in Table I. Three of the parameters are of special interest because they have been obtained using new concepts in operational amplifier design. These are offset voltage drift with temperature (TCV$_{OS}$), closed-loop gain stability, and common-mode rejection ratio (CMRR).

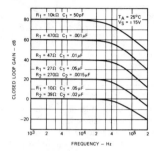

Fig. 5. Frequency response for various closed loop gains.

Minimizing Offset Voltage Drift With Temperature

It is a well known property (see Reference 1) of differential amplifiers, such as shown in Figure 6, that:

$$TCV_{OS} = \frac{V_{OS}(T)}{T}$$

(1)

or

$$TCV_{OS} = 3.3 \ \mu V/°C \quad \text{for every millivolt of offset voltage at } 25°C$$

TABLE I

TYPICAL ELECTRICAL CHARACTERISTICS — T_A = +25°C, V_S = ±15 V (unless otherwise specified)

PARAMETER	CONDITIONS	VALUE	UNITS
Input Offset Voltage	R$_S$ ≤ 10 kΩ	0.6	mV
Temperature Coefficient	External Nulling	0.6	μV/°C
Drift per Day		1.5	μV
Input Offset Current		3	nA
Temperature Coefficient		10	pA/°C
Input Bias Current		45	nA
	T_A = −55°C	115	nA
Large Signal Voltage Gain		4 x 10⁶	
Closed Loop Gain Stability	R$_L$ ≥ 2 kΩ	1000 ±.06	%
Common Mode Rejection Ratio	R$_S$ ≤ 10 kΩ	120	dB
Power Supply Rejection Ratio	R$_S$ ≤ 10 kΩ	120	dB
Output Voltage Swing	R$_L$ ≥ 2 kΩ	±13	V
Common Mode Input Voltage		±14	V
Input Noise Current	f$_o$ = 10 Hz	.7	pA
	ΔF = 1 Hz		
Input Noise Voltage	f$_o$ = 10 Hz	11	nV
	ΔF = 1 Hz		
Input Resistance		1.6	MΩ
	T_A = −55°C	.5	MΩ
Output Resistance		130	Ω
Slew Rate Gain: 10,000	R$_L$ ≥ 2 kΩ	40	V/μs
Gain: 1,000	R$_L$ ≥ 2 kΩ	6	V/μs
Bandwidth (Closed Loop Gain = 1)		600	kHz
(Closed Loop Gain = 1000)		500	kHz
Power Dissipation, Quiescent		90	mW

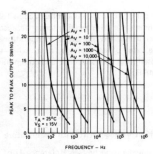

Fig. 6. μA725 maximum undistorted sinusoidal output vs. frequency.

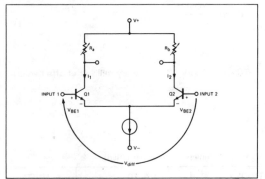

Fig. 7. Differential amplifier.

It follows from Equation 1 that if V_{OS} is adjusted to zero by some nulling procedure, TCV_{OS} will be zero. The offset nulling resistor is external and its temperature coefficient (TC) may differ significantly from the diffused resistor TCs. A parameter Θ can be defined as the difference between the nulling resistor's TC and the diffused resistor's TC. If R_{X1} is used externally to null the amplifier as shown in Figure 8, it can be shown that:

$$TCV_{OS} \cong [V_{OS} \text{ (unnulled)} \times \Theta] + \\ [V_{OS} \text{ (nulled)} \times 3360 \text{ ppm/}^{\circ}\text{C}] \qquad (2)$$

Although the V_{OS}/T term of Equation 1 is indeed eliminated by nulling, a new drift term is introduced. If $\Theta = 2500$ ppm/°C which is typical for film resistors, TCV_{OS} is reduced by only 25% — an insignificant improvement over the initial unnulled drift.

Similarly, if R_{X2} is the nulling potentiometer:

$$TCV_{OS} \cong \frac{R_{X2}}{R_{X2} + 2(R_1 + R_2)} \times V_{OS} \text{ (unnulled)} \times \Theta \qquad (3)$$

This procedure is used to null several of the operational amplifiers available today. Since $R_{X2} \gg R_1 + R_2$ because of other design considerations, the drift is basically the same as in the previous case.

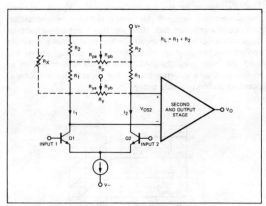

Fig. 8. Three ways of nulling operational amplifiers.

If R_p is used to null in Figure 8, two degrees of design freedom are introduced: the ratios R_1/R_2 and R_p/R_2. The only restriction on these ratios is the capability to null out all possible offset voltages. Depending on the values used, TCV_{OS} can range from $-V_{OS}$ times Θ to $+V_{OS}$ times Θ. Thus a value can be determined such that the drift is zero. A computer evaluation of the rather involved functional relationship between TCV_{OS} and V_{OS} with R_1/R_2 and R_p/R_2 as parameters yields the optimum values shown in the circuit diagram of Figure 1, and ensures that the effect of the TC differential Θ is negligible. A more detailed discussion of temperature drift is presented in Appendix I.

Closed Loop Gain Accuracy

The closed loop gain (A_{CL}) of an amplifier may be expressed as:

$$A_{CL} = -\frac{\alpha}{\beta} \left[\frac{1}{1 + \dfrac{1}{\beta A_{OL}}} \right] \qquad (4)$$

where:

A_{OL} = open loop gain
α = attenuation factor
β = feedback factor
α/β = "ideal" gain

In this expression α/β is the ideal gain. For best noise figure and lowest drift, alpha should be as close to one as possible. Expanding the bracketed expression above in a power series, the accuracy of A_{CL} can be found to be:

$$\epsilon(\%) \cong \frac{100}{\beta A_{OL}} \qquad (5)$$

thus if $\beta = .001$ and the desired ϵ is 0.1% then $A_{OL} = 1,000,000$ min.

Common Mode Rejection

One of the most important parameters of operational amplifiers is common mode rejection ratio (CMRR). If, for example, we wish to amplify a 100 μV differential voltage superimposed on a 1 V common mode signal and the amplifier only has a 100 μV/V (80 dB) CMRR, the output voltage can be zero.

This is not an uncommon requirement, yet most operational amplifiers today do not guarantee more than 80 dB CMRR. Thus very high common mode rejection of over 110 dB is required in instrumentation applications.

It can be shown that CMRR, in volts/volts, in terms of circuit parameters is:

$$CMRR = \frac{kT}{q} \Delta\gamma \tag{6}$$

where γ is the current normalized output conductance of the input devices Q_1 and Q_2 and $\Delta\gamma$ is the difference between the two γs. Equation 6 holds if the output conductance of current source Q_3 is significantly less than that of Q_1 and Q_2 and if the voltage drop across R_1 and R_2 is much larger than any possible second stage offset voltage. The typical 120 dB CMRR for the μA725 has been obtained by the following:

(1) developing a process which features high β, low noise, and low output conductance of the input transistors (gamma);

(2) closely matching the input quad and thereby obtaining a value of $\Delta\gamma$.

Additional details on CMRR theory that include the constraints on Equation 8 are presented in Appendix II.

APPLICATIONS

The μA725 has been designed specifically for low level signal processing applications such as signal conditioners, instrumentation amplifiers, precision measuring equipment, data acquisition systems, telemetry and process controls.

In these applications, it is recommended that stable precision thin film resistors be used to take advantage of the full capabilities of the μA725. In applications where CMRR is important, the input resistor bridge ratios must be trimmed to better than 10 ppm to prevent imbalances and the resulting degradation of CMRR. In addition, the input capacity on each input must be balanced to within 1 pF in order to obtain good CMRR with frequency.

Ground lands and shields should be used as extensively as possible to prevent coupling unwanted signals from the output to the input. If remote zero adjust is desirable (more than 2 inches), leads 1 and 8 should be decoupled with 0.1 μF capacitors to V+ and cables to the remote null pot should be shielded to reduce noise pick up and prevent unwanted coupling to null leads.

CONCLUSIONS

A new instrumentation operational amplifier has been built which makes extensive use of second generation technologies. The low offset drifts, low input currents, low noise performance and massive open loop gain make the device an ideal choice for low level signal processing applications.

APPENDIX I
MINIMIZING OFFSET VOLTAGE DRIFT WITH TEMPERATURE IN MONOLITHIC OPERATIONAL AMPLIFIERS

INTRODUCTION

It is a well known property of differential amplifiers, such as shown in Figure 7, that input offset voltage (V_{OS}) drift with temperature (TCV_{OS}) is substantially reduced by operating the two transistors with equal base-emitter voltages (V_{BE}) instead of with equal collector currents (I_C). To illustrate this simply, the starting point is the standard equation relating I_C to V_{BE}

$$I_C = I_S e^{(q\,V_{BE}/kT)} \tag{1}$$

from which

$$V_{diff} \cong V_{BE1} - V_{BE2} = \frac{kT}{q} \ln\left(\frac{I_1}{I_2} \times \frac{I_{S2}}{I_{S1}}\right) \tag{2}$$

and

$$V_{OS}(T) \cong V_{diff}(T) \Big|_{I_1 = I_2} \tag{3}$$

Differentiating (2) with respect to temperature yields:

$$TCV_{OS} \cong \frac{dV_{diff}}{dT} = \frac{V_{diff}}{T} + \frac{kT}{q} \times \frac{\frac{d}{dT}\left(\frac{I_1}{I_2}\right)}{\frac{I_1}{I_2}} + \epsilon \tag{4}$$

where ϵ is an error term. If $I_1 = I_2$, then $\frac{V_{OS}}{T}$ dominates the equation for TCV_{OS}. The significance of ϵ will be discussed later. Therefore, if V_{diff} is forced to zero by making $V_{BE1} = V_{BE2}$, TCV_{OS} is diminished. This statement hinges on the assumption that the second term of (4) is negligible.

When V_{diff} is set to zero by some external adjustment of the input stage of a monolithic operational amplifier the second term of Equation 4 does become appreciable. The nulling network must optimize for minimum TCV_{OS}. This appendix presents the details of obtaining this optimum nulling method.

NULLING METHODS

The nulling is usually accomplished by shorting the inputs together and therefore forcing V_{diff} to zero. The resulting collector current mismatch is approximately

$$e^{\left(\frac{qV_{OS}}{kT}\right)}$$

or 4% for initial V_{OS} of 1 mV. This is cancelled by adjusting the resistors loading the differential pair to make the input voltage to the following stages zero. This implies that:

$$I_1 R_a = I_2 R_b \quad \text{at } T_O \tag{5}$$

where R_a and R_b are equivalent resistances loading Q_1 and Q_2, respectively; T_O is the temperature at which the nulling is performed, usually room temperature.

From Equations 2, 3 and 5

$$V_{diff}(T_O) = 0 = \frac{kT_O}{q} \ln \frac{I_{S2} I_1}{I_{S1} I_2} \tag{6}$$

$$= \frac{kT_O}{q} \times \ln \left[\frac{I_{S2}}{I_{S1}} \times \frac{R_b}{R_a} (T_O) \right]$$

and

$$V_{OS}(T_O) = \frac{kT_O}{q} \ln \left(\frac{I_{S2}}{I_{S1}} \right) = \frac{kT_O}{q} \ln \left(\frac{R_a}{R_b} \right)$$

by series expansion

$$\approx -\left(\frac{kT_O}{q} \right) \left(\frac{\Delta R}{R_a} \right) \tag{7}$$

$$\approx -\left(\frac{kT_O}{q} \right) \left(\frac{\Delta R}{R_b} \right)$$

where $\Delta R = R_b - R_a$ and $V_{OS} \ll \dfrac{kT}{q}$

If the error term of (4) is neglected, then

$$TCV_{OS} = \frac{dV_{diff}}{dT} \bigg|_{T = T_O} = \frac{kT_O}{q} \times \frac{R_a}{R_b} \times$$

$$\frac{d}{dT} \left(\frac{R_b}{R_a} \right) = \frac{kT_O}{q} \times \frac{R_a}{R_b} \times \frac{d}{dT} \left(\frac{\Delta R}{R_a} \right) \tag{8}$$

Figure 8 shows three different means of nulling operational amplifiers. R_X, R_Y, and R_P are external nulling potentiometers; the R_Ls are well-matched diffused resistors. The temperature coefficients (TC) of the potentiometers and diffused resistors will differ significantly; a new parameter Θ can be defined as this TC difference:

$$\Theta = (\text{TC of } R_L) - (\text{TC of nulling potentiometer}) \tag{9}$$

Θ is typically 2500 ppm/°C for diffused silicon resistors and a thin film potentiometer. If R_X is used to null, and Θ is assumed constant with temperature, then:

$$\frac{R_b}{R_a} (T_O) = \frac{R_L}{R_L \| R_X} = 1 + \frac{R_L}{R_X}; \quad \frac{\Delta R}{R_a} = \frac{R_L}{R_X} \tag{10}$$

and

$$\frac{R_b}{R_a} (T) = 1 + \frac{R_L \left[1 + \Theta (T - T_O) \right]}{R_X} \tag{11}$$

$$\frac{d}{dT} \left[\frac{R_b}{R_a} (T) \right] = \frac{R_L}{R_X} \times \Theta \tag{12}$$

from Equations 7, 8, 10 and 12, nulling with R_X yields:

$$V_{OS} \cong -\frac{kT_O}{q} \times \frac{\Delta R}{R_b} \approx -\frac{kT_O}{q} \times \frac{R_L}{R_L + R_X} \tag{13}$$

if $R_X \gg R_L$

$$TCV_{OS} = \frac{kT_O}{q} \times \frac{R_X}{R_L + R_X} \times \frac{R_L}{R_X} \times \Theta \approx -V_{OS} \times \Theta \tag{14}$$

Although the dominant $\dfrac{V_{OS}}{T}$ term of Equation 4 is indeed eliminated by nulling with R_X, the new drift term due to the resistor TC differential reduces the initial, unnulled drift by only 25%. If R_Y is the nulling potentiometer, an involved but elementary calculation results in:

$$TCV_{OS} \approx -\frac{R_Y}{R_Y + 2R_L} \times V_{OS} \times \Theta \tag{15}$$

Equation 15 is obtained by finding the equivalent expressions to (10), (11) and (12), then substituting into the general Equations 7 and 8. Nulling with R_Y is the method used for several of the operational amplifiers available today. Since $R_Y \gg R_L$, the drift is essentially the same as in the previous case.

THE OPTIMUM NULLING NETWORK

If R_P is used to null, two degrees of design freedom are introduced, namely the ratios R_1/R_2 and R_P/R_2; in the previous two cases there are no degrees of freedom at all. The only constraint on these ratios is the capability to null out all possible offset voltages. An explicit relationship between TCV_{OS} and V_{OS} in the form of Equations 13 and 15 is difficult to obtain, but Equations 7 and 8 can be utilized to develop expressions for V_{OS} and TCV_{OS}. After some considerable algebra, the results are:

$$V_{OS} = \frac{kT}{q} \times \frac{a - 2z}{z \left[1 + (b + 1)(a - z) \right] + b (1 + a)} \tag{16}$$

$$TCV_{OS} = \Theta \times \frac{kT}{q} \times \left[f(a - z) - f(z) \right] \tag{17}$$

where

$$f(z) = \frac{z}{(1 + z)[b(1 + z) + z]} \tag{18}$$

and

$$a = \frac{R_p}{R_2}; \quad b = \frac{R_1}{R_2}; \quad z = \frac{R_{pb}}{R_2} \tag{19}$$

A computer can then evaluate (16) and (17) with z as the independent variable and a and b as parameters and plot TCV_{OS}/Θ vs. V_{OS} for various values of a and b. Depending on the parameter values, TCV_{OS} can range from $-V_{OS}\,\Theta$ to $+V_{OS}\,\Theta$. Thus a and b may be selected such that the nulled drift closely approaches zero.

Figures I.1 and I.2 illustrate the TCV_{OS} variations with V_{OS}, a, and b. Only positive offset voltages are shown; the curves are symmetrical about the origin. If a is between 1.5 and 4, and b lies within 1 and 5, the TCV_{OS}, in general, will be less than 1.0 $\mu V/°C$.

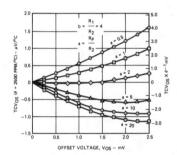

Fig. I.1. Temperature drift of input offset voltage as a function of input offset voltage.

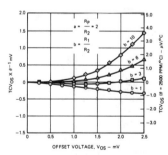

Fig. I.2. Temperature drift of offset voltage as a function of input offset voltage.

DEVIATIONS FROM THEORY

The error term ϵ of Equation 4 represents the difference between the actual TCV_{OS} and that predicted by theory. In function form

$$\epsilon = \frac{kT}{q}\frac{d}{dT}\left(\ln\frac{I_{S2}}{I_{S1}}\right) + TCV_{OS}(\Delta TCR_L) + \tag{20}$$
$$TCV_{OS}(V_{OS2}) + TCV_{OS}(I_{OS2})$$

The definitions and particulars of the various terms of Equation 20 are as follows:

(a) $\dfrac{kT}{q}\dfrac{d}{dT}\left(\ln\dfrac{I_{S2}}{I_{S1}}\right)$ arises from the differentiation of (2) and is typically less than $\pm 0.5\ \mu V/°C$.

(b) $TCV_{OS}(\Delta TCR_L)$ is due to the temperature coefficient mismatch of diffused resistors R_L (ΔTCR_L). From (8)

$$TCV_{OS}(\Delta TCR_L) \approx \frac{kT_0}{q} \times \Delta TCR_L \tag{21}$$

Therefore, a one percent mismatch in TCR_L yields a 0.6 $\mu V/°C$ drift (25 mV x 0.01 x 2500 ppm/$°C \approx 0.6\ \mu V/°C$).

(c) $TCV_{OS}(V_{OS2})$ is the effect of the offset voltage of the second stage (V_{OS2}) which is attenuated by the gain of the input stage, A_{V1}.

$$A_{V1} = \frac{qI_1}{kT} \times R_{eq} \tag{22}$$

where R_{eq} is the equivalent resistance loading Q_1. Hence, from (4)

$$TCV_{OS}(V_{OS2}) = \frac{TCV_{OS2}}{A_{V1}} \approx \frac{V_{OS2}}{T} \times \frac{kT}{qI_1 R_{eq}} \tag{23}$$

For typical operational amplifiers $V_{OS2} < 5$ mV, $I_1 R_{eq} > 500$ mV, therefore $TCV_{OS}(V_{OS2}) < 0.8\ \mu V/°C$.

(d) $TCV_{OS}(I_{OS2})$ is the contribution of the offset current drift of the second stage (TCI_{OS2}) reduced by the first stage gain

$$TCV_{OS}(I_{OS2}) = \frac{TCI_{OS2}R_{eq}}{A_{V1}} = TCI_{OS2}\frac{kT}{qI_1} \tag{24}$$

A survey of the more popular monolithic operational amplifiers indicates that typical values for $TCV_{OS}(I_{OS2})$ range from 0.3 $\mu V/°C$ to 0.8 $\mu V/°C$.

If an operational amplifier with 1.0 $\mu V/°C$ or less TCV_{OS} is required, the error component ϵ is obviously not negligible and can easily exceed 1.0 $\mu V/°C$. With very careful chip layout and second stage design, these error terms cannot be disregarded but can certainly be reduced. Yet ϵ was neglected in (4). The justification for this is that ϵ is random; consequently, no functional relationship can be established between TCV_{OS} and ϵ at the design stage as shown in Figure I.3. The general equation for TCV_{OS}, Equation 8, and the curves of Figures I.1 and I.2 still provide the best available estimate for TCV_{OS}.

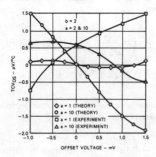

Fig. I.3. Theoretical and experimental offset voltage drift.

CONCLUSION

We have shown that arbitrary nulling does not provide the desired results to compensate externally for changes in input offset voltage with temperature. Optimum nulling networks can be devised to minimize this effect. First and second amplifier stages can be designed very close to ideal conditions necessary to match an external nulling scheme. An amplifier that provides this superior performance with temperature is the μA725.

APPENDIX II
IMPROVING THE COMMON-MODE REJECTION OF OPERATIONAL AMPLIFIERS

One of the most important parameters of operational amplifiers is common mode rejection ratio (CMRR). If, for example, amplification of a 100 μV differential voltage is superimposed on a 1 V common mode signal and the amplifier has only a 100 μV/V (or 80 dB) CMRR, the output voltage could be zero. This is not an unreasonable application, yet most operational amplifiers today do not have more than 80 dB CMRR. CMRR has been the unwanted stepchild parameter of operational amplifiers. Designers aim for other improvements and accept the resulting CMRR. Probably the main reason for this is that simple, workable design formulae have not been developed for CMRR in terms of transistor and processing parameters.

In Reference 4 an expression was developed for CMRR of a differential amplifier as shown in Figure II.1. An extension to include the effects of the load resistor mismatch, ΔR_L, result in

$$CMRR = \frac{g_o}{g_m}\left[\frac{\Delta g_m}{g_m} - \frac{\Delta g_o}{g_o}\right] \times \left[1 + \frac{R_L}{2R_{o3}}\right] + \frac{1}{2R_o3g_m}\left[\frac{\Delta g_m}{g_m} + \frac{\Delta R_L}{R_L}\right] \quad (1)$$

where:

CMRR is in volts/volt
R_o3 is the output resistance of current source Q_3

g_o, g_{o2} are the output conductances of Q_1 and Q_2, respectively

$\Delta g_o = g_{o2} - g_o$ g

g_m, g_{m2} are the transconductances of Q_1 and Q_2, respectively $\left(\cong \dfrac{qI_c}{kT}\right)$

$\Delta g_m = g_{m2} - g_m$

R_L, R_{L2} are the loads on Q_1 and Q_2, respectively, including the input resistance of the second stage. R_L may be a resistor or the output resistance of an active load

$\Delta R_L = R_{L2} - R_L$

Reducing this rather unwieldy equation to a clear, precise form, one may proceed as follows:

Since g_m = constant x I

then:

$$\frac{\Delta g_m}{g_m} = \frac{\Delta I}{I} \quad (2)$$

where

$$\Delta I = I_2 - I$$

From Figure II.1,

$$V_{OS2} = I R_L - I_2 R_{L2} \quad (3)$$

or

$$\frac{V_{OS2}}{I R_L} = 1 - \frac{(I + \Delta I)(R_L + \Delta R_L)}{I R_L} \approx \frac{\Delta I}{I} + \frac{\Delta R_L}{R_L} \quad (4)$$

An expression for g_o can be derived using the fact that

$$I = I_c \text{ and } I_c \approx \frac{1}{W_B} \quad (5)$$

and

$$W_B = W_{BM} - X_{dE} - X_{dC} = (W_{BM} - X_{dE}) - \sqrt{\left(\frac{2K_s\epsilon_o}{q}\right)\left(\frac{N_C}{N_B{}^2}\right)(V_{CB} + V_D)} \quad (6)$$

where:

W_B is the effective base width;
W_{BM} is the metallurgical base width;
X_{dE} is the reduction in base width due to the emitter depletion region;
X_{dC} is the reduction in base width due to the collector depletion region (step junction approximation);
$K_s\epsilon_o$ is the permittivity of silicon;
N_C and N_B are the collector and base concentrations, respectively;
V_{CB} is the collector base voltage;
V_D is the built-in voltage of the collector-base junction.

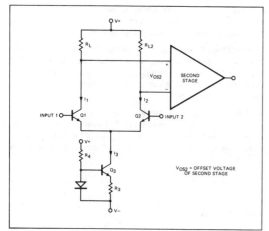

Fig. II.1. Operational amplifier input stage.

From (5) and (6) and since W_{dE} does not change at constant V_{BE}:

$$g_o \left(\frac{dI_C}{dV_{CE}} \right) \bigg|_{V_{BE} = \text{constant}} =$$

$$\left(\frac{dI_C}{dW_B} \right) \left(\frac{dW_B}{dV_{CE}} \right) \bigg|_{V_{BE} = \text{constant}} =$$

$$\frac{dI_C}{dW_B} \times \frac{dW_B}{dV_{CB}} = \frac{I_C}{W_B} \sqrt{\frac{K_s \epsilon_o N_C}{2qN_B^2 (V_{CB} + V_D)}} \qquad (7)$$

If a new parameter γ, the current-normalized output conductance, in volts^{-1}, is defined as

$$g_o = \gamma I$$

$$g_{o2} = \gamma_2 I_2$$

$$\Delta\gamma = \gamma - \gamma_2 \qquad (8)$$

$$\gamma = \frac{1}{W_B} \sqrt{\frac{K_s \epsilon_o N_C}{2qN_B^2 (V_{CB} + V_D)}} \qquad (9)$$

then

$$\frac{g_o}{g_m} = \frac{kT}{q} \gamma \qquad (10)$$

From (2) and (8)

$$\frac{\Delta g_m}{g_m} - \frac{\Delta g_m}{g_o} = \frac{\Delta I}{I} + \frac{\Delta \gamma}{\gamma} - \frac{\Delta I}{I} = \frac{\Delta \gamma}{\gamma} \qquad (11)$$

Substitution of (4), (10) and (11) into (1) yields

$$CMRR = \frac{kT}{q} \times \gamma \times \frac{\Delta\gamma}{\gamma} \times \left[1 + \frac{R_L}{2R_{O3}} \right] +$$

$$\qquad (12)$$

$$\frac{V_{OS2}}{I R_L} \times \frac{1}{2R_{O3}g_m}$$

The output resistance of the current source Q_3 is

$$R_{o3} = \frac{\left(1 + \frac{qI_3}{kT} \times R_3 \right)}{g_{o3}}$$

$$\qquad (13)$$

$$\approx \frac{1 + \frac{qI_3}{kT} \times R_3}{2g_o}$$

where g_{o3} is the output conductance of transistor Q_3. $g_{o3} \approx 2g_o$ because $I_3 \approx 2I$, however, this relationship is only approximate since the collector-base voltages of Q_3 and Q_1 are unequal. Therefore, in (12)

$$\frac{R_L}{2R_{o3}} \ll 1$$

even if R_L is the output resistance of an active load, and consequently its value approaches $1/g_o$. This is true because usually $\frac{qI_3}{kT} R_3 > 1$ in (13).

Also from (10) and (13):

$$\frac{1}{2R_{o3}} g_m \approx \frac{g_o}{g_m \frac{(1 + qI_3 \times R_3)}{kT}}$$

$$= \frac{1}{\left(\frac{1 + qI_3 \times R_3}{kT} \right)} \times \frac{kT}{q} \gamma \qquad (14)$$

For well designed operational amplifiers $V_{os2} < 5mV$, $I R_L > 500$ mV. Hence:

$$\frac{V_{os2}}{I R_L} \times \frac{1}{2R_{o3} g_m} = \frac{V_{os2}}{I R_L} \times$$

$$\qquad (15)$$

$$\frac{1}{1 + \left(\frac{qI_3}{kT} \right) R_3} \times \frac{kT}{q} \gamma \ll \frac{kT}{q} \gamma \frac{\Delta\gamma}{\gamma}$$

even if $\Delta\gamma/\gamma = 0.01$, which is about the best γ matching one can expect. Therefore, (12) further reduces to the simple form

$$CMRR = \frac{kT}{q} \Delta\gamma \qquad (16)$$

CONCLUSIONS

The following can be concluded from Equation 9 and Equation 16:

1. CMRR is independent of operating current if conditions of (9) and (16) are met.

2. Increasing transistor β by narrowing the base width seriously degrades CMRR[1].

From statement 2 above, "punch-through" or collector starvation techniques, which yield "super beta" transistors, will degrade CMRR. But from statement 1, devices may be operated at very low collector currents without degrading CMRR, thus allowing operation with low input currents. The μA725 makes use of the above facts and obtains its low input currents by operating input devices at low collector currents and by using a process which increases bulk lifetimes and eliminates emitter-base pinch-off in the input devices, thus maintaining constant beta at these low current levels.

The excellent CMRR performance has been obtained without the use of complex circuitry such as cascodes or CMRR feedback by developing a low $\Delta\gamma$ process. The resulting simple differential pair also provides excellent input offset voltage and current matching.

This occurs because $\gamma \approx 1/W_B$ and the γ matching of two adjacent transistors deteriorate. For example, a 0.1 micron W_B mismatch is 10% for $W_B = 1$, but is five times as much for $W_B = 0.2$. Figure II.2 illustrates the experimental results which indicate that:

$$CMRR \cong \beta^{-1.25}$$

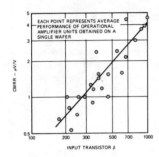

Fig. II.2. Common mode rejection ratio of operational amplifiers as a function of input transistor beta.

REFERENCES

(1) A. H. Hoffait, R. D. Thornton: "Limitations of Transistor DC Amplifiers," *Proceedings of the IEEE, February 1964.*

(2) Fairchild Linear Integrated Circuits Handbook; edited by J. N. Giles.

(3) G. Meyer: Brotz and Akley, "The Common-mode Rejection of Transistor Differential Amplifiers," IEEE Transactions on Circuit Theory, Vol. CT-13, p. 171-175, June 1966.

(4) A. S. Grove: *Physics and Technology of Semiconductor Devices,* New York: Wiley, 1967.

(5) M. V. Joyce and K. K. Clarke: Transistor Circuit Analysis, Massachusetts: Addison - Wesley, 1961.

APPLICATIONS OF THE
μA741 OPERATIONAL AMPLIFIER

INTRODUCTION

A monolithic operational amplifier designed for high performance and ease of application, the μA741 requires no external components for frequency compensation and is fully protected against damage from short circuit conditions occurring at either the input or the output. The amplifier will not "latch-up" and can accept a wide range of both common mode and differential mode input voltages. The μA741 exhibits the high reliability and low cost advantages characteristic of monolithic construction.

APPLICATIONS

The μA741 can be used in a wide variety of applications. Because the amplifier is self protecting and internally compensated, it requires none of the external components usually needed to secure stable and reliable operation from other amplifiers. The following paragraphs describe several applications illustrating the attributes of the μA741.

THE UNITY GAIN VOLTAGE FOLLOWER

Figure 1 is a schematic of the voltage follower which is frequently used as a buffer amplifier to reduce voltage error caused by source loading and to isolate high impedance sources from following circuitry. (The gain of this circuit is unity.) The output duplicates or follows the input voltage, hence the name voltage follower.

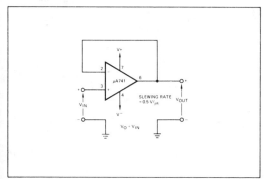

Fig. 1 Unity Gain Voltage Follower

The voltage follower is a "worst case" for stable operation as maximum feedback is applied. Normally, external components are required to reduce the gain below unity at high frequencies to prevent oscillation. The μA741 does not require external stabilizing components as it has an internal monolithic compensation network.

Voltage followers are also subject to latch-up, which may occur if the input common mode voltage limit is exceeded. If the input transistor at the inverting input saturates, then the input to this transistor is fed directly to its collector circuit through the collector base junction. Thus, the inverting input becomes noninverting if the common mode limit is exceeded, resulting in positive feedback holding the amplifier in saturation.

Designed to prevent latch-up, the μA741 input stage requires no external protective circuitry. The μA741 has a larger common mode range than most monolithic operational amplifiers and is therefore capable of larger output voltage excursions. The worst case common mode range of the μA741 is typically ±12 V; thus allowing voltage follower output swings up to ±12 V for V_S = ±15 V.

The accuracy of the voltage follower is determined by the open loop gain of the operational amplifier and by its common mode rejection ratio.

The expression for the accuracy is:

$$\frac{V_{OUT}}{V_{IN}} = \frac{1 + \dfrac{1}{CMRR}}{1 + \dfrac{1}{A}} \tag{1}$$

Note: $CMRR_{dB} = 20 \log_{10} CMRR$

Using typical numbers from the μA741 data sheet (A_{OL} = 200,000 CMRR = 90 dB) the dc accuracy of the voltage follower is found to be better than .003% if V_{OS} is adjusted to 0.

INTEGRATOR

The integrator, shown in Figure 2, provides an output that is proportional to the time interval of the input signal. The gain function for the integrator is given by:

$$V_{OUT} = - \frac{1}{R1\,C1} \int V_{IN}\,dt \tag{2}$$

R1 and C1 are labeled in the figure.

FAIRCHILD

SEMICONDUCTOR

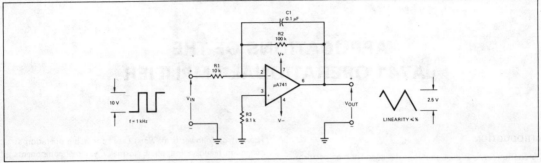

Fig. 2 Integrator

As an example, consider the response of the integrator to a symmetrical square wave input signal with an average value of zero volts. If the input has a peak amplitude of A volts, and period T, then the peak-to-peak output can be calculated by integrating over one-half the input period giving:

$$V_{OUT\ pk-pk} = \frac{1}{R1\ C1} \int_{0}^{T/2} A\ dt$$

$$= \frac{A}{R1\ C1}\left(\frac{T}{2}\right) \quad VOLTS \qquad (3)$$

The waveshape will be triangular corresponding to the integral of the square wave. For the component values shown in the figure, assuming A = 5 volts and T = 1 ms, using equation (2),

$$R1\ C1 = 10^{-3}\ s$$

$$V_{OUT\ pk-pk} = \frac{5\ \times\ 10^{-3}}{10^{-3}\ \times\ 2} = 2.5\ V\ pk-pk$$

The resistor R2 is included to provide dc stabilization for the integrator. Its function is to limit the low frequency gain of the amplifier and thus minimize drift. The frequency above which the circuit will perform as an integrator is given by:

$$f = \frac{1}{2\pi\ R2\ C1}\ Hz \qquad (4)$$

For best linearity, the frequency of the input signal should be at least 10 times the frequency given by equation (4). The linearity of the circuit illustrated is better than 1% with an input frequency of 1 kHz.

Although not immediately obvious, the integrator requires both a large common mode and differential mode input voltage range if it is to operate reliably. There are several ways the input voltage limits may be inadvertently exceeded. The most obvious is that transients occurring at the output of the amplifier can be coupled back to the input by the integrating capacitor, C1. Thus either common mode or differential voltage limits can be exceeded.

Another less obvious problem can occur when the amplifier is driven from fast rising or falling input signals such as square waves. The output of the amplifier cannot instantaneously respond to an input. During the short interval before the output reacts, the summing point at lead 2 of the amplifier may not be held at ground potential. If the input signal change is large enough, the voltage at the summing point could exceed sage limits for the amplifier.

The μA741 is more resistant to this type of damage than other monolithic operational amplifiers because of its large differential input voltage range of ±30 V. The extended common mode range of the μA741 also helps to insure reliable operation.

DIFFERENTIATOR

The differentiator circuit of Figure 3 provides an output proportional to the derivative of the input signal. The gain function of the differentiator is given by:

$$V_{OUT} = -R2\ C1\ \frac{\Delta V_1}{dt} \qquad (5)$$

As the differentiator performs the reverse of the integrator function, a triangular input will produce a square wave output. For a 2.5 V peak-to-peak triangle wave with a period of 1 millisecond for the circuit illustrated we have:

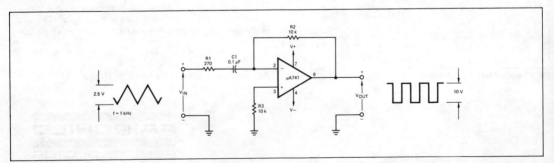

Fig. 3 Differentiator

$$\frac{\Delta V}{dt} = \frac{2.5\,V}{0.5\,ms} = 5\ \frac{V}{ms}$$

$$V_{OUT} = -(10k)\ (0.1\,\mu F)\ 5\ \frac{V}{ms}$$

$$= 5\ V_{\text{pk-pk}}$$

The resistor R1 is needed to limit the high frequency gain of the differentiator. This makes the circuit less susceptible to high frequency noise and assures dynamic stability. The corner frequency where the gain limiting comes into effect is given by

$$f = \frac{1}{2\pi\ R1\ C1} \qquad (6)$$

and should be at least 10 times the highest input frequency for accurate operation. A maximum value for the corner frequency is determined by stability criteria. In general, it should be no larger than the geometric mean between $\frac{1}{2\pi\ R2\ C1}$ and the

gain bandwidth product of the operational amplifier. The $\mu A741$ has a gain bandwidth product of approximately 1 MHz hence the limit on f is given by

$$f < \sqrt{\frac{1\ X\ 10^6}{2\pi\ R2\ C1}} \qquad (7)$$

As in the case with the integrator, the differentiator is subject to damage from fast rising input signals and, as previously discussed, the circuit is also susceptible to high frequency instability. The wide range of input voltages and the built in compensation of the $\mu A741$ are assets when the amplifier is used as a differentiator.

VOLTAGE REGULATOR REFERENCE AMPLIFIER

Operational amplifiers are frequently used as reference amplifiers in voltage regulated power supplies. A typical circuit with variable output voltage is shown in Figure 4. The purpose of the amplifier is to isolate the voltage reference, a Zener diode in Figure 4, from changes in loading at the supply output. This results in lower supply output impedance, hence improved load regulation. Also, because of the high gain of the $\mu A741$, the voltage applied to the inverting input of the amplifier from the output voltage divider is always maintained within a few millivolts of the reference. Thus, the output voltage may be varied

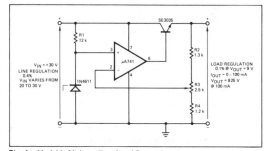

Fig. 4   Variable Voltage Regulated Power Supply

by changing the division ratio of the divider. The 800 kΩ input impedance of the $\mu A741$ keeps loading of the reference Zener to a minimum. The output impedance of the circuit shown is less than 0.1Ω and the line regulation is approximately 0.4% for input voltages varying from 20 to 30 V.

HIGH-VOLTAGE REGULATED POWER SUPPLY

With proper biasing, the $\mu A741$ can be used as a regulated power supply control element. Figure 5 shows a 100 V regulated power supply using the $\mu A741$ as the control amplifier.

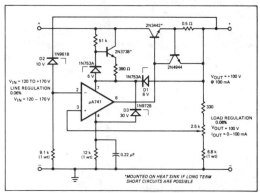

Fig. 5 High Voltage Regulated Power Supply

Zener diodes D1 thru D3 supply proper operating voltages to the $\mu A741$. The diodes reference the amplifier voltages to the power supply output so the bias levels can follow the output voltage over a wide range of adjustment. D1 keeps the positive supply terminal of the $\mu A741$ at 6 V above the regulator output. D2 holds the inverting input at 10 V below the output voltage, while D3 maintains a 30 V drop across the amplifier's supply terminals.

Biased by a Zener-resistor network, the 2N3738 acts as a current source supplying operating current to the amplifier and part of the biasing network.

The regulator output is fed back to the $\mu A741$ amplifier thru a voltage divider. The division ratio is obtained by first selecting the desired output voltage and calculating the division ratio required to make the divider output 10 V less (the Zener voltage of D2 less) than the output from the regulator. For the circuit shown, the desired output is 100 V and D2 is a 10 V diode giving:

$$V_{OUT}\ \frac{R}{R_{total}} = V_{OUT} - V_{D2}$$

$$100\ \frac{R}{R_{total}} = 100 - 10$$

$$\frac{R}{R_{total}} = 0.9 = \text{division ratio}$$

The regulator is short circuit protected by the 2N4944 transistor and the 5 Ω resistor in series with the output. As the output current increases, the voltage drop across the 5 Ω resistor increases turning on the 2N4944. The transistor thus shunts base current away from the 2N3442 pass transistor. If the output current is further increased, the voltage output drops rapidly to zero.

With a 5 Ω resistor, the output current limits at approximately 100 mA. Proportionally, larger and smaller resistor value give other current limits, i. e. 2.5 Ω for a 200 mA limit. It should be remembered that the pass transistor must be capable of dissipating the power generated by the maximum unregulated input voltage, and the short circuit current as it is connected across the input terminals under short circuit conditions.

Line and load regulation in the circuit shown is approximately 0.06% for input voltages ranging from 120 to 170 V and an output voltage of 100 V at 0 to 100 mA.

CLIPPING AMPLIFIER

It is occasionally desirable to limit the output swing of an amplifier to within specific limits. This can be done by adding non-linear elements to the feedback network as shown in Figure 6.

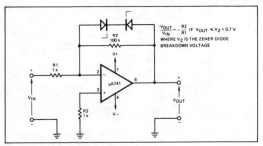

Fig. 6   Clipping Amplifier

The amplifier's gain is quickly reduced by the Zener diodes if the output tries to exceed the limits set by the Zener voltages. When the Zeners are not conducting, the gain is determined by feedback resistors R1 and R2.

It is often overlooked that an amplifier used as a clipper must be frequency compensated for a gain of unity. This is because the gain of the circuit passes through unity as the Zeners begin their clipping action. The µA741 causes no worry in this respect as it is internally compensated for unity gain.

COMPARATOR

Many control functions require a comparison between two voltages and an output indicating which of the two is greater. The µA741 can be used as a comparator in many applications where high speed is not a prerequisite. Since the internal compensation network limits the response time, it cannot compete with comparators designed for high speed operation such as the Fairchild µA710.

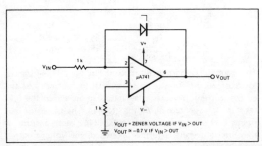

Fig. 7   Comparator

Features of the µA741 that make it attractive as a comparator are its common mode and differential input voltage range. The inputs to be compared may vary over a wide range without the necessity of external protective circuitry.

A typical comparator circuit is shown in Figure 7. The Zener voltage may be compatible with high level DTL or normal CCSL logic levels, with MOS device thresholds, or the amplifier can be used open loop.

OTHER FEATURES

Short Circuit Protection

Short circuit protection is incorporated into the µA741 which limits the maximum output current to approximately 25 mA at room temperature. Should the output inadvertently be shorted either to ground or to the positive or negative power supply, the µA741 will not be damaged.

The maximum permissible input voltage limits are equal to the supply voltages for power supplies of ±15 V or less. Thus the input circuitry will not be harmed even if shorted to the power supplies for supply voltages up to ±15 V.

Offset Adjustment

The input offset of the µA741 may easily be nulled by connecting a 10k potentiometer as shown in Figure 8. Other operational amplifiers similar to the µA741 require a large valued potentiometer of several megohms for offset adjustment. Precision potentiometers of this large a value are costly and difficult to obtain. On the other hand, precision 10k potentiometers are readily available, thus, the µA741 offset can be nulled simply and economically.

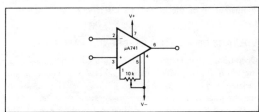

Fig. 8   Voltage Offset Nulling Circuit

Power Consumption

Power consumption of the µA741 is quite low, typically 50 mW with ±15 V supply voltage. Power consumption drops rapidly with supply voltage and a typical device consumes less than 5 mW with ±5 V supplies. With this low power consumption, the µA741 is ideal for satellite and other low power applications.

CONCLUSION

From the few possible applications of the µA741 presented, it can be seen that this device can be used to advantage in many diverse applications. The amplifier is self protecting and difficult to damage either on the bench or in a system. Input offset can be simply nulled by the use of an external potentiometer. The device has low power dissipation making it useful in aerospace systems. The µA741 leads itself to rapid and straight forward application in a wide range of linear circuitry.

2001-21-0008-063 5M

AN IMPROVED SAMPLE AND HOLD CIRCUIT USING THE µA740

INTRODUCTION

Sampled signal processing generally requires a sample and hold circuit, which is basically quite simple *(Figure 1)*. However, it becomes more complex as a practical version of the circuit is developed to provide better than 10 µs acquisition time. To maintain circuit accuracy, sampling offset and input signal isolation problems must be considered.

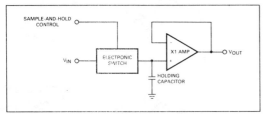

Fig. 1. Basic Sample and Hold Circuit

Before proceeding to the actual circuit design, a basic discussion of acquisition and hold times is presented. The circuit is then developed using the µA740 FET input operational amplifier as the buffer amplifier and the 2N4382 junction FET as the sampling switch. Finally the design is refined to compensate for sampling offset and input signal isolation.

ACQUISITION TIME

Acquisition time is the time required to leave the hold mode, sample the input and return to hold. Several factors influence it: the source resistance, the ON resistance of the sampling switch, the value of the holding capacitor and the transient response of the buffer amplifier.

The charging time-constant for the holding capacitor C is

$$t = (R_S + R_{ON})\, C \qquad (1)$$

The time allowed for settling must be at least 4.6t for 1% accuracy; 6.9t for 0.1%; 9.2t for 0.01%.

If the buffer amplifier slew rate is faster than the maximum slope of the capacitor voltage, the required acquisition time is determined by t. If the amplifier slew rate is slower than the capacitor voltage slope, then the amplifier affects the acquisition time. The capacitor voltage may reach the correct value before the amplifier has settled, but there is little point in considering the signal to be acquired unless a useful output is available from the circuit.

HOLD TIME

Performance in the hold mode is determined by the leakage current of the sampling switch, the bias current of the buffer amplifier, and the size of the holding capacitor. The held voltage will gradually change due to the leakage and bias currents flowing through the holding capacitor. If I_C is the net capacitor current, then the slope of the held voltage is given by:

$$\frac{\Delta v}{\Delta t} = \frac{I_C}{C} \qquad (2)$$

Equation 2 can be used to calculate how long a held voltage will remain within a specified accuracy of its original value.

A PRACTICAL CIRCUIT

In developing the practical sample and hold circuit *(Figure 2)*, Equations 1 and 2 should be kept in mind. The following specifications are assumed:

Signal Range: +5 V
Accuracy: Better than 0.1% of full-scale input
Acquisition Time: Better than 10 µs
Hold Time: 100 µs

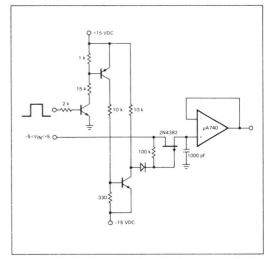

Fig. 2. A Sample and Hold Circuit

SEMICONDUCTOR

The device parameters of most importance in choosing the sampling switch are ON resistance and gate leakage current, I_{GSS}. A 2N4382 junction FET was chosen because maximum ON resistance is 350 Ω and maximum leakage current is 1 nA at 25°C. If the maximum source resistance is 1 kΩ, then from Equation 1:

$$t = (R_S + R_{ON}) C$$

$$t = (1 \, k\Omega + 350\Omega) C$$

Since the settling time for 0.1% accuracy is 6.9t the maximum value for C can be calculated:

$$6.9t = 10 \, \mu s$$

$$t = \frac{10 \times 10^{-6}}{6.9} = 1.45 \, \mu s$$

$$1.45 \, \mu s = (1 \, k\Omega + 350\Omega) C$$

$$C = \frac{1.45 \times 10^{-6} \, s}{1.35 \times 10^3 \Omega} = 1074 \, pF$$

C is chosen to be 1000 pF

The change in capacitor voltage during the hold mode should be small compared with the required system accuracy. The µA740 FET-input operational amplifier is chosen as the buffer amplifier for its good slew rate (6 V/µs) and its low input bias current (2 nA). The FET leakage and the amplifier bias current partially compensate each other in the *Figure 2* circuit. A worst-case estimate of the change in held voltage can be made by assuming that the full amplifier bias current flows from the holding capacitor and that the FET leakage is negligible. Using Equation 2,

$$\frac{\Delta V}{\Delta t} = \frac{2 \times 10^{-9} \, A}{1000 \, pF} = 2 \, V/s$$

Thus the slope of the held voltage will be negligible during the 100 µs hold interval.

REFINING THE DESIGN

Because of the acquisition time requirement, the holding capacitor is relatively small. As a result, the parasitic capacitances associated with the sampling FET are significant in comparison to the holding capacitor. To maintain the required accuracy, the problems of sampling offset and input signal isolation must be investigated.

Sampling Offset

When the FET switch is turned off, a portion of the gate drive signal is coupled onto the holding capacitor. If this coupled voltage were fixed, there would be little problem. A fixed amount of charge could be coupled onto the holding capacitor to compensate the offset. The offset is not fixed but is a function of the input signal, since the gate voltage of the sampling switch is equal to V_{IN} during the sample mode and goes to V+ during hold. Furthermore, the gate-to-source capacitance of the FET is a non-linear function of voltage, and thus has a different effective value depending on signal level.

A compensating scheme that allows for the variation in offset with V_{IN} and with device non-linearity is added to the basic circuit in *Figure 3*. The compensating signal is bootstrapped to the output of the buffer amplifier so that its amplitude is also a function of the input voltage. To compensate for the non-linearity of the FET capacitance, the correction signal is coupled through the gate-to-channel capacitance of another FET which exhibits a non-linearity similar to that of the sampling switch. The amplitude of the compensating signal is reduced by a voltage divider since both the source and drain of the compensating FET are connected to the holding capacitor, giving a larger effective coupling capacitance.

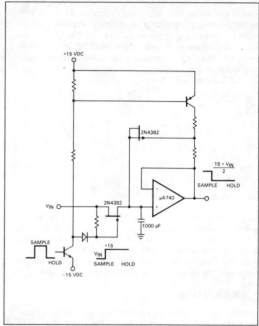

Fig. 3. Sampling Offset Compensation

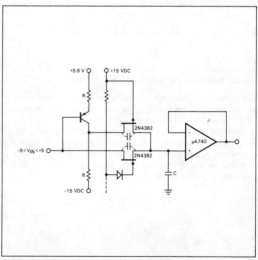

Fig. 4. Hold Mode External Transient Compensation

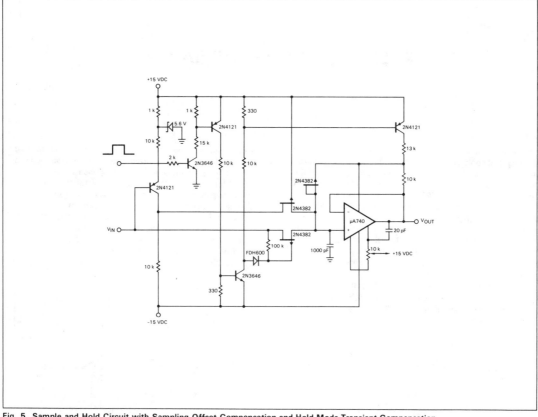

Fig. 5. Sample and Hold Circuit with Sampling Offset Compensation and Hold Mode Transient Compensation

Input Signal Isolation

During the hold mode, transient changes in the input signal, such as would occur if the input were multiplexed, can be coupled onto the holding capacitor through the stray capacitance of the OFF sampling switch. With the holding capacitor at 1000 pF, only 1 pF of combined device and stray capacitance is required to cause a 0.1% error in the held voltage.

Compensation for input transients is accomplished by feeding the input signal through a unity gain inverter and coupling the inverted signal onto the holding capacitor. This cancels the effect of the input transient. The input transient compensation is coupled to the holding capacitor through a FET that is always in the off state, rather than through a discrete capacitor of a fraction of a picofarad, as shown in *Figure 4*. This coupling method provides a capacitance that is very similar to the capacitance of the sampling switch and the coupling FET helps to equalize the effects of stray capacitances.

OVERALL PERFORMANCE

The final circuit for the compensated sample and hold is shown in *Figure 5*. The 20 pF capacitor between the output of the μA740 and its offset null terminal dampens the overshoot of the amplifier which occurs following a large (±5 V) output swing of the μA740.

Circuit performance was measured with a +5 V input excursion and a sampling rate of 10 kHz. Within the acquisition time of 10 μs, the output settled to within 2.5 mV of the input, i.e., 0.05%, with the input maintained at a constant +5 V. Droop at the output was approximately 8 mV over the hold period of 100 μs. Immediately following an input change from –5 V to +5 V, i.e., at the next sample period, the output settled to within 5 mV of the input in the 10 μs acquisition time.

APPLICATIONS OF THE µA777

INTRODUCTION

The µA777 is a versatile monolithic operational amplifier featuring lead connections allowing frequency response to be tailored to the user's needs. It is an improved version of the µA741 with lower offset and bias currents. The 30 pF MOS capacitor, found in the µA741, has been omitted and the circuit nodes have been brought out to external leads. As a result, a 20 times higher gain bandwidth product is possible for the open loop frequency response curve. *Figure 1* shows the open loop voltage gains as a function of frequency for three of the possible gain compensation options. The x1 gain curve (C_C = 30 pF) is precisely the same curve as the open loop voltage gain plot for the µA741. This fact, coupled with the lead compatability between the µA777 and µA741 makes these devices completely interchangeable except in applications using the expanded gain bandwidth feature of the µA777.

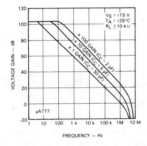

Fig. 1. Open Loop Voltage Gain as a Function of Frequency for Various Gain/Compensation Options

High common mode input voltage range, latch-up protection, short circuit protection and simple frequency compensation make the µA777 easy to use. High speed operation as a result of the individual frequency response tailoring of the µA777 is demonstrated in a pulse amplifier with a feed forward compensation circuit. A Wein bridge oscillator circuit shows how a low distortion value may be attained using the µA777. A variable gain differential amplifier further demonstrates the versatility of the device. Not only can the µA777 be used in signal generation and processing applications, but it may also be efficiently transformed into a power amplifier capable of driving ampere level currents at supply voltages in the ±30 V range or more.

PULSE AMPLIFIER

The x1 amplifier shown in *Figure 2* uses both a feed-forward path and a diode clamp to raise the slew rate and dampen the overshoot in the high-speed pulse response of the µA777. The feed-forward path, consisting of resistor R2 and capacitor C2, bypasses the first stage lateral pnp transistors at frequencies above about 355 kHz and thereby raises the slew rate from the specified 0.5 V/µs to approximately 20 V/µs. The two diodes minimize the overshoot so that it is less than 1% for any output voltage in the tested range of pulse amplitudes from 0.5 to 10.0 V peak-to-peak.

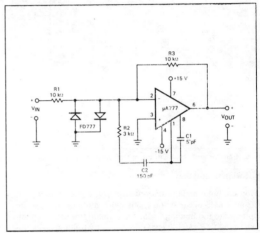

Fig. 2. Pulse Amplifier

WEIN BRIDGE OSCILLATOR

In the Wein bridge oscillator shown in *Figure 3*, a junction field effect transistor, Q1, operates in the linear resistive region to provide automatic gain control. Because the attenuation of the RC network is one-third at the zero phase-shift oscillation frequency, the amplifier gain determined by resistor R2 and equivalent resistor R1 must be just equal to three to make up the unity gain positive feedback requirement needed for stable oscillation. Resistors R3 and R4 are set to approximately 1000 Ω less than the required R1 resistance. The FET dynamically provides the trimming resistance needed to make R1 one-half of the resistance of R2.

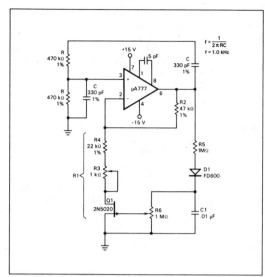

Fig. 3. Wein Bridge Oscillator

The circuit composed of R5, D1, and C1 isolates, rectifies and filters the output sine wave, converting it into a dc potential to control the gate of the FET. For the low drain-to-source voltages used, the FET provides a symmetrical linear resistance for a given gate-to-source voltage. The simplified circuit shown in *Figure 4* dispenses with the isolation, rectification and filtering at the cost of slightly higher distortion.

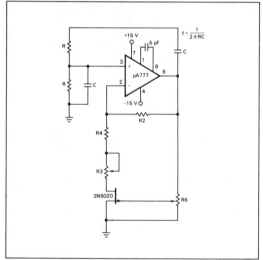

Fig. 4. Simplified Wein Bridge Oscillator

Figure 5 shows the distortion percentages as a function of peak output voltages for each of the two circuits. The curves shown represent data taken with potentiometer R6 set at a fixed position and with potentiometer R3 varied to provide the amplitude control. The lowest distortion values result when the set-up procedure is as follows: set R3 at the midpoint of its range, adjust R6 until output clipping just begins, and finally use R3 to reduce the output amplitude to the desired level. Because of the precise nature of the x3 gain

requirement, the 1% tolerances specified for R, C, R2, and R4 are vital to insure proper circuit operation. The median distortion value in the 1 to 5 V peak output region for the *Figure 3* circuit is approximately 0.025%.

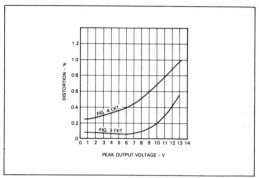

Fig. 5. Distortion vs Output Voltage

VARIABLE GAIN DIFFERENTIAL AMPLIFIER

The differential amplifier shown in *Figure 6* uses the differential form of the resistive T feedback network to achieve a wide variation in gain using a single potentiometer. The differential gain of the circuit is

$$\frac{V_O}{V_B - V_A} = \frac{2\,R2}{R1}\left(1 + \frac{1}{k}\right)$$

where k is less than or equal to unity. The gain control factor $1 + 1/k$ varies in a fairly linear manner for values of k close to unity, but increases very quickly in the high gain region where k is much less than unity. For circuits requiring more linear gain control in the high gain region, a series range resistor and a potentiometer with a lower resistance significantly improve the gain control resolution.

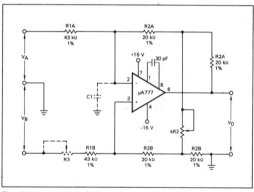

Fig. 6. Variable Gain Differential Amplifier

To achieve good common mode rejection in this circuit, the three A-suffix resistors on the top should be symmetrically balanced with the three B-suffix resistors on the bottom. This is particularly important for the two input resistors, R1A and R1B, and their associated source impedances. Inserting a trimming potentiometer, R3, in either the A or the B side will aid in this balancing. With the addition of a small trimming capacitance, C1, to balance ac impedances at the plus and minus input nodes, the circuit exhibits as much as 60 dB of common mode rejection ratio independent of the value of k and of the frequency of operation. In the actual breadboard circuit, where R3 was 500 Ω, the common mode rejection ratio at the null setting of R3 was only 40 dB until a 1 pF trimmer was added (C1). The rejection ratio then increased to 60 dB, independent of either gain settings or frequency variations.

POWER AMPLIFIER

The circuit in *Figure 7* shows how the µA777 can be used as a power amplifier to drive ampere level currents at supply voltages in the ±30 V range or more. Amplifier response is flat from dc to about 100 kHz with distortion values ranging from 0.05% to 0.1% at 1 kHz, depending on the output current required. Applications include servo drivers, audio amplifiers and many control circuits where flat response and medium power characteristics are an advantage.

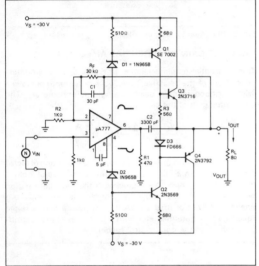

Fig. 7. Power Amplifier

Circuit operation depends largely on the high power supply rejection ratio (typically 13 µV/V) and the Class B configuration in the output stage of the µA777. The effect of these two factors is that any positive current signal flowing through resistor R1 appears in undistorted form at the positive voltage supply terminal (lead 7) and any negative current signal through R1 appears undistorted at the negative voltage supply terminal (lead 4). Capacitor C2 supplies stabilizing negative feedback for the output stages and has no significant effect on the forward current amplification of the circuit. Zener diodes D1 and D2 cause a level shift of the plus and minus current signals from the ±V source requirements of the µA777 to whatever supply voltages are required to drive the load.

Transistors Q1 and Q2 amplify these currents and drive the bases of the Class B output power transistors Q3 and Q4. Diode D3 and resistor R3 develop just enough voltage from the amplified standby current of the µA777 to keep transistors Q3 and Q4 biased ON and thereby minimize crossover distortion when the amplifier output passes through zero volts. Resistors R2 and R_F determine the amplifier's net voltage gain, while capacitor C1 in conjunction with R_F determines the 3 dB high frequency rolloff of the circuit.

The first requirement in using the basic circuit configuration is to choose the appropriate supply voltage and related Zener voltage values for a given load resistance and load power requirement. Allowing a conservative 6 V minimum drop across Q3 and Q4, the equation relating output power, load resistance, and source voltage is;

$$P_{OUT} = \left(\frac{V_S - 6}{\sqrt{2}} \right)^2 \frac{1}{R_L}$$

For example, 35 W through an 8 Ω load yields:

$$V_S = \sqrt{2 R_L P_{OUT}} + 6$$

$$V_S = 30 \text{ V}$$

The Zener voltage should be equal to the source voltage minus the operating voltage of the µA777. Choosing a 15 V supply for the µA777 gives:

$$V_Z = V_S - 15 \text{ V}$$

And for the given example with $V_S = ±30$ V:

$$V_Z = 15 \text{ V}$$

The only remaining requirement is that the four transistors, Q1 through Q4, be capable of handling the two times V_S standoff voltage (in this case 60 V) without breaking down.

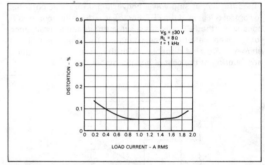

Fig. 8. Distortion vs Load Current

Figure 8 shows distortion versus load current for the circuit. Distortion remains relatively constant at about 0.05%, except at the lower output current levels. This increase at low signal levels is due to the emergence of noise as a factor with respect to the signal level.

The frequency response shown in *Figure 9* demonstrates that the 3 dB down frequency is 180 kHz using an R_F resistor value of 30 kΩ and a parallel capacitance of 30 pF.

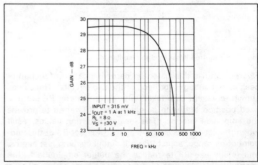

Fig. 9. Frequency Response

OPERATIONAL AMPLIFIERS AS INDUCTORS
Moise Hamaoui

INTRODUCTION

Operational amplifiers are easily modified to act as inductors by simply adding feedback resistance between the output and input V_i, (Figure 1a). In the presence of feedback resistance, the gain roll-off of practical operational amplifiers causes simulated inductive input impedance.

The derivation of the equivalent circuit (Figure 1b) and the necessary component values to obtain inductances from milli-henries to kilohenries are included in this application note. The application of simulated inductances in voltage controlled sinewave oscillators and in bandpass and notch filter designs is also illustrated as are the component values for VCOs at frequencies up to 50 kHz and for filters with center frequencies up to 50 kHz.

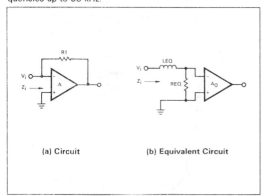

(a) Circuit   (b) Equivalent Circuit

Fig. 1. Simulated Inductive Input Impedance in Operational Amplifiers.

EQUIVALENT CIRCUIT

From Figure 1a

$$Z_i = \frac{R1}{1 - A} \qquad (1) \text{ Miller's Theorem}$$

Most operational amplifiers have a gain (A) given by

$$A = \frac{-A_0}{1 + j\left(\dfrac{w}{w_0}\right)} \qquad (2)$$

where A_0 is the dc open loop gain and w_0 is the 3 dB down roll-off frequency. This neglects the 2nd high frequency pole, (Figure 2).

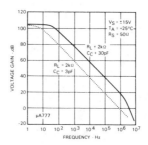

Fig. 2. Open Loop Voltage Gain As A Function of Frequency

Substituting Equation 2 in Equation 1 for A

$$Z_i = \frac{R1}{1 + j\left(\dfrac{w}{w_0}\right) + A_0} + jw\left(\frac{\dfrac{R1}{w_0}}{1 + j\left(\dfrac{w}{w_0}\right) + A_0}\right) \qquad (3)$$

For input frequencies $w \ll (A_0 + 1) \, w_0$, the denominator of Equation 3 can be approximated to be simply $(A_0 + 1)$, introducing very insignificant magnitude or phase angle error. Equation 3 then becomes

$$Z_i = \frac{R1}{1 + A_0} + jw\left(\frac{R1}{w_0 \, (1 + A_0)}\right) \qquad (4)$$

Req and Leq of *Figure 1b* are therefore

$$Req = \frac{R1}{1 + A_O} \cong \frac{R1}{A_O} \qquad (5)$$

$$Leq = \frac{R1}{w_O (1 + A_O)} \cong \frac{R1}{w_O A_O} \qquad (6)$$

since $A_O \gg 1$.

ONE MILLIHENRY TO ONE KILOHENRY INDUCTOR DESIGN

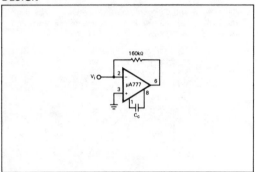

Fig. 3. 1 mH — 1 kH Inductor Circuit

Figure 3 shows a 1 mH to 1 kH inductor circuit. The 3 dB down roll-off frequency f_c of the µA777 is easily controlled with external capacitor C_c. In the following equations, C_c is in Farads, Leq in Henries.

$$f_{c\,(typ)} = \frac{159 \times 10^{-12}}{C_c} \; Hz \qquad (7)$$

With $A_{o(typ)}$ = 250,000 and feedback resistance = 160 kΩ, using Equations 5, 6, and 7:

$$Leq = \frac{R1}{(1 + A_O)\, 2\,\pi\, f_c} = (6.4 \times 10^8) C_c \qquad (8)$$

$$Req = \frac{R1}{1 + A_O} = 0.64\,\Omega \qquad (9)$$

where the maximum input frequency to satisfy $w \gg (A_O + 1)\, w_O$ is given by

$$f_{max} = \left(\frac{1}{1000}\right) \left(\frac{R1}{Leq}\right) = \frac{160}{Leq} \; Hz \qquad (10)$$

Figures 4, 5, and *6* show the necessary capacitor (C_c) and the maximum input signal frequency to attain simulated inductances from 1 mH to 1 kH.

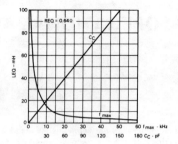

Fig. 4.

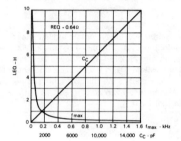

Fig. 5.

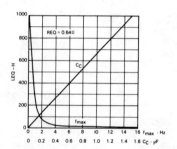

Fig. 6.

MINIMIZING REQ

If it is desired to decrease the value of Req, then feedback resistances R2 and R3 are added to the basic circuit of *Figure 1* to introduce a negative resistance component as shown in *Figure 7a*.

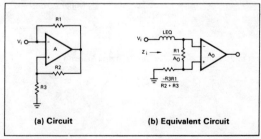

(a) Circuit   (b) Equivalent Circuit

Fig. 7. Minimizing Req

$$Z_i = \frac{R1}{A_O} - \frac{R3R1}{R2 + R3} + jw\left(\frac{R1}{A_O w_c}\right) \quad (11)$$

for $\dfrac{R3}{R2 + R3} \ll 1$ and $w \ll (A_O + 1)\, w_c$

See Appendix A for derivation.

VOLTAGE CONTROLLED VARIABLE INDUCTOR

By replacing R1 of *Figure 1* or *Figure 7* with a FET of drain-to-source resistance R_{DS} in series with R1, *Figure 8*

$$Leq = \frac{R1 + R_{DS}}{A_O w_c} \quad (12)$$

Varying V_i changes R_{DS}, thus varying Leq.

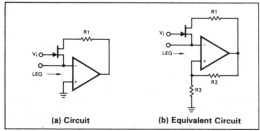

(a) Circuit   (b) Equivalent Circuit

Fig. 8. Voltage Controlled Variable Inductor

APPLICATIONS

Voltage Controlled Sinewave Oscillator

The circuit of *Figure 9a* is the basic voltage controlled variable inductor of *Figure 8b* with a capacitor C at the input.

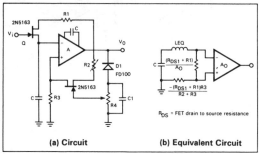

(a) Circuit   (b) Equivalent Circuit

Fig. 9. Voltage Controlled Sinewave Oscillator

Referring to *Figure 9b*, if $\dfrac{R1 + R_{DSI}}{A_O} - \dfrac{(R_{DSI} + R1)\, R3}{R2 + R3}$

is made very close to zero, the result is an LC circuit. When power is turned on, the output of the operational amplifier goes either positive or negative, causing initial charging of the capacitor C to initiate sinusoidal oscillation at the tuned frequency.

$$f_O = \frac{1}{2\pi \sqrt{LC}} = \frac{1}{2\pi\sqrt{\dfrac{(R1 + R_{DS1})\, C}{A_O w_c}}} \quad (13)$$

By varying the voltage at the gate of Q, R_{DS1} changes, thus varying the frequency of oscillation, f_O.

D1, C1, and R4 form a half-wave rectifier and filter to provide an AGC resulting in a constant output amplitude. R2 and R3 are the main controls of distortion of the output waveform. In practice, distortions of less than 1% were easily attainable.

Figure 10 and the charts in *Figure 11* show complete circuit elements for oscillation frequencies up to 50 kHz. The µA777 used in these examples exhibits an A_O of 250,000 typical and typical wave oscillations of 333 rad/s for C_c = 3 pF and 33.3 rad/s for C_c = 30 pF. Due to the wide production distribution of A_O, either R1 or C should be adjustable to allow trimming to the desired output frequency.

$$C \cong \frac{A_O w_c}{4\pi^2\,(R1 + R_{DS1})\, f_O{}^2}$$

$$C = \frac{5.27}{f_O{}^2} \qquad \text{for} \quad f_O > 10\,\text{kHz},\ C_C = 3\,\text{pF}$$

$$C = \frac{52.7}{f_O{}^2} \qquad \text{for} \quad f_O < 10\,\text{kHz},\ C_C = 30\,\text{pF}$$

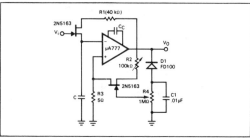

Fig. 10. Voltage Controlled Sinewave Oscillator for Frequencies to 50 kHz

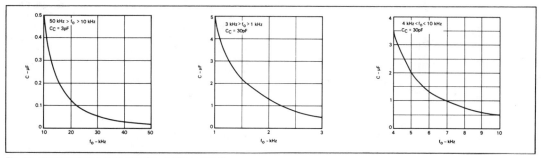

Fig. 11. Capacitor Value Determination, 1 kHz to 50 kHz

335

Bandpass and Notch Filters

The equivalent circuit *(Figure 12b)* shows that *Figure 12a* is an RLC circuit. At the resonant frequency $f_o = \dfrac{1}{2\pi\sqrt{LC}}$ the series impedance of the inductor and capacitor C is zero and all of the signal voltage is divided between the resistances R_S, $\dfrac{R1}{A_o}$, and $\dfrac{-R1R3}{R2+R3}$, resulting in maximum voltage at V_o given by

$$V_O \,(\text{Resonance}) = \frac{-A_o V_S \left(\dfrac{R1}{A_o}\right)}{R_S + \left(\dfrac{R1}{A_o}\right) - \left(\dfrac{R1R3}{R2+R3}\right)} \quad (14)$$

Thus, a bandpass filter at center frequency f_o and a quality factor Q, given by

$$Q = \frac{2\pi\, f_O\, L_{eq}}{R_S + \left(\dfrac{R1}{A_o}\right) - \left(\dfrac{R1R3}{R2+R3}\right)} \quad (15)$$

is realized.

The negative resistance $\dfrac{R1R3}{R2+R3}$ allows designers to obtain very high Q by minimizing the denominator. If it is desired to modify the circuit to a voltage controlled tuned filter, a FET can be added in series with R1 to use the variation of drain to source resistance as a function of gate voltage to effectively vary inductance Leq *(See Figure 8b)*.

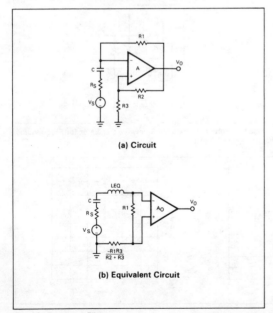

(a) Circuit

(b) Equivalent Circuit

Fig. 12. Bandpass Filter

Figure 13 shows a practical circuit for center frequencies up to 50 kHz. Again, the µA777 is used and values of capacitor C versus f_o are given in *Figure 11*. R2 is adjusted for the desired Q factor.

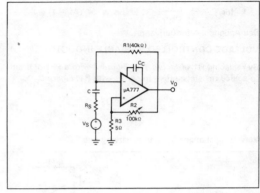

Fig. 13. Bandpass Filter, Center Frequencies to 50 kHz

The bandpass filter of *Figure 13* inverts and amplifies the signals of frequency f_o; when its output is added to the original input V_S, all the signals of frequency f_o are eliminated *(Figure 14)*. The second µA777 performs the additional operation and R3 is adjusted to cancel V_S at V_o at frequency f_o. This circuit assumes small delay in the bandpass filter.

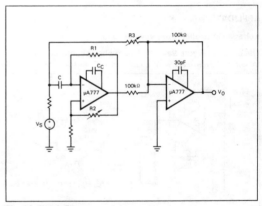

Fig. 14. Notch Filter

CONCLUSION

Within certain limitations (imposed because the circuit depends upon stable and reproducible A_o and w_o for proper operation), the circuit designer now has at his disposal another means for realizing a wide range of inductances. In view of this dependance, however, careful evaluation of the effects of both power supply and temperature upon these parameters is necessary.

ACKNOWLEDGEMENTS

Technical assistance from Norman Doyle, Robert Ricks and Dr. Henry Nettesheim is greatly appreciated.

APPENDIX A: Z_i DERIVATION

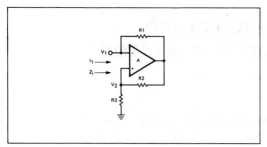

Fig. A1

$$Z_i = \frac{V_1}{I_1} \tag{1}$$

$$I_1 = \frac{V_1 - V_0}{R1} \tag{2}$$

(Assuming negligible input current to the Op Amp)

$$V_0 = A(V_2 - V_1) \tag{3}$$

$$V_2 = \frac{V_0 R3}{R2 + R3} \tag{4}$$

Substituting Equation 4 for Equation 3,

$$V_0 = A\left(\frac{V_0 R3}{R2 + R3} - V_1\right) \tag{5}$$

Rearranging Equation 5,

$$V_0 = \frac{-AV_1}{1 - \left(\dfrac{AR3}{R2 + R3}\right)} \tag{6}$$

Substituting Equation 6 for Equation 2,

$$I_1 = \frac{V_1}{R1}\left(1 + \left[\frac{A}{1 - \left(\dfrac{AR3}{R2 + R3}\right)}\right]\right) \tag{7}$$

From Equation 7,

$$Z_i = \frac{V_1}{I_1} = \frac{R1}{\left[1 + \dfrac{A}{1 - \left(\dfrac{AR3}{R2 + R3}\right)}\right]} \tag{8}$$

Rearranging Equation 8,

$$Z_i = \frac{R1}{1 + A\left(1 - \dfrac{R3}{R2 + R3}\right)} - \frac{R1\,A\left(\dfrac{R3}{R2 + R3}\right)}{1 + A\left(1 - \dfrac{R3}{R2 + R3}\right)} \tag{9}$$

For $\dfrac{R3}{R2 + R3} \ll 1$, Equation 9 simplifies to

$$Z_i = \frac{R1}{1 + A} - \frac{R1R3}{R2 + R3}\left(\frac{A}{1 + A}\right) \tag{10}$$

Substituting $\dfrac{A_0}{1 + j\left(\dfrac{w}{w_c}\right)}$ for A results in

$$\tag{11}$$

$$Z_i = \frac{R1}{1 + \left[\dfrac{A_0}{1 + j\left(\dfrac{w}{w_c}\right)}\right]} - \frac{R1R3}{R2 + R3} \cdot \frac{\dfrac{A_0}{1 + j\left(\dfrac{w}{w_c}\right)}}{1 + \dfrac{A_0}{1 + j\left(\dfrac{w}{w_c}\right)}}$$

Rearranging Equation 11 results in

$$\tag{12}$$

$$Z_i = \frac{R1\left[1 + j\left(\dfrac{w}{w_c}\right)\right]}{1 + j\left(\dfrac{w}{w_c}\right) + A_0} - \frac{R1R3}{R2 + R3} \cdot \frac{\dfrac{A_0}{1 + j\left(\dfrac{w}{w_c}\right)}}{1 + \dfrac{A_0}{1 + j\left(\dfrac{w}{w_c}\right)}}$$

For $A_0 \gg \dfrac{w}{w_c} + 1$, Equation 12 simplifies to

$$Z_i = \frac{R1}{A_0} - \frac{R1R3}{R2 + R3} + jw\left(\frac{R1}{A_0 w_c}\right) \tag{13}$$

Thus, the equivalent input impedance of the circuit in *Figure A1* is:

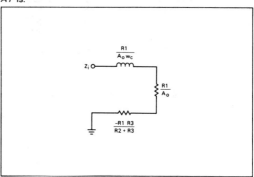

Fig. A2

THE µA760 — A HIGH SPEED
MONOLITHIC VOLTAGE COMPARATOR
Peter Holtham

INTRODUCTION

The basic comparator function produces a digital one or zero output which corresponds to the value of an input signal compared with a reference. This function has been adequately described elsewhere.[1] A new monolithic voltage comparator, the µA760, offers many advantages over earlier designs. Performance features include:

- Complementary outputs with nominally equal delays to each output,

- Typical propagation delay 5 to 10 ns faster than the µA710,

- Operation from symmetrical supplies of ±4.5 to ±6.5 volts,

- A common mode input voltage range of ±4 volts with ±6 volt supplies,

- TTL compatible outputs with current sourcing capability of 5 mA for each output, and current sinking capability of 3.2 mA (2 TTL gate loads).

FUNCTIONAL DESCRIPTION

Figure 1 is a block diagram of the µA760, which has a linear differential amplifier followed by two identical output stages. The output stage design is very similar to standard TTL logic design, providing good current sourcing and current sinking capability with TTL logic compatibility. Figure 2 is a simplified schematic. The first stage (Q_1, Q_2, R_1 and R_2) is biased by the

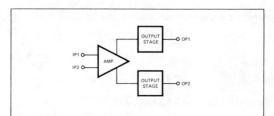

Fig. 1. Block Diagram

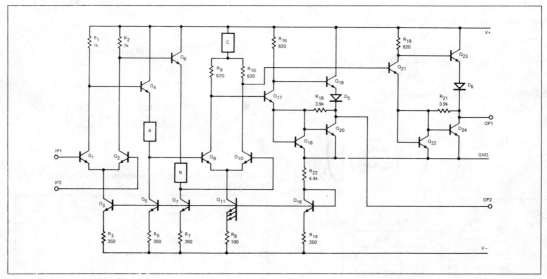

Fig. 2. Simplified Schematic of the µA760

current source Q_3 R_3, at approximately 1 mA. The maximum voltage swing at Q_1 and Q_2 collectors is set at 1 V by R_1 and R_2 and the 1 mA current source. This gives a high common mode input voltage range. The first stage outputs are coupled to transistors Q_9 and Q_{10} of the second stage through emitter followers Q_4 and Q_6 and level shifting elements A and B. The second stage (Q_9, Q_{10}, R_9 and R_{10}) is biased by the current source Q_{11} and R_8 and level shifting element C. The outputs of this stage feed the two output stages which are very similar to TTL gates except that the multi-input (strobe) capability has been omitted to optimize speed. One gate consists of Q_{17}, Q_{18}, Q_{19}, Q_{20}, D_5, R_{16} and R18, and the other is Q_{21}, Q_{22}, Q_{23}, Q_{24}, D_6, R_{19} and R_{21}. In operation, when the input to the base of Q_{17} rises above two base-emitter voltage drops, the collector of Q_{17} falls, Q_{20} is turned on and eventually saturates. The current sinking capability of Q_{20} is determined by the emitter current of Q_{17} and the emitter area ratios of Q_{18} and Q_{20}. These are all designed to insure a low output voltage level of less than 0.4V for sink currents up to 3.2 mA, or the equivalent of two gate loads. When the input to Q_{17} falls below two base-emitter voltage drops, Q_{17} and Q_{20} are no longer saturated and the output rises to a voltage equal to the supply voltage minus two base-emitter voltage drops, which is the normal TTL output level. When the output is high, some current flows through R_{18} and Q_{18}, preventing Q_{20} from completely turning off. This improves switching speed when the output goes low. Switching speed is also enhanced by the small positive feedback through R_{18} and Q_{18} to the emitter of Q_{17}.

Level shifting elements A and B are basically zener diodes, but the zener voltage originally was a little large, which could cause Q_{11} to saturate under worst case supply voltage and temperature conditions. To overcome this problem, the level shifter was modified as shown in Figure 3. The delay introduced by this modification is less than one nanosecond.

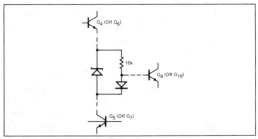

Fig. 3. Level Shifting Elements A and B

Level shifting element C is more complex and is shown in Figure 4. A negative feedback loop formed by Q_{14}, Q_{15}, R_{16}, Q_8 and R_{11} holds the junction of R_{11}, Q_{14}, Q_{12} at two base-emitter voltage levels above ground, which is the threshold of the output stages. Voltage drops across R_9, R_{10} and R_{11} are closely matched by defining their ratios and the ratios of the current sources Q_{11}, R_8, Q_{12} and R_{12}. Resistors R_8 and R_{12} define current sources with a current ratio of 3:1. Q_{11} is a triple emitter device and each emitter is the same size as the Q_{12} emitter providing optimum V_{BE} matching. The current

in R_9 and R_{10} will be nominally one-and-a-half times the current in R_{11}; hence the ratios R_{11} to R_{10} and R_{11} to R_9 should be 1.5:1. The actual ratio is slightly larger because Q_{14} and Q_{15} operate at a lower current than the output stage transistors so their base-emitter voltages are lower.

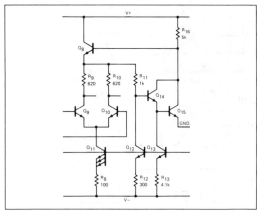

Fig. 4. Level Shifting Element C.

The complete schematic for the μA760 is shown in Figure 5. Speed is optimized by using small geometry devices throughout. Gold doping minimizes recovery time of the saturating elements of the circuit. Also, collector resistors R_1, R_2, R_9 and R_{10} are moderately low in value to minimize time constants which would degrade speed. This also limits gain, but it is still considerably greater than that of the μA710.

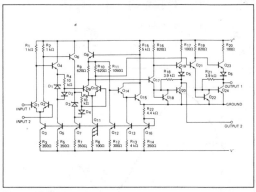

Fig. 5. μA760 Schematic.

PERFORMANCE

Table I lists some typical parameters. Figure 6 shows the voltage transfer characteristic, and pulse responses are shown in Figures 7 and 8. Many applications involve input signals with significant rise and fall times. Performance under such conditions is shown in Figures 9 and 10, where t_{pd+} and t_{pd-} are plotted as a function of the input level of a 10 MHz sinusoidal signal for a device with its input voltage offset nulled. For normal unnulled operation, allowances must be made for the combined effect of device offset and input signal rise and fall times.

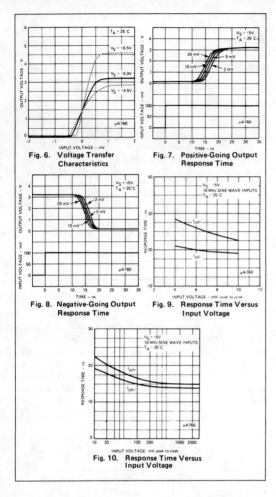

Fig. 6. Voltage Transfer Characteristics

Fig. 7. Positive-Going Output Response Time

Fig. 8. Negative-Going Output Response Time

Fig. 9. Response Time Versus Input Voltage

Fig. 10. Response Time Versus Input Voltage

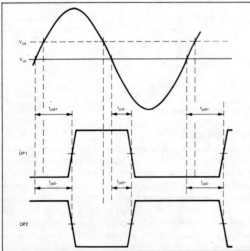

Fig. 11. Effect of Input Offset Voltage on Propagation Delay

TYPICAL PERFORMANCE CHARACTERISTICS

Fairchild's μA760 High Speed Comparator (all data for 25°C Ambient Temperature and V_S = ±4.5V to ±6.5V, unless otherwise specified.)

INPUT OFFSET VOLTAGE	$R_S \leqslant 200\Omega$	1 mV
INPUT OFFSET CURRENT	$V_S = \pm6.5V$	0.5μA
INPUT BIAS CURRENT	$V_S = \pm6.5V$	7 μA
VOLTAGE GAIN	$V_S = \pm5.5V$	5000
OUTPUT RESISTANCE	$V_{OUT} = V_{OH}$	100Ω
INPUT RESISTANCE	f = 1 MHz	12kΩ
INPUT CAPACITANCE	f = 1 MHz	8pF
RESPONSE TIME	V_{IN} = 30mVp-p 10 MHz sine wave	18ns
	100mV pulse with 5mv overdrive	16ns
POSITIVE SUPPLY CURRENT	$V_S = \pm6.5V$	18mA
NEGATIVE SUPPLY CURRENT	$V_S = \pm6.5V$	9mA

Figures 9 and 10 show that the difference between t_{pd+} and t_{pd-} is typically 2 ns and this measurement is very sensitive to input offset voltage since it is made with a sinusoidal input signal. Figure 11 illustrates the effect of input offset which increases t_{pd+} of output 1 and t_{pd-} of output 2, and reduces t_{pd+} of output 1 and t_{pd-} of output 1. For a 10 MHz, 30 mV peak-to-peak input, 1 mV of input offset results in a 1.06 ns change in propagation delay. This also results in a 2.1 ns change in delay difference between t_{pd+} and t_{pd-} of each output, between the two t_{pd+} outputs and between the two t_{pd-} outputs. This sensitivity of delay difference to offset voltage must be considered in some applications. Figure 11 also shows that the effect of offset voltage variations on delay difference is less for inputs with higher frequency or input voltage. The delay difference variation for pulse inputs also is less dependent on input offset. Considering offset voltage as a change in overdrive, the effect of offset voltage on pulse response can be determined from Figures 7 and 8. A change in overdrive from 20 mV to 5 mV (See Figure 7) would increase delay less than 2 ns; a change in overdrive from 5 mV to 20 mV (See Figure 8) would reduce delay less than 2 ns. Thus, for a theoretical 15 mV offset voltage, the delay difference changes less than 4 ns (less than 1/3 ns per millivolt). As shown in Figure 11, the delay difference between t_{pd+} of output 1 and t_{pd-} of output 2 (also typically 2 ns) is virtually unchanged by input offset voltage. This is also true of the delay difference between t_{pd+} of output 2 and t_{pd-} of output 1.

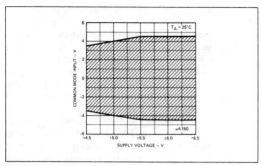

Fig. 12. Common Mode Range Versus Supply Voltage

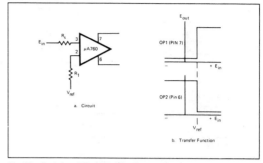

Fig. 13. Basic Level Detector Circuit

Figure 12 shows the typical common mode range, which is within one volt of the supply voltage up to ±5.5 volt supplies - - - ±4.5 volts at greater supply voltages.

APPLICATIONS

LEVEL DETECTOR AND LINE RECEIVERS

A basic level detector circuit is shown in Figure 13. R_1 and R_S should be equal and as low as possible to minimize errors caused by bias and offset currents. To insure satisfactory operation, V_{REF} must be within the common mode range of the amplifier and should be about 0.5 volts less than the typical value shown in Figure 11. There is no foldback in the transfer curve when the common mode range is exceeded. Using positive feedback to create hysteresis in the transfer function is often desirable. For example, this technique could be useful when it is unacceptable for the comparator output to be in the transition region, or when noise is expected at the input which might cause random switching of the comparator and result in misleading operation. Figure 14 shows a simple arrangement for applying hysteresis. The upper and lower trip points of the circuit can be described as follows:

$$V_{UT} = V_{REF} + \left(\frac{R_1}{R_1 + R_2}\right)\left(V_{OH} - V_{REF}\right) \quad (1)$$

and:

$$V_{LT} = V_{REF} + \left(\frac{R_1}{R_1 + R_2}\right)\left(V_{OL} - V_{REF}\right) \quad (2)$$

The hysteresis is:

$$V_H = V_{UT} - V_{LT} = \left(\frac{R_1}{R_1 + R_2}\right)\left(V_{OH} - V_{OL}\right) \quad (3)$$

The effective offset (V'_{OS}) might be defined as the deviation of the algebraic mean of V_{UT} and V_{LT} from zero or:

$$V'_{OS} = \frac{V_{UT} + V_{LT}}{2}$$

$$= V_{REF} + 1/2\left(\frac{R_1}{R_1 + R_2}\right)\left(V_{OH} + V_{OL} - 2V_{REF}\right) \quad (4)$$

$$= V_{REF}\left(\frac{R_2}{R_1 + R_2}\right) + 1/2\left(V_{OH} + V_{OL}\right)\left(\frac{R_1}{R_1 + R_2}\right) \quad (5)$$

Thus, using equation 3 knowing V_{OH} and V_{OL}, $R_1 + R_2$ can be chosen to provide the desired hysteresis. Then equation 4 or 5 can be used to determine the value of V_{REF} to provide the desired offset. The offset of the device is additive, but if the

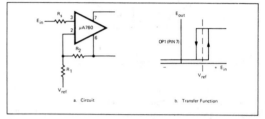

Fig. 14. Level Detector with Hysteresis

hysteresis is large, the contribution will be small. R_S and R_1 should be small, and R_S should be equal to the parallel combination of R_1 and R_2 to minimize errors caused by bias and offset currents. Reliable operation can be obtained with hysteresis down to less than 0.5 mV.

A more versatile method of achieving hysteresis uses the μA760 complementary outputs as shown in Figure 15. This method does not require a V_{REF}, can be used for differential signals and hysteresis and effective offset are both set by resistor ratios. For this circuit:

$$V_{UT} = V_{OH}\left(\frac{R_2}{R_1}\right) - V_{OL}\left(\frac{R_4}{R_3}\right) \quad (6)$$

$$V_{LT} = V_{OL}\left(\frac{R_2}{R_1}\right) - V_{OH}\left(\frac{R_4}{R_3}\right) \quad (7)$$

$$V_H = \left(V_{OH} - V_{OL}\right)\left(\frac{R_2}{R_1} + \frac{R_4}{R_3}\right) \quad (8)$$

$$V'_{OS} = 1/2\left(V_{OH} + V_{OL}\right)\left(\frac{R_2}{R_1} - \frac{R_4}{R_3}\right) \quad (9)$$

These expressions neglect errors caused by R_2 and R_4 being unequal. However, if R_2 and R_4 are small and hysteresis is not too small, these errors are minimal. If $R_1 = R_3$ and $R_2 = R_4$, these errors are virtually eliminated and V'_{OS} equals the device offset. A useful line receiver using this circuit with symmetrical hysteresis is shown in Figure 16. If R_1 and R_2 are chosen to provide moderate hysteresis and are well matched to minimize effective offset, and if R_3 and R_4 are as large as the required sensitivity allows, the upper and lower switching levels are well defined and common mode range is increased.

Suppose, for example, the hysteresis is set by R_1 and R_2 to be 30 mV with an effective offset of 1 mV (7 mV including device

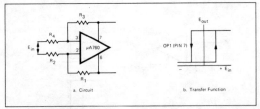

Fig. 15. Modified Level Detector with Hysteresis

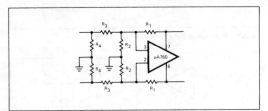

Fig. 16. Line Receiver with Large Common Mode Range

offset). Then the maximum switching level is 22 mV. Assuming the required overall sensitivity is +100 mV, R_3 should be chosen to give attenuation of something less than 100/22, say 4. With careful R_3 matching, the common mode range can be increased as much as four times that of the $\mu A760$ alone. Figure 17 illustrates a special application of this circuit, which conforms to MIL-STD-188C line receiver requirements.

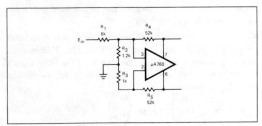

Fig. 17. MIL STD Line Receiver

ZERO CROSSING DETECTORS

A zero crossing detector is a logical application for any comparator. The $\mu A760$ offers superior performance as a zero crossing detector because of its speed and complementary outputs. Figure 18 shows a zero crossing detector using two $\mu A760$s. The outputs of the first $\mu A760$ change state each time the input signal passes through zero. Diodes D_1 and D_2, capacitors C_1 and C_2 and resistors R_3, R_4 and R_5 generate a short, positive pulse which is applied to input one of the second $\mu A760$. A positive pulse results at output one of the second $\mu A760$. This pulse represents the timing of the input zero crossing. The timing measurement error is equal to the circuit dealy, typically 30 ns. Negative pulses are obtained from the other output. The output pulse widths can be adjusted by varying R_6. The circuit functions at frequencies from 300 Hz to 4 MHz with a signal of about 30 mV RMS at 4 MHz rising to about seven volts at 300 Hz. Adjustment of the time constant of the differentiator circuit C_1, C_2, R_3 and R_4 provides satisfactory operation at low frequency with a lower input

voltage. Figure 19 shows a zero crossing detector application which determines the timing of the peak of a pulse. C_1 and R_1 generate the derivative of the input pulse which is applied to the input of the lower comparator. When the input pulse reaches a peak, its derivative passes through zero, the input to the lower $\mu A760$ passes through zero and B, and the comparator output changes from a low to a high state. To prevent transitions on noise, A and B are fed into a NAND gate and A will go to a high state only when the input pulse amplitude exceeds V_{th}. The negative-going edge of output (E_{out}) establishes the peak timing of the input pulse. A slightly different circuit is shown in Figure 20 where outputs B and C are effectively inhibited by output A of the top comparator, except when the input pulse amplitude exceeds V_{th}. As shown in the waveform diagram, pulse peak timing is given by the negative-going edge of C. The advantage of the Figure 20 circuit is that delay is reduced by eliminating the NAND gate, and two complementary outputs are available.

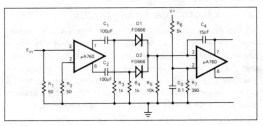

Fig. 18. Zero Crossing Detector

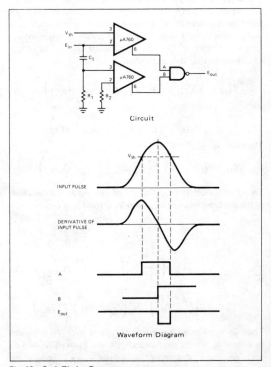

Fig. 19. Peak Timing Detector

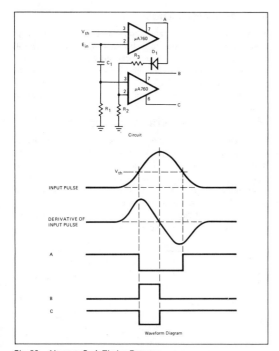

Fig. 20. Alternate Peak Timing Detector

HIGH SPEED A/D CONVERSION

The use of the µA760 for high speed analog to digital conversion is shown in Figure 21. Each µA760 (one through seven) has one input biased to a voltage level at which the digital equivalent of the input signal should change. The use of both outputs of comparators two and four provides a simpler and faster circuit than using comparators with a single output, which would require two inverters. The voltages shown along the resistor chain R_1 to R_8 are the theoretical voltages at which each comparator should switch. Figure 22 illustrates the required analog to digital relationship and the determination of the switching levels. When comparators two, four and six switch, they may affect more than one bit. Hysteresis generated by resistors R_9, R_{10} and R_{11} avoids possible erroneous outputs. The switching levels set by the resistor chain are slightly modified by the effect of bias currents. For example, when comparator three is about to switch, the input supplies the total bias current of comparators one and two. This is equivalent to the sum of the two bias currents since there is a large differential voltage between the inputs. The input also will supply half the total bias current of comparator three, which has a nominally zero differential input voltage. The total bias currents of comparators four, five, six and seven and half the total bias current of comparator three are supplied by the resistor chain R_1 to R_8. Resistors R_9, R_{10} and R_{11} also modify the currents in the resistor chain, introducing additional errors. Determination of the maximum error requires analysis of the circuit for inputs equal to each of the seven switching levels. Assuming resistor tolerances of ±1%, bias currents of 7 µA (total bias current 14 µA) and a supply voltage tolerance of ±2%, the maximum error is less than 0.1 V (or less than one-

fifth of the least significant bit) for the Figure 21 circuit. Obviously some improvement can be obtained, either by adjusting resistor values to compensate for bias currents or by designing independent reference voltages with lower source resistances. The main purpose of the Figure 22 circuit is fast analog to digital conversion without undue emphasis on accuracy. Because of the logic delays, conversion speed depends upon which of the three bits switch. The most significant bit delay is typically 13 ns to 18 ns. The second most significant bit delay is typically 22 ns to 30 ns, and the least significant bit delay is typically 20 ns to 35 ns. Total conversion speed is typically less than 35 ns.

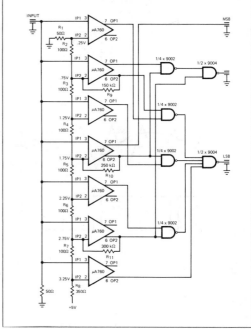

Fig. 21. High Speed A-D Converter

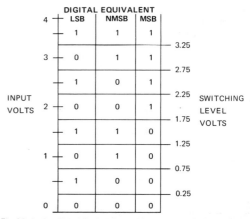

Fig. 22. Analog-Digital Equivalents and Corresponding Reference Levels

	DIGITAL EQUIVALENT			
INPUT VOLTS		LSB	NMSB	MSB	SWITCHING LEVEL VOLTS
4		1	1	1	
					3.25
3		0	1	1	
					2.75
		1	0	1	
					2.25
2		0	0	1	
					1.75
		1	1	0	
					1.25
1		0	1	0	
					0.75
		1	0	0	
					0.25
0		0	0	0	

343

PULSE WIDTH MODULATOR

Figure 23 shows a pulse width modulator using a μA760. The μA715 is connected as a ramp generator and the ramp output is fed into one input of the μA760 while the other input of the μA760 is fed from an audio signal. The μA760 outputs will change state each time the audio input equals the ramp voltage. The μA760 outputs vary in pulse width as a function of the instantaneous value of the audio input. Refer to the waveform in Figure 23.

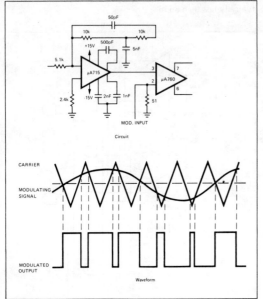

Circuit

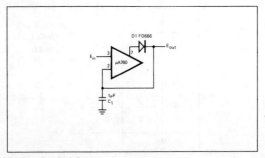

Waveform

Fig. 23. Pulse Width Modulator

FAST PEAK DETECTOR

Figure 24 shows a simple fast peak detector which operates with input pulse widths down to 50 ns. The discharge current for C_1 is simply the bias current for the μA760, typically 14 μA. If a shorter time constant is desired to enable the circuit to follow rapidly varying signals a resistor can be connected between the output and V–. Without this resistor, the decay time of the voltage across C_1 is approximately 50 ns/V.

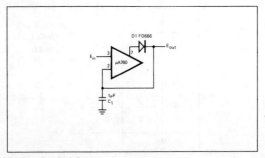

Fig. 24. Fast Peak Detector

HIGH SPEED APPLICATIONS

Phase encoded systems, tape readout systems and similar applications are ideally suited to such characteristics of the μA760 as its low response time, reduced dependance of response time on overdrive level and its nominally equal delays to each output. System speed improvement is possible in some cases by using the complementary outputs to eliminate an inversion stage.

PROVIDING OUTPUT STROBE ON THE μA760

Figure 25 shows an active level low common strobe added to both outputs of the μA760. When the $\overline{\text{STROBE}}$ input is high, outputs A and B are at a logic level low state. When the $\overline{\text{STROBE}}$ input is low, the outputs of the μA760 are passed through the gates. In this state, if input one is more positive than input two, output A will be low while output B will be high. Likewise, if input two is more positive than input one, output A will be high while output B is low.

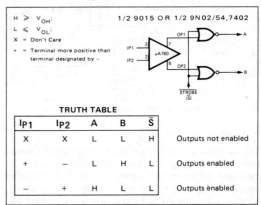

H	≥ V_{OH}:				
L	≤ V_{OL}:				
X	= Don't Care				
+	= Terminal more positive than terminal designated by –				

1/2 9015 OR 1/2 9N02/54,7402

TRUTH TABLE

IP1	IP2	A	B	$\overline{S}$	
X	X	L	L	H	Outputs not enabled
+	–	L	H	L	Outputs enabled
–	+	H	L	L	Outputs enabled

Fig. 25. STROBE Output using NOR Gates

Figure 26 shows the strobe circuit using NAND gates. Note that the logic sense of the strobe has changed to active level high and the inhibited outputs (STROBE = low) are now high instead of low. The truth table shows that the circuit in Figure 26 provides the same response as the circuit in Figure 25 with the exception of STROBE logical sense and output state when inhibited.

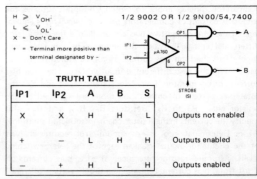

H	≥ V_{OH}:				
L	≤ V_{OL}:				
X	= Don't Care				
+	= Terminal more positive than terminal designated by –				

1/2 9002 OR 1/2 9N00/54,7400

TRUTH TABLE

IP1	IP2	A	B	S	
X	X	H	H	L	Outputs not enabled
+	–	L	H	H	Outputs enabled
–	+	H	L	H	Outputs enabled

Fig. 26. STROBE Output using NAND Gates

CONCLUSION

Various applications have been described which take advantage of the high speed complementary outputs and low supply voltages of the μA760. The speed and current sinking capability of the μA760 provide better performance than the μA710. This circuit is highly versatile because of its complementary outputs, symmetrical supplies and compatibility with most logic forms.

REFERENCES

1. The Operation and Use of a Fast Integrated Circuit Comparator, R.J. Widlar, Fairchild Semiconductor APP-123.

ACKNOWLEDGEMENTS

The author greatefully acknowledges technical contributions and assistance received from J.D. Lieux and Ken True. Thanks are also due to Arnold Salazar who built and tested many of the circuits shown.

THE μA750 DUAL COMPARATOR SUBSYSTEM

H. Ebenhoech and R. Ricks

INTRODUCTION

The μA750 is a dual high current comparator on a single silicon chip. The two comparators are functionally independent. Each has strobing capability, built-in hysteresis for positive switching, output current sinking capability and high current source capability. The device operates over a wide supply range, has a separate reference voltage available for external circuitry bias and has adjustable excess current and chip temperature protection. Both comparator and strobe inputs are TTL compatible, but the comparator inputs require pull up resistors for some applications.

The device is designed primarily for dual comparator functions in systems with high load currents. However as a means of reducing package count, it should be considered for any system using more than one comparator. Specific applications of the device covered here illustrate the capability of the product. Detailed device characteristics are included on the data sheet.

GENERAL CIRCUIT OPERATION

A block diagram of the device is shown in Figure 1. Each side of the μA750 has two amplifier inputs and the strobe input. From the input amplifier, the signal is fed to the flip-flop which switches the output between fully ON and fully OFF positions without permitting a linear transfer function between input and output. During application of a strobe input (positive voltage between 2.3 and 5V) the output remains in its existing state and the input amplifier ignores any change in the comparator input conditions.

The output can be represented by the equivalent circuit shown in Figure 2. When the input differential voltage between the non-inverting and the inverting inputs is greater than the built-in threshold voltage (10 mV), switches S_1 and S_2 are closed. ($V = V_{IN}(+) - V_{IN}(-) \geqslant V_{THRESHOLD}$).

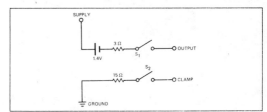

Fig. 2 Output equivalent circuit

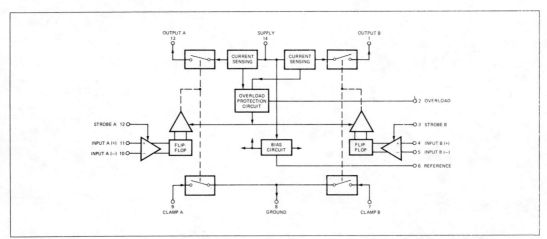

Fig. 1 μA750 block diagram

The output load current is sensed by the current sensing network which, upon reaching an internally defined threshold, causes the overload protection circuit to shut off the bias voltage to the output amplifiers of both sides. After shutdown the device is reset by disconnecting the supply voltage. To preserve memory information stored in the flip-flop of either side, resetting must be done by connecting the OVERLOAD terminal to the SUPPLY terminal. In this case, care should be taken not to damage the device. Refer to the section of designing with the μA750. The reference output voltage (7.8V typical) is not affected by either the strobe signal or the overload shutoff action.

EQUIVALENT CIRCUIT

The equivalent circuit of the μA750 is shown in Figure 3. Both sides of the comparator are identical in function. The subscripts used in the following description refer to side A.

Input Amplifier and Memory Element

The input amplifier is formed by the differentially connected transistors Q_5 and Q_6, and these are biased by current source transistor Q_7. Their collector load resistors, R_1/R_3, and R_2/R_4, together with Q_3 and Q_4, form a flip-flop. Transistors Q_1 and Q_2 serve as buffers and reduce the effective base current of the flip-flop transistors Q_3 and Q_4.

The current through the flip-flop is set by the current

source Q_8 and R_9 so as to prevent Q_4 and Q_3 from saturating, thus minimizing switching time.

When the differential input voltage is $\Delta V = V(+) - V(-) = 0$, Q_5 and Q_6 share the current of the current source Q_7 equally. To change the state of the flip-flop, the ratio of currents has to deviate from unity to a ratio obtained with a differential input voltage typically of 10 mV which is the threshold voltage (positive for turn on, negative for turn off).

Output Amplifier and Output Stage

The signal is taken from the flip-flop via the two emitter resistors R_5 and R_6 and brought to the output amplifier, Q_{10} and Q_{11}. The output signal of Q_{11} is taken at two points from its load resistor. One point is connected to the base of the PNP transistor Q_{13}, which serves as signal inverter for the Darlington-connected source output transistors Q_{15} and Q_{16} (OUTPUT). The other point is connected to the base of transistor Q_{14}. Q_{14}, D_1, Q_{13} and R_{13} form a current source for the sink output transistor Q_{17} (CLAMP). When the flip-flop is in the OFF state, the current in R_{11} is sufficiently low to prevent Q_{13} and Q_{17} from conducting.

Strobe

The strobe terminal is connected to the base of Q_9. A positive voltage of 2.3 to 5V at this point turns off current source Q_7 and thus prevents any signal transfer from the input leads to the flip-flop. Therefore, the output remains in the state it was in prior to the strobe input.

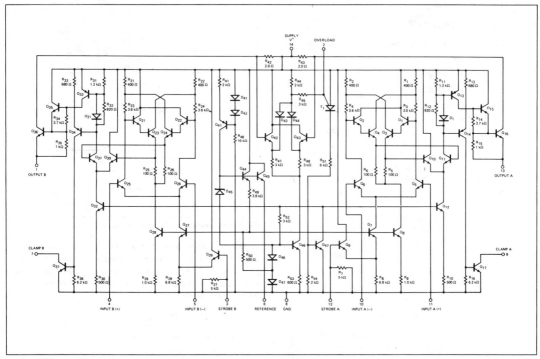

Fig. 3 μA750 equivalent circuit

Bias Section and Overload Protection Circuit

In operation, the only path which carries a current approximately proportional to the supply voltage is composed of D_{41}, D_{42} and R_{46}. Q_{41} provides the current source for the Zener diode D_{45} and the bases of Q_{44} and Q_{45}, the latter being the reference output transistor. The current sources Q_7 and Q_8 in the comparator section and their counterparts on the other side are fed from a resistive divider R_{49}/R_{50}, diodes D_{45}, D_{46}, D_{47} and transistor Q_{44}. The design has minimum voltage V_{HYST} sensitivity to variations in temperature and supply voltage.

The overload protection circuit of the µA750 is sensing resistors R_{42} and R_{43} (one for each side), an OR gate and a switch (SCR). The voltages appearing across the sensing resistors due to load currents are transferred into a voltage drop across resistor R_{44}. The voltage across R_{44} will always be the larger of two voltages across R_{42} or R_{43}. When the threshold voltage of T_1 is reached (about 0.7 volts at 25°C), the SCR conducts and causes transistor Q_{47} to remove the bias voltages of the output stage current sources Q_{12} and Q_{32}. Resetting is accomplished, as mentioned above, by either connecting the OVERLOAD terminal to the supply or by momentarily removing the supply voltage.

The SCR T_1 contains an internal diode connected between the anode and the gate. The negative temperature coefficient of this junction and the positive temperature coefficient of the sensing resistors reduces the output current at which the SCR is triggered into conduction and shuts off the µA750. Thus, an effective temperature protection circuit is built into the device.

DESIGNING WITH THE µA750

When designing with the µA750, two aspects should be given special consideration:

1. the built-in hysteresis of the transistor function and,

2. the total power dissipation of the device.

The hysteresis is defined in Figure 4. This figure shows that the device has no linear region and, therefore, the output voltage will either be zero or about 1.8 volts below the supply voltage. The typical input hysteresis voltage, V_{HYST}, is 20 mV. This voltage can be increased by use of the CLAMP output to vary the differential input voltage as the device output changes. This is indicated in Figure 5. As long as the device is OFF the voltage on the INPUT (–) is determined by the resistive divider including the resistance R_3. When the device is turned ON, R_3 is shunted by the internal resistance of the clamp (about 15 Ω) and thus the voltage on the INPUT (–) lead is lowered. For turn-off, the input voltage $V_{IN(+)}$ now must drop below the lowered voltage on the INPUT (–) by $= |V_{THRESH(-)}|$. The effective hysteresis voltage is therefore increased.

The increase can be described by

$$\Delta_{HYST} = \frac{R_1 (R_3 - R_x) \cdot V_{REF}}{(R_1 + R_2)(R_1 + R_2 + R_3 + R_x)}$$

where R_x is the parallel resistance of R_3 and the internal resistance of the clamp transistor. (Assumed: $R_3 \ll R_1 + R_2$ and $R_x \ll R_1 + R_2$.)

The total effective hysteresis voltage is then

$$V_{HYST_{eff}} = V_{HYST} + \Delta_{HYST}$$

For example:

Assume: $R_1 = 10\ k\Omega$ $V_{REF} = 7.8V$

$R_2 = 10\ k\Omega$

$R_3 = 500\ \Omega$

$R_x = R_3$ in parallel with 15 Ω   (Figure 2)

$= 14.5\ \Omega$

then: $\Delta_{HYST} = \dfrac{10 \times (.486) \times 10^6\ \Omega}{20 \times 20.513 \times 10^6\ \Omega} \times 12V = 0.092V$

and $V_{HYST_{eff}} = 0.020 + 0.092 = 0.112V$

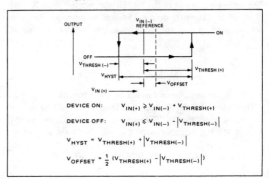

Fig. 4 Hysteresis definitions

$V_{IN(-)}$ REFERENCE

ON

OFF

$V_{THRESH\ (-)}$

V_{HYST}

$V_{THRESH\ (+)}$

$V_{IN\ (+)}$

V_{OFFSET}

DEVICE ON: $V_{IN(+)} \geqslant V_{IN(-)} + V_{THRESH(+)}$

DEVICE OFF: $V_{IN(+)} \leqslant V_{IN(-)} - |V_{THRESH(-)}|$

$V_{HYST} = V_{THRESH(+)} + |V_{THRESH(-)}|$

$V_{OFFSET} = \frac{1}{2} (V_{THRESH(+)} - |V_{THRESH(-)}|)$

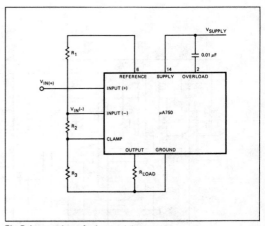

Fig. 5 Input resistors for hysteresis increase

A second special consideration are the relationships among ambient temperature, internal power dissipation and protection sensitivity to output current overloads. Dissipated power is composed of several terms which depend on the applications. These terms are affected by:

   a. BIAS current

   b. REFERENCE current

   c. CLAMP current

   d. OUTPUT current

These factors are described in Figures 6, 7 and 8.

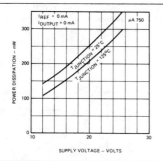

Fig. 6 Power dissipation due to bias current as a function of supply voltage

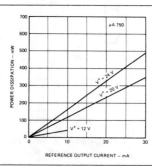

Fig. 7 Power dissipation due to reference output current as a function of supply voltage

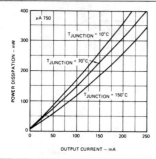

Fig. 8 Power dissipation as a function of output current (one side) and junction temperature

Because of the small clamp saturation voltage, the contribution by the clamp current is small and can be neglected in most applications. Figure 9, with Figures 6, 7, and 8, provide data to determine if, in a particular application, the device will shut itself off unless a heat sink is used.

To determine the highest operating temperature for a device under the following conditions:

Supply Voltage	24V
Output Current	50 mA/side
Clamp Current	20 mA (one side only)
Reference Current	10 mA

First, assume the maximum junction temperature, $150^\circ C$.

Then, from Graph 6:

$$P_{diss} \text{ for } V_{supply} = 24 \text{ V} \qquad 280 \text{ mW}$$

From Graph 7:

$$P_{diss} \text{ for } I_{REF} = 10 \text{ mA, } V^+ = 24 \text{ V} \qquad 170 \text{ mW}$$

From Graph 8:

$$P_{diss} \text{ for 50 mA/side A} \qquad 60 \text{ mW}$$

$$50 \text{ mA/side B} \qquad 60 \text{ mW}$$

for clamp current calculation the maximum saturation voltage given on the data sheet can be taken (= 0.8V)

$$P_{diss} \text{ Clamp} = 20 \text{ mA} \times 0.8V = \qquad 16 \text{ mW}$$

$$\text{Total } P_{diss} \text{ at } T_j = 150^\circ C: \qquad 586 \text{ mW}$$

Figure 9 shows that the device can be operated over the full temperature range up to $70^\circ C$ without requiring a heat sink. When a heat sink is required, then a thermal resistance of $50^\circ C/W$ should be used in the thermal calculations.

In a similar fashion, the OUTPUT CURRENT - TEMPERATURE - HEAT DISSIPATION question can be solved for other load and supply conditions. Figure 10 indicates that with lower junction temperature, the continuous output current can be increased subject to absolute maximum limits.

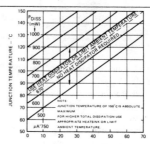

For higher total power dissipation, use external heat sink. To calculate overall thermal resistance, R_{TH} (junction to case) = $50^\circ C/W$ can be used. R_{TH} (junction to ambient) = $120^\circ C/W$.

Fig. 9 Junction temperature as a function of ambient temperature and power dissipation

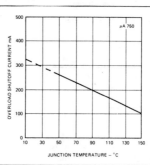

Fig. 10 Minimum overload shut off current as a function of junction temperature

The inputs of an unused comparator section should never be left open and at least one of the terminals, (preferably V_{IN} (-)), should always be connected to a positive voltage in the input voltage range. Connecting this terminal to the REFERENCE terminal is a convenient solution.

OVERLOAD PROTECTION

The overload protection circuit shuts off the device if the current through the sensing resistor reaches the built-in threshold level. This level is mirrored in the turn off threshold voltage between the SUPPLY and the OVERLOAD terminals. To prevent premature shut-down due to load current turn on transients, a .01 μF capacitor, is used between the OVERLOAD and SUPPLY terminals. This capacitor also prevents accidental triggering of the overload protection circuit due to noise. A capacitor value larger than 0.1 μF tends to reduce the effectiveness of the protection circuit and should not be used. A resistor/capacitor network (Figure 11), is recommended for desensitizing the μA750 to longer duration overload transients.

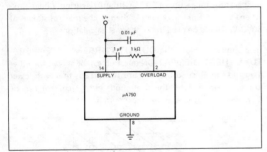

Fig. 11 Overload desensitizing for longer duration overloads

Although a direct connection between the OVERLOAD terminal to the SUPPLY terminal resets the device, it also disables the overload protection circuit which could damage the device. A safer reset circuit (Figure 12), allows the device to return to the shut off condition if an overload condition exists when attempting reset.

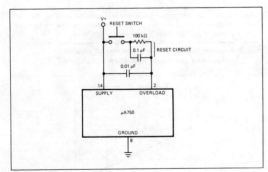

Fig. 12 Overload reset circuit

APPLICATIONS

The μA750 comparator is designed to perform a temperature sensing and direct relay driving function while operating from a single dc power supply. Built-in hysteresis, an on chip reference voltage and several internal chip protection features allow

precise temperature control circuitry with a minimum of external components as shown in the combined heater/air conditioner control in Figure 13.

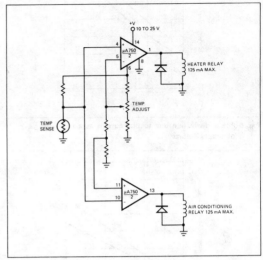

Fig. 13 Combined heater/air conditioner control

If the internal device hysteresis is insufficient, the clamp outputs of the μA750 can be used to increase the switching window (Figure 14).

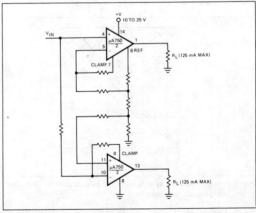

Fig. 14 Increased switching window

In high electrical noise environments, the strobe control leads can be used to advantage (Figure 15). Note that the inhibit does not change the state of the output latch when applied but is only used to preserve the previous information until the next sample time.

MALFUNCTION INDICATOR

The variety of functions built into the μA750 make this device useful over a wide range of applications not normally associated with integrated circuit comparators. One such application is a malfunction indicator with priority override.

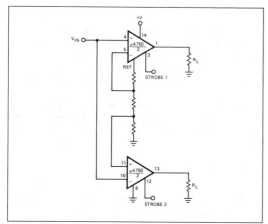

Fig. 15 Inhibit circuit

In any complex system, a variety of possible failures with varying levels of importance exists. With human operators for system control, only the most important problem, or series of problems, should be displayed in case of malfunction.

The malfunction indicator circuit in Figure 16 monitors system parts A, B, C and D with the order of priority starting with A. The outputs of the μA750s drive LEDs and a malfunction is recorded whenever the input voltages V_A, V_B, V_C or V_D exceed their corresponding threshold voltages (V_1, V_2, V_3, V_4). Stable threshold voltages can be obtained using a resistive divider from the reference output of the μA750s (Lead 6). This concept is expandable with additional comparators and gates as required.

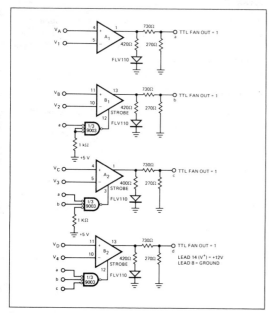

Fig. 16 Malfunction indicator

The malfunction indicator function indicated in Figure 16 can be used in a variety of analog Go/No-Go testing applications as shown in the analog status indicator.

ANALOG STATUS INDICATOR AND DISPLAY

In test equipment, it is often desirable to display certain test voltages when they are above, below or between two threshold voltages. The circuit in Figure 17 uses the source and sink outputs of the μA750 to perform this function.

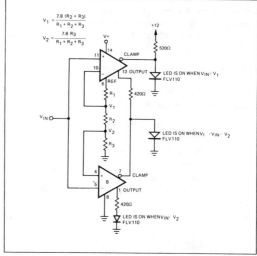

Fig. 17 Analog status indicator

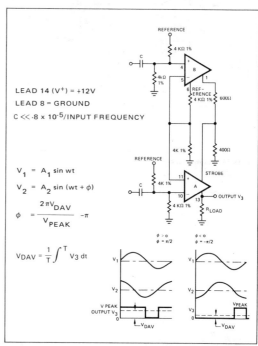

Fig. 18 Input/output examples

LOGIC FUNCTIONS

Simple logic can be performed by using the strobe inputs of the μA750 as shown in this phase meter application. The phase meter circuit in Figure 18 uses the μA750 strobe inputs as an inhibit to produce a pulse duration modulation representation of the input phase. This circuit does not have a coincidence pulse elimination feature, so phase coincidence (0° and 180°) must be avoided. Thus, operation in the $0^\circ - 180^\circ$ phase range is a tradeoff involving maximum input frequency, phase accuracy, and phase range. For example, a frequency of 1 MHz can be processed, but because of a typical 500 ns propagation delay, a static phase error of 10% is present at the output for each 100 ns difference in propagation delay between the two comparators.

MINIMUM FREQUENCY DETECTOR

Each comparator in the μA750 can be used for separate applications which, when connected, provide a total function.

The simple minimum frequency detector shown in Figure 19 uses input pulse conditioning to achieve predictable operation with varying input pulse levels and widths.

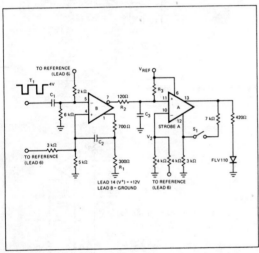

Fig. 19 Minimum frequency detector

When power is applied, capacitor C_3 starts charging towards V_{REF}. If the clamp output of the first comparator (B) goes low causing capacitor C_3 to discharge before the threshold voltage V_2 is reached, the output of comparator A is low and the display is off. However, if the voltage across capacitor C_3 reaches the threshold voltage V_2 before discharging, the output of A is high (ON). With S_1 closed, output A applies three volts to the STROBE A input and maintains drive to the display. The time required for the voltage across C_3 to reach V_2 is given by:

$$t_{Max} = R_3 C_3 \ln 2 \quad \text{or} \quad f_{Min} = \frac{1}{0.69\ R_3 C_3}$$

The LED is off when the frequency f_{IN} is higher than f_{Min} and turns on when f_{IN} has dropped to f_{Min}.

Comparator B is used as a one-shot, triggering on negative going edges with output low (OFF) for a time (t) determined by C_2 and R_1 (charging time of C_3). With R_3 selected as 10kΩ the circuit equations below ensure that C_2 and C_1 have sufficient time to return to the steady state conditions during the charging time of C_3.

CIRCUIT EQUATIONS (Units are Hz, seconds, and farads)

$$C_1 \leqslant 66 \times 10^{-6} T_1$$

$$C_3 \leqslant 0.14 \times 10^{-3}/f_{Min}$$

$$C_2 = 0.46\ C_3$$

CONCLUSION

The μA750 is a versatile integrated circuit with applications including the basic temperature control function and a wide range of circuits which can use to advantage the combination of precision comparison and high drive current.

ACKNOWLEDGEMENT

Appreciation to Mr. Moise Hamoui who did a substantial part of the application work described in this paper.

A MONOLITHIC ZERO-CROSSING AC TRIGGER (TRIGAC) FOR THYRISTOR POWER CONTROLS

Andy Adamian and Larry Blaser

INTRODUCTION

AC power control with thyristors (SCRs and triacs) can be accomplished by phase control or by zero-crossing switching, also referred to as synchronous switching. Both methods of power control are in common use, each with advantages and disadvantages.

Phase control permits continuously variable power to be applied to a load by controlling the conduction period during each half cycle. Consequently, the thyristor may turn on during any portion of a half cycle. The sudden increase in load current when turn-on occurs, especially near peak line voltages, results in high surge currents and considerable RFI (radio frequency interference) generation. In many applications, RFI is troublesome. In some applications, bulky and expensive filtering is required to reduce it to an acceptable level.

Zero-crossing control provides only ON-OFF operation of a load, but because switching between modes occurs at or very near the zero load current point of the ac cycle, RFI generation is reduced to a level where filtering is not normally required. Circuitry for thyristor triggering in zero-crossing controls is usually more complex than comparable phase control circuitry.

A zero-crossing ac trigger integrated circuit has been developed to take over control functions for triggering power thyristors previously performed by specialized discrete circuitry. The Fairchild μA742 zero-crossing ac trigger, or TRIGAC, operates as an interface element between a sensor bridge and a thyristor to provide ON-OFF power control with minimum RFI generation. The TRIGAC is the first monolithic IC to automatically provide zero-crossing control with either resistive or inductive loads; including loads such as motors, which exhibit variable phase angle characteristics during start-up and loading.

The TRIGAC has extremely flexible power supply requirements. The device may be powered through a dropping resistor directly from the ac line or from a dc power supply. A wide range of nominal ac or dc supply voltages can be accommodated by appropriate selection of the dropping resistor. Normal voltage variations in an ac supply or an unregulated dc supply will not adversely affect circuit operation.

CIRCUIT DESCRIPTION

The block diagram of Figure 1 shows a closed-loop control system using the TRIGAC. As indicated in the block diagram

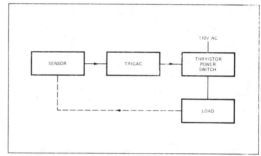

Fig. 1. Closed-Loop Control System Using the TRIGAC

by the dashed lines, feedback is obtained from the load to the TRIGAC via the sensor. Figure 2 shows a TRIGAC control circuit with its internal and external parts operating directly from a single ac supply. There are seven distinct functional sections in the TRIGAC:

1. Power Supply
2. Charge Control
3. Charging Network
4. Zero-Crossing Detector
5. Pulse Generator
6. Hysteresis Switch
7. Proportional Control Switch

Operation From an AC Supply

Figure 3 shows the various waveforms appearing at some of the TRIGAC terminals for both resistive and inductive loads. Note that the horizontal scales are referenced with respect to the ac line, shown on the top, Figure 3(a).

When operated directly from an ac line through dropping resistor, R_{DR}, zener diodes D_2, D_3, D_4 and diodes D_5, D_6 in the Power Supply Section provide a regulated supply of about +24 volts at lead 13 during the positive half cycles, (Figure 2). During the negative half cycles, due to the isolation diode D_1, this potential reverses to about -1.2 V as shown in Figure 3(d).

The Charge Control Section contains a conventional differential amplifier with a matched pair of transistors Q_1 and Q_2 fed by a constant current source, Q_3. Transistor Q_3 begins to

FAIRCHILD

SEMICONDUCTOR

A DIVISION OF FAIRCHILD CAMERA AND INSTRUMENT CORPORATION

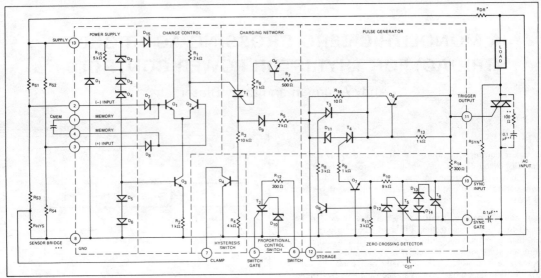

Fig. 2. TRIGAC Control Circuit with Internal and External Parts

conduct only after the supply voltage at lead 13 has exceeded about 15 volts or when diodes D_3 through D_6 conduct.

The inputs of the differential amplifier are connected to the Sensor Bridge Network. If the input to the differential amplifier is such that the voltage at lead two is higher than that at lead three, Q_1 conducts and keeps Q_2 off, the "inhibit" state. When the input to the differential amplifier is offset (lead three at a higher potential than lead two), Q_2 conducts and pulls current out of the anode-gate of thyristor T_1 in the Charging Network, causing T_1 to start conducting during the positive half cycles. This is the "trigger" state. As soon as T_1 conducts, it charges storage capacitor C_{ST} via D_9 and R_5 to a voltage equal to the supply voltage of lead 13 minus the drop across T_1 and D_9, approximately 22 volts. See Figure 3(e).

At the start of the next negative half cycle, Q_7 begins to conduct and causes T_4 to turn on due to the current pulled out of the anode-gate of T_4. Thyristor T_4 provides the base drive to Q_5 and Q_8. Thus, Q_8 turns on and switches part of the energy stored in the capacitor during the positive half cycle into the gate of the triac, thus causing the triac to turn on near the beginning of the negative half cycle, Figure 3(e) and (f).

As soon as the voltage across C_{ST} falls to about 8 volts, the current through T_4 falls below its holding current level and T_4 and Q_8 turn off. C_{ST} maintains this voltage for the remainder of the negative half cycle. At the start of the following positive half cycle, Q_6 is forward-biased again. T_3 and Q_8 conduct and the storage capacitor C_{ST} discharges to about 1 volt through R_{16} and Q_8. The high energy pulse generated triggers the triac near the start of the positive half cycle. As soon as the voltage across the triac collapses, base drive of Q_6 and consequently the current out of the anode-gate of T_3 is stopped. At the start of the next positive half cycle, Q_2 causes T_1 to turn on again. The storage capacitor charges up and thus the cycle continues until Q_1 and Q_2 revert to the inhibit state.

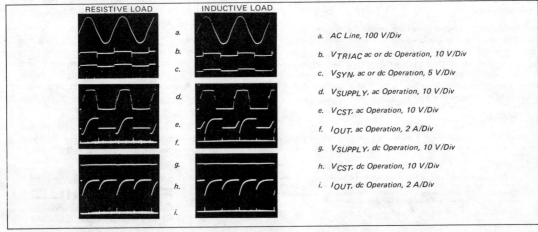

RESISTIVE LOAD	INDUCTIVE LOAD		
		a.	a. AC Line, 100 V/Div
		b.	b. V_{TRIAC} ac or dc Operation, 10 V/Div
		c.	c. V_{SYN}, ac or dc Operation, 5 V/Div
		d.	d. V_{SUPPLY}, ac Operation, 10 V/Div
		e.	e. V_{CST}, ac Operation, 10 V/Div
		f.	f. I_{OUT}, ac Operation, 2 A/Div
		g.	g. V_{SUPPLY}, dc Operation, 10 V/Div
		h.	h. V_{CST}, dc Operation, 10 V/Div
		i.	i. I_{OUT}, dc Operation, 2 A/Div

Fig. 3. TRIGAC Waveforms

Transistors Q_6 and Q_7, thyristors T_5 and T_6 and their associated components form the Zero-Crossing Detector. They provide the necessary control to ensure that trigger output pulses supplied by the Pulse Generator Section are delivered to the thyristor power switch near the zero-crossing of the load current. Early in the positive half cycles, Q_6 is forward-biased via resistors R_{SYN} and R_{10}. When the anode voltage of T_5 exceeds the zener voltage of D_{12}, about eight volts, T_5 switches on and causes the sync input voltage at lead 10 to collapse to about one volt, turning off Q_6 and removing the drive from T_5. See Figure 3(b) and (c). This ensures that if T_3 is to turn on, it does so only within the first few volts of the positive half cycle. The storage capacitor begins to charge only after diodes D_3 through D_6 have started conducting, or when the supply voltage at lead 13 has reached about 15 volts. The charging and discharging of the storage capacitor occur at two distinct times. During the first positive half cycle coinciding with or immediately following the start of conduction of Q_2, current flows out of the anode-gate of T_3 (through Q_6) within the first eight volts of the positive half cycle but does not turn T_3 on due to the absence of voltage on the storage capacitor. A little later during the same positive half cycle, when the supply voltage at lead 13 reaches about 15 volts, the storage capacitor begins to charge. Its voltage rises to about 22 volts during the remainder of the half cycle and retains this value. See Figure 3(e).

The Hysteresis Switch Section contains transistor Q_4. As Figure 2 illustrates, every time T_1 is turned on Q_4 is also turned on, shunts the hysteresis resistor R_{HYS} and enhances the trigger state condition. Transistor Q_2 then turns on harder and supplies positive feedback to the differential amplifier. To supplement the hysteresis function performed by Q_4, memory capacitor C_{MEM} charges during the positive half cycle of the ac line according to the input conditions at leads two and three and "remembers" it for the next cycle. Diodes D_7 and D_8 prevent the charge stored on the capacitor from draining during the next negative half cycle, but at the start of the next positive half cycle, C_{MEM} causes transistor Q_2 to turn on. Therefore, the storage capacitor starts charging at the beginning of that positive half cycle regardless of the condition of the sensor bridge. The transfer characteristic of this mode of operation is given in Figure 4. Note that if the hysteresis feature is not used, Figure 5, S_1 and S_2 in Figure 4 coincide. In this mode of operation, an intermediate state exists as the magnitude of the plus and minus inputs approach each other, and the TRIGAC may supply trigger output pulses in an undetermined manner which could cause skip firing (a few cycles on, a few cycles off) to occur. The width of this band is about 3 mV, and as mentioned, it is eliminated when the hysteresis feature is used.

Proportional control, a means of controlling ON-OFF ratio, is another feature available with the TRIGAC and is shown in Figure 6. It provides the precise control needed in some temperature controls as well as the proportional control function needed for ON-OFF ac flashers. This function is achieved by using thyristor T_2 in the Proportional Control Switch Section to develop a ramp function which is superimposed upon the bridge input signal through the 200 kΩ resistor. Once the voltage on lead six reaches about eight volts, T_2 switches into conduction and lowers the input voltage to lead three, causing Q_2 to turn off. As the ramp voltage on lead six starts to increase again, the input to lead three also increases. The level on the ramp at which Q_2 conducts determines how long the load remains energized.

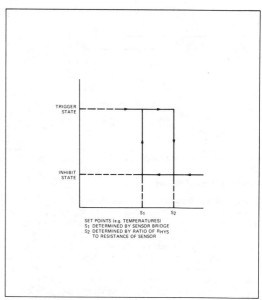

Fig. 4. Transfer Characteristic of Hysteresis Control Operation

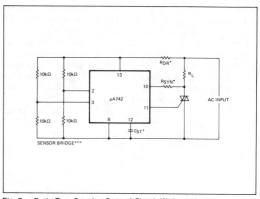

Fig. 5. Basic Zero-Crossing Control Circuit Without Hysteresis

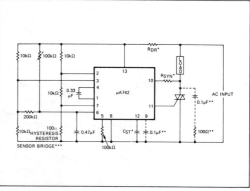

Fig. 6. Zero-Crossing with Proportional Control

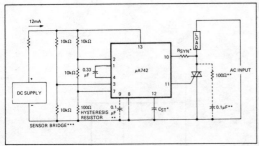

Fig. 7. Zero-Crossing Circuit with dc Supply

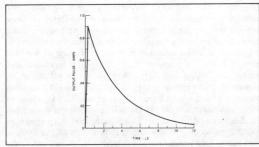

Fig. 8. Typical Trigger Output Pulse (Resistive Load, ac Operation, Beginning of Positive Half Cycles)

Operation from a DC Supply

The connection diagram for dc operation is given in Figure 7 while some of the waveshapes appear in Figure 3(g), 3(h) and 3(i). In this mode, the constant supply voltage keeps the differential amplifier in operation, (Figure 2). Therefore, regardless of the instantaneous polarity of the ac line, the storage capacitor C_{ST} starts charging as soon as T_1 is triggered on by Q_2, see Figure 3(h). Let us now examine the transition from the inhibit state to the trigger state occurring during a positive half cycle of the ac supply. At the beginning of the next negative half cycle, Q_7 is forward-biased, and just as in the ac operation mode, T_4 turns on forward-biasing Q_8 and Q_5. Transistor Q_8 produces an output trigger pulse at the beginning of this half cycle while Q_5 pulls current out of the cathode-gate of T_1, causing it to turn off every time T_3 or T_4 is turned on. Note that in the ac mode of operation, T_1 turns off at the end of each positive half cycle by the natural reversal of the line voltage, and Q_5 does not perform any function. However, since the TRIGAC is powered through a dc supply and Q_2 is assumed conducting, T_1 turns on again as soon as Q_5 turns off and recharges C_{ST} to about 22 volts. With the next half cycle (positive), Q_6 is forward-biased, and similarly, a trigger output pulse is delivered to the triac. Transistor Q_5 pulls current out of the cathode-gate of T_1, turning it off. This time C_{ST} discharges to about one volt. However, when Q_2 turns T_1 on again, C_{ST} recharges to about 22 volts and the cycle continues. See Figure 3(h) and (i).

Assume that the transition from "inhibit" to "trigger" takes place during a negative half cycle of the ac line. At the beginning of the next half cycle, Q_6 is forward-biased and this time T_3 turns on first, forward-biasing Q_8 and Q_5. The triac, therefore, conducts initially at the start of a positive half cycle. The rest of the operation is similar to the previous description. When the input to the differential amplifier reverts back to the inhibit state, the TRIGAC stops delivering output pulses. Then the triac starts blocking, always beginning with a negative half cycle.

INPUT/OUTPUT CHARACTERISTICS OF THE TRIGAC

The typical input bias current of the differential amplifier is on the order of $5\,\mu A$. Because of this low value, the TRIGAC can be used with high impedance sensors such as photocells, thermistors (NTC or PTC) and pressure transducers as well as low impedance networks such as the output of a digital counter or a flip-flop. The exact location of the sensor in the Sensor Bridge legs has deliberately been omitted because this depends on the sensor characteristics and on the type of feedback relationship desired between the load and the sensor.

The magnitude of the trigger output pulse varies with the type of supply, ac or dc, and the type of load used. It should be noted that the storage capacitor voltage switching level determines the peak value of this pulse, see Figure 3(e), 3(f), 3(h) and 3(i). The highest output pulse is obtained in dc operation (with any load) at the beginning of positive half cycles and is typically 2.2 A peak. The lowest pulse is obtained in ac operation with a resistive load, also at the beginning of positive half cycles and it is typically 0.9 A peak. The wave-shape of a 0.9 A output trigger pulse is shown in Figure 8.

APPLICATIONS

In addition to the circuits already described, the TRIGAC can be used with an SCR in a half wave circuit, Figure 9, or with a pair of inverse-parallel SCRs, Figures 10 and 11. Inverse-parallel SCR schemes can be used to extend the capabilities of the TRIGAC beyond present current, voltage and operating frequency limitations of triacs. The inverse-parallel SCRs in Figure 10 are triggered on by the pulse transformer. Those in

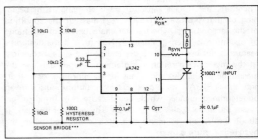

Fig. 9. SCR Firing — Half Wave

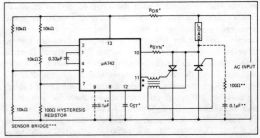

Fig. 10. Inverse-Parallel SCR Pair Firing with a Pulse Transformer

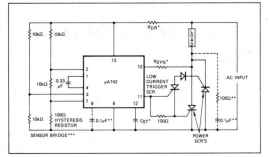

Fig. 11. Inverse-Parallel SCR Pair Firing with a Third SCR

Figure 11 are triggered on via the low current trigger SCR. It is interesting that during the negative half cycles, the low current SCR is used in the remote base operation mode (like a PNP transistor) and supplies the trigger output current from lead 11 through its gate and out of its anode to the gate of the power SCR on the right, turning it on.

Some TRIGAC applications may require complete isolation between the load and the sensor. Figure 12 shows an isolated system connection for a resistive load. Note that the synchronizing input to the TRIGAC is derived directly from the secondary of step down transformer T_2; therefore, this circuit is suitable for use with resistive loads only. Figure 13 shows another isolated system usable with any load but at the expense of an additional current sensing transformer T_3 which supplies the synchronizing input to the TRIGAC.

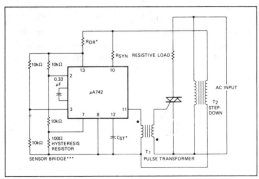

Fig. 12. Isolated System — Resistive Load

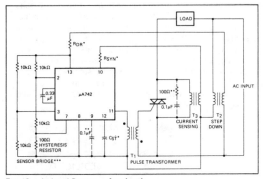

Fig. 13. Isolated System — Any Load

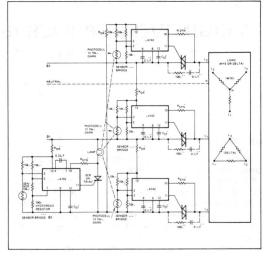

Fig. 14. Zero-Crossing Switching for a Three-Phase System

The TRIGAC can easily be adapted for use with multi-phase power systems. Figure 14 shows a zero-crossing trigger circuit for a three phase system with a wye or delta-connection. The SCR, its associated TRIGAC, sensor and lamp load slave operate as a master control to drive the three main power triacs by coupling the light output of the lamp to the photocells used in the sensor bridges of the slave TRIGACS.

*Recommended Values

AC Supply Voltage 60 Hz Volts - RMS	R_{DR}	R_{SYN}	C_{ST}
24	0.5 kΩ	2.2 kΩ	0.47 μF/25 V
110	10 kΩ	10 kΩ	0.47 μF/25 V
220	22 kΩ	22 kΩ	0.47 μF/25 V

FOR SUPPLY VOLTAGE FREQUENCY OF 400 Hz REDUCE C_{ST} TO .047 μF/25 V

**Necessary with inductive loads.

***The sensor resistance will determine the values of the bridge resistors. For the values of R_{DR} shown, the total current into the bridge should not exceed 5 mA.

CONCLUSION

A monolithic ac trigger or TRIGAC is available for triggering SCRs and triacs in thyristor power control systems which operate in an ON-OFF mode. Because trigger pulses are delivered only during line current zero-crossings, RFI generation is minimized. The TRIGAC may be powered through a dropping resistor directly off an ac line or by a separate ac or dc supply. It provides ON-OFF control to either resistive or inductive loads over a wide range of applications including oven heaters, ac flashers and air conditioners.

A HIGH OUTPUT POWER (5 WATT), LOW DISTORTION, IC AUDIO AMPLIFIER

John W. Chu

INTRODUCTION

The μA706 is an audio power amplifier suited for applications in audio systems which can operate on 14 V nominal supplies. At this voltage, the μA706 can deliver 5.5 W continously, to a 4Ω load. The μA706 is suitable for television receivers, and for industrial applications requiring high output power, low distortion, and reliable performance. Unique features of this circuit include low standby current, direct coupling to input, and self-centering bias at supply voltages from 6 V to 16 V. These features make the μA706 very desirable for almost any portable audio application.

FUNCTIONAL DESCRIPTION

The complete schematic of the μA706 audio power amplifier is shown in Figure 1. The circuit is considered as two sections, the preamplifier and the power amplifier.

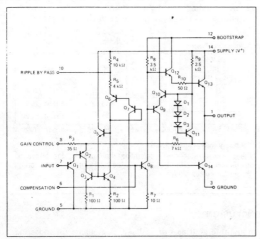

Fig. 1. μA706 Schematic

Basically, the preamplifier is a single stage, common emitter amplifier with an input buffer transistor (Q_1), a gain transistor (Q_2), a current source (Q_3) and associated bias circuitry. Q_1 is a high current gain pnp transistor providing 3 MΩ input resistance and a level shift allowing input signal reference to ground. Q_2 is a high gain, common emitter

amplifier with a high impedance collector load provided by current source Q_3. The voltage gain of the stage can be expressed as:

$$A_{VOL} = \frac{1/[Y_{22(Q_3)} + Y_{11(Q_8)}]}{r_{e(Q_2)}} \quad (1)$$

where $r_e = \dfrac{kT/q}{I_{E(Q2)}}$ = intrinsic emitter resistance of Q_2

$Y_{22(Q_3)}$ = output admittance of the current source transistor Q_3,

$Y_{11(Q_8)}$ = input admittance of transistor Q_8.

Preamplifier gain, using Equation 1, is approximately 100.

The preamplifier output is coupled directly to the power amplifier, which consists of a gain transistor (Q_8), the output transistors, and the bias circuitry. To determine power amplifier gain:

$$A_{VOL} = \frac{R_8}{r_e(Q_8) + R_7} = \frac{3500}{25 + 10} = 100 \quad (2)$$

The output stage is a quasi-complementary Push/Pull amplifier operating in class AB, meaning the transistors are biased to achieve a conduction angle slightly greater than 180°. With a voltage source drive, class AB distortion only results from variations in V_{BE} (ON), negligible during the conduction period, and crossover distortion is minimized. Output power transistors Q_{13} and Q_{14} are buffered by Q_{12} and Q_9, and they are coupled directly to the collector of Q_8. The standby current of the output transistors is controlled by the current through resistor R_9, which sets up a voltage across D_1, D_2, D_3 and Q_{11}. This voltage appears across the emitter base junctions of Q_9, Q_{10}, Q_{12} and

Q_{13}, so the standby current is equal to the current in R_9, multiplying by a geometry factor. The following equations (refer to Figure 1) prove this relationship.

$$V_{D_1} + V_{D_2} + V_{D_3} + V_{BE_{11}} =$$

$$V_{BE_{10}} + V_{BE_9} + V_{BE_{12}} + V_{BE_{13}} \qquad (3)$$

Thus,

$$\frac{kT}{q}\left\{ \ln\frac{I_{R_9}}{A_{D_1}h_{FE_{11}}} + \ln\frac{I_{R_9}}{A_{D_2}h_{FE_{11}}} + \ln\frac{I_{R_9}}{A_{D_3}h_{FE_{11}}} + \ln\frac{I_{R_9}}{A_{11}} \right\} =$$

$$\frac{kT}{q}\left\{ \ln\frac{I_0}{A_9h_{FE_{14}}} + \ln\frac{I_0}{A_{10}h_{FE_{14}}} + \ln\frac{I_0}{A_{12}h_{FE_{13}}} + \ln\frac{I_0}{A_{13}} \right\} \quad (4)$$

where I_0 is the standby current of the complementary output stage and A is the emitter area of a transistor or a diode,

Solving Equation 4 for I_0,

$$I_0 = I_{R_9} \sqrt[4]{\frac{A_9A_{10}A_{12}A_{13}}{A_{D_1}A_{D_2}A_{D_3}A_{11}} \frac{(h_{FE_{13}})(h_{FE_{14}})^2}{(h_{FE_{11}})^3}} \quad (5)$$

where

$$I_{R_9} = \frac{V^+/2 - (V_{D_1} + V_{D_2} + V_{D_3} + V_{BE_{11}})}{R_9} \quad (6)$$

At a supply voltage of 14 V, and at room temperature, I_0 is approximately 15 mA.

A negative feedback is applied from the output of the power amplifier to the emitter of Q_2 through resistor R_6 to achieve good linearity and low distortion. The combined open loop voltage gain of the two stages is typically 10,000 (80 dB). The closed loop voltage gain of the amplifier is determined by resistors R_6 and R_3 and a series R-C network on lead 8, external to the device. This external R-C network provides gain selection options to system designers. The closed loop gain of the amplifier is expressed as:

$$A_V = \frac{R_6}{R_3 + Z_{external}} \quad (7)$$

where $Z_{external}$ is the impedance presented by the the series R-C network. Thus, the maximum voltage gain available is determined.

$$\frac{R_6}{R_3} = 200 \text{ (46 dB)}$$

At the maximum voltage gain of 46 dB, feedback is approximately 35 dB, and total harmonic distortion (THD) is typically less than 0.5% with $R_L = 4\Omega$. With less gain, feedback increases and THD is reduced to approximately 0.2%. To ob-

tain closed loop stability, a dominant single pole response is set by an external capacitor (C_c) from the high impedance collector of Q_3 (lead 6) to ground. The bandwidth of the amplifier is cut by an external R-C network connected between leads 1 and 6.

DESIGN CONSIDERATIONS

For symmetrical clipping and efficiency, the output should be biased at half the supply. To accomplish this bias, Q_3 and Q_4 are identical transistors with identical emitter degeneration resistors. They are located close together on an isothermal line to equalize their temperatures. Their bases are connected together, so obviously their collector currents are equal. The current in Q_4 is set by the voltage across R_4 and R_5, which is the supply voltage minus the voltage drops of the emitter base diodes of Q_6, Q_7, Q_5 and Q_4.

$$I_{Q4} = \frac{V^+ - 4V_{BE}}{R_4 + R_5} \quad (8)$$

The current in Q_3 comes from the output through R_6. If the input is connected to ground, the voltage across R_6 is the output voltage minus two diode voltage drops.

$$I_{Q3} = \frac{V_{OUT} - 2V_{BE}}{R_6} \quad (9)$$

Because Equation 8 and Equation 9 are equal, $(I_{Q3} = I_{Q4})$,

$$\frac{V^+ - 4V_{BE}}{R_4 + R_5} = \frac{V_{OUT} - 2V_{BE}}{R_6} \quad (10)$$

With $R_4 + R_5 = 2 R_6$, the only solution for Equation 10 is

$$V_{OUT} = \frac{V^+}{2} \quad (11)$$

The most significant feature of this design is the device ability to deliver more than 5 W output power with a 14 V supply and a 4Ω load. The voltage swing required is:

$$V = \sqrt{5\,W \times 4\,\Omega} \quad = 4.47\,V \quad (12)$$

$$(12.65\,V \text{ peak-to-peak})$$

Therefore, total loss on the positive and negative excursions of the amplifier output must not exceed 1.3 V for nominal 14 V operation. Now, the voltage swing of the amplifier is limited by the drive circuit to the output devices and the $V_{CE\,(sat)}$ of the output devices (Q_{13} and Q_{14}).

The drive circuit limitation is overcome with a technique known as "boot-strapping". An output voltage of the same polarity as the input voltage injects a current to the input equal to the current drawn from the driving source. Consequently, the source need not supply current and this limitation is eliminated. The collector load of Q_8 and the collectors of Q_{10} and Q_{12} are connected to lead 12. The output load is connected to the positive supply through a capacitor to the amplifier output, so it bears a voltage across it which swings above and below the positive supply. Connecting lead 12 to the load insures sufficient drive to the output transistors and the output swing is then limited only by the saturation voltage of Q_{13} and Q_{14}.

The second voltage swing limitation, the saturation resistance of power transistors, is reduced by a special processing technique. Figure 2 illustrates that the saturation resistance of an integrated power transistor is controlled by three variables:

1. R_{Epi}, epitaxial layer resistance in the emitter region,

2. R_C, collector series resistance, and

3. R_{BL}, the buried layer resistance

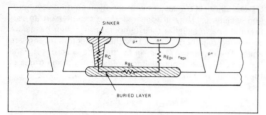

Fig. 2. Diffused Collector Sinker for Power Transistors

R_C and R_{Epi} can both be reduced by using a low resistivity epitaxial material. However, this also reduces collector-to-base breakdown voltage and is not desirable. A better alternative is special diffused collector sinker as shown in Figure 2. The material is highly doped and thus creates a low resistance path for the collector current. R_{BL}, quite small because the sheet resistivity of the buried layer is low, is not an important factor. The $V_{CE\,(sat)}$ of a power transistor made with this technique is more than adequate for the peak-to-peak voltage swing requirements of this circuit. Figure 3 is a photomicrograph of the device. Note that two power transistors occupy about 60% of the 60 x 62 mil chip area.

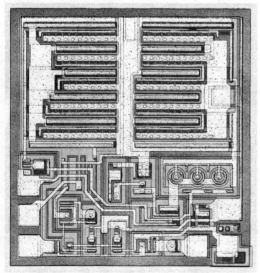

Fig. 3. µA706 Photomicrograph

Table 1 shows performance of the µA706. Figure 4 shows the test circuit. At a supply voltage of 14 V, the device can deliver 5.5 W into a $4\,\Omega$ load with less than 10% total harmonic distortion (THD). The distortion at high output levels is caused by clipping. Figure 5 is a plot of THD as a function of output power. Figure 6 shows THD as a function of frequency.

PARAMETER	CONDITIONS	TYPICAL VALUE
Total Supply Current	$P_{OUT} = 0$	18 mA
Quiescent Current in Output Transistors	$P_{OUT} = 0$	15 mA
Input Bias Current		200 nA
DC Output Level	$R_S = 22\,k$	7 V
Voltage Gain, A_V	$R_B = 0$	46 dB
Output Power, P_{OUT}	THD = 10%, f = 1 kHZ, A_V = 46 dB	5.5 W
Total Harmonic Distortion	f = 1 kHZ, A_V = 46 dB	
	P_{OUT} = 50 mW	0.3 %
	P_{OUT} = 2 W	0.5 %
	P_{OUT} = 4.5 W	3.0 %
Equivalent Input Noise Voltage	$R_S = 22\,k$ B.W. = 10 kHZ	3.5 µV
Total Supply Current	P_{OUT} = 4.5 W	510 mA
Input Impedance	A_V = 46 dB, f = 1 kHZ	3 M
DC Voltage at Ripple By Pass Terminal	$P_{OUT} = 0$	5.9 V
DC Voltage at Gain Control Terminal	$P_{OUT} = 0$	1.3 V
DC Voltage at Compensation Terminal	$P_{OUT} = 0$	0.7 V

Table I Typical Electrical Performance of the uA706 5 Watt Audio Amplifier (V+ = 14 V, $R_L = 4\,\Omega$ T_A = 25°C, ⊖C-A = 13°C/W, Test Circuit 1 unless otherwise specified)

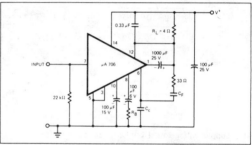

Fig. 4. Test Circuit 1 (A_V = 46 dB, R_B = 0Ω, C_C = 1.5 nF, C_F = 150 pF)

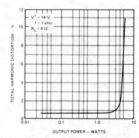

Fig. 5. Total Harmonic Distortion as a Function of Output Power

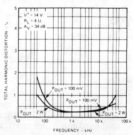

Fig. 6. Total Harmonic Distortion as a Function of Frequency

HEAT SINKING

Generally, μA706 applications require heat sinks. Each use requires a different heat sink capability. A proper evaluation of heat sink requirements must consider the μA706 package. The consumer nature of the device application requires a low cost, reliable package. A modified plastic Dual In-Line package with a copper heat sink, (Figure 7) was selected. The package lead frame is soldered to a copper heat sink. This copper heat sink is exposed at the top of the package allowing the user to further heat sink the device for a specific application. The measured thermal resistance between the junction of the device to the top of the copper slug is 11°C/W. An optional copper bracket may be soldered to the top side of the device to serve as a mechanical support as well as a heat path to a heat sink. Figure 8 is a photograph of the packages.

Figure 9 shows power dissipation as a function of output power, the maximum power dissipation is 3 W for the conditions specified. At an ambient temperature of 85°C, the junction-to-ambient thermal resistance required to insure a junction temperature less than 150°C is

$$\Theta_{J-A} \leq \frac{T_J - T_A}{P_d} = \frac{150°C - 85°C}{3\,W} \simeq 22°C/W \quad (13)$$

The junction-to-ambient thermal resistance for a type A package (without the bracket) is 73°C/W; for a type B package (with the bracket) 55°C/W. These exceed the required 22°C/W. Additional heat sinking is therefore required. A heat sink of 10°C/W is needed in this case, because the Θ_{J-C} of the package (type B) is 12°C/W.

Several heat sink applications are plausible. Figure 10 shows a commercially available heat sink for a type B package. Junction-to-ambient thermal resistance of a type B package improves to approximately 21°C/W with this heat sink.* Another approach uses a 2-sided copper PC board as a radiator for type B packages. The top side acts as a heat radiator for the device and the bottom side carries the usual traces. The bracket is soldered to the top of the PC board. With a PC board 3.5″ x 4.5″ in size, a thermal resistance of 22°C/W

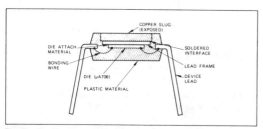

Fig. 7. Profile of the μA706 Power Plastic DIP Package

Fig. 8. High Power Plastic DIP Packages

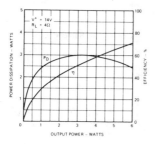

Fig. 9. Power Dissipation and Efficiency as a Function of Output Power

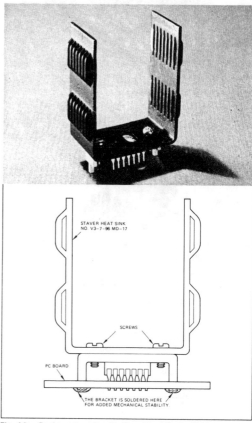

Fig. 10. Package type B with Commercially Available Heat Sink

*V3-7-96MD-17, Staver Company, 41-51 N. Saxon Ave. Bay Shore, N.Y. 11707

361

is achieved. Figure 11, two µA706 devices in an FM stereo receiver, shows that sinks for the devices are incorporated on the top of the PC board.

Figure 12 shows a Thermalloy* DIP heat sink attached directly to a type A package. Although the junction-to-ambient thermal resistance is improved only to about 50°C/W (#6010 Thermalloy), it does serve the purpose of showing how it can be done for applications which only require 50°C/W thermal resistance.

Figures 13 and 14 plot maximum power dissipation as a function of ambient temperature for the type A and B packages, respectively. The effect of heat sinking is clearly indicated.

APPLICATIONS

The most obvious applications of the µA706 are as audio power amplifiers in auto radios and portable radios and TVs or similar applications. It operates at voltages ranging from 6 V to 16 V, allowing direct operation from almost any combination of supply voltages.

5-W Audio Amplifier

Figure 15, an application with the speaker load connected between the output and ground, is a contrast to Figure 4, with the speaker load connected between the output and the supply. This is at the expense of two additional components; a 47Ω resistor and a 220 µF capacitor. These two components accomplish bootstrapping because the load resistors and the coupling capacitors can no longer be shared for this

Fig. 11. µA706 Stereo Amplifier

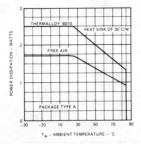

Fig. 12. Package type A with Thermalloy DIP Heat Sink No. 6010

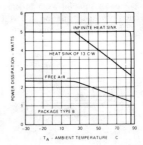

Fig. 14. Maximum Allowable Power Dissipation for Package type B as a Function of Ambient Temperature

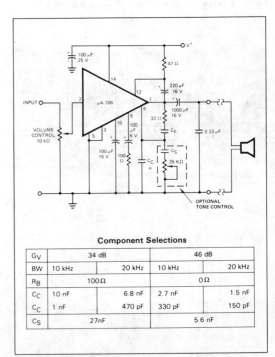

Component Selections

G_V	34 dB		46 dB	
BW	10 kHz	20 kHz	10 kHz	20 kHz
R_B	100Ω		0Ω	
C_C	10 nF	6.8 nF	2.7 nF	1.5 nF
C_C	1 nF	470 pF	330 pF	150 pF
C_S	27nF		5.6 nF	

Fig. 15. 5-Watt Audio Amplifier with Speaker Load Connected to Ground

Fig. 13. Maximum Allowable Power Dissipation for Package type A as a Function of Ambient Temperature

*Thermalloy Company, 8717 Diplomacy Row, Dallas, Texas 75247

purpose. Note that optional tone control is included. The value of C_S is selected for 3 dB gain fall-off at 4 kHz. A guide to component selection for different gain levels and band-widths is included in Figure 15. Figure 16 is a PC board lay-out for this circuit.

The stability of this amplifier is established by a single pole roll-off with an external capacitor (C_C) connected between the high impedance collector of Q_3 (lead 6) and ground. However, high current flow in the ground lead may cause ground loop system instability. Lead inductance and input pick-up (due to high impedance input) can also present a problem. Circuit designers must consider the following when laying out circuit boards.

- Leads three and five (grounds) must be as close as possible to one ground. This avoids possible ground loop problems.

- The output coupling capacitor (1000 µF) must be close to the output terminal to avoid lead in-ductance.

- The capacitor across the speaker terminals (.33 µF) should be close to the output coupling capacitor to insure that speaker and lead inductances are swamped.

- Input and output leads must be separated.

10-W Audio Amplifier

Two µA706 circuits can drive a load in a bridge configuration, increasing output power to 10 W (Figure 17).

High Performance FM Stereo Receiver

Figure 18 is a block diagram of an integrated circuit FM Stereo Receiver. Two µA706s are used as audio output amplifiers, one for each channel. The entire system uses only four transistors and five integrated circuits. Virtually all of the circuit functions from IF to the audio outputs are perform-ed by presently available low cost integrated circuits. Simpli-fied alignment requires only two or three adjustments.

CONCLUSION

The µA706 is an integrated power audio amplifier capable of delivering more than 5 W to a 4Ω load with a nominal 14 V supply voltage. A bootstrapping circuit combined with a spec-ial process technique resulted in a high peak-to-peak output voltage swing. A pair of these devices, connected in bridge configuration, forms a 10 W amplifier. Also, a high quality FM Stereo system (two µA706s) was described.

REFERENCE

"Integrated Circuits for FM Receivers, "David K. Long, pre-sented at SEMINEX, London, Engalnd, April, 1972.

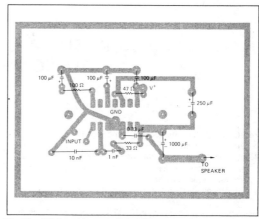

Fig. 16.   PC Board Layout of the 5 Watt µA706 Audio Amplifier

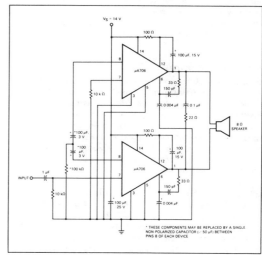

Fig. 17.   10-Watt Audio Amplifier

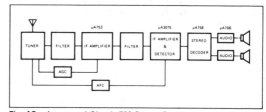

Fig. 18.   Integrated Circuit FM Stereo Receiver

232-21-0004-056   3M

20 W TO 60 W COMPLEMENTARY DARLINGTON AUDIO AMPLIFIERS

Hans Palouda

In recent years, there has been a trend toward higher power and better performance in the traditionally inexpensive record player/amplifier combinations and high fidelity receivers. Two amplifiers are described that are capable of supplying performance and power output specifications superior to any currently available integrated circuits at very low cost.

These amplifiers each use one TO-92 small-signal transistor and two Darlington power transistors. They provide flat frequency response up to 200 kHz with typical harmonic distortion below 0.2%. These performance specifications, along with the low parts count and high power output, illustrate the design advantages of TO-220 Darlingtons.

CIRCUIT DESCRIPTION (Figure 1)

The amplifiers utilize a complementary Darlington push-pull output, Q2 and Q3, driven by a Class A high-gain transistor Q1. Diodes D1 — D3 and R6 provide dc bias for the output transistors and set the idling current to about 20 mA, which reduces crossover distortion. The diodes are thermally connected to the heat sink to compensate for the shift in the base-emitter voltages of Q2 and Q3 with temperature. The diodes thus maintain a stable operating point and prevent thermal runaway of the output pair.

The center point A is fixed at half the supply voltage by the dc feedback consisting of R2, R3 and R4; in fact, the $V_{BE(on)}$ of transistor Q1 is multiplied. The voltage at the center point is adjusted with the potentiometer R4. Transistor Q1 is dc stabilized by local feedback achieved with a 150 Ω emitter resistor R5. To retain the high ac gain of Q1, R5 is bypassed by a 200 µF capacitor C4. The rolloff frequency of this combination is set at 5 Hz which is below the rolloff of the output C5 and R_L and, therefore, does not affect the low frequency response of the amplifier.

The ac gain, about 12, is set by the ratio of R3 and R1. Point B is the tiepoint of the feedback network and its ac potential is essentially held to zero. The 10 kΩ resistor R1 becomes the input resistance of the amplifier. A bootstrap capacitor C3 holds the voltage constant between the points A and C during the up and down swing of the ac output voltage. During the positive halfwave, point C rises above the supply voltage V_C thereby ensuring sufficient base drive into the output transistor Q2. The voltage across R7 differs from the voltage across C3 only by the $V_{BE(on)}$ of Q2 and is therefore also approximately constant, which means that Q2 and Q3 are driven from

a high impedance which acts like a current source. This helps lower the crossover distortion because the output transistors are controlled by their beta characteristics rather than their V_{BE} characteristics. Although the beta vs I_C characteristic is non-linear, it can be made linear by negative feedback, while the V_{BE} characteristic has a threshold below which there is no output at all. In this area, the open loop gain is zero and the feedback is ineffective.

If driven by a current source, the base voltages of the output transistors show a step across the V_{BE} threshold voltage. In practice, ideal steps do not exist in that the current source is not ideal; also, residual capacitances must be charged. Therefore, there is still some crossover distortion. To help the situation, the voltage step, if it cannot be ideal, can be made small; diodes D1 — D3 serve this purpose.

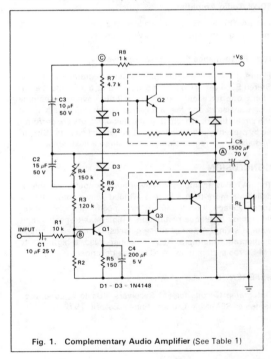

Fig. 1.   Complementary Audio Amplifier (See Table 1)

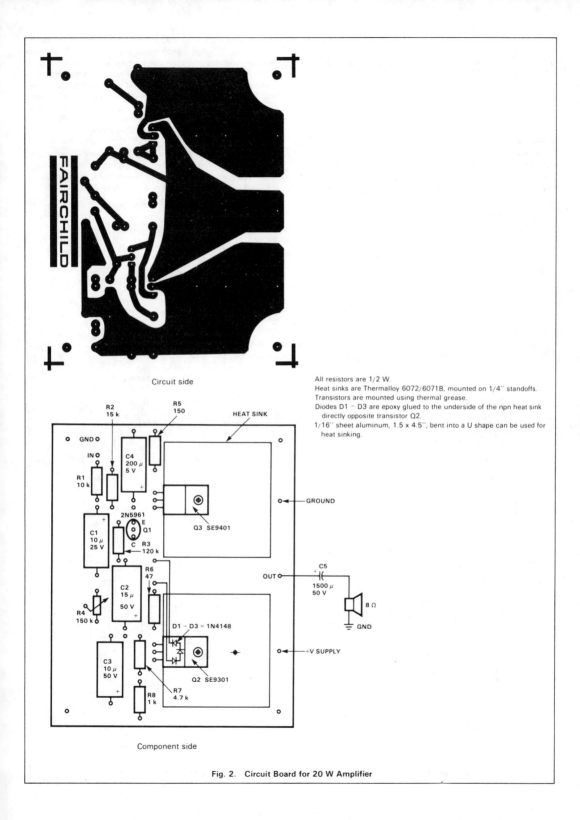

Circuit side

All resistors are 1/2 W.
Heat sinks are Thermalloy 6072/6071B, mounted on 1/4'' standoffs.
Transistors are mounted using thermal grease.
Diodes D1 – D3 are epoxy glued to the underside of the npn heat sink
    directly opposite transistor Q2.
1/16'' sheet aluminum, 1.5 x 4.5'', bent into a U shape can be used for
    heat sinking.

Component side

Fig. 2.   Circuit Board for 20 W Amplifier

Five different amplifiers are described, all using the same circuit with different output transistors and supply voltages. Plastic TO-220 Darlingtons are used to achieve 20 W into an 8 Ω load. With TO-3 packaged devices and increased power supplies, the circuit delivers 40 W into a 4 Ω or an 8 Ω load. With specially SOA-selected output transistors, the circuit becomes a 50 W amplifier into 8 Ω or 60 W into 4 Ω (see *Table 1*). The circuit board is shown in *Figure 2*.

PERFORMANCE

The frequency response is flat within 1 dB from 20 Hz for an 8 Ω load and from 50 Hz for 4 Ω load, up to above 200 kHz (*Figure 3*). The low end is limited by C5, R_L, the high end by the frequency response of the output transistors. Although the response is flat to 200 kHz, distortion increases above 70 kHz due to large-signal crossover distortion. This stems from the inability of Darlington transistors to turn off quickly because of stored base charge. This also leads to higher dissipation due to common-mode conduction. Since audio signals do not carry high amplitudes above 20 kHz, the frequency response is excellent for all practical purposes. For highly inductive loads, an RC circuit placed across the load R_L can be useful to increase stability at high frequencies.

The harmonic distortion is low for such a simple circuit and permits hi-fi reproduction. Between 2% and 50% of the rated output power, the distortion is below 0.2%. It runs below 0.5% up to the rated output power (*Figure 4*).

P_{OUT} Nominal	20	40	40	50	60	W
P_{OUT} (0.5% Distortion)	21.4	43	42	52	60	W
Supply Voltage, V_S	40	55	42	60	50	V
Load Resistance, R_L	8	8	4	8	4	Ω
Input Transistor, Q1	2N5961	2N5830	2N5830	2N5830	2N5830	
Output Transistor, Q2	SE9301	SE9304	SE9304	SE9304	SE9304	
Q3	SE9401	SE9404	SE9404	SE9404	SE9404	
Special SOA Selection of Q2 and Q3	—	—	—	45 V, 2.4 A	30 V, 5A	
Q2, Q3 Package	TO-220	TO-3	TO-3	TO-3	TO-3	
Max Permissible Case Temperature of Q2, Q3, $T_{C(max)}$	103	107	103	118	112	°C
Heat Sink for each Q2, Q3	6.5	3.5	2.3	4.0	2.2	max °C/W
Heat Sink for $T_{C(max)} = 100°C$	6.0	3.2	2.1	2.6	1.4	°C/W
Resistor R2	15	12	15	12	12	kΩ
Input Voltage for Maximum Output	1.2	1.6	1.25	1.75	1.5	V_{RMS}

Table 1. Circuit Specifications

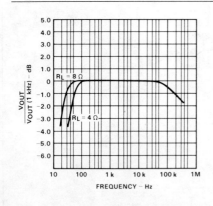

Fig. 3. Normalized Frequency Response

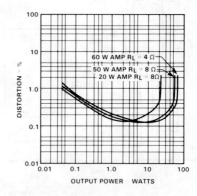

Fig. 4. Total Harmonic Distortion

Excellent square-wave performance at 10 kHz indicates wide bandwidth and very good transient response. The input impedance is 10 kΩ over the entire frequency range. The output impedance is lower than 150 mΩ for most of the range *(Figure 5)* but, at low frequencies, it rises because of the output capacitance C5.

Sensitivity

The amplification is 12 (26 dB), and the necessary input voltage for maximum output power is from 1.2 V for the 20 W amplifier to 1.75 V for the 50 W amplifier (see *Table 1*). The sensitivity can be increased by lowering the input resistance.

Heatsinking

Table 1 shows the maximum allowable case temperatures and the value of the heat sinks for each output transistor. Also listed are heat sinks that will hold the temperature of the transistors below 100°C.

CONCLUSION

This is a simple and, therefore, inexpensive circuit with excellent performance. The high gain of the output Darlingtons results in low harmonic distortion; listening quality is excellent due to low transient distortion.

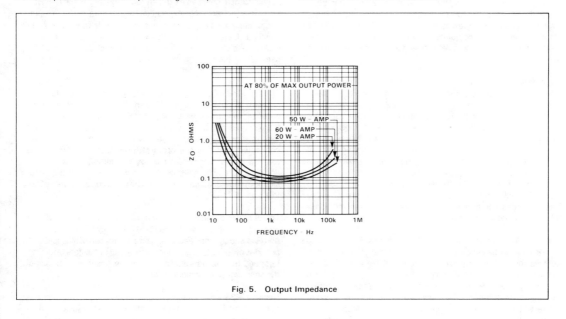

Fig. 5.   Output Impedance

75W HI FI AUDIO AMPLIFIER WITH LOW TRANSIENT INTERMODULATION DISTORTION

Hans Palouda

Until very recently, the trend in hi-fi audio amplifiers has been towards lower harmonic and intermodulation distortion numbers. Surprisingly, these ultra-low distortion amplifiers did not have the high sound quality that the distortion figures would indicate. It was soon discovered that the human ear was right and the traditional measurements were incomplete. What had been overlooked was transient distortion.

Transient distortion is high in an amplifier when there is the combination of high open loop gain and high negative feedback. Although this type of amplifier can be made stable, usually its relative stability is low due to a low gain and phase margin. This results in overshoot for a transient signal, which rings out in a dampened wave to its steady state. Another way to look at it is that the correction capacitances perform an integrating function and delay the signal. The leading edge of a transient signal is amplified with the open loop gain until the feedback takes effect. High transient amplitudes and even clipping are the result. If a second signal is present, it will momentarily disappear while the transient goes into clipping; this results in high transient intermodulation distortion (TIM).

The amplifier described here is designed to have low open-loop distortion and relatively low open-loop gain, therefore low transient distortion. This is achieved by using local negative feedback. Also, there is only 23 dB of loop negative feedback. In addition to the lag-type frequency rolloff that is natural in an amplifier, there is a lead-type rolloff in the feedback leg which acts as a phase correction and increases the phase margin of the loop, thereby increasing the relative stability. The result is an amplifier that has no visible overshoot on transients.

CIRCUIT DESCRIPTION

The amplifier is a complementary design to provide minimum open-loop distortion. The front end consists of two difference amplifiers *(Figure 1);* each amplifies the input signal for one side of the push-pull output. The right sides (bases of Q2 and Q4) serve as tie points for both ac and dc feedback. Local feedback is provided by the emitter resistors (R7, R8, R11, R12) and base resistors (R3, R4, R19, R20); the collector resistors are chosen at 2.7 kΩ to hold gain low and maintain good frequency response. The input impedance of the amplifier is high (>30 kΩ) because R2 need supply only the difference in Q1 and Q3 base currents and can, therefore, be high without creating a large offset voltage. Any offset voltage at this point is reflected into the output and causes dc to flow into the load; therefore, Q1 through Q4 should be matched (15% beta match at $I_c = 5$ mA). Beta matching the remainder of the transistors further reduces offset and distortion.

Input capacitor C1 is large (10 μF) and, together with the high input resistance, gives an extremely low frequency rolloff (0.5 Hz); C1 is used to block off any dc that might come from the input. Large amplitudes at frequencies above 70 kHz require an additional rolloff capacitor C2 in the amplifier input to avoid dynamic crossover distortion in the output transistors. The value of C2 depends on the output resistance of the preamplifier, about 1 nF is a good approximation.

The predrivers Q5 and Q7 have large emitter resistors for local negative feedback. Resistors R25 and R28 are used to lower the collector impedance which would otherwise be extremely high thereby causing high gain that would result in larger negative loop feedback and early open-loop rolloff. Transistor Q6, thermally connected to the heat sink of one of the output transistors, is used as a V_{BE} multiplier to reduce crossover distortion. Capacitors C7 and C8 stop any parasitic oscillations which are small but undesirable in a low distortion amplifier. The idling current is set by R26 to about 20 mA.

The output is a Darlington configuration with fast drivers Q8, Q9 and rugged output transistors Q10, Q11. Emitter resistors R33 and R34 supply local feedback. The combination of R32 and C11 provides off-drive for the bases of the output transistors Q10, Q11 to speed up the turn-off. This raises the onset of large signal dynamic crossover distortion from ~30 kHz to ~70 kHz.

Resistor R35 and capacitor C12 provide a constant high frequency load for the amplifier. Certain speakers (electrostatic) may require an inductance in parallel with a damping resistor at the output; 10 μH and 10 Ω are suitable values. In this case, the feedback should be taken directly from the speaker to compensate for the voltage drop across the LR combination.

The feedback ties back into the two difference amplifiers. DC is coupled back directly; for ac, the blocking capacitor C6 is chosen for low-frequency rolloff (1.5 Hz). This lag-type low-frequency rolloff is the only rolloff within the feedback loop and, therefore, the amplifier is unconditionally stable at low frequencies. At medium frequencies, the amplifier gain is set to R22/R23 = 22. Capacitor C5 parallel to R22 provides a lead-type high-frequency rolloff which is phase-correcting and provides better transient stability.

The supply voltage at the front end is ac-decoupled by R30 and C9 on one side and R31 and C10 on the other. The diodes D1 and D2 prohibit the discharge of C9 and C10 into the output thus providing voltage for the front end to avoid switch-off noise when the amplifier is turned off.

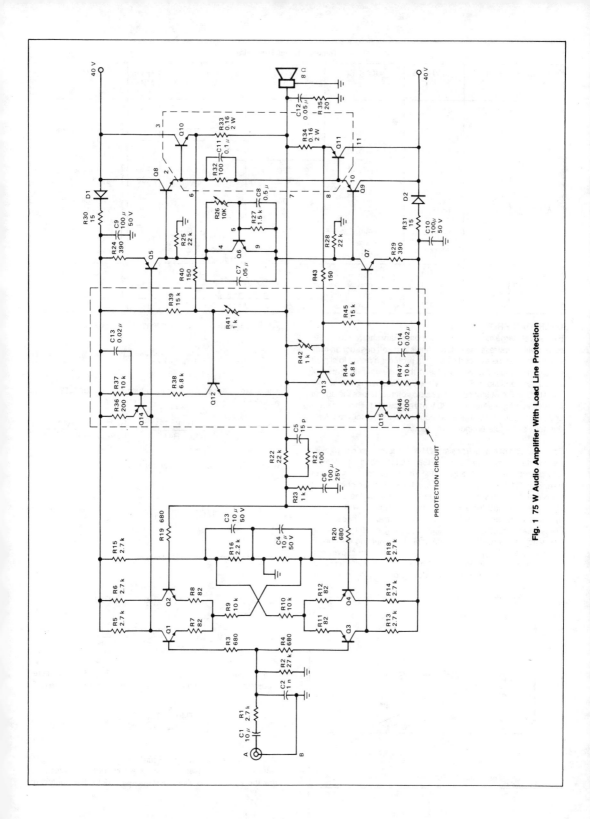

Fig. 1 75 W Audio Amplifier With Load Line Protection

369

Table 1. Recommended Transistors

TRANSISTOR		TYPE	POLARITY	$V_{CEO(sus)}$ Min V	h_{FE} Min @	I_C A	f_T typ MHz	REMARKS
Front End	Q1, Q2	2N5961	npn	60	135	1 m	150	low noise, high gain down to μA, gain linearity
	Q3, Q4	PN4250A-18	pnp	60	250	100 μ	70	
Multiplier	Q6	2N5961	npn	See Above				
Pre driver	Q5	2N5400	pnp	120	40	10 m	200	high voltage, rugged
	Q7	2N5830	npn	100	80	10 m	200	
Driver	Q8	FT317	npn	100	35	1	35	high voltage, fast 40 W, TO-220
	Q9	FT417	pnp	100	35	1	25	
Output	Q10	FT324	npn	140	20	5	6	200 W TO-3, rugged SOA, 50 V, 3.0 A medium speed
	Q11	FT424	pnp	140	20	5	6	
Protection Circuit	Q12	2N5831	npn	140	80	10 m	200	high voltage rugged
	Q13	2N5401	pnp	150	60	10 m	150	
	Q14	PN4250A-18	pnp	See Above				high gain
	Q15	2N5961	npn	60	150	10 m	100	

OVERLOAD PROTECTION

Excessively large input signals or a momentary short circuit in the output will overstress the output transistors and destruction may result. This can be avoided by using a protection circuit to clip off excessive signals that would exceed the safe operating area of the output transistors. The signals are clipped along a load line that starts at 5 A output current for zero voltage across the output transistor and goes linearly to 80 V at zero current. This voltage – double the supply voltage – is required because the speakers normally constitute an inductive load.

For protection of output transistor Q10, the current-sensing resistor R33 determines the 5 A limit, R39 and R40 set the 80 V limit, and potentiometer R41 adjusts the protection to the $V_{BE(on)}$ of transistor Q12. Figure 2 shows the load lines for one output transistor. V_{cc} is the supply voltage for one side of the amplifier, R_L is the load line for a resistive load, in this case 8 Ω. The inductive load lines for an inductive speaker are ellipses of decreasing amplitude and increasing phase-angle φ for increasing frequency. The envelope is a straight line connecting the coordinates 0, I_p and 2 V_{cc}, 0. Speaker systems using crossover networks have similar impedances. The protection circuit clips off any signal beyond this line but does not shut off the signal altogether.

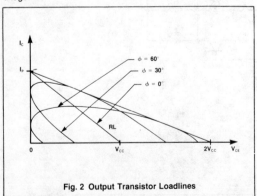

Fig. 2 Output Transistor Loadlines

The load line (envelope of the load ellipses) can be expressed:

$$\frac{I_C}{I_P} + \frac{V_{CE}}{2V_{CC}} = 1 \tag{1}$$

The base voltage of the load sensing transistor Q12 can be expressed by:

$$V_{BE} = I_C R33 \frac{R41}{R40 + R41} + V_{CE} \frac{R40}{R39} \times \frac{R41}{R40 + R41} \tag{2}$$

which is a good approximation for R33 ≪ R40 ≪ R39. Equation (2) can be written as:

$$\frac{I_C}{V_{BE} \dfrac{R40 + R41}{R33 \times R40}} + \frac{V_{CE}}{V_{BE} \dfrac{R40 + R41}{R40} \times \dfrac{R39}{R40}} = 1 \tag{3}$$

Direct comparison with (1) yields

$$I_P = V_{BE} \frac{R40 + R41}{R40} \times \frac{1}{R33} \tag{4}$$

$$2V_{CC} = V_{BE} \frac{R40 + R41}{R40} \times \frac{R39}{R40} \tag{5}$$

In this case I_P = 5 A, $2V_{CC}$ = 80 V. For R33, 0.16 Ω is selected. Substituting in Equation 4, the following results.

$$V_{BE} \frac{R40 + R41}{R40} = 0.80 \text{ V} \tag{6}$$

With this value substituted in Equation (5) and 150 Ω selected for R40, R39 = 15 kΩ. Resistor R41 is a 1 kΩ potentiometer set so that the V_{BE} turn-on voltage of transistor Q12 fulfills Equation (6).

When Q12 is turned on, it activates Q14, which shunts the signal off Q5. Capacitor C13 is used to stabilize the protection loop and suppress oscillations. The high-frequency rolloff for this protection loop is at Q5, as it is for the whole amplifier. The protection for the lower side is complementary and works in the same manner to protect Q11.

PC BOARD LAYOUT

The pc board *(Figures 3, 4)* is laid out as symmetrically as possible with amplification going in one direction. Input and output grounds are decoupled to avoid ground-loop problems. The drivers Q8 and Q9 are TO-220 mounted upright and carry friction-fit

heat sinks of about 20°C/W (Model 106B from Fab-Tec, Danbury, CT). Each output transistor is on a separate heat sink ($\theta =$ 2.7°C/W) mounted with thermal grease. Transistor Q6 is mounted snugly into a hole in one of the output heat sinks. Thermal grease is advisable, but if there is any danger that transistor Q6 could slip out of its hole and lose thermal connection, epoxy should be used.

In case it is necessary to compensate the speaker impedance with a series LR combination, the feedback can be taken directly from the speaker. This is accomplished by drilling a hole at point X and connecting the feedback to the speaker by a separate wire from point Y.

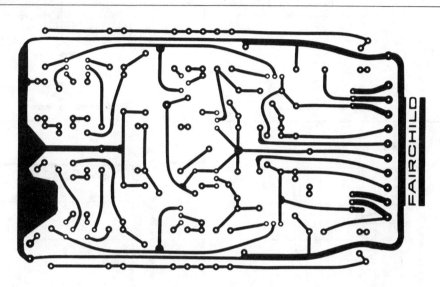

Fig. 3 PC Board, Circuit Side

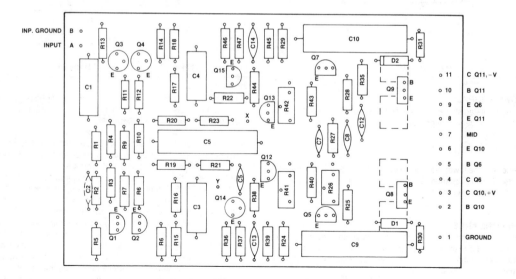

Fig. 4 PC Board, Component Side

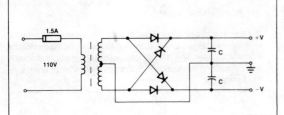

Fig. 5 Power Supply

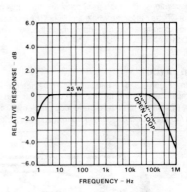

Fig. 6 Frequency Response

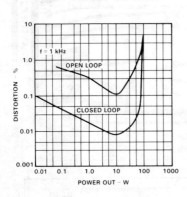

Fig. 7 Total Harmonic Distortion

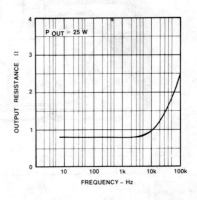

Fig. 8 Open Loop Output Resistance

POWER SUPPLY

An unregulated split supply is used *(Figure 5)*. The transformer is 110 V/56 V center tapped and should be able to deliver

$$P = \frac{V_{CC}^2}{2R_L} \times \frac{4}{\pi} = \frac{40^2}{2.8} \times \frac{4}{\pi} = 128 \text{ W} \qquad (7)$$

Generally, the lower the output resistance of the transformer, the better. The capacitances C were chosen 5000 μF; the bigger the C, the stiffer the supply.

PERFORMANCE

The basic design philosophy was to build an amplifier that works well without a feedback loop, and add a little feedback to get an extremely stable amplifier that has low distortion and wide bandwidth at the same time.

The amplifier without feedback has a linear frequency response far above the audible range; it rolls off 1 dB at 70 kHz *(Figure 6)*. The harmonic distortion is below 1% *(Figure 7)*, and the output resistance typically 0.8 Ω *(Figure 8)*.

With the feedback connected, these performance figures improve drastically. The 1 dB frequency rolloff shifts up to 300 kHz and the rolloff at the low end is 1 dB below 3 Hz *(Figure 6)*. The harmonic distortion has improved by a factor of 10 and is below 0.1% up to 75 W output; in the middle range it is below 0.01% *(Figure 7)*. Distortion vs frequency is below 0.03% up to 35 kHz for 25 W output *(Figure 9)*. Due to the feedback, the output impedance has dropped to typically 20 mΩ *(Figure 10)*; the input resistance is high due to the double differential input, about 30 kΩ. The voltage gain is set to about 23, and the input voltage for full output is below 1.4 V$_{rms}$ which can be handled by any commercial pre-amp. Transient stability of this amplifier is excellent; a 1 kHz square wave shows no visible overshoot or ringing.

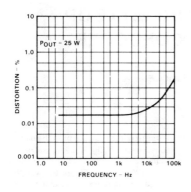

Fig. 9 Total Harmonic Distortion (Closed Loop)

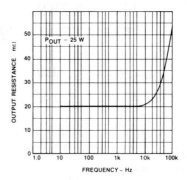

Fig. 10 Total Harmonic Distortion (Closed Loop)

POWER DATA BOOK

In dem neuen Datenbuch stellt Fairchild sein umfangreiches Programm an Leistungstransistoren vor, das auch die populären Vorzugstypen beschreibt. Neben Hinweisen zur richtigen Auswahl und einer Vergleichsübersicht industrieller Typen enthält dieses Buch zusätzlich einen technischen Teil über technologischen Aufbau, sicheren Betriebsbereich (SOAR) Gehäusearten, Kühlung und Zuverlässigkeit. Die richtige Arbeitsunterlage für den Entwickler.

FAIRCHILD

700 Seiten; DIN A5; In engl. Spr.

Best.-Nr. DE 1206   Preis: DM 13,50*

Alle angegebenen Preise verstehen sich inkl. MwSt., zuzügl. Versandspesen

THE μA758, A PHASE LOCKED LOOP FM STEREO MULTIPLEX DECODER

Larry Blaser and Bill Cocke

INTRODUCTION

Phase Locked Loop (PLL) systems have been used for many years in consumer entertainment equipment. They have been used in black and white TV receivers for horizontal sweep synchronization and in color TV receivers for regeneration of the 3.58 MHz chroma subcarrier. However, only recently has the PLL concept been successfully applied to the FM stereo multiplex signal decoding (references 1, 2, 3). Because PLL systems are complex this approach is not practical in multiplex decoder designs using discrete components. However, integrated circuit technology has progressed to the point where such a complex system can economically be built on a single IC chip.

38 kHz SUBCARRIER SIGNAL REGENERATION

In any multiplex decoder it is necessary to reconstruct the 38 kHz subcarrier present in the encoding equipment by using the 19 kHz pilot signal. This pilot signal is part of the composite multiplex signal received and bears a well defined frequency and phase relationship to the 38 kHz subcarrier.

Earlier decoders either doubled the 19 kHz pilot to form the 38 kHz subcarrier or injected the 19 kHz pilot into a 38 kHz oscillator to lock the oscillator at precisely twice the 19 kHz pilot frequency. Both techniques require at least one, but more commonly two, selective 19 kHz filters to extract the pilot from the composite signal. In addition, a 38 kHz tuned circuit is needed to separate the 38 kHz subcarrier from the pilot when using the doubler system or to establish the oscillator frequency when using the injection locked system. Critical phasing is required for good separation so these tuned circuits demand precise alignment which is difficult in volume production. Also, both temperature and aging affect the drift characteristics of coils, degrading long term performance.

A Phase Locked Loop for regenerating the 38 kHz subcarrier eliminates coils, and phase accuracy of the 38 kHz signal is only limited by the loop gain of the system and by the stability of the free-running oscillator frequency. Both of these parameters can be easily controlled, providing easy, rapid adjustment and excellent long term stability.

ADVANTAGES OF THE μA758

For the FM stereo receiver manufacturer, the economic advantages of the PLL multiplex decoder system result from the lack of coils, the minimum parts count, and the simple adjustment. The μA758 offers all of these economic benefits as well as outstanding performance, satisfying both the demanding performance requirements of High Fidelity Stereo component equipment and the cost requirements of lower cost FM stereo receivers. The μA758 system operates over the extreme temperature range encountered in the automobile radio environment and offers superior stability in this application because it lacks coils which are sensitive to the combined effects of temperature, vibration, mechanical shock, and aging.

In addition to the basic function of decoding the multiplex signal into left and right channels, the μA758 offers the following features.

- Automatic Stereo/Mono switching

- Stereo indicator lamp driver with preset hysteresis switch points

- Lamp driver current-limiting to limit turn on current, prolonging lamp life and protecting the integrated circuit against accidental overload

- High impedance input

- Low impedance outputs

- High rejection to SCA (Subsidiary Carrier Authorization) interference without special filtering

The photograph of Figure 1 shows the simplicity of the μA758 system compared to the popular μA732 and its associated components.

Fig. 1.   The μA758 PLL System Compared to a Conventional Decoder Using the μA732

FAIRCHILD

SEMICONDUCTOR

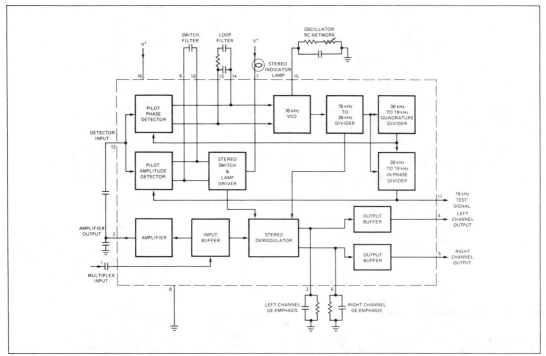

Fig. 2. Decoder Block Diagram

A complete block diagram of the µA758 is shown in Figure 2. The upper row of blocks comprise the Phase Locked Loop which regenerates the 38 kHz suppressed carrier required for demodulation of the multiplex signal. The oscillator is voltage controlled and operates at 76 kHz, twice the subcarrier frequency to insure a perfect 50% duty cycle of the regenerated 38 kHz signal. Perfect symmetry is required for optimum right/left separation and for highest rejection to signals in the SCA (Subsidiary Carrier Authorization) band which, if present, are usually centered at 67 kHz. The 38 kHz signal is divided by two and fed to the phase detector for comparison with the pilot signal contained in the composite multiplex input signal. The error signal from the pilot phase detector passes through the low pass filter and controls the oscillator for phase lock to the pilot. In the phase locked condition, the pilot signal is in quadrature with the internal 19 kHz signal.

Referring next to the second row of blocks in Figure 2, the divide-by-two circuit develops a second 19 kHz signal which is in phase with the pilot (and 90° out of phase with the output of the first 38 kHz to 19 kHz divider). This divider is steered by the other two dividers to prevent 180° phase ambiguity. It drives a detector essentially identical to the pilot phase detector but because of the in-phase relationship of 19 kHz drive with the pilot, this detector operates as a synchronous amplitude detector instead of as a phase detector. The output from the pilot amplitude detector is filtered and drives a switch which has hysteresis to insure fully ON or fully OFF outputs. The stereo switch drives a stereo indicator lamp and also enables the stereo demodulator when a stereo signal is present. The demodulator is disabled in the presence of a monophonic signal to obtain optimum noise performance.

The input buffer and amplifier in the bottom row of Figure 2 have unity gain to the demodulator and a gain of three to the

detectors. The demodulator is a fully balanced synchronous type followed by inverters which allow the output signals to be developed with respect to ground for good supply voltage rejection.

FUNCTIONAL DESCRIPTION

The µA758 circuitry is more complex than that of most linear ICs. To simplify this description, the circuitry is divided into six major groups. An equivalent circuit diagram accompanies each circuit group.

- Input Buffer/Amplifier and Bias Supply–Figure 3
- Demodulator–Figure 4
- Stereo Switch and Lamp Driver–Figure 5
- Voltage Controlled Oscillator–Figure 6
- Frequency Dividers–Figure 7
- Pilot Phase and Amplitude Detectors–Figure 8

The complete equivalent circuit of the µA758, including the associated components for a typical application, is shown in Figure 9.

Input Buffer/Amplifier and Bias Supply

A 6 V bias supply with excellent supply voltage rejection is developed at the emitter of Q_2 by zener diode Z_1, diode D_1, and transistors Q_1 through Q_3. Diode D_1 cancels the voltage variations that appear at the base of Q_3 due to supply voltage modulation. Two additional voltages are derived from the temperature compensated voltage divider chain, R_3, R_4 and R_5. These voltages, both approximately 3 V, are taken from the emitters of Q_4 and Q_5.

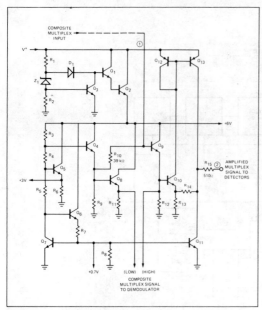

Fig. 3.   Input Buffer/Amplifier and Bias Supply

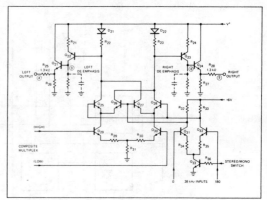

Fig. 4   Demodulator

transistors Q_{22} and Q_{23}. The left and right output signals are developed across external resistors which tie to ground from leads 3 and 6. De-emphasis is accomplished at this point with external capacitors connected across the load resistors. Emitter follower transistors Q_{21} and Q_{24} provide a 1.3 kΩ output impedance to leads 4 and 5 through resistors R_{25} and R_{28}.

Stereo Switch and Lamp Driver

The differential voltage from the pilot amplitude detector is sensed by transistors Q_{41} and Q_{42} which feed amplifier and lamp driver transistors Q_{45} through Q_{50}. Positive switch action (hysteresis) is achieved by feedback from Q_{49} through R_{46} which turns off Q_{44}.

The turn on threshold is the differential input voltage required to overcome the voltage across R_{43} developed by one-half of the total bias current into Q_{43} and Q_{44}. A lower turn off threshold is established by the reduced bias current through R_{43} since Q_{44} is OFF when the lamp is ON.

Transistor Q_7 (driven by Q_6), is the control transistor for several current sources throughout the decoder; Q_{11}, Q_{43}, Q_{44}, Q_{67} and Q_{73}.

The multiplex input signal amplifier, Q_8 through Q_{13}, provides a high input impedance at lead 1. The demodulator is driven differentially from Q_9, which is the signal path, and from Q_8 for dc biasing.

The multiplex signal is amplified by Q_{10} through Q_{13} to drive the pilot phase detector and the amplitude detector. The gain of this amplifier is determined by feedback resistors R_{13} and R_{14} and is independent of supply voltage.

Demodulator

The basic demodulator, Q_{25} through Q_{30}, is a fully balanced synchronous detector type identical to the one in the μA732 (Reference 4). The composite multiplex signal is fed to transistor Q_{29}. Transistor Q_{30} is dc biased at the same potential as Q_{29}. The resistor network R_{29}, R_{30} and R_{31} between the two emitters introduces a small multiplex signal in the collector of Q_{30}. This signal is necessary to compensate for the cross-talk components inherent in the process of synchronous switching demodulation.

The multiplex signal is switched to its left and right components by transistors Q_{25} and Q_{26}. Transistors Q_{27} and Q_{28} provide the cross-talk correction component as well as an equal dc current to that flowing in switches Q_{25} and Q_{26}, eliminating the large 38 kHz switching component which would otherwise be present in the demodulator output.

Balanced 38 kHz drive to switches Q_{25} through Q_{28} is developed at the collectors of Q_{31} and Q_{32} when Q_{33} is ON. Turning Q_{33} OFF places a dc bias on the bases of the switch transistors and converts the decoder to monophonic operation.

To obtain supply voltage rejection at the demodulator outputs, the currents from the switching transistors are inverted in

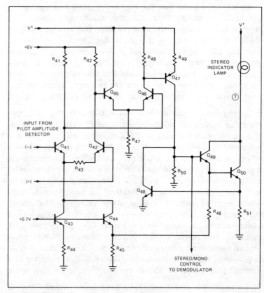

Fig. 5.   Stereo Switch and Lamp Driver

Transistor Q_{48} senses the voltage across R_{51} and limits lamp turn on current into lead 7 prolonging lamp life and providing overload current protection to the IC. The automatic Mono/Stereo switch signal for the demodulator is taken from the base of Q_{49}.

Voltage Controlled Oscillator (VCO)

The dc amplifier in the VCO converts the differential error voltage from the pilot phase detector to a bidirectional, single ended current drive to the oscillator. The output currents from the differential amplifier (Q_{65} and Q_{66}), are mirrored in Q_{61} and Q_{64} respectively, and the current in Q_{61} is in turn, mirrored in Q_{69}. The overall transconductance of the amplifier is therefore equal to the transconductance of the differential input pair, and the nominal dc output current to lead 15 is zero when the differential input voltage is zero.

The oscillator, Q_{71} through Q_{79}, is an R-C relaxation type which generates a positive, low duty cycle, 76 kHz output. The oscillator frequency is established by the controlled charge and discharge of the external capacitor (on lead 15) between two well defined set voltages, V_H and V_L.

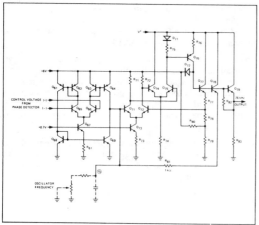

Fig. 6a. Voltage Controlled Oscillator (VCO)

The heart of the oscillator is a comparator, Q_{71} through Q_{76}, which senses when the voltage on the capacitor reaches one of the two set voltages, then causes the direction of charge to be reversed, and simultaneously switches the set voltage. The voltage on the capacitor is compared with the set voltages by the differential input stage, Q_{71} and Q_{72}. This feeds a second differential stage, Q_{74} and Q_{75}. The single ended output from Q_{75} drives a PNP inverter, Q_{76}. Diode D_{71} tracks the temperature dependence of the base emitter drop of Q_{76} to maintain relatively constant current in the collector of Q_{76}, which is the comparator output.

The lower set voltage, V_L, is determined by the division of the 6 V regulated supply through resistors R_{79} and R_{80}. The upper set voltage, V_H, involves two additional resistors, R_{77} and R_{78} and is established when Q_{77} is turned on by the comparator output Q_{76}. The base of Q_{77} is clamped at one V_{BE} above the 6 V supply so that resistor R_{77}, which connects to the emitter of Q_{77}, is brought to the same potential as the 6 V supply. Because of this, both set points are a fixed percentage of the 6 V supply, and these percentages are dependent only on resistor ratios.

Capacitor charge from the lower to upper set voltage is through Q_{78} and R_{81}. Similar to R_{77}, R_{81} is brought to the 6 V supply potential during the charge period. The charge period occupies less than 10% of the total cycle time to minimize the effect of the positive temperature dependence of the internal charge resistor R_{81}.

The capacitor discharges from the upper to lower set voltage through the external fixed resistor in series with the potentiometer. The discharge period occupies over 90% of the total cycle time and thus predominantly determines oscillator frequency. This discharge period is controlled by adjustment of the external potentiometer for initial set up of free-running frequency and is controlled in the locked condition by the net error current from the dc amplifier. A positive error current (from lead 15 into the external R-C network) decreases the discharge rate and thus decreases oscillator frequency. Conversely, a negative error current from the dc amplifier increases oscillator frequency.

The capacitor and set voltage waveforms shown in Figure 6b include the first order expressions for the charge and discharge periods. Note the independence to variations in the 6 V supply.

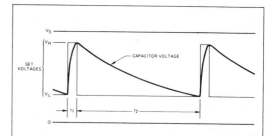

BASIC TIMING EQUATIONS:

$$t_1 = R_{81}C \ln \frac{V_s - V_L}{V_s - V_H}$$

$$t_2 = RC \ln \frac{V_H}{V_L}$$

where R and C are external components on Lead 15, R_{81} is on the chip, and V_H and V_L are set voltages which are a fixed percentage of V_s, the internally regulated 6 Volt supply.

Fig. 6b. Oscillator Waveforms

A positive output pulse from the oscillator is taken from the emitter of Q_{79}. All transistors in the oscillator operate in their linear mode thus eliminating storage effects associated with saturation which could affect oscillator stability.

Frequency Dividers

Transistors Q_{91} through Q_{94} form a simple divide-by-two circuit which converts the pulse output from the 76 kHz oscillator to a 38 kHz square wave (reference 5).

The divider changes state during the positive excursion of the input pulse supplied from the emitter of Q_{79} in the oscillator. Initially, when the input is low, Q_{91} and Q_{92} are OFF and we may arbitrarily assume Q_{93} is ON and Q_{94} is OFF.

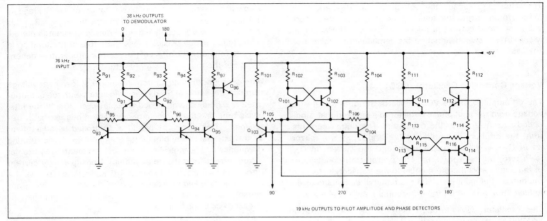

Fig. 7. Frequency Dividers

As the potential on the input rises, Q_{91} starts conduction before Q_{92} because the emitter of Q_{91} is at a lower potential than the emitter of Q_{92}. (The emitter of Q_{91} is connected through R_{95} to the collector of Q_{93} which is in saturation, whereas the emitter of Q_{92} is at the $V_{BE(ON)}$ potential of Q_{93}). Since Q_{91} is ON, the current from both R_{92} and R_{93} flows through the emitter of Q_{91} into R_{95}. As this current increases, the rising voltage at the emitter of Q_{91} turns Q_{94} ON which removes base drive to Q_{93} and turns it OFF, thus producing a change of state in the divider. Even though the relative potentials at the emitters of Q_{91} and Q_{92} are now reversed, current continues to flow in Q_{91} for the duration of the positive input because Q_{92} is held OFF by Q_{91}. When the input returns to a low potential, Q_{91} turns OFF. The divider remains in its present state until driven by the next positive going input.

Oppositely phased 38 kHz outputs to the demodulator are taken from the collectors of Q_{93} and Q_{94}. Transistors Q_{95} and Q_{96} are used to drive the two 38 kHz dividers.

The 38 kHz Quadrature Divider has an identical configuration to the 76 kHz divider. A change of state occurs with each positive excursion of the 38 kHz input signal from the emitter of Q_{96}.

The 38 kHz In-Phase divider contains a bistable pair, Q_{113} and Q_{114}, steered by inputs into Q_{111} and Q_{112}, (a 38 kHz input from the collector of Q_{95}, and 19 kHz inputs from the bases of Q_{103} and Q_{104}). If the 19 kHz input to the base of Q_{111} is high when the 76 kHz divider turns Q_{95} ON, Q_{111} conducts and removes drive to Q_{114}, changing the state of the bistable pair, Q_{113} and Q_{114}. The bistable remains in this state until the next 38 kHz turn on of Q_{95} which, this time, turns Q_{112} ON, removes drive to Q_{113} and resets the bistable pair. The resulting 19 kHz output from Q_{113} and Q_{114} is at 90 degrees to the Quadrature Divider output with no ambiguity in phasing.

Pilot Phase and Amplitude Detectors

The pilot phase detector and pilot amplitude detector are synchronous, balanced chopper types which develop differential output signals across external filters. Back-to-back NPN transistor pairs are used for each switch to insure minimum drop regardless of signal polarity without reliance on inverse NPN beta characteristics.

The chopper transistors (Q_{121} through Q_{124}), in the phase detector are driven from the 38 kHz Quadrature Divider through transistors Q_{125} and Q_{126}. The input signal is supplied from lead 12 through resistors R_{125} and R_{126}. A differential output is developed across the loop filter, comprised of resistors R_{123} and R_{124} and the external R-C network between leads 13 and 14.

The pilot amplitude detector (Q_{131} through Q_{136}), has an identical configuration to the phase detector. Since it operates with drive which is in phase with the pilot signal (90 degrees from the drive to the phase detector), its output is proportional to the amplitude of the pilot component of the multiplex signal. The differential output at leads 9 and 10 is filtered by the external capacitor on these two leads.

A reference 19 kHz square wave signal is taken from the collector of drive transistor Q_{136} through resistor R_{137} to lead 11. It has the same phasing as the pilot contained in the multiplex input signal.

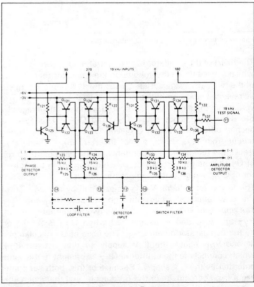

Fig. 8. Pilot Phase and Amplitude Detectors

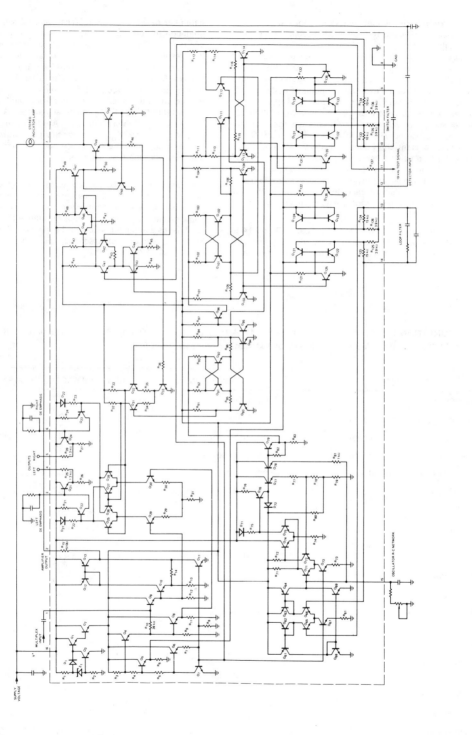

Fig. 9. µA758 Equivalent Schematic

OPERATING CHARACTERISTICS

Typical performance obtained when using the external components shown in Figure 10 is outlined in Table 1 and Figures 11 through 18. The graphs in Figures 11 and 12, show that the free-running oscillator frequency is relatively independent of temperature, varying less than 1% over a range from -30°C to +85°C, and is almost completely independent of supply voltage. Selection of the external components in the oscillator R-C network provides a convenient means of adjusting the loop gain of the PLL by controlling the sensitivity of the VCO. The loop gain is proportional to R^2C whereas the oscillator frequency is proportional to $1/RC$. As long as the R-C product is held constant, the values of R and C can be varied to change the loop gain. Changing C_6 from 390 pF to 510 pF decreases the loop gain by approximately 25% and improves both separation and distortion performance by a few dB. However, capture range also decreases by approximately 25% and separation becomes more sensitive to oscillator mistuning. (Refer to Figure 19.)

The loop filter network shown between leads 13 and 14 in Figure 10 provides optimum separation and distortion performance over a wide range of audio frequencies. The alter-nate filter network in Figure 20 can be used with a slight degradation in performance; at high audio frequencies this is due to phase jitter and at low audio frequencies this is due to loop resonance. C_4 connected from lead 2 to ground (Figure 10), introduces a phase lag in the 19 kHz pilot signal to compensate for the delays in the 76 kHz to 19 kHz divider chain in the integrated circuit. If the filter network in Figure 20 is used and if the coupling capacitor from lead 2 to lead 12 is increased to 0.068 uF, C_4 can be eliminated. A small phase error results as shown in Figure 21. Any further increase in the coupling capacitor, C_5, decreases this phase error but it also seriously degrades the separation performance at audio frequencies near the loop resonance.

Separation at low audio frequencies can be degraded because of phase shifts in the left plus right component of the stereo signal due to the high pass network formed by the input coupling capacitor (C_1), and the input resistance of the IC. This establishes a minimum value for the input coupling capacitor. Separation versus audio frequency is shown as a function of C_1 in Figure 17.

Table I

TEST CONDITIONS: T_A = 25°C, V+ = +12V, 19 kHz pilot level = 30 mV, Multiplex signal (L = R, pilot OFF) = 300 mV RMS, Modulation frequency = 400 kHz or 1 kHz unless otherwise specified.

PARAMETER	CONDITION	MIN	TYPICAL	MAX	UNITS
Supply Current	Lamp OFF		26		mA
Maximum Available Lamp Current			150		mA
Voltage at Lamp Driver Terminal	I_{LAMP} = 50 mA		1.3		V
Voltage Shift at Either Output Terminal	Stereo to Mono Operation		30		mV
Power Supply Ripple Rejection	200 Hz, 200 mV		45		dB
Input Impedance			35		kΩ
Output Impedance			1.3		kΩ
Channel Separation	100 Hz		40		dB
	1 kHz		45		dB
	10 kHz		45		dB
Channel Balance			0.3		dB
Voltage Gain			0.9		V/V
Pilot Input Level	Lamp Turn On		15		mV
	Lamp Turn Off		7		mV
Capture Range			4.0		%
Total Harmonic Distortion	Multiplex Level = 600 mV, Pilot Off		0.4		%
19 kHz Rejection			35		dB
38 kHz Rejection			45		dB
SCA Rejection			70		dB

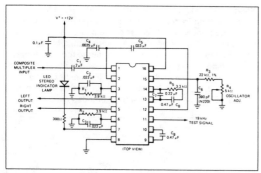

Fig. 10.   Typical Application

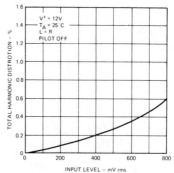

Fig. 14.   Total Harmonic Distortion as a Function of Input Level

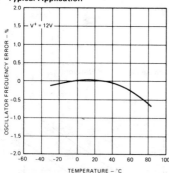

Fig. 11.   Oscillator Free Running Frequency Error as a Function of Temperature

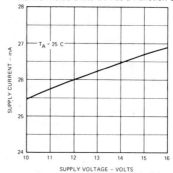

Fig. 15.   Supply Current as a Function of Supply Voltage

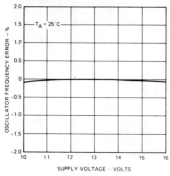

Fig. 12.   Free Running Oscillator Frequency Error as a Function of Supply Voltage

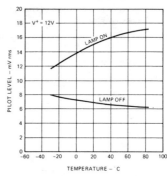

Fig. 16.   Lamp Turn On and Turn Off Sensitivity as a Function of Temperature

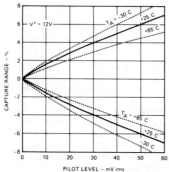

Fig. 13.   Capture Range as a Function of Pilot Level

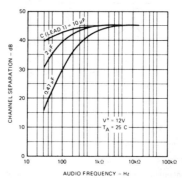

Fig. 17.   Channel Separation as a Function of Audio Frequency

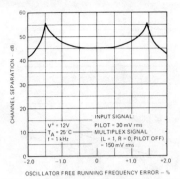

Fig. 18. Channel Separation as a Function of Oscillator Free Running Frequency Error

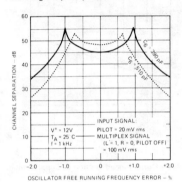

Fig. 19. Channel Separation as a Function of Oscillator Free Running Frequency Error

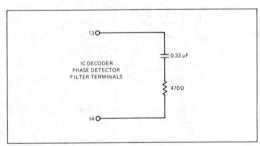

Fig. 20. Alternate Phase Detector Filter

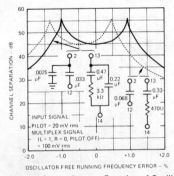

Fig. 21. Channel Separation as a Function of Oscillator Free Running Frequency Error

When the decoder is installed in an actual stereo FM receiver, some reduction in separation will be observed, especially at high audio frequencies, because of the phase response of the IF amplifier. This effect can be compensated by adding an R-C lead network in series with the input to the decoder. The exact component values of the R-C network will vary depending on the response of the particular IF amplifier being used. Figure 22 shows an RC network which can be used in conjunction with a µA3075 IF amplifier and detector.

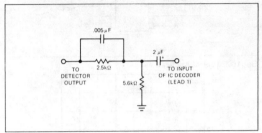

Fig. 22. Input Phase Correction Network

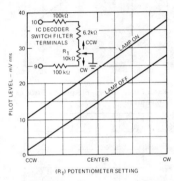

Fig. 23. Lamp Turn On and Turn Off Sensitivity as a Function of R_1 Setting

Because of different receiver design characteristics, the amount of recovered audio voltage available at the input to the µA758 can vary. Therefore, it may be desirable in some receivers to change the sensitivity of the lamp driver switching circuitry. This sensitivity may be changed by adding a resistive divider between the switch filter terminals (leads 9 and 10) and ground. A suggested circuit and typical performance is shown in Figure 23.

The quality of the audio signal under weak signal conditions can sometimes be improved by manually switching the stereo decoder to the monaural mode. This is easily accomplished with the µA758 by connecting a 10 kΩ resistor from lead 9 to ground.

All of the critical circuitry in the µA758 is biased from an internally regulated bias supply. Hence, the device can be operated with supply voltages ranging from 10 V to 16 V without any noticeable change in performance. Because the output currents are essentially independent of supply voltage, the external load resistor values may be increased at higher voltages to increase the voltage gain. If the load resistor values are changed from those shown in Figure 10, the de-emphasis capacitor values must also be changed to maintain a 75 us de-emphasis characteristic. The recommended values for load resistors and capacitors are listed in Table 2.

 Table II

Minimum Supply Voltage	Load Resistors (R_1 & R_2)	De-Emphasis Capacitors (C_2 & C_3)	Typical 1 kHz Voltage Gain
10 V	3.9 kΩ	0.02	1.0 V/V
12 V	4.7 kΩ	0.015	1.2 V/V
14 V	6.2 kΩ	0.015	1.3 V/V

The μA758 can supply up to 100 mA to a stereo indicator lamp such as a FLV102 light emitting diode or a Chicago Miniature 756 incandescent lamp. If the LED is used, a 300 Ω resistor must be connected in series to limit the forward current of the LED to 50 mA.

TESTING AND ALIGNMENT

A test circuit, useful for testing small quantities of devices, is shown in Figure 24. Prior to testing, align the circuit as follows. Place all switches in the positions indicated in Figure 24. With no signal input, apply 12 V to the V_{CC} terminal. Adjust R_1 until the frequency of the test signal at lead 11 is 19 kHz $\pm$ 10 Hz.

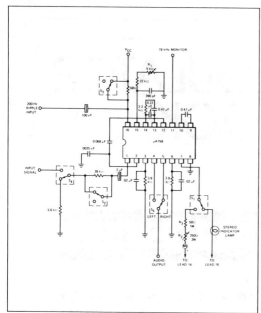

Fig. 24. Test Circuit

Each parameter is tested as follows.

Stereo Lamp Sensitivity and Hysteresis

1. Operate S_4 so that the input signal is coupled to lead 1.

2. Apply a low level 19 kHz pilot signal to the multiplex input. Slowly increase the amplitude of this signal until the lamp lights. Decrease the signal level until the lamp extinguishes. Typically, the lamp turns on at 15 mV and turns off at 7 mV.

Maximum Lamp Current

1. Adjust R_2 for maximum resistance.

2. Operate S_1, connecting R_3 to lead 7.

3. Decrease the resistance of R_2 until the lamp driver current, displayed on M_1, no longer increases. The current level at this point is typically 150 mA.

4. Return S_1 to its original position.

Demodulator Gain and Channel Balance

1. With a stereo generator, such as the Radiometer SMG-1, apply a 300 mV, 1 kHz, L = R, pilot = 0, composite signal to the multiplex input. The signal level at either the left or right output is typically 300 mV.

2. Compare the left and right outputs; the difference is typically 0.4 dB.

Input Impedance

1. Record the output voltage (E_1) measured in the preceding step.

2. Operate S_2 inserting 39 kΩ in series with the input and record the measured output voltage (E_2). The input impedance is calculated by the equation:

$$R_{IN} = \frac{39 \text{ k}\Omega}{\frac{E_1}{E_2} - 1}$$

3. Close S_2

Distortion

1. Increase the input level to 600 mV rms. Measure THD using a distortion analyzer such as the HP 334A. THD at either output is typically 0.4%.

Stereo Separation

1. With a left only, 1 kHz signal and the pilot = 0, adjust the output of the stereo generator to 150 mV rms. Remove the modulation and adjust the pilot level to 30 mV rms. Reinsert the 1 kHz modulation. The composite signal level will be approximately 156 mV rms.

2. With a selective voltmeter such as the HP 302A Wave Analyzer, measure the 1 kHz component in the left output. Change the modulation to the right channel and again measure the left channel output. The ratio of these two readings is the left channel separation.

3. Repeat for the right channel. The separation for both channels is typically 45 dB.

19 kHz and 38 kHz Rejection

1. Apply the same input signal as in step 1 of the previous test, use the selective voltmeter to measure the left output, and compare the 1 kHz component with the 19 kHz and 38 kHz components in the output signal. The 19 kHz and 38 kHz components are typically 35 dB below the 1 kHz component.

2. Repeat for the right channel.

Stereo to Mono dc Level Shift

1. Apply a 20 mV pilot signal to the input and measure the dc voltage at the left output. Remove the pilot signal and note the change in output voltage. This dc level shift is typically 30 mV.

Power Supply Rejection

1. Operate S_3 to connect the 68 Ω resistor in series with the supply voltage. Adjust V_{CC} for 12 V dc on lead 16. Apply a 200 Hz, 200 mV rms signal to lead 16. Terminate the input with 5.6 k Ω (S_4), and measure the 200 Hz signal at either output with the selective voltmeter. This signal is typically 45 dB below the applied signal

CONCLUSION

The µA758 Phase Locked Loop FM Stereo Multiplex Decoder operates with a minimum number of external components and requires no coils. It is aligned with a single potentiometer adjustment. The µA758 is applicable to a wide variety of home and automotive stereo FM receivers.

REFERENCES

1. "An Inductorless Monolithic Stereo Demodulator", O. A. Kolody and W. P. Haynes, General Electric Application Information 300.051.

2. "Integrated-Circuit Stereo Decoder Does Everything", L. A. Kaplan, H. M. Kleinman and A. L. Limberg, IEEE Transactions on Broadcast and Television Receivers, Vol. BTR-17, No. 3, Aug. 1971.

3. "A Monolithic Phase-Lock-Loop Stereo Decoder", M. J. Gay, IEEE Transactions on Broadcast and Television Receivers, Vol. BTR-17, No. 4, Nov. 1971.

4. "The µA729, µA732 and µA767 Integrated Circuit Stereo Multiplex Decoders", J. Feit, Fairchild Application Note 286/1, 1974.

5. "New Binary Counter Circuit", A. Richardson and R. C. Foss, Electronic Letters, The Institute of Electrical Engineers, Vol. 1, No. 10, Dec. 1965.

USING THE µA79HG NEGATIVE ADJUSTABLE VOLTAGE REGULATOR

INTRODUCTION

The µA79HG is an adjustable negative voltage regulator that can supply a minimum of 5 A at externally programmable output voltages of from -2.3 V to -24 V, nominal. It is supplied in a 4-lead, hermetically sealed TO-3 package capable of dissipating 50 W at a case temperature of 25° C. The TO-3 package is electrically isolated to allow direct mechanical contact to a heat sink.

STABILITY CONSIDERATIONS

Solid tantalum input and output bypass capacitors are recommended for most applications to insure stable operation. A 1 µF capacitor should be used to bypass the output and should be connected as closely as possible to the output terminal. A 2 µF input bypass capacitor is necessary unless the rectifier filter capacitor is located within four inches of the input terminal.

INPUT VOLTAGE REQUIREMENTS

Minimum input voltage required for regulation is -7 V, and a minimum input/output differential of 2.5 V must be maintained. Because the µA79HG has good line regulation, it can be used with an unregulated input having considerable ripple. Peak ripple voltage, illustrated in *Figure 1*, should not exceed these limits.

MOUNTING

The regulator package is isolated from the circuit, eliminating the need for electrical insulation. Good thermal contact must be established between the package and a heat sink to take advantage of the full power capability of the device. Also, using thermal compounds such as GE 662 or Dow Corning DC-340 insures maximum heat transfer. The power/temperature derating chart, *Figure 2*, shows guaranteed capability.

SHORT CIRCUIT PROTECTION

Current limiting and thermal shutdown are used by the µA79HG to achieve device protection. The device continues to regulate voltage until the established current limit is reached or the die temperature exceeds safe limits. If the ratings shown in *Figure 2* are exceeded, the device limits internal power dissipation to a non-destructive level by reducing output current.

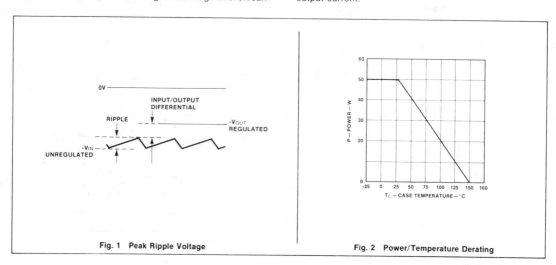

Fig. 1   Peak Ripple Voltage

Fig. 2   Power/Temperature Derating

CONTROL INPUT CONSIDERATIONS

The control pin is one of the inputs to the internal error amplifier. The high gain of the amplifier makes this input sensitive to any capacitance added by external circuitry. It is not advisable to use the control input with remote sensing schemes. Also, wiring from the resistor divider to the control pin must be kept short, and distributed capacitances should be minimized, to avoid oscillation problems.

INPUT SHORT CIRCUIT PROTECTION

In applications requiring large capacitances connected to the regulator output, reverse current through the regulator should be prevented. As shown in the functional block diagram (Figure 3), the emitter of the output transistor is connected to the regulator output. This junction avalanches at approximately 10 V and the device may be damaged if the input voltage is shorted out suddenly. Under normal circumstances, a 1 μF bypass capacitor at the regulator output does not store enough energy to cause damage.

OUTPUT VOLTAGE

The μA79HG can be used as a fixed output regulator (Figure 4) or as a variable output regulator (Figure 5). Basic regulation is achieved by comparing the resistance-divided output voltage appearing on the control input to an internal reference voltage. An internal feedback circuit (shown in Figure 3) adjusts the output voltage so that the control input is equal to the reference voltage, normally -2.23 V ±5%. This tolerance is reflected in the output voltage and increased by the resistor divider tolerance.

To determine the divider resistor values, it is convenient to use 2.21 kΩ for R2. This is an available 1% value resistor, and since the control voltage is -2.23 V, approximately 1 mA flows through R2. This current is sourced from the output voltage through R1, so that the numerical value of the output voltage is equal to R1 + R2 in kilohms:

$$V_{OUT} = 1 \text{ mA } (R1 + R2) \text{ in kilohms.}$$

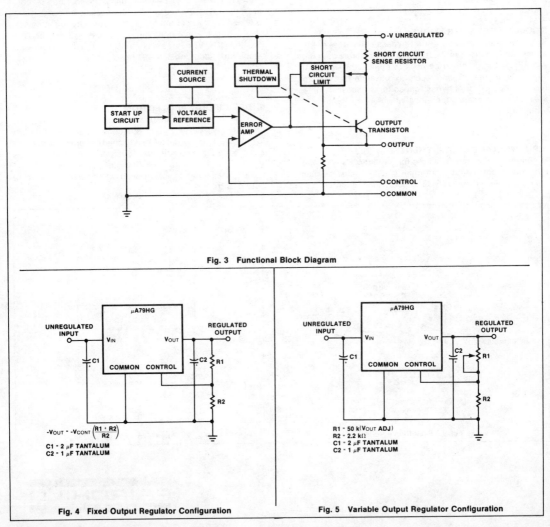

Fig. 3   Functional Block Diagram

Fig. 4   Fixed Output Regulator Configuration

Fig. 5   Variable Output Regulator Configuration

INTERFACE CIRCUITS

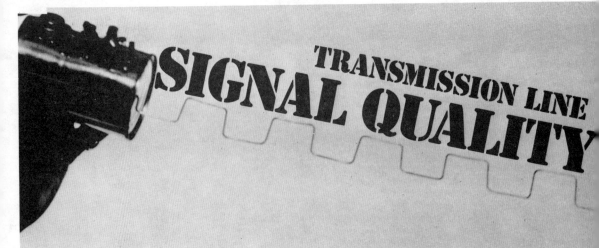

TRANSMISSION LINE SIGNAL QUALITY

by Ken True

The world of data transmission divides neatly into two primary areas. One area is concerned with the *physical aspects* of information transmission; *e.g.,* line drivers/ receivers, transmission lines, pulse codes, modems, etc. The other area centers about the *mechanics* of information transmission: handshaking protocol, data rates, information codes, error detection/correction, etc. These specific areas diverge somewhat from each other in spite of their common goal of facilitating the movement of information from one location to another. In these two areas, different terms have evolved describing similar phenomena. This can lead to confusion.

The intent here is to provide some background on the terms used when the physical aspects of information transmission via digital baseband techniques is of primary interest.

Signal Quality—Terms

Data transmission has as its objective the transfer of *information* from one location to another. This information is *digital* in nature; *i.e.,* a finite number of separate states or choices. This is in contrast to *analog* which has an infinite number of separate states or a continuous range of choices. The digital information here is *binary* or two-valued; thus two different, recognizable electrical states/levels are used to symbolize the digital information. A binary symbol is commonly called a binary-digit or *bit*. A single binary symbol or bit, by itself, can represent only one of two possible things. To represent alphabetic or numeric characters, a group of bits is arranged to provide the necessary number of unique combinations. This arrangement of bits which is then considered as an information unit is called a *byte*. In the same manner that a group of bits can be called a byte, a collection of bytes, considered as a unit, is called a *word*. Selective arrangement of seven bits will provide 2^7 (or 128) distinct character combinations (unique bytes). The American Standard Code for Information Interchange (ASCII) is an excellent example of just such an arrangement—upper and lower case alphabetic, zero to nine numeric, punctuation marks, and miscellaneous information-code control functions.

Now with the means for representing information as bits or bytes, and the means for transmission of the bits (symbols) from one location to another (transmission line), the remaining task is to ensure that a particular bit arriving at its destination is interpreted in the proper context. To achieve this, both the sender and receiver of the data must accomplish the five following requirements.

1. Agree upon the nominal rate of transmission; or how many bits are to be emitted per second by the sender.

2. Agree upon a specified information code providing a one-to-one mapping ratio of information-to-bit pattern and vice versa.

3. Establish a particular scheme whereby each bit can be properly positioned within a byte by the receiver of the data.

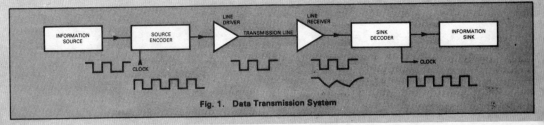

Fig. 1. Data Transmission System

4. Define the protocol (handshaking) sequences necessary to ensure an orderly flow of information.

5. Agree to the electrical states representing the logic values of each bit and the particular pulse code to be used.

These are by no means all of the points that must be agreed upon by sender and receiver—but these are probably the most important. Items 2, 3 and 4 are more or less "software" type decisions, because the actual signal flow along the transmission line is usually independent of these decisions. Because items 1 and 5 are much more dependent on the characteristics of line drivers, line receivers, and transmission lines, they are the primary concern here.

Figure 1 represents the components of a typical data transmission system. The *information source* can be a computer terminal or a digitized transducer output, or any device emitting a stream of bits at the rate of one bit every t_B seconds. This establishes the *information rate* of the system at $1/t_B$ bits per second. The information source in the figure feeds a *source encoder* which performs logic operations not only on the data, but also on the associated clock and, perhaps, the past data bits. Thus, the source encoder produces a binary data stream controlling the *line driver*. The line driver interfaces the internal logic levels (TTL, MOS, etc.) with transmission line current/voltage requirements. The transmission line conveys signals produced by the line driver to the line receiver. The line receiver makes a decision on the signal logic state by comparing the received signal to a decision threshold level, and the *sink decoder* performs logic operations on the binary bit stream recovered by the line receiver. For example, the sink decoder may extract the clock from the data or perhaps detect and correct errors in the data. From the optional sink decoder, the recovered binary data passes to the *information sink*—the destination for the data produced by the information source.

Assume for the moment, that the source encoder and sink decoder are "transparent"; that is, they will not modify the binary data presented to them in any way. Line driver signals, then, have the same timing as the original bit stream. The data source emits a new bit every t_B seconds. The *pulse code* produced by the source encoder and line driver is called Non-Return to Zero (NRZ), a very common signal in TTL logic systems. A sample bit pattern with its NRZ representation is shown in *Figure 2*. The arrows at the top represent the *ideal instants,* or the times the signal can change state. The term *unit interval* is used to express the time duration of the shortest signaling element. The shortest signaling element for NRZ data is one bit time t_B, so the unit interval for NRZ data is also t_B. The rate at which the signal changes is the *modulation rate* (or signaling speed), and *baud* is the unit of modulation rate. A modulation rate of one baud corresponds to the transmission of one unit interval per second. Thus the modulation rate, in baud, is just the reciprocal of the time for one unit interval. A unit interval of 20 ms, therefore, means the signaling speed is 50 baud.

The reason for differentiating between the information rate in bits per second and the modulation rate in baud is necessary for adequate treatment of the minimum pulse width appearing on the line when pulse codes other than NRZ are used. For example, self-clocking pulse codes such as Bi-Phase Level (Manchester) or Polar Return to Zero have a minimum pulse width (unit interval) of 0.5 t_B for a given bit rate. So the pulses occurring on the transmission line with such a coding scheme will have a much shorter duration than predicted by simply using the information rate in bits per second. Since the minimum pulse width has a great deal

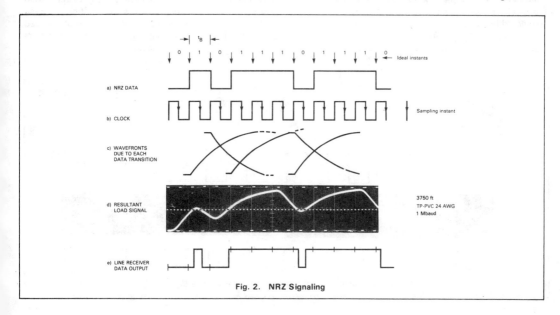

Fig. 2. NRZ Signaling

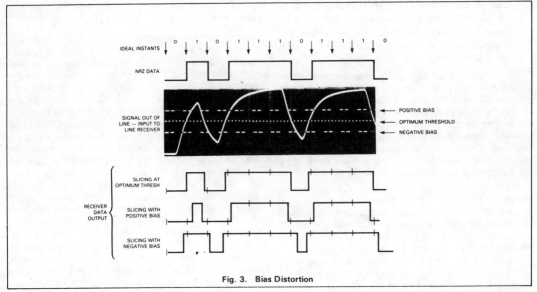

Fig. 3. Bias Distortion

to do with the recoverability of the binary data stream at the end of a lossy, dispersive transmission line, it behooves the designer to forego information rate in favor of modulation rate. This is because modulation rate is solely dependent upon the actual characteristics of the signal to be transmitted/received, yet independent of the information content and rate of events causing signals on the line. (See Progress Vol. I, No. 4, Sept. 73)

NRZ data should always be accompanied by a clock signal, *Figure 2b,* which tells the receiver when to sample the data signal and thus determine the current logic state. For the example in *Figure 2b,* the falling edge of the clock corresponds to the middle of the data bits, so it could be used to transfer the line receiver data output into a binary latch. The falling edge of the clock is

thus the *sampling instant* for the data. The line receiver does have a *decision threshold* or slicing point so that voltages above that threshold level produce one logic state output, while voltages below the threshold produce the other logic state at the receiver output. The receiver may incorporate positive feedback to produce *hysteresis* in its transfer function. This reduces the possibility of oscillation in response to slow rise or fall time signals applied to the receiver inputs.

It is well known that a real transmission line exhibits attenuation and dispersion. This causes each fast rise time signal to be slowed down and "rounded out" as it travels down the line. The resultant signal at the load end of the line consists of the superposition of these transformed transitions. The waves arriving at the load end of the line are shown in *Figure 2c* and their super-

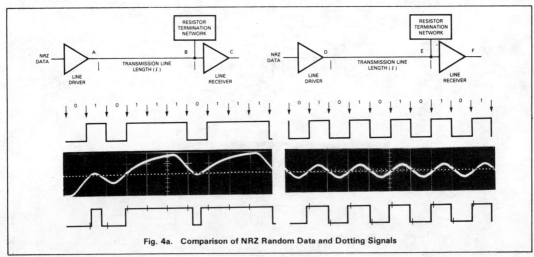

Fig. 4a. Comparison of NRZ Random Data and Dotting Signals

position is shown in *Figure 2d.* It is assumed that the line is terminated in its characteristic resistance so that reflections are not present. The receiver's threshold level is shown here, superimposed on the resultant load signal, and the re-converted data input of the line receiver is shown in *Figure 2e* along with the ideal instants for the data transitions.

Comparing the original data *(Figure 2a)* to the recovered data *(Figure 2e)* shows that the actual recovered data transitions may be displaced from their ideal instants (arrows below *Figure 2e*). This time displacement of the transitions is due to a new wave arriving at the receiver site before the previous wave has reached its final value. Since the wave representing a previous data bit is *interfering* with the wave representing the present data bit, this phenomenon is called *intersymbol interference* (in telegraphy it is called *characteristic distortion*). The intersymbol interference can be reduced to zero by making the unit interval of the signal quite long in comparison to the rise/fall time of the signal at the receiver site. This can be accomplished by either reducing the modulation rate for a given line length, or by reducing the line length for a given modulation rate.

Signal quality is concerned with the variance between the ideal instants of the original data signal and the actual transition times for the recovered data signal.

For synchronous signaling, such as NRZ data, the *isochronous distortion* of the recovered data is the ratio of the unit interval to the maximum measured difference irrespective of sign between the actual and theoretical significant instants. The isochronous distortion is, then, the peak-to-peak time jitter of the data signal expressed as a percentage of the unit interval. A 25% isochronous distortion means that the peak-to-peak time jitter of the transition is .25 unit interval (max).

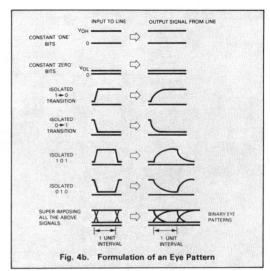

Fig. 4b.   Formulation of an Eye Pattern

If the receiver threshold is shifted up toward the *1 signal level,* then the time duration of the *1*-bits shortens with respect to the duration of the *0-bits,* and vice versa. This is called *bias distortion* in telegraphy and can be due to receiver threshold offset (bias) asymmetrical output levels of the driver, or a combination of both. This effect is shown in *Figure 3.*

Bias distortion and characteristic distortion (intersymbol interference) together are called *systemic distortion,* because their magnitudes are determined by characteristics within the data transmission system. The other variety of time distortion is called *fortuitous distortion* and is due to factors outside the data transmission system such as noise and crosstalk, which may occur randomly with respect to the signal timing.

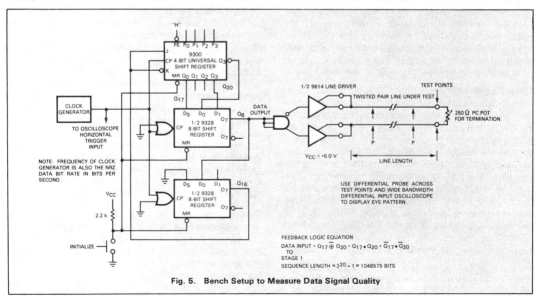

Fig. 5.   Bench Setup to Measure Data Signal Quality

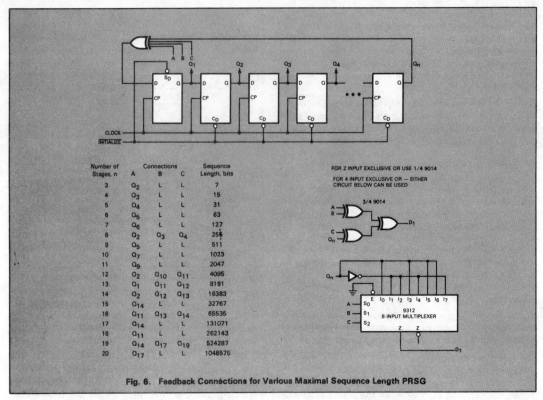

Fig. 6. Feedback Connections for Various Maximal Sequence Length PRSG

Signal Quality Measurement—The Eye Pattern

To examine the relative effects of intersymbol interference on random NRZ data and a "dotting"* pattern, see *Figure 4a*. The top two graphs represent the NRZ data and dotting pattern as outputs into two identical long transmission lines. The middle two traces illustrate the resultant signals at the line outputs and the bottom two traces show the data output of the line receivers. The respective thresholds are shown as dashed lines on the middle two traces. The arrows indicate the ideal instants for both random data and dotting signals.

Notice that the dotting signal (D) is symmetrical, *i.e.*, every One is preceded by a Zero and vice versa, while the NRZ data is random. The resultant dotting signal out of the line is also symmetrical. Because, in this case, the dotting half-cycle time is less than the rise/fall time of the line, the resultant signal out of the line (E) is a partial response—it never reaches its final level before changing. The dotting signal, due to its symmetry, does not show intersymbol interference in the same way that random NRZ data does. But it does show bias distortion, manifesting itself as a change in duty cycle for the recovered dotting pattern. The NRZ data shows intersymbol interference due to its unpredictable bit sequence. Thus, whenever feasibility of a data trans-

mission system is to be tested, a random data sequence should be used. This is because a symmetrical dotting pattern or clock signal could not show the effects of possible intersymbol interference.

A very effective method of measuring time distortion through a data transmission system is based on the eye pattern. The eye pattern, displayed on an oscilloscope, is simply the superposition—over one unit interval—of all the Zero-to-One and One-to-Zero transitions, each preceded and followed by various combinations of One and Zero, and also a constant One and Zero level. The name eye pattern comes from the resemblance of the pattern center to an eye. The diagramatic construction of an eye pattern is depicted in *Figure 4b*. The data sequence can be generated by a pseudo-random sequence generator, which is a digital shift register with feedback connected to produce a maximum length sequence. The PRSG, requiring only two devices. shown in *Figure 5*, generates a sequence that repeats after $2^{20}-1$ bits. Feedback connections for PRSG shift registers from 4 to 20 bits in length are shown in *Figure 6*.

Several features of the eye pattern make it a useful tool for measuring data signal quality. *Figure 7* shows a typical binary eye pattern for NRZ data. The spread of traces crossing the receiver threshold level (dotted line) is a direct measure of the peak-to-peak transition jitter—isochronous distortion in a synchronous system—of the data signal. The rise and fall time of the signal can be

*The term dotting pattern is from telegraphy and means an alternating sequence of 1-bits and 0-bits. Note that an NRZ dotting pattern generates a signal which has a 50% duty cycle and a frequency of $1/2\ t_B$ (Hz).

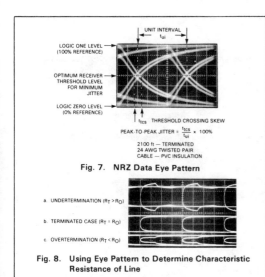

Fig. 7. NRZ Data Eye Pattern

a. UNDERTERMINATION ($R_T > R_O$)

b. TERMINATED CASE ($R_T = R_O$)

c. OVERTERMINATION ($R_T < R_O$)

Fig. 8. Using Eye Pattern to Determine Characteristic Resistance of Line

conveniently measured by using the built-in 0% and 100% references produced by long strings of Zeros and Ones. The height of the trace above or below the receiver threshold level at the sampling instant is the noise margin of the system. If no clear transition-free space in the eye pattern exists, the eye is closed. This indicates that error-free data transmission is not possible at that data rate and line length with that particular transmission line without resorting to equalizing techniques. In some extreme cases, error-free data recovery may not be possible even with equalization. The eye pattern can also be used to find the characteristic resistance of a transmission line. The 250 Ω printed circuit-type potentiometer termination resistor (Figure 5) can be adjusted to yield the minimum overshoot and undershoot of the data signal. Figure 8 shows the NRZ data eye patterns for $R_T > R_O$, $R_T = R_O$ and $R_T < R_O$. The 100% and 0% reference levels are again provided by long strings of Ones and Zeros, and any overshoot or undershoot is easily discernible. The termination resistor is adjusted so that the eye pattern transitions exhibit the minimum perturbations (Figure 8b). The resistor is then removed from the transmission line, and its measured value is the characteristic resistance of the line.

By using the eye pattern to measure signal quality at the load end of a given line, a graph can be constructed showing the tradeoffs in signal quality—peak-to-peak jitter—as a function of line length and modulation rate for a specific pulse code. An example graph for NRZ data is shown in Figure 9. The graph was constructed using eye pattern measurements on a 24 AWG twisted pair line (PVC insulation) driven by a differential voltage source driver (9614) with the line parallel-terminated in its characteristic resistance (96 Ω). The oscilloscope photographs in Figure 10 show the typical eye patterns for NRZ data with various amounts of isochronous distortion. The straight lines represent a "best fit" to the actual measurement points. Since the twisted

pair line used was not specifically constructed for pulse service, the graph probably represents a reasonably good worst-case condition insofar as signal quality vs line length is concerned. Twisted pair lines with polyethylene or Teflon* insulation have shown better performance at a given length than the polyvinyl chloride insulation. Likewise, larger conductors (20 AWG, 22 AWG) also provide better performance at a given length. Thus, the graph in Figure 9 can be used to estimate feasibility of a data transmission system when the actual cable to be used is unavailable for measurement purposes. The arbitrary cutoff of 4000 feet on the graph was due to an observed signal amplitude loss of 6 dBV (1/2 voltage) of the 24 AWG line at that distance. The cutoff of 10 Mbaud is based on the propagation delays of the typical TTL line drivers and receivers. Field experience has shown that twisted pair transmission systems using TTL drivers and receivers have operated essentially error-free when the line length and modulation rate are kept to within the shaded recommended operating region shown in Figure 9. This has not precluded operation outside this region for some systems, but these systems must be carefully designed with particular attention paid to defining the required characteristics of the line, the driver, and the receiver devices. The use of coaxial cable instead of twisted pair lines almost always yields better performance, i.e., greater modulation rate at a given line length and signal quality. This is because most coaxial cable has a wider bandwidth and reduced attenuation at a given length than twisted pair line (one notable exception is RG 174/U cable).

It should be remembered that, in some ways, the eye pattern gives the *minimum* peak-to-peak transition jitter for a given line length, type, pulse code, and modulation rate. This is because the eye pattern transition spread is the result of intersymbol interference and reflection effects (if present) and this minimum jitter is only obtainable if the following conditions are met.

*Teflon is a registered trademark of E.I. du Pont de Nemours Company

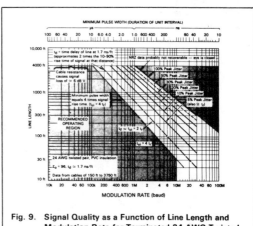

Fig. 9. Signal Quality as a Function of Line Length and Modulation Rate for Terminated 24 AWG Twisted Pair (PVC Insulation)

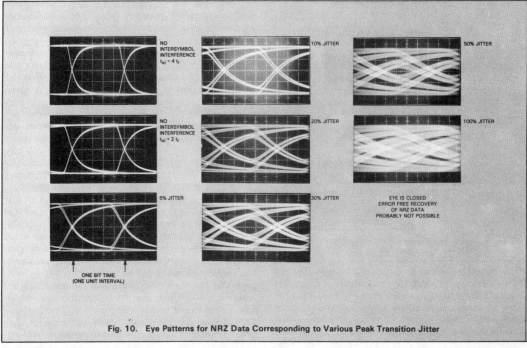

Fig. 10.   Eye Patterns for NRZ Data Corresponding to Various Peak Transition Jitter

- The One and Zero signal levels produced by the line driver are symmetrical, and the line receiver's decision threshold (for NRZ signaling) is set to coincide with the mean of those two levels.

- The line is perfectly terminated in its characteristic resistance to prevent reflections from altering the signal threshold crossings.

- The time delays through driver and receiver devices for both logic states is symmetrical and there is no relative skew in the delays (difference between L → H and H → L propagation delays = 0). This is especially important when the device propagation delays become significant fractions of the unit interval for the applicable modulation rate.

If any one of these conditions is not satisfied, the signal quality is reduced (more distortion). The effects of receiver bias or threshold ambiguity and driver offset can be determined by location of the decision threshold(s) on the oscillograph of the eye pattern for that driver/ cable modulation rate combination. For eye patterns displaying more than 20% isochronous distortion, the slope of the signal in the transition region is relatively small. Therefore, a small amount of bias results in a large increase in net isochronous distortion. See *Figure 11* for a graphic illustration of this effect. In the interest of optimizing design practices, systems should always be designed with less than 5% transition spread in the eye pattern. This allows the detrimental effects due to bias to be minimized, thus simplifying construction of line drivers and receivers.

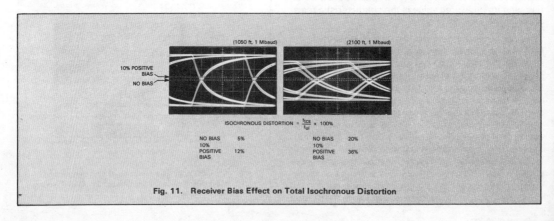

Fig. 11.   Receiver Bias Effect on Total Isochronous Distortion

Signal Quality Estimation

FOR COAXIAL CABLES

by Ken True

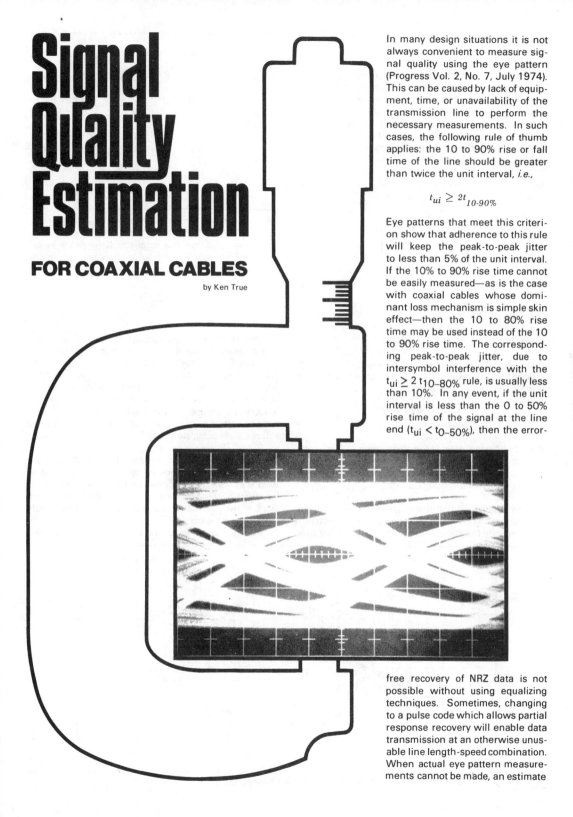

In many design situations it is not always convenient to measure signal quality using the eye pattern (Progress Vol. 2, No. 7, July 1974). This can be caused by lack of equipment, time, or unavailability of the transmission line to perform the necessary measurements. In such cases, the following rule of thumb applies: the 10 to 90% rise or fall time of the line should be greater than twice the unit interval, *i.e.*,

$$t_{ui} \geq 2t_{10\text{-}90\%}$$

Eye patterns that meet this criterion show that adherence to this rule will keep the peak-to-peak jitter to less than 5% of the unit interval. If the 10% to 90% rise time cannot be easily measured—as is the case with coaxial cables whose dominant loss mechanism is simple skin effect—then the 10 to 80% rise time may be used instead of the 10 to 90% rise time. The corresponding peak-to-peak jitter, due to intersymbol interference with the $t_{ui} \geq 2\,t_{10\text{–}80\%}$ rule, is usually less than 10%. In any event, if the unit interval is less than the 0 to 50% rise time of the signal at the line end ($t_{ui} < t_{0\text{–}50\%}$), then the error-

free recovery of NRZ data is not possible without using equalizing techniques. Sometimes, changing to a pulse code which allows partial response recovery will enable data transmission at an otherwise unusable line length-speed combination. When actual eye pattern measurements cannot be made, an estimate of feasibility can still be obtained by calculating the signal transition time.

N.S. Nahman[1,2] presented a simple method to predict the transient response of a coaxial cable from the cable attenuation. The procedure was based on a graphical analysis technique allowing prediction of the step response of a network from a graph of the imaginary part of the transfer function, in this case the imaginary part of γ (s). The normalized step responses *(Figure 1)* are plotted with the abscissa in normalized time (x)

$$x = t/a \qquad (1)$$

where

$$a = \frac{1}{2\pi f_O} \left[\frac{\alpha(f_O)}{cos(m\pi/2)} \right]^{\frac{1}{m}} \qquad (2)$$

and

t = real time,

$\alpha(f_O)$ = attenuation of the coaxial cable in nepers at frequency (f_O) for length l. If $\alpha(f_O)$ is known in dB, then division by 8.686 will convert the dB/length into nepers/length (1 neper = 8.686 dB).

m = slope of the attenuation vs frequency curve for the particular coaxial cable when plotted on log-log graph paper (log dB vs log frequency).

$$m = \frac{\log \alpha(f_2) - \log \alpha(f_1)}{\log (f_2) - \log (f_1)}$$

where $f_2 > f_1$ and $\alpha(f_2)$ is the attenuation at frequency (f_2), and log ( ) is common (base 10) logarithm.

Slope m will have a range of $0 \leq m \leq 1$.

Nahman pointed out that this method applies to cables where either the attenuation *or* the phase characteristic can specify the transfer function. This implies that

NORMALIZED TIME			
m	x50%	x10–90%	x10–80%
0.4	1.30	*	14.5
0.5	1.15	*	7.1
0.6	1.00	*	3.5
0.7	0.92	6.6	2.4
0.8	0.89	3.0	1.4
0.9	0.89	1.0	0.7

*90% points not given on graph for these values (Figure 4[1])

Fig. 2.   Normalized Time to Reach Various Percentages of Signal Final Value for Various Values of m

knowledge of either characteristic alone provides sufficient information for the other characteristic; in particular, the Bode condition must be met.

$$\lim_{s \to \infty} \frac{\gamma(s)}{s} = 0$$

For details, see Nahman's paper[1]. In general, a reasonably accurate modified transfer function may be specified satisfying Bode's condition for coaxial cables. Twisted pair and parallel wire lines cannot usually be fully characterized by either attenuation or phase characteristics. This is because each has a significant contribution to the overall transfer function. Thus Bode's condition cannot usually be met, so Nahman's method will not yield accurate results.

In a more recent paper[2], he asserted that the primary contributors to the shape of the step response waveform are those frequency components transmitted with less than 20 dB of attenuation. Thus, the predominant slope of the attenuation curve up to 20 dB at that cable length should be used. For short cables (1000 ft) the 20 dB attenuation may occur in the 10 to 100 MHz

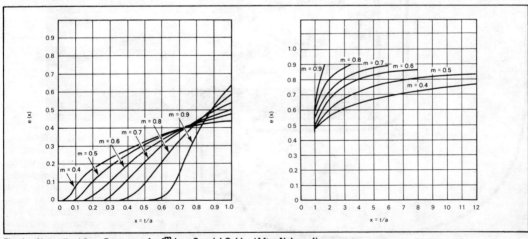

Fig. 1.   Normalized Step Responses for f^m Law Coaxial Cables (After Nahman[1])

region. *Equation 2* may be modified by factoring out the cable length to produce

$$a = \frac{1}{2\pi f_0} \left[\frac{\alpha_1(f_0)}{cos(m\pi/2)}\right]^{\frac{1}{m}} \cdot \left[l\right]^{\frac{1}{m}} \quad (3)$$

where $\alpha_1(f_0)$ is now the attenuation (in nepers) per unit length and l is the line length. The time for the line signal to rise to 50% is obtained by combining *Equations 1* and *3 (Equations 5* and *7* in Reference 2).

$$t_{50\%} = \frac{x_{50\%}}{2\pi f_0} \left[\frac{\alpha_1(f_0)}{cos(m\pi/2)}\right]^{\frac{1}{m}} \cdot \left[l\right]^{\frac{1}{m}} \quad (4)$$

where $x_{50\%}$ is obtained from *Figure 1* or the table in *Figure 2*. Likewise, combining the expressions for $x_{10\%}$ and $x_{80\%}$ and subtracting gives

$$t_{10\text{-}80\%} = \frac{x_{80\%} - x_{10\%}}{2\pi f_0} \left[\frac{\alpha_1(f_0)}{cos(m\pi/2)}\right]^{\frac{1}{m}} \cdot \left[l\right]^{\frac{1}{m}} \quad (5)$$

The 10 to 90% rise time can be found similarly by substituting $x_{90\%}$ for $x_{80\%}$ in *Equation 5*.

As an example of the use of these equations to predict step response of a coaxial cable, consider RG59A/U cable. The listed attenuation for RG59A/U is[3]

f_0	$\alpha(f_0)/100$ ft (dB)
10 MHz	1.07
100 MHz	3.4
400 MHz	7.0

The slope of the attenuation curve is

$$m = \frac{log\ 7.0 - log\ 1.07}{log\ (400\ x\ 10^6) = log\ (10\ x\ 10^6)} = \frac{.82}{1.60} = 0.51$$

The attenuation per unit length (in nepers) at 400 mHz is

$$\alpha_1\ (400\ MHz) = \frac{7.0}{8.686} \cdot \frac{1}{100\ ft.} = 0.008059\ nepers/ft$$

Thus, the normalization constant, a, is

$$a = \frac{1}{2\pi(400\ X\ 10^6)} \left[\frac{.008059}{cos[(.51)\pi/2]}\right]^{\frac{1}{.51}} = 6.355\ X\ 10^{-14}$$

A 140-foot length of line, therefore, should have a $t_{50\%}$ time

$$t_{50\%} = (1.15)\ (6.355\ X\ 10^{-14})\ (140)^{\frac{1}{.51}} = 1.18\ ns$$

and the 10% to 80% rise time is

$$t_{10\text{-}80\%} = (7.1)\ (6.355\ X\ 10^{-14})\ (140)^{\frac{1}{.51}} = 7.29\ ns$$

For 1000 ft of RG59A/U, the previous results for 140 ft can be scaled.

$$t_{50\%} = 1.18 \cdot \left[\frac{1000}{140}\right]^{\frac{1}{.51}} = 55.7\ ns$$

and

$$t_{10\text{-}80\%} = 7.29 \cdot \left[\frac{1000}{140}\right]^{\frac{1}{.51}} = 344.2\ ns$$

If the desired modulation rate is 1 Mbaud (t_{ui} = 1.0 µs) and the line length is 1000 feet, then the system using RG59/U cable would probably operate satisfactorily. Be aware, however, that if the single slope (m) does not accurately approximate the actual attenuation characteristic of the coaxial cable, then Nahman's method will show considerable error in predicting the signal transition time. RG174/U is a coaxial cable with an attenuation characteristic that has a slope in the 0.3 to 0.65 range depending on the frequency. Thus the method cannot be accurately applied to RG174/U cable.

Also, Nahman's method cannot be applied to commonly available twisted pair or parallel wire lines. This is because knowledge of either the line attenuation or its phase characteristics is not normally sufficient to completely specify the transfer function. Thus, the previously mentioned Bode condition is not satisified, and the analysis previously used cannot be applied satisfactorily.

Experimental tests on various twisted pair cables from 10 to 4000 feet in length have revealed that these cables show a law of $m \cong 0.6$ for attenuation, but follow an almost linear increase in rise time as cable length is increased. The 10 to 90% rise time usually falls in the following range.

$$\tau \leq t_{10\text{-}90\%} \leq 2\tau$$

where τ is the time delay of the cable per unit length times the cable length. Combining this with the suggestion that the unit interval should be at least twice the 10–90% rise time of the line, then the minimum unit interval should be

$$t_{ui} \geq 4\tau$$

This corresponds with a boundary for recommended operating regions shown in *Figure 3* (next page). Experience has shown that adherence to the above relationship with twisted pair cables results in less than 10% peak-to-peak jitter due to intersymbol interference.

REFERENCES

1. N.S. Nahman; "A Discussion on the Transient Analysis of Coaxial Cables Considering High Frequency Losses", IRE Trans. on Circuit Theory, VOL CT-9, No. 2, June 1962, pp. 144-152.

2. N.S. Nahman; "A Note on the Transition (Rise) Time Versus Line Length in Coaxial Cables", IEEE Trans. on Circuit Theory (correspondence), VOL CT-20, No. 2, Mar. 1973, pp. 165-167.

3. Standard Wire and Cable Co., Catalog, Third Edition, Mar. 1971, pp. 62-74.

TYPICAL NRZ DATA EYE PATTERNS

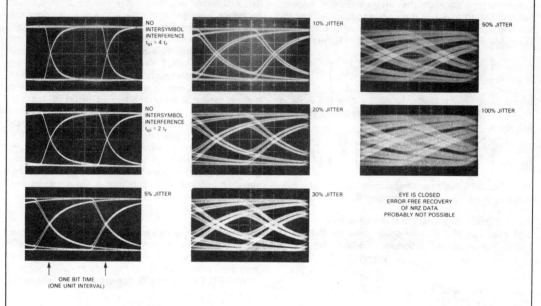

NO INTERSYMBOL INTERFERENCE $t_{ui} = 4 t_r$

10% JITTER

50% JITTER

NO INTERSYMBOL INTERFERENCE $t_{ui} = 2 t_r$

20% JITTER

100% JITTER

5% JITTER

30% JITTER

EYE IS CLOSED
ERROR FREE RECOVERY
OF NRZ DATA
PROBABLY NOT POSSIBLE

ONE BIT TIME
(ONE UNIT INTERVAL)

SIGNAL QUALITY AS A FUNCTION OF LINE LENGTH AND MODULATION RATE

MINIMUM PULSE WIDTH (DURATION OF UNIT INTERVAL)

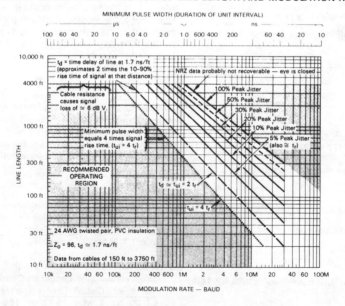

t_d = time delay of line at 1.7 ns/ft
(approximates 2 times the 10-90%
rise time of signal at that distance)

NRZ data probably not recoverable — eye is closed

Cable resistance
causes signal
loss of $\simeq$ 6 dB V.

100% Peak Jitter
50% Peak Jitter
30% Peak Jitter
20% Peak Jitter
10% Peak Jitter

Minimum pulse width
equals 4 times signal
rise time. ($t_{ui} = 4 t_r$)

5% Peak Jitter
(also $\simeq t_r$)

RECOMMENDED
OPERATING
REGION

$t_d \simeq t_{ui} = 2 t_r$

$t_{ui} = 4 t_r$

24 AWG twisted pair, PVC insulation

$Z_0 = 96$, $t_d \simeq 1.7$ ns/ft

Data from cables of 150 ft to 3750 ft

LINE LENGTH

MODULATION RATE — BAUD

Figure 3

398

A MICROPROCESSOR-COMPATIBLE A/D CONVERTER

by Russell J. Apfel and John Conover

The growth of low-cost microprocessors has led to the conversion of many data control systems from an all-analog to a digital controller form. These systems, using high-speed digital processing, offer the higher accuracy, greater flexibility, and other benefits that derive from software control. However, the real world is basically an analog world and the input signals to the system are generally of an analog nature, requiring conversion to a digital form for the processor. An analog-to-digital (A/D) converter performs this function.

In a typical data acquisition system *(Figure 1)*, the A/D converter is normally preceded by an analog multiplexer (MUX) that enables multiple signals to be processed by one converter, and by a sample-and-hold amplifier that holds the input constant during the conversion. Most present systems require separate integrated circuits for each of these functions; with the new μA9708 device, however, the MUX, sample-and-hold, and A/D-converter functions are all performed by a single monolithic integrated circuit.

DEVICE ARCHITECTURE

The μA9708 is a 6-channel, 8-bit A/D converter, designed to be used with microprocessor-based data control systems, that provides 8-bit, 1/2-LSB conversion in 300 μs with automatic zero and built-in full-scale calibration. It consists of an 8-channel multiplexer with a 1-of-8 address decoder, a sample and ramp amplifier, a constant current source, a reference current generator, and an output comparator *(Figure 2)*. Because two channels are reserved for system correction features, only six data channels are actually available.

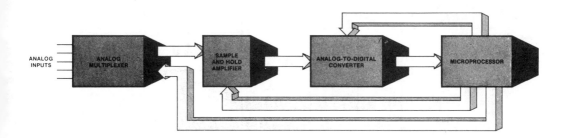

Fig. 1 Typical Data Acquisition System

The address decoder accepts an input from the microprocessor (MPU) and selects one of the eight multiplexer channels. The input signal is fed into the sample and ramp amplifier, which stores the signal in the external holding capacitor, C_H. When C_H is fully settled, the device is ready to perform the A/D conversion.

A start command from the MPU begins the conversion by disabling the sample and ramp amplifier, enabling the constant current source to discharge the holding capacitor. The capacitor discharges at a linear rate of I_{REF}/C_H until the voltage on C_H crosses one V_{BE}, at which time the output comparator changes state, signifying a completed conver-

sion. This stop command is sent to the MPU. The time from start to stop signal is a linear function of the input voltage amplitude (V_{IN}); therefore, the technique is called analog-to-pulse width (A/PW) conversion. If a counter is connected so that it is enabled by the start command and disabled by the stop command, its count would be a digital representation of the analog input.

ANALOG-TO-PULSE WIDTH CONVERSION

The key to the μA9708 is the simple analog-to-pulse width technique used to achieve high-accuracy conversions at moderate speeds with no critical external components. The sample and ramp amplifier, shown in Figure 3 with the

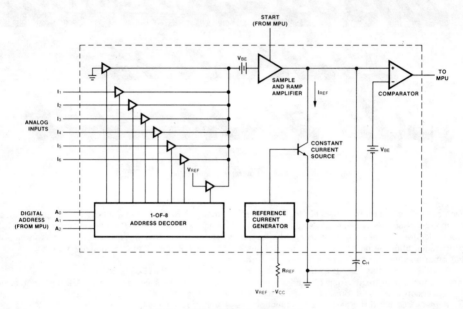

Fig. 2 μA9708 6-Channel A/D Converter

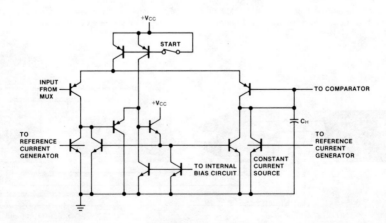

Fig. 3 Sample and Ramp Amplifier

400

holding capacitor and the constant current source, is simply a switched voltage follower that is active during sampling periods. This forces the voltage on C_H to be equal to the input and provides the current for the constant current source. The start command disables the bias current source and turns the amplifier off, making its output look like a high impedance. When this occurs, the constant current source starts discharging the holding capacitor.

The reference current generator and constant current source are shown in *Figure 4*. The generator uses an internal amplifier to force the voltage across the external reference resistor, R_{REF}, to be equal to $V_{CC}-V_{REF}$. V_{REF} may be a fixed external reference or, as shown in the figure, a ratio-metric reference that makes possible the use of V_{CC} as the reference for the sensors and provides tracking compensation for changes in V_{CC}. Two reference currents are generated to balance the loading of the sample and ramp amplifier.

The constant current source cannot discharge C_H from a single supply, so the MUX shifts the level of the input signal one V_{BE} and the output comparator detects a level on C_H of one V_{BE}. The output comparator is a high-speed, differential comparator with an open-collector output to simplify interfacing with any MPU or logic family.

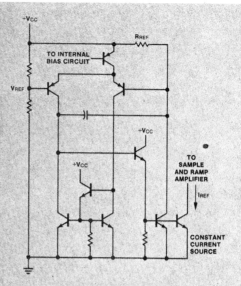

Fig. 4   Reference Current Generator

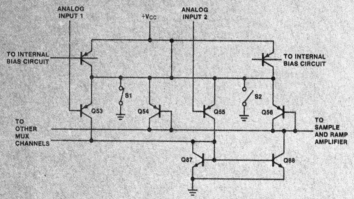

Fig. 5   Simplified Schematic of Two Multiplexer Channels

CONVERSION ERRORS

The major potential sources of error in the analog-to-pulse width technique are switching feedthrough of the sample and ramp amplifier, nonlinearity due to finite output impedance in the constant current source, and offset voltages in the sample and ramp amplifier and the output comparator. However, the sample and ramp amplifier switching feedthrough is better than 80 dB, which reduces its error contribution; likewise, the output impedance of the constant current source, while finite, is still sufficiently high to easily achieve 12-bit resolution.

The offset voltages represent a dc error that can readily be corrected by using the arithmetic capability of the resident microprocessor for automatic calibration. In these processes, the MUX input addressed by (000) is internally connected to ground and the input addressed by (111) is internally connected to V_{REF}. By converting ground and V_{REF} to digital pulses, data corresponding to zero volts and to a known fraction of full-scale input can be stored in the MPU memory for use by automatic zero and calibration programming. Using this process, a typical system exhibits 10-bit accuracy with a sample time of 40 μs and a maximum resolution time of 256 μs, which corresponds to a 12-V full-scale input.

MUX ERRORS

A simplified schematic of two multiplexer channels *(Figure 5)* shows that, with S1 closed and S2 open, no current flows through Q53 and Q54, while current flows through the other input pair. The current through Q55 and Q56 is routed to the common current mirror (Q87 and Q88), causing the output to the sample and ramp amplifier to assume the potential of analog input 2. Since Q55 and Q56 have different emitter-collector voltages, the finite transistor output conductances make a MUX error contribution in the range of 2 mV.

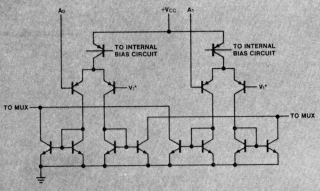

*$V_t \approx 1.6$ V (DIGITAL THRESHOLD)

Fig. 6 Simplified Schematic of One-of-Eight Address Decoder

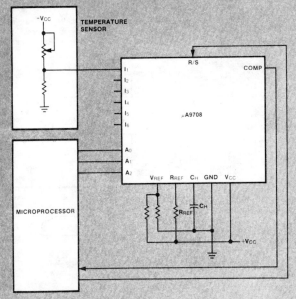

Fig. 7 Typical μA9708 Application

A second MUX error contribution, typically about 4 mV, is made by the relative base-emitter match of all the transistors. The base-emitter match contribution of the common current mirror transistors is common to all MUX channels.

ADDRESS DECODING
The inputs to the 1-of-8 address decoder (Figure 6) are buffered through a differential pair; decoding is accomplished by ORing the mirror transistor collectors. The digital threshold (V_t) for the 1-of-8 decoder is TTL compatible, simplifying interface considerations.

APPLICATION
A typical use of the μA9708 is in conjunction with a microprocessor as a temperature controller (Figure 7). Through an I/O port, the MPU selects the analog channel input to be converted. After issuing the start command, the MPU executes a register increment operation until the comparator output assumes a logic '0', signifying that the conversion is complete. The processor is then free to return to the main program control with the temperature information, converted to a digital form, stored in the internal register.

As this application illustrates, the μA9708 requires only a single voltage rail and includes ground potential in its dynamic range. The device also exhibits 8-bit non-corrected and 10-bit corrected precision. With incorporation of several functions into a single integrated circuit added to these advantages, the μA9708 A/D converter represents a sensible, cost-effective approach to multi-channel microprocessor-based data acquisition systems. □

DIGITAL DISPLAY SYSTEMS

by
Eric G. Breeze

INTRODUCTION

Automation continues to demand better display readout devices for point of sale equipment, DVMs, frequency meters, counters, etc. The result is a wide variety of shapes, sizes, input drive requirements and principles of operation of display units. Most electronic readout devices use neon, fluorescent, incandescent, electroluminescent or gallium arsenide methods to form or illuminate the readout display.

A display decoder/driver takes 4-bit (usually BCD) input data and decodes it into the correct format for the particular display being activated. Outputs must be of sufficient current and voltage and correct polarity to drive the display. Such decoder/drivers are now available for many display types in a single integrated circuit.

DISPLAYS

One of the oldest electronic numeric readouts is the one-of-ten display such as the NIXIE* tube. An inherent disadvantage is that each of the numbers within the tube is not on the same plane. This is very evident when a number of displays are used side by side. Additionally, the red illumination of the displays makes it difficult to change the readout color. Also, they are difficult to multiplex because of relatively high voltage requirements. Seven-segment displays have become popular due to their lower prices and pleasant, modern numeral format. These displays are available in a wide variety of size, color and type.

Incandescent displays can be made in a wide range of sizes and colors and are among the brightest available depending upon the lamps used. Until recently their main disadvantage was reliability due to segment failure. New materials, packages and methods however, have improved their reliability.

Many newer incandescent displays have all seven segment filaments contained within a single vacuum envelope and are compatible with standard DTL and TTL voltages. Multiplexing incandescent readouts doesn't offer much advantage in part count as each of the display segments requires a diode to stop sneak electrical paths.

Cold cathode displays, also known as *neon, gas discharge,* or *plasma* displays are improved nixie-type displays with seven segments instead of 10 numeral cathodes. Easily read and red-orange in color, they are available in sizes up to 0.75 inches high. They do have a disadvantage in that a high anode potential is required making them difficult to multiplex.

Fluorescent displays are blue-green, available to approximately 0.6 inch character height, and are used primarily in imported calculators. Their relatively low current and voltage requirements make them easy to multiplex.

The *light emitting diode* is a modern technology, solid state device using either gallium arsenide or gallium arsenide phosphide. Generally, the advantage of these displays lies in their smaller size, more reliable operation under severe mechanical conditions, and voltage current compatibility with standard integrated circuit technology. LEDs are available from 0.1 inch to 0.8 inch heights and are typically red in color; however, yellows and greens are offered at a price. Most of the smaller 0.1 inch LEDs are used in domestic hand calculators.

Liquid crystal displays are unique because they scatter, rather than generate, light. There are two basic types: reflective which requires front illumination, and transmissive which requires rear illumination. Liquid crystal display devices have the lowest power requirements of any display; however, they require an ac drive system which makes them difficult to multiplex. Short operating life, low reliability, and sensitivity to ultraviolet light have impeded the progress of these displays.

Other technologies for making 7-segment displays are electroluminescent and light emitting thin films with very high voltage requirements, but IC decoder/drivers for these displays are cumbersome and difficult to make.

*NIXIE is a registered trademark of Burroughs Corporation

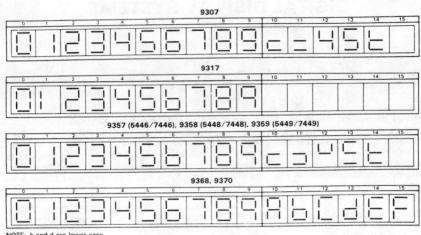

9307

9317

9357 (5446/7446), 9358 (5448/7448), 9359 (5449/7449)

9368, 9370

NOTE: b and d are lower case.

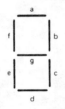

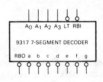

SEGMENTS ACTIVE HIGH RESISTIVE PULL-UP OUTPUT CIRCUIT

SEGMENT DESIGNATION

SEGMENTS ACTIVE LOW OPEN COLLECTOR OUTPUT CIRCUIT

INPUTS						OUTPUTS								DECIMAL OR FUNCTION
LT	RBI	A0	A1	A2	A3	a	b	c	d	e	f	g	RBO	
L	X	X	X	X	X	H	H	H	H	H	H	H	H	TEST
H	L	L	L	L	L	L	L	L	L	L	L	L	L	BLANK
H	H	L	L	L	L	H	H	H	H	H	H	L	H	0
H	X	H	L	L	L	L	H	H	L	L	L	L	H	1
H	H	L	H	L	L	H	H	L	H	H	L	H	H	2
H	H	H	H	L	L	H	H	H	H	L	L	H	H	3
H	H	L	L	H	L	L	H	H	L	L	H	H	H	4
H	H	H	L	H	L	H	L	H	H	L	H	H	H	5
H	H	L	H	H	L	L	L	H	H	H	H	H	H	6
H	H	H	H	H	L	H	H	H	L	L	L	L	H	7
H	H	L	L	L	H	H	H	H	H	H	H	H	H	8
H	H	H	L	L	H	H	H	H	L	L	H	H	H	9
H	H	L	H	L	H	L	L	L	H	H	L	H	H	10
H	H	H	H	L	H	L	L	L	L	H	L	H	H	11
H	H	L	L	H	H	L	L	L	H	L	L	H	H	12
H	H	H	L	H	H	L	H	H	L	L	H	H	H	13
H	H	L	H	H	H	H	L	L	H	L	H	H	H	14
H	X	H	H	H	H	L	L	L	L	L	L	L	H	15

INPUTS						OUTPUTS								DECIMAL OR FUNCTION
LT	RBI	A0	A1	A2	A3	ā	b̄	c̄	d̄	ē	f̄	ḡ	RBO	
L	X	X	X	X	X	L	L	L	L	L	L	L	H	TEST
H	L	L	L	L	L	H	H	H	H	H	H	H	H	BLANK
H	H	L	L	L	L	L	L	L	L	L	L	H	H	0
H	X	H	L	L	L	H	L	L	H	H	H	H	H	1
H	H	L	H	L	L	L	L	H	L	L	H	L	H	2
H	H	H	H	L	L	L	L	L	L	H	H	L	H	3
H	H	L	L	H	L	H	L	L	H	H	L	L	H	4
H	H	H	L	H	L	L	H	L	L	H	L	L	H	5
H	H	L	H	H	L	H	H	L	L	L	L	L	H	6
H	H	H	H	H	L	L	L	L	H	H	H	H	H	7
H	H	L	L	L	H	L	L	L	L	L	L	L	H	8
H	H	H	L	L	H	L	L	L	H	H	L	L	H	9
H	H	L	H	L	H	H	H	H	L	L	H	L	H	10
H	H	H	H	L	H	H	H	H	H	L	H	L	H	11
H	H	L	L	H	H	H	H	H	L	H	H	L	H	12
H	H	H	L	H	H	H	L	L	H	H	L	L	H	13
H	H	L	H	H	H	L	H	H	L	H	L	L	H	14
H	X	H	H	H	H	H	H	H	H	H	H	L	L	15

Decoder/drivers for 7-segment displays accept a 4-bit BCD 8421 input code and produce the appropriate outputs for selection of segments in a 7-segment matrix display used for representing the decimal numbers 0—9 and alpha characters when necessary. The seven outputs (a, b, c, d, e, f, g) of the decoder select the corresponding segments in the matrices shown. The numeric designations chosen to represent the decimal numbers are shown in the decode fonts above.

The 9368 and 9370 devices have built-in latch circuits for data storage. Latches are activated by a single active Low Enable input. When the Enable is Low, the latches are transparent; when High, the data present at the inputs prior to the Enable going High is stored.

When decoders have active Low input Lamp Test LT, this input overrides all other conditions and enables a check on possible display malfunctions. The RBO terminal of the decoder can be OR-tied with a modulating signal via isolating buffer for either pulse duration intensity modulations or display blanking.

9357A,B / 7446,47

SEGMENTS ACTIVE LOW
OPEN COLLECTOR OUTPUT CIRCUIT

LT	RBI	A0	A1	A2	A3	ā	b̄	c̄	d̄	ē	f̄	ḡ	BI OR RBO	DECIMAL OR FUNCTION
L	X	X	X	X	X	L	L	L	L	L	L	L	H	TEST
H	L	L	L	L	L	H	H	H	H	H	H	H	L	BLANK
H	H	L	L	L	L	L	L	L	L	L	L	H	H	0
	X	H	L	L	L	H	L	L	H	H	H	H	H	1
	L	H	L	L	L	L	L	H	L	L	H	L	H	2
	H	H	L	L	L	L	L	L	L	H	H	L	H	3
	L	L	H	L	L	H	L	L	H	H	L	L	H	4
	H	L	H	L	L	L	H	L	L	H	L	L	H	5
	L	H	H	L	L	H	H	L	L	L	L	L	H	6
	H	H	H	L	L	L	L	L	H	H	H	H	H	7
	L	L	L	H	L	L	L	L	L	L	L	L	H	8
	H	L	L	H	L	L	L	L	H	H	L	L	H	9
	L	H	L	H	L	H	H	H	L	L	H	L	H	10
	H	H	L	H	L	H	H	L	L	H	H	L	H	11
	L	L	H	H	L	L	H	H	H	H	L	L	H	12
	H	L	H	H	L	L	H	H	L	H	L	L	H	13
	L	H	H	H	L	H	H	H	L	L	L	L	H	14
H	X	H	H	H	H	H	H	H	H	H	H	H	L	15

9358 / 7448

SEGMENTS ACTIVE HIGH
RESISTIVE PULL-UP OUTPUT CIRCUIT

LT	RBI	A0	A1	A2	A3	a	b	c	d	e	f	g	BI OR RBO	DECIMAL OR FUNCTION
L	X	X	X	X	X	H	H	H	H	H	H	H	H	TEST
H	L	L	L	L	L	L	L	L	L	L	L	L	L	BLANK
H	H	L	L	L	L	H	H	H	H	H	H	L	H	0
	X	H	L	L	L	L	H	H	L	L	L	L	H	1
	L	H	L	L	L	H	H	L	H	H	L	H	H	2
	H	H	L	L	L	H	H	H	H	L	L	H	H	3
	L	L	H	L	L	L	H	H	L	L	H	H	H	4
	H	L	H	L	L	H	L	H	H	L	H	H	H	5
	L	H	H	L	L	L	L	H	H	H	H	H	H	6
	H	H	H	L	L	H	H	H	L	L	L	L	H	7
	L	L	L	H	L	H	H	H	H	H	H	H	H	8
	H	L	L	H	L	H	H	H	L	L	H	H	H	9
	L	H	L	H	L	L	L	L	H	H	L	H	H	10
	H	H	L	H	L	L	L	H	H	L	L	H	H	11
	L	L	H	H	L	H	L	L	L	L	H	H	H	12
	H	L	H	H	L	H	L	L	H	L	H	H	H	13
	L	H	H	H	L	L	L	L	H	H	H	H	H	14
H	X	H	H	H	H	L	L	L	L	L	L	L	L	15

9359 / 7449

SEGMENTS ACTIVE HIGH
OPEN COLLECTOR OUTPUT CIRCUIT

BI	A0	A1	A2	A3	a	b	c	d	e	f	g	DECIMAL OR FUNCTION
L	X	X	X	X	L	L	L	L	L	L	L	BLANK
H	L	L	L	L	H	H	H	H	H	H	L	0
	H	L	L	L	L	H	H	L	L	L	L	1
	L	H	L	L	H	H	L	H	H	L	H	2
	H	H	L	L	H	H	H	H	L	L	H	3
	L	L	H	L	L	H	H	L	L	H	H	4
	H	L	H	L	H	L	H	H	L	H	H	5
	L	H	H	L	L	L	H	H	H	H	H	6
	H	H	H	L	H	H	H	L	L	L	L	7
	L	L	L	H	H	H	H	H	H	H	H	8
	H	L	L	H	H	H	H	L	L	H	H	9
	L	H	L	H	L	L	L	H	H	L	H	10
	H	H	L	H	L	L	H	H	L	L	H	11
	L	L	H	H	H	L	L	L	L	H	H	12
	H	L	H	H	H	L	L	H	L	H	H	13
	L	H	H	H	L	L	L	H	H	H	H	14
H	H	H	H	H	L	L	L	L	L	L	L	15

9368 7-SEGMENT DECODER DRIVER/LATCH

LATCH ENABLE	OUTPUTS
L	Data follows input
H	Store

SEGMENTS ACTIVE HIGH
CURRENT LIMITED
OPEN EMITTER OUTPUT CIRCUIT

9368

	RBI	A3	A2	A1	A0	a	b	c	d	e	f	g	RBO	DISPLAYS
*	X	X	X	X	X	L	L	L	L	L	L	L	L*	BLANK
0	L	L	L	L	L	L	L	L	L	L	L	L	L	BLANK
0	H	L	L	L	L	H	H	H	H	H	H	L	H	0
1	X	L	L	L	H	L	H	H	L	L	L	L	H	1
2		L	L	H	L	H	H	L	H	H	L	H	H	2
3		L	L	H	H	H	H	H	H	L	L	H	H	3
4		L	H	L	L	L	H	H	L	L	H	H	H	4
5		L	H	L	H	H	L	H	H	L	H	H	H	5
6		L	H	H	L	H	L	H	H	H	H	H	H	6
7		L	H	H	H	H	H	H	L	L	L	L	H	7
8		H	L	L	L	H	H	H	H	H	H	H	H	8
9		H	L	L	H	H	H	H	L	L	H	H	H	9
10		H	L	H	L	H	H	H	L	H	H	H	H	A
11		H	L	H	H	L	L	H	H	H	H	H	H	b
12		H	H	L	L	H	L	L	H	H	H	L	H	C
13		H	H	L	H	L	H	H	H	H	L	H	H	d
14		H	H	H	L	H	L	L	H	H	H	H	H	E
15	X	H	H	H	H	H	L	L	L	H	H	H	H	F

*RBO used as an input

9370 7-SEGMENT DECODER DRIVER LATCH

LATCH ENABLE	OUTPUTS
L	Data follows input
H	Store

SEGMENTS ACTIVE LOW
OPEN COLLECTOR OUTPUT CIRCUIT

	RBI	A3	A2	A1	A0	ā	b̄	c̄	d̄	ē	f̄	ḡ	RBO	DISPLAY
*	X	X	X	X	X	H	H	H	H	H	H	H	L*	BLANK
0	L	L	L	L	L	H	H	H	H	H	H	H	L	BLANK
0	H	L	L	L	L	L	L	L	L	L	L	H	H	0
1	X	L	L	L	H	H	L	L	H	H	H	H	H	1
2		L	L	H	L	L	L	H	L	L	H	L	H	2
3		L	L	H	H	L	L	L	L	H	H	L	H	3
4		L	H	L	L	H	L	L	H	H	L	L	H	4
5		L	H	L	H	L	H	L	L	H	L	L	H	5
6		L	H	H	L	L	H	L	L	L	L	L	H	6
7		L	H	H	H	L	L	L	H	H	H	H	H	7
8		H	L	L	L	L	L	L	L	L	L	L	H	8
9		H	L	L	H	L	L	L	H	H	L	L	H	9
10		H	L	H	L	L	L	L	H	L	L	L	H	A
11		H	L	H	H	H	H	L	L	L	L	L	H	b
12		H	H	L	L	L	H	H	L	L	L	H	H	C
13		H	H	L	H	H	L	L	L	L	H	L	H	d
14		H	H	H	L	L	H	H	L	L	L	L	H	E
15	X	H	H	H	H	L	H	H	H	L	L	L	H	F

*RBO used as an input

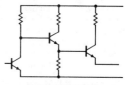

Vcc

RESISTIVE PULL-UP OUTPUT CIRCUIT   **OPEN COLLECTOR OUTPUT CIRCUIT**

CURRENT LIMITED
OPEN EMITTER OUTPUT CIRCUIT

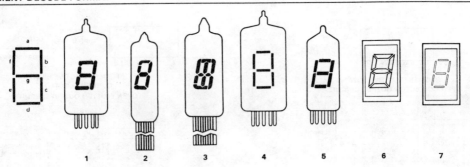

Decoder/driver logic for 7-segment displays is based on four basic decode formats. Output drive capability and polarity are adjusted to suit the display device. The decoder/drivers listed are grouped by logic decode format.

- 9307
- 9317
- 9357 (7445 & 7446), 9358 (7448), 9359 (7449)
- 9368, 9370

Decode format is an important consideration for 7-segment displays, not only for appearance and reliability, but also because certain segment shapes selected by manufacturers do not represent certain numerals well. For example, a left-hand one or a six without a tail would be difficult to decipher using the displays in 1, 2, and 3 above.

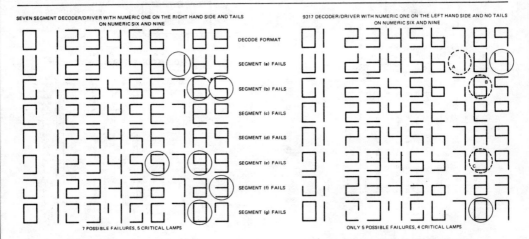

CONSIDERING A, B & C FAILURES FOR THE 9317 FORMAT ON THE RIGHT ABOVE, THERE IS A READABLE NUMBER. FAILURES A ①, B ⑥, AND C ⑨ ARE IN THE WRONG DECODE FONT. A CAREFUL OBSERVER WOULD NOTICE THAT THESE ARE THE WRONG NUMBERS. OF COURSE, THEY SHOULD READ 7 FOR A, 8 FOR B, AND 8 FOR C.

Another consideration involves possible failures and critical lamp considerations for both formats (decimal one on right segments with tails on six and nine and decimal one on left segments without tails on six and nine). Note that for the 9317 font, dotted circles show actual numerals even with segment failures but the numeric formats are wrong. Thus, there are actually only two possible failures and two critical lamps if the viewer realizes that the numbers 1, 6 and 9 are in the wrong format. Considering all readable numerals, there are five failures and four critical lamps.

The elimination of the tails on the six and nine provides the greatest single contribution to reliability. Placing the decimal one on the left hand segments also increases

reliability. This is because the distribution of segment use for all ten numerals is more equal.

LAMP SEGMENT USED	SEGMENT USE DISTRIBUTION NUMERIC ONE POSITION ON	
	L.H. SIDE	R.H. SIDE
B	7	8
C	8	9
E	5	4
F	7	6

Because of improved segment use distribution and fewer critical lamps, the 9317 format is an advantage in military or other applications where there is increased concern with erroneous readout.

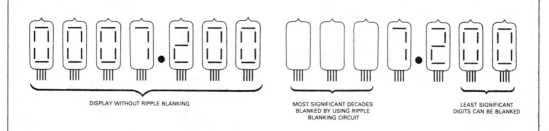

DISPLAY WITHOUT RIPPLE BLANKING

MOST SIGNIFICANT DECADES BLANKED BY USING RIPPLE BLANKING CIRCUIT

LEAST SIGNIFICANT DIGITS CAN BE BLANKED

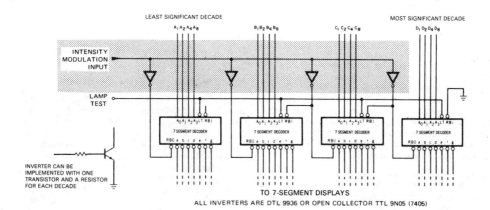

LEAST SIGNIFICANT DECADE

MOST SIGNIFICANT DECADE

INTENSITY MODULATION INPUT

LAMP TEST

INVERTER CAN BE IMPLEMENTED WITH ONE TRANSISTOR AND A RESISTOR FOR EACH DECADE

TO 7-SEGMENT DISPLAYS

ALL INVERTERS ARE DTL 9936 OR OPEN COLLECTOR TTL 9N05 (7405)

Leading or trailing edge zero suppression is particularly valuable in multidigit displays with a decimal point. Legibility is enhanced by blanking irrelevant decades. All devices except the 9359 have provision for automatic blanking of the leading and/or trailing edge zeros in a multidigit decimal number, resulting in an easily readable decimal display, conforming to normal writing practice. In an 8-digit, mixed integer, fraction decimal representation, using the automatic blanking capability, 0007.200 would be displayed as 7.2. Leading edge zero suppression is obtained by connecting the Ripple Blanking Output RBO of a decoder to the Ripple Blanking Input RBI of the next lower stage device. The most significant decoder stage should have the RBI input grounded. Since the suppression of the least significant integer zero in a number is not usually desired, the RBI input of this decoder stage should be left open. A similar procedure for the fractional part of a display provides automatic suppression of trailing edge zeros.

The 9368 and 9370 devices have built-in latch circuits for data storage. Latches are activated by a single active Low Enable input. When the Enable is Low, the latches are transparent; when High, the data present at the inputs prior to the Enable going High is stored. Note that with the 9368 and 9370, the RBI and RBO are activated by data stored within their latch functions.

As shown, the RBI of the most significant decade decoder is grounded. If a BCD zero is present on this decade's inputs, this display is blanked and RBO is Low. The remainder of the decoders operate in the same manner; consequently, this system is called Ripple Blanking.

The RBO of these decoders has two functions: In addition to its use as an active Low output to detect BCD zeros when RBI is Low, it can also be used as an OR-tied input for either blanking the entire display or controlling brightness by applying pulse duration intensity modulation. The OR-tie capability of the RBO is tied to open collector TTL, DTL or discrete device inverters to control brightness shown in shaded area.

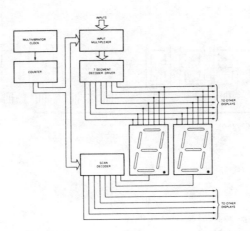

Typically, multiplexing is a result of economic considerations such as requirements for simple drive circuitry, or minimum interconnections between the displays and the system providing the data to be displayed. The multiplexed or direct drive display selection is based upon each system's design characteristics. Overall circuit complexity and cost are primary considerations in the majority of consumer and industrial design efforts as opposed to military applications where the priority is more commonly maximum reliability.

In some systems, this choice is quite clear. For example, the popular pocket calculators use a single chip producing data in a serialized format while multiple digit LED displays employ data bussing for ease of manufacturing and to reduce connections. Therefore, the connections and drive units between display and chip are held to a minimum.

Conversely, in a system where the data is presented in parallel format and close to the display, multiplexing the data would greatly increase system complexity and cost. Any data sent a considerable distance should be sent on a single cable and serialized (an advanced form of multiplexing). However, a display subsystem located a few feet away may warrant a simpler form of multiplexing using fewer wires. Even though purchase price and maintenance costs of cables, connectors and joints is increasing, the cost of MSI per function is decreasing. Multiplexing and the degree of multiplexing, therefore, is to be considered carefully.

Five units are used in this basic multiplexing circuit.

- A decoder/driver usually decoding BCD input data to the code requirements of the display device, normally 7-segment or 1-of-10 decode.

- An input address selector (multiplexer or shift register) taking the BCD input data to be displayed to the decoder/driver.

- A scan decoder selecting the display to be energized.

- A scan counter addressing the scan decoder and input address selector.

- A clock input determining the multiplexing rate.

Multiplexing a small number of displays is not economical unless the data input is in serial form. Multiplexing can offer advantages after about four digits for some display types. The maximum number of digits is about 12 (except with LED displays). Beyond this number, it becomes difficult to power each display unit for its diminishing share of time. For a given brightness the display will require a given power whether or not it is multiplexed. When multiplexed, this power is supplied to the display in pulses for a fraction of the complete scan cycle. Hence, voltage and/or current must be increased over that required for the dc conditions. Multiplexing incandescent displays is less attractive because each filament of the display requires a diode to stop sneak electrical paths.

Advantages:

- Fewer parts—lower system cost.

- Easier printed circuit layout.

- Reduced interconnection wiring when readout is remote from display logic.

- System hook-up requires fewer parts.

Disadvantages:

- Higher operating voltages or current required for equivalent brightness.

- Scan rate must be above 1 kHz to reduce flicker.

- Careful decoupling of power supplies to stop switching transients is required.

- A clock is required to drive multiplexed systems.

- Clock failure results in full power to displays, damaging an unprotected system.

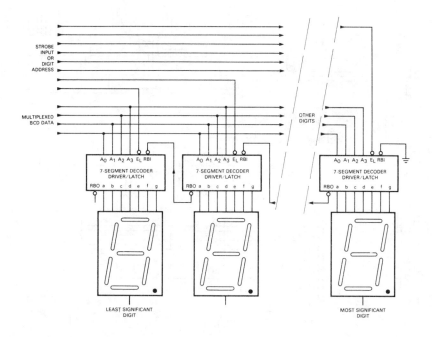

9368 Sources 19 mA at 1.7 V, Drives FND 70 Directly
9370 Sinks 25 mA, $V_{CC\ MAX}$ 7 V

This system takes advantage of the storage capabilities of the 7-segment decoder/driver/latch combination. The input data is in multiplexed form while the displays operate in the static mode.

The principle advantage of this system is that 5 V incandescent or FND 70 LED displays are driven directly without any other components using the existing 5 V supply. There are other advantages over the standard multiplex system.

- Low multiplexing rates can be used without flicker.

- Relatively low power line spiking.

- Economically sound on many systems up to 5 digits (incandescents allow even more).

- Clock failure does not cause excessive voltage or currents to be applied to any one display.

Some disadvantages include:

- BCD data and strobe timing (digit address) is critical.

- PC layout can be slightly more difficult depending on display mounting configuration.

The input BCD data must be stable during the last 30 ns of the active Low enable pulse. All strobe pulse glitches must be avoided.

This method is particularly advantageous in the case of 5 V incandescent displays because the total cost of the decoder/driver/latches compares with the standard multiplex system which uses seven diodes (high insertion cost) per display, two power supply voltages, and a clock failure detection system.

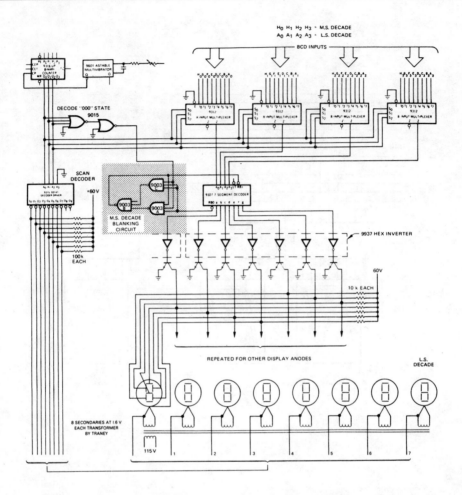

This circuit illustrates one of the simpler and more straightforward methods of a multiplexing system. Four 9312 8-input multiplexers select the BCD input data for the 9307 decoder. Address for the multiplexers and the scan decoder from the 9316 binary counter uses only the first three bits. Each 3-bit address selects the BCD input data to be displayed and the scan decoder energizes the correct display readout device. The counter progresses through all eight counts and repeats, activating each display unit for 1/8th of the scanning cycle. Higher operating voltage must be applied for the displays to have the same brightness as displays in a static mode (dc). The circuit as shown uses fluorescent diode displays. Other displays may be substituted with the appropriate drive circuitry.

MOST SIGNIFICANT DECADE BLANKING

The objective of the shaded circuit is to hold $\overline{RBI}$ Low

during a scan period until a decimal number other than zero appears and then shift $\overline{RBI}$ High for the rest of the scan period. The most significant decade is at the start of the scan period; the least significant is at the end.

When $\overline{RBI}$ is Low, any BCD zeros to the decoder will be blanked on the display, however any BCD number is displayed. Control of this input achieves most significant digit blanking.

The circuit sets the flip-flop (gates A and B) so gate B output is Low at the start of the scan period (zero count on scan decoder, active Low). With $\overline{RBI}$ Low and BCD zeros into the decoder, $\overline{RBO}$ is Low. With the first decimal number of the scan period, $\overline{RBO}$ goes High. As the reset line is also High, gate C output goes Low setting flip-flop, (gate B output High, therefore $\overline{RBI}$ is High). This sequence repeats each scan period.

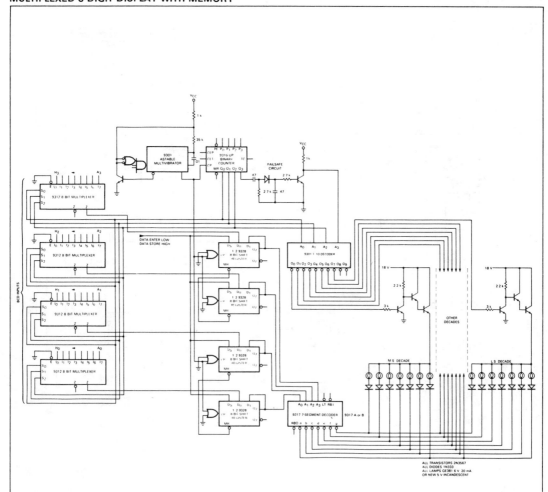

This multiplexing system has storage capability. Each bit of the 4-bit BCD code input is supplied to one of the four 9312 multiplexers. The multiplexer input addresses are selected by a 3-bit binary output from 9316 counter. The multiplexer outputs are fed into four 8-bit shift registers when Data Select D_S is Low. The multiplexer steps from one input address to the next on each clock pulse. Simultaneously, information is propagated through the shift registers to the decoder/driver. With D_S High, shift register output information is returned to the input to form a recirculating memory. Information continues to circulate as long as D_S is High and power is applied. Information must be present at the inputs for at least one complete scan period to insure that the multiplexers sample all inputs.

The failsafe circuit detects clock failure and disables the address to avoid excessive voltage to any one display. Incoming clock pulses are applied to a diode and C2 is charged to the peak voltage of the incoming pulse, which, through the transistor base resistor, supplies sufficient drive to maintain the transistor on. For protection, ac coupling is used in case the clock fails in the High state. The transistor output is applied to the most significant bit of the scan decoder and in normal operation stays Low. If the clock fails, the transistor output goes High and the scan decoder addresses the two unused outputs. As shown, it operates satisfactorily from 1 kHz up with duty cycle pulse widths down to 10%. This circuit uses incandescent displays. Other displays may be substituted with appropriate drive circuitry.

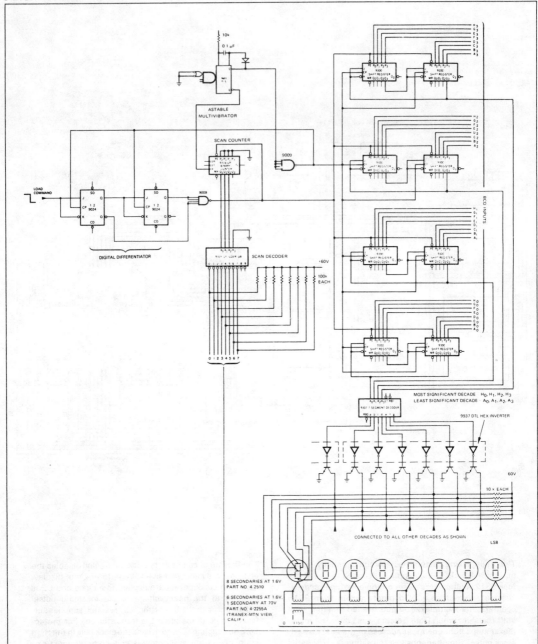

Four rows of 8-bit, parallel loadable shift registers with outputs fed back to inputs form a recirculating memory, storing the four BCD bits in parallel and the eight characters serially. The four lines of serial information are fed into the 7-segment decoder circuitry which drives the display tubes. All tube anodes are in parallel. Multiplexing is achieved by sequentially switching the cathodes (filaments) to ground with the scan decoder. Eight BCD digits of parallel data are entered into the shift register when the Load input goes from High to Low. This transition is detected by the digital differentiator and activates the PE inputs for one clock period.

INCANDESCENT DIGITAL DISPLAY SYSTEMS

Seven-segment incandescent displays are the oldest of all digital displays and have been used extensively for many military applications. They are available with character heights from 1/4 inch to several feet in a variety of colors.

Since these displays employ incandescent lamps, high brightnesses can be achieved and they are available in a wide range of voltages and currents. The simplest 7-segment display is lamps placed behind seven slots on some opaque material. Incandescent displays using seven aligned filaments to comprise a 7-segment character within one package are now available. One package is a small vacuum tube envelope; while another is a special, miniature flat package which inserts directly into a standard 16-lead Dual In-line socket. Many of the incandescent displays can be driven directly from a wide range of available decoder drivers (see selection guide).

MULTIPLEXING 7-SEGMENT INCANDESCENT DISPLAYS

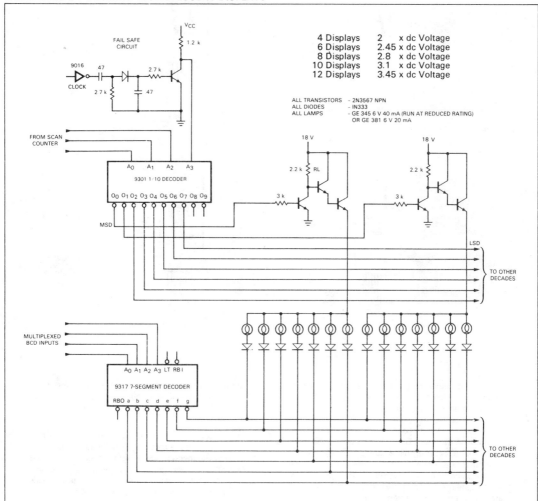

4 Displays	2	x dc Voltage
6 Displays	2.45	x dc Voltage
8 Displays	2.8	x dc Voltage
10 Displays	3.1	x dc Voltage
12 Displays	3.45	x dc Voltage

ALL TRANSISTORS – 2N3567 NPN
ALL DIODES – 1N333
ALL LAMPS – GE 345 6 V 40 mA (RUN AT REDUCED RATING)
OR GE 381 6 V 20 mA

Multiplexed incandescent displays receive power in pulses for only a fraction of the complete scan period. For adequate brightness, voltage must be increased. The wattage for an incandescent lamp at a stated brightness will remain constant regardless of duty cycle or waveform shape, providing the multiplexing rate is faster then the time-constant of the filament. Power dissipation for a constant load is proportional to the square of the input voltage. Therefore, calculation of the required supply voltage for multiplexed operation is possible.

Multiplexed voltage $=\sqrt{\text{Number of displays}}$ x dc voltage of lamps, i.e., eight digits of multiplexed display readouts—6.3 volt lamps $\equiv \sqrt{8}$ x 6.3 = 17.5 volts.

This table gives the factors for common numbers of multiplexed units. Voltage drops across the integrated circuits and switching transistors must be added to these figures. Some of the more advanced types use fiber optics or light-carrying beams to illuminate the seven segments.

DIGIVAC
CONVENTIONAL
7 SEGMENT
FORMAT

SYLVANIA
FLUOROTRON

LEGI
DG10
NEC

LEGI
DG12
DG19
NEC
LD

Fluorescent displays are basically vacuum tube diodes or triodes in which the anodes form a visible 7 or 8-segment character. Each anode is coated with phosphor. A positive potential between anode and cathode (filament) accelerates electrons to the anode phosphor causing the anode to glow. The light emitted by the phosphors is a wide spectrum in the blue/green region which can be filtered to certain other colors with little light loss. The cathode (filament) is suspended in front of the display segments and is hardly visible since it is only heated sufficiently for electron emission.

Of the two types of fluorescent displays, triodes are somewhat easier to operate in a multiplexed mode because they have an extra, almost invisible control grid electrode between the filament and the anode. Multiple digit displays of up to ten digits in a single glass and metal enclosure are available using fluorescent triodes.

The main advantages of fluorescent displays are their economy, low power requirements, wide viewing angle, single plane readout, and minimum likelihood of erroneous readout with display failures. Two disadvantages are the need for a filament supply and their fragile structure.

The selection of a decoder for fluorescent displays should take into account the fact that some displays have altered segment shapes as shown. Some decode formats provided by the decoders generate aesthetically unpleasant characters. Following are some points to note when selecting a fluorescent display decoder/driver.

9307   The decoder format is acceptable for all types of 7-segment displays. The decimal one appears on the right hand segments.

9358/9359   With these decoders, the decimal six looks poor on all except the Digivac* display. The decimal one is shown on the right hand side.

*Digivac is a registered trademark of Tung-Sol division of Wagner.

414

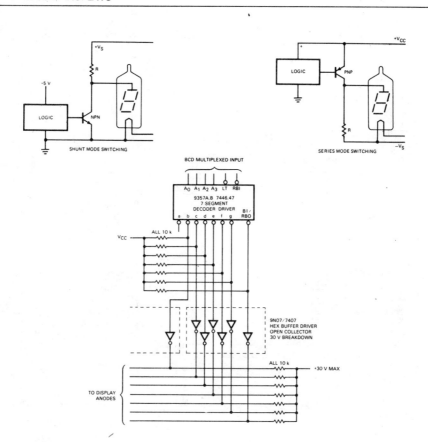

Driving fluorescent displays requires a 7-segment decoder and extra components. There are two basic methods of switching, the shunt method and the series method. As seen, the shunt method has a slightly better cost/part count when supply voltages of less than 30 V are involved because an open collector, hex inverter integrated circuit can be used. With supplies above 30 V, both systems require approximately the same number of parts; however, the series method is superior for power consumption. The shunt method shown draws maximum current when the display is blanked while the series method draws maximum current when all segments are illuminated.

The value of the load resistor selected for use with the shunt method is the result of a compromise between resistor power dissipation in the segments On and Off states. When the display is Off, the full supply voltage is across the resistor and maximum power is dissipated. While On, however, the only voltage drop is due to the segment current. Typical operating conditions for a non-multiplexed fluorescent display are 25 V and 0.5 mA to 1 mA per segment. The following example shows a driving method for 30 V supplies.

With a 30 V supply, allowing for a 5 V drop across the resistors at 0.5 mA per segment, $R = 10 \text{ k}\Omega$. For displaying a decimal eight (all segments illuminated) total current = 7 segments x 0.5 mA = 3.5 mA. This means 105 mW supply power is required. In a blanked display, the current is 3 mA per segment (7) or 21 mA requiring 630 mW supply power. The Off to On power ratio is 630:105 or 6:1, worst case.

This would indicate that supply voltage regulation is required to maintain even brightness for all numerals displayed. A substantially better On to Off ratio is obtainable with a higher supply voltage.

With a supply voltage of 60 V, allowing for a 35 V drop across R, 0.5 mA per segment = $70 \text{ k}\Omega$. When displaying a decimal eight (3.5 mA), W = 60 x 3.5 or 210 mW. With the display blanked, current per segment is .85 mA or 6 mA. W = 60 x 6 or 360 mW. The Off to On power ratio is 360:210 or 1.7:1.

The higher supply voltage with larger resistance provides a more constant current source.

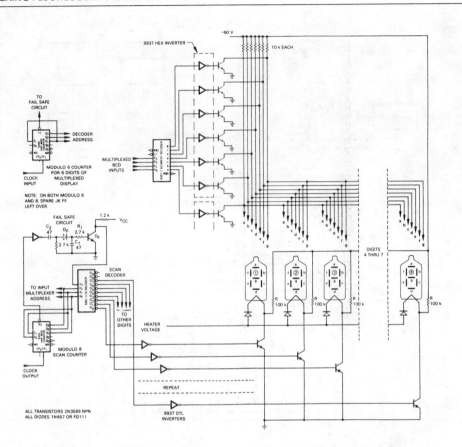

The multiplexing system shown supplies the display heaters from convenient +5 V logic levels using a 1/8 (eight digit display) duty cycle. Heater power to the displays is supplied in pulse form and the thermal inertial of the filaments keeps them hot during the off period. Each of the display heaters has a transistor and a diode. The display is active when the transistor is conducting. When the transistor is Off, active resistor R pulls up the cathode to a +V potential, reverse biasing the diode leaving no potential across the display tube.

All the logic operates from a +5 V supply and thus it dictates a positive display voltage and a shunt method of switching. Because the display filaments are resistive, they have a given resistance value for a given emission value (ignoring switching losses) for either a pulsed or a dc power supply. The listed dc current and voltage specifications allow the calculation of the pulsed values.

$$V_P = (\sqrt{N} \times V_F) + \text{diode and switching losses}$$

where: V_P = required voltage

N = number of parts in scan cycle

V_F = dc filament voltages of the display

Current is determined by substituting I_F filament current

For the 8-digit example shown, the required pulsed voltage calculation is given.

$$V_P = (\sqrt{8} \times 1.4 \text{ V}) + .9 \text{ V} = 4.9 \text{ V}$$

where: 8 = number of digits,

1.4 = filament voltage,

.9 = diode/switching loss (.7 V/diode and .2 V/transistor)

This circuit is easily changed to a 6-digit system by changing the scan counter to a Modulo 6.

A failsafe circuit is added to the most significant digit of the scan decoder to prevent full filament supply voltage from being applied to any one heater should the clock fail. With the counter operating, pulses are supplied to diode D_F and the R-C network, biasing transistor Q_F on. Failure removes the bias on Q_F and the input code to the scan decoder addresses unused outputs 8 and 9. This circuit operates with clock frequencies up to 20 kHz.

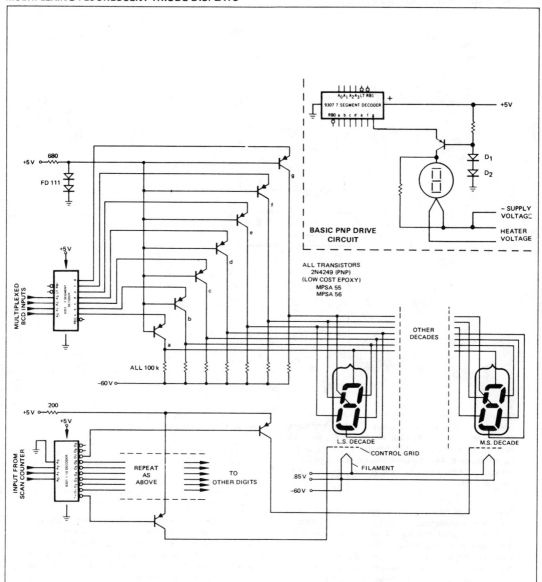

The only decoder/driver which provides the correct decode format for fluorescent triode displays is the 9307 and it requires the use of extra drive components. The most economical method uses pnp drive transistors with negative supply voltage. The active high output of the 9307 biases the transistor emitter more positive than the base, turning the transistor on. Diodes D1 and D2 insure that the transistor is back biased in the Off position (right). Collector resistors are used so anode

capacitance charges can be leaked off quickly.

Control grids of fluorescent displays are activated to the same potential as the anodes to obtain full brightness. They are activated by a pnp switch transistor. This is driven directly by the output of the 9301 scan decoder which has active low outputs. The base-emitter current on the pnp transistor is limited by a single resistor in common with all the pnp emitters.

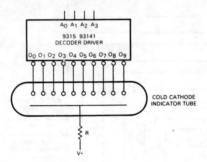

Gas discharge displays, otherwise known as cold cathode, are available in a wide variety of shapes and sizes. The oldest and most familiar is the NIXIE*, with the newest sample being the Burroughs Panaplex or the Sperry displays. All of these displays require a high supply voltage in the range of 80 to 200 V to cause ionization for display.

The nixie-type tube is not a 7-segment display but a 1-of-10 multiplane display with ten stacked cathodes shaped as characters mounted behind an almost invisible anode in a glass envelope filled with neon gas. A high potential between the anode and one of the cathode characters causes an ionization to occur and the character glows a dull red. These displays are available in a wide variety of shapes and sizes from miniature sizes with character heights of just over 1/4 inch to jumbo sizes with 2 inch characters.

The advantages of this type of display are: availability, reliability, wide selection of sizes and styles, and low power consumption. Special characters are available.

Some disadvantages of this display system are: high voltage requirements, multiplexing difficulty, multiplane display readout, and limited color selection.

Cold cathode displays require a 1-of-10 decoder/driver with high voltage breakdown npn transistors on the outputs. The transistors must have low leakage characteristics in the Off mode since leakage causes a background glow. Voltage across the displays after ionization is controlled by a series resistor, as shown above. This resistance value is given by the display manufacturers.

*NIXIE is a registered trademark of Burroughs Corporation

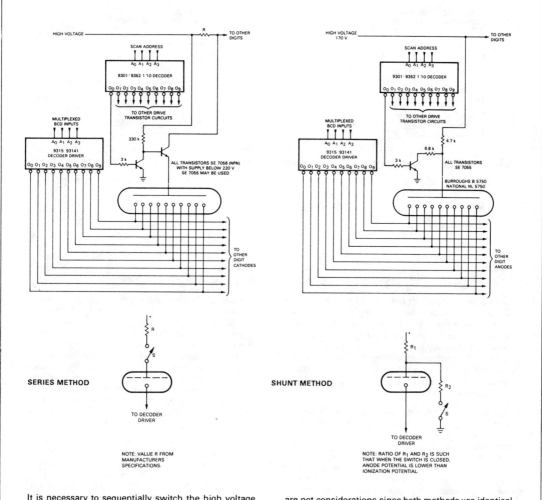

SERIES METHOD

NOTE: VALUE R FROM
MANUFACTURERS
SPECIFICATIONS.

SHUNT METHOD

NOTE: RATIO OF R_1 AND R_2 IS SUCH
THAT WHEN THE SWITCH IS CLOSED,
ANODE POTENTIAL IS LOWER THAN
IONIZATION POTENTIAL.

It is necessary to sequentially switch the high voltage anode supply when multiplexing this type of display so that only one digit is addressed at a time. There are two basic approaches for accomplishing this, the series method and the shunt method. Part count and economy are not considerations since both methods use identical hardware. The series method offers an advantage with lower power dissipation but places higher voltage and leakage requirements on the transistors. Leakage is not as important in the shunt method.

There are several different 7-segment gas discharge displays available, ranging widely in configuration and complexity. The oldest type are simply seven neon lamps arranged behind seven slots in an opaque material. Another form of 7-segment gas discharge displays is a small tube envelope which encloses a specially constructed 7-segment unit with a character height of 7/16 of an inch. The newer types are Burroughs Panaplex and the Sperry units. Burroughs Panaplex is a multi-digit unit and, therefore, must be multiplexed. Special drive considerations are required, best obtained from the manufacturer's literature. Sperry displays can be either driven directly or can be multiplexed if desired.

Neon 7-segment displays require a resistor in series with each of the cathodes. A separate resistor is required because the ionization start-up voltage required is higher than that needed to maintain ionization. Once ionization takes place the resistor lowers the voltage applied between segment cathode and anode thus maintaining correct segment current. Neon 7-segment displays can be multiplexed with the same techniques used for 1-of-10 cold cathode displays previously described.

LIGHT EMITTING DIODE DISPLAYS

COMMON CATHODE
(DECODER/DRIVER SOURCES CURRENT)

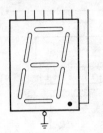

COMMON ANODE
(DECODER/DRIVER SINKS CURRENT)

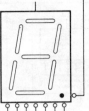

SINGLE DIODE LED DISPLAY CIRCUIT

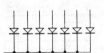

SINGLE DIODE LED DISPLAY CIRCUIT

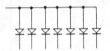

DUAL DIODE LED DISPLAY CIRCUIT

	GaP	GaAsP
1 DIODE	≃2.1 V	≃1.65 V

	GaP	GaAsP
1 DIODE	≃2.1 V	≃1.54 V

	GaP	GaAsP
2 DIODES	≃4.2 V	≃3.4 V

Light emitting diodes (LEDs) are now found in a wide variety of portable electronic equipment including pocket calculators, electronic stop watches, thermometers, digital voltmeters, and similar equipment. They have gained popularity by virtue of their compact size, voltage and current compatibility with integrated circuit technology, and solid-state reliability. Typically small in character size, they can be made up to 0.8 inch using hybrid construction techniques.

The standard LED display color is a bright, penetrating monochromatic red with sharply defined characters which appear about twice as large as their actual size. Green and yellow displays are also offered, but are somewhat more expensive. The primary disadvantage inherent with LEDs is a narrow spectrum of light output. This makes them not only difficult to filter for high ambient light applications, but impossible to filter for alternate colors. A polarized filter improves viewing under normal light circumstances. See the Selection Guide for a list of currently available LED displays.

LED displays use either gallium phosphide (GaP) or gallium arsenide phosphide (GaAsP). Both types seem to have equal advantages and disadvantages. They are available in two character formats, a 5 x 7 dot matrix which can display alphanumerics and lower cost, 7-segment displays. LED 7-segment displays use either common anode or common cathode techniques. The 0.1 inch character height calls for the common cathode. Hybrid construction can be either, but the common anode has more popularity. With the common cathode method, the decoder/driver must be able to source current into the display. The common anode variety requires the decoder/driver to sink current, which is presently easier.

Electrically, the LED is the same as the familiar solid-state diode with its inherent characteristics although with a higher forward voltage drop. Below the knee of the I/V curve, they pass little current. Above the knee, current increases linearly with voltage. Thus, uniform brightness of each segment and digit requires a constant current source rather than constant voltage. Light output increases linearly with current for low values until light saturation is reached and further current does not increase light output. Current should be limited to avoid device failure.

LED DISPLAY TERMINOLOGY

I_{PEAK}. Absolute maximum pulse current that can be passed through a segment without damaging the display. This is usually specified for some pulse width generally within 500 us to 1 ms. I_{PEAK} determines the maximum number of displays that can be multiplexed within a system array.

$I_{AVERAGE}$. Peak pulsed current x duty cycle*. Sometimes referred to as average segment current. It is generally specified as a typical value and a max limit.

$I_{AVERAGE (TYP)}$. Current for given light output (Luminous Intensity) at which the display is typically operated.

$I_{AVERAGE (MAX)}$. Maximum average current per segment the display can tolerate without overheating. Usually derated for ambient temperature.

LUMINOUS INTENSITY. Brightness and readability. There are many methods for measuring the light outputs of displays but, unfortunately, no one standard exists among manufacturers. Comparing light output specifications of various displays from different manufacturers will not indicate whether or not the displays have identical readability under the same ambient light conditions. This is because of the different materials and colors used for backgrounds and lens material, which affect contrast ratio between the illuminated segment and reflected ambient light from the display background. The best method for comparison is to try different displays under equal conditions.

*Duty Cycle = 1/N where N is the number of parts in a scan cycle.

INTENSITY MODULATION

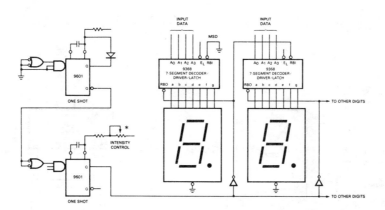

Applying intensity modulation to direct drive LEDs can result in a 15 to 20% power saving for essentially the same brightness. This is because LEDs operate most efficiently in the pulse mode and the eye tends to peak detect intensity changes. An added advantage: when a photo resistor* is used as a replacement for the intensity control potentiometer, it compensates for ambient light changes.

Using the 9368 decoder/driver and FND 70 LED display combination, an 80% duty cycle saves 20% of the LED drive power. Although this circuit is common cathode, intensity modulation applies also to common anode circuits.

POWER SAVING CONCEPT

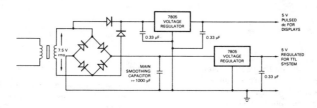

In some small line operated systems using TTL/MSI and LED or incandescent displays, a significant portion of the total dc power is consumed to drive the displays. Since it is irrelevant whether displays are driven from unfiltered dc or pulsed dc (at fast rates), a dual power system can be used that makes better utilization of transformer rms ratings. Using the system shown, the displays are driven by rectified and regulated, but unsmoothed voltage, while the rest of the system is driven by the conventional dc.

With the standard capacitor filter circuit, the rms current (full wave) loading of the transformer is approximately twice the dc output. Therefore the removal of a large portion of the filtered dc current requirement (display power) substantially reduces the transformer loading. Even more power is saved because the unfiltered display section appears as a constant current to the transformer after 6–8 V regulator voltage conduction level is reached, and then only consumes current at the rms input value.

Most commercial transformer manufacturers rate transformers with capacitive input filters as follows:

Full Wave Bridge Rectifier Circuit
 Transformer rms current = 1.8 x dc current required

Full Wave Center Tapped Rectifier Circuit
 Transformer rms current = 1.2 x dc current required

When this system is used with multiplexed displays, the multiplexed frequency must be chosen such that it does not beat with the 120 Hz rectified power frequencies.

The main advantages of this system are

- Reduced transformer rating
- Small smoothing capacitor
- Increased LED light output due to pulsed operation

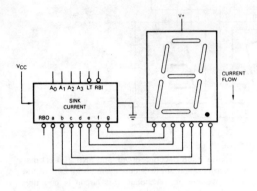

COMMON ANODE

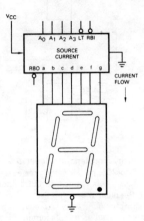

COMMON CATHODE

LED displays have electrical and light output rise times in the nanosecond region. This means they can be operated at a low duty cycle with high scanning rates when multiplexed. Scanning rates above 1 kHz are recommended. As many as 24 or more displays can be multiplexed. Because the human eye tends to peak-detect, a low duty cycle with high peak current pulsed into LED displays provides high apparent brightness.

Drive requirements for 7-segment decoder/drivers are not as stringent as those for character or digit address where the total pulsed current of all seven segments must pass through. Ideally, the decoder/driver is a constant current source or sink, depending upon the device. The digit address is a low resistance switch. Resistors may be required for current control to the displays,

depending on displays and decoders used.

In some applications, a common cathode LED display, when driven by the fixed current output of a 9368 decoder/driver/latch, is too bright. Since the 9368 has no provision for output current adjustment, an intensity modulation technique is used to reduce both brightness and power dissipation — and thus, heat. Because the human eye tends to peak detect, and because decreasing current to the display would decrease its efficiency, a pulsed duty cycle technique is superior to a "brute force" current reduction. A thirty percent savings in power can be realized without a significant loss of brightness. When a reduction in brightness is desired, further savings of power is possible.

MULTIPLEXING LED DISPLAYS

Segment and Strobe Driver Requirements

The drive requirements for multiplexed arrays are not only roughly proportional to the number of devices that are multiplexed, but vary also with the brightness required for each application. Operation in ambient sunlight requires considerably higher current than operation under normal interior lighting conditions.

Intensity

The efficiency and light output of LEDs, even with identical part numbers and from the same manufacturer, differ widely. The LED devices used in a multiplexed array should therefore always be purchased as a matched set or with the same intensity coding.

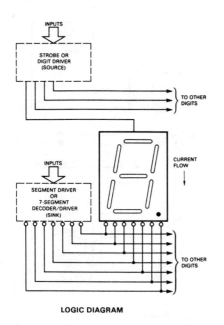

LOGIC DIAGRAM

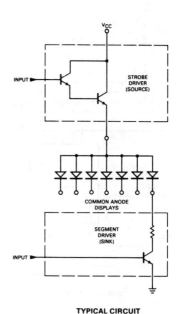

TYPICAL CIRCUIT

FND 507	Fairchild Optoelectronics
7730 Series	Hewlett Packard
DL 1A, 6, 8, 10A, 62, 707	Litronix
MAN 1, 6A, 10, 1001	Monsanto
TIL 302	Texas Instrument
SLA 1, 3, 4, 7	Opcoa

7-SEGMENT DECODER/DRIVERS (SINK CURRENT)

9317 7-segment decoder/driver sinks 40 mA and requires seven current limiting resistors. TTL inputs.

9357 7-segment decoder/driver sinks 40 mA and requires seven current limiting resistors. TTL inputs.

9370 7-segment decoder/driver/latch sinks 40 mA and requires seven current limiting resistors. TTL inputs.

SEGMENT DRIVERS (SINK CURRENT)

9662 Quad LED digit/lamp driver sinks 600 mA has Inverting Enable input control for inverting or non-inverting operation. If used as a segment driver, two 9662 devices and seven current limiting resistors are

needed to drive 7-segment displays. MOS/TTL compatible inputs.

9663 Hex LED digit/lamp driver sinks 600 mA is the same as 9662 but with six outputs.

STROBE OR DIGIT DRIVERS (SOURCE CURRENT)

9661 Programmable current quad segment driver sources 5-75 mA. MOS/TTL compatible inputs.

75491 Quad segment driver sinks or sources 50 mA. Each section has two transistors, Darlington connected, with uncommitted emitter and collector.

Transistors, High current npn or pnp transistors with resistors can be used for strobe or digit drive.

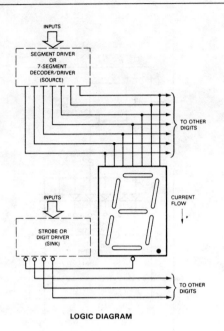

LOGIC DIAGRAM

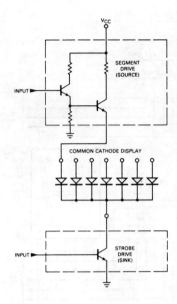

TYPICAL CIRCUIT

FND 70, 500	Fairchild Optoelectronics
FNA 30, 45	Fairchild Optoelectronics
DA 1007, DA 1009	Antex
R7M	Bowmar
4700 Series	Hewlett Packard
DL 4, 33, 34, 704	Litronix
NSN 33, 133	National Semiconductor
MAN 3, 4	Monsanto

7-SEGMENT DECODER/DRIVERS (SOURCE CURRENT)

9368 7-segment decoder/driver/latch sources 19 mA @ 1.7 V output. Hexadecimal decode format. TTL inputs.

9369 7-segment decoder/driver/latch sources 50 mA @ 3.4 V output and requires current limiting resistors. TTL inputs.

9660 7-segment decoder/driver with decimal point drive, sources 5-50 mA. Output current is controlled by one external resistor. MOS/TTL compatible inputs.

SEGMENT DRIVERS (SOURCE CURRENT)

9661 Programmable current quad segment driver (two per system required) sources 5-75 mA @ 3 V output. One output can be reduced by approximately 1/2 for decimal point drive. One external resistor determines the output currents of both devices.

75491 Quad segment driver sinks or sources 50 mA. Inverting when used in sink mode. Two devices and seven current limiting resistors are required to drive seven segments. Each section has two transistors, Darlington connected, with uncommitted emitter and collector.

75492 Hex LED/lamp driver sinks 250 mA. Each section has two transistors, Darlington connected, with uncommitted collector.

STROBE OR DIGIT DRIVERS (SINK CURRENT)

9662 Quad LED digit/lamp driver sinks 600 mA, has Inverting Enable input control for inverting or non-inverting operation. MOS/TTL compatible inputs.

9663 Hex LED digit/lamp driver sinks 600 mA is the same as 9662 with six outputs.

9345, 7445 1-of-10 decoder/driver sinks 80 mA. TTL inputs.

93145, 74145 1-of-10 decoder/driver sinks 80 mA. TTL inputs.

75491 Quad segment driver sinks or sources 50 mA. Each section has two transistors, Darlington connected, with uncommitted emitter and collector.

75492 Hex LED/lamp driver sinks 250 mA. Each section has a Darlington transistor with uncommitted collector.

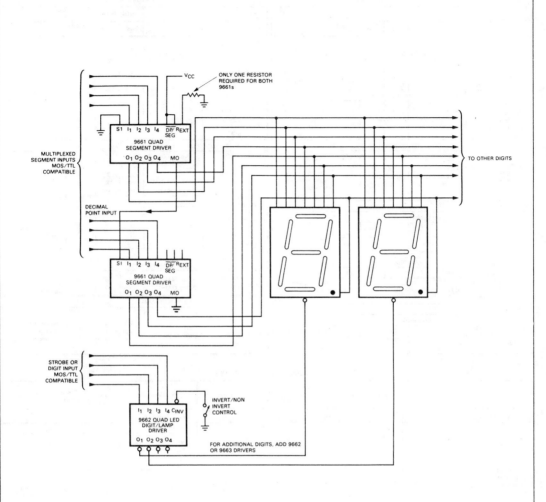

The multiplexing circuit shown uses two 9661 quad segment drivers. The four outputs of the first unit drive segments a, b, c, and d of each display. The four outputs of the second 9661 drive segments e, f, g, and the decimal point of each display.

In this circuit, the two 9661 segment drivers can be replaced with one 9660 7-segment decoder/driver when current required is less than 50 mA @ 3 V and BCD to 7-segment decoding is required.

Other segment/digit/lamp drivers can be used depending on display requirements.

9661 — Programmable current quad segment driver can source current from 5 to 75 mA @ 3 V. Output current is determined by one external resistor R_{EXT} to ground. If the DP/Segment inputs are not connected to V_{CC}, the current at O_4 is reduced by 50%, which is suitable for driving the decimal point. All inputs are TTL/MOS compatible.

9662 — Quad LED digit/lamp driver is capable of sinking 600 mA on each of four outputs and all inputs are TTL/MOS compatible. Inverting operation is selected by grounding the Control Invert input.

9663 — Hex LED digit/lamp driver is the same as the 9662 but with six outputs.

DIGITAL DISPLAY SELECTION GUIDE

DIRECT DRIVE DISPLAYS

Display	Driver	Output Drive mA	Output Drive Volts	Input Compat.	Remarks
LED Common Cathode					
All the following Common Cathode LEDs may be driven by the 9660	7-Segment Decoder/Driver: 9660* Constant Current Source Outputs	5 to 50		MOS	Output current programmable with a single resistor
FND 500*, 70 Fairchild / DL 704 Litronix / HP 5082-7740 Hewlett-Packard	7-Segment Decoder/Driver/Latch: 9368 Constant Current Source Outputs	19 @ 1.7 Constant Current		TTL	Direct drive. No resistors or transistors.
DL 4, 402 Litronix / MAN 3, 4 Monsanto	7-Segment Decoder/Driver/Latch: 9368 Constant Current Source Outputs	19 @ 1.7 Constant Current		TTL	Requires either resistor current limiting or pulse width modulation to reduce current output
LED Common Anode					
FND 507* Fairchild / DL 1A. 6,8,10,707 Litronix / MAN 1,6,10 Mansonto / HP 5082-7730 Hewlett-Packard / SLA 1, 2, 7—Opcoa / TIXL Texas Instruments	7-Segment Decoder/Driver: 9317B	40	20	TTL	Requires 7 current limiting resistors per display
	9317C	20	30	TTL	
	9357A (7446A)	40	30	TTL	
	9358B (7447A)	40	15	TTL	
	7-Segment Decoder/Driver/Latch: 9370	25	7	TTL	No resistors or transistors. Low power consumption
	9371*	15	5	TTL	
Fluorescent					
GE Y1938, Y4075 Y4102, 05 General Electric	7-Segment Decoder/Driver: 9307	2.0 @ 0.85 to drive npn transistors		TTL	Requires either transistors or interface units

DIRECT DRIVE DISPLAYS

Display	Driver	Output Drive mA	Output Drive Volts	Input Compat.	Remarks
Fluorescent (continued)					
Ligitron DG 1Q 12 H, 19C / Legi Electronics (Iseden, Japan) / NEC DG12E/ LD915, DG10E, LD938 / Nippon Electric / Digivac—Tung Sol / Fluorotron / Sylvania	7-Segment Decoder/Driver: 9307	2.0 @ 0.85 to drive npn transistors		TTL	Requires either transistors or interface units
Incandescent					
Alco Inc. "Appollo" / Diametrics Inc. / Dialight Corp. / EDP Corp. / Pinlights / Luminetics Inc. / Mesa "Minitron"® / Readouts, Inc. "Numitron"® / RCA Corp.	7-Segment Decoder/Drivers: 9317B	40	20	TTL	No additional components required
	9317C	20	30	TTL	
	9357A (7446A)	40	30	TTL	
	9358B (7447A)	40	15	TTL	
	7-Segment Decoder/Driver/Latch: 9370	25	7	TTL	9371 is constant current sink, low power consumption
	9371*	15	5	TTL	
Gas Discharge					
1-of-10 Type Nixie®—Burroughs Most Types	1-of-10 Decoder/Drivers: 9315 (7441)	7	65	TTL	No additional components required
	93141 (74141)	7	55	TTL	
7-Segment Type Panaplex® Burroughs / SP Series—Sperry / Elfin—Alco	7-Segment Decoders: 9307	2.0 @ 0.85 to drive npn transistors		TTL	Requires 7 npn transistor interface devices
	9358 (7448)			TTL	

MULTIPLEXED LED DISPLAYS

Display	Segment Drivers	Output Drive mA	Output Drive Volts	Input Compat.	Remarks	Strobe Drivers	Output Drive mA	Input Compat.	Remarks
Common Cathode	**Segments (Current Source)**					**Strobe (Current Sink)**			
FNA 30, 35, 37 — Fairchild / FND, 500*, 70 — Fairchild / MAN 3, 4 — Monsanto / DL 4, 33, 34, 704 — Litronix / HP 5082-7740 / HP 7402-7415 — Hewlett-Packard	7-Segment Decoders: 9307			TTL	Requires interface units such as 9661	Decoder Drivers: 9345 1-of-10 Decoder	80	TTL	
						93145 1-of-10 Decoder	80	TTL	
	7-Segment Decoder/Drivers: 9660*	50 @ 3.0		MOS	Output Current programmable with one resistor	Strobe Drivers: 75492 Hex LED/Lamp Driver	250	MOS	Inverting (sink only)
	7-Segment Decoder/Driver/Latch: 9368	16 @ 2.1		TTL		75491 Quad Segment Driver	50	MOS	Inverting (sink only)
	Segment Drivers: 9661* Quad Segment Driver	5-75 @ 3.0 Constant Current		MOS	Output Current programmable with one resistor	9662* Quad LED Digit/Lamp Driver	600	MOS	Inverting or non-inverting selection pin
	75491 Quad Segment Driver	50		MOS	Requires current limiting resistors	9663* Hex LED Digit/Lamp Driver	600	MOS	Inverting or non-inverting selection pin
Common Anode	**Segments (Current Sink)**					**Strobe (Current Source)**			
FND 507* — Fairchild / MAN 1, 6A, 10 — Monsanto / DL 6, 10, 707 — Litronix / HP 5082-7730 — Hewlett-Packard / TIXL — Texas Instruments / SLA 1, 3, 7 — Opcoa	7-Segment Decoder/Drivers: 9317B	40		TTL	Require current limiting resistors	Strobe Drivers: 9661* Quad Segment Driver	75	MOS	Non-inverting
	9357B (7447) or (7446)	40		TTL		75491 Quad Segment Driver Transistors	50	MOS	Non-inverting
	7-Segment Decoder/Driver/Latch: 9370	25		TTL					

*To be announced.

FAIRCHILD
SEMICONDUCTOR

2006-21-0001-083   10 M

9616/9617 EIA INTERFACE DRIVER AND RECEIVER

John Petrilla and Ken True

INTRODUCTION

Two Fairchild integrated circuits provide the necessary interface for DTL/TTL systems to meet EIA RS 232-C and CCITT V.24 signal interchange specification: the 9616 Triple Line Driver and the 9617 Triple Line Receiver (See *Figure 2* for typical application). This driver/receiver pair also reduces external component count and is more flexible than other available devices. The line driver, an AND/OR/INVERT function, provides inhibit (*i.e.,* forcing the output to a V_{OL} or MARK state) without external gating and also incorporates internal slew rate control eliminating the need for external capacitors. The line receiver offers either hysteresis or slicing operation with individual response control leads for increased ac noise immunity. The input/output signal waveforms for both devices are shown in *Figure 1.*

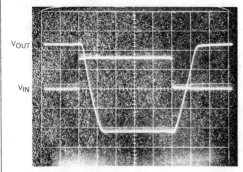

Typical 9616 Response:

(V_{CC} + = +12 V, Output Unloaded,
V_{EE} – = –12 V)

Channel A (V_{IN}) – 2.5 V/cm

Channel B (V_{OUT}) –2.5 V/cm

Sweep –0.5 μs/cm

PARAMETERS		TYPICAL VALUES
Output High Voltage		+6.0 V
Output Low Voltage		–6.0 V
Output Short Circuit Current		
Positive		–17 mA
Negative		+17 mA
Input Low Current		–1.2 mA
Positive Supply Current		7.5 mA
Negative Supply Current		–7.5 mA

Typical 9617 Response:

(V_{CC} + = +5 V, Output Unloaded, and Hysteresis Leads Shorted.)

Channel A (V_{IN}) – 1.0 V/cm

Channel B (V_{OUT}) – 1.0 V/cm

Sweep –0.2 μs/cm

PARAMETERS	TYPICAL VALUES
Output High Voltage (I_L = –200 μA)	3.0 V
Output Low Voltage (I_L = 8 mA)	0.3 V
Upper Input Threshold Voltage (Hysteresis)	2.0 V
Lower Input Threshold Voltage (Hysteresis)	0.85 V
Input Threshold Voltage (Non-Hysteresis)	1.0 V
Output Short Circuit Current	2.5 mA
Supply Current	12 mA

Fig. 1. 9616/9617 Performance Characteristics

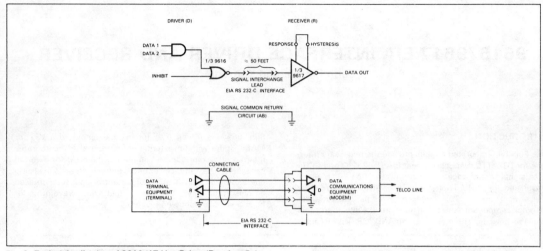

Fig. 2. Typical Application of 9616/17 Line Driver/Receiver Pair

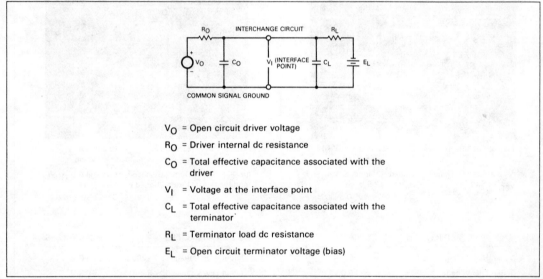

V_O = Open circuit driver voltage

R_O = Driver internal dc resistance

C_O = Total effective capacitance associated with the driver

V_I = Voltage at the interface point

C_L = Total effective capacitance associated with the terminator

R_L = Terminator load dc resistance

E_L = Open circuit terminator voltage (bias)

Fig. 3. RS 232-C Equivalent Circuit, Driver and Terminator

WHAT IS EIA RS 232-C?

The Electronic Industries Association Recommended Standard 232-C defines the electrical and functional characteristics for data, timing and control signal interchange between data communications equipment (modems, etc.) and data terminal equipment (teletypewriters, CRT terminals, etc.). The standard actually specifies the "handshaking" necessary to allow a terminal device and an attached modem to operate as a single unit. RS 232-C applies only to data communication equipment using serial binary data interchange at rates from one to 20,000 baud*, (See equivalent circuit, *Figure 3*). This standard specifies the equivalent electrical characteristics for the drivers and terminators (receivers) of the interchange circuits (*Table 1*) and recommends the lead assignment and logic functions of the control, timing, and data circuits. Each interchange circuit is single-ended (all voltage levels are referenced to a common return), polar (positive and negative voltage signal levels), and simplex (uni-directional, non-reversible data flow from driver to receiver). In addition, the signal lead is not terminated in its characteristic impedance, but is bridged by a high impedance load (3 kΩ to 7 kΩ) in the receiver. Short interconnect cables (≤50 feet) and a controlled slew rate on the driver minimize reflection effects on the signal waveforms in the interchange circuits. This phenomenon is based on a ratio of >3:1 between signal rise time and time delay of the transmission line. In such cases, the reflection effects due to low impedance drivers and a high impedance line termination are masked by the superposition of ramps rather than the unit steps used in classical transmission line analysis. This same effect is used for writing wiring rules in such logic families as ECL and TTL.

*See last section on BPS vs baud

TABLE I
RS 232-C ELECTRICAL CHARACTERISTICS

		MIN	MAX	UNIT
DRIVER OUTPUT VOLTAGE, OPEN CIRCUIT	V_O, OUTPUT HIGH		25	V
	V_O, OUTPUT LOW	-25		V
DRIVER OUTPUT VOLTAGE WITH 3 kΩ to 7 kΩ LOAD	V_O, OUTPUT HIGH	5	15	V
	V_O, OUTPUT LOW	-15	-5	V
DRIVER OUTPUT IMPEDANCE WITH POWER OFF	MEASURED FOR RANGE OF -2 V TO+2 V APPLIED TO DRIVER OUTPUT	300		Ω
DRIVER OUTPUT SHORT CIRCUIT I_O	MAGNITUDE		0.5	A
SLEW RATE[1] $\dfrac{dV_I}{dt}$	ALL INTERCHANGE CIRCUITS		30	V/μs
	CONTROL CIRCUITS	6		V/μs
	TIMING CIRCUITS	4		V/μs
RECEIVER INPUT RESISTANCE R_L	V_I = $\pm$3 V to $\pm$25 V	3	7	kΩ
RECEIVER OPEN CIRCUIT INPUT VOLTAGE E_L	MAGNITUDE		2	V
RECEIVER INPUT VOLTAGE V_I	OUTPUT = MARK	3	25	V
	OUTPUT = SPACE	-25	-3	V
FAILSAFE REQUIREMENTS (on control circuits CA, CC, CD, SCA, when these leads are used) RS 232-C, Section 2.5	RECEIVER INPUT OPEN — MARK OUTPUT RECEIVER INPUT GROUNDED —MARK OUTPUT			

NEITHER A DRIVER NOR A RECEIVER IS TO BE DAMAGED BY A SHORT OCCURRING BETWEEN ANY TWO INTERCHANGE LEADS, INCLUDING SIGNAL GROUND[2].

NOTE 1:
Since the maximum data rate specified by RS 232-C is 20,000 baud, the duration of the minimum signaling element is 1/20,000 baud = 50 μs. The timing or data signal is required to pass through the transition region (-3 V to +3 V) in 4% or less of this interval (.04 x 50 μs = 2 μs). Thus, slew rate must be greater than 6 V/2 μs or 3 V/μs. For control interchange signals, the time required for the signal to pass through the transition region (-3 V to +3 V) is 1 ms or less, yielding a slew rate of 6 V/ms. The CCITT V.24 recommendation specifies (Section V-5.4) that the signal shall pass through the transition region in 3% of the unit interval or less which at 20,000 baud yields a minimum slew rate of 6 V/ (.03 x 50 μs) = 4 V/μs at the interchange point. Since this slew rate is greater than that required by RS 232-C, all slew rate requirements in both standards may be satisfied if the driver output slew rate is greater than 4 V/μs and less than 30 V/μs. The 30 V/μs maximum slew rate specified minimizes cross talk. The internal slew rate control in the 9616 guarantees these parameters with the driver output unloaded to fully loaded with 3 kΩ shunted by 2500 pF.

NOTE 2:
RS 232-C requires that driver and receiver circuits not be damaged by shorts between any two interchange leads including signal and protective grounds. This implies that two driver outputs could be shorted together. Since the output impedance of the driver (R_O in Figure 2) is not directly specified, some interpretation is required to determine minimum R_O. The maximum open circuit source voltage (V_O) is specified at +25 V, and the maximum LOADED OUTPUT interface voltage (V_I) is +15 V. This requires R_O to be a minimum of 4.667 kΩ (R_O = (25 V/15 V x 7 kΩ) − 7 kΩ). If V_O is assumed to be 15 V, R_O must be 30Ω to meet the 0.5 A maximum short circuit current specification. Thus a driver output may be represented by either a 25 V source with a series resistance of 4.667 kΩ or by a 15 V source with a series resistance of 30Ω. Under the fault condition described, a driver output must withstand a hard 15 V source (i.e., 30Ω series resistance) or a soft 25 V source (i.e., 4,667 kΩ series resistance), but not a hard 25 V source which was allowed by the former issue of the standard, (RS 232-B).

9616 TRIPLE LINE DRIVER

The 9616 Line Driver is an AND/OR/INVERT GATE with special output characteristics. The device features DTL/TTL compatible inputs, a current source/sink arrangement to determine output slew rate, Zener clamps to determine output voltage levels, and an output stage providing current limiting and high stand-off voltages. The logic diagram, truth table and schematic are shown in *Figure 4*.

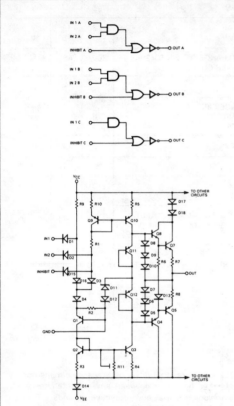

NOTE: Above circuit is one of three identical circuits.

9616 TRUTH TABLE

IN1	IN2	Inhibit	Out	Logic State of Output
L	L	L	H	Space
H	L	L	H	Space
L	H	L	H	Space
H	H	L	L	Mark
L	L	H	L	Mark
H	L	H	L	Mark
L	H	H	L	Mark
H	H	H	L	Mark

NOTE: Truth Table entries are not valid for Channel C.

Fig. 4. 9616 Logic Diagram, Schematic and Truth Table

The input stage provides the AND/OR logic function with diode gating, (D1/D2/D15); the INVERT function is provided by the current sink, Q3. The input stage uses Q1 to form the necessary level shifting of the input logic levels to the required output interface levels. The proper input conditions $(IN_1 \cdot IN_2) + INHIBIT$ High) allow current to flow through common base connected pnp transistor Q1 supplying a bias current to current sink Q3 and its bias circuit, Q2/R3/R4.

Current source Q10 and its bias circuit (Q9/R5/R10), and current sink Q3 are arranged so the sink drains the current supplied from the source. The sink is biased to demand approximately twice the current that the source is biased to supply. If the sink is biased on, its collector voltage falls toward V_{EE}, pulling the source collector voltage down. If the sink bias is not supplied by the input stage, the sink is biased off by R11, and the collector voltages are pulled toward V_{CC}. The voltage swing range is determined by Zener diodes D11 and D12.

The output stage contains complementary Darlington emitter-follower pairs (Q8/Q7 and Q4/Q5). When current sink Q3 is off, current from the source, Q10, supplies the necessary base drive to the Q8/Q7 pair. Because the composite gain of the pair is high, most of the source current flows through Q11, through D11, (forcing it to zener), and through forward-biased D12 to ground. Therefore the output level is determined essentially by V_{D11}.

Similarly, when the current sink is on, D11 becomes forward biased and D12 zeners to clamp the output voltage. Therefore, Q3 must sink enough current to remove the base drive from the Q8/Q7 pair, provide base drive to the Q4/Q5 pair, and provide operating current to D12. The dependency of V_{OUT} on V_Z permits output voltage levels to be independent of power supply variation and allows symmetry with respect to ground.

In addition to controlling output level, the current source/sinking arrangement controls output slew rate by charging and discharging known capacitances with a constant current. Thus, output slew rate, dV_{OUT}/dt, can be specified to RS232-C slew rate requirements without external capacitors. The input and output waveforms of an unloaded 9616 driver are shown in *Figure 1*.

Another feature, current limiting, uses diodes D5—D10 and resistors R7, R8. Current limiting occurs when the voltage drop across the emitter-base junction of the output transistor pair, (Q8/Q7) plus the current drop in the output resistor (R7) equals the turn-on voltage of the current limiting diodes, $(V_{BEQ8} + V_{BEQ7} + R7 \, I_{OUT} = V_{D8F} + V_{D9F} + V_{D10F})$. This occurs when the base drive, normally flowing into the base of Q8, flows through D8, D9, D10 removing this base drive from the output stage.

Similar operation occurs in both halves of the output stage. Current limiting determines minimum output slew rate by fixing the maximum output current available for charging external load capacitances.

During a V_{OUT} High-to-Low transition, R6 and D13 permit a high $I_{BQ7(OFF)}$, resulting in a turn-off much faster than recombination alone can provide. This is also true in V_{OUT} Low/High transitions. These fast switching times insure that the output slew rate is determined by the current source/sinking technique.

9617 TRIPLE LINE RECEIVER

The 9617 triple line receiver was designed to satisfy EIA RS 232-C. The logic diagram and schematic are shown in *Figure 5*. The circuit is DTL/TTL compatible, has three cascaded common-emitter stages and offers optional positive feedback providing a hysteresis mode. This hysteresis provides the option of improved ac noise immunity over that of a slicing mode.

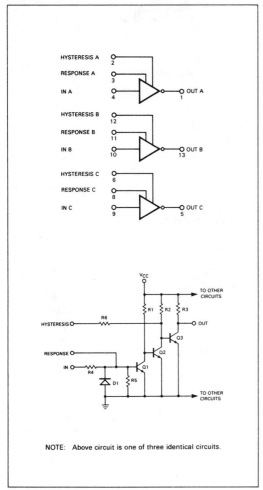

NOTE: Above circuit is one of three identical circuits.

Fig. 5. 9617 Logic and Schematic Diagrams

RS 232-C requires (on certain interchange leads) that the receiver assume a MARK state when any of the following three conditions exist.

- Transmitter power is off

- Receiver is open-circuited (disconnected from the inter-change circuit)

- Receiver input is shorted to signal common return or ground

To accomplish this, input transistor Q1 is biased off when the input is open or when $V_{IN} = 0$ V, meeting the failsafe

requirement of RS 232-C. The 9617 open circuit input bias meets the +2 V requirement. The input impedance, R_{IN}, is held to the 3 – 7 kΩ range allowed for input voltages in the 3 – 25 V range.

The hysteresis mode is enabled by connecting the Response and the Hysteresis leads providing positive feedback from the Q2 collector to the Q1 base. With Q1 off, Q2 saturates and shunts the Q1 base resistor R5 and the feedback resistor R6 to ground. This lowers the impedance at the base of Q1, forcing V_{IN} high enough to turn on Q1. If Q1 is on, Q2 is off and Q1 receives additional base drive through R5 and can stay on with a smaller V_{IN}. External resistance added between the Hysteresis and Response leads reduces the amount of hysteresis.

In the hysteresis mode, a cpacitor connected between the Response lead and ground improves ac noise immunity without reducing rise and fall times of the output signal. However, in a slicing mode, large capacitors can cause some time distortion of the output signal, (*i.e.*, degradation of rise and fall times). The merits of increased ac noise immunity must be weighed against the decreased signal quality at the receiver output.

BITS PER SECOND vs BAUD

Contrary to the popular interpretation, the two terms "bps" (bits per second) and "baud" are not necessarily synonyms. In certain cases, considering them synonyms can cause serious problems with data signal quality.

Bits per second (bps) is the unit of *information* rate. It expresses the number of binary digits passed through a channel per second.

Baud is the unit of *modulation* rate (or signalling speed). It is defined as the reciprocal of the duration of the minimum signalling element (pulse).

The four waveforms in *Figure 6* illustrate the difference between "bps" and "baud". The Non Return to Zero (NRZ) signal *(a)* has 1 unit of information occuring every T seconds, thus its information rate is 1/T bits per second. Its minimum signalling element is also T seconds in duration, so the modulation rate is 1/T baud. For NRZ signalling, the modulation rate in baud equals the information rate in bits per second.

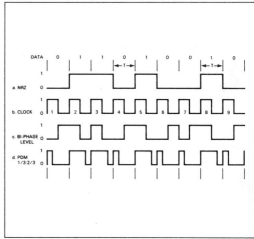

Fig. 6. Three Types of Pulse Codes

Bi-phase level signalling (sometimes called Manchester code) is digital phase shift keying. It is produced by performing an Exclusive NOR on the NRZ data and clock *(b)*. The information rate for the bi-phase L code shown is the same as for the NRZ data: $1/T$ bits per second. However, the modulation rate is not the same. The minimum signalling element is now $1/2$ clock cycle $(T/2)$ so the modulation rate is $2/T$ or twice the modulation rate as the NRZ signal. Likewise, a study of Pulse Duration Modulation (PDM) shown in *d* shows that the information rate in bps is the same as the NRZ signal, while the modulation rate is now $3/T$ (three times the modulation rate of NRZ), since the minimum pulse width is $T/3$.

As a final example, consider a 1 kHz audio tone. The presence or absence of the tone is the method of expressing one bit of information. If the tone can be turned on or off only once per hour, then the information rate is one bit per hour. Since each half cycle of the 1 kHz tone constitutes a minimum signalling element, the modulation rate is a constant $1/0.5 \times 1$ ms = 2000 baud.

A designer, concerned with signal quality (how much the ideal signal will shrink, expand or be displaced in time) at the output of a transmission medium such as a twisted pair of wires, is really not interested in the information rate, but in the modulation rate of the signal source. The modulation rate gives the minimum pulse width that will be sent; from that plus the characteristics of the transmission medium, the amount of time jitter which the signal accumulates by the time it arrives at the destination can be determined.

To eliminate confusion and possible system malfunctions, designers of transmission systems should ignore bps in favor of the modulation rate in baud as the tool for system data quality estimation.

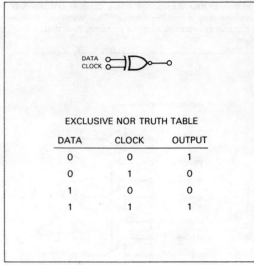

EXCLUSIVE NOR TRUTH TABLE

DATA	CLOCK	OUTPUT
0	0	1
0	1	0
1	0	0
1	1	1

Fig. 7. Exclusive NOR Gate

QUALITY–RELIABILITY–HIGH REL

AQL or LTPD

THEY ARE NOT THE SAME

AQLs and LTPDs, What's the Difference?

All too often, both manufacturers and customers use the terms AQL and LTPD interchangeably. By doing so, they have created an air of confusion as to what exactly is expected from a given sampling plan. The two terms do not mean the same thing and it is very important to understand the difference. Of course, QA people are intimately familiar with AQLs and LTPDs including the statistics behind them, but for others, it is well to review the definitions and meanings.

AQL (Acceptable Quality Level) is a statistically defined quality level, in terms of percent defective, *accepted* on an average of 95% of the time. In other words, a sampling plan with 1% AQL passes (accepts) lots 1% defective, 95% of the time.

LTPD (Lot Tolerance Percent Defective) is again a statistically defined quality level, in percent defective, which is *rejected* on an average, 90% of the time. Thus, a lot which is truly 5% defective is rejected 90% of the time when a 5% LTPD is used.

What is a Sampling Plan and an OC Curve?

The sampling plan is the specific criteria used in the sampling process. Besides defining how many samples to be selected from a lot and how many rejects are required to reject the lot, it also defines the AQL and LTPD.

Every sampling plan has an operating characteristic curve (OC curve) that defines the probability of accepting a lot, with a given percent defective, using a particular sampling plan. Typical OC curves are shown. Both OC curves have an AQL of 1% and an LTPD of 2.5 and 5%. Both are 1% AQL curves

from MIL-STD-105 and differ only in sample size. The solid curve results from a sample of 200 pieces with a maximum of 5 rejects. The dotted curve results from a sample of 500 pieces with a maximum of 10 rejects. These sample sizes are used for lot sizes of 5,000 and 50,000 pieces respectively. Note that the AQL is the same for both curves but that the LTPD decreases as the sample size is increased. When the sample plan is changed, the OC curve also changes, for every sampling plan has its own OC curve.

Because of these factors, there is a high probability of lots being accepted which are much more than 1% defective. For instance, with the 200 piece sample, a lot 2% defective will be accepted 75% of the time and a lot 4% defective will be accepted 25% of the time. The 50% acceptance levels are 3% and 1.8% for the two curves. The 50% acceptance level indicates there is a 50/50 chance

the lots will be accepted. In other words, if the lot is 3% bad there is a 50/50 chance that it will be accepted. Another way to look at this is that the manufacturer has a 50/50 chance of shipping the lot and the customer has a 50/50 chance of rejecting it during incoming inspection.

Many customers believe a 1% AQL assures them the product will not have more than 1% defectives. This is just not true, particularly if one looks at any individual lot.

How to use AQL and LTPD Tables

Some confusion when interpreting AQL and LTPD tables can be clarified by analyzing various sections of the tables and giving some examples.

Figure 2 is a combination of parts of Table 1 and Table 2 of MIL-STD-105D. There are columns for lot size, inspection levels, sample size code letter, sample size, and an accept/reject (A/R)

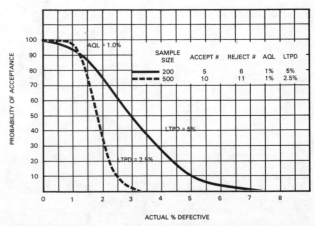

FIGURE 1   OC CURVE

434

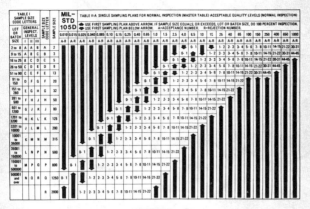

FIGURE 2

number shown in each column for that particular AQL. This table is arranged for general inspection level II, normally used for semiconductor acceptance plans. To use the table, two things must be known—lot size and AQL level.

Example – a lot size of 1,000 pieces and a 1% AQL. Reading across horizontally, the sample size required is 80 pieces and the accept/reject number is 2/3 (i.e., 2 rejects accepts the lot and with 3 rejects, the lot is rejected).

A number of arrows are also shown in certain columns. These mean that it is impossible to make a valid statistical determination for the required AQL using that sample size. Therefore, go to the sample size and accept number below or above arrow, as the case may be.

Example – a lot size of 500 pieces and a 0.65% AQL. The chart indicates a sample size of 50 pieces but there is an arrow pointing downward in the column. Therefore, the correct sample plan for this lot would be found in the next column which is 80 pieces, accept on 1, reject on 2.

The general inspection levels I, II, and III are used when less discrimination, normal or more discrimination is required, respectively. More or less discrimination refers to the slope of the OC curve. A more discriminating sample plan (Level III) has a more nearly vertical slope and therefore a tighter (lower) LTPD even though the AQL is the same. If an inspection level other than II is specified, read the code letter under the proper inspection level for that lot size. The sample size may then be selected by finding the sample

size code letter corresponding to the code letter shown under the general inspection levels and using that sample size.

Example – Level III on a 5,000 piece lot; the indicated code letter is M. To perform this inspection, the sample size would be selected for code letter M, which requires a 315-piece sample for the appropriate AQL.

Figure 3 is the same LTPD table used in both MIL-M-38510 and MIL-S-19500E. Notice that lot sizes are not included in the LTPD table. The horizontal numbers across the top indicate the LTPD number and the vertical numbers on the left indicate the accept numbers. The reject number is one more than the accept number. To use the LTPD table, two things must be known—the LTPD and the maximum accept number.

Example – LTPD of 7, maximum accept number of 3. The sample plan requires a sample of 94 pieces with no more than 3 rejects.

Customer specifications sometimes specify lambda (λ) which by definition, is the LTPD per 1000 hours. The LTPD table may then be used by multiplying the sample size by 1000 to obtain the total device hours required.

Example – Lambda of 10, accept number of 3. This requires 65,000 unit hours of test data with no more than 3 failures. In effect, this says there is a 90% confidence that the failure rate per 1000 hours will not exceed 10%.

Tightened sampling is often referred to in both manufacturers' and customers' specifications. When tightened inspection is in effect for both AQL and LTPD tables, the next tighter sampling plan is used. For instance, if normal operation is to a 1% AQL, under tightened inspection operation would be to a 0.65% AQL with the same sample size but with the accept/reject number corresponding to the 0.65% AQL level. If normal operation is to a 7% LTPD, under tightened inspection an LTPD of 5 is used, keeping the same accept number but increasing the sample size.

CONCLUSION

This discussion is intended as a primer, certainly not a complete explanation, of the statistically defined quality levels commonly used in R&QA sampling plans. A basic understanding of AQL and LTPD, their meanings and usage, can help clear up some of the confusion surrounding them.

MIL-M-38510 – Table B-1
MIL-S-19500E – Table C-1   **LTPD Sampling Plans[1]**

Minimum size of sample to be tested to assure, with a 90 percent confidence, that a lot having percent-defective equal to the specified LTPD will not be accepted (single sample).

Max. Percent Defective (LTPD) or λ	50	30	20	15	10	7	5	3	2	1.5	1	0.7	0.5	0.3	0.2	0.15	0.1
Acceptance Number (c) (r = c + 1)	Minimum Sample Sizes (For device-hours required for life test, multiply by 1000)																
0	5	8	11	15	22	32	45	76	116	153	231	328	461	767	1152	1534	2303
1	8	13	18	25	38	55	77	129	195	258	390	555	778	1296	1946	2592	3891
2	11	18	25	34	52	75	105	176	266	354	533	759	1065	1773	2662	3547	5323
3	13	22	32	43	65	94	132	221	333	444	668	953	1337	2226	3341	4452	6681
4	16	27	38	52	78	113	158	265	398	531	798	1140	1599	2663	3997	5327	7994
5	19	31	45	60	91	131	184	308	462	617	927	1323	1855	3090	4638	6181	9275
6	21	35	51	68	104	149	209	349	528	700	1054	1503	2107	3509	5267	7019	10533
7	24	39	57	77	116	166	234	390	589	783	1178	1680	2355	3922	5886	7845	11771
8	26	43	63	85	128	184	258	431	648	864	1300	1854	2599	4329	6498	8660	12995
9	28	47	69	93	140	201	282	471	709	945	1421	2027	2842	4733	7103	9468	14206
10	31	51	75	100	152	218	306	511	770	1025	1541	2199	3082	5133	7704	10268	15407

[1]Sample sizes are based upon the Poisson exponential binomial limit.

FIGURE 3

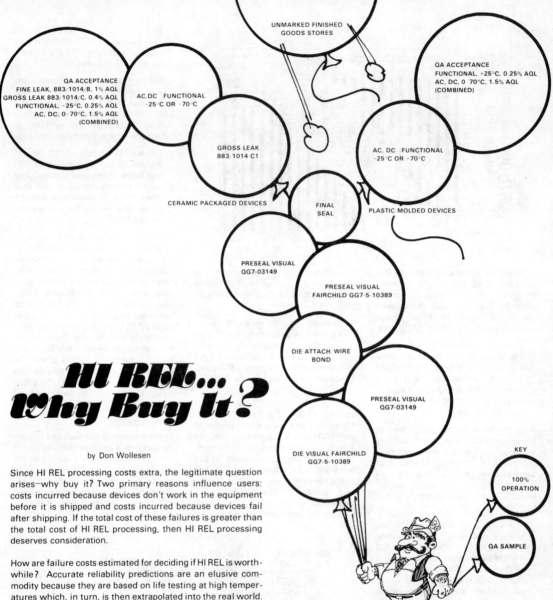

Figure labels (balloon diagram):

UNMARKED FINISHED GOODS STORES

QA ACCEPTANCE
FINE LEAK, 883/1014/B, 1% AQL
GROSS LEAK 883/1014/C, 0.4% AQL
FUNCTIONAL, -25°C, 0.25% AQL
AC, DC, 0-70°C, 1.5% AQL
(COMBINED)

AC,DC FUNCTIONAL
-25°C OR -70°C

QA ACCEPTANCE
FUNCTIONAL, +25°C, 0.25% AQL
AC, DC, 0-70°C, 1.5% AQL
(COMBINED)

GROSS LEAK
883/1014 C1

AC, DC FUNCTIONAL
-25°C OR -70°C

CERAMIC PACKAGED DEVICES

FINAL SEAL

PLASTIC MOLDED DEVICES

PRESEAL VISUAL
QG7-03149

PRESEAL VISUAL
FAIRCHILD GG7-5-10389

DIE ATTACH/WIRE BOND

PRESEAL VISUAL
QG7-03149

DIE VISUAL FAIRCHILD
GG7-5-10389

KEY

100% OPERATION

QA SAMPLE

HI REL... Why Buy it?

by Don Wollesen

Since HI REL processing costs extra, the legitimate question arises—why buy it? Two primary reasons influence users: costs incurred because devices don't work in the equipment before it is shipped and costs incurred because devices fail after shipping. If the total cost of these failures is greater than the total cost of HI REL processing, then HI REL processing deserves consideration.

How are failure costs estimated for deciding if HI REL is worthwhile? Accurate reliability predictions are an elusive commodity because they are based on life testing at high temperatures which, in turn, is then extrapolated into the real world. By the time users have actual data, chances are the device in question is either no longer manufactured or the manufacturing process is substantially changed. Progress is the life blood of the semiconductor industry but it makes accurate reliability predictions difficult. Calculations probably won't be good past the first significant digit.

WHAT IS HI REL?

HI REL processing entails additional, more stringent processing than that normally required for commercial grade products. More stringent processing results in improved incoming quality and reliability for the user. Although HI REL processing increases the cost of integrated circuits, in most cases it lowers final system cost and significantly cuts expensive field failures.

Two separate MOS HI REL processing procedures are available—Unique 38510/883A for military requirements, and Matrix VI for commercial and industrial requirements.

UNIQUE 38510/883A PROCESSING FOR MILITARY APPLICATIONS

This method establishes procedures for total lot screening to assist in achieving high levels of quality and reliability in devices intended for military applications. There are three standard processing flows provided by Fairchild — QA, QB and QC — which coincide with classes A, B and C of MIL STD 883A. These processing flows allow the user to choose a reliability level commensurate with the cost or risk involved in potential electronic system failures.

HI REL PROCESSING FOR COMMERCIAL AND INDUSTRIAL APPLICATIONS

The Fairchild Matrix VI program offers a broad spectrum of screens, packages and high technology/high volume integrated circuit products to meet quality and reliability requirements typically associated with the commercial and industrial market.

There are six screening options, each with a separate degree of reliability and cost level. To simplify a cost effective analysis, reliability factors have been assigned to each of the six screening levels shown on the opposite page.

It is the goal of Matrix VI to achieve the highest possible reliability consistent with the user's needs and cost constraints. Cost effective reliability is the essence of Matrix VI.

Matrix VI is the most comprehensive program of its kind now offered to the industrial/commercial market. The MOS Matrix VI processing differs slightly from that of other Fairchild product lines because of minor procedural differences and the use of Sentry 600 testers to perform ac, dc and functionality tests simultaneously.

CALCULATING THE PROBABILITY OF FAILURE

The most important issue here is the rate of failure per system; system failure rate is determined by the number of components in the system and component failure rate. For example, for a given component quality level, a circuit board with 500 components is less likely to work at the outset and will not be as reliable as a circuit board with 17 components. If the average component failure rate is 0.3%, the probability that the component will work is 0.997 and the probability of circuit board failure is:

for n = 500
$$P_{fail} = 1 - 0.997^{500} = 1 - 0.22 = 0.78$$
for n = 17
$$P_{fail} = 1 - 0.997^{17} = 1 - 0.95 - 0.05$$

where

n = number of components
P = Probability
$$P_{fail} = 1 - P^n_{success}$$

So, for the same component failure rate, the 500-component board will experience a 78% failure rate where the simple 17-component board will experience a 5% failure rate. It is also important to note that the 500-component board will most likely cost a lot more to repair because of the greater difficulty in finding the fault.

CALCULATING THE COST OF AN IN-HOUSE FAILURE

The cost of the technician, his equipment and overhead should be reduced to an hourly cost. For a 500-component board, it may take the technician eight hours with simple bench equipment or one hour with a $100,000 automatic board-fault tester. A technician at $7.00/hour and 300% overhead rate costs $28.00 per hour. For a five year life, 250 working days/year, 2 shifts, $10,000.00 of bench equipment would cost $.50 per hour; the $100,000 automatic

board-fault tester would cost $5.00 per hour. For a $2.00 component, using an automatic tester, the cost per failure is as follows:

$$cost/fault = (hours\ to\ repair)$$
$$(\frac{tech\ cost}{hour} + \frac{equipment\ depreciation}{hour})$$
$$+ component\ cost.$$
$$= (1\ hr)\ (\$28 + \$5) + \$2 = \$35$$

For the 17-component board, it might take 15 minutes with simple bench equipment for a cost of $9.13 per board fault.

CALCULATING THE COST OF A FIELD FAILURE

The cost of the field engineer and his equipment cost should be reduced to an hourly cost. At $10/hour and 400% overhead, his cost would be $50/hour. By comparison, equipment cost and component cost is likely to be trival. Transportation and lodging must also be accounted for; assume it is $50.00 per day. If the field engineer averages two calls per day, the cost per field failure is about $250.00. Assuming a 0.3%/1000 hour mean time between failures, 12 hours/day operation and a 3 month warranty (about 1000 hr operating time), probability of device failure will be 0.3%. For a 6 month warranty, assume probability of device failure is 0.6%.

$$P_{fail} = 1 - .994^{500}$$
$$= 0.95$$

If field failures are excessive, good will and business will also be lost. The estimation of this cost is quite subjective, but it is definitely a consideration over and above the simple arithmetic analysis presented here.

COST PER UNIT

The cost per unit is the cost of repair times the probability of repair divided by the number of units in question. In-house and field repair costs are additive.

$$cost/unit = (\$35.00)\ (.78)/500 + (250.00)\ .95/500$$
$$= \$.055 + \$0.475 = \$0.53/unit$$

Because most of the cost is due to field failures, reliability-oriented processing may be in order. Burn-in is the most cost effective method for reducing field failures since it has a greater long-term effect although in-house failure rate is also improved.

If the above failure rate were observed on Matrix VI level-3 parts on the 500-component circuit board, improved reliability could be achieved by using Matrix VI level-6 parts instead. Comparing Reliability Factors (see bottom of figure) of 2 for level 3 and 14 for level 6, the comparative reliability factor is 14/2 = 7. Expected failure rate is seven times lower, hence the cost/unit is reduced. If half of the in-house units initially work, then fail, these would be considered in the reliability factor.

$$cost/unit\ saving = cost/unit\ (1 - 1/Reliability\ Factor)$$
$$= (\frac{.055}{2} + 0.475)\ (1 - 1/7)$$
$$= \$0.43/unit\ saving$$

Thus, if the additional Matrix VI level-6 cost is less than $0.43 per unit, it pays to buy level 6 over level 3.

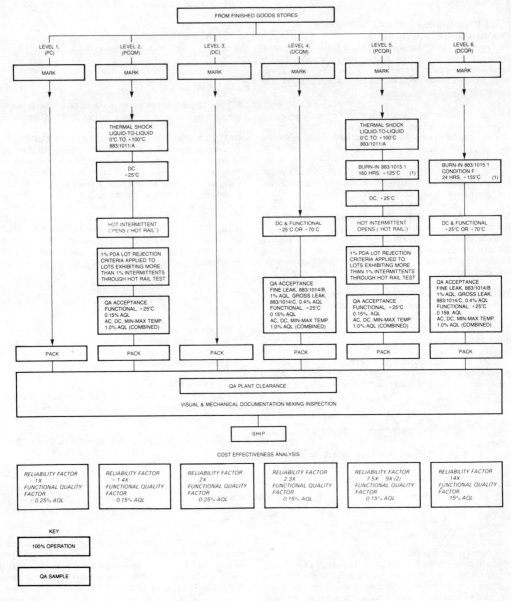

Matrix VI Process Flow Options and Cost Effectiveness

CONCLUSION

When considering HI REL processing, the cost/reliability trade-offs must be analyzed carefully, taking into consideration the specific application for the part and the unfortunate fact that some reliability factors may be quite subjective in nature. While failure rates theoretically may be calculated, the degree to which a company's reputation suffers from field failures is difficult to determine objectively. The decision to go HI REL then must be based not only on hard, calculable facts, but also on considerations that only experience and

judgment can evaluate. Certainly the decision to go HI REL can only – at worst – cost a bit more. However, the decision to use a less reliable part in a critical or marginally critical application can result in a risk of unacceptable field failure and – conceivably – a possible realignment of the system manufacturer's status in the marketplace.

For a more detailed discussion of HI REL processing procedures, write for the new MOS HI REL brochure.

Are Your Plastic PROMs Protected ?

by Joseph Ferro

NICHROME LINKS

The fabrication of nichrome link programmable read only memories in plastic packages requires good process control to assure device reliability. Moisture penetration in plastics could lead to electrolysis causing corrosion of the nichrome fuses. Fuse protection is provided by the surface glassivation layer applied to the chip, and a reliable method of evaluating the effectiveness of this glassivation is necessary. The testing method used should provide meaningful reliability prediction data in a short time.

Biased Pressure Temperature Humidity (BPTH) testing is an effective process control method for plastic encapsulated nichrome link PROMs. With the control limit established, reliability is *better than 0.001%/1,000 hours*. Both chemical vapor-desposited phosphovapox and plasma-deposited silicon nitride glassivation techniques were evaluated. Silicon-nitride protected devices proved to have a life three times that of the phosphovapox devices and five times that of unglassivated devices.

The PROMs tested are high-power devices (typically 0.5 W) creating a problem in terms of humidity bias testing. Chip temperature is approximately 50° C higher than ambient temperature, driving the moisture away from the chip. For moisture to permeate the chip surface, a 50% duty cycle was used.

At 85°C and 85% relative humidity, the *Bias Temperature Humidity test* requires at least 2000 hours to obtain meaningful reliability data, not timely enough for process control. *Unbiased* autoclave humidity tests (pressure cooker tests) are meaningless for process control, since failures cannot be produced because of the absence of a voltage gradient across the devices under test. In more than 44,000 device hours of testing, no failures occurred.

BPTH DEVICE TESTING IS EFFECTIVE

Considering these factors, *Biased Pressure Temperature Humidity* testing is conducted with biased units in an autoclave. Environment at the device surface is maintained at 100% relative humidity, 121°C, and 15 psig with the power cycled. Two important objectives are accomplished with the BPTH test: fast results are available for process control and reliability predictions of device life times are possible.

Evaluations were made on PROMs manufactured with the Isoplanar Schottky process, meaning the semiconductor elements are separated by an insulating film of thermally grown oxide, *Figure 1*. The device has a dual-layer metallization system of aluminum doped with silicon and copper with a dielectric layer of phosphovapox. A surface-protecting glassivation layer is deposited on top of the device, which is then encapsulated in epoxy.

Resistance of the nichrome fuse in these devices is approximately 300 Ω. Devices under test are biased to draw read current through each selected bit (fuse), with a power supply voltage of 5 V. When selected, the unprogrammed fuse typically draws 1 mA. Therefore, an addressed unprogrammed fuse has a typical potential drop of 300 mV.

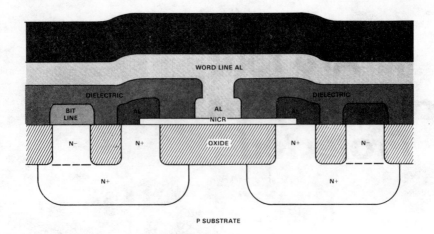

Fig. 1   Cross Section of Isoplanar Schottky PROM.

PHOSPHOVAPOX GLASSIVATION

An acceleration factor between Biased 85° C/85% Relative Humidity and Biased Pressure Temperature Humidity testing was established. Devices from five different assembly lots were evaluated using 85° C/85% RH and BPTH tests. These lots were all glassivated with a single layer of phosphovapox from 1.2 to 1.4 μm thick. Results of both tests are plotted in *Figure 2*. The dominant failure mode for both tests was nichrome fuse corrosion. However, with the BPTH test, aluminum corrosion became the primary failure mode for units surviving beyond 336 hours. The time required to obtain 50% cumulative failure for the 85° C/85% RH test was 4,000 hours. For the BPTH test, only 200 hours were necessary, indicating an acceleration factor of 20.

NON-GLASSIVATED DEVICES

A group of devices without any surface glassivation was subjected to both tests, with the results of the 85° C/85% RH test also plotted in *Figure 2*. Time to 50% cumulative failure was 2,350 hours with the primary failure mode being nichrome fuse corrosion. With the BPTH test, the primary failure mode was corrosion of the top layer of aluminum metallization at the point of greatest potential difference between adjacent metal lines. A possible explanation is that the non-glassivated surface becomes moisture saturated, causing the aluminum metallization to corrode before any moisture can reach the nichrome fuses beneath the dielectric layer. Because the failure modes of the two tests were different, BPTH testing cannot be used effectively for non-glassivated nichrome PROMs, although this technique may still be appropriate for other non-glassivated devices not employing nichrome links.

SILICON-NITRIDE GLASSIVATION

Silicon nitride has been shown to be an excellent ionic contamination and moisture barrier. Several devices with a 6000 ±500 A° coating of silicon nitride were evaluated with both tests. The results of these tests compared to the BPTH tests of the phosphovapox devices are shown in *Figure 3*. Time to 50% cumulative failure for the silicon-nitride glassivated units was 660 hours compared to 200 hours for the

phosphovapox glassivated units. The primary failure mode for the silicon-nitride devices in the BPTH tests was corrosion of the aluminum at the bonding pads and at cracks in the glassivation. No corrosion failures at all occurred until the 400-hour point. This aluminum corrosion is consistent with the results obtained with the phosphovapox glassivated devices that survived beyond 336 hours of testing. Failure of the silicon-nitride glassivated devices because of nichrome fuse corrosion was limited to less than 5%. With the 85° C/85% RH test, *no corrosion failures at all occurred in 7,000 hours*. Based on the acceleration factor determined for the BPTH test, a projected 50% cumulative failure level would be in excess of 13,000 *hours* for the 85° C/85% RH test.

The silicon-nitride glassivation demonstrates excellent protection against nichrome fuse corrosion. Results indicate that device life times are improved a factor of more than three when using silicon nitride instead of phosphovapox. Compared to unglassivated device, the improvement is fivefold. The results are tabulated below.

GLASSIVATION	TIME TO 50% CUMULATIVE FAILURE	
	BPTH TEST	85°C/85% RH TEST
Non-glassivation		2350
Phosphovapox	200	4000
Silicon Nitride	660	13000?

PROCESS CONTROL MEANS LIMITS

There is little agreement as to the relationship between 85° C/85% RH bias testing and actual field performance. Acceleration factors ranging from 50 to 10^6 have been reported. Assuming that an acceptable field failure rate (for electrolytic corrosion failures) is 1% in one million operating hours or about 114 years, the failure rate per 1,000 hours is 0.001%. With an acceleration factor of 1,000, this field failure rate goal can be met if the failure rate per 1,000 hours of operation at 85° C/85% RH is less than 1%. Because of the

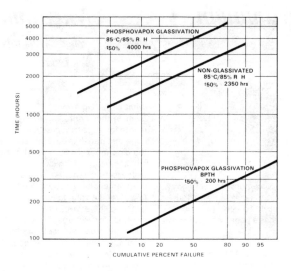

Fig. 2   85°C/85% RH versus BPTH Test Results for Phosphovapox Glassivated Devices.
85°C/85% RH Test Results for Unglassivated Units are Shown for Comparison.

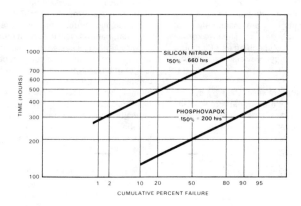

Fig. 3   BPTH Test Results for Silicon Nitride versus Phosphovapox Glassivation.

power cycling, and to be conservative, a failure rate of 1% per 2,000 hours of 85°C/85% RH testing was established.

The process control limit for the BPTH testing was based on the same factors, taking into account the acceleration factor of 20. Thus, the acceptable failure limit for the BPTH test was established at 1% per 100 hours of operation under BPTH conditions. To avoid the cost of large sample sizes and to minimize sensitivity to sampling variations by allowing more failures, a limit of 20% failure in 175 hours was determined to be an appropriate test condition by extrapolating a line parallel to those in Figure 2 through the 1% failure per 100 hours point. Beyond the 20% failure per 175 hours limit, the devices can be assumed to have reached a wear out condition because of humidity effects.

ACCURATE RESULTS FASTER

Biased Pressure Temperature Humidity testing is an effective process control test providing meaningful reliability prediction data in a relatively short period of time. By conducting controlled tests of nichrome link PROMs, BPTH test were shown to have an acceleration factor of 20 over normal 85°C/85% Relativity Humidity tests. In addition, by testing devices without glassivation, with phosophovapox glassivation, and with silicon-nitride glassivation, it was possible to conclude that the silicon-nitride glassivation offers more than three times the protection against corrosion than that provided by phosophovapox glassivation for plastic encapsulated nichrome link devices. In fact, the plastic PROMs with the silicon-nitride glassivation proved to be as reliable as hermetic PROMs. ☐

441

When Is A Minimum A Maximum?

by Peter Alfke

It All Depends On Your Point Of View

"When I use a word," Humpty Dumpty said, in rather a scornful tone, "it means just what I choose it to mean — neither more nor less." "The question is," said Alice, "whether you can make words mean so many different things." "The question is," said Humpty Dumpty, "what is to be master — that's all."

— Lewis Carroll from "Through The Looking Glass"

When is a Minimum Larger Than a Maximum? In every day life the meaning of Minimum and Maximum is fairly obvious. Max 55 MPH means that a speed up to 55 miles per hour is legal. Minimum balance $300 indicates a penalty if a balance drops below this set value.

Lewis Carroll had many a word reverse in Alice in Wonderland and Through the Looking Glass. Sometimes semiconductor data sheets also use words in less than obvious ways, such as the terms Min and Max. The reason is that data sheets are prepared from two points of view for two entirely different purposes.

From the semiconductor manufacturer's point of view, they are used to specify device limits and are essentially legal documents determining acceptable devices. The breakdown voltage of a transistor is thus usually specified as a Minimum value, indicating that all acceptable devices exceed this minimum value.

On the other hand, data sheets are also used by system designers, who must be sure that different parts of systems work together. They interpret the Minimum breakdown voltage of the transistor as the absolute Maximum voltage that may be applied to the devices.

Very few designers are confused by something as simple as breakdown voltage, but they may be puzzled by memory timing values specified as follows:

	MIN	TYP
93415 tw - minimum write pulse width - ns	30	25

How Can the Minimum Value Be Larger Than the Typical Value?

This strange manner of specifying stems from the misguided attempt on the part of semiconductor manufacturers to specify *system requirements* rather than *component parameters*. The specification above must therefore be interpreted to mean . . . "All 93415 devices function properly with a write pulse width of at least 30 ns." This 30 ns is therefore the minimum *system requirement* for a worst case design. Typically, a device reacts to a 25 ns write pulse, but this is not guaranteed so it is not a very meaningful value.

Obviously, it would be more logical to specify the *component parameter* itself, not its *system* implication. The longest time would then become a *maximum*, and confusion would be *minimized*. Unfortunately, all semiconductor manufacturers use such reverse specifications, and it is too late to change.

What is Set-Up Time?

Even further confusion exists around set-up time requirements for edge triggered flip-flops and registers. It is a clock edge that transfers data into such devices, and it is the level of the data input (D, P, J, or K) a short time *prior* to the active clock edge that is clocked into the device. This short time is called set-up time. As with all other parameters, this time requirement has a production tolerance, a temperature coefficient, and a voltage coefficient. The semiconductor manufacturer, therefore, guarantees predictable operation of a flip-flop, for example, only if the data input lines are held stable over the *spread* of possible *set-up time values* ranging from a long time — early enough for the slowest part — to a short time — late enough so that even a fast device does not recognize a subsequent input change.

Component specification would label these time requirements as a set-up time with a minimum (short) and a maximum (long) value. A very sophisticated specification might even provide two sets of values, one for a LOW-to-HIGH change and another for a HIGH-to-LOW change. Unfortunately, semiconductor manufacturers have far greater creative imaginations. The prevalent method specifies the set-up requirements as a system parameter, placing the longest set-up value in the minimum column, because it is the minimum length of time before the next clock edge that the inputs must be stable. This is the same reverse specification as used for memory write pulse widths. The shortest set-up time value has fared even worse. Many years ago, Fairchild called it — logically enough — a release time, since all requirements on the input are released after this time. In many data sheets, however, this shortest set-up time is listed as a negative hold time.

What is Negative Hold Time?

In the 7470, one of the oldest TTL flip-flops, the designer managed to achieve an on-chip clock delay longer than the data delay. Instead of correcting this mistake, an impressive name was selected and a flip-flop with a "hold time" requirement was announced. In other words, the data inputs must be held at their level even a short time *beyond* the clock edge. Any system designer immediately recognizes the ugly clock skew problems this generates.

The world has become enlightened since then. No modern flip-flop or register has this hold time requirement, but the 7400 series perpetuates the confusion by continuing to call the shortest set-up time a "negative hold time," rather than giving it a more logical label such as minimum set-up time or release time.

What Does This Mean to Designers?

Modern semiconductor components are specified with an impressive number of parameter values, providing the user with a large amount of useful and reliable information. The user can have confidence in these figures, but he must also use judgement and common sense to interpret the *intent* of the maximum or minimum labels. □

The Second Generation TO-92

TWNTWNTWN

by Jules Farago and Gene Thomas

There is much more to the TO-92 package than is apparent in the JEDEC registered drawing. The internal structure, hidden by the encapsulation, the packaging materials themselves, and the methods used in assembling the chip and package determine the ultimate product quality and performance.

TWN, the Fairchild second generation TO-92 package, is the result of a two-year development program during which twenty different material systems and designs were thoroughly evaluated. The result is a package that incorporates the best features of all these systems. Designed for maximum reliability, TWN is a significant step forward in plastic transistor packaging. Tests performed during development show it to be clearly superior to previous Fairchild and competitors' TO-92 products.

The TWN package features a monoplane (flat) copper lead frame for maximum power dissipation (nominally up to 625 mW) and epoxy encapsulation to ensure mechanical integrity and resistance to moisture penetration. Die attach is a gold eutectic system employing a scrub process for optimum mechanical strength and high thermal dissipation. Gold bond wires are attached using a thermal compression ball-bonding system.

Dice are fabricated using the Planar* process, metalized with aluminum and then passivated with a proprietary process during wafer fabrication. This manufacturing procedure assures a high degree of device stability that is evident in the High Temperature Reverse Bias (HTRB) and Intermittent Operating Life (IOPL) test data presented in Table 1.

*Planar is a patented Fairchild Process

Stress Test	Total Samples or Accum. Hours	Failure Rate
	Samples	Percent
Thermal Intermittency (Both Methods Combined)	325K	0.002
Thermal Shock	8.5K	0.14
Moisture Resistance	5.7K	0.47
HTRB	1480	0.3
	Hours	Percent/ 1000 Hrs
WHTRB	276K	0.4
HTS	885K	0.0
IOPL	1774K	0.07

Failures are defined as:
Catastrophic opens or shorts
Intermittent opens or shorts
Changes in h_{FE} greater than 25%, measured at the nominal conditions specified*
I_{CES} or I_{CBO} readings greater than 1 μA or the specification limit plus the initial readings whichever is greater*
$V_{CE(sat)}$ and $V_{BE(sat)}$ changes greater than 25% measured at the nominal conditions.

*Not to be used for the moisture stress, since it is a test for corrosion.

Table 1. Consumer Reliability Test Results

TWNTWNTWNTWNTWNTWN

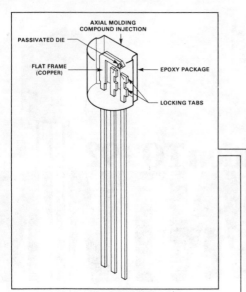

Fig. 1.   TWN TO-92 Package

Labels in figure:
AXIAL MOLDING COMPOUND INJECTION
PASSIVATED DIE
FLAT FRAME (COPPER)
EPOXY PACKAGE
LOCKING TABS

Fig. 2.   TWN Flat Frame

Fig. 3.   After Lead Bonding

WHY IS TWN MORE RELIABLE?

Flat Frame The TWN monoplane frame with double locking tabs *(Figure 1)* increases lead-pull strength and virtually eliminates separation of the lead frame and encapsulant. The wire-bond areas are coined to flatten the surface for ease and consistency of wire bonding *(Figure 2)*. Combined with top side injection of the encapsulant, flat frame construction *(Figure 3)* greatly reduces wire wash/thermal intermittency problems since the encapsulant flows in the same axis as the bond wires. This process yields consistent wire placement and reduces the possibility of wire sag *(Figure 4)*.

Improved Frame Metallurgy The TWN lead frame is copper with a nickel/gold cladding of uniform thickness and density in the die attach and wire bond areas. With the elimination of unpredictable variables (density, porosity, thickness) associated with electroplating, process control is significantly improved. *Figures 5* and *6* contrast the gold cladding and electroplating processes. *Figure 5* shows a cross-section of a TWN copper lead frame on which a uniformly thick gold layer is clad to an underlayer of nickel. The gold layer in *Figure 6* is electroplated to a barrier layer deposited on a copper lead frame. In these two figures, note the contrast of density and thickness in the two gold layers. The TWN metallurgical improvements give a uniformly high-quality die attach and consistently high thermal dissipation which significantly increase overall reliability.

Die Passivation The passivation applied during wafer fabrication eliminates the need for a junction coat, one of the major causes of bond-wire failure in other TO-92 packages. *Figures 7* and *8* show a die before and after passivation. The bond pad cut-outs in *Figure 8* are etched through after the passivation layer is deposited. Passivated dice have HTRB and IOPL test results that surpass those of silicone or junction-coated devices. Passivation also protects the dice from scratching and metal smearing during assembly.

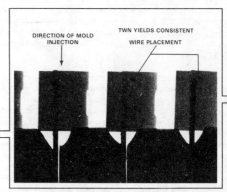

Fig. 4.   TWN Yields Consistent Wire Placement

Labels in figure:
DIRECTION OF MOLD INJECTION
TWN YIELDS CONSISTENT WIRE PLACEMENT

NTWNTWNTWNTWNTWNTWNTWN

Epoxy Package Compared to other TO-92 package materials, epoxy encapsulant has significantly improved Wet High Temperature Reverse Bias (WHTRB) test results, and gives thermal shock and temperature cycle performance unsurpassed by other TO-92 products. The high cleanliness level of epoxy, coupled with die surface passivation, provides an optimized die environment.

TEST PROCEDURES AND OUTGOING INSPECTION LEVELS

All TWN products are subjected to two 100% tests. The first is performed to the basic Fairchild test specs which meet or exceed either JEDEC or customer requirements. The second tests the devices to the customer drawing or 2N specs and checks any additional parameters imposed by Fairchild to guarantee performance and reliability in the customer's application. In addition to these 100% tests, all products are subjected to a post-assembly sample inspection to identify and segregate lots with potential thermal intermittency or mixed device problems. A 100% test at an elevated temperature is available as a test option.

The figures below show that the outgoing inspection levels at Fairchild are currently the tightest in the industry. They represent the minimum quality levels for all TWN products and are the tightest AQL levels offered for standard products in the industry.

DC Electricals	0.4%	AQL Level II
Catastrophic Failures	0.065%	AQL Level II
Visual Mechanicals	0.65%	AQL Level II

The TWN process also includes a continuous reliability monitor called Consumer Reliability Testing. This program subjects the products to continuous evaluation so that trends or potential product problems are identified before they reach the end user. The test conditions for this program are as follows; test results are summarized in *Table 1*.

Thermal Intermittents: Two test methods are used: a 150°C op/non-op test and a high current $V_{BE(fwd)}$ test. Performed on a curve tracer, the $V_{BE(fwd)}$ test checks for electrical instability and evidence of resistance in the V_{BE} diode.

Thermal Shock: Stress is formed by subjecting the devices to −65°C liquid for 5 minutes and immediately transferring them to a liquid at 125°C for a 5 minute duration. The devices are cycled 10 times.

Intermittent Operating Life (IOPL): This test is performed at an ambient temperature of 25°C and at the rated power level with an applied collector-emitter voltage of approximately 75% of the rated LV_{CEO}. The device is on for 5 minutes and then off for 5 minutes for a total duration of 1,000 hours.

Moisture Stress (WHTRB): The devices are at ambient conditions of 85°C, 85% relative humidity and an applied bias across the collector-base of approximately 80% of the rated BV_{CBO}. Test duration is 168 hours.

High Temperature Storage (HTS): The devices are stored at a temperature of 150°C for a total of 1,000 hours.

Moisture Resistance: Moisture penetration is performed in a pressure chamber using distilled water heated to a temperature sufficient to obtain an internal pressure of 15 pounds per square inch. Total chamber time is 24 hours.

Temperature/Voltage Stress (HTRB): The product is tested at 150°C with approximately 80% of the rated BV_{CBO} applied to the collector-base. Test duration is 168 hours.

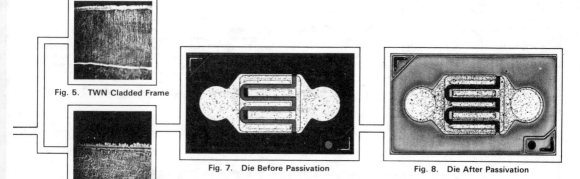

Fig. 5.   TWN Cladded Frame

Fig. 6.   Electroplated Frame

Fig. 7.   Die Before Passivation

Fig. 8.   Die After Passivation

CONCLUSION

The improvements in frame construction and metallurgy, die passivation and encapsulant composition have increased TWN TO-92 reliability to the point that the outgoing inspection levels for TWN products represent an industry breakthrough.

The lower AQL levels, higher power dissipation capability and cost effectiveness of TWN TO-92 products will create application niches for transistors in plastic packages that were unimaginable just a few years ago.

NTWNTWNTWNTWNTWNTWNTWN

Fachliteratur

VON FAIRCHILD

DATENBÜCHER

FULL LINE CONDENSED CATALOGUE (78)

Auswahltabellen mit den wichtigsten Parametern und Anschlußdiagramme für das gesamte Halbleiterspektrum von Fairchild: Dioden, Transistoren, Optoelektronik, CCD-Bildsensoren + Analoge Schieberegister, Hybrid, Linear, Interface, Digital (TTL, CMOS, ECL), Speicher (RAMs, ROMs, PROMs, EPROMs) und Mikroprozessoren (F8, F6800, 8-/16-Bit-Bipolarspeicher).
JAN QPL-Qualifikationsliste und Gehäuseabmessungen.

(1978) 528 Seiten, in engl. Spr.   Best.-Nr. DE 1201   DM 15,50*

ECL DATABOOK (78)

Neben den herkömmlichen Serien F10K und F95K ist die neue Subnanosekunden-Logik F100K und die bis in den GHz-Bereich arbeitende Serie F11C (Teiler, Prescaler, Synthesizer) enthalten. Ebenso RAMs (bis 4K) und PROMs (1K). 100 Seiten Design-Regeln.

(1978) 512 Seiten, in engl. Spr.   Best.-Nr. DE 1210   DM 15,50*

CMOS DATABOOK (77)

Industrie-Standardserie 4000 B. Periphere LSI und Bit-Slice-Bausteine (Macrologic). Schaltungscharakteristiken und Design-Regeln für die CMOS-Familie.

(1977) 528 Seiten, in engl. Spr.   Best.-Nr. DE 1211   DM 15,50*

MACROLOGIC DATABOOK (76)

LSI-Bausteine in Bipolar und CMOS-Technologie zur Bildung von 8-Bit μP-Systemen einschließlich der Peripherie. 44 Seiten Applikationen (Hardware + Software). Bausteine: Bit Rate Generatoren, Stacks, Microprogram Sequencer, FIFOs, Data Access Register, CRC-Generator Checker.

(1976) 240 Seiten, in engl. Spr.   Best.-Nr. DE 1209   DM 12,50*

BIPOLAR MEMORY DATABOOK (76)

TTL-und ECL-Speicher für schnelle Anwendungen. RAMs (bis 4K), ROMs/PROMs (bis 8K) und FPLAs. FIFOs und LIFOs.
24 Seiten Design-Regeln für RAMs; 22 Seiten ROM-/PROM-Applikationen.

(1976) 304 Seiten, in engl. Spr.   Best.-Nr. DE 1208   DM 12,50*

LPS DATABOOK (77)

Industrie-Standardserie 54/74LS. Schaltungscharakteristiken und Design-Regeln für die LPS-Familie.

(1977) 342 Seiten, in engl. Spr.   Best.-Nr. DE 1202   DM 12,50*

VOLTAGE REGULATOR HANDBOOK (78)

Positive und negative, feste und einstellbare Spannungsregler für Ausgangsströme bis 10 A (Hybrid-Technik). Getaktete Spannungsregler speziell für batterieversorgte Systeme.
87 Seiten Applikationen, 21 Seiten Test- und Zuverlässigkeitskriterien.

(1978) 366 Seiten, in engl. Spr.   Best.-Nr. DE 1212   DM 13,50*

POWER DATABOOK (76)

Neben ausführlichen Datenangaben der Leistungstransistoren von Fairchild, gibt das Buch Einzelheiten über deren Technologie; Montage und Wärmeableitung der Gehäuse; und Hinweise zur Safe Operating Area.

(1976) 384 Seiten, in engl. Spr.   Best.Nr. DE 1206   DM 13,50*

OPTO-DATA BOOK '78

INHALT:
Lampen-, Ziffern-, Uhren- und Skalenanzeigen aus verschiedenfarbigen LED-Elementen. Phototransistor-, IR Emitter und Sensorarrays. Optokoppler bis 5 kV. Angaben über Technologie, Fabrikation, Test und Zuverlässigkeit.

(1978) 304 Seiten, in engl. Spr.   Best.Nr. DE 1213   DM 12,50*

TTL APPLICATIONS HANDBOOK (73)

Umfassendes Buch für den TTL-Anwender mit den Kapiteln: Multiplexer (19 Seiten), Decoder (22 Seiten), Display-Systeme (24 Seiten), Encoder (14 Seiten), Recheneinheiten (61 Seiten), Latches (25 Seiten), Speicher (20 Seiten), Register (25 Seiten), Zähler (40 Seiten), Monostabile Multivibratoren (25 Seiten). Ausführliches Kapitel über Charakteristiken und Übertragungseigenschaften der Standard-TTL-Familie.

(1978) 368 Seiten, in engl. Spr.   Best.-Nr. AE 1302   DM 16,50*

MIKROPROZESSOR-LITERATUR-KITS

BIPOLAR μP KIT

Das Kit enthält neben dem Macrologic-Datenbuch (8-Bit-Slice und periphere LSI-Bausteine) den neuen 16-Bit μP 9440 (Microflame) mit einer Reihe von Broschüren für die Software-Entwicklung.

In engl. Sprache   Best.-Nr. KIT 103   DM 35,—*

F8 KIT

Das Kit enthält neben den Büchern F8 User's Guide (F8 Hardware), F8 Guide to Programming (F8 Software) und Formulator User's Guide (F8 Entwicklungssystem) den neuen Einchip-Microprozessor F3870 (Micromachine) sowie eine Reihe von Broschüren für die Software-Entwicklung.

In engl. Sprache   Best.-Nr. KIT 102   DM 35,—*

* Alle Preise verstehen sich inkl. 6% MwSt., zuzügl. Versandspesen.

FAIRCHILD SALES OFFICES — INTERNATIONAL

AUSTRALIA
Fairchild Australia Pty Ltd.
72 Whiting Street
Artarmon 2064
New South Wales
Australia
Tel: Sydney (02)-438-2733

(mailing address)
P.O. Box 450
North Sydney 2060
New South Wales
Australia

AUSTRIA AND EASTERN EUROPE
Fairchild Electronics
A-1010 Wien
Schwedenplatz 2
Tel: 0222 635821 Telex: 75096

BRAZIL
Fairchild Semicondutores Ltda
Caixa Postal 30407
Rua Alagoas, 663
01242 Sao Paulo, Brazil
Tel: 66-9092 Telex: 011-23831
Cable: FAIRLEC

FRANCE
Fairchild Camera & Instrument S.A.
121, Avenue d'Italie
750013-Paris, France
Tel: 00331-584 55 66
Telex: 0042 200614 or 260937

GERMANY
Fairchild Camera and Instrument (Deutschland)
Daimlerstr 15
8046 Garching-Hochbrück
W-Germany
Tel: (089) 320031 Telex: 52 4831 fair d

Fairchild Camera and Instrument (Deutschland)
Koenigsworther Strasse 23
3000 Hannover
W-Germany
Tel: 0511 17844 Telex:09 22922

Fairchild Camera and Instrument (Deutschland)
Poststrasse 37
7251 Leonberg
W-Germany
Tel: 07152 41026 Telex: 07 245711

Fairchild Camera and Instrument (Deutschland)
Waldluststrasse 1
8500 Nuernberg
W-Germany
Tel: 0911 407005 Telex: 06 23665

HONG KONG
Fairchild Semiconductor (HK) Ltd.
135 Hoi Bun Road
Kwun Tong
Kowloon, Hong Kong
Tel: K-890271 Telex: HKG-531

ITALY
Fairchild Semiconduttori, S.P.A.
Via Flamenia Vecchia 653
00191 Roma, Italy
Tel: 06 327 4006 Telex: 63046 (FAIR ROM)

Fairchild Semiconduttori S.P.A.
Via Rosellini, 12
20124 Milano, Italy
Tel: 02 6887451 Telex: 36522

JAPAN
TDK-Fairchild
Pola Bldg. 7th Floor 1-15-21 Shibuya
Tokyo 150, Japan
Tel: 03 400 8351 Telex: 242173

KOREA
Fairchild Semikor Ltd.
K2 219-6 Kari Bong Dong
Young Dung Po-Ku
Seoul 150-06, Korea
Tel: 86-6751 through 55 Telex: FAIRKOR 22705

(mailing address)
Central P.O. Box 2806

MEXICO
Fairchild Mexicana S.A.
Blvd. Adolfo Lopez Mateos No. 163
Mexico 19, D.F.
Tel: 905-563-5411 Telex: 017-71-038

SCANDINAVIA
Fairchild Semiconductor AB
Svartengsgatan 6
S-11620 Stockholm
Sweden
Tel: 8-449255 Telex: 17759

SINGAPORE
Fairchild Semiconductor Pty Ltd.
No. 11, Lorong 3
Toa Payoh
Singapore 12
Tel: 531-066 Telex: FAIRSIN-RS 21376

TAIWAN
Fairchild Semiconductor (Taiwan) Ltd.
Hsietsu Building, Room 502
47 Chung Shan North Road
Sec. 3 Taipei, Taiwan
Tel: 573205 thru 573207

BENELUX
Fairchild Semiconductor
Paradijslaan 39
Eindhoven, Holland
Tel: 00-31-40-446909 Telex: 00-1451024

UNITED KINGDOM
Fairchild Camera and Instrument (UK) Ltd.
Semiconductor Division
230 High Street
Potters Bar
Hertfordshire EN6 5BU
England
Tel: 0707 51111 Telex: 0051 262835·

Fairchild Semiconductor Ltd.
Shiel House
Craigshill
Livingston
West Lothian, Scotland
Tel: Livingston 0589 32891 Telex: 72629

FAIRCHILD SALES OFFICES — UNITED STATES AND CANADA

ALABAMA
Huntsville Office*
Executive Plaza
Suite 107
4717 University Drive, N.W.
Huntsville, Alabama 35805
Tel: 205-837-8960

ARIZONA
Phoenix Office
4414 N. 19th Avenue 85015
Suite G
Tel: 602-264-4948 TWX: 910-951-1544

CALIFORNIA
Los Angeles Office*
Crocker Bank Bldg.
15760 Ventura Blvd. Suite 1027
Encino 91436
Tel: 213-990-9800 TWX: 910-495-1776

Santa Ana Office*
2101 East Forth St. 92705
Bldg. B, Suite 185
Tel: 714-558-1881 TWX: 910-595-1109

Santa Clara Office*
3212-3214 Scott Blvd.
Santa Clara, 95050
Tel: 408-244-1400 TWX: 910-338-0241

FLORIDA
Ft. Lauderdale Office
Executive Plaza
Suite 300-B
1001 Northwest 62nd Street
Ft. Lauderdale, Florida 33309
Tel: 305-771-0320 TWX: 510-955-4098

Orlando Office*
Crane's Roost Office Park
303 Whooping Loop
Altamonte Springs 32701
Tel: 305-834-7000 TWX: 810-850-0152

GEORGIA
Atlanta Office*
1641 Wellshire Lane
Dunwoody, Ga. 30338
Tel: 404-394-5298

ILLINOIS
Chicago Office*
The Tower - Suite 610
Rolling Meadows 60008
Tel: 312-640-1000

INDIANA
Ft. Wayne Office
2118 Inwood Drive 46805
Suite 111
Tel: 219-483-6453 TWX: 810-332-1507

Indianapolis Office*
Room 205
7202 N. Shadeland 46250
Tel: 317-849-5412 TWX: 810-260-1793

KANSAS
Kansas City Office
Corporate Woods·
10875 Grandview, Suite 2255
Overland Park 66210
Tel: 913-649-3974

MARYLAND
Bladensburg Office
5801 Annapolis Road 20710
Suite 500
Tel: 301-779-0954 TWX: 710-826-9654

MASSACHUSETTS
Boston Office*
888 Worcester Street
Wellesley Hills 02181
Tel: 617-237-3400 TWX: 710-348-0424

MICHIGAN
Detroit Office*
Johnston Building, Suite 24
20793 Farmington Road
Farmington Hills 48024
Tel: 313-478-7400 TWX: 810-242-2973

MINNESOTA
Minneapolis Office*
7600 Parklawn Avenue
Room 251
Edina 55435
Tel: 612-835-3322 TWX: 910-576-2944

NEW JERSEY
Wayne Office
580 Valley Road 07490
Suite 1
Tel: 201-696-7070

NEW MEXICO
Albuquerque Office
2403 San Mateo N.E. 87110
Plaza 13
Tel: 505-265-5601 TWX: 910-989-1186

NEW YORK
Melville Office*
275 Broadhollow Road 11746
Tel: 516-293-2900 TWX: 510-224-6480

Poughkeepsie Office
15 College View Ave. 12603
Tel: 914-452-4200 TWX: 510-248-0030

Rochester Office*
260 Perinton Hills Office Park
Fairport 14450
Tel: 716-223-7700

OHIO
Dayton Office
4812 Frederick Road 45414
Suite 105
Tel: 513-278-8278 TWX: 810-459-1803

PENNSYLVANIA
Philadelphia Office*
2500 Office Center
2500 Maryland Road
Willow Grove, Pa. 19090
Tel: 215-657-2711

TEXAS
Dallas Office*
13771 N. Central Expressway 75231
Suite 809
Tel: 214-234-3391 TWX: 910-867-4757

Houston Office*
6430 Hillcroft 77081
Suite 102
Tel: 713-771-3547 TWX: 910-881-6278

CANADA
Toronto Regional Office
Fairchild Semiconductor
1590 Matheson Blvd, Unit 26
Mississauga, Ontario L4W 1J1, Canada
Tel: 416-625-7070 TWX: 610-492-4311